ENGLAND, WALES & CH

Turn to the page

ENGLAND

WALES

Channel Islands

Scotland & Ireland

Turn to the page shown for the start of each county

INTRODUCTION

Andrew Warren, Managing Director, Condé Nast Johansens Ltd.

Many of the hotels that we recommended when we commenced publishing in 1983, remain with us today. Their continued presence in this Guide has been assured by their ability to almost seamlessly reinvent themselves to meet your needs as a guest in the twenty first century.

Our team of hotel inspectors are pleased to report that some things never change, at the top of their list is quality and excellence throughout plus good old fashioned hospitality.

All our recommended hotels and spas now accept 'Gift Vouchers'. These make a very acceptable present for special occasions. Details can be found in this Guide.

We encourage your comments as they help us to compile a more useful Guide each year and they also contribute directly to the nominations for our Annual Awards. You may wish to complete a 'Guest Survey Report' printed at the back of this Guide or on our website www.johansens.com, if you have first taken advantage of our e-club free membership. Attractive 'Special Offers' are also available to everyone using our website.

Above all please remember to mention 'Johansens' when you make an enquiry or reservation and again when you arrive. You will be especially welcome.

THE CONDÉ NAST JOHANSENS PROMISE

Condé Nast Johansens is the most comprehensive illustrated reference to annually inspected, independently owned accommodation and meetings venues throughout Great Britain, Europe, the Mediterranean, the Americas, Atlantic, Caribbean and Pacific.

It is our objective to maintain the trust of guide users by recommending by annual inspection a careful choice of accommodation offering quality, excellent service and value for money.

Our team of over 50 dedicated Regional Inspectors visit thousands of hotels, country houses, inns, resorts and spas throughout the world to select only the very best for recommendation in the 2006 editions of our Guides.

No hotel or spa can appear unless it meets our exacting standards.

Condé Nast Johansens Guides

Recommending only the finest hotels and spas in the world

As well as this Guide, Condé Nast Johansens also publishes the following titles:

Recommended Country Houses, Small Hotels & Inns, Great Britain & Ireland

Smaller, more rural properties, ideal for short breaks or more intimate stays

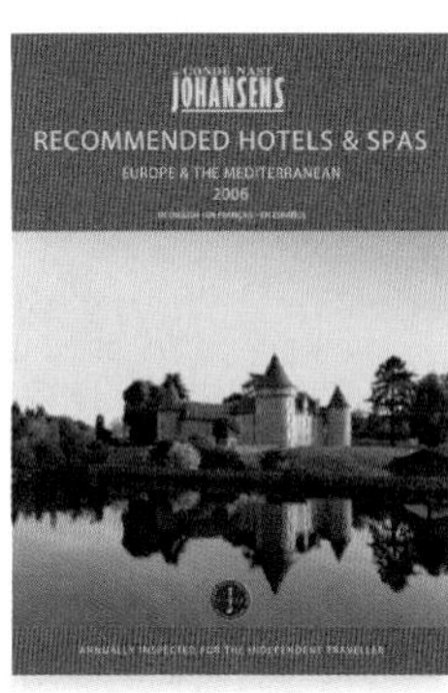

Recommended Hotels & Spas, Europe & the Mediterranean

A wonderful choice of properties including châteaux, resorts, charming countryside hotels and stylish city hotels.

Recommended Hotels, Inns, Resorts & Spas The Americas, Atlantic, Caribbean, Pacific

A diverse collection of properties across the region, including exotic ocean-front resorts, historic plantation houses and traditional inns.

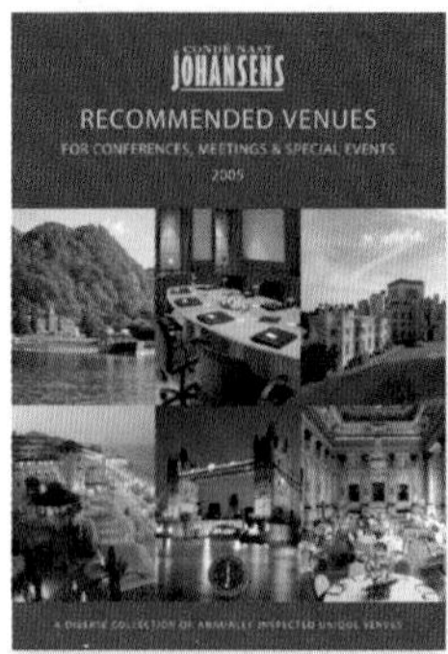

Recommended Venues, For Conferences, Meetings & Special Events

Venues that cater specifically for business meetings, conferences, product launches, events and celebrations.

When you purchase 2 Guides or more we will be pleased to offer you a reduction in the cost.

The complete set of 5 Condé Nast Johansens Guides may be purchased as "The International Collection".

To order any Guides please complete the order form on page 425, call FREEPHONE 0800 269 397 or visit our Bookshop at www.johansens.com

How to use this Guide

To find a hotel by location:

- Use the county maps at the front to identify the area of the country you wish to search.
- Turn to the relevant county section where hotels are featured alphabetically by location.
- Alternatively use the maps on pages 413–424 at the rear of the Guide. These maps cover all regions of Great Britain & Ireland and each hotel is marked.

There are over 45 properties which did not feature in our last (2005) edition and these are identified with a "NEW" symbol at the top of the page.

To find a hotel by its name or the name of its nearest town look in the indexes on pages 401–407.

The indexes also list recommended hotels by their amenities such as spa, swimming pool, golf on-site, etc.

If you cannot find a suitable hotel where you wish to stay, you may decide to choose one of the properties within the Condé Nast Johansens Recommended Country Houses, Small Hotels and Inns Guide as an alternative. These more intimate establishments are listed by place names on pages 371–375.

Once you have made your choice please contact the hotel directly. Rates are per room, including VAT and breakfast (unless stated otherwise) and are correct at the time of going to press but you should always check with the hotel before you make your reservation. **When making a booking please mention that Condé Nast Johansens was your source of reference.**

We occasionally receive letters from guests who have been charged for accommodation booked in advance but later cancelled. Readers should be aware that by making a reservation with a hotel, either by telephone, e-mail or in writing, they are entering into a legal contract. A hotelier under certain circumstances is entitled to make a charge for accommodation when guests fail to arrive, even if notice of the cancellation is given.

All Guides are obtainable from bookshops, by calling Freephone 0800 269397, by using the Order Forms on pages 425–431 or at our Bookshop at www.johansens.com

Condé Nast Johansens

Condé Nast Johansens Ltd, 6-8 Old Bond Street, London W1S 4PH
Tel: +44 (0)20 7499 9080 Fax: +44 (0)20 7152 3565
Find Condé Nast Johansens on the Internet at: www.johansens.com
E-mail: info@johansens.com

Publishing Director:	Janie Coppen-Gardner
PA to Publishing Director:	Amelia Dempster
Hotel Inspectors:	Jean Branham
	Geraldine Bromley
	Robert Bromley
	Pat Gillson
	Marie Iversen
	Pauline Mason
	John O'Neill
	Mary O'Neill
	Fiona Patrick
	Liza Reeves
	John Sloggie
	Nevill Swanson
	David Wilkinson
	Helen Wynn
Production Manager:	Kevin Bradbrook
Production Editor:	Laura Kerry
Senior Designer:	Michael Tompsett
Copywriters:	Clare Barker
	Sasha Creed
	Norman Flack
	Sarah Koya
	Debra O'Sullivan
	Rozanne Paragon
	Leonora Sandwell
Marketing and Sales Promotions Executive:	Eloise Mallen
Marketing Coordinator:	Siobhan Smith
Client Services Director:	Fiona Patrick
PA to Managing Director:	Siobhan Smith
Managing Director:	Andrew Warren

Condé Nast Johansens Ltd. is part of The Condé Nast Publications Ltd.

ISBN 1 903665 23 X

Printed in England by St Ives plc
Colour origination by Wyndeham Graphics

Distributed in the UK and Europe by Portfolio, Greenford (bookstores).
In North America by Casemate Publishing, Havertown (bookstores).

2005 Awards For Excellence

The winners of the Condé Nast Johansens 2005 Awards for Excellence

The Condé Nast Johansens 2005 Awards for Excellence were presented at the Awards Luncheon held at The Dorchester hotel, London, on November 8th, 2004. Awards were offered to those properties worldwide that represented the finest standards and best value for money in luxury independent travel. An important source of information for these awards was the feedback provided by guests who completed Johansens Guest Survey reports. Guest Survey forms can be found on page 426.

Most Excellent London Hotel

51 Buckingham Gate – London, England, p184

"A hotel that offers everything the discerning guest could wish for — contemporary style and luxury on a grand scale."

Most Excellent City Hotel

One Devonshire Gardens – Glasgow, Scotland, p333

"The attention to detail in this hotel just gets better each year and it's tranquil atmosphere belies it's proximity to Glasgow's city centre."

Most Excellent Service

East Lodge Country House Hotel – Derbyshire, England, p78

"The Hardman family take tremendous pride in their hotel. This is truly represented in its ambiance and attention to detail."

Most Excellent Restaurant

The Lake Country House – Powys, Wales, p370

"Consistently good, well balanced menus offering variety and wonderful old fashioned values. It has a touch of old theatre and the wine list is a real treasure with many bottles to raise a squeal of delight."

Most Excellent Spa

Whatley Manor – Wiltshire, England, p255

"A real retreat to get away from it all with sumptuous décor, sophisticated understated elegance and the most amazing spa."

Most Excellent Country Hotel

Cotswold House Hotel – Gloucestershire, England, p118

"State of the art style and luxury in the heart of the Cotswolds – the bathrooms are stunning and you may not even wish to leave your room."

The Perfect Gift...

Condé Nast Johansens Gift Vouchers

Condé Nast Johansens Gift Vouchers make a unique and much valued present for birthdays, weddings, anniversaries, special occasions or as a corporate incentive.

Vouchers are available in denominations of £100, £50, €140, €70, $150, $75 and may be used as payment or part payment for your stay or a meal at any Condé Nast Johansens 2006 recommended property.

To order, call Amelia Dempster on +44 (0)207 152 3558
or purchase direct at www.johansens.com

Laura Bailey photographed by David Slijper

2005 Awards For Excellence

The winners of the Condé Nast Johansens 2005 Awards for Excellence

The following award winners are featured within Condé Nast Johansens 2006 Guides to Country Houses – Great Britain & Ireland; Hotels & Spas – Europe & The Mediterranean; Hotels & Resorts – Americas, Atlantic, Caribbean, Pacific. See page 2 for details. Also listed are the winners of the Knight Frank Award and Taittinger Wine List Award.

Most Excellent Country House
Ford Abbey – Herefordshire, England,

Most Excellent Traditional Inn
The Falcon Hotel – Northamptonshire, England

Most Excellent Coastal Hotel
The White House – Herm Island, Channel Islands

Most Excellent Value for Money
The Mill At Gordleton – Hampshire, England

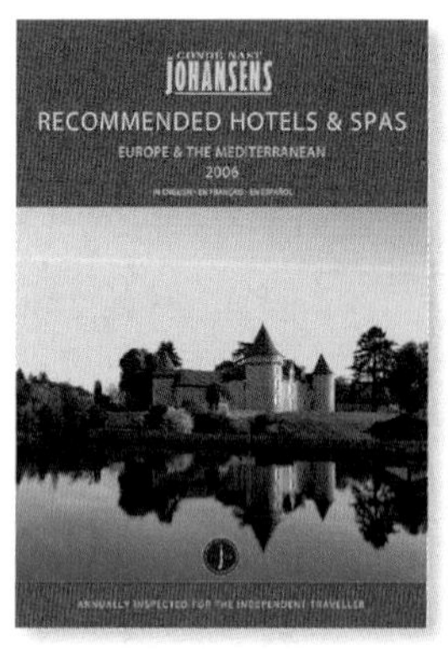

Europe: Most Excellent City/Town Hotel
Hostellerie Le Maréchal – Alsace~Lorraine, France

Europe: Most Excellent Countryside Hotel
Hotel La Bobadilla – Andalucía, Spain

Europe: Most Excellent Waterside Hotel
La Posta Vecchia Hotel Spa – Lazio, Italy

Europe: Most Excellent Value for Money Hotel
Le Manoir Les Minimes – Loire Valley, France

Europe: Most Excellent Spa Hotel
Hotel Byblos Andaluz – Andalucía, Spain

Europe: Most Excellent Resort Hotel
St Nicolas Bay Hotel – Crete, Greece

Europe: Most Romantic Hotel
Hotel Cocumella – Campania, Italy

Americas, Atlantic, Caribbean, Pacific: Most Outstanding Inn
The Emerson Inn & Spa – New York, USA

Americas, Atlantic, Caribbean, Pacific: Most Outstanding Small Inn
The Inn at Irving Place – New York, USA

Americas, Atlantic, Caribbean, Pacific: Most Outstanding Hotel
Hotel Villa Del Sol – Zihuatanejo, Mexico

Americas, Atlantic, Caribbean, Pacific: Most Outstanding Lodge
Rough Creek Lodge – Texas, USA

Americas, Atlantic, Caribbean, Pacific: Most Outstanding Spa
Ballantyne Resort – North Carolina, USA

Americas, Atlantic, Caribbean, Pacific: Most Outstanding Resort
Grand Velas All Suites & Spa Resort – Nuevo Vallarta, Mexico

Knight Frank for Outstanding Excellence & Innovation
The Goodwin Family, Bailiffscourt Hotel & Health Spa – West Sussex, England, p237

Taittinger Wine List of the Year
The Devonshire Arms Country House Hotel – North Yorkshire, England, p269

spa
developments
"Shaping world-class spa business
solutions for Condé Nast Johansens
recommended hotels and resorts"
www.spadevelopments.com

ENGLAND

Recommendations in England appear on pages 14-289

Images from www.britainonview.com

For further information on England, please contact:

Cumbria Tourist Board
Ashleigh, Holly Road, Windermere, Cumbria LA23 2AQ
Tel: +44 (0)15394 44444
Web: www.golakes.co.uk

East of England Tourist Board
Toppesfield Hall , Hadleigh, Suffolk IP7 5DN
Tel: +44 (0)1473 822922
Web: www.visiteastofengland.com

Heart of England Tourism
Larkhill Road, Worcester, Worcestershire WR5 2EZ
Tel: +44 (0)1905 761100
Web: www.visitheartofengland.com

Visit London
6th Floor, 2 More London Riverside, London SE1 2RR
Tel: 0870 156 6366
Web: www.visitlondon.com

One North East Tourism Team
Stelle House, Gold Crest Way, Newburn Riverside,
Newcastle-Upon-Tyne, N15 8NY
Tel: +44 (0)191 375 3000
Web: www.visitnorthumbria.com

North West Tourist Board
Swan House, Swan Meadow Road, Wigan, Lancashire WN3 5BB
Tel: +44 (0)1942 821 222
Web: www.visitnorthwest.com

Tourism South East
40 Chamberlayne Road, Eastleigh, Hampshire, SO50 5JH
Tel: +44 (0)23 8062 5400
Web: www.visistsoutheastengland.com

South West Tourism
Woodwater Park, Exeter, Devon EX2 5WT
Tel: +44 (0)1392 360 050
Web: www.visitsouthwest.co.uk

Yorkshire Tourist Board
312 Tadcaster Road, York, Yorkshire YO24 1GS
Tel: +44 (0)1904 707961
Web: www.ytb.org.uk
Yorkshire and North & North East Lincolnshire.

English Heritage
Customer Services Department , PO Box 569, Swindon SN2 2YP
Tel: +44 (0) 870 333 1181
Web: www.english-heritage.org.uk

Historic Houses Association
2 Chester Street, London SW1X 7BB
Tel: +44 (0)20 7259 5688
Web: www.hha.org.uk

The National Trust
Heelis, Kemble Drive, Swindon, SN2 2NA
Tel: 0870 242 6620
Web: www.nationaltrust.org.uk

or see pages 376-378 for details of
local attractions to visit during your stay.

The Bath Priory Hotel and Restaurant

WESTON ROAD, BATH, SOMERSET BA1 2XT

Standing in 4 acres of gardens, The Bath Priory Hotel is close to some of England's most famous and finest architecture. Within walking distance of Bath city centre, this Georgian, mellow stone building dates from 1835, when it formed part of a row of fashionable residences on the west side of the city. Visitors will sense the luxury as they enter the hotel; antique furniture, many superb oil paintings and objets d'art add interest to the 2 spacious reception rooms and the elegant drawing room. Well-defined colour schemes lend an uplifting brightness throughout, particularly in the tastefully appointed bedrooms. Enjoy Michelin-starred Mediterranean cuisine in the charming restaurant, under the direction of restaurant manager Vito Scaduto M.C.A, served in 3 interconnecting dining rooms which overlook the gardens. An especially good selection of wines can be recommended to accompany meals. Private functions can be accommodated both in the terrace, pavilion and the Orangery. The Roman Baths, Theatre Royal, Museum of Costume and a host of bijou shops offer plenty for visitors to see. The Garden Spa consists of a fitness suite, swimming pool, sauna, steam room and health and beauty spa.

Our inspector loved: *The beautiful drawing room with blazing fire and wonderful paintings.*

Directions: 1 mile west of the centre of Bath. Please contact the hotel for precise directions.

Web: www.johansens.com/bathpriory
E-mail: mail@thebathpriory.co.uk
Tel: 0870 381 8345
International: +44 (0)1225 331922
Fax: 01225 448276

Price Guide: (incl. full English breakfast)
double/twin from £245

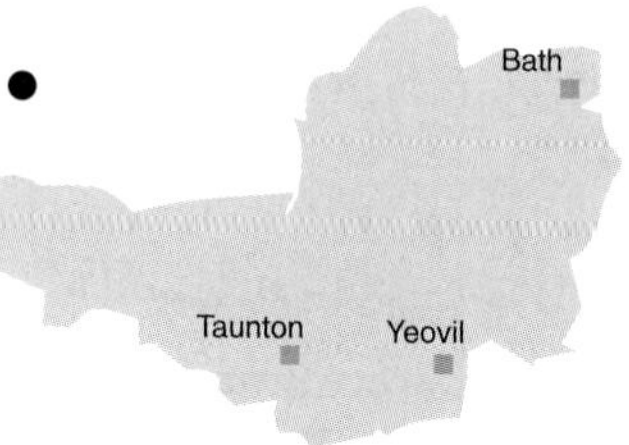

The Bath Spa Hotel

SYDNEY ROAD, BATH, SOMERSET BA2 6JF

Nestling in 7 acres of mature grounds dotted with ancient cedars, formal gardens, ponds and fountains, The Bath Spa Hotel's elegant Georgian façade can only hint at the warmth, style, comfort and attentive personal service. It is a handsome building in a handsome setting with antique furniture, richly coloured carpeting and well defined colour schemes lending an uplifting brightness throughout. The bedrooms are elegantly decorated; the bathrooms are luxuriously appointed in mahogany and marble. The Bath Spa Hotel offers all amenities that guests would expect of a 5-star hotel, for example WiFi, whilst retaining the character of a homely country house. Chef Andrew Hamer's imaginative, contemporary style is the primary inspiration for the award-winning cuisine served in the 2 restaurants. For relaxation there is a fully equipped health and leisure spa which includes an indoor swimming pool, gymnasium, sauna, Jacuzzi, 3 treatment rooms, hair salon and croquet lawn. Apart from the delights of Bath, there is motor racing at Castle Combe and hot air ballooning nearby.

Our inspector loved: *The warm welcome, grand entrance and the magnificent floral display.*

Directions: Exit M4 jct 18 onto A46, follow signs to Bath for 8 miles until major roundabout. Turn right onto A4 follow city centre signs for a mile, at first major set of traffic lights turn left towards A36. Over Cleveland Bridge, past Fire Station, turn right at the traffic lights after the pedestrian crossing then next left after Holburne Museum into Sydney Place. The Hotel is 200 yards up the hill on the right.

Web: www.johansens.com/bathspa
E-mail: sales@bathspahotel.com
Tel: 0870 381 8346
International: +44 (0)1225 444424
Fax: 01225 444006

Price Guide:
double/twin £270–£340
4-poster £390–£460

104 130

COMBE GROVE MANOR HOTEL & COUNTRY CLUB

BRASSKNOCKER HILL, MONKTON COMBE, BATH, SOMERSET BA2 7HS

Directions: Set south-east of Bath, off the A36 near the University. A map can be supplied on request.

Web: www.johansens.com/combegrovemanor
E-mail: info@combegrovemanor.com
Tel: 0870 381 8438
International: +44 (0)1225 834644
Fax: 01225 834961

Price Guide:
single from £130
double/twin from £130
suite from £300

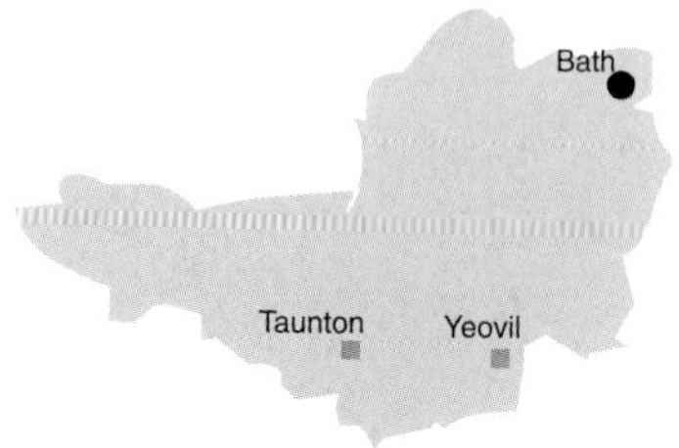

This exclusive 18th-century Country House Hotel is conveniently located just 2 miles from the beautiful city of Bath. Built on the hillside site of an ancient Roman settlement, Combe Grove Manor is set in 69 acres of beautiful private gardens and woodlands, with awe-inspiring panoramic views over the magnificent Limpley Stoke Valley and surrounding areas. The Manor House features luxurious four-poster rooms and suites with Jacuzzi baths, whilst the rooms in the Garden Lodge have spectacular views, some with private balconies. All 42 bedrooms are lavishly appointed and individual in design with superb en-suite facilities. Within the hotel's grounds are some of the finest leisure facilities in the south west, including indoor and outdoor heated pools, hydrospa beds and steam room, 4 all-weather tennis courts, a 5-hole par 3 golf course and a 16-bay driving range. Guests may use the fully-equipped gym, aerobics studio, sauna and solaria or simply indulge in the full range of treatments offered by professionally trained staff in the Clarins beauty rooms. There is also a choice of 2 superb restaurants; the elegant Georgian restaurant features delicious traditional style cuisine and fine wines, whereas the informal Eden Bistro offers an exciting contemporary international menu.

Our inspector loved: *The extensive spa and lesiure facilities and of course the beautiful views.*

DUKES HOTEL

GREAT PULTENEY STREET, BATH, SOMERSET BA2 4DN

Upon entering the elegant entrance topped with half-moon shaped decorative glass ornamentation edged by slim, black, wrought-iron railings, guests are immediately introduced to the charm, character, style and understated luxury of this Grade I listed town house hotel. Situated in one of the finest and most majestic boulevards in Europe, in the heart of the best preserved Georgian city in Britain, Dukes Hotel is a former Palladian mansion, built from Bath stone and now transformed to its original splendour. The front guest rooms overlook façades inspired by Palladio and rear rooms have views of rolling hills. Each en-suite bedroom and suite is the essence of quality; most have original features such as intricate plasterwork and large sash windows. Fine furniture and fabrics abound throughout. The newly introduced and refurbished Cavendish Restaurant is a light, airy and relaxing venue in which to enjoy superb cuisine prepared by talented chef Richard Allen. The very best of organic and free-range British ingredients, including Cornish lamb, Angus beef and seafood delivered daily from Salcombe, are on the menu. There are 2 further, smaller dining rooms, complemented by a secluded, walled patio garden, which provides an enviable setting for summer al fresco dining.

Our inspector loved: *The lovely patio garden for alfresco dining.*

Directions: Exit the M4, junction 18 and follow signs for Bath. Turn left at the traffic lights towards Warminster then right at the next traffic lights into Sydney Place. Great Pulteney Street is on the right after approx 150 yards.

Bath

Taunton

Yeovil

Web: www.johansens.com/dukesbath
E-mail: info@dukesbath.co.uk
Tel: 0870 381 8357
International: +44 (0)1225 787960
Fax: 01225 787961

Price Guide:
single £95
double/twin £125–£145
suite £185–£205

The Francis Hotel

QUEEN SQUARE, BATH, SOMERSET BA1 2HH

Directions: The Francis is located on Queen Square, a short distance from The Circus. Simply follow the A4 through route, which forms the north side of Queen Square.

Web: www.johansens.com/francis
E-mail: sales.francis@macdonald-hotels.co.uk
Tel: 0870 381 8728
International: +44 (0)1225 424105
Fax: 01225 319715

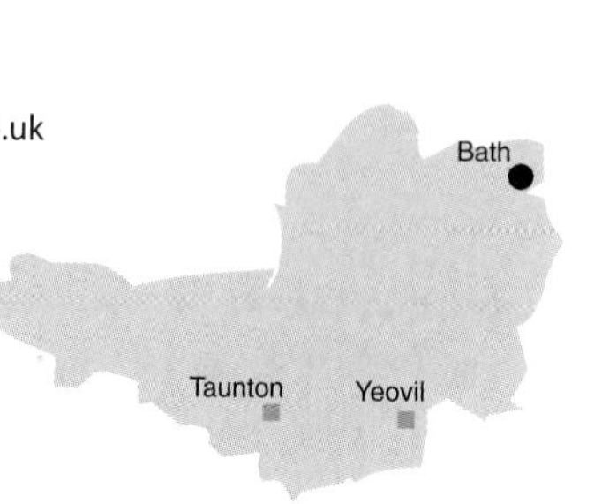

Price Guide:
double £130-£150
suite £190-£210

This classic Regency town house lies in the very centre of this striking and exciting city, and minutes away from the many attractions that it has to offer. The stunning Abbey, historical Roman Baths and Pump Room are all within a stone's throw, making The Francis the ideal base from which to explore, not just the historical tourist trail, but also the many fine shops, cafés and restaurants. The hotel itself has some 95 air conditioned en-suite bedrooms, each of which is decorated with careful flair – Regency stripes pay homage to the building's Georgian origins, but are brought up to date with exciting chenilles, damasks, stripes and checks. This modern approach is echoed by the style of food, sample dishes such as fresh aparagus, parma ham, poached egg, hollandaise sauce or grilled yellow fin tuna, slow roasted tomatoes grilled aubergine and mozzarella, are served in The Square Restaurant, whilst more informal suppers are available in the Caffébar. There are 2 well-equipped meeting rooms available for conferences, product launches and meetings; and with London Paddington being less than 2 hours away, The Francis is a great location for the business traveller as well as weekenders. Weddings can also be organised and catered for.

Our inspector loved: *The great location, right in the heart of Bath, with an easy walk to all sights and shops.*

 95  80       

The Royal Crescent Hotel

16 ROYAL CRESCENT, BATH, SOMERSET BA1 2LS

The Royal Crescent Hotel is a Grade I listed building of the greatest historical and architectural importance and occupies the central 2 houses of one of Europe's finest masterpieces. The Royal Crescent is a sweep of 30 houses with identical façades stretching in a 500ft curve. Built by 1775, the hotel was completely refurbished in 1998 and the work undertaken has restored many of the classical Georgian features with all the additional modern comforts. Each of the 45 bedrooms is equipped with air conditioning, the Cliveden bed, video/compact disc player and personal facsimile machine. Pimpernel's restaurant offers a relaxed and informal dining atmosphere, presenting a contemporary menu. Comprehensively equipped, the secure private boardroom provides self-contained business meeting facilities. Exclusive use of the hotel can be arranged for a special occasion or corporate event. Magnificent views of Bath and the surrounding countryside may be enjoyed from the hotel's vintage river launch or by hot air balloon upon arrangement. The Bath House is a unique spa, in which to enjoy both complementary therapies and holistic massage. Adjacent to this tranquil setting is the gym with cardio-vascular and resistance equipment.

Our inspector loved: *The amazing architecture of this wonderful building and the spacious elegant suites and drawing room.*

Directions: Detailed directions are available from the hotel on booking.

Bath
Taunton
Yeovil

Web: www.johansens.com/royalcrescent
E-mail: info@royalcrescent.co.uk
Tel: 0870 381 8874
International: +44 (0)1225 823333
Fax: 01225 339401

Price Guide:
(including continental breakfast)
double/twin from £290
suite from £530

Homewood Park

HINTON CHARTERHOUSE, BATH, SOMERSET BA2 7TB

Directions: On the A36, 6 miles from Bath towards Warminster.

Web: www.johansens.com/homewoodpark
E-mail: info@homewoodpark.co.uk
Tel: 0870 381 8605
International: +44 (0)1225 723731
Fax: 01225 723820

Price Guide:
single from £120
double/twin from £165
suites from £295

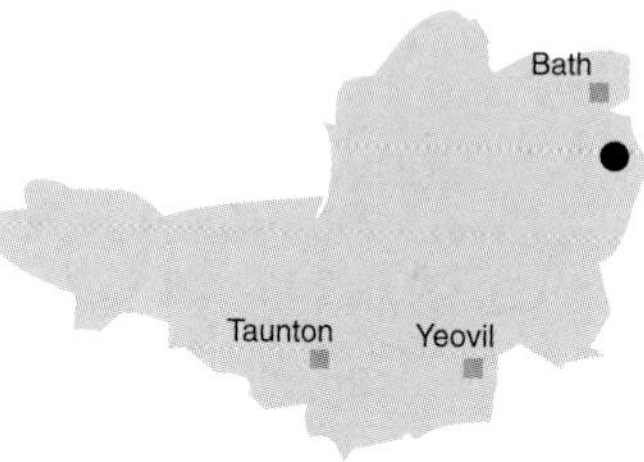

Standing amid 10 acres of beautiful grounds and woodland on the edge of Limpley Stoke Valley, designated area of outstanding natural beauty is Homewood Park, one of Britain's finest privately-owned smaller country house hotels. This lovely 19th-century building has an elegant interior, adorned with beautiful fabrics, antiques, oriental rugs and original oil paintings. Lavishly furnished bedrooms offer the best in comfort, style and privacy. Each of them has a charm and character of its own and most have good views over the Victorian garden. The outstanding cuisine has won the hotel an excellent reputation and the à la carte menu uses, wherever possible, produce from local suppliers. A range of carefully selected wines, stored in the hotel's original medieval cellars, lies patiently waiting to augment lunch and dinner. Before or after a meal guests can enjoy a drink in the comfortable bar or drawing rooms, both of which have a log fire during the cooler months. The hotel is well placed for guests to enjoy the varied attractions of the wonderful city of Bath with its unique hot springs, Roman remains, superb Georgian architecture and American Museum. Further afield but within reach are Stonehenge and Cheddar caves.

Our inspector loved: *This lovely house set in beautiful gardens with its peaceful and relaxing atmosphere.*

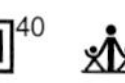

Hunstrete House

HUNSTRETE, NR BATH, SOMERSET BS39 4NS

In a classical English landscape on the edge of the Mendip Hills stands Hunstrete House. This unique hotel, surrounded by lovely gardens, is largely 18th century, although the history of the estate goes back to 963AD. Each of the bedrooms is individually decorated and furnished to a high standard, combining the benefits of a hotel room with the atmosphere of a charming private country house. Many offer uninterrupted views over undulating fields and woodlands. The reception areas exhibit warmth and elegance and are liberally furnished with beautiful antiques. Log fires burn in the hall, library and drawing room through the winter and on cooler summer evenings. The Terrace dining room looks out on to an Italianate, flower-filled courtyard. A highly skilled head chef offers light, elegant dishes using produce from the extensive garden, including organic meat and vegetables. The menu changes regularly and the hotel has an excellent reputation for the quality and interest of its wine list. In a sheltered corner of the walled garden there is a heated swimming pool for guests to enjoy. For the energetic, the all-weather tennis court provides another diversion. The hotel is also available for exclusive use wedding and corporate events with a marquee to seat up to 120 people.

Our inspector loved: *The spacious light airy bedrooms with a true country house feel.*

Directions: From Bath take the A4 towards Bristol and then the A368 to Wells.

Web: www.johansens.com/hunstretehouse
E-mail: reception@hunstretehouse.co.uk
Tel: 0870 381 8630
International: +44 (0)1761 490490
Fax: 01761 490732

Price Guide:
single from £135
double/twin from £170
suite from £265

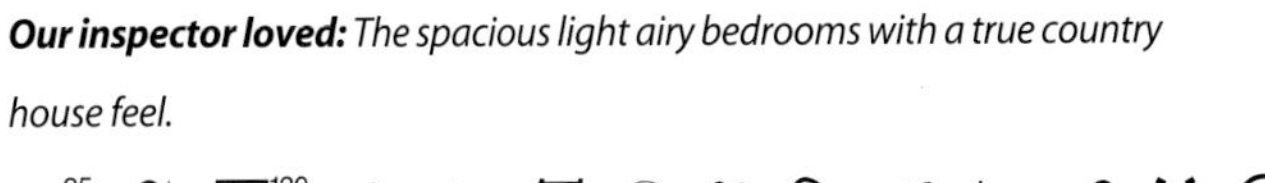

The Park

WICK, NEAR BATH BS30 5RN

Nestling in 240 acres of historic natural parkland, The Park is conveniently located between Bristol and the magnificent city of Bath, just 4 miles away. Within the hotel's grounds are 2 championship golf courses filled with mature trees, lakes and modern specification greens. Completely refurbished in 2005, the bedrooms in the picturesque courtyard have been decorated to a very high standard and offer the best in comfort and style; some have four-poster beds. The Park's restaurant, Oakwood, has an open-plan kitchen under the instruction of Chef Mark Treasure, and was originally an old stone Masonic temple. The menu specializes in simple treatment of roasted meats and fish cooked in a wood burning oven accompanied by a particularly interesting organic wine, beer and cider list. The Park has 8 conference and syndicate rooms that can accommodate up to 150 delegates, and the attractive Park Room, with views over the golf course, can seat up to 150 for a private banquet or wedding reception. This is an ideal location for golf enthusiasts, weekend breaks and corporate stays.

Our inspector loved: *The wonderful setting: a golfer's paradise.*

Directions: From the M4 take junction 18, then the A46 and A420. The entrance to The Park is just off the A420.

Web: www.johansens.com/thepark
E-mail: info@tpresort.com
Tel: 0870 381 8394
International: +44 (0)117 937 2251
Fax: 0117 937 4288

Price Guide:
single from £130
double from £195

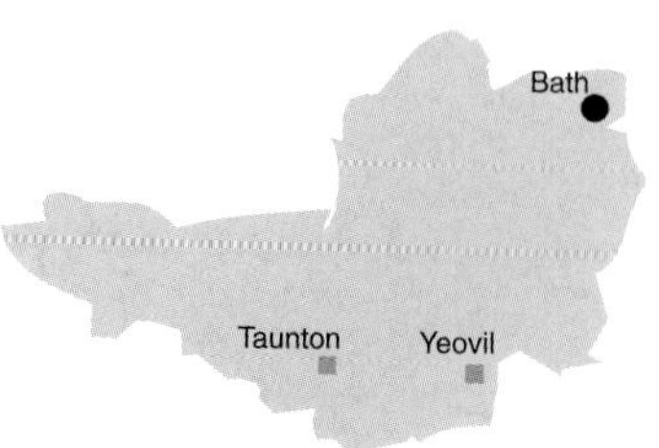

MOORE PLACE HOTEL

THE SQUARE, ASPLEY GUISE, MILTON KEYNES, BEDFORDSHIRE MK17 8DW

Built in 1786, Moore Place Hotel is a delightful country house hotel set in the centre of the peaceful village of Aspley Guise, and only 1.5 miles from the M1. Sympathetically extended to create extra accommodation, the new wing frames the attractive patio courtyard, rock garden, lily pool and waterfall. In May 2003, an additional 10 guest rooms were opened in the converted, listed cottage; each maintaining a very special character of its own. All 62 bedrooms are well-appointed and offer little extras such as trouser press, hairdryer, welcome drinks and large towelling bathrobes to make each visit special, for both business and leisure travellers alike. The attractive Victorian-style conservatory houses the highly acclaimed Greenhouse Restaurant, which is open to residents as well as non-residents, and serves cuisine rated amongst the best in the area. The menu is traditional English with European influences and is enhanced by a selection of fine wines; private dinners, conferences and special celebrations can be accommodated in 4 private function rooms. Moore Place Hotel is ideally situated for exploring the surrounding countryside and places of interest such as Bletchley Park, Waddesdon Manor, Woburn Abbey and Whipsnade Zoo to name but a few.

Our inspector loved: *The newly available spacious and attractive rooms in the cottage.*

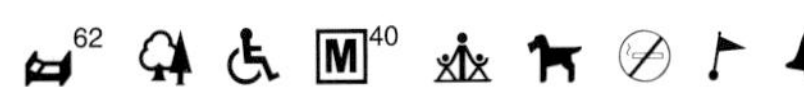

Directions: Only a 2-minute drive from the M1/junction 13.

Web: www.johansens.com/mooreplace
E-mail: manager@mooreplace.com
Tel: 0870 381 8745
International: +44 (0)1908 282000
Fax: 01908 281888

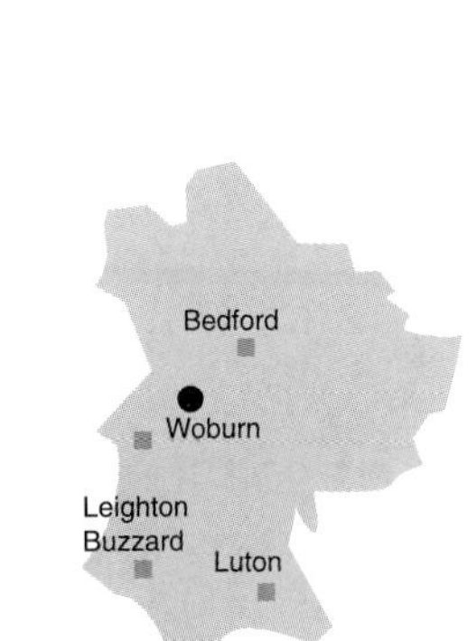

Price Guide:
single £58–£114
double/twin £79–£145
suite £150–£211

Fredrick's – Hotel Restaurant Spa

SHOPPENHANGERS ROAD, MAIDENHEAD, BERKSHIRE SL6 2PZ

'Putting people first' is the guiding philosophy behind this sumptuously equipped deluxe hotel. Guests can expect to receive uncompromising service from this second generation family-run establishment. Extensive landscaped gardens furnished with an array of contemporary artwork overlook the fairways and greens of Maidenhead Golf Club. The spectacular addition of Fredrick's exclusive Spa offers the ultimate in relaxation and is the first in the UK equipped with its own private flotation suite. Guests can indulge in restorative treatments such as Rasul or LaStone therapies. In the hotel, minute attention to detail is evident in the luxurious bedrooms, all immaculate with gleaming, marble bathrooms, whilst some of the suites have their own patio or balcony. A quiet drink can be enjoyed in the light airy wintergarden lounge, and in warmer weather on the patio, before entering the 3 AA Rosette air-conditioned restaurant. Gourmet cuisine, which has received recognition from leading guides for many years, is served in elegant surroundings enhanced by a collection of fine art and sculpture. As well as being suitable for relaxation, leisurely spa breaks, romantic stays and fine dining, Fredrick's is perfectly located for conferences and corporate hospitality. Fredrick's is easily accessible from London, Heathrow and the West Country and near to Windsor, Henley, and Ascot .

Our inspector loved: *The all indulging spa as well as a wonderful welcome.*

Directions: Leave M4 at junction 8/9, take A404(M) and leave at first exit 9A signed Cox Green/White Waltham. Turn left into Shoppenhangers Road towards Maidenhead. the entrance to Fredrick's is on the right.

Web: www.johansens.com/fredricks
E-mail: reservations@fredricks–hotel.co.uk
Tel: 0870 381 8531
International: +44 (0)1628 581000
Fax: 01628 771054

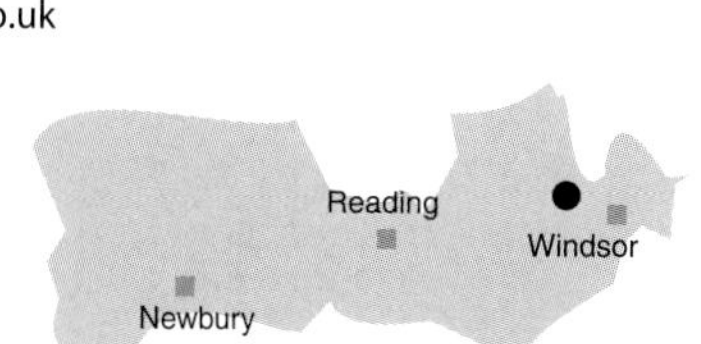

Price Guide:
single from £215
double/twin from £285
suite from £430

      SPA   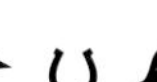

Cliveden

TAPLOW, BERKSHIRE SL6 0JF

Cliveden is Britain's only 5 Red AA Star hotel that is also a stately home. Set in 376 acres of gardens and parkland on an elevated position overlooking the Thames, Cliveden has been home to a Prince of Wales, 3 dukes, an earl and the Astor family, and has been at the centre of Britain's social and political life for over 300 years. Exquisitely furnished in an English country house style, original works of art and antiques abound, and the French Dining Room is one of the most stunning examples of an 18th-century interior in this country. Guests seeking privacy may stay in Spring Cottage on the edge of the River Thames, where unrivalled peace is guaranteed. Sample fine dining in the award-winning restaurants, either Waldo's or The Terrace, which overlooks the Parterre. Enjoy being pampered with treatments in the Pavilion Spa, roam the estate or partake in a river cruise on one of the hotel's vintage launches. Leisure activities include indoor and outdoor swimming, tennis, squash, a gymnasium, golf, horse riding and shooting. 2 well-equipped private boardrooms provide self-contained business meeting facilities. Luxury transfers via helicopter, a Rolls Royce Phantom or Bentley can be arranged. Cliveden is part of the von Essen hotel collection.

Our inspector loved: *The splendid approach to Cliveden along the wide and imposing drive.*

Directions: From the M4, jct 7 take the A4 towards Maidenhead. After a few miles, turn right into Berry Hill and follow the road for ¾ mile. Cliveden's drive is on the left-hand side via a grand entrance. Follow the "House Guests"signs.

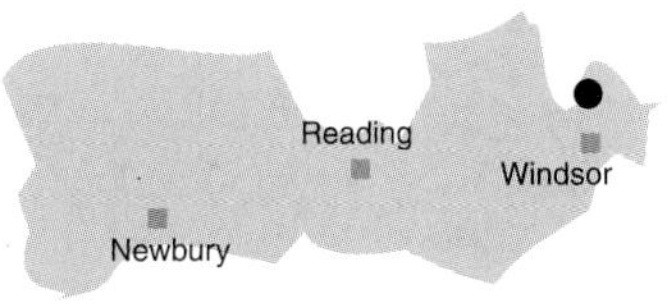

Web: www.johansens.com/cliveden
E-mail: Reservations@clivedenhouse.co.uk
Tel: 0870 381 8432
International: +44 (0)1628 668561
Fax: 01628 661837

Reading
Windsor
Newbury

Price Guide:
double/twin from £295

suites from £480

DONNINGTON VALLEY HOTEL & GOLF CLUB

OLD OXFORD ROAD, DONNINGTON, NEWBURY, BERKSHIRE RG14 3AG

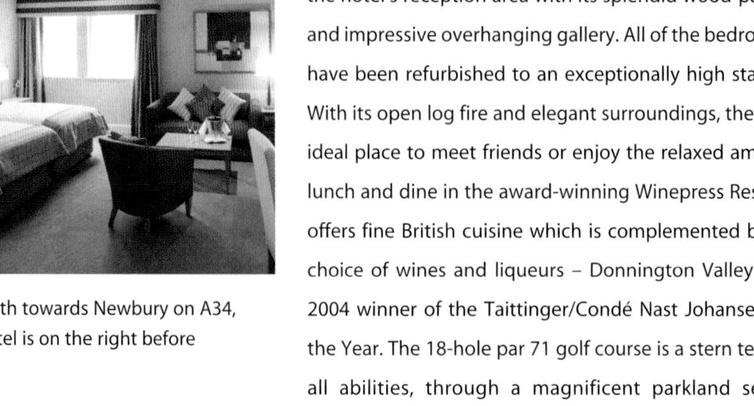

Uncompromising quality is the hallmark of this award winning hotel built in contrasting styles in 1991 with its own golf course. The grandeur of the Edwardian era has been captured by the interior of the hotel's reception area with its splendid wood-panelled ceilings and impressive overhanging gallery. All of the bedrooms and suites have been refurbished to an exceptionally high standard in 2005. With its open log fire and elegant surroundings, the Piano Bar is an ideal place to meet friends or enjoy the relaxed ambience. Guests lunch and dine in the award-winning Winepress Restaurant, which offers fine British cuisine which is complemented by an extensive choice of wines and liqueurs – Donnington Valley Hotel was the 2004 winner of the Taittinger/Condé Nast Johansens wine List of the Year. The 18-hole par 71 golf course is a stern test for golfers of all abilities, through a magnificent parkland setting. Special corporate golfing packages are offered and golf days can be arranged. The hotel also makes the perfect venue for golf breaks away.

Our inspector loved: *The friendly welcome and versatile facilities.*

Directions: Leave the M4 at junction 13, go south towards Newbury on A34, then follow signs for Donnington Castle. The hotel is on the right before reaching the castle.

Web: www.johansens.com/donningtonvalley
E-mail: general@donningtonvalley.co.uk
Tel: 0870 381 8484
International: +44 (0)1635 551199
Fax: 01635 551123

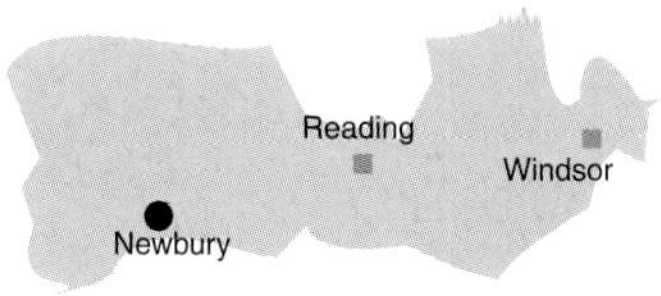

Reading
Windsor
Newbury

Price Guide:
single from £165
double/twin £165–£190
suite from £230

The Vineyard At Stockcross

NEWBURY, BERKSHIRE RG20 8JU

The Vineyard at Stockcross, Sir Peter Michael's "restaurant-with-suites" is a European showcase for the finest Californian wines including those from the Peter Michael Winery. Head Sommelier, Joao Pires, has selected the best from the most highly-prized, family-owned Californian wineries, creating one of the widest, most innovative, international wine lists. Awarded 5 Red Stars and 4 Rosettes by the AA, the modern British cuisine matches the calibre of the wines. Pure flavours, fresh ingredients and subtle design blend harmoniously with the fine wines. A stimulating collection of paintings and sculpture includes the keynote piece,"Fire and Water" by William Pye FRBS and "Deconstructing the Grape", a sculpture commissioned for The Vineyard Spa. A vine-inspired steel balustrade elegantly dominates the restaurant and the luxurious interior is complemented by subtle attention to detail throughout with stunning china and glass designs. The 49 well-appointed bedrooms include 31 suites offering stylish comfort with distinctive character. The Vineyard Spa features an indoor pool, spa bath, sauna, steam room, gym and treatment rooms.

Our inspector loved: *This sophisticated light and airy hotel with its very special feel.*

Directions: From M4, exit Jct13, A34 towards Newbury, then Hungerford exit. 1st roundabout Hungerford exit, 2nd roundabout Stockcross exit. Hotel on right.

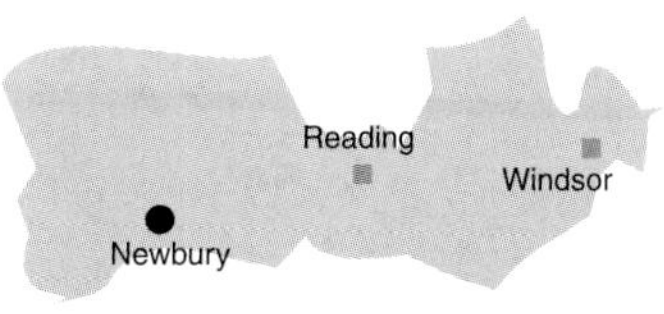

Web: www.johansens.com/vineyardstockcross
E-mail: general@the-vineyard.co.uk
Tel: 0870 381 8965
International: +44 (0)1635 528770
Fax: 01635 528398

Price Guide: (excluding VAT)
single/double/twin £169–£240
suite £310–£630

The Regency Park Hotel

BOWLING GREEN ROAD, THATCHAM, BERKSHIRE RG18 3RP

Directions: Between Newbury and Reading. Leave M4 at Jct12 or 13; the hotel is signposted on A4, on the western outskirts of Thatcham.

Web: www.johansens.com/regencypark
E-mail: info@regencyparkhotel.co.uk
Tel: 0870 381 8852
International: +44 (0)1635 871555
Fax: 01635 871571

Price Guide:
single £95–£229
double/twin £110–£229
suite £233–£385

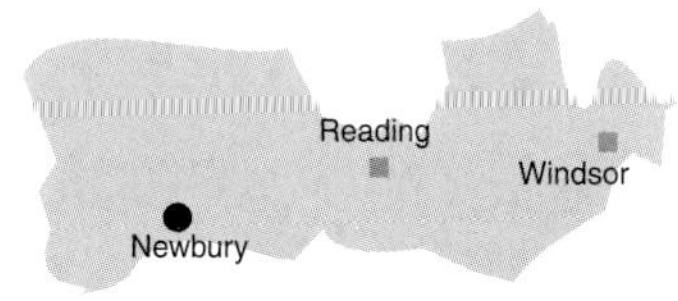

Ideally situated for access to both London and the South West, the Regency Park is a modern hotel that takes great pride in providing not only the most sophisticated facilities but combining them with the most attentive service and care. The style is neat and crisp with an understated elegance throughout, from the airy and spacious bedrooms to the array of meeting venues housed in the Business Centre. The Parkland Suite is a beautiful setting for any occasion, and with its own entrance and facilities for up to 200 guests it is the ideal place for wedding receptions and parties, as well as conferences and launches. "escape" is the name of the leisure complex, and true to its name it really is a place where state-of-the-art technology and sheer luxury meet to form a special feature. The serenity of the 17m swimming pool and the large health and beauty salon create an instantly relaxing atmosphere where fully qualified staff offer holistic health and beauty treatments. The Watermark Restaurant again has a contemporary elegance and attractive views over the waterfall gardens, reflected in its excellent menu of modern flavours and fusions. There is even a children's menu to ensure all guests are catered for. Weekend breaks available.

Our inspector loved: *The friendly, helpul staff in the cool, contemporary surround.*

       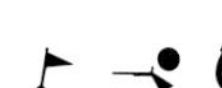 

The French Horn

SONNING-ON-THAMES, BERKSHIRE RG4 6TN

For over 150 years The French Horn, nestling beside the Thames near the historic village of Sonning with its pretty riverside walks,has provided a charming riverside retreat. Today, although busier on this stretch of the river, it continues that fine tradition of comfortable accommodation and outstanding cuisine in a beautiful setting. It is as ideal for a midweek or weekend break as it is for an executive meeting or private dinner. The bedrooms and suites are comfortable and homely and many have river views. The old panelled bar provides an intimate scene for pre-dinner drinks and the Condé Nast Johansens award winning restaurant with its' speciality of locally reared duck, spit roasted here over an open fire. By day the restaurant is a lovely setting for lunch, while by night diners can enjoy the floodlit view of the graceful weeping willows which fringe the river. Dinner is served by candlelight and the cuisine is a mixture of French and English cooking using the freshest ingredients, complemented by The French Horn's fine and extensive wine list. Places of interest in the area include Henley, Windsor Stratfield Saye, and Mapledurham. There are numerous golf courses, equestrian centres and fishing. Shooting can be arranged at Bisley, there are leisure facilities at the local nearby spa as well as local theatre to enjoy.

Our inspector loved: *The comfortable and charming atmosphere in a glorious setting.*

Directions: Leave the M4 at J8/9. Follow A404/M then at Thickets Roundabout turn left on A4 towards Reading for 8 miles. Turn right for Sonning. Cross Thames on B478. Hotel is on right.

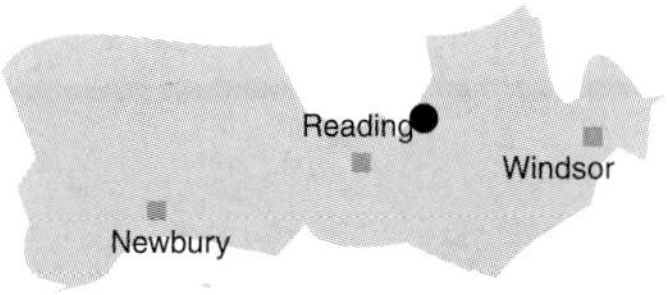

Web: www.johansens.com/frenchhorn
E-mail: info@thefrenchhorn.co.uk
Tel: 0870 381 8532
International: +44 (0)1189 692204
Fax: 01189 442210

Price Guide:
single £120–£165
double/twin £150–£205

NEW

The Great House

THAMES STREET, SONNING-ON-THAMES, NEAR READING, BERKSHIRE RG4 6UT

The enchanting village of Sonning lies on a beautiful stretch of the river, with the Thames path heading towards Oxford and London Bridge in either direction. One of the oldest villages in England it is steeped in history and is surprisingly accessible from London, Heathrow, Reading and the West Country. History enthusiasts will love its proximity to Windsor and bustling Henley, and the hotel itself has an interesting story of its own. Bedrooms are located in the original White Hart Hotel, the 16th-century Palace Yard and Hideaway Buildings, 17th-century Coach House and 19th-century Manor House. Each is individually designed and reflective of its period. One room has a four-poster bed, some are large enough to accommodate families and have river views. The Regatta Bar and Restaurant has a more contemporary feel and serves dishes influenced by the Mediterranean and Pacific Rim; al fresco dining is available in the summer. The Ferrymans Bar has an ambience of a traditional inn with warm fires in winter and regular Friday barbecues during the summer. There are moorings for up to 4 boats and boat owners are most welcome. The house has a "something for everyone" attitude and is popular for weddings, parties, functions and corporate meetings alike.

Our inspector loved: *The contemporary yet comfortable feel of this riverside hotel.*

Directions: From the M4 exit either at junction 8, 9 or 10 and take the A4. Sonning is situated 10 minutes from the A4 on the B478. The hotel is on the right just before the bridge.

Web: www.johansens.com/greathouse
E-mail: greathouse@btconnect.com
Tel: 0870 381 8374
International: +44 (0)118 9692277
Fax: 0118 9441296

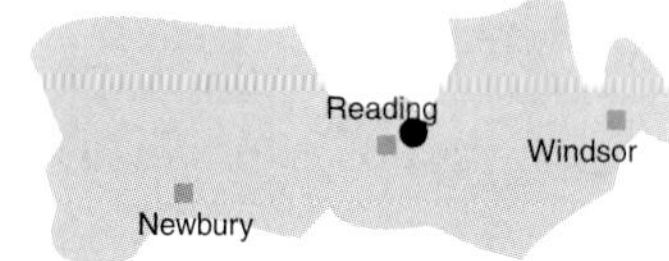

Price Guide:
single £59.50–£139
double £99–£169
suite £129–£189

Sir Christopher Wren's House Hotel & Wren's Club

THAMES STREET, WINDSOR, BERKSHIRE SL4 1PX

A friendly and welcoming atmosphere makes Sir Christopher Wren's House a perfect location for guests wanting to combine shopping and sightseeing with leisure. Built by the famous architect in 1676, it nestles beneath the ramparts and towers of Windsor Castle, beside the River Thames and Eton Bridge. The hotel combines antique furnishings with contemporary modern design. Additions to the original house, include a light and airy pavilion overlooking the Thames and Riverside "Champagne" terrace. There are 90 bedrooms available for guests, all beautifully and richly furnished – some feature a balcony and river view, others overlook the famous castle and there are character rooms in the mews. All offer a full range of amenities, including state-of-the-art technology. For longer stays guests may wish to use the hotels' apartments. Stroks Riverside Restaurant and attractive open terrace offers a good selection of beautifully cooked and well-presented meals. The hotel also has an excellent health and fitness gym with outdoor spa pool, and indulging beauty treatments. The Windsor area has a great deal to offer, among the many attractions within easy reach are Windsor Castle, Eton College, river excursions, Royal Ascot, Windsor racecourse, Thorpe Park, Henley, Savill Gardens and Legoland.

Our inspector loved: *The sumptuous rooms, the character and wonderful welcome.*

Directions: Windsor is just 2 miles from Jct 6 of the M4. Follow one-way system with River Thames on your left towards Datchet. Turn left into Thames Street. (Thames Street is pedestrianised).

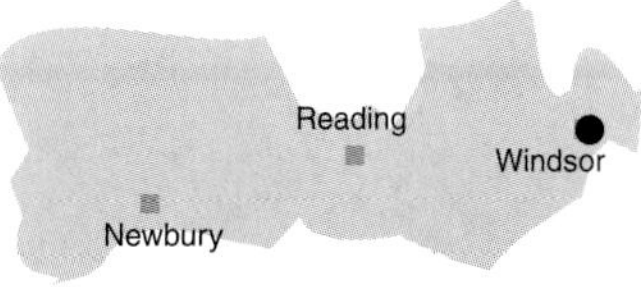

Web: www.johansens.com/sirchristopher
E-mail: reservations@wrensgroup.com
Tel: 0870 381 8896
International: +44 (0)1753 861354
Fax: 01753 860172

Price Guide:
single from £70–£160
double/twin from £80–£239
suite from £200–£292

NEW HALL

WALMLEY ROAD, ROYAL SUTTON COLDFIELD, WEST MIDLANDS B76 1QX

Reputedly the oldest moated manor house in England, generations have left their mark on New Hall, and the stonework, windows and ceilings are liberally sprinkled with coats of arms, emblems and inscriptions of those that have owned and cherished the property for nearly 800 years. Set on the edge of the Royal town of Sutton Coldfield and surrounded by 26 acres of private gardens and open parkland, the hotel strives to offer a taste of aristocratic living with a modern twist. The 60 beautifully furnished bedrooms include a number of suites and studios, and some have four-poster beds. Each guest room in the original house is named after a species of lily, some of which cover the moat in a blaze of colour from spring. Other special touches include a nightcap by the bed and luxurious marble tiled bathrooms with fluffy towels and complimentary toiletries. In the Bridge Restaurant, with its crackling log fire, exquisite English cuisine is served, created from quality local produce and with a flair that has earned it AA Rosettes. There is also an excellent choice of wines, both traditional and New World. Activities at the hotel include golf, tennis, archery, croquet and there is also a leisure spa.

Our inspector loved: *The grounds, the topiary and the moat, with its abundance of lilies.*

Directions: From exit 9 of the M42, follow the A4097 (ignoring signs to the A38 Sutton Coldfield). At the B4148 turn right at the traffic lights. New Hall is 1 mile on the left.

Web: www.johansens.com/newhall
E-mail: info@newhalluk.com
Tel: 0870 381 8756
International: +44 (0)121 378 2442
Fax: 0121 378 4637

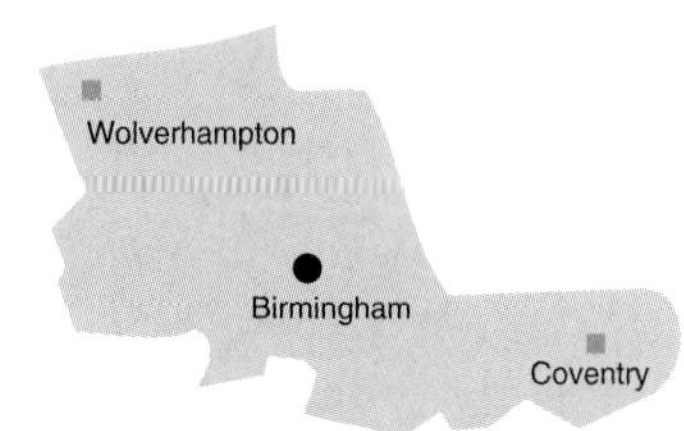

Price Guide:
single from £150
double/twin from £160
suite from £270

Hartwell House Hotel, Restaurant & Spa

OXFORD ROAD, NEAR AYLESBURY, BUCKINGHAMSHIRE HP17 8NL

Standing in 90 acres of gardens and parkland landscaped by a contemporary of Capability Brown, Hartwell House has both Jacobean and Georgian facades. This beautiful country house is a Grade 1 listed building, and was the residence in exile of King Louis XVIII of France from 1809 to 1814. The large ground floor reception rooms, with oak panelling and decorated ceilings, have antique furniture and fine paintings that evoke the elegance of the 18th century. There are 46 individually designed bedrooms and suites, 30 of which are non smoking in the main house and 16 in the Hartwell Court, the restored 18th century stables. The dining room at Hartwell is the setting for excellent food awarded 3 AA Rosettes and there are also 2 private dining rooms. The Old Rectory, Hartwell with its 2 acres of gardens, tennis court and swimming pool, provides superb accommodation and offers great comfort and privacy. The recently refurbished Hartwell Spa adjacent to the hotel includes an indoor heated pool, whirlpool spa bath, steam room, saunas, gymnasium and 4 beauty salons. Situated in the Vale of Aylesbury, the hotel is only 45 minutes from London Heathrow, one hour from London and 20 miles from Oxford. Blenheim Palace, Waddesdon Manor and Woburn Abbey are just some of the nearby attractions. Dogs are permitted only in Hartwell Court bedrooms. Owned and restored by Historic House Hotels Limited

Directions: Off the A418 between Oxford and Aylesbury. 2 miles from Aylesbury, 20 minutes from M40, Junction 7

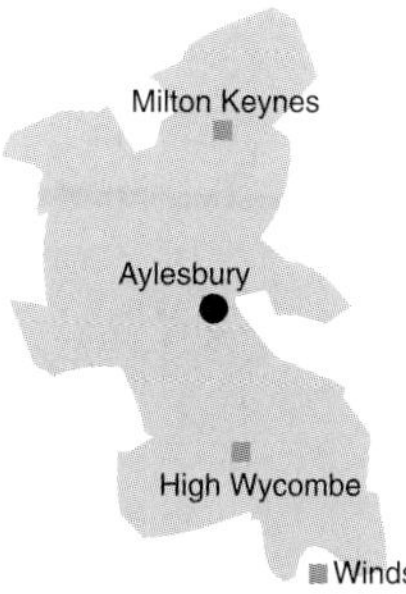

Web: www.johansens.com/hartwellhouse
E-mail: info@hartwell-house.com
Tel: 0870 381 8585
International: +44 (0)1296 747444
Fax: 01296 747450

Price Guide: (inc continental breakfast)
single from £165
double/twin from £270
suites from £370

Our inspector loved: *The grand old country house hotel "specialness".*

              SPA

DANESFIELD HOUSE HOTEL AND SPA

HENLEY ROAD, MARLOW-ON-THAMES, BUCKINGHAMSHIRE SL7 2EY

Danesfield House Hotel and Spa is set within 65 acres of gardens and parkland overlooking the River Thames, and boasts panoramic views across the Chiltern Hills. It is the third house since 1664 to occupy this lovely setting and was designed and built in sumptuous style at the end of the 19th century. The house has recently been fully refurbished and combines Victorian splendour with contemporary touches. The luxury bedrooms are all beautifully and richly decorated and furnished to include many facilities. Guests may relax in the magnificent Grand Hall, with its galleried library, in the sun-lit atrium or comfortable bar before taking dinner in one of the 2 restaurants. The 2 Rosette-awarded Oak Room and Orangery Brasserie both offer a choice of delicious cuisine. Leisure facilities include the award-winning spa with 20m pool, sauna, steam room, gymnasium and superb treatment rooms. Windsor Castle, Marlow, Henley and London are nearby, and the main motorway networks and Heathrow Airport are easily accessible. The hotel has 6 private banqueting and conference rooms.

Our inspector loved: *The sumptuous yet comfortable interior and glorious setting.*

Directions: Danesfield is situated between Henley-on-Thames and Marlow and is easily accessed by the M4 junction 8/9 and the M40.

Web: www.johansens.com/danesfieldhouse
E-mail: sales@danesfieldhouse.co.uk
Tel: 0870 381 8474
International: +44 (0)1628 891010
Fax: 01628 890408

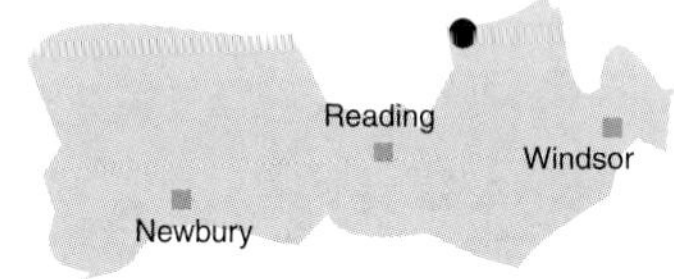

Price Guide:
single £215
double/twin £260
suites £300

STOKE PARK CLUB

PARK ROAD, STOKE POGES, BUCKINGHAMSHIRE SL2 4PG

Amidst 350 acres of sweeping parkland and gardens, Stoke Park Club is the epitome of elegance and style. For more than 900 years the estate has been at the heart of English heritage, playing host to lords, noblemen, kings and queens. History has left an indelible mark of prestige on the hotel and today it effortlessly combines peerless service with luxury. The magnificence of the Palladian mansion is echoed by the stunningly decorated interior where intricate attention to detail has been paid to the décor with antiques, exquisite fabrics and original paintings and prints ensuring that each room is a masterpiece of indulgence. All 21 individually furnished bedrooms and suites are complemented by marble en-suite bathrooms and some open onto terraces where an early evening drink can be enjoyed as the sun descends over the lakes and gardens. The Park Restaurant, and 8 beautiful function rooms, perfect for entertaining, also continue the theme of tasteful elegance. Since 1908 the hotel has been home to one of the finest 27-hole championship parkland golf courses in the world, Stoke Poges, and the addition of an all indulging spa, health and racquet pavilion re-affirms the hotel's position as one of the country's leading sporting venues. Luxury facilities include 11 beauty treatment rooms, indoor swimming pool, state-of-the-art gymnasium and studio and 13 tennis courts.

Our inspector loved: *The elegant bedrooms and fabulous spa.*

Directions: From the M4 take junction 6 or from the M40 take junction 2 then the A344. At the double roundabout at Farnham Royal take the B416. The entrance is just over 1 mile on the right.

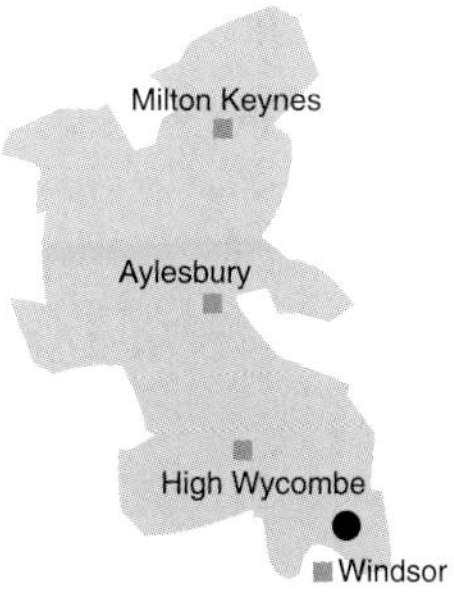

Milton Keynes
Aylesbury
High Wycombe
Windsor

Web: www.johansens.com/stokepark
E-mail: info@stokeparkclub.com
Tel: 0870 381 8915
International: +44 (0)1753 717171
Fax: 01753 717181

Price Guide:
single £285
suite from £595

21 120 SPA

HOTEL FELIX

WHITEHOUSE LANE, HUNTINGDON ROAD, CAMBRIDGE CB3 0LX

Hotel Felix combines Victorian and modern architecture and sits in landscaped gardens offering peaceful surroundings, yet is within minutes' reach of Cambridge with its famous contrast of high-tech science parks and beautiful medieval university buildings. The furniture in the hotel's public areas is bespoke and the décor is softly neutral with splashes of colour and carefully selected sculptures and artwork. All of the 52 en-suite bedrooms comprise king-sized beds and state-of-the-art communication facilities. Rooms have elegant proportions and are light and airy with high ceilings and views over the gardens. A restaurant and adjacent Café Bar act as a focal point and guests experience modern cuisine with a strong Mediterranean influence or continental coffees and pastries, fine teas, wine and champagne by the glass. Hotel Felix specialises in private corporate and celebration dining and its 4 meeting rooms with natural daylight and ISDN connections will accommodate 34 boardroom and 60 theatre style. Other activities to be enjoyed in Cambridge are visits to Kings College, the Botanical Gardens, Fitzwilliam Museum and punting on the River Cam. Nearby places of interest include Ely, Bury St Edmunds and the races at Newmarket.

Our inspector loved: *The romantic bedroom hidden away in the top of the house.*

Directions: 1 mile north of Cambridge city centre.

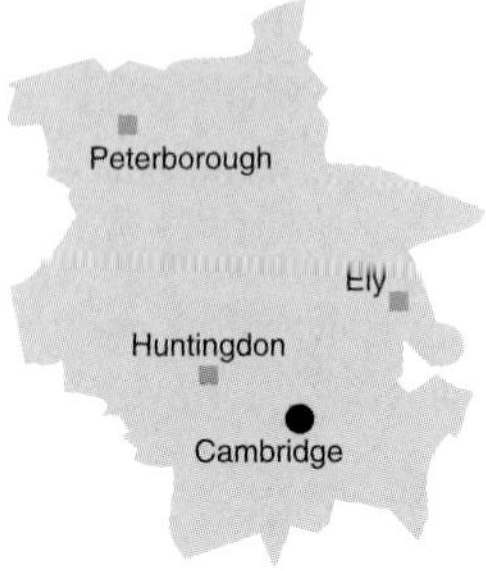

Peterborough
Ely
Huntingdon
Cambridge

Web: www.johansens.com/felix
E-mail: help@hotelfelix.co.uk
Tel: 0870 381 9056
International: +44 (0)1223 277977
Fax: 01223 277973

Price Guide:
single £132–£182
double/twin £163–£270

THE HAYCOCK

WANSFORD, PETERBOROUGH, CAMBRIDGESHIRE PE8 6JA

A traditional warmth and welcome invites guests to The Haycock, a beautiful 16th-century coaching inn steeped in history with great charm and character. The host to royal guests over the centuries, notable visitors include Mary Queen of Scotts in 1586, Princess Alexandra, Queen Victoria in 1832 and Princess Diana. Overlooking the historic bridge, which spans the River Nene, the hotel is set in a delightful village of unspoilt cottages. The Haycock's combination of sympathetic design and fine craftsmanship has created rooms that delight and relax in equal measure. All bedrooms are individually designed and equipped with modern amenities. Bentley's Fine Dining, and the more informal Orchards restaurant, offer superb food of international standard complemented by an interesting and outstanding wine selection. A purpose-built ballroom, with oak beams and private walled garden, is a popular venue for balls, weddings, product launches and conferences. The Business Centre is well equipped with every facility for the discerning businessman and offers flexibility. Places of interest nearby: Stamford, Burghley House, Nene Valley Railway, Elton Hall, Rutland Water and Peterborough Cathedral and Showground.

Our inspector loved: *The clever marriage of the traditional historic building with the stunning new interior.*

Directions: Clearly signposted on the A1, a few miles south of Stamford, on the A1/A47 intersection west of Peterborough.

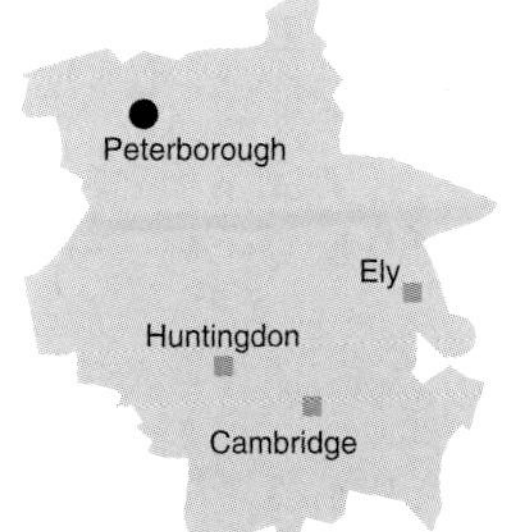

Web: www.johansens.com/haycock
E-mail: sales@thehaycock.co.uk
Tel: 0870 381 8587
International: +44 (0)1780 782223
Fax: 01780 783031

Price Guide:
single from £85
double/twin room from £119
four posters from £175
junior suite from £195

The Alderley Edge Hotel

MACCLESFIELD ROAD, ALDERLEY EDGE, CHESHIRE SK9 7BJ

Directions: Follow M6 to M56 Stockport. Exit Jct 6, take A538 to Wilmslow. Follow signs 1½ miles to Alderley Edge. Turn left at end of the main shopping area on to Macclesfield Rd (B5087). The hotel is 200 yards on the right. From M6 take Jct 18 and follow signs for Holmes Chapel and Alderley Edge.

Web: www.johansens.com/alderleyedge
E-mail: sales@alderleyedgehotel.com
Tel: 0870 381 8307
International: +44 (0)1625 583033
Fax: 01625 586343

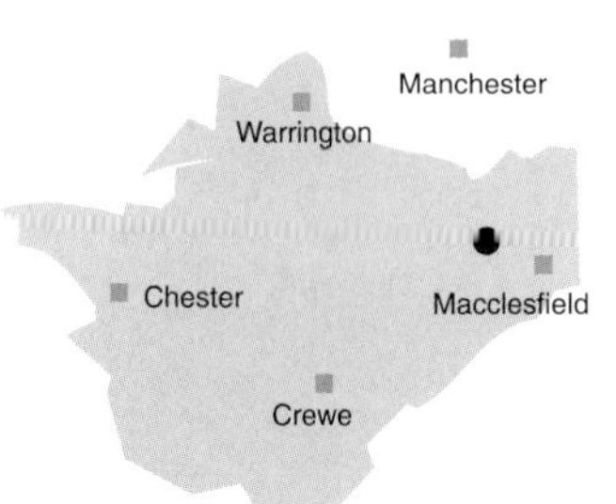

Price Guide:
single £55–£180
double £99–£260
suite from £250

This privately owned award-winning hotel has 52 bedrooms including the Presidential and Bridal Suites, which are beautifully decorated to a high standard. Located in the sumptuous conservatory, the restaurant offers exceptional views and the highest standards of cooking; fresh produce, including fish delivered daily, is provided by local suppliers. Specialities include hot and cold seafood dishes, puddings served piping hot from the oven and a daily selection of unusual and delicious breads, baked each morning in the hotel bakery. The food is complemented by an extensive wine list, featuring a wide range of champagnes and wines. Special wine and champagne dinners are held quarterly. In addition to the main conference room there is a suite of meeting and private dining rooms. The famous Edge walks are nearby, as are Tatton and Lyme Parks, Quarry Bank Mill and Dunham Massey. Manchester's thriving city centre is 15 miles away and the airport is a 20-minute drive.

Our inspector loved: *The dining experience in the Alderley Restaurant with its extensive list of champagnes and wines.*

The Chester Grosvenor and Spa

EASTGATE, CHESTER, CHESHIRE CH1 1LT

Located in the centre of Chester, this Grade II listed building has a black and white half timbered façade that belies the modern elegance of the interior. Awarded 5 Red Stars from the AA and 5 Stars from the RAC, this highly acclaimed hotel is just a short walk from the medieval galleried streets known as the "Rows", Roman Walls, Chester Cathedral and one of the oldest race courses in England. Each of the air-conditioned 80 guest bedrooms and suites is individually decorated and features a queen or king-size bed. Morning coffee, lunch and afternoon tea are all served in the relaxing and comfortable Library. The Arkle restaurant offers contemporary dining in an atmosphere of supreme elegance and features French cuisine with a modern twist. The restaurant has retained its Michelin Star for the fifteenth consecutive year and has one of the most extensive wine cellars in England. The less formal, Parisian-style La Brasserie provides an alternative dining option. The Grosvenor Spa offers both Western and Eastern treatments and comprises 5 treatment rooms. Facilities include: thermal suite, salt grotto, crystal steam room, ice fountain and herb sauna. For the more athletic, there is a fitness centre adjacent to the spa. Conference facilities for up to 250 delegates can be accommodated.

Our inspector loved: *The new innovative spa, which is an excellent addition to Chester's finest hotel.*

Directions: In the centre of Chester on Eastgate. 24-hour NCP car parking available – follow signs to Grosvenor Shopping Centre Car Park

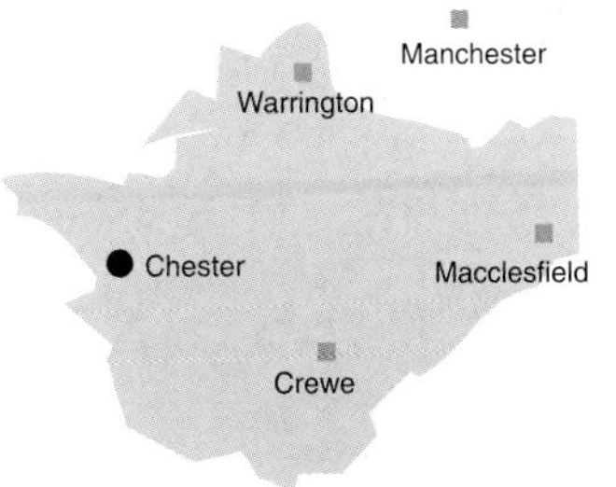

Web: www.johansens.com/chestergrosvenor
E-mail: hotel@chestergrosvenor.com
Tel: 0870 381 9264
International: +44 (0)1244 324024
Fax: 01244 313246

Price Guide:
double/twin from £190
suite from £340

Green Bough Hotel

60 HOOLE ROAD, CHESTER, CHESHIRE CH2 3NL

Proprietors Janice and Philip Martin have worked ceaselessly to create this friendly, relaxing haven, which is now Chester's premier small luxury hotel. The 15 sumptuous bedrooms and suites have been completely refurbished using Italian wall coverings and fabrics in keeping with the Roman theme which is evident throughout the hotel. Original oil paintings depicting scenes from a bygone era in Pompeii add to the exclusive ambience. Bedrooms feature original antique cast-iron beds and some have four-posters, plasma televisions, CD players and Jacuzzi baths. There are 7 deluxe bedrooms and 1 master suite in the Lodge. This totally non-smoking hotel enjoys an outstanding reputation reflected in the prestigious awards it has accumulated: Regional Small Hotel of the Year 2005, RAC Gold Ribbon, ETC Gold Award, Excellence in England Finalist 2003. The Olive Tree restaurant offers a fine dining experience bringing together an eclectic mix of aromas and flavours to produce imaginative and innovative dishes for the daily changing table d'hôte menu, which is complemented by wines from the extensive cellar. The hotel is located within walking distance of the ancient and historic city of Chester and centrally placed for easy access to Snowdonia, Cumbria, Manchester and Liverpool. There is ample off-road free parking.

Directions: Leave M53 at Jct12. Take A56 into Chester for 1 mile. The Green Bough Hotel is on the right.

Web: www.johansens.com/greenbough
E-mail: luxury@greenbough.co.uk
Tel: 0870 381 8571
International: +44 (0)1244 326241
Fax: 01244 326265

Price Guide:
single from £95
double/twin from £130
suites from £185

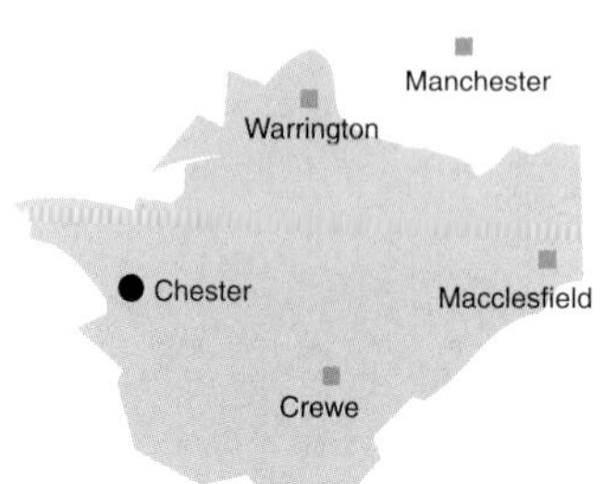

Our inspector loved: *The Roman theme prevalent throughout the hotel.*

Nunsmere Hall

TARPORLEY ROAD, OAKMERE, NORTHWICH, CHESHIRE CW8 2ES

Set in peaceful Cheshire countryside and surrounded on three sides by a lake, Nunsmere Hall epitomises the elegant country manor where superior standards of hospitality still exist. Wood panelling, antique furniture, exclusive fabrics, Chinese lamps and magnificent chandeliers evoke an air of luxury. The 29 bedrooms and 7 junior suites, most with spectacular views of the lake and gardens, are beautifully appointed with king-size beds, comfortable breakfast seating and marbled bathrooms containing soft bathrobes and toiletries. The Brocklebank, Delamere and Oakmere business suites are air-conditioned, soundproofed and offer excellent facilities for boardroom meetings, private dining and seminars. The restaurant has a reputation for fine food and uses only fresh seasonal produce. Twice County Restaurant of the Year in the Good Food Guide. A snooker room is available and there are several championship golf courses nearby. Oulton Park racing circuit and the Cheshire Polo Club are next door. Golf pitch and putt is available in the grounds. Archery and air rifle shooting by arrangement. Although secluded, Nunsmere is convenient for major towns and routes. AA 3 Red Star and 2 Rosettes.

Our inspector loved: *This elegant country house surrounded by its own lake.*

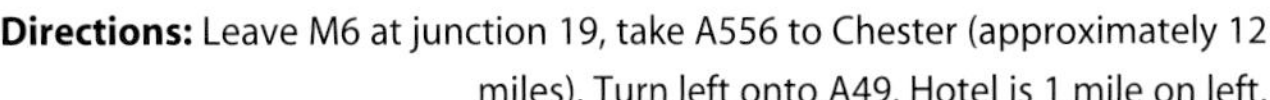

Directions: Leave M6 at junction 19, take A556 to Chester (approximately 12 miles). Turn left onto A49. Hotel is 1 mile on left.

Web: www.johansens.com/nunsmerehall
E-mail: reservations@nunsmere.co.uk
Tel: 0870 381 8772
International: +44 (0)1606 889100
Fax: 01606 889055

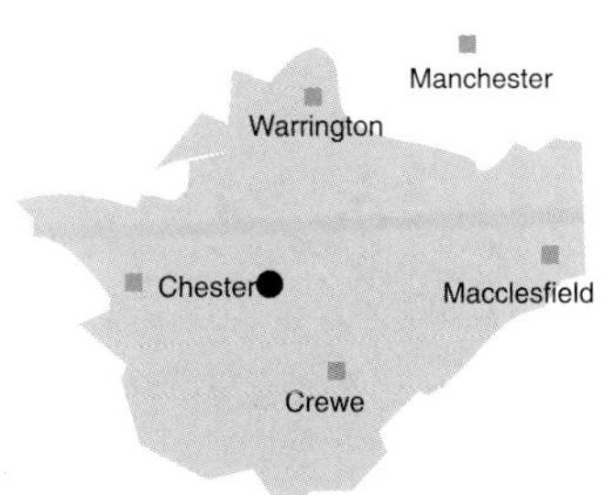

Price Guide:
single £145–£170
double/twin £200–£237
junior suites £260–£360

Rowton Hall Hotel, Health Club & Spa

WHITCHURCH ROAD, ROWTON, CHESTER, CHESHIRE CH3 6AD

Set in over 8 acres of award-winning gardens, Rowton Hall is located at the end of a leafy lane, only a mile from Chester. Built as a private residence in 1779, it retains many of its original features, including extensive oak panelling, a self-supporting hand-carved staircase, an original Inglenook fireplace and an elegant Robert Adam fireplace. Each luxury bedroom is individually and tastefully decorated with attention to detail, and is equipped with every modern amenity, including private bathroom, satellite television, broadband and voice mail, personal safe, luxury bathrobes, trouser press and hostess tray. Dining in the oak-panelled Langdale Restaurant is a delight; every dish is carefully created by head chef, Matt Hulmes, who uses the finest ingredients from local markets and the Hall's gardens to produce exquisite cuisine. Guests can enjoy the Health Club with swimming pool and spa, relax in the Jacuzzi, sauna and steam room. For the more energetic, a workout in the well-equipped gymnasium and dance studio is available and 2 floodlit all-weather tennis courts are within the grounds. Four main conference and banqueting suites make the Hall an ideal venue for meetings, weddings, private dining or conferences and corporate events for up to 200 guests. Marquee events can be arranged in the gardens. Special offers available.

Our inspector loved: *The new health club, gym and spa.*

Directions: From the centre of Chester, take A41 towards Whitchurch. After 3 miles, turn right to Rowton village. The hotel is in the centre of the village.

Web: www.johansens.com/rowtonhall
E-mail: rowtonhall@rowtonhall.co.uk
Tel: 0870 381 8871
International: +44 (0)1244 335262
Fax: 01244 335464

Price Guide:
single £135–£375
double/twin £145–£385
suites £335–£500

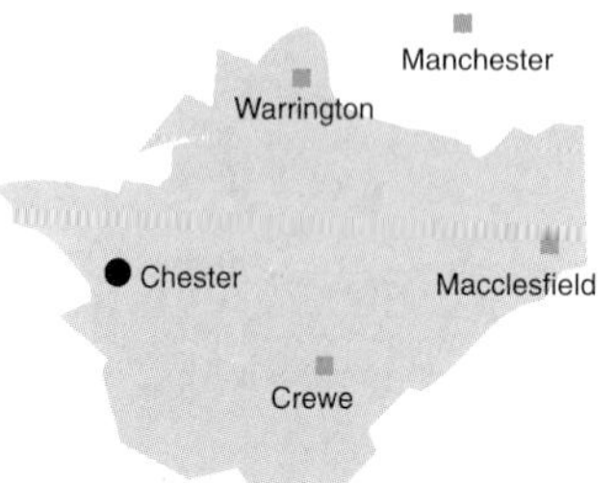

Crewe Hall

WESTON ROAD, CREWE, CHESHIRE CW1 6UZ

Set in vast, impressive grounds, the magnificent Crewe Hall is the jewel of Cheshire. Once the seat of the Earls of Crewe and owned by the Queen as part of the estate of the Duchy of Lancaster, this stately home transports guests back to an age of splendour and luxury where quality and service were imperative. An exquisite Jacobean carving, which adorns the lavish main entrance, is reflected over the whole exterior from the balustraded terraces to the tip of the tall West Wing Tower. Crewe Hall's beautiful interior boats a confident juxtaposition between the traditional and modern. The newly refurbished and air-conditioned west wing, with its stylish, contemporary décor, is contrasted with the traditional home rooms, which have magnificent panelling and marble, huge stone fireplaces, intricate carvings, stained glass and antique furniture. Regarded as one of the finest specimens of Elizabethan architecture, the staircase in the East Hall climbs majestically upwards. Guests can dine in the quiet, elegant dining room or the informal Brasserie, which has a unique revolving bar (whose smooth motion means you will not notice you are moving until the view has suddenly changed) and offers imaginative, delicious meals complemented by international beers and wines.

Our inspector loved: *The eclectic mix of the traditional and modern in this Jacobean mansion.*

Directions: From the M6, exit at junction 16 and follow the A500 towards Crewe. At the first roundabout take the last exit. At the next roundabout take the first exit. After ¼ mile turn right into the drive.

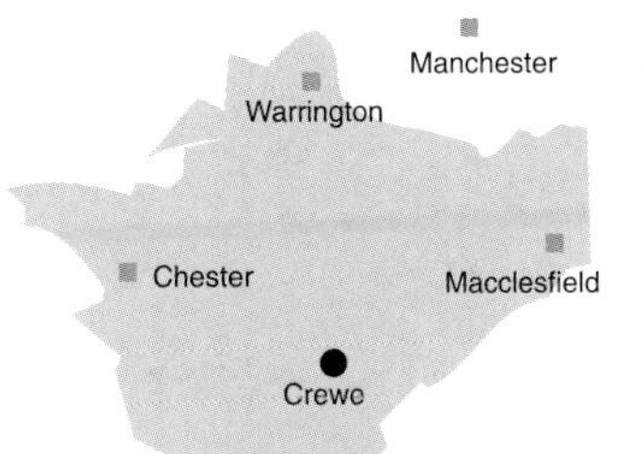

Web: www.johansens.com/crewehall
E-mail: crewehall@marstonhotels.com
Tel: 0870 381 8458
International: +44 (0)1270 253333
Fax: 01270 253322

Price Guide:
single £219–£440
double/twin £233–£459
suite £270–£459

HILLBARK HOTEL

ROYDEN PARK, FRANKBY, WIRRAL CH48 1NP

Directions: Take M53, jct 3 for A552. Then take A551 towards Upton. After the hospital turn left onto Arrowe Brook Road then left onto Arrowe Brook Lane. Travel over the roundabout and Hillbark is on the left.

Web: www.johansens.com/hillbark
E-mail: enquiries@hillbarkhotel.co.uk
Tel: 0870 381 9128
International: +44 (0)151 625 2400
Fax: 0151 625 4040

Price Guide:
single from £175
double/twin £175–£250
suite £250–£500

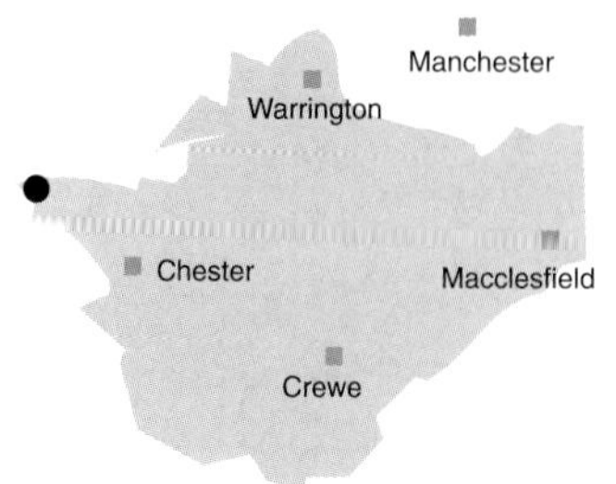

In the heart of the beautiful Wirral Peninsula, just 15 minutes, yet seeming a million miles away, from vibrant Liverpool and historic Chester, this Grade II listed hotel provides the finest luxury coupled with discreet yet friendly service. Set in 250 acres of beautiful parkland overlooking the scenic Dee Estuary across to the hills of North Wales, Hillbark's character appearance hides a fascinating history. The house was originally built in 1891 in Birkenhead for the soap manufacturer Robert William Hudson, a founder of Lever Fabergé. It was sold in 1921 to Cunard shipping magnate Sir Ernest Royden, and was then moved in 1928 to its present site, brick by brick, finally being completed in 1931.The house contains many interesting features: the Great Hall has a 1527 Jacobean fireplace from Sir Walter Raleigh's house in Ireland; a set of William Morris stained-glass windows and a pair of 13th-century church screen doors; the library was originally in a stately home in Gloucestershire; and the Yellow Room restaurant contains a 1795 Robert Adam fire surround. Delicious, imaginative haute cuisine is served in the opulent Yellow Room restaurant and stylish Hillbark Grill, with a 300-bin cellar. Suites and bedrooms are individually designed and lavishly furnished. Leisure activities include world-class golf and windsurfing. Rolls-Royce and Bentley cars are available to collect guests from airports and rail stations.

Our inspector loved: *The oak panelling in this Elizabethan-style house.*

Mere Court Hotel

WARRINGTON ROAD, MERE, KNUTSFORD, CHESHIRE WA16 0RW

This attractive Edwardian house stands in 7 acres of mature gardens and parkland in one of the loveliest parts of Cheshire. Maintained as a family home since being built in 1903, Mere Court has been skilfully restored into a fine country house hotel offering visitors a peaceful ambience in luxury surroundings. Comforts and conveniences of the present mix excellently with the ambience and many original features of the past. The bedrooms have views over the grounds or ornamental lake. All are individually designed and a number of them have a Jacuzzi spa bath and mini bar. Facilities include safes, personalised voice mail telephones and modem points. Heavy ceiling beams, polished oak panelling and restful waterside views are features of the elegant Aboreum Restaurant, which serves the best of traditional English and Mediterranean cuisines. Lighter meals can be enjoyed in the Lounge Bar. The original coach house has been converted into a designated conference centre with state-of-the-art conference suites and syndicate rooms accommodating up to 120 delegates. The addition of the lakeside Conservatory gives the hotel added space for weddings and functions accommodating up to 180 guests. Warrington, Chester, Manchester Airport and many National Trust properties are within easy reach.

Our inspector loved: *The oak-panelled restaurant overlooking the ornamental lake.*

Directions: From M6, exit at junction 19. Take A556 towards Manchester. After 1 mile turn left at traffic lights onto A50 towards Warrington. Mere Court is on the right.

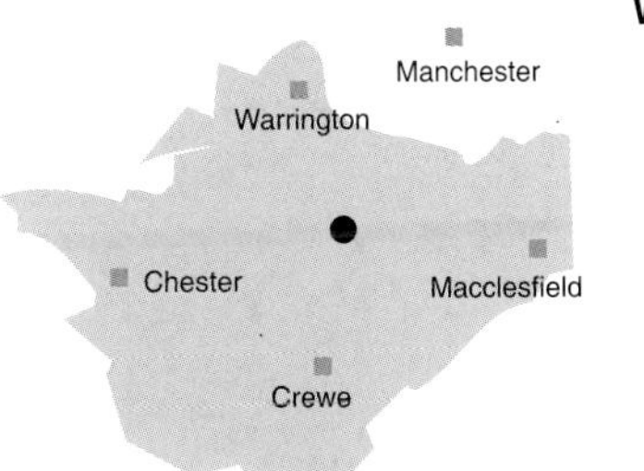

Web: www.johansens.com/merecourt
E-mail: sales@merecourt.co.uk
Tel: 0870 381 8727
International: +44 (0)1565 831000
Fax: 01565 831001

Price Guide:
single £130–£147
double/twin £154–£200

THE NARE HOTEL

CARNE BEACH, VERYAN-IN-ROSELAND, TRURO, CORNWALL TR2 5PF

Peace, tranquillity and stunning sea views make The Nare a real find. Superbly positioned, the hotel overlooks the fine sandy beach of Gerrans Bay, facing south and sheltered by The Nare and St Mawes headlands. In recent years extensive refurbishments have ensured comfort and elegance without detracting from the country house charm of this friendly family-run hotel. All bedrooms are close to the sea, many with patios and balconies taking advantage of the spectacular outlook. In the main dining room guests can enjoy the sea views from 3 sides of the room where local seafood, such as lobster and delicious homemade puddings, are served with Cornish cream, complemented by an interesting range of wines. The Quarterdeck Restaurant is open all day serving morning coffee, light luncheons, cream teas and offers relaxed dining in the evening. The Nare remains the highest rated AA 4 star hotel in the south west with 2 Rosettes for its food. Surrounded by subtropical gardens and National Trust land the hotel's seclusion is ideal for exploring the coastline and villages of the glorious Roseland Peninsula. It is also central for many of Cornwall's beautiful houses and gardens including the famous Heligan. Guests arriving by train or air are met, without charge, by prior arrangement, at Truro Station or Newquay Airport. The hotel is open throughout the year, including Christmas and New Year.

Our inspector loved: *The location , year round facilities and fine dining .*

Directions: Follow the road to St Mawes. 2 miles after Tregony Bridge turn left for Veryan. The hotel is 1 mile beyond Veryan.

Web: www.johansens.com/nare
E-mail: office@narehotel.co.uk
Tel: 0870 381 8755
International: +44 (0)1872 501111
Fax: 01872 501856

Price Guide:
single £96-£183
double/twin £182-£336
suite £324-£530

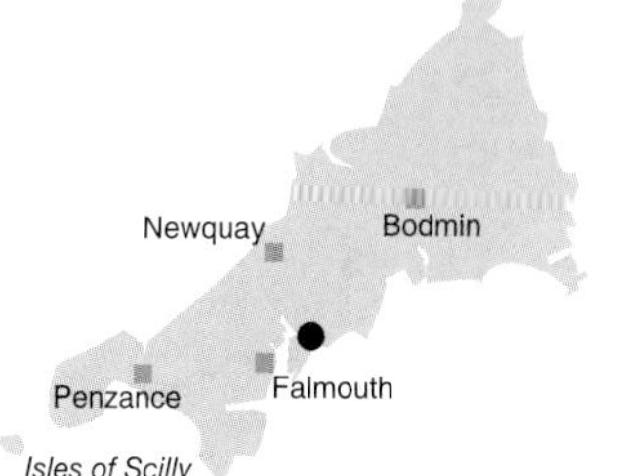

40 60 SPA

THE GREENBANK HOTEL

HARBOURSIDE, FALMOUTH, CORNWALL TR11 2SR

Surrounded by the vibrant atmosphere of Falmouth, the Greenbank is the only hotel on the banks of one of the world's largest and deepest natural harbours. Because of its position as a ferry point to Flushing, its history stretches back to the 17th century, and visitors have included Florence Nightingale and Kenneth Grahame, whose letters from the hotel to his son formed the basis for his book "The Wind in the Willows". Seaward views from the hotel are stunning, and reaching out from each side are lovely clifftop paths leading to secluded coves where walkers can relax while enjoying a paddle in clear blue waters and breathing in fresh, clean sea air. Most of the charming, delightfully furnished and well equipped en-suite bedrooms enjoy panoramic views across the harbour to Flushing and St Mawes. Recently granted 3 Dining Awards by the RAC, the Harbourside Restaurant will satisfy the keenest of appetites with a variety of dishes which include local seafood landed at the hotel's private quay . There are opportunities locally for golf, sailing, riding and fishing. Interesting places nearby include Cornwall's National Maritime Museum, several heritage sites and many National Trust properties and gardens.

Our inspector loved: *The magnificent location and breathtaking views across Falmouth harbour's ever changing scenery.*

Directions: Take the A39 from Truro and on approaching Falmouth join the Old Road going through Penryn. Turn left at the second roundabout where the hotel is signposted.

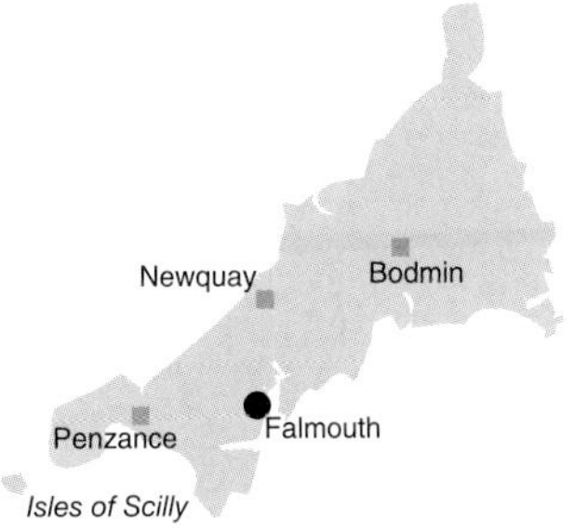

Newquay
Bodmin
Penzance
Falmouth
Isles of Scilly

Web: www.johansens.com/greenbank
E-mail: sales@greenbank-hotel.com
Tel: 0870 381 8573
International: +44 (0)1326 312440
Fax: 01326 211362

Price Guide:

single £70–£100
double/twin £110–£185
suite £195–£245

St Michael's Hotel & Spa

GYLLYNGVASE BEACH, FALMOUTH, CORNWALL TR11 4NB

Directions: Take A39 to Falmouth then follow signs for beaches and hotels. Travel over the first roundabout and turn right at the second. At the end turn left into Spernen Road, then left into Stracey. The hotel is 400m on the right.

Web: www.johansens.com/stmichaelsfalmouth
E-mail: info@stmichaelshotel.co.uk
Tel: 0870 381 8399
International: +44 (0)1326 312707
Fax: 01326 211772

Price Guide:
single £40–£100
double/twin £80–£195
suite £110–£270

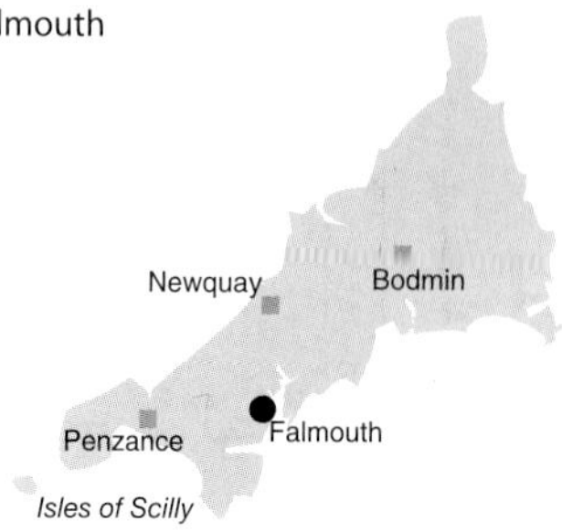

Newquay
Bodmin
Penzance
Falmouth
Isles of Scilly

Set in 4 acres of tranquil, subtropical gardens, with stunning views of the beautiful Cornish coastline, St Michael's Hotel & Spa is a place that guests return to time and time again. The property has undergone an extensive £2 million refurbishment programme that has resulted in a state-of-the-art health club and spa, award-winning restaurants and modernized bedrooms, bars and conference suites. The main restaurant, Oyster Bay, focuses on fresh fish and seafood, with a menu that regularly changes to utilize the best seasonal Cornish produce. The informal Flying Fish Bar and Grill serves fresh, exciting dishes in contemporary surroundings, and also provides a superb children's menu. The exotic grounds form the perfect backdrop for a magical wedding, and the hotel offers a variety of rooms to suit large conferences or small meetings. Set within the gardens, the newly created St Michael's Spa provides an impressive range of health, beauty and relaxation treatments. Guests can also enjoy the sauna, Jacuzzi and steam room, take a dip in the large heated indoor swimming pool or relax on the timber sundeck overlooking the sea. Visitors will find plenty to do in the surrounding area with a sandy blue flag beach directly opposite the hotel, the National Maritime Museum a short walk away, and the Eden Project within an hour's drive.

Our inspector loved: *The location, and superb nautical presentation.*

SPA

Budock Vean - The Hotel on the River

NEAR HELFORD PASSAGE, MAWNAN SMITH, FALMOUTH, CORNWALL TR11 5LG

This family-run, 4-star Cornwall Tourist Board Hotel of the Year 2002, 2003 and 2004, is nestled in 65 acres of award-winning gardens and parkland with a private foreshore on the tranquil Helford River. Set in a designated area of breathtaking natural beauty, the hotel is a destination in itself with outstanding leisure facilities and space to relax and be pampered. The AA Rosette restaurant offers excellent cuisine using the finest local produce to create exciting and imaginative 5-course dinners, with fresh seafood being a speciality. On site are a golf course, large indoor swimming pool, tennis courts, a billiard room, boating, fishing, and the Natural Health Spa. Awarded the South West Tourism Large Hotel of the Year 2003. The local ferry will take guests from the hotel's jetty to waterside pubs, to Frenchman's Creek or to hire a boat. The hotel also takes out guests on its own 32-foot "Sunseeker". A myriad of magnificent country and coastal walks from the wild grandeur of Kynance and the Lizard to the peace and tranquillity of the Helford itself, as well as several of the Great Gardens of Cornwall, are in the close vicinity.

Our inspector loved: *The latest refurbished bedrooms and as always the peace and tranquillity in a magnificent location.*

Directions: From the A39, Truro to Falmouth road, follow the brown tourist signs for Trebah Garden. Budock Vean appears ½ mile after passing Trebah on the left-hand side.

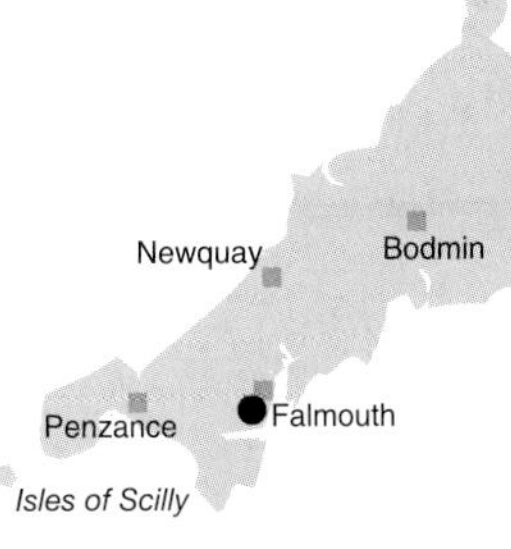

Web: www.johansens.com/budockvean
E-mail: relax@budockvean.co.uk
Tel: 0870 381 8392
International: reservations+44 (0)1326 252100
Fax: 01326 250892

Price Guide: (including dinner)
single £70–£115
double/twin £140–£230
suites £236–£300

57 50

MEUDON HOTEL

MAWNAN SMITH, NR FALMOUTH, CORNWALL TR11 5HT

Set against a delightfully romantic backdrop of densely wooded countryside between the Fal and Helford Rivers, Meudon Hotel is a unique, family-run, superior retreat with sub-tropical gardens leading to its own private sea beach. The French name originates from a nearby farmhouse built by Napoleonic prisoners of war and called after their eponymous home village in the environs of Paris. 9 acres of sub-tropical gardens are coaxed into early bloom by the Gulf Stream and mild Cornish climate; Meudon is safely surrounded by 200 acres of beautiful National Trust land and the sea. All bedrooms are in a modern wing, have en-suite bathrooms and each enjoys spectacular garden views. Many a guest is enticed by the cuisine to return; in the restaurant fresh seafood, caught by local fishermen, is served with wines from a judiciously compiled list. Rich in natural beauty with a myriad of watersports and country pursuits to indulge in, you can play golf free at nearby Falmouth Golf Club and 5 others in Cornwall, sail aboard the hotel's skipperd 34-foot yacht or just laze on the beach.

Our inspector loved: *The newly presented en-suite bedrooms and magnificent gardens.*

Directions: From Truro A39 torwards Falmouth at Hillhead roundabout take 2nd exit. The hotel is 4 miles on the left.

Web: www.johansens.com/meudon
E-mail: wecare@meudon.co.uk
Tel: 0870 381 8730
International: +44 (0)1326 250541
Fax: 01326 250543

Price Guide: (including dinner)
single £120
double/twin £240
suite £330

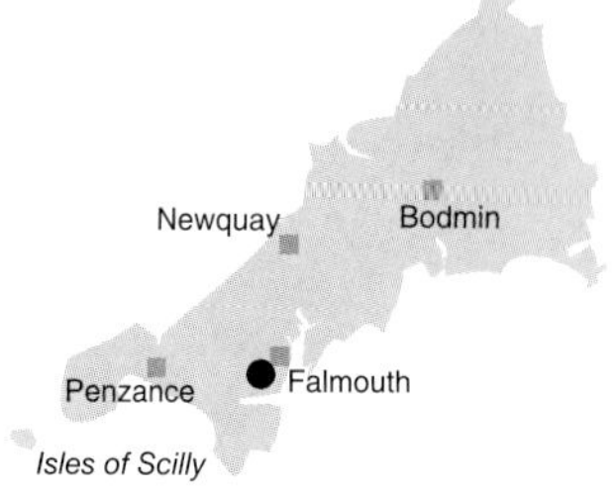

25

Fowey Hall Hotel & Restaurant

HANSON DRIVE, FOWEY, CORNWALL PL23 1ET

Situated in five acres of beautiful grounds overlooking the Estuary, Fowey Hall Hotel is a magnificent Victorian mansion renowned for its excellent service and comfortable accommodation. The fine panelling and superb plasterwork ceilings add character to the spacious public rooms. Located in either the main house or the Court, the 24 bedrooms include 12 suites and interconnecting rooms. All are well-proportioned with a full range of modern comforts. The panelled dining rooms provide an intimate atmosphere where guests may savour the local delicacies. Using the best of regional produce, the menu comprises tempting seafood and fish specialities. The hotel offers a full complimentary crèche service. Guests may swim in the indoor swimming pool or play croquet in the gardens. Older children have not been forgotten and "The Garage" in the courtyard is well-equipped with table tennis, table football and many other games. Also a new cinema room with a 42" plasma screen showing the latest childrens movies. Outdoor pursuits include sea fishing, boat trips and a variety of water sports such as sailing, scuba-diving and windsurfing. There are several coastal walks for those who wish to explore Cornwall and its beautiful landscape.

Our inspector loved: *This wonderful friendly hotel for families and all the other first class facilities offered.*

Directions: On reaching Fowey, go straight over 3 mini roundabouts and follow the road all the way eventually taking a sharp right bend, take the next left turn and Fowey Hall drive is on the right.

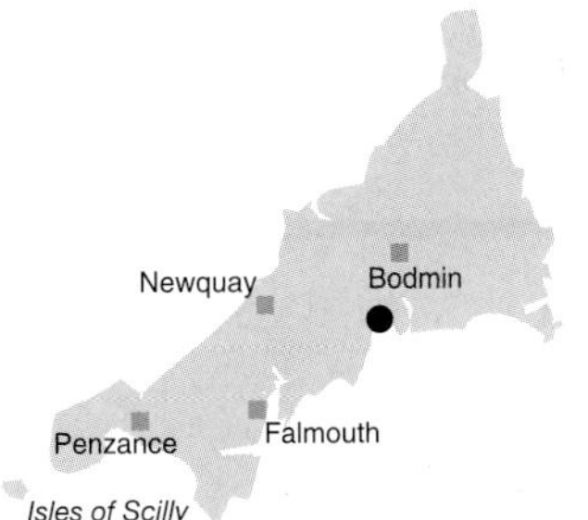

Web: www.johansens.com/foweyhall
E-mail: info@foweyhall.com
Tel: 0870 381 8529
International: +44 (0)1726 833866
Fax: 01726 834100

Price Guide: (min 2 nights incl dinner)
double/twin £160–£285 per night
suite £195–£450 per night

Trenython Manor Hotel & Spa

TYWARDREATH, NEAR FOWEY, CORNWALL PL24 2TS

Standing in one of the premier locations on the Cornish coast, set in beautiful grounds overlooking St Austell Bay, Trenython Manor Hotel & Spa offers fine dining, luxurious accommodation and total relaxation. This 17th-century manor has a unique ambience, and a tasteful renovation, completed to the highest standard, has successfully combined Italian style with English charm. Originally commissioned by Giuseppe Garibaldi, Trenython was awarded to Colonel Peard, who commanded the "English Thousand Legion" and in 1891, Bishop Gott, the third bishop of Truro, bought the house and it remained a Bishop's palace for 15 years. Guests may dine in the contemporary bistro or in the fine dining restaurant where magnificent oak panelling, sourced from York Minster and Worcester Cathedral, dates from the 16th century. Guests may also admire General Wolf's headboard, Lord Nelson's sea chest and fine Italian marbles, sent over by Garibaldi. The hotel is located 3.5 miles from the Eden Project and is ideally situated for visiting Cornwall's National Trust properties, gardens and spectacular coastline. Numerous outdoor activities can be arranged by the hotel including fishing shooting and private guided tours, alternatively, visit the hotel's health and beauty salon and indoor leisure facilities.

Directions: From Exeter join the A30 towards Cornwall then the B3269 signposted Lostwithiel. Take the A390 St Austell/Fowey B3269 and follow signs to Fowey for approximately 4 miles. The hotel is then signposted.

Web: www.johansens.com/trenython
E-mail: enquiries@trenython.co.uk
Tel: 0870 381 9139
International: +44 (0)1726 814797
Fax: 01726 817030

Price Guide:
single from £110
double £130-£240

Our inspector loved: *The location, comfort and superb cuisine.*

Hell Bay

BRYHER, ISLES OF SCILLY, CORNWALL TR23 0PR

Bryher is the smallest community of the Isles of Scilly, 28 miles west of Land's End, and Hell Bay its only hotel. It stands in a spectacular and dramatic setting in extensive lawned grounds on the rugged West Coast overlooking the unbroken Atlantic Ocean. Described as a "spectacularly located getaway-from-it-all destination that is a paradise for adults and children alike" .. and it is. Outdoor heated swimming pool, gym, sauna, spa bath, children's playground, games room and par 3 golf course ensure there is never a dull moment. Daily boat trips are available so that you can discover the islands, the world famous tropical Abbey Garden is on the neighbouring island of Tresco. White sanded beaches abound with an array of water sports available. Dining is an integral part of staying at Hell Bay and the food will not disappoint; as you would expect, seafood is a speciality. Out of season breaks available and open for Christmas and New Year.

Our inspector loved: *From stepping off the boat on arrival - the perfect haven*

Directions: The Isles of Scilly are reached by helicopter or boat from Penzance or fixed-wing aircraft from Southampton, Bristol, Exeter, Newquay and Lands End. The hotel can make all necessary travel arrangements and will co-ordinate all transfers to Bryher on arrival.

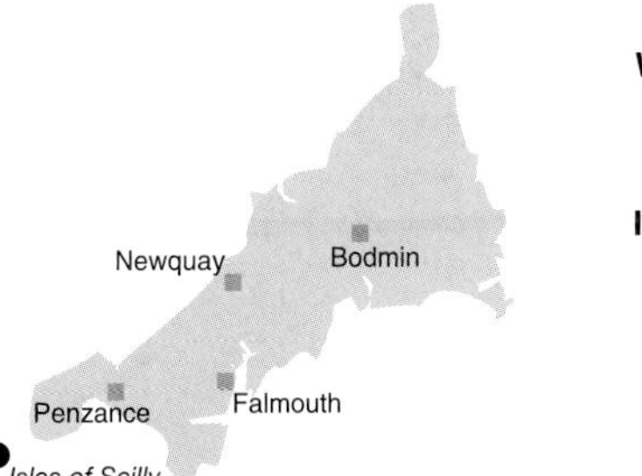

Web: www.johansens.com/hellbay
E-mail: contactus@hellbay.co.uk
Tel: 0870 381 8591
International: +44 (0)1720 422947
Fax: 01720 423004

Price Guide: (including dinner)
suites £220–£440

Talland Bay Hotel

PORTHALLOW, CORNWALL PL13 2JB

Directions: The hotel is signposted from the A387 Looe–Polperro road.

Web: www.johansens.com/tallandbay
E-mail: info@tallandbayhotel.co.uk
Tel: 0870 381 8937
International: +44 (0)1503 272667
Fax: 01503 272940

Price Guide:
single £90–£145
double/twin £130–£195

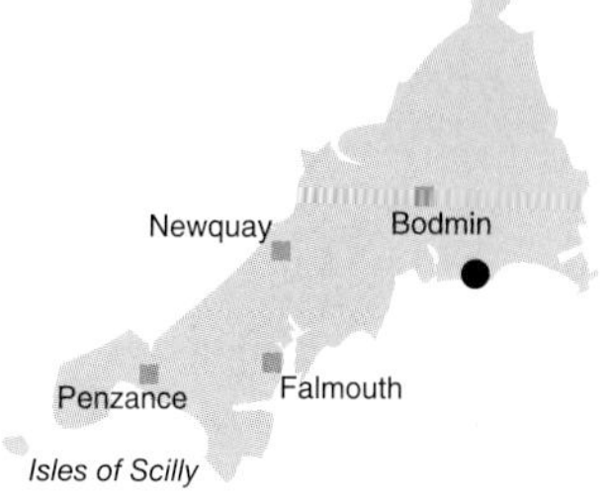

Surrounded by 2 acres of beautiful sub-tropical gardens and with dramatic views over Talland Bay, this lovely old Cornish manor house is a real gem. Each of the 23 bedrooms has its own individual character and is traditionally furnished. Many offer stunning views of the sea and the garden's magnificent Monterey pines. In the bathrooms, fluffy bathrobes and Molton Brown toiletries are just some of the extra touches that are the hotel's hallmark. The award-winning, 2 AA Rosetted restaurant, has recently gained the accolade Restaurant Newcomer of the Year for Cornwall from the Good Food Guide. The menu is essentially modern British and incorporates high quality, fresh local produce complemented by fine wines specially selected by the owners. The hotel organises a number of exclusive weekends combining gourmet food with superb entertainment – such as an evening of jazz or classical music or a wine masterclass with one of the world's leading experts. Talland Bay is also noted for its splendid Christmas and New Year "house party" breaks. There are fabulous coastal walks all year round while, in summer, putting and croquet can be played on the beautiful lawns and the heated outdoor swimming pool, with its south-facing terrace, is a constant temptation. In the winter, there is a chance to read that favourite book by a roaring log fire.

Our inspector loved: *The tasteful menus sourced from local produce.*

The Rosevine Hotel

PORTHCURNICK BEACH, PORTSCATHO, ST MAWES, TRURO, CORNWALL TR2 5EW

At the heart of Cornwall's breathtaking Roseland Peninsula, the Rosevine is an elegant and gracious late Georgian hotel that offers visitors complete comfort and peace. The Rosevine stands in its own landscaped grounds overlooking Portscatho Harbour, a traditional Cornish fishing village. The superbly equipped bedrooms are delightfully designed, with some benefiting from direct access into the gardens and from their own private patio. This is the only hotel in Cornwall to hold the awards of 3 AA Red Stars and the RAC Blue Ribbon and Triple Dining Rosettes. The restaurant serves exceptional food, using the freshest seafood and locally grown produce. After dining, guests can relax in any of the 3 tastefully and comfortably presented lounges, bathe in the spacious indoor heated pool, or read in the hotel's well stocked library. Visitors to the region do not forget the walks to the charming villages dotted along the Roseland Peninsula, and the golden sand of the National Trust maintained beach, which immediately faces the hotel. Children and family holdays are especially catered for. Visitors can also take river trips on small ferries, once the only means of travel around the peninsula. The hotel is ideally placed for the Eden Project, Heligan, National Trust gardens and the beautiful Cathedral city of Truro.

Our inspector loved: *The wonderful welcome – the mouthwatering cuisine and the total peace.*

Directions: From Exeter take A30 towards Truro. Take the St Mawes turn and the hotel is signed to the left.

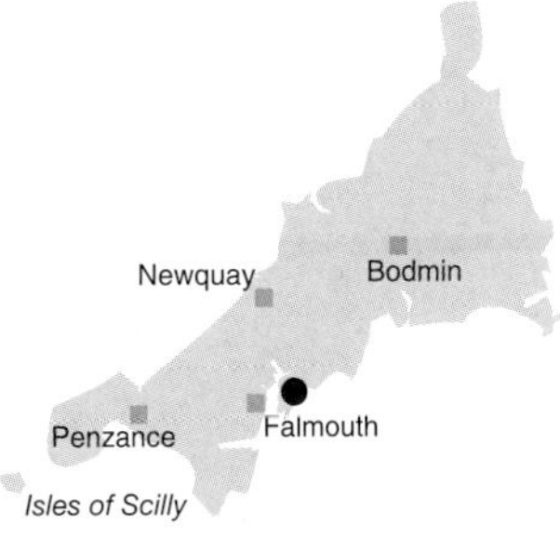

Web: www.johansens.com/rosevinehotel
E-mail: info@rosevine.co.uk
Tel: 0870 381 8867
International: +44 (0)1872 580206
Fax: 01872 580230

Price Guide:
single £90–£190
double/twin £175–£250
suite £250–£360

THE LUGGER HOTEL

PORTLOE, NR TRURO, CORNWALL TR2 5RD

Set on the water's edge and sheltered on three sides by green rolling hills tumbling into the sea, this lovely little former inn is as picturesque as any you will come across. Reputedly the haunt of 17th-century smugglers The Lugger Hotel overlooks a tiny working harbour in the scenic village of Portloe on the unspoilt Roseland Peninsula. It is a conservation area of outstanding beauty and an idyllic location in which to escape the stresses of today's hectic world. Seaward views from the hotel are stunning and reaching out from each side are lovely coastal paths leading to secluded coves. Welcoming owners Sheryl and Richard Young have created an atmosphere of total comfort and relaxation whilst retaining an historic ambience. The 21 bedrooms have every amenity; each is en suite, tastefully decorated and furnished, whilst some are situated across an attractive courtyard. A great variety of dishes and innovative dinner menus are offered in the restaurant overlooking the harbour. Local seafood is a specialty with crab and lobster being particular favourites. For beach lovers, the sandy stretches of Pendower and Carne are within easy reach, as are many National Trust properties and gardens, including the Lost Gardens of Heligan and the Eden project.

Our inspector loved: *This little gem so idyllically tucked away.*

Directions: Turn off A390 St Austell to Truro onto B3287 Tregony. Then take A3048 signed St Mawes, after 2 miles take left fork following signs for Portloe.

Web: www.johansens.com/lugger
E-mail: office@luggerhotel.com
Tel: 0870 381 8708
International: +44 (0)1872 501322
Fax: 01872 501691

Price Guide: (including dinner)
double/twin £200–£310

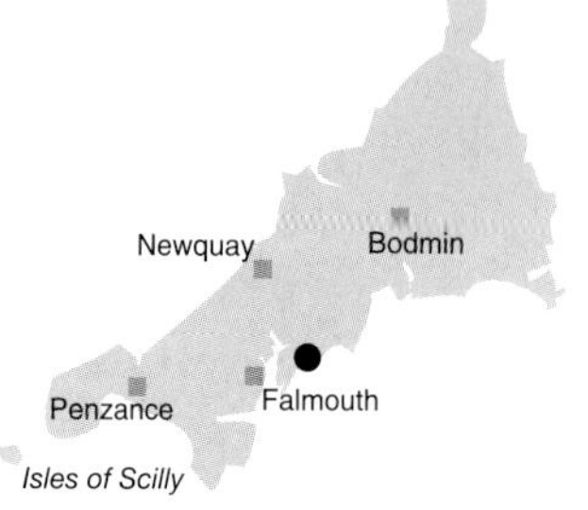

THE GARRACK HOTEL & RESTAURANT

BURTHALLAN LANE, ST IVES, CORNWALL TR26 3AA

This family-run hotel, secluded and full of character, ideal for a family holiday, is set in 2 acres of gardens with fabulous sea views over Porthmeor Beach, the St Ives Tate Gallery and the old town of St Ives. The bedrooms in the original house are in keeping with the style of the building. The additional rooms are modern in design. All rooms have private bathrooms. Enhanced rooms have either four-poster beds or whirlpool baths. A ground-floor room has been fitted for guests with disabilities. Visitors return year after year to enjoy informal yet professional service, good food and hospitality. The restaurant specialises in seafood especially fresh lobsters. The wine list includes over 70 labels from ten regions. The lounges have books, magazines and board games for all and open fires. The small attractive leisure centre contains a small swimming pool with integral spa, sauna, solarium and fitness area. The hotel has its own car park. Porthmeor Beach, just below the hotel, is renowned for surfing. Riding, golf, bowls, sea-fishing and other activities can be enjoyed locally. St Ives, with its harbour, is famous for artists and for the new St Ives Tate Gallery. Gateway to coastal footpaths. Dogs are welcome by prior arrangement

Our inspector loved: *This family-run relaxed informal hotel overlooking Porthmeor Beach.*

Directions: A30–A3074–B3311–B3306. Go ½ mile, turn left at mini-roundabout, hotel signs are on the left as the road starts down hill.

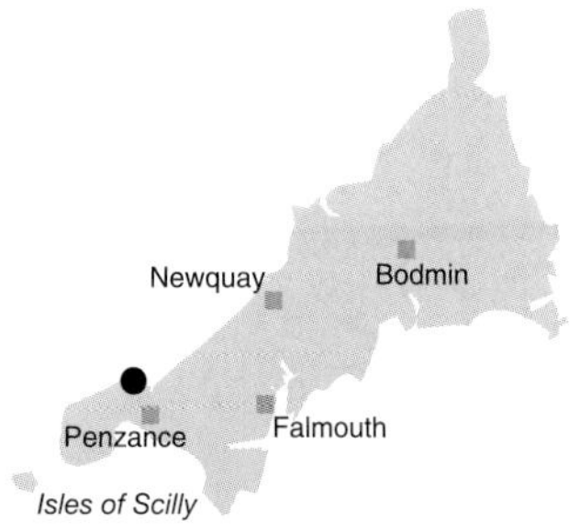

Web: www.johansens.com/garrack
E-mail: djenquiry@garrack.com
Tel: 0870 381 8536
International: +44 (0)1736 796199
Fax: 01736 798955

Price Guide:
single £68–£75
double/twin £117–£180

THE WELL HOUSE

ST KEYNE, LISKEARD, CORNWALL PL14 4RN

The West Country is one corner of England where hospitality and friendliness are at their most spontaneous and nowhere more so than at The Well House, just beyond the River Tamar. New arrivals are entranced by their first view of this lovely Victorian country manor. Its façade, wrapped in rambling wisteria and jasmine trailers is just one of a continuous series of delights including top-quality service, modern luxury and impeccable standards of comfort and cooking. The hotel is professionally managed by proprietor Nick Wainford and manager Chris Swire, whose attention to every smallest detail has earned their hotel numerous awards, among them AA 2 Red Stars and the restaurant 3 Rosettes. From the tastefully appointed bedrooms there are fine rural views and each private bathroom offers luxurious bath linen, soaps and gels. Continental breakfast can be served in bed – or a traditional English breakfast may be taken in the dining room. Chef Glenn Gatland selects fresh, seasonal produce to create his balanced and superbly presented cuisine. Tennis and swimming are on site and the Cornish coastline offers matchless scenery for walks. The Eden Project and the Lost Gardens of Heligan are a short drive away.

Our inspector loved: *The beautiful newly presented bar and restaurant complementing the fine cuisine.*

Directions: Leave the A38 at Liskeard and take the A390 to town centre. Then take the B3254 south to St Keyne Well and hotel.

Web: www.johansens.com/wellhouse
E-mail: enquiries@wellhouse.co.uk
Tel: 0870 381 8975
International: +44 (0)1579 342001
Fax: 01579 343891

Price Guide:
single from £80
double/twin £125–£185
family suite from £195

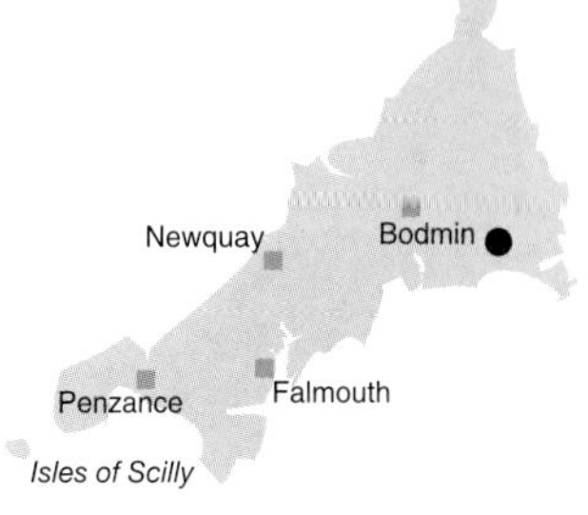

THE IDLE ROCKS HOTEL

HARBOURSIDE, ST MAWES, CORNWALL TR2 5AN

Set on the harbourside of St Mawes, a former fishing village on the tip of Cornwall's Roseland Peninsular, The Idle Rocks Hotel boasts a tranquil location for guests in need of a peaceful environment. From the narrow lanes of fisherman's cottages to the verdant fields leading down to the Cornish beaches, this waterside property enjoys idyllic surrounds. Food is the key criterion and the Water's Edge Restaurant has retained its 2 Rosettes consistently for over 13 years. Every table enjoys picturesque harbour views and serves a menu that is heavily influenced by Cornish sourced produce and seafood specialities. Also, available at lunch time and in the evening, the "On the Rocks" Plain & Simple menu, a selection of individually priced dishes. During the day, the best place to be is "On The Rocks" terrace, enjoy morning coffee or an afternoon Cornish cream tea. After a sumptuous dinner, the well-appointed bedrooms, most of which offer a sea view, are a pleasure to discover. Housed in either the original building, a restored fisherman's cottage or a Georgian house, the 33 rooms are well-appointed with every modern comfort. Attractions in the nearby area include St Mawes Castle, the Eden Project, Lost Gardens of Heligan, Trelissick and Trebah Gardens. Sea lovers wishing to get closer to nature should take the foot ferry from St Mawes to Falmouth or try a day trip with the local ferry operator.

Our inspector loved: *The wonderfully relaxing ambience.*

Directions: From St Austell take the A390 signposted Truro then turn left onto the A3287 signposted Tregony. Drive through Tregony then join the A3078 for St Mawes.

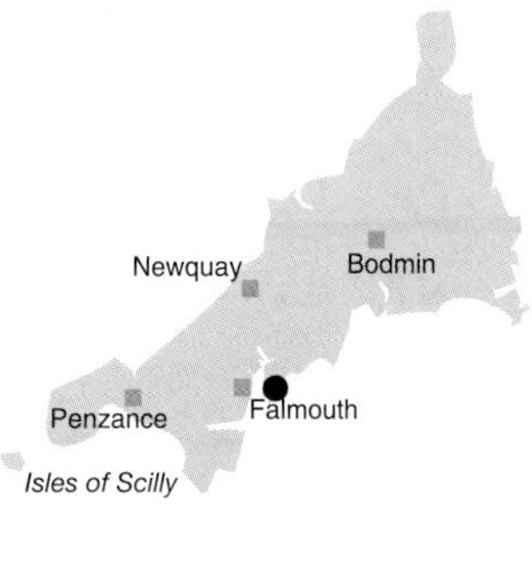

Web: www.johansens.com/idlerocks
E-mail: reception@idlerocks.co.uk
Tel: 0870 381 8324
International: +44 (0)1326 270771
Fax: 01326 270062

Price Guide: (including dinner)
single £69–£99
double/twin £138–£298
suite £228–£258

Alverton Manor

TREGOLLS ROAD, TRURO, CORNWALL TR1 1ZQ

Standing in the heart of the cathedral city of Truro and rising majestically over immaculate surrounds, Alverton Manor, awarded 2 AA Rosettes, is the epitome of a mid-19th-century family home. With its handsome sandstone walls, mullioned windows and superb Cornish Delabole slate roof, this elegant and gracious hotel is reminiscent of the splendour of a bygone era and proudly defends its claim to a Grade II* listing. Built for the Tweedy family over 150 years ago, it was acquired by the Bishop of Truro in the 1880s and later occupied by the Sister of the Epiphany before being taken over and restored to its former glory. Owner Michael Sagin and his talented and dedicated staff take pride in not only providing a high standard of service and modern English cuisine but also in enthusiastically maintaining a welcoming and relaxing ambience that attracts guests time and again. A superb entrance hall with a huge, decorative York stone archway leads to rooms that are comfortable in a quiet, elegant way. Lounges are restful, finely furnished, tastefully decorated and warmed by open fires in winter. The dining room is exquisite, and each of the 33 bedrooms has been individually designed to provide a special character, from the intimate to the grand. Golf, sailing and fishing nearby. Special golf and garden breaks available.

Our inspector loved: *The peace and tranquillity throughout this former beautiful nunnery.*

Directions: Exit the M5, junction 30 and join the A30 through Devon into Cornwall at Fraddon and join the A39 to Truro.

Web: www.johansens.com/alverton
E-mail: reception@alvertonmanor.co.uk
Tel: 0870 381 9152
International: +44 (0)1872 276633
Fax: 01872 222989

Price Guide:
single £75
double £125-£140
suite £160

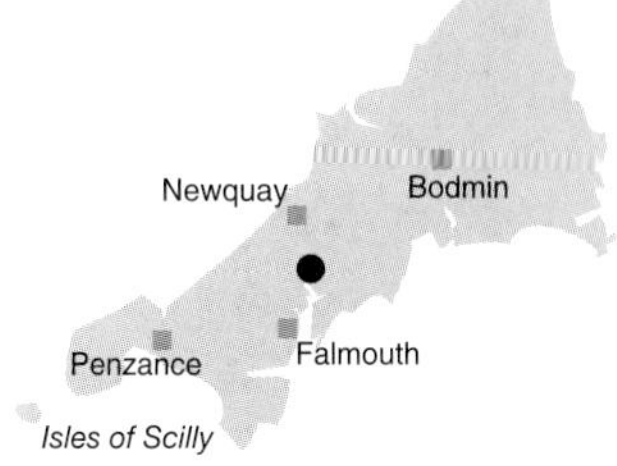

LOVELADY SHIELD COUNTRY HOUSE HOTEL

NENTHEAD ROAD, ALSTON, CUMBRIA CA9 3LF

Reached by the A646, one of the worlds 10 best drives and 2½ miles from Alston, England's highest market town, Lovelady Shield, nestles in 3 acres of secluded riverside gardens. Bright log fires in the library and drawing room enhance the hotel's welcoming atmosphere. Owners Peter and Marie Haynes take great care to create a peaceful and tranquil haven where guests can relax and unwind. The 5-course dinners prepared by master chef Barrie Garton, rounded off by homemade puddings and a selection of English farmhouse cheeses, have consistently been awarded AA Rosettes for the past 10 years for food. Many guests first discover Lovelady Shield en route to Scotland. They then return to explore this beautiful and unspoilt part of England and experience the comforts of the hotel. Golf, fishing, shooting, pony-trekking and riding can be arranged locally. The Pennine Way, Hadrian's Wall and the Lake District are within easy reach. Facilities for small conferences and boardroom meetings are available. Open all year, Special Christmas, New Year, and short breaks are offered with special rates for 2 and 3-day stays.

Our inspector loved: *This informal relaxing hotel set in a picturesque valley.*

Directions: The hotel's driveway is by the junction of the B6294 and the A689, 2¼ miles east of Alston.

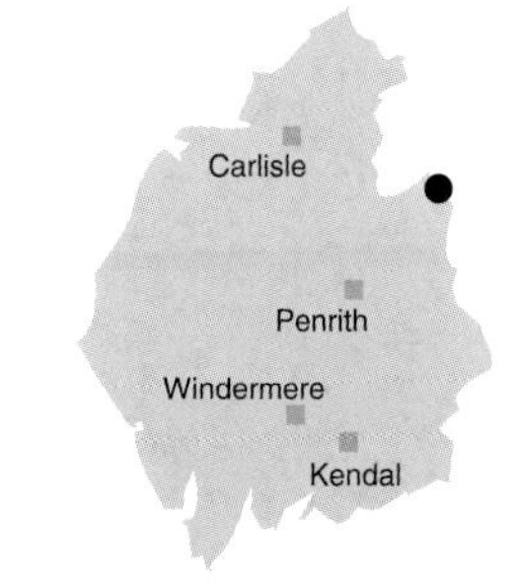

Web: www.johansens.com/loveladyshield
E-mail: enquiries@lovelady.co.uk
Tel: 0870 381 8705
International: +44 (0)1434 381203
Fax: 01434 381515

Price Guide:
single £70–£120
double/twin £140–£240

HOLBECK GHYLL COUNTRY HOUSE HOTEL

HOLBECK LANE, WINDERMERE, CUMBRIA LA23 1LU

Directions: From Windermere, pass Brockhole Visitors Centre, then after $\frac{1}{2}$ mile turn right into Holbeck Lane. Hotel is $\frac{1}{2}$ mile on left.

Web: www.johansens.com/holbeckghyll
E-mail: stay@holbeckghyll.com
Tel: 0870 381 8601
International: +44 (0)15394 32375
Fax: 015394 34743

Price Guide: (including 4 course dinner)
single from £140
double/twin £190–£380
suite £240–£380

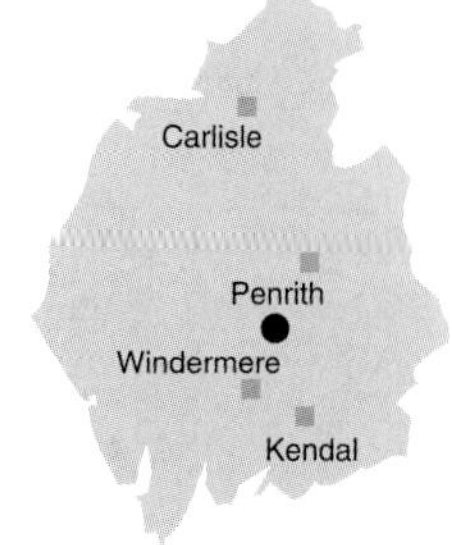

The saying goes that all the best sites for building a house in England were taken long before the days of the motor car. Holbeck Ghyll has one such prime position. It was built in the early days of the 19th century and is superbly located overlooking Lake Windermere and the Langdale Fells. Today this luxury hotel has an outstanding reputation and is managed personally and expertly by its proprietors, David and Patricia Nicholson. As well as being awarded the RAC Gold Ribbon and 3 AA Red Stars they are among an élite who have won an AA Courtesy and Care Award, Holbeck Ghyll was 2002 Country Life Hotel of the Year. The majority of bedrooms are large and have spectacular and breathtaking lake views. All are recently refurbished to a very high standard and include decanters of sherry, fresh flowers, fluffy bathrobes and much more. There are 6 suites in the lodge. The oak-panelled restaurant, awarded a coveted Michelin star and 3 AA Rosettes, is a delightful setting for memorable dining and the meals are classically prepared, with the focus on flavours and presentation, while an extensive wine list reflects quality and variety. The hotel has an all-weather tennis court and a health spa with gym, sauna and treatment facilities.

Our inspector loved: *The delicious dinner in the oak-panelled restaurant with extensive views over Lake Windermere.*

20 50 SPA

Rothay Manor

ROTHAY BRIDGE, AMBLESIDE, CUMBRIA LA22 0EH

A short walk from the centre of Ambleside and ¼ mile from Lake Windermere, this Regency country house hotel, set within landscaped gardens, has been personally managed by the Nixon family for over 35 years. Renowned for its relaxed, comfortable and friendly atmosphere, each of the 16 bedrooms in the hotel is individually designed, some with balconies overlooking the garden, and there are 3 spacious, private suites, 2 of which are situated within the grounds. Family rooms and suites are also available, and a ground-floor bedroom and one suite designed with particular attention to the comfort of those with disabilities. A varied menu is prepared with flair and imagination using local produce whenever possible, complemented by a personally compiled wine list. Guests are entitled to free use of nearby Low Wood Leisure Club with swimming pool, sauna, steam room, gym, Jacuzzi, squash courts, sunbeds and a health and beauty salon. Local activities such as walking, sightseeing, cycling, sailing, horse riding, golf and fishing (permits available) can be arranged. Alternatively, spend the day cruising on Lake Windermere. Special interest holidays from October-May include: gardening, antiques, walking, photography, bridge, music, painting and Lake District heritage. Small functions and conferences can be catered for and short breaks are available all year.

Our inspector loved: *The delicious home-made cakes and biscuits.*

Directions: ¼ mile from Ambleside on the A593 to Coniston. Closed 3rd-28th January.

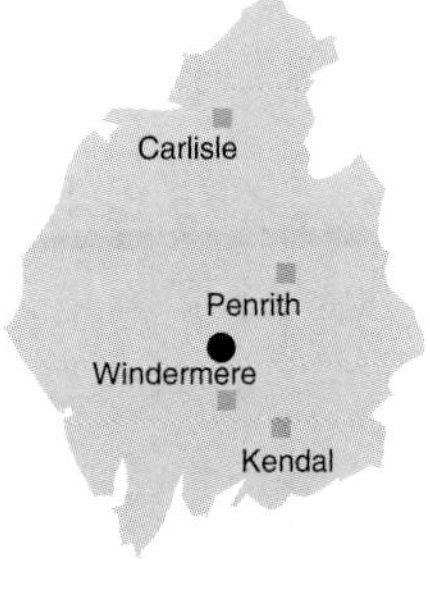

Carlisle
Penrith
Windermere
Kendal

Web: www.johansens.com/rothaymanor
E-mail: hotel@rothaymanor.co.uk
Tel: 0870 381 8869
International: +44 (0)15394 33605
Fax: 015394 33607

Price Guide:
single £85–£125
double/twin £145–£175
suite £190–£215

Tufton Arms Hotel

MARKET SQUARE, APPLEBY-IN-WESTMORLAND, CUMBRIA CA16 6XA

This distinguished Victorian coaching inn, owned and run by the Milsom family, has been refurbished to provide a high standard of comfort. The bedrooms evoke the style of the 19th century, when the Tufton Arms became one of the premier hotels in Victorian England. The kitchen is run under the auspices of David Milsom and Shaun Atkinson, who spoil guests for choice with a gourmet dinner menu as well as a grill menu, the restaurant being renowned for its fish dishes. Complementing the cuisine is an extensive wine list. There are conference and meeting rooms including the air-conditioned Hothfield Suite which can accommodate up to 100 people. Appleby, the historic county town of Westmorland, stands in splendid countryside and is ideal for touring the Lakes, Yorkshire Dales and Pennines. It is also a convenient stop-over en route to Scotland. Members of the Milsom family also run The Royal Hotel in Comrie. Superb fishing for wild brown trout on a 24-mile stretch of the main River Eden, salmon fishing can be arranged on the lower reaches of the river. Shooting parties for grouse, duck and pheasant are a speciality. Appleby has an 18-hole moorland golf course.

Our inspector loved: *Being taken fishing by Nigel Milsom on the River Eden.*

Directions: In centre of Appleby (bypassed by the A66), 38 miles west of Scotch Corner, 13 miles east of Penrith (M6 junction 40), 12 miles from M6 junction 38.

Web: www.johansens.com/tuftonarms
E-mail: info@tuftonarmshotel.co.uk
Tel: 0870 381 8956
International: +44 (0)17683 51593
Fax: 017683 52761

Price Guide:
single £72.50–£107.50
double/twin £98–£140
suite £160

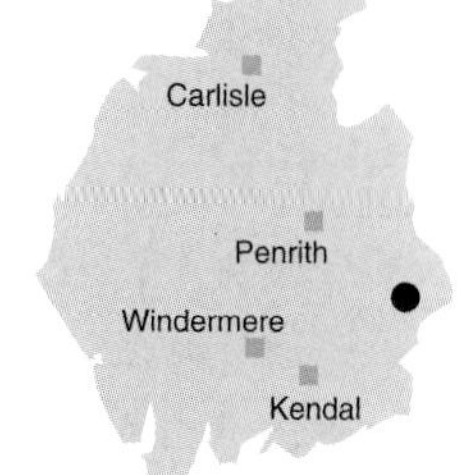

NETHERWOOD HOTEL

LINDALE ROAD, GRANGE-OVER-SANDS, CUMBRIA LA11 6ET

This dramatic and stately residence was built as a family house in the 19th century, and still retains its family ambience in the careful hands of its long - standing owners, the Fallowfields. Impressive oak panelling is a key feature of the property and provides a marvellous backdrop to the public areas – the lounge, lounge bar and ballroom, where log fires roar in the winter months. All of the bedrooms have en-suite facilities, and many have been furnished to extremely high modern standards; all have picturesque views of the sea, woodland or gardens. The light and airy restaurant is housed in the conservatory area on the first floor of the property, maximising the dramatic views over Morecambe Bay. Here, a daily changing menu of freshly prepared specialities caters for a wide variety of tastes and is complemented by an extensive selection of fine wines. A stunning indoor swimming pool and fitness centre is a delightful haven and a keen favourite with families – the pool even has toys for younger guests - whilst an extensive range of beauty treatments, massage and complementary therapies is available at "Equilibrium", the hotel's health spa. Special breaks available.

Our inspector loved: *The oak panelling in the hall and lounge and the stunning views over Morecambe Bay.*

Directions: Take the M6, exit 36 then the A590 towards Barrow-in-Burness. Then the B5277 into Grange-Over-Sands. The hotel is on the right before the town.

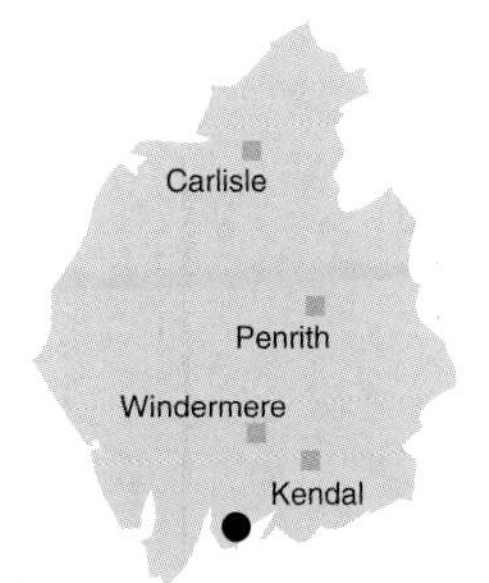

Web: www.johansens.com/netherwood
E-mail: enquiries@netherwood-hotel.co.uk
Tel: 0870 381 8729
International: +44 (0)15395 32552
Fax: 015395 34121

Price Guide:
single £80–£110
double £120-£180

32 200 SPA

Armathwaite Hall Hotel

BASSENTHWAITE LAKE, KESWICK, CUMBRIA CA12 4RE

With an awe-inspiring backdrop of Skiddaw Mountain and the surrounding Lakeland fells, on the shores of Bassenthwaite Lake, the romantic Armathwaite Hall is the perfect location for lovers of boating, walking and climbing. Amidst 400 acres of deer park and woodland, this 4-star country house is a tranquil hideaway for those wishing to relax and escape from modern day living, where comfort is intensified by an emphasis on quality and old-fashioned hospitality, as you would expect of a family-owned and run hotel. The timeless elegance of this stately home is complemented by original features such as wood panelling, magnificent stonework, artworks and antiques. Beautiful bedrooms are decorated in a warm, traditional style and guests can arrange to have champagne, chocolates and flowers on their arrival. The Rosette restaurant offers exceptional cuisine created by Master Chef Kevin Dowling, who uses the finest local seasonal produce. In the Spa there is a gym, indoor swimming pool and a holistic Beauty Salon. Clay pigeon shooting, quad bike safaris, falconry, mountain biking, tennis and croquet are all available, with sailing, fishing and golf nearby. Family friendly with a programme of activities for children and the attraction of Trotters World of Animals on the estate, home to many traditional favourites and endangered species.

Our inspector loved: *The spectacular views over Bassenthwaite Lake.*

Directions: Take the M6 to Penrith. At J40 take the A66 to Keswick roundabout then the A591 towards Carlisle. Go 8 miles to Castle Inn junction, turn left and Armanthwaite Hall is 300 yards ahead.

Web: www.johansens.com/armathwaite
E-mail: reservations@armathwaite-hall.com
Tel: 0870 381 8478
International: +44 (0)17687 76551
Fax: 017687 76220

Price Guide:
single £75–£175
double/twin£150–£330

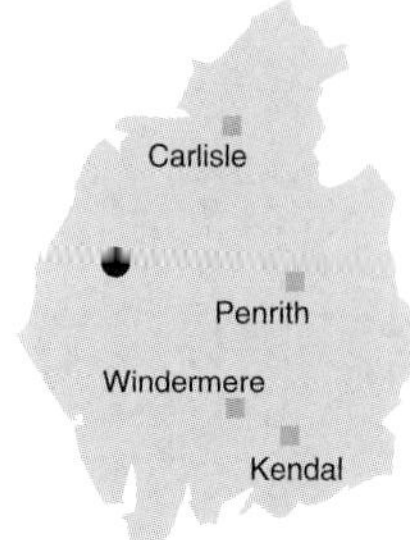

42 80 SPA

The Lodore Falls Hotel

BORROWDALE, KESWICK, CUMBRIA CA12 5UX

Imagine a place with stunning lake and mountain views – the Lodore Falls Hotel is such a place. Situated in the picturesque Borrowdale Valley with 20 acres of lake frontage and landscaped gardens and with the famous Lodore waterfalls in the grounds, this hotel offers not only a magnificent setting in the heart of the Lake District, but also the very best in hospitality. The 71 en-suite Fell and Lake View Rooms, including family rooms and luxurious suites, some with balconies, have every modern amenity, such as Playstations and Internet access. Light meals and coffee can be enjoyed in the comfortable lounges, whilst the cocktail bar is the ideal venue for a pre-dinner drink. The superb Lake View restaurant serves the best in English and Continental cuisine accompanied by fine wines after a long day exploring the surroundings. Free midweek golf is available at nearby Keswick Golf Club, and the hotel's leisure facilities include an indoor and outdoor swimming pool, sauna, gymnasium, tennis and squash court and beauty salon. In addition to an outdoor children's playground an activity programme is also available for 2 hours daily during school holidays. The hotel's large function suites can accommodate up to 200 guests – ideal for weddings, conferences and meetings.

Our inspector loved: *Having a stroll up to the Lodore Falls before dinner.*

Directions: Take the M6 at junction 40. Take the A66 into Keswick then the B5289 to Borrowdale. After 3 minutes, the hotel is on the left-hand side. The nearest railway station is Penrith.

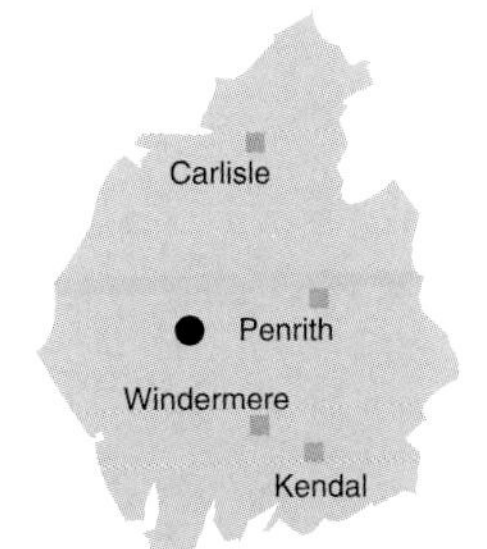

Web: www.johansens.com/lodorefalls
E-mail: info@lodorefallshotel.co.uk
Tel: 0870 381 9314
International: +44 (0)17687 77285
Fax: 017687 77343

Price Guide:
single from £72
double from £132
suite from £234

SHARROW BAY COUNTRY HOUSE HOTEL

HOWTOWN, LAKE ULLSWATER, PENRITH, CUMBRIA CA10 2LZ

Now in its 57th year, Sharrow Bay is known to discerning travellers the world over, who return again and again to this magnificent lakeside hotel. It wasn't always so. The late Francis Coulson arrived in 1948, he was joined by the late Brian Sack in 1952 and the partnership flourished, to make Sharrow Bay what it is today. All the bedrooms are elegantly furnished and guests are guaranteed the utmost comfort. In addition to the main hotel, there are 2 cottages nearby, the Gate House Lodge and Bank House which offer similarly luxurious accommodation. All the reception rooms are delightfully decorated. Sharrow Bay is universally renowned for its wonderful cuisine. The team of chefs, led by Johnnie Martin and Colin Akrigg, ensure that each meal is a special occasion, a mouth-watering adventure! With its private jetty and 12-acres of lakeside gardens Sharrow Bay offers guests boating, swimming and fishing. Fell-walking is a challenge for the upwardly mobile. Sharrow Bay is the oldest British member of Relais et Châteaux.

***Our inspector loved:** The newly refurbished bedrooms up at Bank House with their stunning views across Lake Ullswater.*

Directions: Take the M6, junction 40, A592 to Lake Ullswater, into Pooley Bridge, then take Howtown road for 2 miles.

Web: www.johansens.com/sharrowbaycountryhouse
E-mail: info@sharrowbay.co.uk
Tel: 0870 381 8891
International: +44 (0)17684 86301/86483
Fax: 017684 86349

Price Guide: (including 6-course dinner and full English breakfast)
single £160–£225
double/twin £350–£440
suites from £460

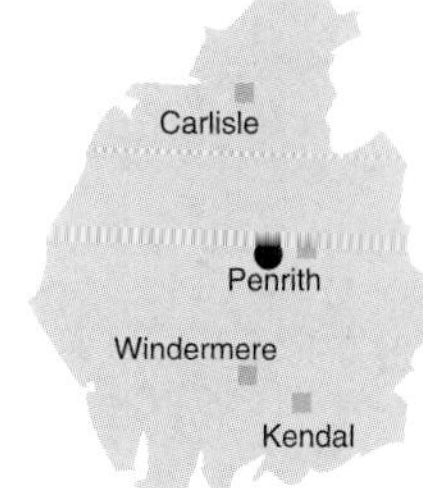

The Inn on the Lake

LAKE ULLSWATER, GLENRIDDING, CUMBRIA CA11 0PE

With its 15 acres of lawns sweeping down to the shore of Lake Ullswater, The Inn on the Lake boasts one of the most spectacular settings in the Lake District. Recently bought and refurbished by the Graves family, this lovely 19th-century hotel offers a wide range of excellent facilities including sailing from its private jetty, pitch and put and croquet. Guests may relax with a drink in the calm comfort of the lounges downstairs or visit The Rambler's Bar in the grounds for the informal ambience of a Lakeland pub. Superb food is served in the Lake View restaurant. Most of the 46 en-suite bedrooms have stunning views across the Lake or face the dramatic Helvellyn mountain range. The lake-view four-poster rooms are particularly romantic. The hotel can host marriage ceremonies and wedding receptions, and can cater for exclusive private functions as well as conference facilities for up to120 delegates. The list of local activities for children and adults alike is endless: rock climbing, pony trekking, canoeing, windsurfing and fishing. Trips aboard the Ullswater steamers can be organised, and many stunning Lake District walks start from Glenridding.

Our inspector loved: *Strolling across the immaculate garden down to Lake Ullswater.*

Directions: Leave the M6 at junction 40, then take the A66 west. At the first roundabout, by Rheged Discovery Centre, head towards Pooley Bridge then follow the shoreline of Lake Ullswater to Glenridding.

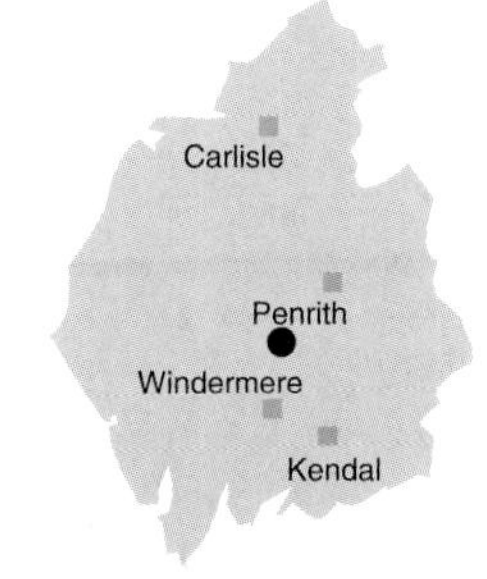

Web: www.johansens.com/innonthelake
E-mail: info@innonthelakeullswater.co.uk
Tel: 0870 381 8640
International: +44 (0)17684 82444
Fax: 017684 82303

Price Guide:
single £72
double from £132
four poster £184

46 120

RAMPSBECK COUNTRY HOUSE HOTEL

WATERMILLOCK, LAKE ULLSWATER, NR PENRITH, CUMBRIA CA11 0LP

A beautifully situated hotel, Rampsbeck Country House stands in 18 acres of landscaped gardens and meadows leading to the shores of Lake Ullswater. Built in 1714, it first became an hotel in 1947, before the present owners acquired it in 1983. Thomas and Marion Gibb, with the help of Marion's mother, Marguerite MacDowall, completely refurbished Rampsbeck with the aim of maintaining its character and adding only to its comfort. Most of the well-appointed bedrooms have lake and garden views. Three have a private balcony and the suite overlooks the lake. In the elegant drawing room, a log fire burns and French windows lead to the garden. Guests and non-residents are welcome to dine in the intimate candle-lit restaurant. Imaginative menus offer a choice of delicious dishes, carefully prepared by Master Chef Andrew McGeorge and his team. A good bar lunch menu offers light snacks as well as hot food. Guests can stroll through the gardens, play croquet or fish from the lake shore, around which there are designated walks. Lake steamer trips, riding, golf, sailing, wind-surfing and fell-walking are available nearby. Closed January to mid-February. Dogs by arrangement only.

***Our inspector loved:** The wonderful views of Lake Ullswater and the beautiful landscaped gardens.*

Directions: Leave M6 at junction 40, take A592 to Ullswater. At T-junction at lake turn right; hotel is 1½ miles on left.

Web: www.johansens.com/rampsbeckcountryhouse
E-mail: enquiries@rampsbeck.fsnet.co.uk
Tel: 0870 381 8848
International: +44 (0)17684 86442
Fax: 017684 86688

Price Guide:
single £75–£150
double/twin £120–£260
suite £260

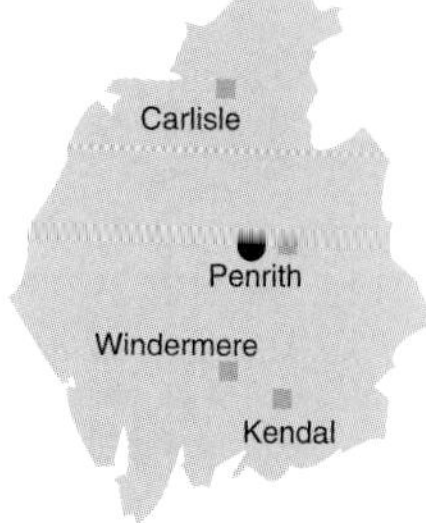

STORRS HALL

LAKE WINDERMERE, CUMBRIA LA23 3LG

From this magnificent listed Georgian manor house not another building can be seen, just a spectacular, seemingly endless view over beautiful Lake Windermere. Built in the 18th century for a Lancashire shipping magnate, Storrs Hall stands majestically in an unrivalled peninsular position surrounded by 17 acres of landscaped, wooded grounds which slope down to half a mile of lakeside frontage. Apart from Wordsworth, who first recited "Daffodils" in the Drawing Room at Storrs, the hotel was frequented by all the great Lakeland poets and Beatrix Potter. Furnished with antiques and objets d'art including a private collection of ship models, it reflects the maritime fortunes which built it. Now part of the English Lakes Hotels group the Hall has 30 beautifully furnished bedrooms, each en suite, spacious and with every comfort. Most of the rooms have views over the lake, and equally splendid views are enjoyed from an exquisite lounge, study and cosy bar. The Terrace Restaurant is renowned for the superb cuisine prepared by head chef Craig Sherrington. Guests receive complimentary use of leisure club facilities at sister hotel, Low Wood, just 3 miles away. Special breaks available.

Our inspector loved: *Strolling in the gardens on the shore of Lake Windermere.*

Directions: Situated on the A592, 2 miles south of Bowness and 5 miles north of Newby Bridge.

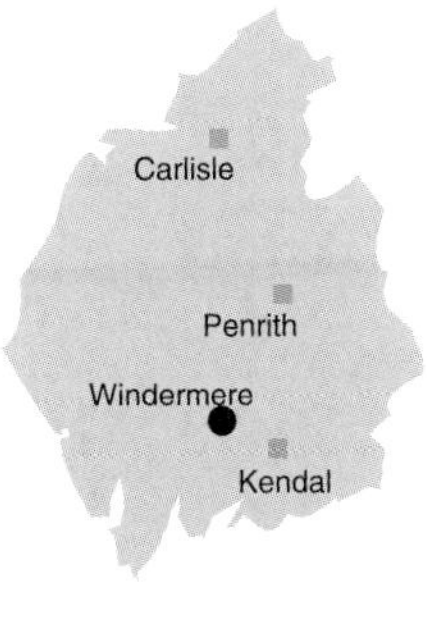

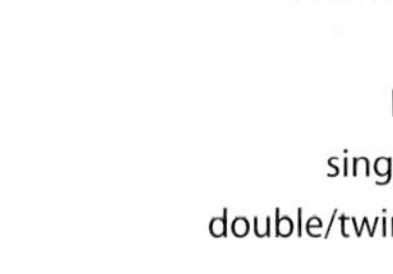

Web: www.johansens.com/storrshall
E-mail: storrshall@elhmail.co.uk
Tel: 0870 381 8919
International: +44 (0)15394 47111
Fax: 015394 47555

Price Guide:
single from £125
double/twin £150–£310
suite £310

LINTHWAITE HOUSE HOTEL

CROOK ROAD, BOWNESS-ON-WINDERMERE, CUMBRIA LA23 3JA

Directions: From the M6, junction 36 follow Kendal by-pass for 8 miles. Take the B5284, Crook Road, for 6 miles. 1 mile beyond Windermere Golf Club, Linthwaite House is signposted on the left.

Web: www.johansens.com/linthwaitehouse
E-mail: admin@linthwaite.com
Tel: 0870 381 8694
International: +44 (0)15394 88600
Fax: 015394 88601

Price Guide:
single £125–£150
double/twin £140–£290
suite £250–£310

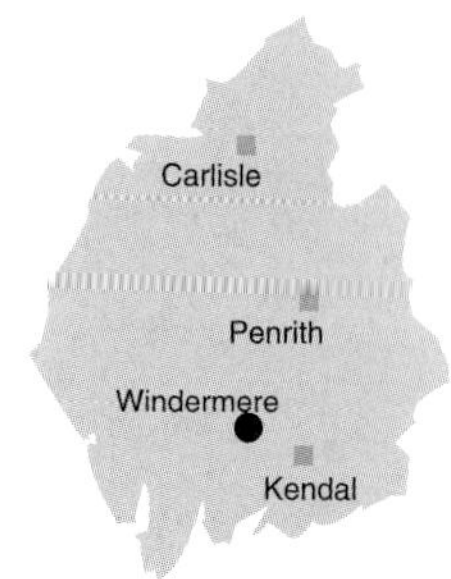

Situated in 14 acres of gardens and woods in the heart of the Lake District, Linthwaite House overlooks Lake Windermere and Belle Isle, with Claife Heights and Coniston Old Man beyond. Here, guests will find themselves amid spectacular scenery, yet only a short drive from the motorway network. The hotel combines stylish originality with the best of traditional English hospitality. Superbly decorated en-suite bedrooms, most of which have lake or garden views. The comfortable lounge is the perfect place to unwind and there is a fire on winter evenings. In the restaurant excellent cuisine features the best of fresh, local produce, accompanied by a fine selection of wines. Within the hotel grounds, there is a 9-hole putting green and a par-3 practice hole. Fly fishermen can fish for brown trout in the hotel tarn. Guests have complimentary use of a private swimming pool and leisure club nearby, while fell walks begin at the hotel's front door. The area around Linthwaite abounds with places of interest: this is Beatrix Potter and Wordsworth country, and there is much to interest the visitor.

Our inspector loved: *Walking through the landscaped gardens up to the tarn with its spectacular views of Lake Windermere.*

27 30

Lakeside Hotel on Lake Windermere

LAKESIDE, NEWBY BRIDGE, CUMBRIA LA12 8AT

Lakeside Hotel offers you a unique location on the water's edge of Lake Windermere. It is a classic, traditional Lakeland hotel offering 4-star facilities and service. All the bedrooms are en suite and enjoy individually designed fabrics and colours, many of the rooms offer breathtaking views of the lake. Guests may dine in either the award-winning Lakeview Restaurant or Ruskin's Brasserie, where extensive menus offer a wide selection of dishes including Cumbrian specialities. The Lakeside Conservatory serves drinks and light meals throughout the day – once there you are sure to fall under the spell of this peaceful location. Berthed next to the hotel there are cruisers which will enable you to explore the lake from the water. To enhance your stay, there is a leisure club including a 17m indoor pool, gymnasium, sauna, steam room and health and beauty suites. The hotel offers a fully equipped conference centre and many syndicate suites allowing plenty of scope and flexibility. Most of all you are assured of a stay in an unrivalled setting of genuine character. The original panelling and beams of the old coaching inn create an excellent ambience, whilst you are certain to enjoy the quality and friendly service. Special breaks available.

Our inspector loved: *Enjoying a delicious afternoon tea in the Lakeside conservatory watching the boats sail by.*

Directions: From the M6, junction 36 join the A590 to Newby Bridge then turn right over bridge towards Hawkshead. The hotel is 1 mile on the right.

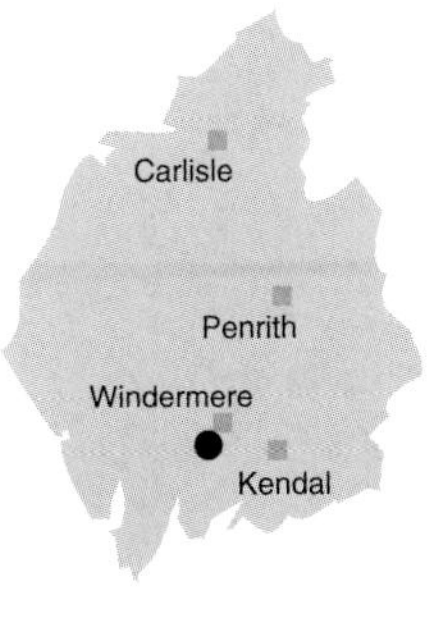

Carlisle
Penrith
Windermere
Kendal

Web: www.johansens.com/lakeside
E-mail: sales@lakesidehotel.co.uk
Tel: 0870 381 8672
International: +44 (0)15395 30001
Fax: 015395 31699

Price Guide:
single from £150
double/twin £185–£295
suite from £325

CALLOW HALL

MAPPLETON ROAD, ASHBOURNE, DERBYSHIRE DE6 2AA

The approach to Callow Hall is up a tree-lined drive through the 44-acre grounds. On arrival visitors can take in the splendid views from the hotel's elevated position, overlooking the valleys of Bentley Brook and the River Dove. The majestic building and Victorian gardens have been restored by resident proprietors, David, Dorothy, son Anthony and daughter, Emma Spencer, who represent the fifth and sixth generations of hoteliers in the Spencer family. The famous local Ashbourne mineral water and homemade biscuits greet guests in the spacious period bedrooms. Fresh local produce is selected daily for use in the kitchen, where the term "homemade" comes into its own. Well hung and personally selected meat, home-cured bacon, sausages, fresh bread, traditional English puddings and melt-in-the-mouth pastries are among the items prepared on the premises, which can be enjoyed by non-residents. Visiting anglers can enjoy a rare opportunity to fish for trout and grayling along a mile-long private stretch of the Bentley Brook, which is mentioned in Izaak Walton's "The Compleat Angler". Callow Hall, as excellent mainline train links from Derby station, and is ideally located for some of England's finest stately homes. Closed at Christmas. East Midlands Airport is 35 minutes away.

Our inspector loved: *Callow Hall, it is very special, so warm and welcoming, truly unspoilt.*

Directions: Take the A515 through Ashbourne towards Buxton. At the Bowling Green Inn on the brow of a steep hill, turn left, then take the first right, signposted Mappleton and the hotel is over the bridge on the right.

Web: www.johansens.com/callowhall
E-mail: stay@callowhall.co.uk
Tel: 0870 381 8400
International: +44 (0)1335 300900
Fax: 01335 300512

Price Guide:
single £98–£120
double/twin £145–£195
suite £225

THE IZAAK WALTON HOTEL

DOVEDALE, NEAR ASHBOURNE, DERBYSHIRE DE6 2AY

This charming farmhouse dates back to the 17th century, and is idyllically situated with glorious views over the Derbyshire countryside. The River Dove meanders in the valley below and the atmosphere is one of peace and tranquillity. The hotel takes its name from the author of "The Compleat Angler," and great care has been taken to retain the building's character. The bedrooms are individually designed to incorporate interesting period features; the original farmhouse building features oak beams and traditional décor. The AA Rosette-awarded Haddon Restaurant serves a diverse menu of creative interpretations on traditional dishes, which is enhanced by an excellent selection of fine wines from respected worldwide vineyards. The warm and welcoming Dovedale Bar is located in the oldest part of the building and its walls are adorned with interesting fishing memorabilia. Here, guests can enjoy light snacks and informal meals. The hotel has permanent rods on the River Dove and private tuition can be arranged. The Peak District National Park is close by and Chatsworth House, Haddon Hall, Staffordshire Potteries and Alton Towers are within easy access. The hotel welcomes families and is ideal for weddings, family parties, meetings and conferences.

Our inspector loved: *The relaxing atmosphere, and location.*

Directions: Dovedale is 2 miles north-west of Ashbourne between the A515 and A52.

Web: www.johansens.com/izaakwalton
E-mail: reception@izaakwaltonhotel.com
Tel: 0870 381 8642
International: +44 (0)1335 350555
Fax: 01335 350539

Price Guide:
single £110
double/twin £135–£175

Riverside House

ASHFORD-IN-THE-WATER, NR BAKEWELL, DERBYSHIRE DE45 1QF

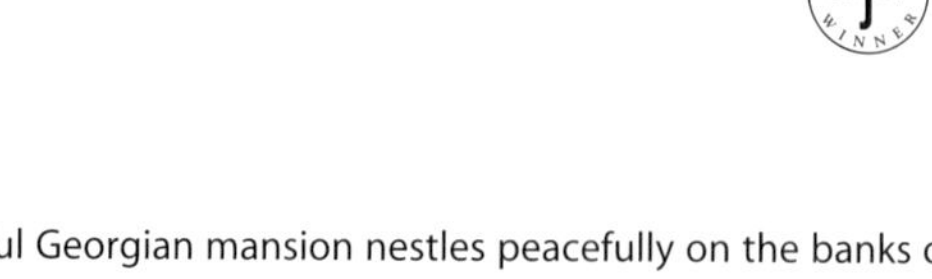

This graceful Georgian mansion nestles peacefully on the banks of the river Wye in one of the Peak District's most picturesque villages. It is an intimate gem of a country hotel, a tranquil rural retreat in the finest traditions of classic hospitality and friendliness. Small and ivy-clad, Riverside House sits majestically in the heart of secluded grounds that feature exquisite landscaped gardens and lawns. Elegance, style, intimacy and informality abound within its interior. Individually designed en-suite bedrooms have their own distinctive character and are comfortably and delightfully furnished with rich fabrics and antique pieces. An atmosphere of complete relaxation is the hallmark of the welcoming public rooms whose large windows offer superb views. Guests can enjoy a distinctive fusion of modern English, International and local cuisine in the excellent and charming 2 AA Rosette awarded restaurant where service is of the highest quality. As well as being conveniently situated to explore the glories of the Peak District, Chatsworth House and Haddon Hall, the hotel is also an ideal base for guests wishing to visit the Derbyshire Dales, Lathkill and Dovedale.

Our inspector loved: *The charm and enthusiasm generated from this very intimate house.*

Directions: Exit M1 at junction 29. Take A617 to Chesterfield, then A619 to Bakewell, then take A6 to Ashford-in-the-Water. Riverside House is at the end of the village main street next to the Sheepwash Bridge.

Web: www.johansens.com/riversidehouse
E-mail: riversidehouse@enta.net
Tel: 0870 381 8860
International: +44 (0)1629 814275
Fax: 01629 812873

Price Guide:
single £90–£120
double/twin £135–£160

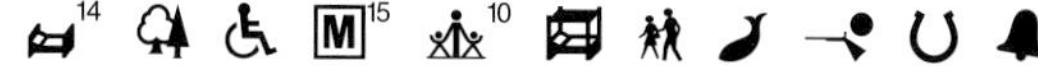

Hassop Hall

HASSOP, NEAR BAKEWELL, DERBYSHIRE DE45 1NS

The recorded history of Hassop Hall reaches back 900 years to the Domesday Book, to a time when the political scene in England was still dominated by the power struggle between the barons and the King, when the only sure access to that power was through possession of land. By 1643, when the Civil War was raging, the Hall was under the ownership of Rowland Eyre, who turned it into a Royalist garrison. It was the scene of several skirmishes before it was recaptured after the Parliamentary victory. Since purchasing Hassop Hall in 1975, Thomas Chapman has determinedly pursued the preservation of its outstanding heritage. Guests can enjoy the beautifully maintained gardens as well as the splendid countryside of the surrounding area. The bedrooms, some of which are particularly spacious, are well furnished and comfortable. A four-poster bedroom is available for romantic occasions. A comprehensive dinner menu offers a wide and varied selection of dishes, with catering for most tastes. As well as the glories of the Peak District, places to visit include Chatsworth House, Haddon Hall and Buxton Opera House. Christmas opening – details on application. Inclusive rates available on request.

Our inspector loved: *So many special points here. For 30 years the Chapmans have delighted and pampered, never faltering on its style.*

Directions: From the M1, exit 29 (Chesterfield), take the A619 to Baslow, then the A623 to Calver. Turn left at the lights to B6001. Hassop Hall is 2 miles on the right.

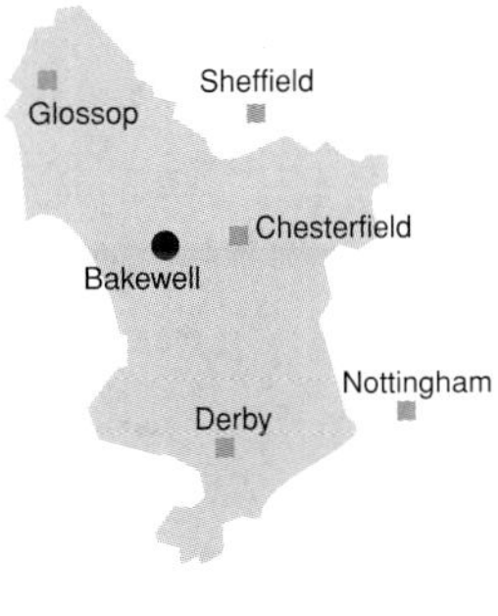

Glossop
Sheffield
Chesterfield
Bakewell
Nottingham
Derby

Web: www.johansens.com/hassophall
E-mail: hassophallhotel@btinternet.com
Tel: 0870 381 8586
International: +44 (0)1629 640488
Fax: 01629 640577

Price Guide: (excluding breakfast)
double/twin £79–£195

EAST LODGE COUNTRY HOUSE HOTEL

ROWSLEY, NR MATLOCK, DERBYSHIRE DE4 2EF

A glorious tree-lined driveway guides visitors to this elegant country house hotel set in the heart of the Peak District National Park. Upon entering the reception hall of this award-winning property, guests are immediately enveloped by a warm, hospitable ambience that prevails throughout the property. The surrounding 10 acres of magnificent grounds create a haven of tranquil privacy making East Lodge an excellent location for weddings and corporate gatherings. David and Joan Hardman, together with their son Iain, will endeavor to meet any request and ensure that no attention to detail is spared. A no smoking policy operates throughout the hotel including the en-suite bedrooms, which are thoughtfully designed and fuse traditional features and contemporary facilities. The luxurious bathrooms boast oversized baths, Pascal Morobito toiletries and soft, sumptuous towels. In the restaurant, which has been awarded 2 AA Rosettes for the seventh consecutive year, chef Marcus Hall creates interesting and stylish dishes. A romantic garden room and attractive terrace merely add to the rustic charm of this property, easily accessible from Sheffield, Manchester, Nottingham, Derby and London, and is the nearest hotel to the historic Chatsworth House.

Our inspector loved: *This quintessential English retreat - delightful.*

Directions: Set back from the A6 in Rowsley village, 3 miles from Bakewell. The hotel entrance is adjacent to the B6012 junction to Sheffield/Chatsworth.

Web: www.johansens.com/eastlodgecountryhouse
E-mail: info@eastlodge.com
Tel: 0870 381 8496
International: +44 (0)1629 734474
Fax: 01629 733949

Price Guide:
single £80
double/twin from £100

The Peacock at Rowsley

ROWSLEY, NEAR MATLOCK, DERBYSHIRE DE4 2EB

Once the Dower House for Haddon Hall, this superb 17th-century country inn has returned to the Haddon estate after nearly 50 years and remains a renowned historic fishing hostelry with a 3-star AA rating. An exciting refurbishment has been overseen by Lord Edward Manners of Haddon Hall, and today the hotel's eclectic mix of ancient and modern is carried off with great style and charisma. Interiors have been created by the magnificent French designer India Mahdavi, and furnishings are bold, featuring contemporary colours and textures. Attractive gardens lead down to the River Derwent and fishermen are spoilt for choice as the River Wye is the only river in the country with wild rainbow trout and brown trout. Fishing reservations and tuition are available at the hotel, along with a purpose-built drying room. The Peacock's 2 AA Rosette-awarded restaurant offers fine British cuisine, with a modern influence, and a good selection of bar food is available. A warm welcome extends to dogs and children, however it is requested that children dine before 8 o'clock. Guests may use the nearby gym and enjoy beauty treatments at Woodlands Fitness Centre, and complimentary golf on the scenic Bakewell golf course can be arranged. Haddon Hall, Chatsworth House, Peak District National Park and Sheffield are all on the doorstep. Transfers to and from nearby East Midlands Airport can be organised.

Directions: M1/exit 28, head for A6. Rowsley is midway between Matlock and Bakewell.

Web: www.johansens.com/peacockrowsley
E-mail: reception@thepeacockatrowsley.com
Tel: 0870 381 8805
International: +44 (0)1629 733518
Fax: 01629 732671

Price Guide:
single £75
double/twin £135

Our inspector loved: *The transition from 1652 to the present day.*

Cavendish Hotel

BASLOW, DERBYSHIRE DE45 1SP

This enchanting hotel offers visitors the opportunity to stay on the famous Chatsworth Estate, close to one of England's greatest stately houses, and home of the Duke and Duchess of Devonshire. 30 years after the hotel became the Cavendish, the Dowager Duchess of Devonshire still enjoys designing and personally supervising the creative décor, and this year has truly enhanced its feeling of calm and tranquillity with the recent refurbishment of the restaurant and bedrooms. Every bedroom features fine art and antiques and has a view across the estate. In the kitchen, chef Chris Allison takes a modern approach to cooking and has received various accolades for his cuisine, which is served by attentive and friendly, yet unobtrusive staff. Breakfast is prepared everyday until lunchtime and informal meals are available from morning to late evening in The Garden Room. The hotel provides a delightful environment during the changing seasons, and there are many fabulous walks to partake in from the doorstep. Enjoy the solitude of the estate when the house is closed or experience the house and gardens of Chatsworth when they are open. Climbing The Peak, exploring The Dales, fishing, golf and Sheffield's Crucible Theatre are among the many leisure pursuits nearby.

Our inspector loved: *The new restaurant, which offers relaxed dining and wonderful views. Very calming and peaceful - a great place to unwind.*

Directions: Take the M1, junction 29, then the A617 to Chesterfield and A619 west to Baslow.

Web: www.johansens.com/cavendish
E-mail: info@cavendish-hotel.net
Tel: 0870 381 8412
International: +44 (0)1246 582311
Fax: 01246 582312

Price Guide: (room only)
single from £103
double/twin from £135

FISCHER'S

BASLOW HALL, CALVER ROAD, BASLOW, DERBYSHIRE DE45 1RR

Situated on the edge of the magnificent Chatsworth Estate, Baslow Hall enjoys an enviable location surrounded by some of England's finest stately homes, and is within easy reach of the Peak District's many cultural and historical attractions. Leisure and business guests alike will find this a welcome retreat that successfully combines the standards of good hotel-keeping with the hospitality and style of country house living. Baslow Hall has been Max and Susan Fischer's home for 16 years. Max is one of the most dedicated chef-patrons in the country, supported since 2002 by Head Chef Rupert Rowley. Using the best available ingredients and his culinary craftsmanship, Max, alongside Rupert's dazzling technique, produces what has been described by one leading national food critic as "gastronomic fireworks." There is plenty to do and see within the vicinity: Chatsworth House, Haddon Hall, Hardwick and Kedleston are only minutes away, and the nearby open countryside is beautiful. This is an ideal venue for intimate weddings, small boardroom meetings and family celebrations.

Our inspector loved: *The experience of Fischer's. So welcoming and truly special.*

Directions: Baslow is within 12 miles of the M1, Chesterfield and Sheffield. Fischer's is on the A623 in Baslow.

Web: www.johansens.com/fischers
E-mail: m.s@fischers-baslowhall.co.uk
Tel: 0870 381 8523
International: +44 (0)1246 583259
Fax: 01246 583818

Price Guide:
single £100-£130
double/twin £140-£180
suite £160

Ringwood Hall Hotel

RINGWOOD ROAD, BRIMINGTON, CHESTERFIELD, DERBYSHIRE S43 1DQ

With its excellent location close to Chesterfield yet in a peaceful setting on the edge of the Peak District, Ringwood Hall Hotel is one of the finest country house hotels in north-east Derbyshire. The Hall has undergone sensitive refurbishment and still retains its charming Grade II exterior, which welcomes guests into an impressive reception area with intricate plaster frieze work, a galleried landing and glazed dome ceiling. The surrounding 29 acres of magnificent gardens and parkland feature original Victorian gardens that have been meticulously restored and provide vegetables and herbs for the kitchen. Each of the 59 bedrooms and suites is traditionally appointed and some have Jacuzzi baths. Fully-equipped 3-room apartments are also available. Finest local produce is used for the extensive menus in the Expressions Restaurant, and numerous conference packages can be arranged, which may include sporting country pursuits such as quad biking, clay pigeon shooting and archery. This is a also a wonderful setting for wedding receptions and civil ceremonies. A superb health and fitness club, which opened in 2002, offers a fitness room, sauna and tanning booth as well as a beauty salon where guests can enjoy treatments such as massages, facials and body wraps. Chesterfield Museum, Hardwick Hall and Bolsover Castle are nearby and families may enjoy a trip to Alton Towers.

Our inspector loved: *The historic gardens, such an enchanting feature.*

Directions: From junction 30 of the M1 take the A619 towards Chesterfield, passing through Mastin Moor and Staveley. Continue on the A619 and rising out of the valley the hotel is set back on the left.

Web: www.johansens.com/ringwood
E-mail: ringwood-hall-reception@lyrichotels.co.uk
Tel: 0870 381 8857
International: +44 (0)1246 280077
Fax: 01246 472241

Glossop
Sheffield
Chesterfield
Bakewell
Nottingham
Derby

Price Guide:
single from £80
double/twin from £100
suite from £120

Riber Hall

MATLOCK, DERBYSHIRE DE4 5JU

There could be few more picturesque settings than this stately Elizabethan manor house standing in its own walled garden in the foothills of the Pennine range. Views over the Peak National Park are outstanding and the atmosphere is one of total tranquillity. Privately owned and managed by the same family for over 30 years the latest round of awards stands testament to their skill and high standards of service. 14 spacious bedrooms are each furnished with period antiques and elegant beds, the majority of which are antique four-poster. Log fires and oak beams of the lounge convey an instant sense of intimacy and timelessness. The restaurant is renowned for its attentive service, game (when in season) and inspired French classical and modern English cuisine. The excellent wine list has also been rated AA Wine Award Finalist in the Top 25 in the UK for 3 consecutive years and was finalist for the Tattinger Condé Nast Johansens wine list award for 2005. This is the perfect setting for both weddings and conferences and there is much to see in the surrounding area for delegates or wedding guests with time to spare. Chatsworth House, Haddon Hall and many world heritage sites are within easy reach. The beautiful Peak District scenery is breathtaking. East Midlands, Sheffield and Birmingham Airports are all nearby.

Our inspector loved: *The ticking of the clock breaking the silence over a warm fire in this timeless historic gem.*

Directions: 20 minutes from junction 28 of the M1, off the A615 at Tansley; 1 mile further to Riber.

Web: www.johansens.com/riberhall
E-mail: info@riber-hall.co.uk
Tel: 0870 381 8854
International: +44 (0)1629 582795
Fax: 01629 580475

Price Guide:
single £95–£105
double/twin £123–£165

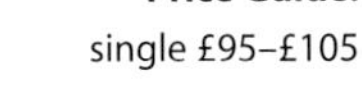

Northcote Manor Country House Hotel

BURRINGTON, UMBERLEIGH, DEVON EX37 9LZ

This 18th-century manor with grounds high above the Taw River Valley offers an ambience of timeless tranquillity. Situated in 20 acres of peaceful Devonshire countryside, Northcote Manor provides complete relaxation and refreshment. Extensive refurbishment has created 11 luxury bedrooms and suites, resulting in a total redesign of the décor in the spacious sitting rooms, hall and restaurant. One of the south west's leading country houses, the Manor has received a series of accolades. In 2002: Condé Nast Johansens Country Hotel of the Year; and AA 3 Red Stars. In 2004: the RAC Gold Ribbon Award; The Which? Hotel Guide; Tourist Board Silver Award; Michelin 2 Red Turrets Award; RAC Cooking Award level 3; and AA 2 Rosettes. Exmoor and Dartmoor are within easy reach and guests may visit RHS Rosemoor and the many National Trust properties nearby. A challenging 18-hole golf course is next door whilst outstanding fishing from the Taw River, at the bottom of the drive, can be arranged with the Gillie. The area also hosts some of the best shoots in the country. A tennis court and croquet lawn are on site. Helicopters can land at Eaglescott Airfield, approximately 2 miles away. Special breaks are available.

Our inspector loved: *The new conservatory, with oak flooring and slate roof, and beautiful water gardens.*

Directions: From Exeter stay on the A377 towards Barnstaple (do not enter Burrington village). The driveway to Northcote Manor is opposite the Portsmouth Arms pub on the A377.

Web: www.johansens.com/northcotemanor
E-mail: rest@northcotemanor.co.uk
Tel: 0870 381 8767
International: +44 (0)1769 560501
Fax: 01769 560770

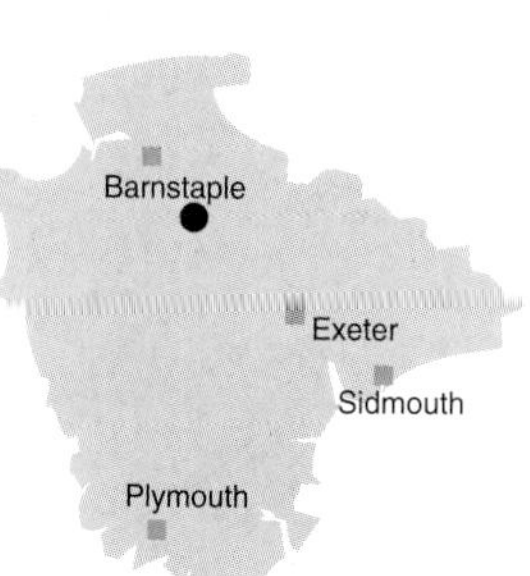

Price Guide:
single from £99
double/twin from £150
suite from £240

Gidleigh Park

CHAGFORD, DEVON TQ13 8HH

Gidleigh Park enjoys an outstanding international reputation among connoisseurs for its comfort and gastronomy. It has collected a clutch of top culinary awards including 2 Michelin stars for its imaginative cuisine and the Gidleigh Park wine list is one of the best in Britain. Service throughout the hotel is faultless. The en-suite bedrooms – 2 of them in a converted chapel – are luxuriously furnished with antiques. The public rooms are elegantly appointed and during the cooler months, a fire burns merrily in the lounge's impressive fireplace. Set amid 45 secluded acres in the Teign Valley, Gidleigh Park is 1½ miles from the nearest public road. 2 croquet lawns, an all-weather tennis court, a bowling lawn and a splendid water garden can be found in the grounds. A 360 yard long, par 52 putting course designed by Peter Alliss was opened in 1995. Guests can swim in the river or explore Dartmoor on foot or in the saddle. There are 14 miles of trout, sea trout and salmon fishing, as well as golf facilities nearby. Gidleigh Park is a Relais & Châteaux member.

Our inspector loved: *The total peace and tranquillity surrounding this superb hotel.*

Directions: Approach from Chagford: go along Mill Street from Chagford Square. Fork right after 150 yards, cross into Holy Street at factory crossroads and follow lane for 2 miles.

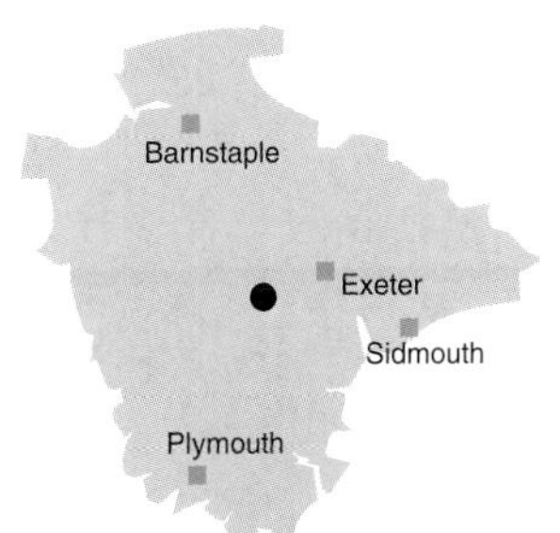

Web: www.johansens.com/gidleighpark
E-mail: gidleighpark@gidleigh.co.uk
Tel: 0870 381 8545
International: +44 (0)1647 432367
Fax: 01647 432574

Price Guide: (including dinner)
single £375–£500
double/twin £450–£600

15 22

Mill End

DARTMOOR NATIONAL PARK, CHAGFORD, DEVON TQ13 8JN

Gleaming white under slate grey roof tiles and with windows and doors opening onto a beautiful English country garden, Mill End, within top 200 AA Hotels, is an idyllic hideaway in Dartmoor's National Park. The lawned garden with its wide, deeply shrubbed and colourful borders runs down to the languid waters of the River Teign, a water wheel slowly turns in the courtyard to the enjoyment of guests and diners. Built in the mid 1700s the hotel was a former flour mill, and inside there are numerous little corner nooks, paintings and old photographs that imbue a feeling of seclusion, enhanced by the smell of wood smoke and polished wood. The delightful en-suite bedrooms have undergone major refurbishment incorporating excellent décor, lovely fabrics and attractive local hand-crafted furniture. Plus, of course, every facility one would expect. The elegance of the dining room is matched by the delicious award-winning cuisine of Master Chef of Great Britain, Barnaby Mason. His menus are full and varied; one shouldn't miss, for example, lobster ravioli with seared scallops and lemon grass broth followed by grilled turbot with aubergine caviar and a dark chocolate tort with burnt orange sauce and rosewater ice cream. An 18-hole golf course is nearby and pony trekking and shooting can be arranged.

Our inspector loved: *The superb upgrading to the entrance and grounds, and as always the stunning location.*

Directions: From the M5 exit at junction 31 towards Okehampton. Take the A382 at Merrymount roundabout towards Moretonhampstead. Mill End is on the right.

Web: www.johansens.com/millend
E-mail: info@millendhotel.com
Tel: 0870 381 8734
International: +44 (0)1647 432282
Fax: 01647 433106

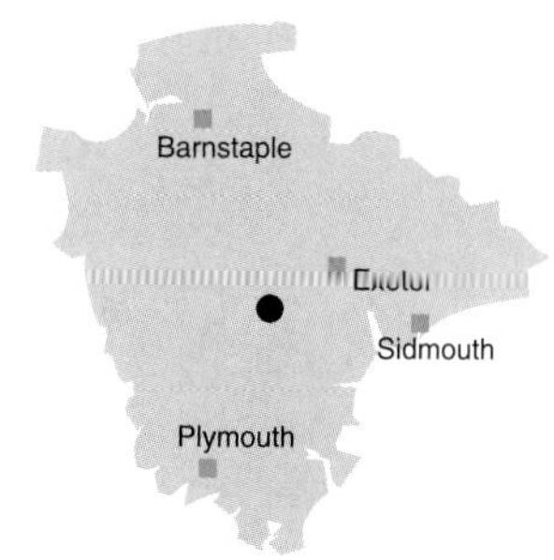

Price Guide:
single £80–£120
double/twin £120–£170
suite £170–£210

Bovey Castle

NORTH BOVEY, DARTMOOR NATIONAL PARK, DEVON TQ13 8RE

Ideally situated within the 368 square miles of Dartmoor National Park and surrounded by moorland, woodlands and rivers, Bovey Castle offers guests the utmost in style, elegance and tranquillity. Built in 1906 for Viscount Hambleden, son of the business baron WH Smith, and transformed into a grand country estate by the 1920s it is now owned by Peter de Savary. Focus on returning this great house to its former glory was then undertaken and remaining true to the standards that the art deco period aspired to has created relaxed luxury and glamour. Sumptuous accommodation in 65 individually designed rooms range from Valley View rooms, with their outlook across Dartmoor, to the triple aspect Chairman's Suites, with views over the gardens, moors and the 1st and 18th holes of the estate's challenging golf course, designed in 1926 to rival Gleneagles and Turnberry. The castle interior is very special with grand oak panelled drawing rooms, ornate broad stairways, a magnificently restored Cathedral Room, with vaulted ceiling, and a superbly crafted Great Hall, which opens onto stone balustraded terraces. The main dining room, where exceptional cuisine is served, is equally impressive in the style of an original art deco Palm Court. Fully equipped spa, indoor swimming pool and many leisure pursuits from riding and shooting to falconry and 25 miles of fishing.

Our inspector loved: *This majestic castle and magnificent location.*

Directions: Take the M5 and exit at junction 30, join the A38 to Newton Abbot and pick up signs for Moretonhampstead. Follow signs for Princetown - Castle Drive and the hotel is 3 miles on the left-hand side.

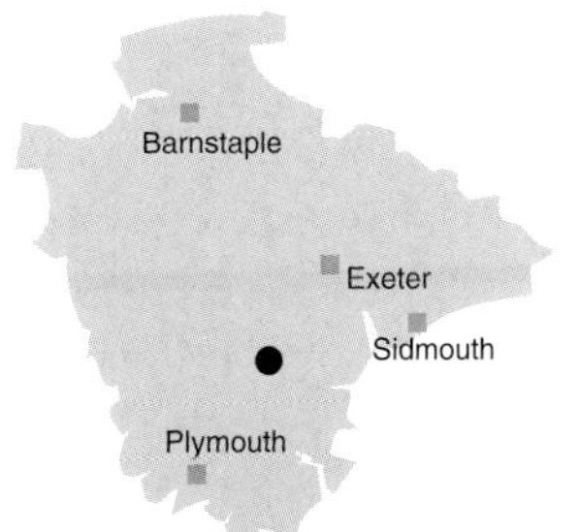

Web: www.johansens.com/boveycastle
E-mail: enquiries@boveycastle.com
Tel: 0870 381 9286
International: +44 (0)1647 445016
Fax: 01647 445020

Price Guide:
single from £180
double from £250
suite from £565

Combe House Hotel & Restaurant

GITTISHAM, HONITON, NEAR EXETER, DEVON EX14 3AD

Awarded 'Best Country House Hotel 2004' (Sunday Times Travel Magazine), Combe House is a wildly romantic, Grade 1 Elizabethan Manor, hidden in 3,500 acres of private Devon estate, yet close to the World Heritage coastline. Arabian horses and pheasants roam freely beside the mile of winding drive leading from the pretty thatched village of Gittisham. The alluring combination of heritage and a welcoming lived-in feel make this a special place for an indulgent mix of eating, drinking and relaxing in the country. Log fires, treasured antiques and fresh flowers abound and 15 bedrooms and suites, many with breathtaking views, exude style and individuality. In the Restaurant, guests are treated to innovative contemporary cuisine created by Master Chef of Great Britain, Philip Leach, who draws extensively on the West Country's bounteous larder and Combe's own kitchen garden to weave his culinary magic. Add this to interesting wines from the ancient cellars, including a specialist Chablis collection and it's easy to understand why Combe was awarded 'Best Restaurant of the Year 2005' in the Devon Life Food and Drink Awards.

Our inspector loved: *The warmth of welcome, the overall feeling of being a friend and wanting to return.*

Directions: M5 exit 28 to Honiton and Sidmouth or exit 29 to Honiton. Follow signs to Fenny Bridges and Gittisham (20 mins). A303/A30 exit Honiton, 5 mins.

Web: www.johansens.com/combehousegittisham
E-mail: stay@thishotel.com
Tel: 0870 381 8440
International: +44 (0)1404 540400
Fax: 01404 46004

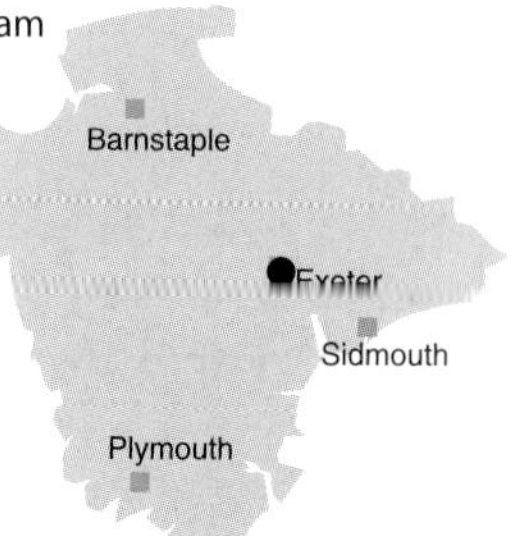

Price Guide:
single £128–£188
double/twin £148–£210
suite £298–£330

Ilsington Country House Hotel

ILSINGTON VILLAGE, NEAR NEWTON ABBOT, DEVON TQ13 9RR

The Ilsington Country House Hotel stands in 10 acres of beautiful private grounds within the Dartmoor National Park. Run by friendly proprietors, Tim and Maura Hassell, the delightful furnishings and ambience offer a most comfortable environment in which to relax. Stylish bedrooms all boast outstanding views across the rolling pastoral countryside and every comfort and convenience to make guests feel at home. The distinctive candle-lit dining room is perfect for savouring the superb cuisine, awarded 2 AA Rosettes, created by talented chefs from fresh local produce. The library is ideal for an intimate dining party or celebration whilst the conservatory or lounge is the place for morning coffee or a Devon cream tea. There is a fully-equipped, purpose-built gymnasium, heated indoor pool, sauna, steam room and spa. Some of England's most idyllic and unspoilt scenery surrounds Ilsington, with the picturesque villages of Lustleigh and Widecombe-in-the-Moor close by. Guests have easy access to the moors from the hotel. Riding, fishing and many other country pursuits can be arranged. Special breaks are available.

Our inspector loved: *The outstanding and beautiful location, and all the facilities offered.*

Directions: From the M5 join the A38 at Exeter following Plymouth signs. After approximately 12 miles, exit for Moretonhampstead and Newton Abbot. At the roundabout follow signs for Ilsington.

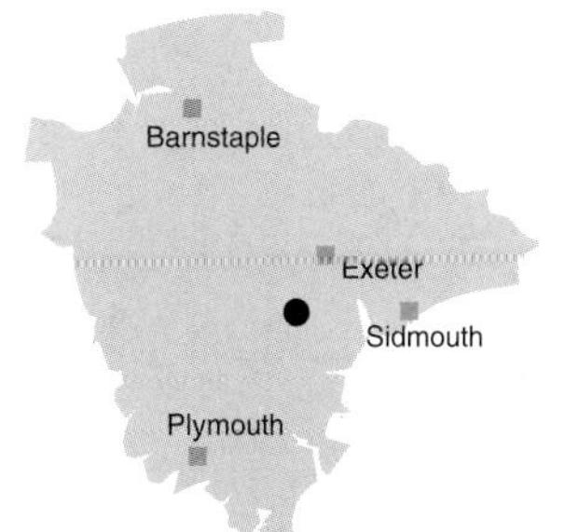

Web: www.johansens.com/ilsington
E-mail: hotel@ilsington.co.uk
Tel: 0870 381 8635
International: +44 (0)1364 661452
Fax: 01364 661307

Price Guide:
single £85–£92
double/twin £128–£135
inclusive dinner rates available

Burgh Island

BIGBURY-ON-SEA, SOUTH DEVON TQ7 4BG

Burgh Island, off the south Devon coast, is a unique and romantic location boasting more proposals of marriage per square inch then any other place in Britain. Linked to the mainland by a tidal beach it has been decorated in genuine art deco design throughout, and is steeped in the style of the 20s and 30s, from the magnificent glass peacock dome of the Palm Court to the cinema room playing black and white classics. Over the years it has welcomed esteemed guests such as Edward VIII and Wallis Simpson, Noel Coward and Agatha Christie, and today, its owners and staff are experts at staging relaxed yet memorable events. Dressing for dinner is expected and when bands are in the house, dancing is encouraged. All of the bedrooms have breathtaking views and beds are fitted with crisp white linen; televisions are only available upon request. The restaurant serves modern international dishes, using local suppliers and traditional produce. The nearby 14th-century Pilchards Inn is also available for informal meals. Outdoor pursuits include swimming in the Mermaid natural rock pool, coastal walks, tennis and golf on the Bigbury course.

Our inspector loved: *The breathtaking location and magnificent atmosphere of a bygone era combined with the superb facilities of the 21st century.*

Directions: From the M5 take the A38 towards Plymouth then exit at Wrangton Cross for the A379 and go through Modbury. Follow signs to Bigbury and Bigbury-on-Sea. At St Anne's Chapel call for further directions.

Web: www.johansens.com/burghisland
E-mail: reception@burghisland.com
Tel: 0870 381 9207
International: +44 (0)1548 810 514
Fax: 01548 810 243

Price Guide:
single £200
double/twin £290
suite £320–£480

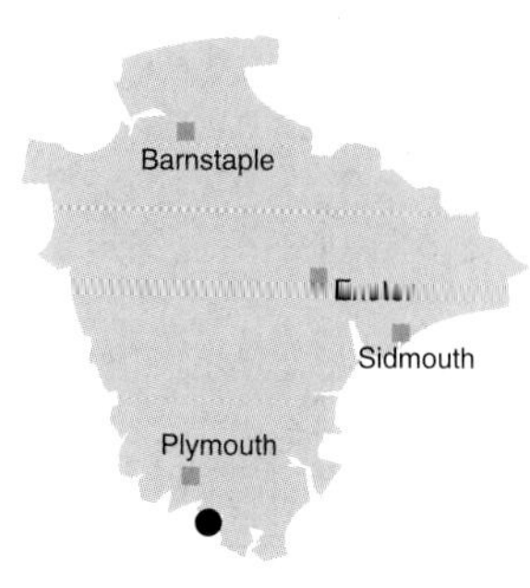

LEWTRENCHARD MANOR

LEWDOWN, NEAR OKEHAMPTON, DEVON EX20 4PN

This beautiful Jacobean manor is tucked away within its own estate on rolling Devon hills, and with just 14 exquisite bedrooms is a delightful retreat from city life. Built in 1600 by the Monk family it was later embellished by the Victorian hymn writer Rev Sabine Baring Gould, and today is a stunning example of ornate ceilings, elegant carved oak staircases and leaded light windows. Carefully incorporated family antique pieces and elegant soft furnishings to create a sense of luxury combined with a warmth that is truly welcoming. Each of the bedrooms looks out over the valley, and the oak-panelled dining room with its coffered ceiling provides a stunning backdrop for some excellent cooking and superb wines. The restaurant has won 3 Rosettes for its exquisitely prepared and artistically presented cuisine, which is based on the freshest of local ingredients. The estate offers clay pigeon shooting and rough shooting and fishing, making this an ideal place for weekend parties, as well as an idyllic setting for weddings and functions. Exeter is on the doorstep with its cathedral and sophisticated shops, whilst Devon's numerous tourist attractions are all within easy reach.

Our inspector loved: *The new courtyard, spacious rooms and the Tower wedding suite.*

Directions: Take A30 (Okehampton–Bodmin) from Exeter. After 25 miles take the road to Tavistock / Plymouth follow signs to Lewdown from there the Lewtrenchard hotel is signposted .

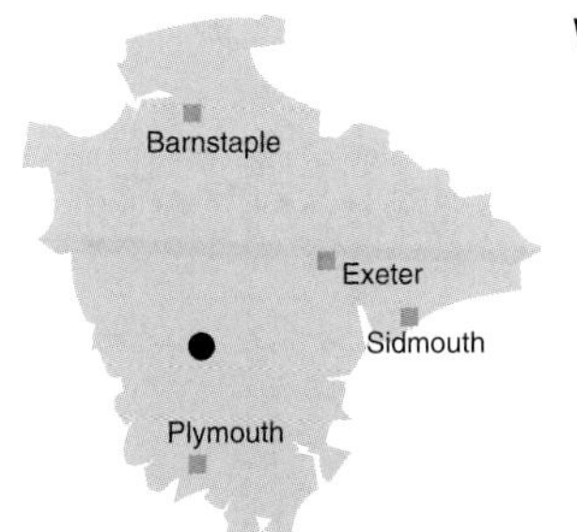

Web: www.johansens.com/lewtrenchard
E-mail: info@lewtrenchard.co.uk
Tel: 0870 381 9177
International: +44 (0)1566 783222
Fax: 01566 783332

Price Guide:
single £100–£130
double/twin £150–£210
suite £220–£250

The Arundell Arms

LIFTON, DEVON PL16 0AA

In a lovely valley close to the uplands of Dartmoor, The Arundell Arms is a former coaching inn, which dates back to Saxon times. Its flagstone floors, cosy fires, paintings and antiques combine to create a haven of warmth and comfort in an atmosphere of Old World charm. One of England's best-known sporting hotels for more than half a century, it boasts 20 miles of exclusive salmon and trout fishing on the Tamar, and 5 of its tributaries, and a famous school of fly fishing. Guests also enjoy a host of other country activities, including hill walking, shooting, riding and golf. The hotel takes great pride in its elegant AA Rosette awarded restaurant, whose gourmet cuisine has gained an international reputation. A splendid base from which to enjoy the wonderful surfing beaches nearby, The Arundell Arms is also well placed for visits to Tintagel and the historic houses and gardens of Devon and Cornwall and the Eden Project. Only 45 minutes from Exeter and Plymouth, it is also ideal for the business executive, reached by major roads from all directions. A spacious conference suite is available.

Our inspector loved: *All 21 totally refurbished bedrooms and en-suites – so tasteful – so striking.*

Directions: Lifton is approximately ¼ mile off the A30, 2 miles east of Launceston and the Cornish Border.

Web: www.johansens.com/arundellarms
E-mail: reservations@arundellarms.com
Tel: 0870 381 8323
International: +44 (0)1566 784666
Fax: 01566 784494

Price Guide:
single from £95
double/twin from £150
suite from £180

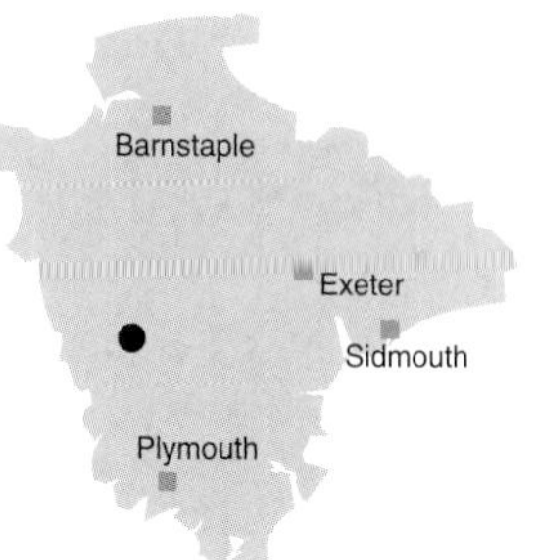

Soar Mill Cove Hotel

SOAR MILL COVE, SALCOMBE, SOUTH DEVON TQ7 3DS

Owned by the Makepeace family for over 25 years, Soar Mill Cove is situated midway between the historic Port of Dartmouth and The Pilgrim Steps of Plymouth, and is easily accessed by road, rail and regional airlines. Nothing is too much trouble at Soar Mill Cove, where guests are invited to enjoy pampering that only a family-owned hotel can offer. Set within 2,000 acres of National Trust countryside this is arguably the most dramatic seaside setting, with breathtaking views; a hidden gem with a warmth that makes guests return again and again. Idylically located for peaceful strolls along the golden sand beach, fishing in rock pools and exploring local caves, memories of the beachside holidays Enid Blyton's Famous Five experienced comes to life! Trek the spectacular coastal path or sit back in the passenger seat of the hotel's free tandem whilst sipping from a complimentary flask of hot toddy. Take advantage of the hotel's number of swimming pools and relax with a massage in "The Ocean Spa" before dining on a feast of lobster and crab accompanied by fine wines.

Our inspector loved: *The superb new rooms with striking sensual fabrics and presentation and as always the breathtaking location.*

Directions: A384 to Totnes, then A381 to Soar Mill Cove.

Web: www.johansens.com/soarmillcove
E-mail: info@soarmillcove.co.uk
Tel: 0870 381 8897
International: +44 (0)1548 561566
Fax: 01548 561223

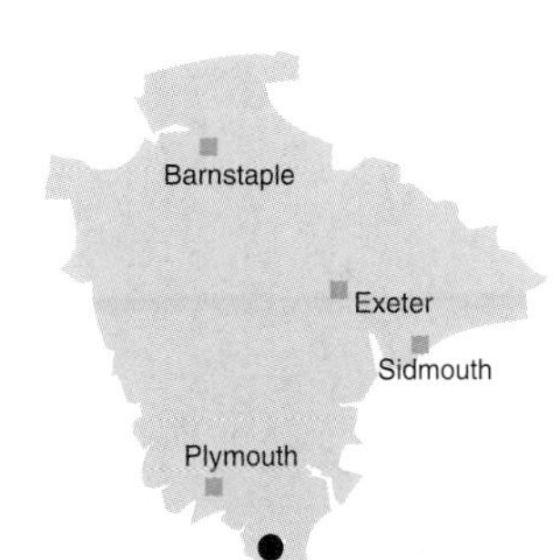

Price Guide:
single £94–£160
double/twin £180–£220
suite from £216

THE TIDES REACH HOTEL

SOUTH SANDS, SALCOMBE, DEVON TQ8 8LJ

Directions: From the M5, exit at junction 30 and join the A38 towards Plymouth. Exit for Totnes and then take the A381.

Web: www.johansens.com/tidesreach
E-mail: enquires@tidesreach.com
Tel: 0870 381 8947
International: +44 (0)1548 843466
Fax: 01548 843954

Price Guide: (including dinner)
single £75–£150
double/twin £140–£300

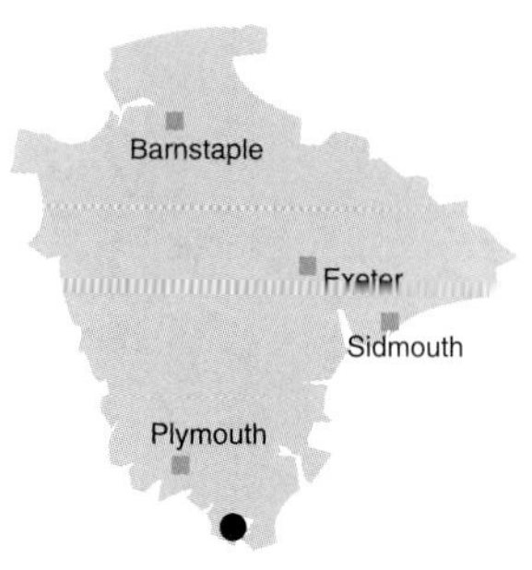

This luxuriously appointed hotel is situated in an ideal position for those wishing to enjoy a relaxing or fun-filled break. Facing south in a tree-fringed sandy cove just inside the mouth of the Salcombe Estuary it has an extensive garden on one side, the sea and a safe bathing sandy beach a few steps opposite and, to the rear, a sheltering hill topped by the subtropical gardens of Overbecks. The Tides Reach has been under the supervision of owners, the Edwards family, for more than 35 years and they have built up a reputation for hospitality and courteous service. The atmosphere is warm and friendly, the décor and furnishings tasteful and comfortable. All 35 spacious bedrooms are en suite, well equipped and decorated with flair and originality. The lawned garden centres around an ornamental lake with waterfall and fountain which is surrounded by landscaped tiers of colourful plants, shrubs and palms. Overlooking it is the restaurant where chef Finn Ibsen's excellent gourmet cuisine has earned AA Rosettes. A superb indoor heated swimming pool is the nucleus of the hotel's leisure complex which includes a sauna, solarium, spa bath, gymnasium, squash court, snooker room and hair & beauty salon . The hotel has facilities for windsurfing, sailing and canoeing.

Our inspector loved: *The location literally on the beach , the warmth of welcome and the facilities.*

Hotel Riviera

THE ESPLANADE, SIDMOUTH, DEVON EX10 8AY

A warm welcome awaits guests arriving at this prestigious award-winning hotel. With accolades such as the AA Courtesy and Care Award and more recently, the Which? Hotel Guide's Hotel of the Year, it comes as no surprise that Peter Wharton's Hotel Riviera is arguably one of the most comfortable and most hospitable in the region. The exterior, with its fine Regency façade and bow fronted windows complements the elegance of the interior comprising handsome public rooms and beautifully appointed bedrooms, many with sea views. Perfectly located at the centre of Sidmouth's historic Georgian esplanade and awarded 4 stars by both the AA and the RAC, the Riviera is committed to providing the very highest standard of excellence which makes each stay at the property a totally pleasurable experience. Guests may dine in the attractive salon, which affords glorious views across Lyme Bay, and indulge in the superb cuisine, prepared by Swiss and French trained chefs. The exceptional cellar will please the most discerning wine connoisseur. Activities include coastal walks, golf, bowling, croquet, putting, tennis, fishing, sailing, riding and exploring the breathtaking surroundings with its gardens, lush countryside and stunning coastline. Short breaks are available.

Our inspector loved: *The location, friendly helpful staff and the imaginative menus – very tempting.*

26 85

Directions: The hotel is situated at the centre of The Esplanade.

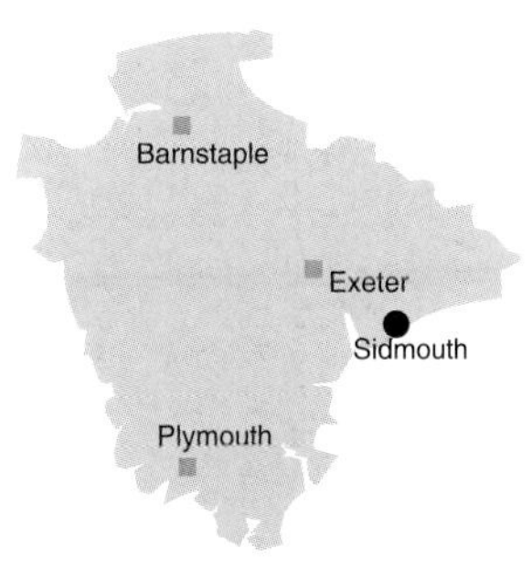

Web: www.johansens.com/riviera
E-mail: enquiries@hotelriviera.co.uk
Tel: 0870 381 8624
International: +44 (0)1395 515201
Fax: 01395 577775

Price Guide: (including 6 course dinner):
single £99–£150
double/twin £198–£278
suite £298–£318

The Palace Hotel

BABBACOMBE ROAD, TORQUAY, DEVON TQ1 3TG

Directions: From seafront follow signs for Babbacombe. Hotel entrance is on the right.

Web: www.johansens.com/palacetorquay
E-mail: info@palacetorquay.co.uk
Tel: 0870 381 8798
International: +44 (0)1803 200200
Fax: 01803 299899

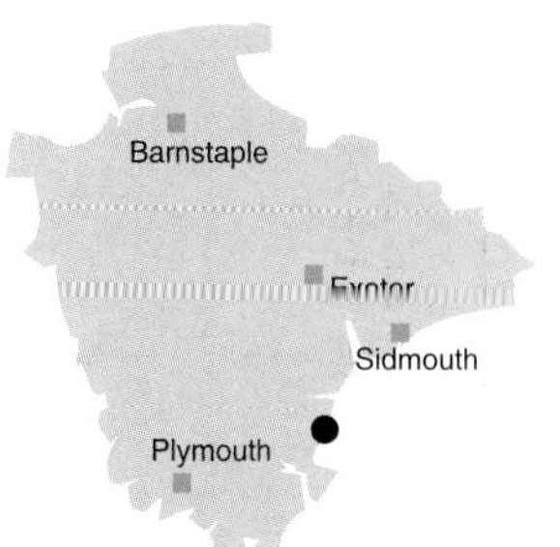

Price Guide:
single £69–£84
double/twin £138–£168
executive £228
suite £248–£290

Once the residence of the Bishop of Exeter, the privately owned Palace Hotel is a gracious Victorian building set in 25 acres of beautifully landscaped gardens and woodlands. The comfortable bedrooms are equipped with every modern amenity and there are also elegant, spacious suites available. Most rooms overlook the hotel's magnificent grounds. The main restaurant provides a high standard of traditional English cooking, making full use of fresh, local produce, as well as offering a good variety of international dishes. The cuisine is complemented by a wide selection of popular and fine wines. Light meals are also available from the lounge and during the summer months, a mediterranean-style menu is served on the terrace. A host of sporting facilities has made this hotel famous. These include a short par 3 9-hole championship golf course, indoor and outdoor swimming pools, 2 indoor and 4 outdoor tennis courts, 2 squash courts, saunas, snooker room and a well-equipped fitness suite. Places of interest nearby include Dartmoor, South Hams and Exeter. Paignton Zoo, Bygone's Museum and Kent's Cavern are among the local attractions.

Our inspector loved: *This gracious hotel - beautiful grounds and the fact one can stay on-site and forget the car.*

Orestone Manor & The Restaurant at Orestone Manor

ROCKHOUSE LANE, MAIDENCOMBE, TORQUAY, DEVON TQ1 4SX

Stylishly refurbished as a Colonial manor house, this luxury country house hotel and restaurant is located on the rural fringe of Torquay, with stunning views across the Torbay coastline and Lyme Bay. Built in 1809 this was once the home of painter John Calcott Horsley RA, whose celebrated portrait of his brother-in-law, Isambard Kingdom Brunel, hangs in the National Gallery. He is also renowned for having painted the very first Christmas card. Each guest room has its own décor and character with full amenities and luxury en-suite bathrooms; some have a terrace or balcony. Excellent service and superb food and wine can be enjoyed in the 2 AA Rosette-awarded restaurant. Using only the best seasonal local produce – some from Orestone's gardens – light lunches, snacks and afternoon teas are served in the conservatory or on the terrace, whilst a full set lunch and à la carte dinner menu are available in the restaurant. A number of accolades have been forthcoming: listed in the AA's Top 200 with 83% (the highest in the southwest), recipient of a RAC Blue Ribbon, award winner of the English Riviera Hotel of the Year and Les Routiers Southwest Hotel of the Year. Numerous places of interest close by include Dartmoor, Exmoor and National Trust properties and gardens. There is also a wide range of activities and picturesque coastal walks to enjoy.

Our inspector loved: *The beautiful setting, and fine dining – quite superb.*

Directions: About 3 miles north of Torquay on the A379 (Formerly B3199). Take the coast road towards Teignmouth.

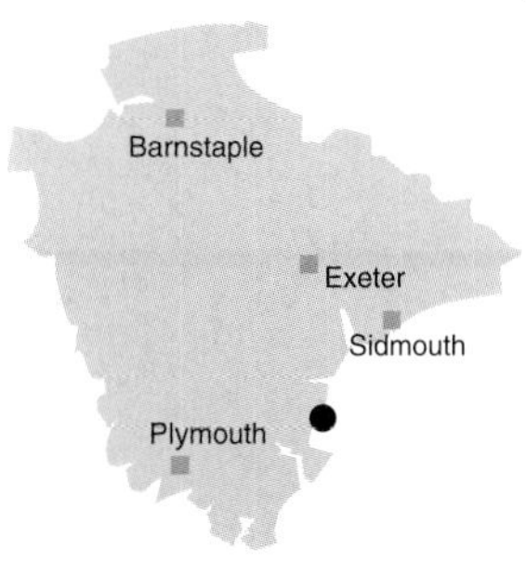

Barnstaple
Exeter
Sidmouth
Plymouth

Web: www.johansens.com/orestonemanor
E-mail: enquiries@orestonemanor.com
Tel: 0870 381 8794
International: +44 (0)1803 328098
Fax: 01803 328336

Price Guide:
single £89–£149
double/twin £125–£225

The Osborne Hotel & Langtry's Restaurant

MEADFOOT BEACH, TORQUAY, DEVON TQ1 2LL

The combination of Mediterranean chic and the much-loved Devon landscape has a special appeal, which is reflected at The Osborne. The hotel is the centrepiece of an elegant Regency crescent in Meadfoot, a quiet location within easy reach of the centre of Torquay. Known as a "country house by the sea", the hotel offers the friendly ambience of a country home complemented by the superior standards of service and comfort expected of a hotel on the English Riviera. Most of the 32 bedrooms have magnificent views and are decorated in pastel shades. Overlooking the sea, Langtry's acclaimed award-winning restaurant provides fine English cooking and tempting regional specialities, whilst the Brasserie has a menu available throughout the day. Guests may relax in the attractive 6-acre gardens and make use of indoor and outdoor swimming pools, gymnasium, sauna, tennis court and putting green – all without leaving the grounds. Sailing, archery, clay pigeon shooting and golf can be arranged. Devon is a county of infinite variety, with its fine coastline, bustling harbours, tranquil lanes, sleepy villages and the wilds of Dartmoor. The Osborne is ideally placed to enjoy all these attractions.

***Our inspector loved:** The magnificent location and the superbly refurbished lounge. A country house by the sea.*

Directions: The hotel is in Meadfoot, to the east of Torquay.

Web: www.johansens.com/osborne
E-mail: enq@osborne-torquay.co.uk
Tel: 0870 381 8795
International: +44 (0)1803 213311
Fax: 01803 296788

Price Guide:
single £55–£100
double/twin £95–£225
suite £120–£250

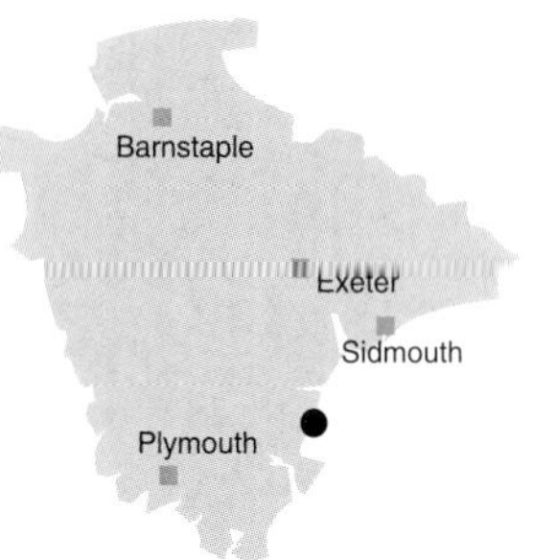

Percy's Country Hotel & Restaurant

COOMBESHEAD ESTATE, VIRGINSTOW, DEVON EX21 5EA

Percy's delivers the unexpected. The 130 acres of unspoilt Devon countryside offers a sanctuary of mixed woodland, orchards, lakes and an abundance of stunning wildlife to explore. Jacob lambs frolic, the Percy brood mares nurture their foals and roe deer are to be seen grazing at dawn and dusk. As guests watch spectacular sunsets, Percy's 4 energetic black labradors insist on sharpening pre-dinner appetites. 8 consecutive years of accolades for cuisine reflects the integrity of the home grown produce and organic ingredients. Fish is bought from Looe quayside, pork and lamb are hand-reared and crisp salad leaves are picked just before sevice. The refreshingly light style of seasonal cooking creates a memorable experience and the breakfast menu echoes this, offering a choice of home produced chicken, duck or goose eggs. Comfort and luxury are evident in the stylish bedrooms, equipped with whirlpool baths and DVD players, comfortable sofas, cafetieres and king-size beds. Important occasions can be celebrated with added privacy by taking exclusive use of the newly refurbished luxury, 3-bedroom Coombeshead cottage.

Our inspector loved: *This beautiful hideaway and its totally organic produce.*

Directions: From Okehampton take the A3079 to Metherell Cross. After 8.3 miles turn left. The hotel is 6.5 miles on the left. See website for more comprehensive details.

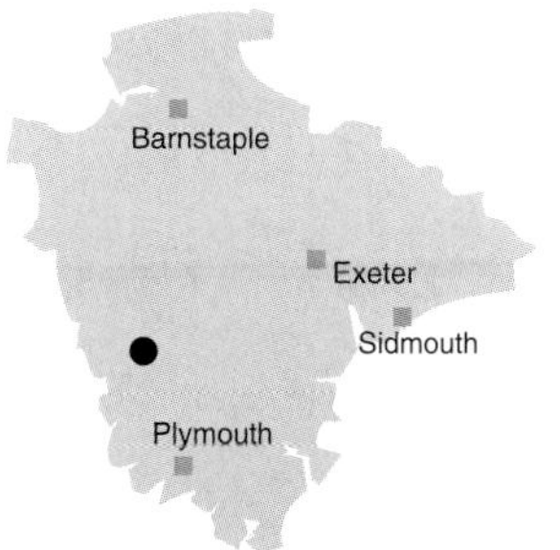

Web: www.johansens.com/percys
E-mail: info@percys.co.uk
Tel: 0870 381 8817
International: +44 (0)1409 211236
Fax: 01409 211460

Price Guide:
single from £90
double from £150

Langdon Court Hotel & Restaurant

DOWN THOMAS, PLYMOUTH, DEVON PL9 0DY

Originally built for Katherine Parr, the sixth wife of Henry VIII, this Grade II listed Tudor manor has even earlier origins, evidence of which can be found in its cellars. Rebuilt in 1648, the house is now surrounded by fields and woodland and has its own Jacobean walled gardens and well-kept lawns. Behind its impressive grey façade lie tiled floors, warmly painted stone walls and classic, uncluttered furnishings. Some of the 12 bedrooms are simply stunning; many have views of the countryside or the gardens. Three function suites: Calmady, Cory and Courtney, are available for wedding receptions, shooting and house parties. An impressive menu is served in the modern brasserie, the bar or on the terrace, specialising in fish and seafood. Throughout the year, the finest produce and organically farmed meats are selected from local suppliers, while the hotel's own kitchen garden provides an assortment of vegetables and herbs, and the cellar holds well-established favourites along with wines from the New World. The hotel has a direct path to the beach at Wembury, access to the coastal paths and is ideally placed for exploring the South Hams countryside, numerous National Trust properties and the Eden project.

Our inspector loved: *The 12 beautifully presented en-suite bedrooms and the imaginative, comprehensive cuisine.*

Directions: From Exeter join the A38 towards Plymouth then take the exit signed Plymouth, Yelverton Plymstock into Brixton. Follow Brixton Tor/Otter Nurseries and carry on the Leyford Lane. Turn left into the hotel's drive.

Web: www.johansens.com/langdon
E-mail: enquiries@langdoncourt.co.uk
Tel: 0870 381 9157
International: +44 (0)1752 862358
Fax: 01752 863428

Price Guide:
single from £85
double from £120

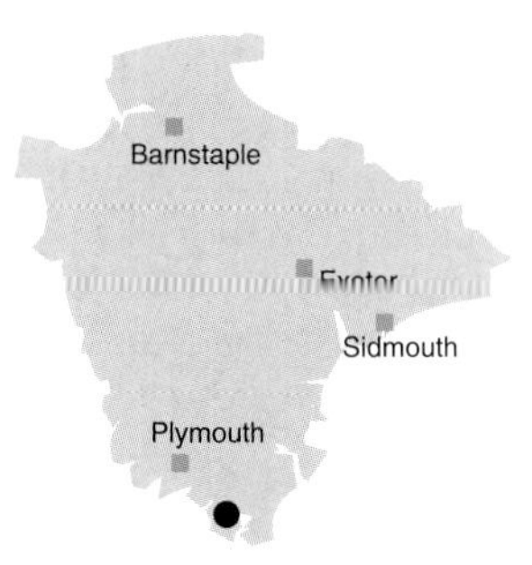

 12   50      

Woolacombe Bay Hotel

SOUTH STREET, WOOLACOMBE, DEVON EX34 7BN

Woolacombe Bay Hotel stands in 6 acres of grounds, leading to 3 miles of golden sand. Built by the Victorians, the hotel has an air of luxury, style and comfort. All rooms are en-suite with satellite TV, baby listening device, ironing centre, some with a balcony. Traditional English and French dishes are offered in the dining room. Superb recreational amenities on-site include unlimited free access to tennis, squash, indoor and outdoor pools, billiards, bowls, croquet, dancing and films, a health suite with steam room, sauna, spa bath with high impulse shower. Power-boating, fishing, shooting and riding can be arranged and preferential rates are offered for golf at the Saunton Golf Club. There is a "Hot House" aerobics studio, beauty salon, cardio vascular weights room, solariums, masseur and beautician. However, being energetic is not a requirement for enjoying the qualities of Woolacombe Bay. Many of its regulars choose simply to relax in the grand public rooms and in the grounds, which extend to the rolling surf of the magnificent bay. A drive along the coastal route in either direction will guarantee splendid views. Exmoor's beautiful Doone Valley is an hour away by car. Closed January.

Our inspector loved: *The first-class upgraded en-suites in all rooms and the superb facilities offered to all guests.*

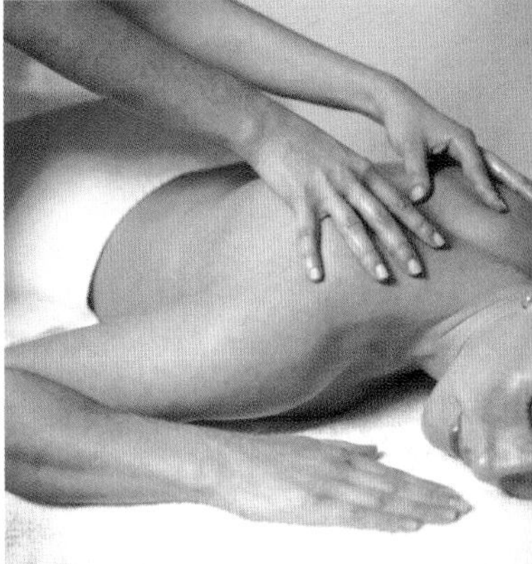

Directions: At the centre of the village, off main Barnstaple–Ilfracombe road.

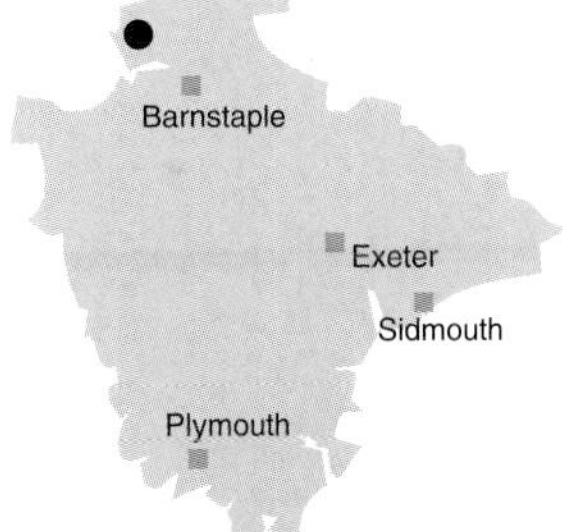

Web: www.johansens.com/woolacombebay
E-mail: woolacombe.bayhotel@btinternet.com
Tel: 0870 381 9007
International: +44 (0)1271 870388
Fax: 01271 870613

Price Guide: (including dinner)
single £92–£152
double/twin £184–£304

65 350 SPA

WATERSMEET HOTEL

MORTEHOE, WOOLACOMBE, DEVON EX34 7EB

In a setting of incomparable beauty the Watersmeet is situated in one of the finest and most dramatic locations in the South West, it commands an elevated position at the waters edge above Combesgate Beach with steps leading directly to the sandy beach. The magnificent views of the rugged coastline to Lundy Island can be enjoyed from the large picture windows in the reception rooms ensuring that guests can admire the ever-changing coastline. Under the ownership of Michael and Amanda James a tasteful refurbishment has transformed the bedrooms, consistent with the high standard of the hotel, to include all accoutrement for luxury living. All boast superb uninterrupted sea views and many have balconies. Award winning imaginative menus combine the use of the finest quality local ingredients with thoughtfully balanced dishes, taken in the pavilion AA Rosette restaurant while admiring the sunsets by candlelight. Lunch and tea may be taken alfresco on the terrace or in the picturesque tea garden. Recreational facilities include heated outdoor and indoor pool with a hot spa and steam room. Scenic coastal walks along National Trust land and Saunton Sands Championship Golf Course are nearby. The excellent reputation of the hotel with the impeccable service, relaxation theme and home from home ambiance continues to attract guests all year round.

Directions: From the M5, junction 27, follow the A361 towards Ilfracombe. Turn left at the roundabout and follow signs to Mortehoe.

Web: www.johansens.com/watersmeet
E-mail: info@watersmeethotel.co.uk
Tel: 0870 381 8972
International: +44 (0)1271 870333
Fax: 01271 870890

Price Guide: (including dinner)
single £98–£150
double/twin £140–£285

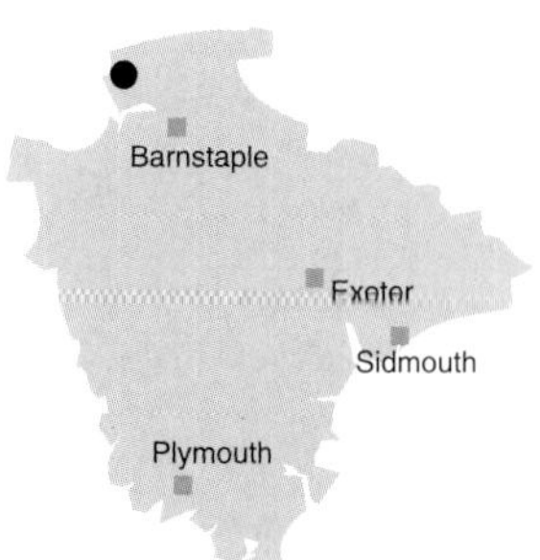

Our inspector loved: *The breathtaking location and relaxing ambience.*

NORFOLK ROYALE HOTEL

RICHMOND HILL, BOURNEMOUTH, DORSET BH2 6EN

Bournemouth has long been a popular seaside resort and has not lost its unique character. The RAC 4 Star Norfolk Royale Hotel is a fine example of the elegant buildings that grace the town. It is a splendid Edwardian house, once the holiday home of the Duke of Norfolk, after whom it is named. Extensive restoration work throughout the hotel, while enhancing its comfort, has not eliminated the echoes of the past and new arrivals are impressed by the elegant furnishings and courtesy of the staff. The designs of the spacious bedrooms reflect consideration for lady travellers, busy business executives, non-smokers and the disabled. The rich fabrics of the delightful colour schemes contribute to their luxurious ambience. Guests relax in the lounge or attractive club bar, in summer enjoying the gardens or patio – all with waiter service – and delicious breakfasts, lunches and candle-lit dinners are served in the Echoes Restaurant, which has an excellent wine list. The good life includes the pleasures of a pool and spa whilst Bournemouth offers golf courses, tennis, water sports, a casino and theatre. It has a large conference and exhibition centre. Poole Harbour, The New Forest, Thomas Hardy country and long sandy beaches are nearby.

Our inspector loved: *The high standards of room provision coupled with friendly and professional service.*

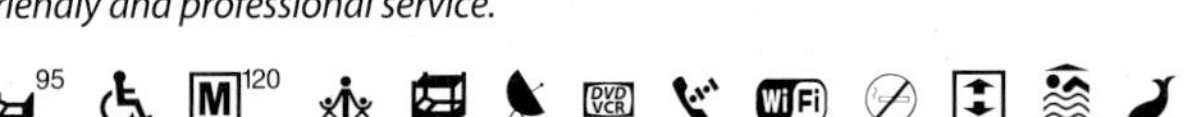

Directions: From the M27, A31 & A338 find the hotel on the right, halfway down Richmond Hill approaching the town centre.

Sherborne
Shaftesbury
Bridport
Dorchester
Bournemouth

Web: www.johansens.com/norfolkroyale
E-mail: norfolkroyale@englishrosehotels.co.uk
Tel: 0870 381 8765
International: +44 (0)1202 551521
Fax: 01202 299729

Price Guide:
single from £105
double/twin £150–£195
suite from £225

THE AVONMOUTH HOTEL AND RESTAURANT

95 MUDEFORD, CHRISTCHURCH, DORSET BH23 3NT

Built in the 1830s as a gentleman's residence, this charming, Grade II listed hotel stands in extensive grounds on a quiet area of the waterfront with magnificent views over Mudeford Quay, Hengistbury Head and Christchurch Estuary. Privately owned, it has undergone sympathetic refurbishment, awarded an AA Rosette and offers the highest standards of accommodation, service and cuisine. Each en-suite bedroom is distinctively styled, tastefully furnished and has every home comfort. Guests have a choice of bedrooms in the Georgian main house or in the Orchard Wing, situated in the landscaped garden, which slopes gently down to the harbour edge. Dining in the delightful Quays Restaurant, with its panoramic window views and sunny terrace, is a real pleasure; classic dishes, with a touch of imagination, are prepared by talented executive chef Nigel Popperwell, formerly personal chef to fashion designers Tommy Hilfiger and Valentino and Ainsley Harriott's successor at London's Westbury Hotel. A heated outdoor swimming pool is popular with visitors (June to August) and for the more energetic there are sailing and windsurfing in the estuary. Bournemouth and Christchurch's attractions are within easy reach while the lovely walks, rambling trails and villages of the New Forest are just 15 minutes away.

Our inspector loved: *The airy dining room with delightful waterside views and delicious cuisine.*

Directions: From the M25/M3/M27, take the A35 Lyndhurst to Christchurch. At Sainsbury roundabout follow signs to Mudeford. Continue on the main route through the village, past a parade of shops on the right and the hotel is on the left.

Web: www.johansens.com/avonmouth
E-mail: info@avonmouth-hotel.co.uk
Tel: 0870 381 9333
International: +44 (0)1202 483434
Fax: 01202 479004

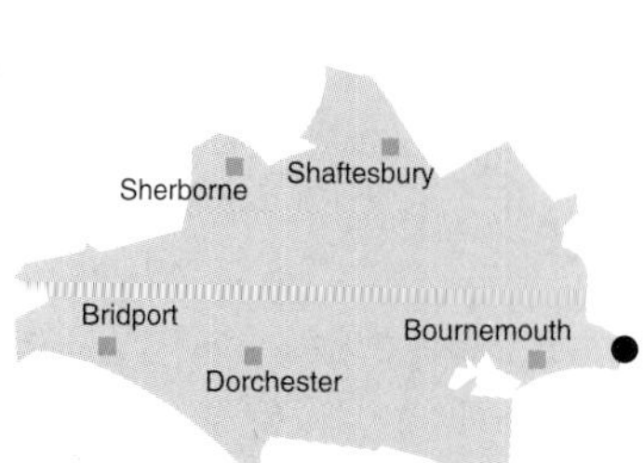

Price Guide:
single from £90
double/twin from £120
double/twin with water view £150

Summer Lodge Country House Hotel, Restaurant & Spa

SUMMER LANE, EVERSHOT, DORSET DT2 0JR

Tucked away amidst 4 private, walled acres and the quaint thatched cottages of Wessex, the luxurious Summer Lodge hails back to 1789. Built for the 2nd Earl of Ilchester, Thomas Hardy was commissioned to draw plans for a second floor by the 6th Earl in 1893. Just 2 hours from London by train and 20 minutes from Dorset's Jurassic coast, the impeccably restored 24 gorgeous rooms, suites and cottages - many with fireplaces - combine finest English furnishings and classical art with the latest technology, such as flat-screen televisions and Wi-Fi, and the highest standards of impeccable, friendly service. The award-winning restaurant, under Head Chef Steven Titman and Sommelier of the Year Eric Zweibel, is a delight and the Lodge's own vegetable garden and extensive wine cellar complement the culinary experience. Lighter meals are available in the cosy, well-stocked bar. A sumptuous Dorset cream tea with delights by the 2 pastry chefs is served each afternoon. The new spa boasts an indoor heated pool, gymnasium, sauna, beauty salon, whirlpool spa and treatment rooms offering Matis products. Civil weddings, small business meetings and private dining are meticulously catered for. Activities arranged, include golf, shooting, tennis, sailing, fishing, horse riding, racing, scuba diving and visits to various museums and country estates.

***Our inspector loved:** This garden takes some beating! Bring notebooks and pencils to take home wonderful ideas.*

Directions: The turning to Evershot leaves the A37 halfway between Dorchester and Yeovil. Once in the village, turn left into Summer Lane and the hotel entrance is 150 yards on the right.

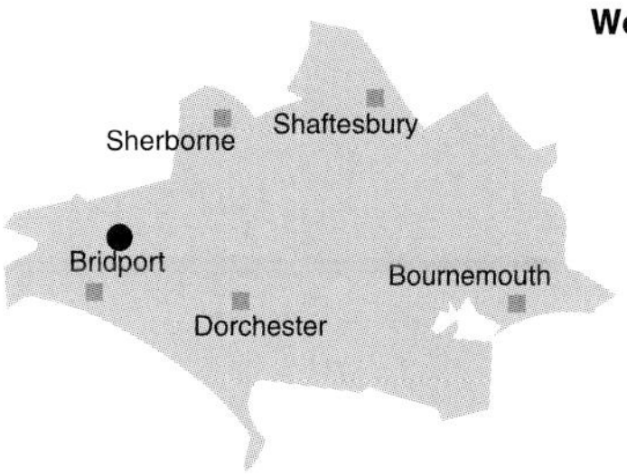

Web: www.johansens.com/summerlodge
E-mail: summer@relaischateaux.com
Tel: 0870 381 8926
International: +44 (0)1935 482000
Fax: 01935 482040

Price Guide:
single from £152.50
double/twin from £185
suite/master bedroom from £330

Plumber Manor

STURMINSTER NEWTON, DORSET DT10 2AF

An imposing Jacobean building of local stone, occupying extensive gardens in the heart of Hardy's Dorset, Plumber Manor has been the home of the Prideaux-Brune family since the early 17th century. Leading off a charming gallery, hung with family portraits, are 6 very comfortable bedrooms. The conversion of a natural stone barn lying within the grounds, as well as the courtyard building, has added a further 10 spacious bedrooms, some of which have window seats overlooking the garden and the Develish stream. 3 interconnecting dining rooms comprise the restaurant, where a good choice of imaginative, well-prepared dishes is presented, supported by a wide-ranging wine list. Chef Brian Prideaux-Brune's culinary prowess has been recognised by all the major food guides. Open for dinner every evening and Sunday lunch. The Dorset landscape, with its picture-postcard villages such as Milton Abbas and Cerne Abbas, is close at hand, while Corfe Castle, Lulworth Cove, Kingston Lacy and Poole Harbour are not far away. Riding can be arranged locally; however, if guests wish to bring their own horse to hack or hunt with local packs, the hotel provides free stabling on a do-it-yourself basis. Closed during February.

Our inspector loved: *This real country house – dogs, horses, good food, quiet nights.*

Directions: Plumber Manor is 2 miles south-west of Sturminster Newton on the Hazelbury Bryan road, off the A357.

Web: www.johansens.com/plumbermanor
E-mail: book@plumbermanor.com
Tel: 0870 381 8829
International: +44 (0)1258 472507
Fax: 01258 473370

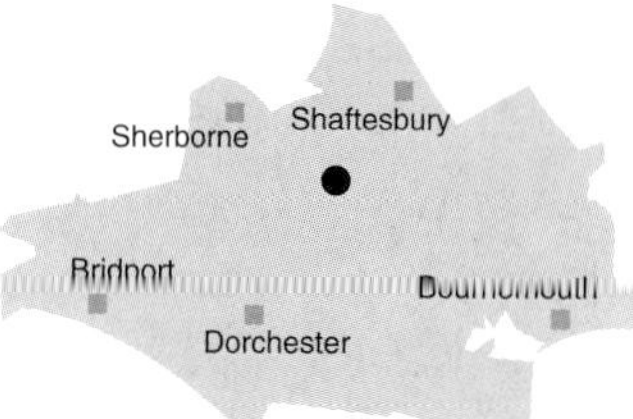

Price Guide:
single from £90
double/twin £110–£170

The Priory Hotel

CHURCH GREEN, WAREHAM, DORSET BH20 4ND

Dating from the early 16th century, the one-time Lady St Mary Priory has, for hundreds of years, offered sanctuary to travellers. In Hardy's Dorset, "Far From the Madding Crowd", it placidly stands on the bank of the River Frome in 4½ acres of immaculate gardens. Steeped in history, The Priory has undergone a sympathetic conversion to a hotel, which is charming yet unpretentious. Each bedroom is distinctively styled, with family antiques lending character and many rooms have views of the Purbeck Hills. A 16th-century clay barn has been transformed into the Boathouse, consisting of 4 spacious luxury suites at the river's edge. Tastefully furnished, the drawing room, residents' lounge and intimate bar together create a convivial atmosphere. The Garden Room Restaurant is open for breakfast and lunch (alfresco lunches are served on the terrace in the summertime), while splendid dinners are served in the vaulted stone cellars. There are moorings for guests arriving by boat. Dating back to the 9th century, the market town of Wareham has more than 200 listed buildings. Corfe Castle, Lulworth Cove, Poole and Swanage are all close by with superb walks and beaches.

Our inspector loved: *This truly beautiful building housing everything excellent for guests' satisfaction.*

Directions: Wareham is on the A351 to the west of Bournemouth and Poole. The hotel is beside the River Frome at the southern end of the town near the parish church.

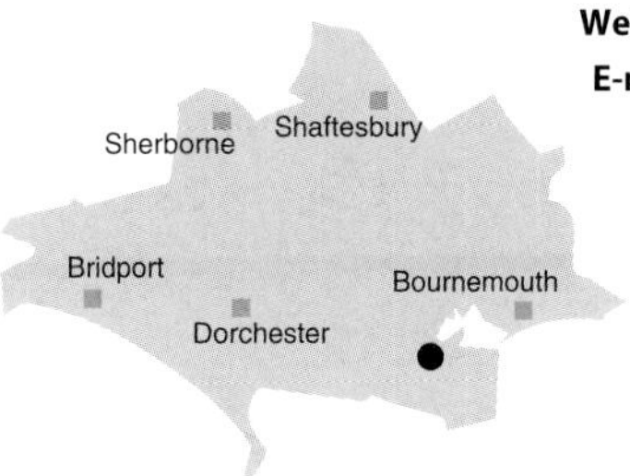

Sherborne
Shaftesbury
Bridport
Dorchester
Bournemouth

Web: www.johansens.com/priorywareham
E-mail: reservations@theprioryhotel.co.uk
Tel: 0870 381 8841
International: +44 (0)1929 551666
Fax: 01929 554519

Price Guide:
single from £110
double/twin from £170
suite from £260

Moonfleet Manor

FLEET, WEYMOUTH, DORSET DT3 4ED

Overlooking Chesil Beach, a unique feature of the Dorset coast, Moonfleet Manor is both a luxury hotel and a family resort. The owners have applied the same flair for design evident in their other family friendly properties, Woolley Grange, The Ickworth Hotel and Fowey Hall in Cornwall. The use of a variety of unusual antiques and objects from around the world lends a refreshing and individual style to this comfortable and attractive hotel. Bedrooms are beautifully decorated and furnished and a range of amenities ensures that guests enjoy standards of maximum comfort and convenience. Enthusiastic and attentive staff work hard to ensure that guests feel at home, whatever their age. Moonfleet's dining room, whose décor and style would do credit to a fashionable London restaurant, offers an excellent and varied menu based on fresh local produce but bringing culinary styles from around the world. Facilities at the hotel include an indoor swimming pool with squash and tennis courts for the more energetic. Key places of interest nearby include Abbotsbury, Dorchester, Corfe Castle and Lulworth Cove, whilst in Weymouth itself the Sea Life Park, The Deep Sea Adventure and The Titanic Story are worth a visit.

Our inspector loved: *Its uniquely, stylish provision for discerning families with children.*

Directions: Take the B3157 Weymouth to Bridport Road, then turn off towards the sea at the sign for Fleet.

Web: www.johansens.com/moonfleetmanor
E-mail: info@moonfleetmanor.com
Tel: 0870 381 8744
International: +44 (0)1305 786948
Fax: 01305 774395

Price Guide:
single from £95
double/twin £135–£285
suite £285–£385

Headlam Hall

HEADLAM, NR GAINFORD, DARLINGTON, COUNTY DURHAM DL2 3HA

This magnificent 17th-century Jacobean mansion stands in 4 acres of formal walled gardens. The grand main lawn, ancient beach hedges and flowing waters evoke an air of tranquillity. Located in the picturesque hamlet of Headlam and surrounded by over 200 acres of its own rolling farmland, Headlam Hall offers guests a special ambience of seclusion and opulence. The traditional bedrooms are all en-suite and furnished to a high standard, many with period furniture. The restaurant offers the very best of modern English and Continental cuisine with the kitchen team enjoying a fine reputation for their dishes. An extensive well-chosen wine list highlights the dining experience. Guests may dine in the tasteful surroundings of either the Panelled room, the Victorian room, the Patio room or Conservatory. The main hall features huge stone pillars and the superb original carved oak fireplace, which has dominated the room for over 300 years. The elegant Georgian drawing room opens on to a stepped terrace overlooking the main lawn. The hotel also offers extensive conference facilities and a fine ballroom, the Edwardian Suite with its oak floor and glass ceiling, suitable for up to 150 people. The vast range of leisure facilities include an indoor pool, sauna, gym, tennis court, croquet lawn, course fishery, a snooker room and a new 9-hole golf course, driving range and golf shop. A new leisure spa is due to open in the autumn.

Directions: Headlam is 2 miles north of Gainford off A67 Darlington–Barnard Castle road.

Web: www.johansens.com/headlamhall
E-mail: admin@headlamhall.co.uk
Tel: 0870 381 8590
International: +44 (0)1325 730238
Fax: 01325 730790

Price Guide:
single £80–£110
double/twin £100–£130
suite from £140

Our inspector loved: *The four-poster and antique beds in this family hotel.*

Five Lakes Resort

COLCHESTER ROAD, TOLLESHUNT KNIGHTS, MALDON, ESSEX CM9 8HX

Set in 320 acres, the superb Five Lakes Resort successfully combines leisure, health and sports activities with excellent conference and banqueting facilities. Each of the 194 bedrooms are furnished to a high standard offering every comfort and convenience. With two 18-hole golf courses – one of which, the Lakes Course, was designed by Neil Coles MBE and was used annually for the PGA European Tour - Five Lakes Resort is one of East Anglia's leading golf venues. Guests can take advantage of the indoor and outdoor championship-standard tennis courts; squash and badminton courts; an indoor pool with spa bath, steam room and sauna; gymnasium; jogging trail, snooker and a luxurious Health & Beauty Spa. Two restaurants offer a choice of good food which is complemented by excellent service. Comfortable lounges and 2 bars provide convivial surroundings in which to relax and enjoy a drink. The extensive facilities for conferences, meetings and exhibitions include 18 meeting rooms, a 3,500m^2 exhibition hall holding over 2,000 guests and a dedicated activity field.

Our inspector loved: *The glass staircase and water features in the Atrium style lounge.*

Directions: From M25 jct 28 to A12, turn left at the Fox pub at Gt Braxted /Silver End exit or A12 from north, exit at Kelvedon. Follow brown tourist signs to the resort, on the B1026.

Web: www.johansens.com/fivelakes
E-mail: enquiries@fivelakes.co.uk
Tel: 0870 381 8524
International: +44 (0)1621 868888
Fax: 01621 869696

Price Guide: (room only)
single £110
double/twin £155
suites £225

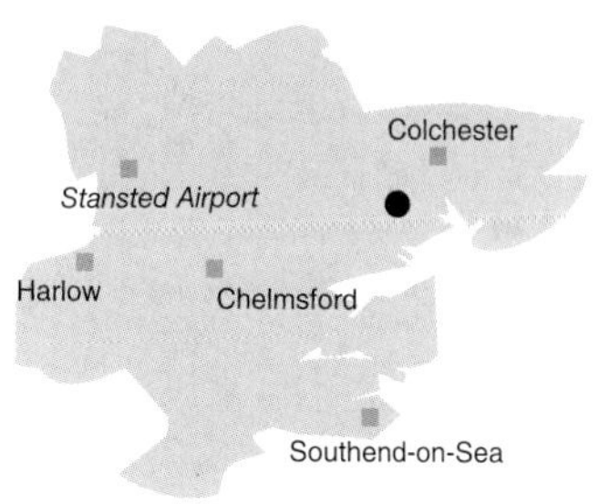

 194    2000     SPA    

MAISON TALBOOTH

STRATFORD ROAD, DEDHAM, COLCHESTER, ESSEX CO7 6HN

In the north-east corner of Essex, where the River Stour borders with Suffolk, is the Vale of Dedham, an idyllic riverside setting immortalised in the early 19th century by the paintings of John Constable. One summer's day in 1952, Gerald Milsom founder of the Pride of Britain group, enjoyed a "cuppa" in the Talbooth tearoom and soon afterwards took the helm at what would develop into Le Talbooth Restaurant. Business was soon booming and the restaurant built itself a reputation as one of the best in the country. In 1969 Maison Talbooth was created in a nearby Victorian rectory, to become, as it still is, a standard bearer for Britain's premier country house hotels. With its atmosphere of opulence, Maison Talbooth has 10 spacious guest suites all have an air of quiet luxury and which 2 have outside hot tubs. Every comfort has been provided. Breakfast is served in the suites. The original Le Talbooth Restaurant is about ½ mile upstream on a riverside terrace reached by leisurely foot or courtesy car. New for this year is the heated outdoor swimming pool. The hotel arranges special Constable tours. Maison Talbooth is also available for exclusive use – take over the hotel for your own private house party to celebrate a special occasion or just for an excuse for a 'get together' with family and friends. Please call for details. Special short breaks also available.

Our inspector loved: *The welcoming greeting on the front steps.*

       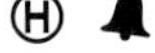

Directions: Dedham is about a mile from the A12 between Colchester and Ipswich.

Web: www.johansens.com/maisontalbooth
E-mail: maison@milsomhotels.com
Tel: 0870 381 8712
International: +44 (0)1206 322367
Fax: 01206 322752

Price Guide:
single £120–£160
double/twin £165–£325

Greenwoods Hotel, Spa & Retreat

STOCK ROAD, NEAR CHELMSFORD, ESSEX CM4 9BE

For rest, relaxation and rebuilding energy, few places better this luxury hotel, spa and peaceful retreat situated in the Essex countryside, 40 minutes from London and Stansted Airport. Greenwoods Estate stands on a high point at the edge of the village of Stock, famed for its church belfry whose beams originate from Spanish galleons. It is a beautifully restored and extended Grade II listed manor house with a combination of Georgian and Victorian architecture. Located in 42 acres of parkland, Greenwoods has 4 acres of formal gardens including a beautiful sunken herb garden. The highly skilled chef offers an imaginative and creative combination of fine dining and a balanced menu. Guests are offered opulence without intimidation, character, charm and welcoming hospitality. Public areas are lavishly decorated with sumptuous panelling, original fireplaces and comfortable sofas. Bedrooms are individually designed and furnished to the highest standard; most have panoramic views and all premier rooms have antique beds. The spa facilities include over 50 beauty and holistic treatments, sauna, steam and spa bath facilities, a fully equipped gym and a 20m lap swimming pool. Discounts are available at the neighbouring golf course. Ideal for weddings, meetings, conferences and teambuilding activities; delegates can enjoy free use of the spa facilities during their stay.

Directions: From the A12 take the B1007.

Web: www.johansens.com/greenwoods
E-mail: info@greenwoodsestate.com
Tel: 0870 381 8575
International: +44 (0)1277 829990
Fax: 01277 829899

Price Guide: (room only)
single from £85
double/twin from £105
suite from £115

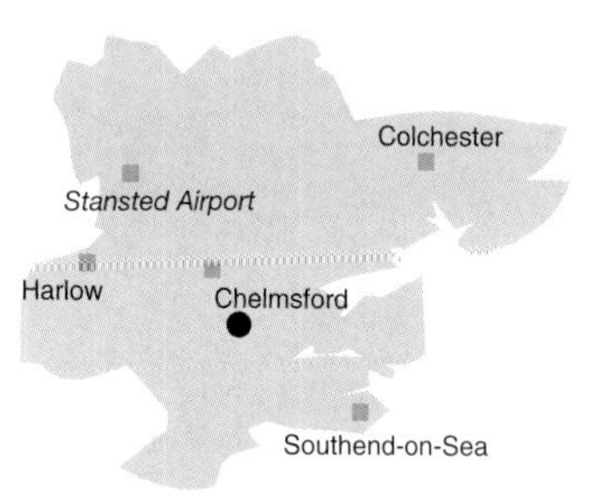

Our inspector loved: *The original hand-painted graphics in the new wing.*

    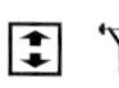 SPA    

THE SWAN HOTEL AT BIBURY

BIBURY, GLOUCESTERSHIRE GL7 5NW

The Swan Hotel at Bibury in the South Cotswolds, a 17th-century coaching inn, is a perfect base for both leisurely and active holidays which will appeal especially to motorists, fishermen and walkers. The hotel has its own fishing rights and a moated ornamental garden encircled by its own crystalline stream. Bibury itself is a delightful village, with its honey-coloured stonework, picturesque ponds, the trout-filled River Coln and its utter lack of modern eyesores. When Cotswold Inns and Hotels acquired the Swan they gained a distinctive hotel in the English countryside which acknowledges the needs of the sophisticated modern-day traveller. Oak panelling, plush carpets and sumptuous fabrics create the background for the fine paintings and antiques that grace the interiors. The 18 eccentric bedrooms are superbly appointed with luxury bathrooms and comfortable furnishings. Guests may dine in the Café Swan and the unique Gallery Restaurant. Midweek special rates available. The luxurious Swan Sanctuary beauty treatment facility is located next to the hotel.

Our inspector loved: *The lovely riverside location in a very pretty English village.*

Directions: Bibury is signposted off A40 Oxford–Cheltenham road, on the left hand side. Secure free parking now available next to the hotel.

Web: www.johansens.com/swanhotelatbibury
E-mail: info@swanhotel.co.uk
Tel: 0870 381 8931
International: +44 (0)1285 740695
Fax: 01285 740473

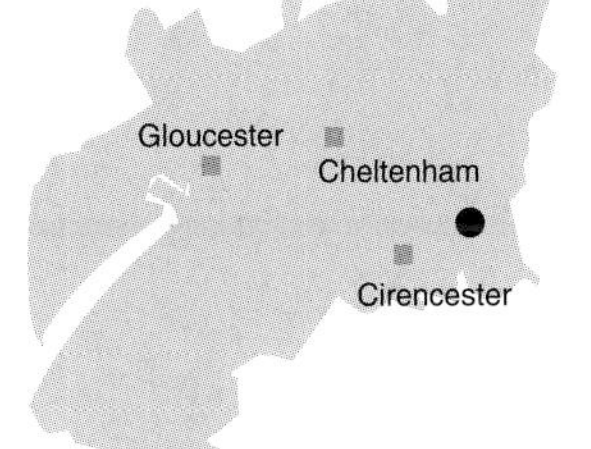

Price Guide:
single £99–£155
double/twin £140–£260

THE DIAL HOUSE

THE CHESTNUTS, HIGH STREET, BOURTON-ON-THE-WATER, GLOUCESTERSHIRE GL54 2AN

Built in 1698 from traditional Cotswold stone, The Dial House is the essence of sophisticated English country style offering guests peace and tranquillity, charm, and a spacious, luxurious interior filled with period furnishings such as large inglenook fireplaces, exposed timber beams, monks' chairs, poor boxes, secret cupboards, water wells and stone arches. Surrounded by a secluded lawned garden, highlighted by aromatic flowers and colourful shrub-filled borders and beds, this privately owned, family-run hotel is idyllically situated in a picturesque and unspoiled village where the little River Windrush flows down the main street under "toy town" low bridges beside trees and lawns. Each of the hotel's 13 bedrooms has every detail and accessory to make a guest's stay comfortable and memorable: hand-painted wallpaper, lavish big beds, deep baths, exquisite fabrics, together with television, video, direct dial telephone and state-of-the-art communication links. Mouth-watering cuisine, created from the finest and freshest of local and national produce, is served in intimate dining rooms whose innovative style and high standards have been recognised by 2 AA Rosettes and Which? Hotel of the Year 2005 Most Ravishing Restaurant with Rooms Award. Blenheim Palace, Warwick Castle, the Roman antiquities at Bath and all the delights of Shakespeare country are nearby.

Directions: From the A40 take the A429 north towards Stow-on-the-Wold for approximately 3.5 miles.

Web: www.johansens.com/dialhouse
E-mail: info@dialhousehotel.com
Tel: 0870 381 9296
International: +44 (0)1451 822244
Fax: 01451 810126

Price Guide:
single £55–£89
double £120–£160
suite £180

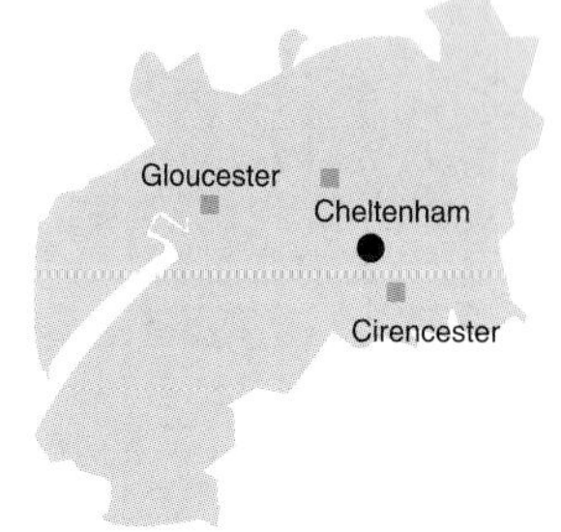

Our inspector loved: *The attention to detail throughout this stylish hotel.*

      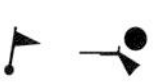 

Hotel On The Park

EVESHAM ROAD, CHELTENHAM, GLOUCESTERSHIRE GL52 2AH

Situated in the refined, Regency spa town of Cheltenham, this attractive wisteria-clad town house hotel combines the elegance and attentive, quality service of the past with an impressive 21st-century standard of accommodation and facilities. The imposing white façade, with grand pillared doorway, leads visitors into a charming, luxurious interior, which has a very welcoming, relaxed atmosphere. Bedrooms are traditional with a contemporary twist and delightfully furnished with antiques. The bathrooms are very special and range from an infinity spa bathroom, through to state-of-the-art whirlpool bathrooms and a spa bathroom with aromatherapy/chromatherapy, which either energises or relaxes bathers with aromatics and mood lighting. The infinity bath, with gently cascading water enhanced by a spectrum cycle of colours that can be controlled according to guests' moods. Parkers the brasserie takes a contemporary approach to food and décor; menus feature imaginative, vibrant cuisine complemented by an unusual and carefully chosen wine list. The public rooms offer comfort and style, and the well-stocked library is popular with those seeking quiet contemplation, a peaceful read or private chat. The town's attractive promenade, exclusive boutiques, theatres and historic attractions are within walking distance, and the Cheltenham National Hunt Racecourse is nearby.

Our inspector loved: *The new bathrooms. This place gets better and better.*

Directions: The hotel is opposite Pittville Park, a 5-minute walk from the town centre.

Web: www.johansens.com/hotelonthepark
E-mail: stay@hotelonthepark.co.uk
Tel: 0870 381 8623
International: +44 (0)1242 518898
Fax: 01242 511526

Price Guide:
single from £94.25
double/twin from £128.50

THE GREENWAY

SHURDINGTON, CHELTENHAM, GLOUCESTERSHIRE GL51 4UG

Set amidst gentle parkland with the rolling Cotswold hills beyond, The Greenway is an Elizabethan country house with a style that is uniquely its own – very individual and very special. Renowned for the warmth of its welcome, its friendly atmosphere and its immaculate personal service, The Greenway is the ideal place for total relaxation. The public rooms with their antique furniture and fresh flowers are elegant and spacious yet comfortable, with roaring log fires in winter and access to the formal gardens in summer. The 21 bedrooms all have private bathrooms and are individually decorated with co-ordinated colour schemes. Eleven of the rooms are located in the main house with a further ten rooms in the converted Georgian coach house immediately adjacent to the main building. The award-winning conservatory dining room overlooks the sunken garden, providing the perfect backdrop to superb cuisine of international appeal complemented by an outstanding selection of wines. Situated in one of Britain's most charming areas, The Greenway is well placed for visiting the spa town of Cheltenham, the Cotswold villages and Shakespeare country.

Our inspector loved: *A delightful getaway, lovely bedrooms, beautiful grounds and great food.*

Directions: On the outskirts of Cheltenham off the A46 Cheltenham–Stroud road, 2½ miles from the town centre.

Web: www.johansens.com/greenway
E-mail: greenway@btconnect.com
Tel: 0870 381 8574
International: +44 (0)1242 862352
Fax: 01242 862780

Price Guide:
single from £99
double/twin £150–£240

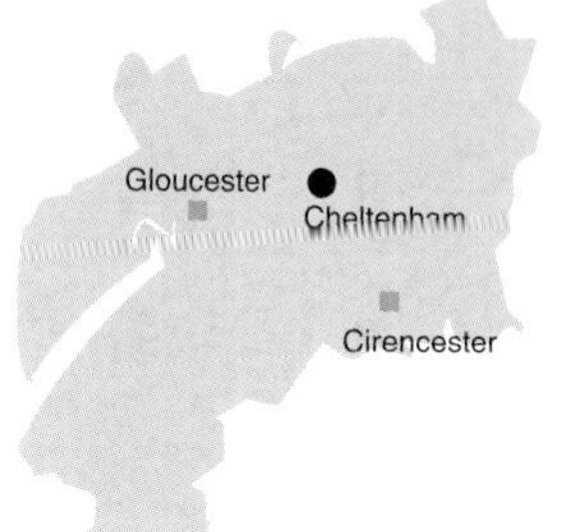

Charingworth Manor

NR CHIPPING CAMPDEN, GLOUCESTERSHIRE GL55 6NS

The ancient manor of Charingworth lies amid the gently rolling Cotswold countryside, just a few miles from the historic towns of Chipping Campden and Broadway. Beautiful old stone buildings everywhere recall the flourishing wool trade that gave the area its wealth. The 14th-century manor house overlooks its own 50-acre grounds and offers peace and enthralling views. Inside, Charingworth is a historic patchwork of intimate public rooms with log fires burning during the colder months. There are 26 individually designed bedrooms, including a limited number of non smoking rooms and a new contemporary style suite called the Ebrington Suite, all furnished with antiques and fine fabrics. Outstanding cuisine is regarded as being of great importance and guests at Charingworth are assured of imaginative dishes. The chef and his team create exciting, mouth-watering cuisine with great emphasis placed on strictly using the finest produce. There is an all-weather tennis court within the grounds, while inside, a beautiful swimming pool, sauna, steam room, solarium and gym are available, allowing guests to relax and unwind. Warwick Castle, Hidcote Manor Gardens, Batsford Arboretum, Stratford-upon-Avon, Oxford and Cheltenham are all within easy reach. Short break rates are available on request.

Our inspector loved: *The beautiful setting surrounded by Cotswold countryside.*

Directions: Charingworth Manor is on the B4035 between Chipping Campden and Shipston-on-Stour.

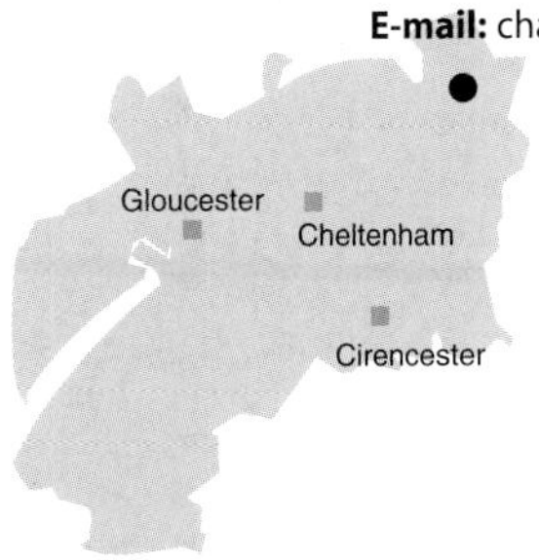

Web: www.johansens.com/charingworthmanor
E-mail: charingworthmanor@englishrosehotels.co.uk
Tel: 0870 381 8414
International: +44 (0)1386 593555
Fax: 01386 593353

Gloucester
Cheltenham
Cirencester

Price Guide: (including full breakfast)
limited double sole occupancy from £125
double/twin from £180

Cotswold House Hotel

HIGH STREET, CHIPPING CAMPDEN, GLOUCESTERSHIRE GL55 6AN

Directions: Chipping Campden is 2 miles north-east of A44, on the B4081.

Web: www.johansens.com/cotswoldhouse
E-mail: reception@cotswoldhouse.com
Tel: 0870 381 8449
International: +44 (0)1386 840330
Fax: 01386 840310

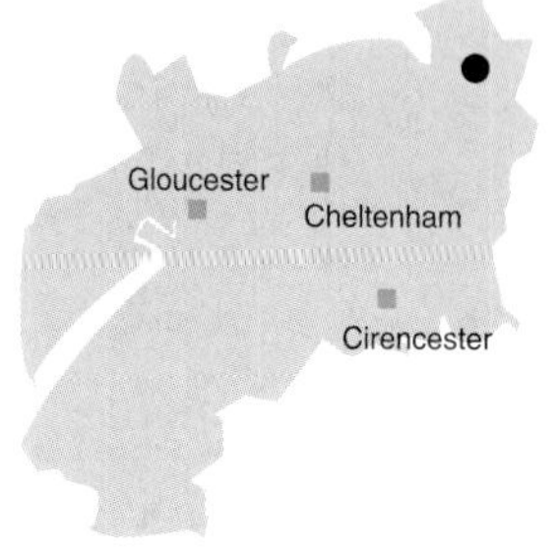

Price Guide:
single from £130
double/twin from £265
four poster from £275
cottage rooms from £395
grammar school 2-bed suite from £650

Chipping Campden is a nostalgic Cotswold town, unspoilt by the 21st-century, and Cotswold House Hotel is a splendid Regency mansion facing the town square, impressive with colonnades flanking the front door and built in soft local stone. The interior successfully contrasts a witty mix of modern style with the surrounding splendid architecture, including a signature spiral staircase. Original pieces of artwork adorn every room, and modern glass sculptures and award-winning lighting are a feast for the senses. The peaceful bedrooms are individually designed, decorated in warm tones and furnished with contemporary furniture of the utmost quality. Most guest rooms, particularly those in the recently opened Montrose House, include state-of-the-art technology, bathroom TVs, feature lighting, huge baths and luscious toiletries. Cotswold House Hotel is deservedly proud of its kitchen, which has won many accolades. The elegant Juliana's Restaurant serves locally sourced cuisine alongside a cellar book of 150 wines. Informal meals are provided in Hicks' Brasserie. Private functions and conferences for up to 100 can be held in the bespoke Montrose Suite or the intimate Grammar School Suite. Guests can enjoy exploring Chipping Campden's intriguing shops and alleyways. The hotel is a ideal base for Stratford-on-Avon and Oxford, and has parking facilities.

***Our inspector loved:** The new bedrooms in Montrose House – pure luxury!*

The Noel Arms Hotel

HIGH STREET, CHIPPING CAMPDEN, GLOUCESTERSHIRE GL55 6AT

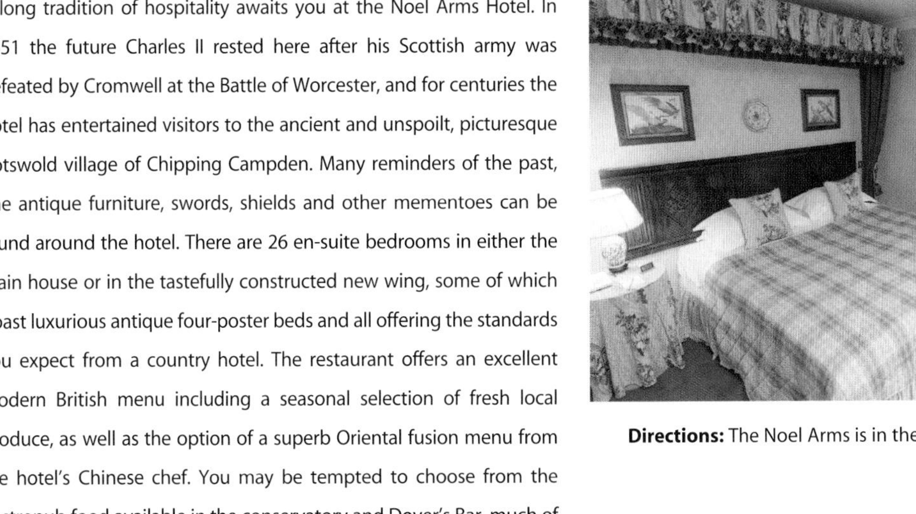

A long tradition of hospitality awaits you at the Noel Arms Hotel. In 1651 the future Charles II rested here after his Scottish army was defeated by Cromwell at the Battle of Worcester, and for centuries the hotel has entertained visitors to the ancient and unspoilt, picturesque Cotswold village of Chipping Campden. Many reminders of the past, fine antique furniture, swords, shields and other mementoes can be found around the hotel. There are 26 en-suite bedrooms in either the main house or in the tastefully constructed new wing, some of which boast luxurious antique four-poster beds and all offering the standards you expect from a country hotel. The restaurant offers an excellent modern British menu including a seasonal selection of fresh local produce, as well as the option of a superb Oriental fusion menu from the hotel's Chinese chef. You may be tempted to choose from the gastropub food available in the conservatory and Dover's Bar, much of which is Cotswold produce. The fine selection of wines from around the world are a delicious accompaniments to any meal. Try some of the traditional cask ales and keg beers. Browse around the delightful array of shops in Chipping Campden or many of the enchanting honey-coloured Cotswold villages, Hidcote Manor Gardens, Cheltenham Spa, Worcester, Oxford and Stratford-upon-Avon which are all close by.

Our inspector loved: *The civil war weaponry hanging in the entrance hall.*

Directions: The Noel Arms is in the centre of Chipping Campden, which is on the B4081, 2 miles east of the A44.

Web: www.johansens.com/noelarms
E-mail: reception@noelarmshotel.com
Tel: 0870 381 8763
International: +44 (0)1386 840317
Fax: 01386 841136

Price Guide:
single £90
double £125–£195

Lower Slaughter Manor

LOWER SLAUGHTER, GLOUCESTERSHIRE GL54 2HP

With a history that spans nearly a thousand years, this Grade II listed Manor stands in complete tranquillity within private grounds on the edge of one of the Cotswold's prettiest villages. Visitors are warmly welcomed by a team of dedicated staff, and enjoy elegant, spacious surroundings. All rooms are beautifully furnished, with carefully chosen antiques, fine china and original paintings. Outside the wonderful grounds reveal a croquet lawn and tennis court, and, within the delightful walled garden, a unique 2-storey dovecote dating back to the 15th century when the Manor was a convent. The award-winning cuisine is prepared using the best local and continental ingredients, and an outstanding wine list offers a range of 800 specially selected wines from the Old and New Worlds. An excellent setting for business meetings, The Sir George Whitmore Suite accommodates up to 16 people, and offers phone line, full secretarial services and audio-visual equipment. For more leisurely pursuits, visitors can explore the Cotswolds, Cheltenham, Stratford, and Warwick and Sudeley Castles.

Our inspector loved: *A beautiful manor house in one of the Cotswold's most idyllic villages.*

Directions: The Manor is on the right as you enter Lower Slaughter from A429.

Web: www.johansens.com/lowerslaughtermanor
E-mail: info@lowerslaughter.co.uk
Tel: 0870 381 8706
International: +44 (0)1451 820456
Fax: 01451 822150

Price Guide:
single £175–£375
double/twin £200–£400
suite £350–£400

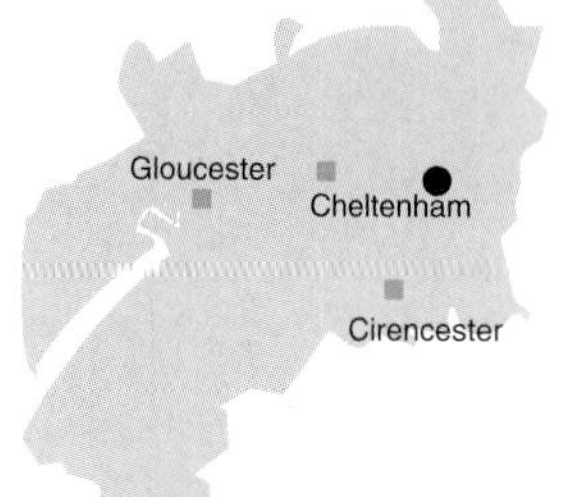

Washbourne Court Hotel

LOWER SLAUGHTER, GLOUCESTERSHIRE GL54 2HS

Washbourne Court Hotel is in the heart of the tranquil and beautiful Cotswold village of Lower Slaughter, set on the bank of the River Eye. The 4 acres of private gardens have been lovingly re-landscaped with lawns and many delightful features. With just 28 bedrooms, it has parts dating back to the 17th century. The recent additions to the hotel, a spacious new dining room and a further 6 guest rooms with comfortable and elegant furnishings, blend in perfectly with the original building. Always full of freshly picked flowers and planted bowls, the hotel has the feel of a private house with its many personal touches. The modern English cuisine offers an abundance of fresh local produce, concentrating on good textures and intense flavours combined with outstanding presentation. Head chef Matthew Pashley now oversees the running of the kitchen. Drinks, light lunches and traditional afternoon tea are also served on the garden terrace during the summer months.

Our inspector loved: *The beautiful setting right next to the river.*

Directions: The hotel is situated ½ a mile from the main A429 Fosseway between Stow-on-the-Wold and Bourton-on-the-Water (signed To the Slaughters).

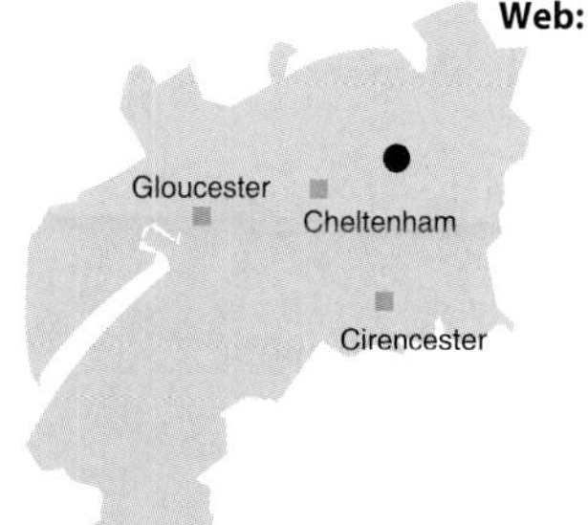

Web: www.johansens.com/washbournecourt
E-mail: info@washbournecourt.co.uk
Tel: 0870 381 8970
International: +44 (0)1451 822143
Fax: 01451 821045

Price Guide: (including dinner)
single from £115
double/twin from £170

Burleigh Court

BURLEIGH, MINCHINHAMPTON, NEAR STROUD, GLOUCESTERSHIRE GL5 2PF

Built in the 18th century, Burleigh Court Hotel is a former gentleman's manor house nestling on the edge of a steep hillside overlooking the Golden Valley in the heart of the Cotswolds. Comfortable surroundings, quality service, the ambience of a bygone era and a tranquil, relaxed atmosphere are combined with 3½ acres of beautifully tended gardens featuring terraces, ponds, pools, hidden pathways and Cotswold stone walls to create an idyllic setting. All the bedrooms are individually and delightfully furnished, with the highest standard of facilities and stunning scenic views. The coach house bedrooms, located by a Victorian plunge pool, and those within the courtyard gardens provide versatile accommodation for families. The elegant restaurant has a reputation for classical cuisine which utilises only the best local produce, whilst an extensive cellar produces a wine list to satisfy the most demanding palate. For special occasions a private dining room overlooking the rear terrace is available. Burleigh Court is perfectly situated to explore the famous honey-stoned villages of the Cotswolds, the market towns of Minchinhampton, Tetbury, Cirencester, Painswick and Bibury and attractions such as Berkely Castle and Chavenage House.

Our inspector loved: *The newly refurbished bedrooms and lovely gardens.*

Directions: Leave Stroud on A419 towards Cirencester. After approximately 2½ miles turn right, signposted Burleigh and Minchinhampton. After a further 500 yards turn left and the hotel is signposted.

Web: www.johansens.com/burleighgloucestershire
E-mail: info@burleighcourthotel.co.uk
Tel: 0870 381 8664
International: +44 (0)1453 883804
Fax: 01453 886870

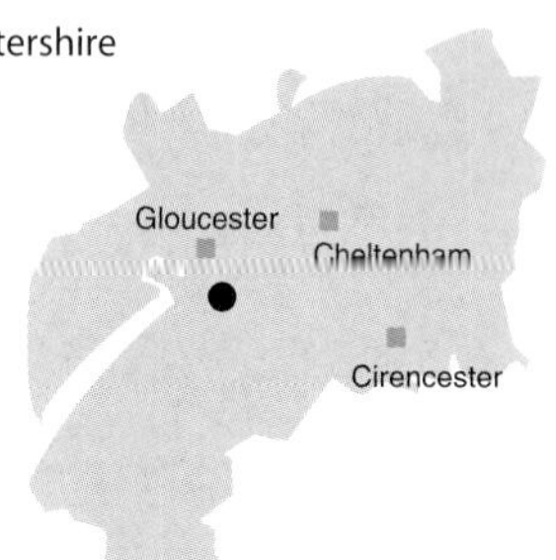

Price Guide:
single £80-£100
double £105-£145
suite £145

The Painswick Hotel

KEMPS LANE, PAINSWICK, GLOUCESTERSHIRE GL6 6YB

The village of Painswick stands high on a hill overlooking the beautiful rolling valleys of the Cotswolds. Dating back to the 14th century, the village was an old wool community; medieval cottages mingle gracefully with elegant Georgian merchants' houses. A feature of the village is the church, with its ancient churchyard graced by 99 Yew trees planted in 1792 and 17th-century table tombs in memory of the wealthy clothiers. Situated majestically within these architectural gems is the Palladian-style Painswick Hotel, built in 1790 and formerly the home of affluent village rectors. Each of the luxury en-suite bedrooms have modern amenities, beautiful fabrics, antique furniture and objets d'art, creating a restful atmosphere and the impression of staying in a comfortable private house. The stylish restaurant, with its pine panelling, offers delicious cuisine with an emphasis upon regional produce such as locally reared Cotswold meat, game, wild Severn salmon and Gloucestershire cheeses. The private Dining Room accommodates quiet dinner parties, wedding occasions and business meetings.

Our inspector loved: *Beautiful place, great location and fabulous food.*

Directions: M5 Jct13. Painswick is on A46 between Stroud and Cheltenham, turn into road by the church and continue round the corner, taking the first right. The hotel is at the bottom of the road on the right hand side.

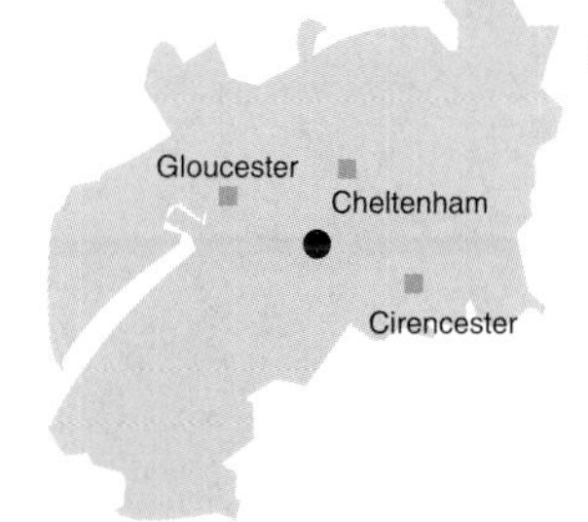

Web: www.johansens.com/painswick
E-mail: reservations@painswickhotel.com
Tel: 0870 381 8797
International: +44 (0)1452 812160
Fax: 01452 814059

Price Guide:
single from £95
double/twin from £145–£220

Fosse Manor

FOSSE WAY, STOW-ON-THE-WOLD, GLOUCESTERSHIRE GL54 1JX

Set in the heart of the Cotswolds, just outside Stow-on-the-Wold, this former rectory, set in 5 acres, combines contemporary style with country charm to provide the perfect place to relax and unwind. Set back from the Fosse Way, the ancient Roman road from which the hotel takes its name, Fosse Manor is ideally located for visiting the famous Cotswold towns and villages and the Spa town of Cheltenham. The bedrooms are individually designed using natural tones and fabrics and each one features either a DVD player or a Playstation with plenty of films and games to choose from. The restaurant and the more informal Green Room, offer an extensive menu ranging from traditional to contemporary English cuisine using the highest quality local produce and ingredients. As well as a comprehensive wine list, a selection of wines from the proprietor's cellar is also available. The new conference suite, situated in the garden with views over the rolling countryside, can cater for discreet meetings and small parties.

Our inspector loved: *The clean, crisp, spacious bedrooms and the great location for exploring the Cotswolds.*

Directions: Fosse Manor is located adjacent to the A429 just south of Stow-on-the-Wold.

Web: www.johansens.com/fossemanor
E-mail: enquiries@fossemanor.co.uk
Tel: 0870 381 9324
International: +44 (0)1451 830354
Fax: 01451 832486

Price Guide:
single £95
double £130–£225

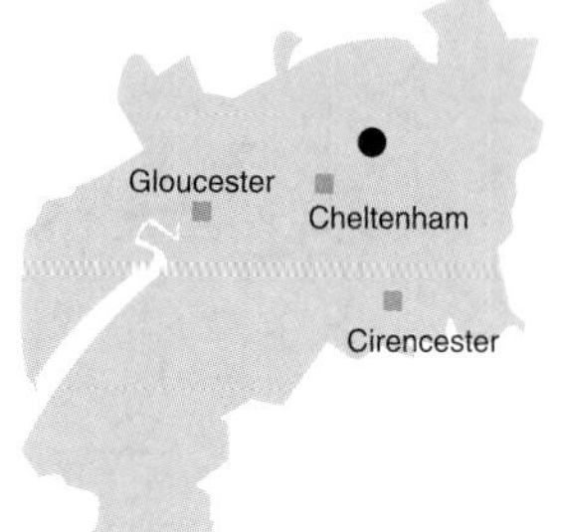

The Unicorn Hotel

SHEEP STREET, STOW-ON-THE-WOLD, GLOUCESTERSHIRE GL54 1HQ

Low oak-beamed ceilings and large stone fireplaces pay tribute to The Unicorn's lengthy past. Over the last 300 years, the inn has changed its standards of accommodation, incorporating the latest modern facilities, yet many vestiges of the former centuries remain. The recently refurbished interior is decorated in a stylish manner featuring Jacobean furniture and antique artefacts whilst log fires abound. Enhanced by floral quilts and comfortable armchairs, the 20 en-suite bedrooms are simple yet charming. Fine paintings adorn the walls of the public rooms and the cosy bar offers hand-carved wooden chairs and rich carpets. Modern British cooking is served in the elegant surroundings of the Shepherd's restaurant from an imaginative à la carte menu. The hotel is well frequented on Sundays by guests wishing to indulge in the delicious lunchtime roast. Local leisure facilities include horse riding and the golf course. Shooting and fishing are popular outdoor pursuits. Many historic buildings and castles are within easy reach including the magnificent Blenheim Palace and Warwick Castle. Nature enthusiasts will be delighted with the splendid gardens at Sudeley Castle.

Our inspector loved: *The great location and value for money.*

Directions: The nearest motorway is the M40 junction 10. Then take the A44 or the A436 in the direction of Stow-on-the-Wold. The hotel is located on the A429.

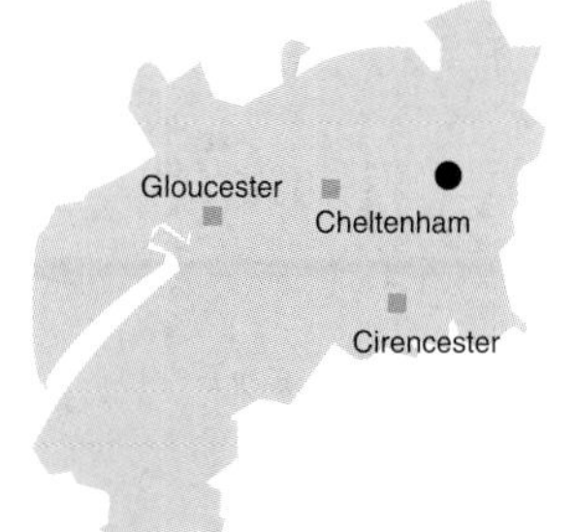

Web: www.johansens.com/unicorn
E-mail: reception@birchhotels.co.uk
Tel: 0870 381 8960
International: +44 (0)1451 830257
Fax: 01451 831090

Price Guide:
single £65–£75
double/twin £105–£125

NEW

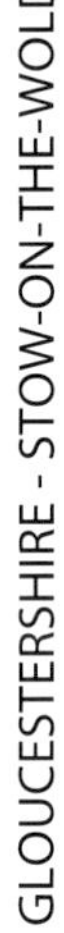

WYCKHILLHOUSE

WYCK HILL, STOW-ON-THE WOLD, GLOUCESTERSHIRE GL54 1HY

Directions: 1½ miles south of Stow-on-the-Wold on the A424 Stow-Burford road.

Web: www.johansens.com/wyckhillhouse
E-mail: enquiries@wyckhillhouse.com
Tel: 0870 381 9014
International: +44 (0)1451 831936
Fax: 01451 832243

Price Guide:
single £128.75–£180.25
double/twin £180.25–£260.59
suite £286.34

wyckhillhouse is part of the Niche Hotels portfolio, and embraces their philosophy of providing the best night's sleep with a comfortable mattress and luxurious linens and furnishings. An 18th-century hilltop manor set in the Cotswolds, the hotel is peaceful and elegant with an attentive staff. The award-winning daytime menus include light meals such as griddled Cotswold sausages and Wyck Hill afternoon tea, whilst dinner menus offer wonderful dishes featuring Cornish scallops, wild seabass, wood pigeon and English lamb as well as a superb cheese board. The 32 bedrooms are situated in the Manor House, Coach House and the Orangery. All fuse the 18th-century canvas with contemporary design, and are fitted with Egyptian cotton bedlinen, DVD players, waffle robes, power showers and deep bath tubs. Some have Parisian-style balconies with views over the Windrush Valley. There are 6 conference, event and private dining rooms, which can accommodate between 10 and 80 people. The hotel's marquee can cater for up to 300 guests for a reception or 200 for a seated dinner. wyckhillhouse has a civil wedding licence for up to 80 guests.

***Our inspector loved:** The wonderful views of the Windrush Valley from the Conservatory Restaurant.*

Lords of the Manor Hotel

UPPER SLAUGHTER, NR BOURTON-ON-THE-WATER, GLOUCESTERSHIRE GL54 2JD

Situated in the heart of the Cotswolds, on the outskirts of one of England's most unspoilt and picturesque villages, stands the Lords of the Manor Hotel. Built in the 17th century of honeyed Cotswold stone, the house enjoys splendid views over the surrounding meadows, stream and parkland. For generations the house was the home of the Witts family, who historically had been rectors of the parish. It is from these origins that the hotel derives its distinctive name. Charming, walled gardens provide a secluded retreat at the rear of the house. Each bedroom bears the maiden name of one of the ladies who married into the Witts family; each room is individually and imaginatively decorated with period furniture. The reception rooms are magnificently furnished with fine antiques, paintings, traditional fabrics and masses of fresh flowers. Log fires blaze in cold weather. The heart of this English country house is its dining room, where truly memorable dishes are created from the best local ingredients. Nearby are Blenheim Palace, Warwick Castle, the Roman antiquities at Bath and Shakespeare country.

Our inspector loved: *The individual luxurious bedrooms and wonderfully peaceful setting.*

Directions: Upper Slaughter is 2 miles west of the A429 between Stow-on-the-Wold and Bourton-on-the-Water.

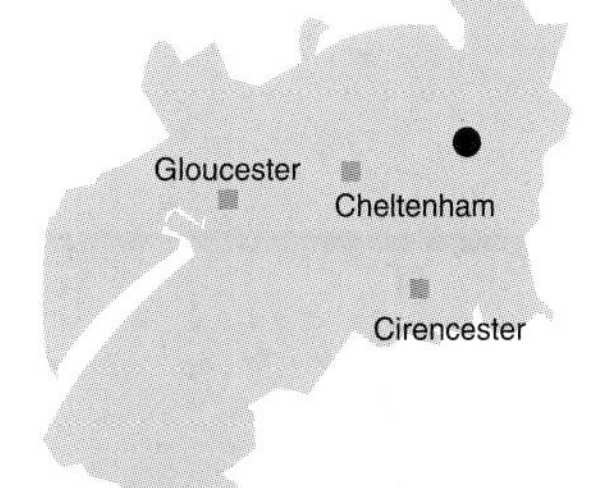

Web: www.johansens.com/lordsofthemanor
E-mail: enquiries@lordsofthemanor.com
Tel: 0870 381 8704
International: +44 (0)1451 820243
Fax: 01451 820696

Price Guide:
single from £100
double/twin £160–£310

THE GRAPEVINE HOTEL

SHEEP STREET, STOW-ON-THE-WOLD, GLOUCESTERSHIRE GL54 1AU

Directions: Sheep Street is part of A436 in the centre of Stow-on-the-Wold.

Web: www.johansens.com/grapevine
E-mail: enquiries@vines.co.uk
Tel: 0870 381 8564
International: +44 (0)1451 830344
Fax: 01451 832278

Price Guide:
single from £85
double/twin from £140

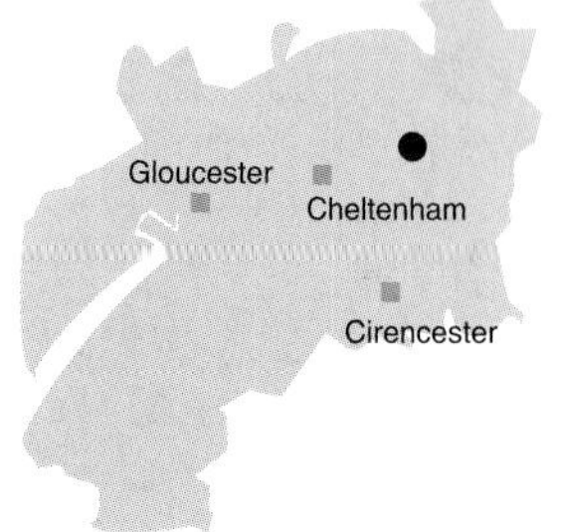

Set in the pretty town of Stow-on-the-Wold, regarded by many as the jewel of the Cotswolds, The Grapevine Hotel has an atmosphere which makes visitors feel welcome and at ease. The outstanding personal service provided by a loyal team of staff is perhaps the secret of the hotel's success. The hotel has 22 beautifully furnished bedrooms, including 6 superb garden rooms across the courtyard and offer every facility. Imaginative cuisine is served in the relaxed atmosphere of the Conservatory Restaurant. Awarded 1 AA Rosette for food, the restaurant, like all of the bedrooms, is non-smoking. In addition to fine dining in the Conservatory Restaurant, the recently opened Mediterranean bistro, La Vigna, offers a fabulous range of pizza, pasta, tapas and meze dishes. La Vigna is fast becoming a lively and popular restaurant in its own right, and al fresco dining is available during the summer months. Whether travelling on business or pleasure, guests will wish to return to The Grapevine Hotel time and again. The local landscape offers unlimited scope for exploration to the numerous picturesque villages in the Cotswolds or to the towns of Oxford, Cirencester and Stratford-upon-Avon. Nature enthusiasts will enjoy the beautiful gardens of Hidcote, Kifsgate and Barnsley House nearby. Open over Christmas.

Our inspector loved: *The friendly and welcoming staff.*

Calcot Manor Hotel & Spa

NEAR TETBURY, GLOUCESTERSHIRE GL8 8YJ

This delightful hotel, built of Cotswold stone, offers guests tranquillity amidst acres of rolling countryside. Situated in the southern Cotswolds close to the historic town of Tetbury, the building dates back to the 15th century and was a farmhouse until 1983. Its beautiful stone barns and stables include one of the oldest tithe barns in England, built in 1300 by the Cistercian monks from Kingswood Abbey. These buildings form a quadrangle and the stone glistening in the dawn or glowing in the dusk is quite a spectacle. Professional service is complemented by cheerful hospitality without any hint of over-formality. Excellent facilities for families include a number of family suites complete with bunk beds and baby listening devices. A play facility to keep older children entertained with Playstation, X boxes and a small cinema, and an Ofsted registered care crèche for younger children is open 7 days a week. Parents can escape to the state-of-the-art spa with 16-metre pool, steam room and sauna, gym and outdoor hot tub. The spa also offers a full range of beauty treatments. In the elegant conservatory restaurant dinner is very much the focus of a memorable stay and the congenial Gumstool Bistro and Bar offers a range of simpler traditional food and local ales. A discreet conference facility is available.

Our inspector loved: *The wonderful mix of cosy and contemporary throughout.*

Directions: From Tetbury, take the A4135 signposted Dursley; Calcot Manor is on the right after 3½ mile

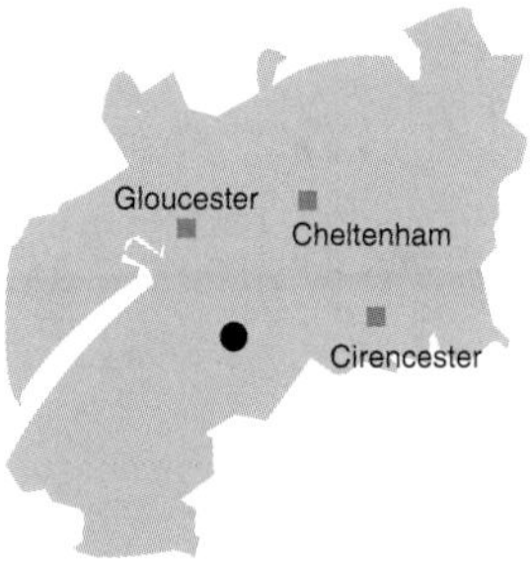

Gloucester
Cheltenham
Cirencester

Web: www.johansens.com/calcotmanor
E-mail: reception@calcotmanor.co.uk
Tel: 0870 381 8398
International: +44 (0)1666 890391
Fax: 01666 890394

Price Guide:
double/twin £185–£225
family room £225
family suite £260

30 100 SPA

The Hare and Hounds Hotel

WESTONBIRT, NEAR TETBURY, GLOUCESTERSHIRE GL8 8QL

This charming and extremely welcoming country hotel stands next to the well-known Westonbirt Arboretum, home to approximately 18,000 specimens of trees and 17 miles of meandering paths. The location makes an idyllic setting for quiet getaways; spring and autumn are the most spectacular months for visiting the Arboretum. Historic Bath is only 21 miles away and excellent road and rail links make The Hare and Hounds Hotel accessible from any corner of the UK. The hotel lies in acres of well-tended grounds, and a combination of blazing log fires, polished parquet floors and club-like public rooms lend a particularly convivial atmosphere. There is a choice of elegant, carefully appointed suites, as well as interconnecting, ground floor and large family bedrooms. The delightful Westonbirt Restaurant offers a well-planned menu that will provide something to suit the most varied of palates, and traditional favourites influenced with a Continental flavour. Licenced for civil wedding ceremonies, the Ballroom, adorned with amazing historic tapestries, is a beautiful setting for any reception or dinner dance. There are also a number of well-designed and stylish meeting rooms and suites that cater for up to 200 delegates – most with direct access from both the car park and gardens.

Our inspector loved: *The wonderful location right next to Westonbirt Arboretum and the well tended grounds.*

Directions: 10 miles from the M4, junction 17, Malmesbury, Tetbury and the A433. The hotel is on the right-hand side 2½ miles outside Tetbury.

Web: www.johansens.com/hareandhounds
E-mail: enquiries@hareandhoundshotel.com
Tel: 0870 381 8302
International: +44 (0)1666 880233
Fax: 01666 880241

Price Guide:
single £88–£98
double/twin £105–£117
suite £130–£140

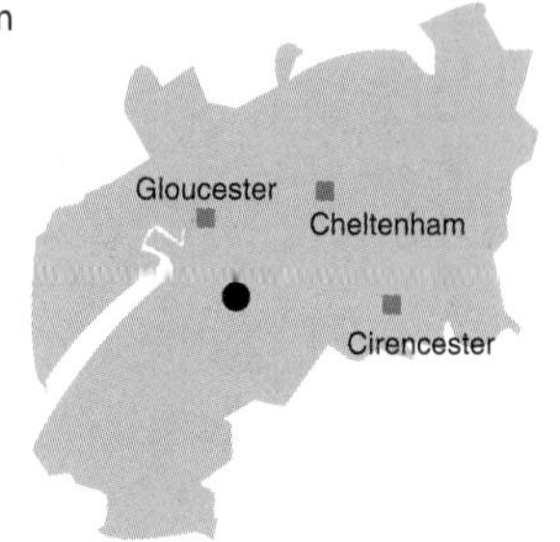

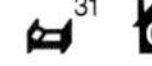

Corse Lawn House Hotel

CORSE LAWN, NR TEWKESBURY, GLOUCESTERSHIRE GL19 4LZ

Although only 6 miles from the M5 and M50, Corse Lawn is a completely unspoilt, typically English hamlet in a peaceful Gloucestershire backwater. The hotel, an elegant Queen Anne listed building set back from the village green, stands in 12 acres of gardens and grounds and still displays the charm of its historic pedigree. Visitors can be assured of the highest standards of service and cooking: Baba Hine is famous for the dishes she produces. The service here, now in the hands of son Giles, is faultlessly efficient, friendly and personal. As well as the renowned restaurant, there are 3 comfortable drawing rooms, a large lounge bar, a private dining-cum-conference room for up to 45 persons and a similar, smaller room for up to 20. A tennis court, heated indoor swimming pool and croquet lawn adjoin the hotel and most sports and leisure activities can be arranged. Corse Lawn is ideal for exploring the Cotswolds, Malverns and Forest of Dean. Short break rates are always available.

Our inspector loved: *The relaxing and comfortable atmosphere and very good food.*

Directions: Corse Lawn House is situated on the B4211 between the A417 (Gloucester–Ledbury road) and the A438 (Tewkesbury–Ledbury road).

Web: www.johansens.com/corselawn
E-mail: enquiries@corselawn.com
Tel: 0870 381 8448
International: +44 (0)1452 780479/771
Fax: 01452 780840

Price Guide:
single £87.50
double/twin £135
four-poster £155

Thornbury Castle

THORNBURY, SOUTH GLOUCESTERSHIRE BS35 1HH

Built in 1511 by Edward Stafford, third Duke of Buckingham, Thornbury Castle was later owned by Henry VIII, who stayed here in 1535 with Anne Boleyn. Today it stands in 15 acres of regal splendour with its vineyard, high walls and the oldest Tudor garden in England. Rich furnishings are displayed against the handsome interior features, including ornate oriel windows, panelled walls and large open fireplaces. The 25 carefully restored bedchambers retain many period details. Thornbury Castle has received many accolades for its luxurious accommodation and excellent cuisine, which includes such delights as Gloucestershire old spot pork, the freshest of south coast fish with local seasonal vegetables, local cheeses and local organic free-range eggs and you will often see the chef picking fresh herbs from the Castle garden. The Castle also provides peaceful and secluded meeting facilities. Thornbury is an ideal base from which to explore Bath, Wales and the Cotswolds. Personally guided tours are available to introduce guests to the little-known as well as the famous places which are unique to the area. In addition, golf may be enjoyed locally and day clay pigeon shooting and archery can be arranged locally.

Our inspector loved: *A unique property with an abundance of historic features and charm.*

Directions: The entrance to the Castle is left of the Parish Church at the lower end of Castle Street which is off Thornbury high street. Look for brown historic signs.

Web: www.johansens.com/thornburycastle
E-mail: info@thornburycastle.co.uk
Tel: 0870 381 8944
International: +44 (0)1454 281182
Fax: 01454 416188

Price Guide:
single from £110
double/twin from £130
suite from £295

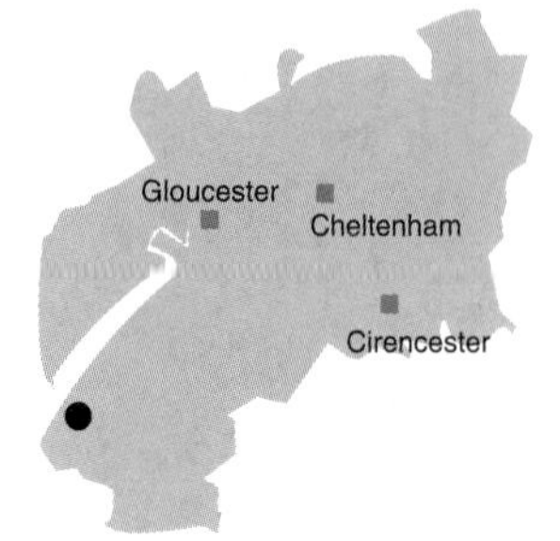

Esseborne Manor

HURSTBOURNE TARRANT, ANDOVER, HAMPSHIRE SP11 0ER

Esseborne Manor is small and unpretentious, yet stylish. The present house was built at the end of the 19th century and carries the name used to record details of the local village in the Domesday Book. It is set in a pleasing garden amid the rich farmland of the North Wessex Downs in a designated area of outstanding natural beauty. Ian and Lucilla Hamilton, who own the house, have established the restful atmosphere of a private country home where guests can unwind and relax. There are now 20 bedrooms including a luxurious suite with a giant sunken Jacuzzi bath; some of the rooms are reached via a courtyard. There are delightful cottage rooms with their own patio overlooking the garden. The pretty sitting room and cosy library are comfortable areas in which to relax. Danny Bozic's fine 2 AA Rosette-awarded cooking is set off to advantage in the new dining room and adjoining bar. There is a spacious meeting and function facility. In the grounds there is a herb garden, an all-weather tennis court, a croquet lawn and plenty of good walking beyond. Nearby Newbury racecourse has a busy programme of steeple-chasing and flat racing. Places to visit include Highclere Castle, Stonehenge, Salisbury, Winchester and Oxford.

Our inspector loved: *The excellent food and fine wine – try the exciting menu du vin.*

Directions: Midway between Newbury and Andover on the A343, 11/2 miles north of Hurstbourne Tarrant.

Web: www.johansens.com/essebornemanor
E-mail: info@esseborne-manor.co.uk
Tel: 0870 381 8506
International: +44 (0)1264 736444
Fax: 01264 736725

Price Guide:
single £95–£135
double/twin £120–£180

TYLNEY HALL

ROTHERWICK, HOOK, HAMPSHIRE RG27 9AZ

Approaching this hotel in the evening, with its floodlit exterior and forecourt fountain, it is easy to imagine arriving for a party in a private stately home. Grade II listed and set in 66 acres of ornamental gardens and parkland, Tylney Hall typifies the great houses of a bygone era. Apéritifs are taken in the wood-panelled library bar; haute cuisine is served in the glass-domed Oak Room restaurant. The hotel holds RAC and AA food awards and also AA 4 Red Stars and RAC Gold Ribbon. The health and leisure facilities include 2 heated pools and whirlpool, solarium, fitness studio, beauty and hairdressing, sauna, tennis, croquet and snooker, whilst hot-air ballooning, archery, clay pigeon shooting, golf and riding can be arranged. Surrounding the hotel are wooded trails ideal for jogging. Functions for up to 100 people are catered for in the Tylney Suite or Chestnut Suite; more intimate gatherings are available in one of the other 10 private banqueting rooms. Tylney Hall is licenced to hold wedding ceremonies on-site. The cathedral city of Winchester and Stratfield Saye House are nearby. Legoland and Windsor Castle are a 40-minute drive away.

Our inspector loved: *Coming up the winding drive, through the stately trees into 66 acres of garden and to a wonderful welcome.*

Directions: M4/jct 11 towards Hook and Rotherwick, follow signs to the hotel. M3/jct 5, A287 towards Newnham, over the A30 into Old School Road. Left for Newnham then right onto Ridge Lane. Hotel is on the left after 1 mile.

Web: www.johansens.com/tylneyhall
E-mail: reservations@tylneyhall.com
Tel: 0870 381 8958
International: +44 (0)1256 764881
Fax: 01256 768141

Price Guide:
single £135–£200
double/twin £165–£230
suite £260–£450

THE MONTAGU ARMS HOTEL

BEAULIEU, NEW FOREST, HAMPSHIRE SO42 7ZL

An AA Top 200 Hotel with 3 Red Stars in the heart of the New Forest, yet close to the M27, The Montagu Arms is a delightful hotel that takes great pride in its outstanding service. With 23 beautifully decorated bedrooms and suites, the hotel is a small oasis of luxury, winner of the AA's Courtesy and Care Award England 2003/2004 for its attentive levels of service. Available for exclusive use, the hotel lends itself ideally to both weddings and conferences, able to cater for anything between 10 and 100 people. The Terrace Restaurant overlooks the beautiful and secluded gardens, and head chef Scott Foy is happy to cater for specific occasions and tastes. Under the guidance of Shaun Hill, Director of Cooking, the Oakwood and Paris Rooms provide a more intimate setting for board meetings, family celebrations and private dining. The New Forest is well known for both sailing on the Solent and good riding in the forest; both of these activites are easily arranged by the hotel. The Montagu Arms Hotel has its own fully-crewed luxury 84ft yacht that can accommodate up to 12 guests for a day's sail, possibly reaching Cowes on the Isle of Wight or the famous Needles. The hotel also has strong links with a number of nearby estates where clay pigeon shooting, fishing, and other country pursuits can take place.

***Our inspector loved:** The calming ambience of this beautiful conservation village hotel; the perfect base from which to explore the surrounding area.*

Directions: The village of Beaulieu is well signposted and the hotel commands an impressive position at the foot of the main street.

Web: www.johansens.com/montaguarms
E-mail: reservations@montaguarmshotel.co.uk
Tel: 0870 381 8743
International: +44 (0)1590 612324
Fax: 01590 612188

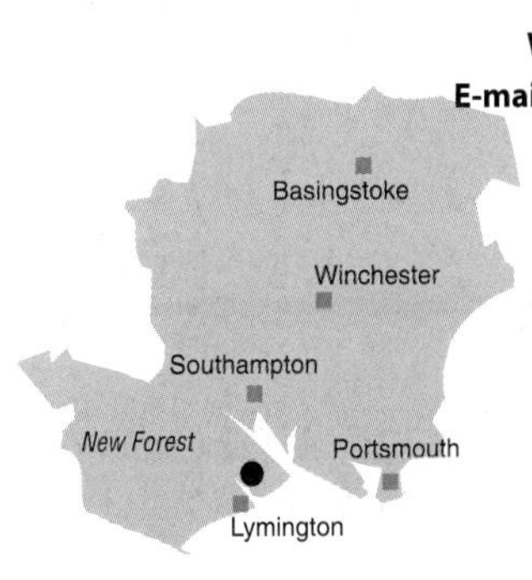

Price Guide: (inclusive terms available)
single £125–£145
double/twin £180–£255
suites £210–£295

Careys Manor Hotel & Senspa

BROCKENHURST, NEW FOREST, HAMPSHIRE SO42 7RH

Careys Manor dates from 1888 and is built on the site of a royal hunting lodge used by Charles II. Situated close to the glorious New Forest countryside, the hotel is proud of the personal welcome and care it extends to its visitors. The bedrooms are comfortably appointed and furnished in a range of styles. In the modern Garden wing some of the rooms have balconies and others open directly onto lawns and borders. The restaurant offers a hearty breakfast and an English and French influenced cuisine at dinner. The superb new Oriental Spa is set within the grounds and linked to the hotel through charming corridors. The spa offers a variety of treatments performed by Eastern and Western therapists and features a state-of-the-art hydrotherapy pool with several experience rooms and showers, which include amongst others, a mud room, blizzard shower, ice room, tepidarium, laconium and Vichy shower. Windsurfing, riding and sailing can all be enjoyed locally, whilst Stonehenge, Beaulieu, Broadlands, Salisbury and Winchester are a short distance away. Business interests can be catered for; there are comprehensive self-contained conference facilities.

Our inspector loved: *The stunning new spa provision with its stylish Zen Garden Restaurant.*

Directions: From the M27, junction 1, follow the A337 signed to Lymington. Careys Manor is on the left after the 30 mph sign at Brockenhurst.

Web: www.johansens.com/careysmanor
E-mail: stay@careysmanor.com
Tel: 0870 381 8405
International: +44 (0)8707 512305
Fax: 08707 512306

Price Guide:
double/twin £129–£199

Le Poussin at Whitley Ridge

Beaulieu Road, Brockenhurst, New Forest, Hampshire SO42 7QL

Set in 25 acres of secluded parkland in the heart of the New Forest, this privately owned Georgian house was once a Royal hunting lodge visited by the Queen Mother. Today it has the ambience of a true country house with the accent on relaxation. The bedrooms are individually decorated, and most have lovely views over open forest. The public rooms are similarly luxurious and elegant and log fires burn on cool evenings. Internationally acclaimed chef patron Alex Aitken, awarded Hampshire Chef of the Year by Hampshire Life Magazine, has re-located his famous Le Poussin restaurant, which holds a Michelin Star and 3 AA Rosettes, in to Whitley Ridge whilst nearby Parkhill undergoes extensive refurbishment and expansion; his innovative, imaginative cuisine is a joy not to be missed. Guests can relax in the grounds or enjoy a game of tennis. Some of the country's best woodland walks are directly accessible from the gardens. Whichever pastime you choose, Whitley Ridge guarantees a restful and enjoyable stay. A number of stately homes, including Broadlands and Wilton House, are within easy reach. Lord Montague's Motor Museum, Buckler's Hard and historic Stonehenge are also within driving distance.

Our inspector loved: *The new cottage suite created in the former stable, simplicity and sophistication combined in a very appealing way.*

Directions: M27 junction 1. Situated on the B3055, Brockenhurst – Beaulieu

Web: www.johansens.com/poussinwhitleyridge
E-mail: whitley@lepoussin.co.uk
Tel: 0870 381 8994
International: +44 (0)1590 622354
Fax: 01590 622856

Price Guide:
single from £70
double £90–£200
cottage suite £200–£220

18 20

New Park Manor

LYNDHURST ROAD, BROCKENHURST, NEW FOREST, HAMPSHIRE SO42 7QH

Escape from the pressures of a hectic lifestyle in this Grade II listed former hunting lodge of Charles II that dates from the 16th century. The house stands within its own clearing in the heart of the New Forest, yet is easily accessed from the main Lyndhurst/Lymington road. All bedrooms boast fine views of the surrounding parklands and forest and are individually decorated, in-keeping with the historic nature of the house. The New Forest rooms are contemporary in style and even have LCD TV screens in the bathrooms! Wandering ponies and wild deer can be viewed from the hotel and on the many walks and paths that run through the forest. The hotel's Equestrian Centre, with BHS trained stable crew, heated outdoor pool and tennis court, affords a perfect starting point from which to explore the countryside and to visit the nearby coast and sailing of the Solent. The new Bath House Spa provides a variety of treatments that take their inspiration from the rural setting such as hay and moss wraps as well as holistic natural therapies, thermal spa treatments and a techno-gym. The lively Polo Bar serves light meals throughout the day whilst the romantic restaurant provides a more extensive menu of traditional British cuisine with a continental twist. The views from the New Forest room, with its picture windows, provides a wonderful location for tailor-made parties or functions.

Our inspector loved: *The setting, home to the annual New Forest show.*

Directions: New Park Manor is ½ mile off the A337 between Lyndhurst and Brockenhurst, easily reached from the M27, junction 1.

Web: www.johansens.com/newparkmanor
E-mail: info@newparkmanorhotel.co.uk
Tel: 0870 381 8761
International: +44 (0)1590 623467
Fax: 01590 622268

Price Guide:
single from £90
double/twin from £120
four poster from £210

Passford House Hotel

MOUNT PLEASANT LANE, LYMINGTON, HAMPSHIRE SO41 8LS

Set in 9 acres of picturesque gardens and rolling parkland, the Passford House Hotel lies midway between the charming New Forest village of Sway and the Georgian splendour of Lymington. Once the home of Lord Arthur Cecil, it is steeped in history and the traditions of leisurely country life. Pleasantly decorated bedrooms include a number of superior rooms, whilst comfort is the keynote in the 4 public lounges. The hotel prides itself on the standard and variety of cuisine served in its delightful restaurant and the extensive menu aims to give pleasure to the most discerning of palates. Meals are complemented by a speciality wine list. The hotel boasts a compact leisure centre, catering for all ages and activities. In addition to 2 heated swimming pools, there is a multi-gym, sauna, pool table, croquet lawn, pétanque and tennis court. Just a short drive away are Beaulieu, the cathedral cities of Winchester and Salisbury and ferry ports to the Isle of Wight and France. The New Forest has numerous golf courses, riding and trekking centres, cycling paths, beautiful walks, and of course sailing on the Solent. Milford-on-Sea, 4 miles away, is the nearest beach.

Our inspector loved: *The peaceful tranquility - yet so close to the bustle of Lymington.*

Directions: Exit 1/M27, A337 to Brockenhurst. The road runs beneath a railway bridge just before a mini roundabout. Straight over this roundabout, taking the next right immediately before the Tollhouse Pub. Continue along Sway Road for about 3/4 mile and bear right into Mount Pleasant Lane.

Web: www.johansens.com/passfordhouse
E-mail: sales@passfordhousehotel.co.uk
Tel: 0870 381 8804
International: +44 (0)1590 682398
Fax: 01590 683494

Price Guide:
single from £80
double/twin from £130

CHEWTON GLEN

NEW MILTON, NEW FOREST, HAMPSHIRE BH25 6QS

Directions: Take A35 from Lyndhurst towards Bournemouth. Turn left at Walkford, then left before roundabout. The hotel is on the right.

Web: www.johansens.com/chewtonglen
E-mail: reservations@chewtonglen.com
Tel: 0870 381 8427
International: +44 (0)1425 275341
US toll free: 1 800 344 5087
Fax: 01425 272310

Price Guide: (room only)
double £205–£445
suites £445–£780

Voted Best Country House Hotel in the World by Gourmet magazine, Chewton Glen is set in 130 acres of gardens, woodland and parkland on the edge of the New Forest, close to the sea. Owners Martin and Brigitte Skan have created a haven of tranquillity, luxury and comfort. The wonderful setting of the restaurant, which overlooks the landscaped gardens, adds to the sublime culinary experience created by head chef Luke Matthews, who uses fresh local produce to create surprising and delicious dishes, complemented by an impressive wine list. The 58 sumptuous bedrooms, all individually designed with carefully chosen fabrics, are the ultimate in luxury with fantastic marble bathrooms, cosy bathrobes and views over the surrounding parkland. The stunning Spa opened in spring 2002. In addition to the magnificent 17 metre pool, there are now improved changing rooms with their own steam room and sauna, more treatment rooms, larger gym, hydrotherapy pool and a totally new lounge, buffet and bar with a conservatory and sun terrace. There are indoor and outdoor tennis courts, a 9-hole par 3 golf course and an outdoor swimming pool. Fishing, shooting and riding can be arranged locally.

Our inspector loved: *The spacious, superbly styled ambience of the stunningly beautiful spa – here is your opportunity for total indulgence.*

NEW

THE DOLPHIN

HIGH STREET, SOUTHAMPTON, HAMPSHIRE SO14 2HN

Originally built in 1390, The Dolphin has attracted a number of esteemed guests including Queen Victoria and Jane Austen. The new owner took inspiration from the eclectic 16th, 17th and 18th-century architecture and created a stylish, elegant and uniquely furnished hotel: contemporarily-styled bedrooms feature bespoke headboards, each one designed by a different artist and bathrooms are adorned with a custom-made piece of artwork. Unique in shape, size and décor, all of the guest rooms are well appointed and have fine Frette Egyptian bed linen and LCD televisions. In the heart of the Old Town, the hotel is close to the banking community and commercial port, and is just minutes from the shopping centre. Enjoy an apéritif in the Oak Bar, with its oak floor and modern glass and stainless steel bar, overlooking the High Street or in Fruit Southampton's only champagne bar and club. Dine at the bleu grill and wine gallery where classic food is complemented by surprisingly inexpensive wine. The Jane Austen Assembly Rooms, the main assembly rooms in the city during the 1700s, where "Jane" celebrated her 18th birthday, are available for meetings and functions. The beautiful New Forest is a 5-mile drive and the Isle of Wight ferry and the International Boat Show, held in September, are a walk away.

***Our inspector loved:** The radical transformation complete with an innovative approach to hotel-keeping.*

Directions: From the M3/M27 exit at junction 3 and follow the brown signs to "Waterfront" and "Red Funnel Isle of Wight Ferry". At Red Funnel termial turn off at Town Quay into the High Street. The hotel is 200 yards on the right.

Basingstoke
Winchester
Southampton
New Forest
Portsmouth
Lymington

Web: www.johansens.com/dolphinhampshire
E-mail: enquiries@thedolphin.co.uk
Tel: 0870 381 9200
International: +44 (0)23 8033 9955
Fax: 023 8033 3650

Price Guide:
single from £137.50
double £137.50-£157.50
suite from £180

Botley Park Hotel, Golf and Country Club

WINCHESTER ROAD, BOORLEY GREEN, BOTLEY, SOUTHAMPTON SO32 2UA

This exquisite hotel is situated within a 176-acre of Hampshire's rolling countryside. Botley Park Hotel prides itself on the relaxing ambience, generous hospitality and homely environment it provides. The spacious bedrooms are decorated in warm, natural hues and are furnished with comfortable ample-sized beds draped in luxurious linens. The property also boasts 3 luxurious suites. For wedding ceremonies, function rooms are available and the extensive grounds provide an enchanting backdrop for photographs, whilst business conferences can be held in one of 13 modern and spacious conferencing and banqueting suites. The romantic atmosphere of the Winchester restaurant is perfect for sumptous dining and fine wines whilst the Plus Fours offers a more casual and light menu and overlooks the 18th green. The 18-hole, 70 par parkland golf course is one of the best in the region and possesses a covered driving range, a Steven Hunter golf shop and experienced staff on hand for guidance on equipment or technique. For guests who prefer to be pampered, the Vital Health & Leisure Club which offers pool, poolside, steam room, sauna and spa. Nearby attractions include Beaulieu Motor Museum, Marwell Zoo, Paultons Park, Winchester Cathedral and the historic naval town of Portsmouth.

Directions: From M27, jct 7, follow the A334 towards Fair Oak. At the first mini-roundabout turn left past the M&S store and continue over the next 4 roundabouts. At the fifth roundabout turn right and the hotel is on the left.

Web: www.johansens.com/botleypark
E-mail: botleypark@macdonald-hotels.co.uk
Tel: 0870 381 8395
International: +44 (0)1489 780888
Fax: 01489 789242

Price Guide:
single £65–£115
double/twin £130–£160
suite from £180

Our inspector loved: *This transformed and now very stylish hotel.*

Chilworth Manor

CHILWORTH, SOUTHAMPTON, HAMPSHIRE SO16 7PT

A long, sweeping, tree-lined drive leads visitors to this imposing Edwardian manor house situated in 12 landscaped acres of glorious Hampshire countryside. The mellow, cream coloured stone exterior is highlighted by tall, slim, sparkling wide sash windows and an attractive balustrade. Heavy, dark oak-front doors open into a magnificent galleried hall, which sets the pattern for a rich and gracious interior overhung with a wealth of historical ambience, charm and comfort. There are 26 bedrooms with panoramic estate views in the Manor and 69 in the Garden Wing; all have been refurbished to a high standard, are pleasantly decorated and have every comfort, including 24-hour room service. Dining in the elegant restaurant is a delight, to be sampled leisurely whilst enjoying views over and beyond manicured lawns and colourful flower beds. The hotel's cuisine is innovative and imaginative and complemented by an extensive international wine list. For the energetic there is a jogging route within the grounds and a hard tennis court. Southampton's splendid shopping facilities and nightlife are within easy reach, as is Portsmouth and the cathedral city of Winchester. Extensive purpose-built conference and meeting facilities are available.

Our inspector loved: *Its lovely grounds and its surprising proximity to the town of Romsey and the urban and maritime delights of Portsmouth and Southampton.*

Directions: Take the M3 and exit at junction 14. At the roundabout take the third exit towards Romsey (A27). Chilworth Manor is on the left after Clump Inn.

Web: www.johansens.com/chilworth
E-mail: sales@chilworth-manor.co.uk
Tel: 0870 381 9057
International: +44 (0)23 8076 7333
Fax: 023 8076 6392

Price Guide:
single from £49.50
double £95-£140
suite £170

LAINSTON HOUSE HOTEL

SPARSHOLT, WINCHESTER, HAMPSHIRE SO21 2LT

Standing majestically in 63 acres of glorious parkland, this exquisite country house hotel provides a perfect retreat for rest and relaxation. Guests are attended to by courteous staff whose service is discreet yet always impeccable. Designed with comfort in mind, each of the elegant bedrooms and suites enjoys a distinctive character and luxurious en-suite facilities. The hotel is able to cater for all manner of special events from small business meetings to large family functions, and exclusive use of the property can be arranged. The principal reception room is the Dawley Barn, which is an attractively converted 17th-century barn, as well as 4 other charming meeting rooms. An unpretentious menu is on offer at The Avenue Restaurant and Al fresco Terrace, where guests dine on succulent, modern English cuisine, in opulent surroundings. For leisure pursuits, patrons have exclusive use of the well-equipped gym and mountain bikes for exploring the local area. Alternatively, laser clay shooting, quad biking or, for those with a head for heights, a flight in a hot-air balloon can be arranged. Lainston House Hotel is easily reached from Waterloo station, Heathrow Airport and central London.

Our inspector loved: *This splendid hotel's timeless quest for always trying to improve room and bathroom provisions.*

Directions: Lainston House is well signposted off the B3049 Winchester–Stockbridge road, at Sparsholt 2½ miles from Winchester.

Web: www.johansens.com/lainston
E-mail: enquiries@lainstonhouse.com
Tel: 0870 381 8667
International: +44 (0)1962 863588
Fax: 01962 776672

Price Guide:
single from £100
double/twin from £150
suite from £285

Castle House

CASTLE STREET, HEREFORD, HEREFORDSHIRE HR1 2NW

A simply stunning example of Georgian architecture, this elegant hotel lies in the centre of Hereford, 100m from the cathedral, overlooking the old moat. The stately façade is both impressive and immaculate, yet as soon as one steps off the street and into the hotel there is an immediate sense of serene tranquillity undisturbed by the bustling town outside. A grand staircase greets guests in the lobby, which has been attentively decorated in welcoming warm yellows and furnished with traditional pieces of furniture. Each of the bedrooms is individually designed and offers the utmost luxury, and the chic public rooms provide comfort in a stylish environment. La Rive restaurant serves exciting and carefully presented food, with a menu that perfectly balances traditional English ingredients with a European twist such as the fillet of Hereford beef with sweet potato dauphinoise, caramelised shallots and wild mushroom compote. The Left Bank Village is 100 yards from the hotel and is an ideal venue for functions, whilst Castle House itself is the perfect base from which to explore the city, returning to enjoy afternoon tea in the delightful gardens. The staff are welcoming, friendly and thoughtful, ensuring guests' complete relaxation and total enjoyment during their stay.

Our inspector loved: *The elegant luxury in a lovely setting.*

Directions: Follow signs for Hereford's City Centre and then City Centre East. From St Owen's Street turn right into St Ethelbert Street and veer right into Castle Street. Hereford Train Station is 1 mile away.

Leominster
Hereford
Ross-on-Wye

Web: www.johansens.com/castlehse
E-mail: info@castlehse.co.uk
Tel: 0870 381 9206
International: +44 (0)1432 365321
Fax: 01432 365909

Price Guide:
single £113.50
double £200
suite £210–£245

THE GROVE HOTEL

CHANDLER'S CROSS, HERTFORDSHIRE WD3 4TG

This magnificent 18th-century former home of the Earls of Clarendon stands in 300 acres of Hertfordshire countryside. Painstakingly restored and transformed into an impressive cosmopolitan country estate, just 45 minutes from the centre of London, it has been awarded AA Hotel of the Year 2005, Best UK Spa Retreat 2005, by readers of Condé Nast Traveller, and is host to the World Golf Championships American Express Championships 2006. Providing the best of 21st-century living within peaceful countryside, a personal welcome and sense of sanctuary and refuge is guaranteed. Great attention to detail and quality is balanced with the ethos of pleasure and wellbeing of guests, and the gardens, grounds and woodland walks are superb. The grand interior displays antiques set against modern elegance, fine pictures and quirky touches. Guest rooms and suites are luxuriously appointed: many have balconies or terraces, some have working fireplaces and all boast panoramic garden and parkland views. There are 3 bars, 3 restaurants and a spa with 13 treatment rooms, a saltwater vitality pool, fitness and exercise studios and an 18-hole golf course. The Walled Garden features 2 tennis courts and outdoor pool, croquet lawn and herb garden. Families will benefit from Anouska's Kid's Club, a crèche and day nursery open to children aged 3 months and over.

Our inspector loved: *The diverse elements that both surprise and delight.*

Directions: From M25 clockwise junction 19, anti-clockwise junction 20.

Web: www.johansens.com/thegrove
E-mail: info@the grove.co.uk
Tel: 0870 381 8646
International: +44 (0)1923 807807
Fax: 01923 221008

Price Guide: (excluding VAT)
single £240–£550
double/twin £240–£320
suite £700–£1,000

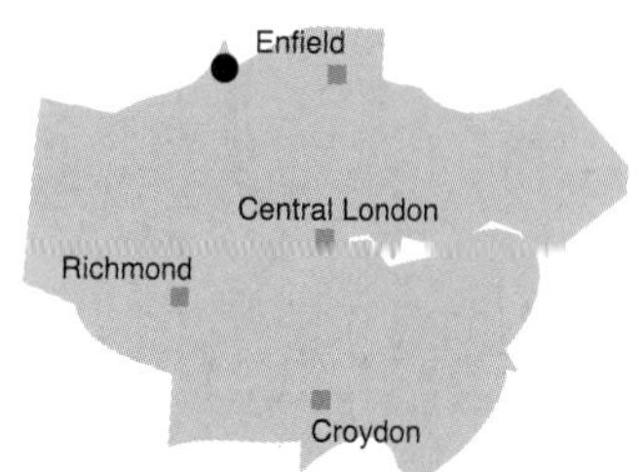

Down Hall Country House Hotel

HATFIELD HEATH, NEAR BISHOP'S STORTFORD, HERTFORDSHIRE CM22 7AS

Set in 110 acres of parkland, this Italianate mansion is the perfect choice for those wishing to escape the pressures of everyday life. A peaceful ambience pervades this tastefully restored country house hotel. The well-appointed bedrooms all feature period furnishings; and afford picturesque views across the grounds. Gastronomes will be pleased with the excellent cuisine served in the Downham and the new Ibbetsons 2 AA Rosette restaurant. Here, English and French dishes are prepared with only the finest fresh ingredients. The superb on-site sporting facilities include croquet lawn, swimming pool, sauna and whirlpool. Clay pigeon shooting, horse-riding and golf can be arranged nearby. Day excursions include visits to Cambridge, horse racing at Newmarket, Constable Country and the old timbered village of Thaxted. This is an ideal venue for board meetings, conferences, award dinners and corporate hospitality in a secluded environment. The rooms accommodate from 10 delegates boardroom style, up to 180 theatre style and a maximum of 500 for a dinner dance. An executive shuttle is available to and from Stansted Airport.

Our inspector loved: *The grandeur of the fresh aromatic flowers and sparkling chandeliers in the lounge.*

Directions: The hotel is 14 miles from the M25, 7 miles from the M11 and Bishop's Stortford Station. Heathrow Airport is 60 miles away; Stansted is 9 miles. There is ample free parking.

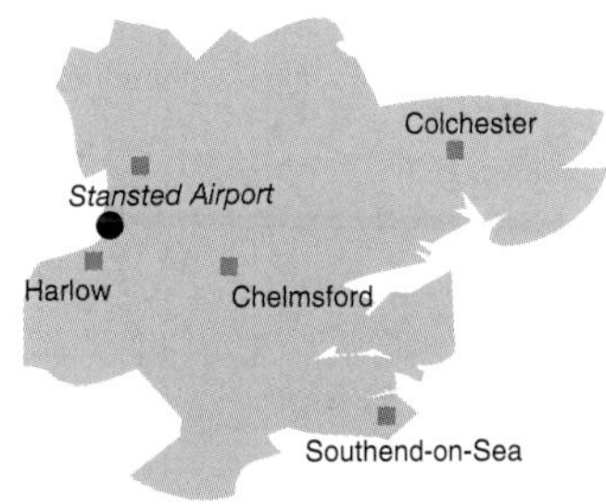

Web: www.johansens.com/downhall
E-mail: sales@downhall.co.uk
Tel: 0870 381 8489
International: +44 (0)1279 731441
Fax: 01279 730416

Price Guide:
single £140
double/twin £175
suite £235

St Michael's Manor

ST MICHAEL'S VILLAGE, FISHPOOL STREET, ST ALBANS, HERTFORDSHIRE AL3 4RY

Owned and run by the Newling Ward family for the past 40 years, St Michael's Manor is a rare gem – peaceful, intimate, and set in delightful landscaped grounds. It is also within the historic village of St Michael's and a stone's throw from the magnificent St Albans Abbey. Each of the 30 bedrooms has been individually designed – some have four-poster beds and some are sitting-room suites – and all have an elegance and charm. Many of the bedrooms overlook the award-winning grounds, set in 5 acres, with wide sweeping lawns and a beautiful lake that hosts a variety of wildlife. The Georgian lounge and the award-winning conservatory dining room also overlook the gardens and make a wonderful setting for a tantalising dinner. There is also an excellent variety of vegetarian dishes. Coffee may be served in the Oak Lounge, which dates from 1586, with its fine panelled walls and original Elizabethan ceiling. Hatfield House, the Roman remains of Verulamium and Verulam golf course – the Home of the Ryder Cup – are within easy reach, as is London, which is only 20 minutes away by train. Weekend rates from £60 per person are available.

Our inspector loved: *The gardens and the lake; they are wonderful.*

Directions: Easy access to the M1, junction 6/7, M25, junction 21a - 10 minutes; M4/M40 - 25 minutes; Luton Airport - 20 minutes.

Web: www.johansens.com/stmichaelsmanor
E-mail: reservations@stmichaelsmanor.com
Tel: 0870 381 8906
International: +44 (0)1727 864444
Fax: 01727 848909

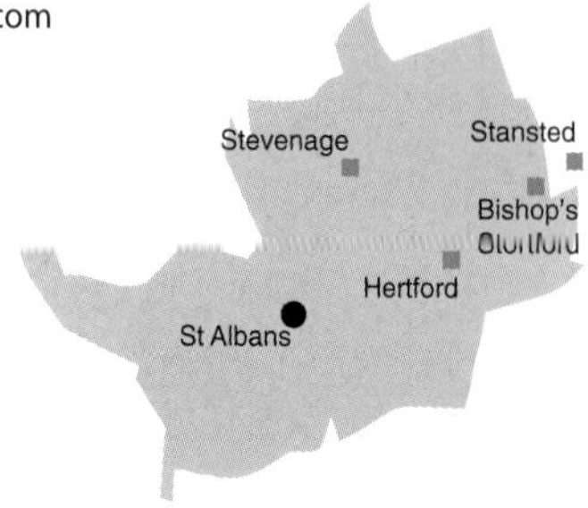

Price Guide:
single £145–£230
double/twin £180–£250
suite £250–£310

Sopwell House

COTTONMILL LANE, SOPWELL, ST ALBANS, HERTFORDSHIRE AL1 2HQ

Once the country home of Lord Mountbatten's family and surrounded by a peaceful verdant 12-acre estate, Sopwell House is an oasis just minutes from the motorways. The classic reception rooms reflect its illustrious past and the grand panelled ballroom opens out onto the terraces and gardens. The bedrooms, some with four-posters, are spacious and well-equipped. Beautifully designed Mews Suites are ideal for long-stay executives and bridal parties. Superb modern British and International cuisine, complemented by fine wines, are served in the enchanting 2 AA Rosette Magnolia Restaurant amidst the trees after which it is named, whilst Bejerano's Brasserie offers an informal ambience. The conference and banqueting suites, overlooking the splendid gardens and terrace, are a popular venue for weddings, conferences and special events. The Country Club & Spa, dedicated to health and relaxation, has a full range of fitness facilities and qualified beauty therapists use E'SPA, Clarins and Aromatherapy Associates products.

Our inspector loved: *The huge entrance lobby with sofas and open fire set in a French chateâu fireplace.*

Directions: Close to M25, M1, M10, A1(M). 28m from Heathrow Airport. From M25 or A414 take A1081 to St Albans. Cross roundabout and turn left after the third set of traffic lights. Hotel is ¼ mile on left.

Web: www.johansens.com/sopwellhouse
E-mail: enquiries@sopwellhouse.co.uk
Tel: 0870 381 8898
International: +44 (0)1727 864477
Fax: 01727 844741

Price Guide: (room only)
single £99–£129
double/twin £169–£185
suites from £217

129 400 SPA

The Pendley Manor Hotel

COW LANE, TRING, HERTFORDSHIRE HP23 5QY

The Pendley Manor was commissioned by Joseph Grout Williams in 1872. His instructions, to architect John Lion, were to build it in the Tudor style, reflecting the owner's interest in flora and fauna on the carved woodwork and stained-glass panels. The bedrooms are attractively furnished and well equipped and the restaurant boasts AA and RAC awards. Pendley Manor offers flexible conference facilities for up to 350 people. 9 purpose-built conference suites and 8 syndicate rooms, all with natural daylight, are available. Team-building and multi-activity days within the grounds can be arranged as well as marquee events. On the estate, which lies at the foot of the Chiltern Hills, sporting facilities include tennis courts, gymnasium, a snooker room with full-size table, games rooms, buggy riding, laser shooting, archery and hot-air balloon rides. Special events, include the annual flower show with Charlie Dimmock and the outdoor Shakespeare festival. The hotel's new health and leisure facilities has an indoor heated swimming pool, Jacuzzi, sauna and solarium. The beauty spa now offers a full range of Clarins treatments. Places of interest nearby include Woburn, Winslow Hall, Chenies Manor, Tring Zoological Museum and Dunstable Downs.

Our inspector loved: *The exotic peacocks in the grounds, especially the white ones with their bridal like display.*

Directions: Leave the M25 at junction 20 and take the new A41. Take the exit marked "Tring". At the roundabout take the A4251, then 1st left turn into Cow Lane.

Web: www.johansens.com/pendleymanor
E-mail: sales@pendley-manor.co.uk
Tel: 0870 381 8812
International: +44 (0)1442 891891
Fax: 01442 890687

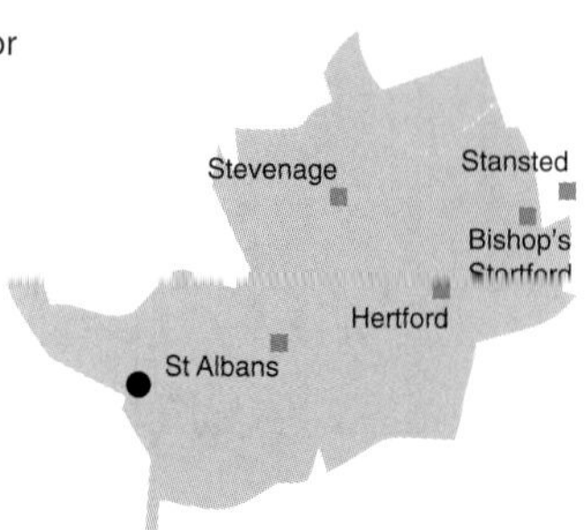

Price Guide:
single £110
double/twin £130–£150
suites £160

74 350 SPA

The Priory Bay Hotel

PRIORY DRIVE, SEAVIEW, ISLE OF WIGHT PO34 5BU

From decades gone by this beautiful site has been built upon by Medieval monks, Tudor farmers and Georgian gentry. Now its medley of buildings has been sympathetically restored and brought to life as a splendid hotel. Situated in a gorgeous open coastal setting to the south of Seaview, the Priory Bay overlooks its own private beach. Everything about it is stylish and elegant, from the impressive arched stone entrance with magnificent carved figures to the delightful, flower-filled gardens with their shady corners and thatched roofed tithe barns. The public rooms are a delight, exquisitely and comfortably furnished, with tall windows framed by rich curtains and liberally filled with vases of flowers. Log fires blaze in open fireplaces during colder months. Each of the 18 comfortable bedrooms is individually decorated and has picturesque views over the gardens. The dining room is establishing a reputation for first-class gastronomy, complemented by a fine wine list. Guests can relax under shady umbrellas in the garden or on the surrounding terraces. For the more energetic guest, there is an outdoor pool and the hotel's adjoining 9-hole golf course. The islands' coastal paths for walking and riding passes the gate, Carisbrooke Castle and Osborne House are nearby.

Our inspector loved: *Its very individual style and the safe, secluded sandy beach.*

Directions: Ferry from Portsmouth, Lymington or Southampton to Fishbourne, Yarmouth. Ryde, East or West Cowes. The hotel is on the B3330.

Web: www.johansens.com/priorybayiow
E-mail: reception@priorybay.co.uk
Tel: 0870 381 8839
International: +44 (0)1983 613146
Fax: 01983 616539

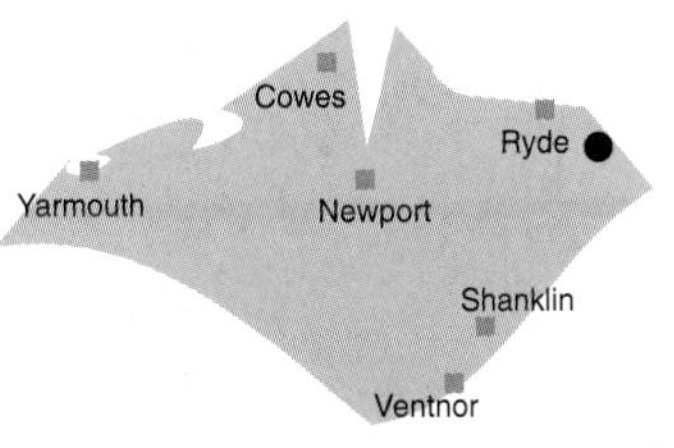

Price Guide:
single £80–£220
double/twin £150–£260
suite £250–£375

The Royal Hotel

BELGRAVE ROAD, VENTNOR, ISLE OF WIGHT PO38 1JJ

Directions: Take the ferry from Portsmouth, Lymington or Southampton to Fishbourne, Yarmouth, Ryde or East/West Cowes. Take the A3054 to Newport, the A3055 to Sandown then the A5056 to Arreton/Sandown. Finally, take the B3327 to Ventnor.

Web: www.johansens.com/royalhoteliow
E-mail: enquiries@royalhoteliow.co.uk
Tel: 0870 381 8389
International: +44 (0)1983 852186
Fax: 01983 855395

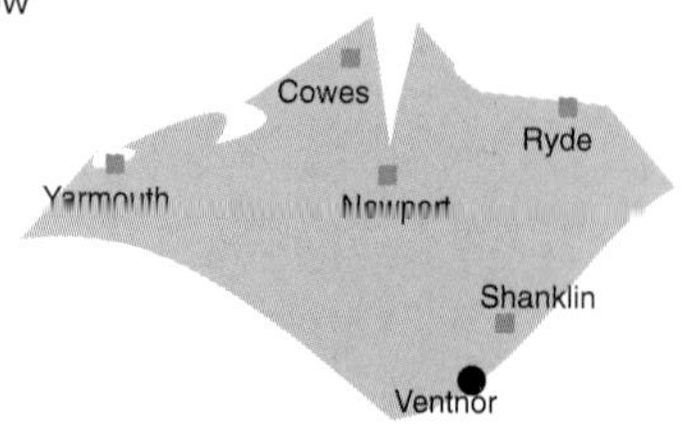

Price Guide:
single £70–£130
double/twin £120–£190

This family-run hotel is lauded as the Isle of Wight's premier location, boasting 4 stars, and 2 AA Rosettes for excellent food. Steeped in Victorian history, The Royal Hotel has 55 comfortable en-suite rooms of varying styles; some have views across the beautiful gardens and the island's coastline. Relaxing lounges and a cosy candle-lit bar are perfect places to enjoy a drink and relax, and on certain evenings the resident pianist provides pleasant background music. There is also a bright, airy conservatory, and the expertly tended gardens, complete with swimming pool, waterfall and cricket net, are tranquil havens. The hotel's head chef Alan Stanley and his team of 9 use the finest local produce such as Ventnor lobster, island lamb, Godshill free-range chicken and asparagus from the Arreton Valley. Superb menus are complemented by an impressive wine list. The island is awash with history and The Royal provides the ideal base from which to explore. Not only can guests visit Queen Victoria and Prince Albert's home, Osborne House, and Carisbrooke Castle, where Charles I was imprisoned, they can make the most of numerous leisure pursuits and places of natural beauty such as Steephill Cove, the Needles, Freshwater Bay, and the linseed fields near Chale.

Our inspector loved: *This very stylish, yet traditional hotel, and the fabulous climbing geranium on the front wall.*

Eastwell Manor

BOUGHTON LEES, NEAR ASHFORD, KENT TN25 4HR

Set in the "Garden of England", Eastwell Manor has a past steeped in history dating back to the 16th century when Richard Plantagenet, son of Richard III, lived on the estate. Surrounded by impressive grounds it encompasses a formal Italian garden, scented rose gardens and attractive lawns and parkland. The magnificent exterior is matched by the splendour of the interior. Exquisite plasterwork and carved oak panelling adorn the public rooms whilst throughout the Manor interesting antique pieces abound. The individually furnished bedrooms and suites, some with fine views across the gardens, feature every possible comfort. There are 19 courtyard apartments giving 39 more bedrooms, all with en-suite facilities. The new health and fitness spa features an indoor and outdoor heated 20m pool, hydrotherapy pool, sauna, steam room, technogym and 15 beauty treatment rooms. Guests can enjoy a choice of dining experiences, fine British cuisine in the Manor Restaurant, and a similar standard of food at the less formal Brasserie. Nearby attractions include the cathedral city of Canterbury, Leeds Castle and several charming market towns. Situated near Ashford Eurostar station, Eastwell is perfect for trips to Paris and Brussels.

***Our inspector loved:** The newly styled bar with its amazing collection of malt and classic whisky and the freshly planted rose garden.*

Directions: M20, junction 9. Turn left into Trinity Road over 4 roundabouts turn left onto the A251. The hotel is 1 mile, on the left.

Web: www.johansens.com/eastwellmanor
E-mail: enquiries@eastwellmanor.co.uk
Tel: 0870 381 8498
International: +44 (0)1233 213000
Fax: 01233 635530

Price Guide:

single From £110
double/twin £140–£285
suites £230–£395

62 150 SPA

CHILSTON PARK

SANDWAY, LENHAM, NR MAIDSTONE, KENT ME17 2BE

This magnificent Grade I listed mansion, one of England's most richly decorated hotels, was built in the 13th century and remodelled in the 18th century. Now sensitively refurbished, the hotel's ambience is enhanced by the lighting, at dusk each day, of over 200 candles. The drawing room and reading room offer guests an opportunity to relax and to admire the outstanding collection of antiques. The entire hotel is a treasure trove full of many interesting objets d'art. The opulently furnished bedrooms are fitted to a high standard and many have four-poster beds. Good, fresh English cooking features on outstanding menus supported by an excellent wine list. Several intimate and delightful rooms afford wonderful opportunities for private dining parties. In keeping with the traditions of a country house, a wide variety of sporting activities are available, golf and riding nearby, fishing in the natural spring lake and punting.

Our inspector loved: *The astonishing collections of objets d'art.*

Directions: Take junction 8 off the M20, then A20 towards Lenham. Turn left into Boughton Road. Go over the crossroads and M20; Chilston Park is on the left.

Web: www.johansens.com/chilstonpark
E-mail: chilstonpark@handpicked.co.uk
Tel: 0870 381 8428
International: +44 (0)1622 859803
Fax: 01622 858588

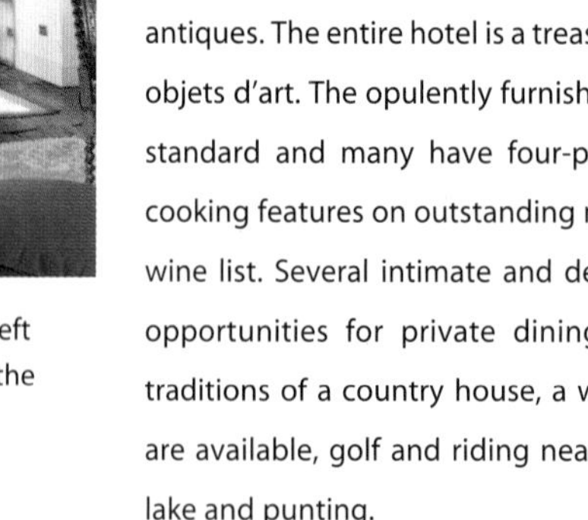

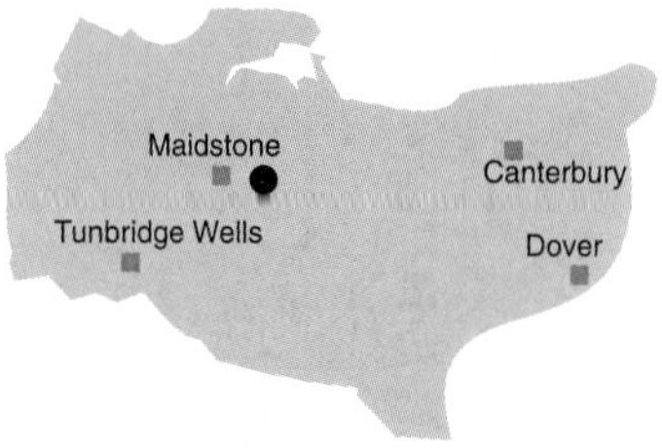

Price Guide:
single from £90
double/twin from £130
suite from £295

THE SPA HOTEL

MOUNT EPHRAIM, ROYAL TUNBRIDGE WELLS, KENT TN4 8XJ

The Spa Hotel was originally built in 1766 as a country mansion with its own landscaped gardens and 3 beautiful lakes. A hotel for over a century now, it retains standards of service reminiscent of life in Georgian and Regency England. All the bedrooms are individually furnished and many offer spectacular views. Above all else, The Spa prides itself on the excellence of its cuisine. The grand, award-winning Chandelier restaurant features the freshest produce from Kentish farms and London markets complemented by a carefully selected wine list. Within the hotel is Sparkling Health, a magnificent health and leisure centre, which is equipped to the highest standards. Leisure facilities include an indoor heated swimming pool, a fully equipped state-of-the-art gymnasium, cardio-vascular gymnasium, steam room, sauna, beauty and hairdressing salons, floodlit hard tennis court and ½ mile jogging track. The newly established stables include gentle trails and safe paddocks for children to enjoy pony-riding under expert guidance. Special half-board weekend breaks are offered, for a minimum 2-night stay, with rates from £91 per person per night – full details available upon request.

Our inspector loved: *The beautiful new look in the dining room – blue and gold decor perfectly complement the excellent cuisine.*

Directions: The hotel faces the common on the A264 in Tunbridge Wells.

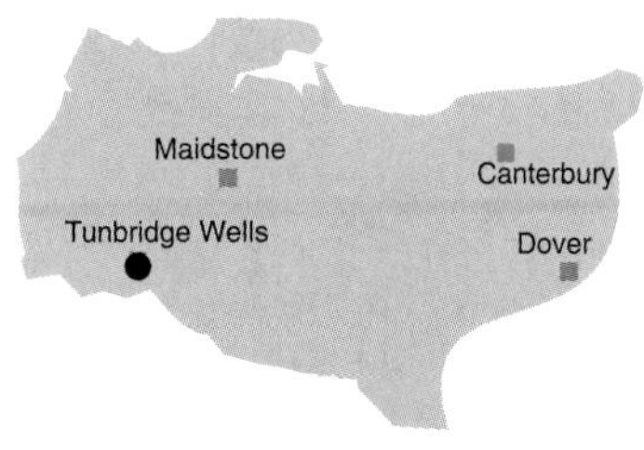

Web: www.johansens.com/spahotel
E-mail: reservations@spahotel.co.uk
Tel: 0870 381 8901
International: +44 (0)1892 520331
Fax: 01892 510575

Price Guide: (room only)
single £96–£106
double/twin £130–£190

        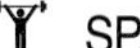 SPA   

Northcote Manor

NORTHCOTE ROAD, LANGHO, BLACKBURN, LANCASHIRE BB6 8BE

Large, redbrick and typically Victorian, this attractive and externally decorative hotel stands in the foothills of the Ribble Valley amidst some of Lancashire's most spectacular countryside. Excellently run by joint proprietors Craig Bancroft, a wine connoisseur, and Nigel Haworth, an award-winning chef, Northcote Manor has been an esteemed restaurant with rooms since 1983. Its high standards of hospitality, comfort, décor and food has earned it the prestigious award of "The Independent Hotel of the Year" by the Caterer and Hotelkeeper. Nigel, proud member of the Academy of Culinary Arts, trained in Switzerland and London and his gourmet cuisine has received innumerable accolades, including a Michelin Star and Egon Ronay's 1995 Chef of the Year distinction. His superb local and creative International dishes are presented with professionalism and aplomb in a delightful restaurant. Each meal is complemented by a superb wine list that is 400 bin strong. The hotel has 14 beautifully furnished, en-suite bedrooms that offer every comfort. Nearby are the Trough of Bowland and the Roman town of Ribchester, and 4 golf courses are within a 10 mile radius. The Yorkshire Dales and Lake District are within easy reach.

Our inspector loved: *The delicious cuisine featuring local and home grown produce.*

Directions: From M6 junction 31 take A59 towards Glitheroe. After 8 miles turn left into Northcote Road, immediately before the Langho roundabout.

Web: www.johansens.com/northcotelancs
E-mail: sales@northcotemanor.com
Tel: 0870 381 8766
International: +44 (0)1254 240555
Fax: 01254 246568

Price Guide:
single £110–£160
double/twin £140–£190

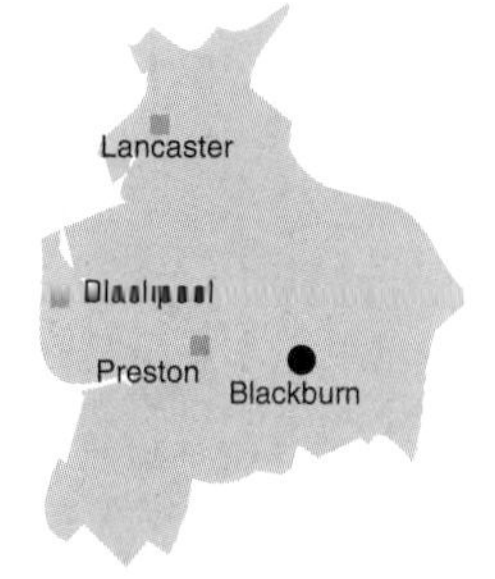

        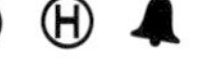

THE PINES HOTEL

CLAYTON–LE–WOODS, CHORLEY, LANCASHIRE PR6 7ED

Built in 1895, this Victorian-style hotel proudly stands within landscaped gardens and mature woodlands. Owner and managing director, Betty Duffin, takes an active role in the day-to-day running of the hotel. Each of the 37 guest rooms has en suite facilities and are individually decorated. De luxe rooms boast Jacuzzi showers, Jacuzzi baths and 4-poster beds whilst telephone, Internet access and voice mail are standard in all bedrooms. Before adjourning to haworth's bar & grill or the more intimate Crystal Room, which is perfect for private dining, guests are welcome to relax in the lounge and visit the well-equipped bar and sample many of the 150 bottles of wine on offer. The highly respected kitchen brigade creates a varied à la carte menu and creates imaginative daily specials. Private dinners, parties and weddings can be accommodated in the Dixon Suite with attentive staff on-hand to provide support; weekly cabaret and dinner dances are also very popular. Haydock Park Race Course and Blackpool are nearby.

Our inspector loved: *The relaxed and informal atmosphere in haworth's bar & grill.*

Directions: Take junction 28 off the M6 then the B5256 towards Chorley. At the roundabout turn right onto the A6 towards Chorley and the hotel is immediately on the left.

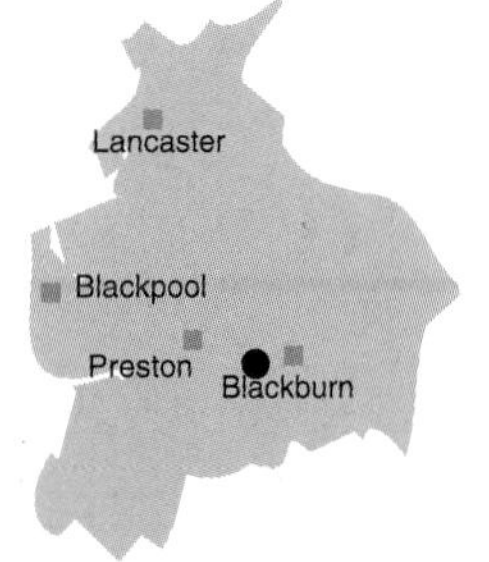

Web: www.johansens.com/thepines
E-mail: mail@thepineshotel.co.uk
Tel: 0870 381 9274
International: +44 (0)1772 338551
Fax: 01772 629002

Price Guide:
single £75–£100
double/twin £85–£110
suite £110–£140

36 M 400

NEW

Eaves Hall

EAVES HALL LANE, WADDINGTON, CLITHEROE, LANCASHIRE BB7 3JG

Set in the heart of the breathtaking Ribble Valley and within 7 acres of beautiful landscaped gardens, this luxurious Georgian-style manor house hotel is the ideal getaway for both leisure and business travellers. The original building was constructed in the mid-19th century, and has been altered considerably over the following 50 years to create the grand red brick building of today. The bedrooms and suites are of the highest standard; many offer superb views over the gardens. There are also 2 self-catering cottages within the grounds, Peels Cottage and The Lodge, which sleep 4 to 5 people and come with fully-equipped kitchens. A sophisticated, modern à la carte menu based on the finest and freshest ingredients can be enjoyed in the warm and inviting ambience of the restaurant, which is decorated with exquisite artworks and affords splendid views across the picturesque surroundings. Eaves Hall is the ideal location for weddings and small meetings, with a ballroom and a further meeting room accommodating up to 60 people. Guests can enjoy the hotel's first-class bowling green, its pitch 'n' putt and tennis courts, and a snooker room with bar billiards. Set within a 2-hour drive from the Lake District, the hotel is ideally located to explore the numerous attractions of this beautiful corner of the country, such as the historic city of York, Skipton Castle or Camelot Theme Park.

Our inspector loved: *The manicured gardens and grounds.*

Directions: M6/junction 31 then A59 towards Clitheroe. At A761 roundabout take Clitheroe bypass, third left for Clitheroe, North and West Bradford and pass through West Bradford. Turn left at T-junction then right into Eaves Hall Lane.

Web: www.johansens.com/eaveshall
E-mail: eaveshall@csma.uk.com
Tel: 0870 381 9198
International: +44 (0)1200 425 271
Fax: 01200 425 131

Price Guide:
single £78–£90
double/twin £120–£140
suite £143–£175

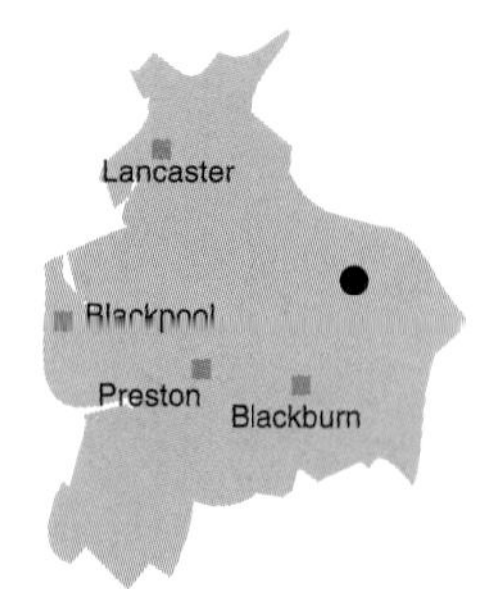

The Gibbon Bridge Hotel

NEAR CHIPPING, FOREST OF BOWLAND, LANCASHIRE PR3 2TQ

This award-winning hotel in the heart of Lancashire in the Forest of Bowland is a welcoming and peaceful retreat. The area, a favourite of the Queen, is now officially recognised as the Centre of the Kingdom! Created in 1982 by resident proprietor Janet Simpson and her late Mother, Margaret, the buildings combine traditional architecture with interesting Gothic masonry. Individually designed and equipped to the highest standard, the 7 bedrooms and 22 suites include four-posters, half-testers, Gothic brass beds and whirlpool baths. The restaurant overlooks the garden and is renowned for traditional and imaginative dishes incorporating home-grown vegetables and herbs. The garden bandstand is perfect for musical repertoires or civil wedding ceremonies. Elegant rooms, lounges and a unique al fresco dining area are available for private dinner parties and wedding receptions. For executive meetings and conference facilities the hotel will offer that "something a bit different". Leisure facilities include a gymnasium, steam room and an all-weather tennis court.

Our inspector loved: *The spectacular landscaped gardens surrounding the bandstand.*

Directions: From the south: M6 Exit 31A, follow signs for Longridge. From the north: M6 Exit 32, follow A6 to Broughton and B5269 to Longridge. At Longridge follow signs for Chipping for approx 3 miles, then follow Gibbon Bridge brown tourism signs.

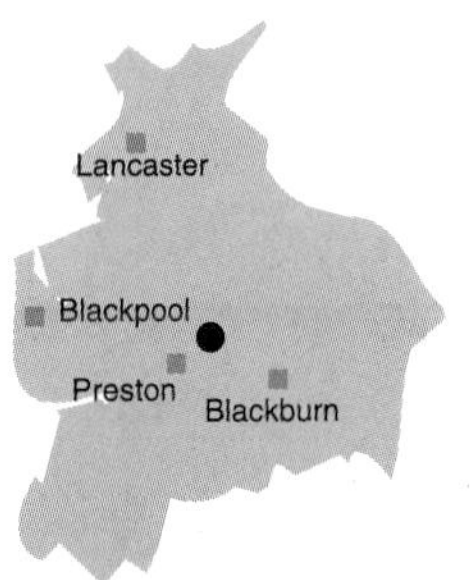

Web: www.johansens.com/gibbonbridge
E-mail: reception@gibbon-bridge.co.uk
Tel: 0870 381 8544
International: +44 (0)1995 61456
Fax: 01995 61277

Price Guide:
single £80-£120
double/twin £120
suite £150-£250

STAPLEFORD PARK HOTEL, SPA, GOLF & SPORTING ESTATE

NR. MELTON MOWBRAY, LEICESTERSHIRE LE14 2EF

Directions: By train Kings Cross/Grantham in 1 hour. Take the A1 north to Colsterworth then the B676 via Saxby.

Web: www.johansens.com/staplefordpark
E-mail: reservations@stapleford.co.uk
Tel: 0870 381 8912
International: +44 (0)1572 787 000
Fax: 01572 787 001

Price Guide:
double/twin £250–£465
suites from £560

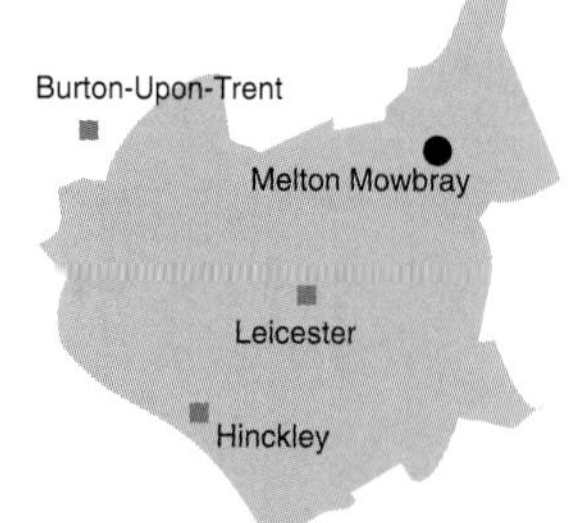

A stately home and sporting estate where casual luxury is the byword. This 16th-century house was once coveted by Edward, Prince of Wales, but his mother Queen Victoria forbade him to buy it for fear that his morals would be corrupted by the Leicestershire hunting society! Today, Stapleford Park offers guests and club members a "lifestyle experience" to transcend all others in supreme surroundings with views over 500 acres of parkland. Stapleford was voted Top UK Hotel for Leisure Facilities by Condé Nast Traveller, Johansens Most Excellent Business Meeting Venue 2000 and holds innumerable awards for its style and hospitality. Individually designed bedrooms and a 4-bedroom cottage have been created by famous names such as Mulberry, Wedgwood, Zoffany and Crabtree & Evelyn. The British with European influences cuisine is carefully prepared to the highest standards and complemented by an adventurous wine list. Sports include fishing, shooting, falconry, riding, tennis and an 18-hole championship golf course designed by Donald Steel. The luxurious Clarins Spa with indoor pool, Jacuzzi, sauna and fitness room offers an array of health therapies. 11 elegant function and dining rooms are suited to private dinners, special occasions and corporate hospitality.

Our inspector loved: *The splendid first floor bedrooms, such as Zoffany, where you can enjoy views of the buildings and the glorious grounds.*

SPA

THE LINCOLN HOTEL

EASTGATE, LINCOLN LN2 1PN

Historic Lincoln, with its Roman remains, second largest cathedral in England, Norman castle, Medieval buildings and cobbled streets surround this extremely modern hotel, with its subtle décor and 21st-century freshness that delights the senses. The Lincoln Hotel is situated opposite the majestic, triple-towered 12th-century cathedral with views of its 365ft high, honey-coloured stone walls from the comfortable lounge and brasserie. Carefully selected furnishings and the finest of fabrics have been judiciously chosen to enrich the hotel's appeal and big beds together with chic bathrooms feature prominently in the spacious bedrooms. Excellent cuisine, incorporating the freshest Lincolnshire produce, can be enjoyed in the coolly elegant restaurant or informal brasserie while pre and after dinner drinks, mid-morning coffee and afternoon tea can be taken in the small, tranquil garden set within Roman walls; a scenic setting for a special celebration. In addition to sightseeing and shopping in the city there are many delightful villages to explore in the nearby area and numerous historic properties such as the Elizabethan Manor House, Doddington Hall and the Norman Boothby Park Manor. There is motor racing at Cadwell Park and horse racing at Market Rasen.

Our inspector loved: *The shark in the lounge - is it Jaws?*

Directions: From the A1 take the A46 at Newark and follow signs to the historic city centre.

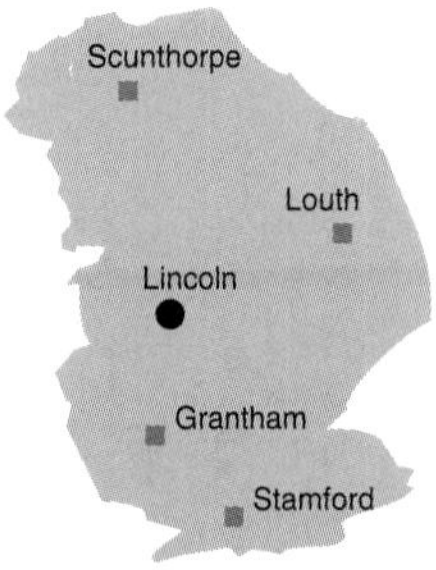

Scunthorpe
Louth
Lincoln
Grantham
Stamford

Web: www.johansens.com/lincolnhotel
E-mail: sales@thelincolnhotel.com
Tel: 0870 381 9288
International: +44 (0)1522 520348
Fax: 01522 510780

Price Guide:
single £75–£95
double £80–£110

41

41 BUCKINGHAM PALACE ROAD, LONDON SW1W 0PS

This intimate, AA 5 Red Star Hotel is quietly situated, overlooking the Royal Mews and Buckingham Palace Gardens. Adjacent also to St James's Park it is perfectly positioned for access to the City and West End. The hotel reflects a remarkable attention to detail, from its discreet and secluded guest entrance and magnificent architectural features to the beautiful furniture and club-like qualities of its superb day rooms. The 18 de luxe bedrooms and 2 split-level suites are furnished with traditional mahogany and black leather décor. With affordable 5-star service, continental breakfast and a variety of tasty snacks are served in the Executive Lounge. Flooded with natural daylight and comfortable chairs, the Lounge is the perfect place to read, meet or just take a moment to unwind. "41" has the world's most comfortable, handmade English mattresses and pure wool carpets throughout, bathrooms are in marble with bespoke bath and beauty products. Every room features an on-demand entertainment system with movie, music and Internet access with Wi-Fi broadband available. A state-of-the-art boardroom offers ISDN teleconferencing and private dining. 41 offers secretarial support, chauffeur driven cars, butler and chef services. Trafalgar Square, the Houses of Parliament and West End theatres are all nearby.

Our inspector loved: *The feeling you are staying in a private club.*

Directions: Victoria Station and Underground links are within minutes' walk; Gatwick Express 30 minutes; Heathrow 40 minutes.

Web: www.johansens.com/41buckinghampalaceroad
E-mail: book41@rchmail.com
Tel: 0870 381 8300
International: +44 (0)20 7300 0041
Fax: 020 7300 0141

Price Guide:
king bedded from £295
junior suite from £495
master suite from £695

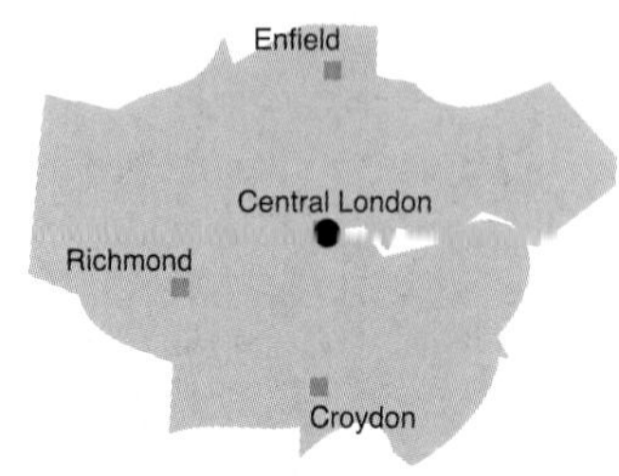

Draycott House Apartments

10 DRAYCOTT AVENUE, CHELSEA, LONDON SW3 3AA

Draycott House is an attractive period town house, standing in a quiet, tree-lined avenue in the heart of Chelsea. Housed in an attractive period building, the apartments have been designed in traditional styles to provide the ideal surroundings and location for a leisure or business visit, combining comfort, privacy and security with a convenient location. All are spacious, luxury suites with a kitchen and a wonderful alternative to a hotel, with 1, 2 or 3 bedrooms. Some have private balconies, a roof terrace and overlook the private courtyard garden. Each apartment is fully equipped with all home comforts; cable television, video, DVD, CD/hi-fi, private direct lines for own telephone/fax/answer machine/data, provisions/continental breakfast on arrival. A complimentary membership to an exclusive nearby health club, maid service, covered garage parking and laundry service. Additional services include airport transfers, transport, catering, travel, theatre tickets, dry cleaning/laundry, childminding and secretarial services. The West End and the City are within easy reach. Knightsbridge within walking distance. Long term reservations may attract preferential terms.

Our inspector loved: *These well appointed apartments, which are perfect for a long stay in London.*

Directions: Draycott House is situated on the corner of Draycott Avenue and Draycott Place, close to Sloane Square.

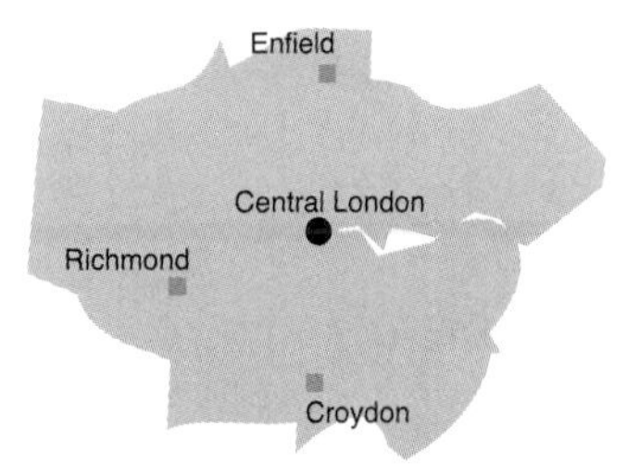

Web: www.johansens.com/draycotthouseapartments
E-mail: sales@draycotthouse.co.uk
Tel: 0870 381 8490
International: +44 (0)20 7584 4659
Fax: 020 7225 3694

Price Guide: (excluding VAT)
£188–£235 per night
£1178–£2948 per week

The Mayflower Hotel

26-28 TREBOVIR ROAD, LONDON SW5 9NJ

Directions: Between Earls Court Road and Warwick Road. The nearest underground station is Earls Court.

Web: www.johansens.com/mayflower
E-mail: info@mayflower-group.co.uk
Tel: 0870 381 9195
International: +44 (0)20 7370 0991
Fax: 020 7370 0994

Price Guide:
double £109
family room £130

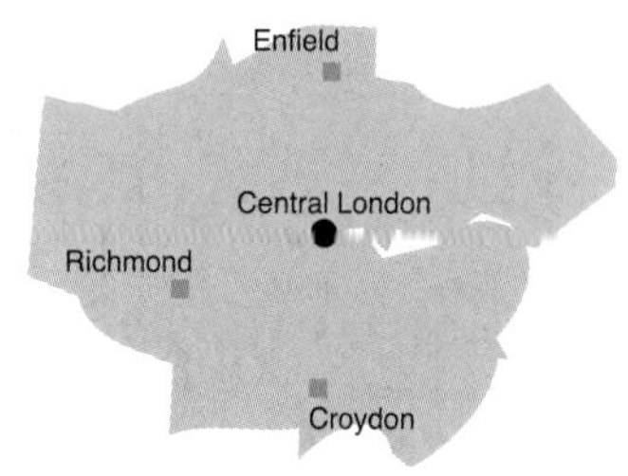

This recently renovated hotel is located in 2 Edwardian town houses conveniently situated in central London. The interior has been designed in a unique style with a fusion of eastern influences. Pale stone and wood floors, rich, vibrant fabrics with Indian and oriental antiques abound in 48 individually decorated bedrooms, 4 of which have balconies. The elegant light rooms have high ceilings and fans, enhanced by beautiful hand-carved wardrobes and bedside tables with ornate beds covered in luxurious Andrew Martin fabrics. All rooms offer broadband Internet access, CD players, safes and tea and coffee making facilities. The en-suite bathrooms are stylish and sparkling in marble and chrome with walk-in showers. Guests can enjoy a complimentary continental buffet breakfast in the new basement dining room or in the patio garden, before venturing out to explore the nearby fashionable shopping areas of Knightsbridge and Chelsea or visit the V&A and The Natural History and Science Museum. The Mayflower's proximity to the famous Earl's Court Exhibition Centre makes it perfectly located to suit business travellers and corporate events. Earl's Court underground station is only a minute's walk away and provides direct access to Heathrow Airport, the City and the West End.

Our inspector loved: *The recently renovated reception and new breakfast room.*

West Lodge Park Country House Hotel

COCKFOSTERS ROAD, HADLEY WOOD, BARNET, HERTFORDSHIRE EN4 0PY

West Lodge Park is a country house hotel which stands in 34 acres of green belt parklands and gardens. These include a lake and an arboretum with hundreds of mature trees. Run by the Beale family for over 60 years, West Lodge Park was originally a gentleman's country seat, rebuilt in 1838 on the site of an earlier keeper's lodge. In the public rooms, antiques, original paintings and period furnishings create a restful atmosphere. All the bright and individually furnished bedrooms, many of which enjoy country views, have a full range of modern amenities. Well presented cuisine is available in the elegant restaurant. Beauty rooms feature Elemis products. Residents enjoy free membership and a free taxi to the nearby leisure centre, which has excellent facilities. Hatfield House and St Albans Abbey are a 15-minute drive away. The hotel is credited with AA 4 stars and 2 Rosettes, RAC 4 stars plus 3 merit awards. Top rating in Hertfordshire, Bedfordshire and North London. Enquire about special offers available.

Our inspector loved: *The stunning arboretum and the diverse programme of special events.*

Directions: The hotel is on the A111, 1 mile north of Cockfosters underground station and 1 mile south of junction 24 on the M25.

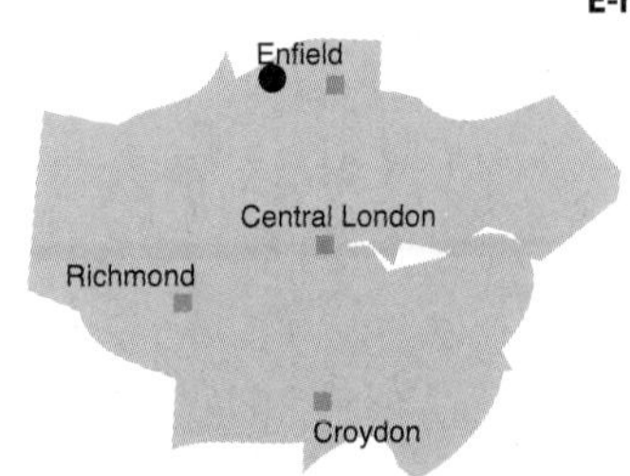

Web: www.johansens.com/westlodgepark
E-mail: westlodgepark@bealeshotels.co.uk
Tel: 0870 381 8978
International: +44 (0)20 8216 3900
Fax: 020 8216 3937

Price Guide:
single £90–£160
double/twin from £115–£180

59 80 WiFi

Kensington House Hotel

15-16 PRINCE OF WALES TERRACE, KENSINGTON, LONDON W8 5PQ

This attractive hotel with its architecturally splendid tall, ornate windows and pillared entrance stands grandly on a 19th-century site long associated with style and elegance. Just off Kensington High Street, this charming town house is an ideal base from which to explore London's attractions. Views cover delightful mews houses, leafy streets and out across the City rooftops. The emphasis is on providing informal, professional service in an atmosphere of relaxation and comfort. Each of the 41 intimate bedrooms offers en-suite facilities. Rooms are bright and airy with modern furniture and fittings adding to the fresh, contemporary treatment of a classic design. Home-from-home comforts include crisp linen, duvets and bathrobes. Other features offered: courtesy tray, ceiling fan, voicemail, modem connection and in-room safe. The 2 junior suites can convert into a family room. The stylish Tiger Bar is a popular venue for coffee or cocktails prior to enjoying a delicious dinner, with a menu that draws on a range of influences offering both traditional and modern dishes. The serenity of Kensington Gardens is just a gentle stroll away and some of the capital's most fashionable shops, restaurants and cultural attractions are within walking distance. Weekend rates are available.

Our inspector loved: The light bright airy rooms and location in Kensington.

Directions: The nearest underground station is High Street Kensington.

Web: www.johansens.com/kensingtonhouse
E-mail: reservations@kenhouse.com
Tel: 0870 381 8648
International: +44 (0)20 7937 2345
Fax: 020 7368 6700

Price Guide:
single £150
double/twin £175-£195
junior suites £215

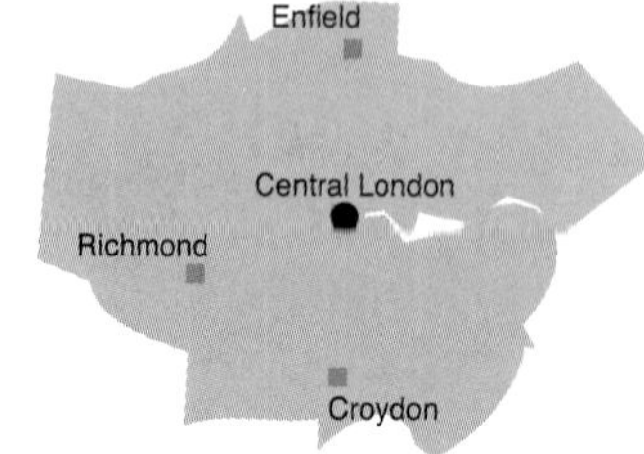

THE MILESTONE HOTEL & APARTMENTS

1 KENSINGTON COURT, LONDON W8 5DL

The beautifully appointed Condé Nast Johansens award winning Milestone Hotel is situated opposite Kensington Palace with views over Kensington Gardens and Hyde Park. A Victorian showpiece, this unique hotel has been carefully restored to its original splendour whilst incorporating every modern facility. The 57 bedrooms include 12 suites and 6 apartments; all are individually designed with antiques, elegant furnishings and some have private balconies. Guests may relax in the comfortable, panelled Park Lounge which, in company with all other rooms, provides a 24-hour service. The hotel's restaurant, Cheneston's, the early spelling of Kensington, has an elaborately carved ceiling, original fireplace and ornate windows. The Windsor Suite is a versatile function room, perfect for private dining and corporate meetings. The fitness centre offers guests the use of a new resistance infinity pool, spa treatment room, sauna, and gymnasium. The traditional bar, Stables, on the ground floor as well as the bright and airy black and white conservatory are ideal for meeting and entertaining friends. The Milestone is within walking distance of some of the finest shopping in Kensington and in Knightsbridge, such as Harrods, and is a short taxi ride to the West End, the heart of London's Theatreland. The Royal Albert Hall and all the museums in Exhibition Road are a short walk away.

Our inspector loved: *The themed rooms and attention to detail throughout.*

Directions: Opposite to Kensington Palace and adjacent to Hyde Park.

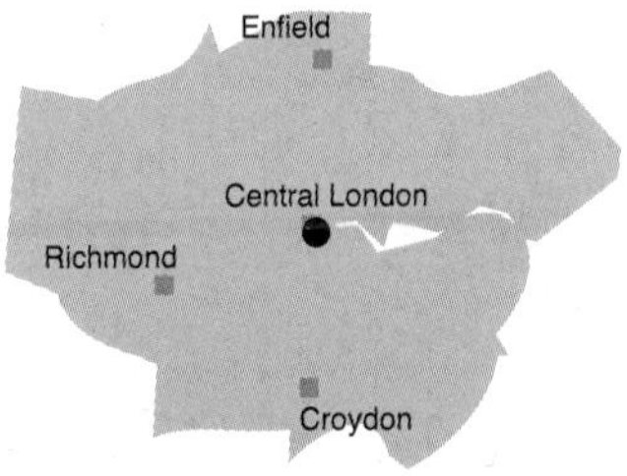

Web: www.johansens.com/milestone
E-mail: bookms@rchmail.com
Tel: 0870 381 8732
International: +44 (0)020 7917 1000
Fax: 020 7917 1010

Price Guide:
double/twin £310–£490
suites £570–£910

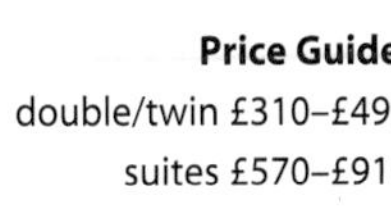

Millennium Bailey's Hotel

140 GLOUCESTER ROAD, LONDON SW7 4QH

Directions: Directly opposite Gloucester Road tube station (Circle, District and Piccadilly lines). Heathrow Airport is 40 minutes direct by underground.

Web: www.johansens.com/millenniumbaileys
E-mail: baileys@mill-cop.com
Tel: 0870 381 9379
International: +44 (0)20 7373 6000
Fax: 020 7370 3760

Price Guide:
single £115
double £150
suite £330

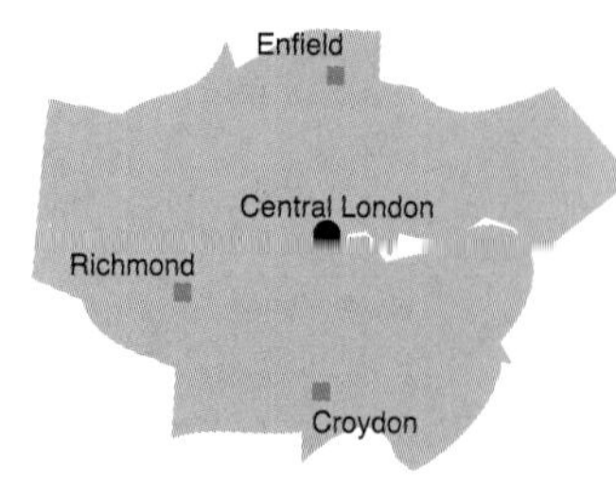

This magnificently restored 19th-century town house hotel is ideally situated in the heart of London close to Hyde Park and Kensington Palace & Gardens as well as some of the capital's most fashionable shops and restaurants. The formality of a traditional hotel has been replaced by the creation of an atmosphere that is as refreshing as it is relaxing. Filled with character, retained over the years since its doors first opened as a purpose-built hotel in 1876, guests enter the stately hall, with its grand curved staircase, into an authentic Victorian interior. Warm muted tones, comfortable seating, fine furnishings and rich fabrics combine with glorious dark woods that create an enchanting ambience alongside the excellent service. Each of the 211 individually decorated and stylish guest rooms is a peaceful and quiet retreat from the City's bustle, with modern comforts and every facility from air-conditioning to a complimentary coffee and tea service. Exceptional cuisine is served in the elegant and welcoming restaurant, which is just one of a range of dining experiences available. As well as enjoying the nearby shopping areas of Knightsbridge and Chelsea, London's other major attractions are easily accessible.

Our inspector loved: *The warm welcome from the staff and wealth of original Victorian features.*

Twenty Nevern Square

20 NEVERN SQUARE, LONDON SW5 9PD

A unique experience in hospitality awaits guests at this elegant 4-star town house hotel. Sumptuously restored, the emphasis is on natural materials and beautiful hand-carved beds and furniture. The hotel overlooks a tranquil garden square and has its own delightful restaurant, Café Twenty, which is also available for small dinner and cocktail parties. Each of the 20 intimate bedrooms provides white marble, compact en-suite facilities, and is individually designed echoing both Asian and European influences. You can choose the delicate silks of the Chinese Room or a touch of opulence in the Rococo Room. The grandeur of the Pasha Suite, complete with four-poster bed and balcony, makes an ideal setting for a special occasion. All rooms have full modern facilities including wide-screen digital TV, CD player, private safe and a separate telephone and Internet/fax connection. Gym facilities are available by arrangement. The location is ideal – close to Earl's Court and Olympia exhibition centres and the tube. The Picadilly Line brings guests arriving at Heathrow in just over 30 minutes. Guests are a mere 10 minutes from London's most fashionable shopping areas, restaurants, theatres and cultural attractions such as the V&A and Science Museums.

***Our inspector loved:** This charming hotel reflecting it's Eastern origins.*

Directions: 2 minutes from Earls Court station.

Web: www.johansens.com/twentynevernsquare
E-mail: hotel@twentynevernsquare.co.uk
Tel: 0870 381 8957
International: +44 (0)20 7565 9555
Fax: 020 7565 9444

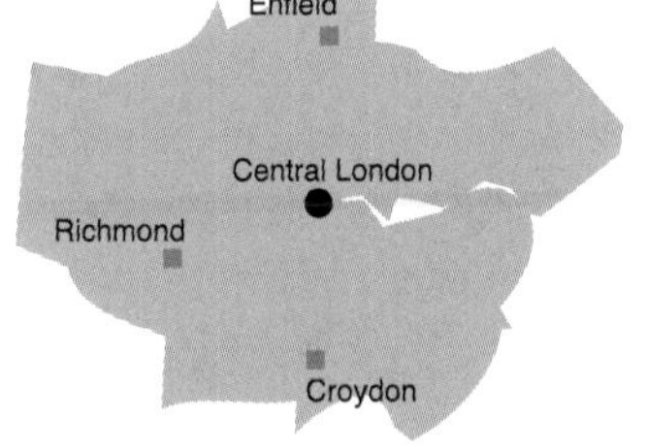

Price Guide:
double/twin £130–£165
suite £275

 20  25     

Beaufort House

45 BEAUFORT GARDENS, KNIGHTSBRIDGE, LONDON SW3 1PN

Directions: Beaufort Gardens leads off Brompton Road near Knightsbridge underground station. There is a 24hr car park nearby.

Web: www.johansens.com/beauforthouseapartments
E-mail: info@beauforthouse.co.uk
Tel: 0870 381 8350
International: +44 (0)20 7584 2600
Fax: 020 7584 6532

Price Guide: (excluding VAT)
£230–£650

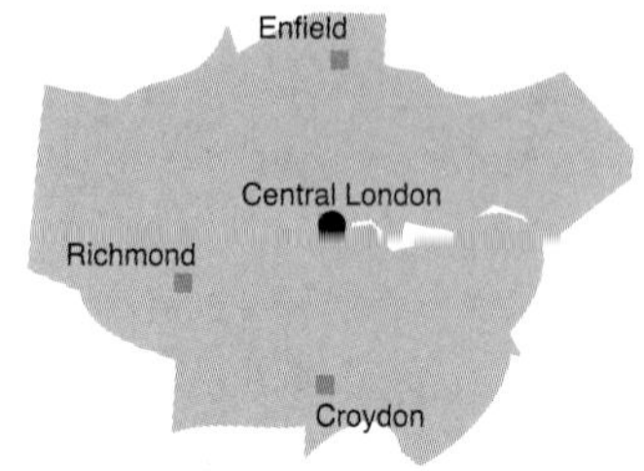

Situated in Beaufort Gardens, a quiet tree-lined Regency cul-de-sac in the heart of Knightsbridge, 250 yards from Harrods, Beaufort House is an exclusive establishment comprising 21 self-contained fully serviced luxury apartments. All the comforts of a first-class hotel are combined with the privacy, discretion and relaxed atmosphere of home. Accommodation ranges in size from an intimate 1- bedroom to a spacious 4-bedroom apartment. Each apartment has been individually and traditionally decorated to the highest standard. All apartments have direct dial telephones with voice mail, personal safes, satellite television, DVD players and high speed Internet access. Some apartments benefit from balconies or patios. The fully equipped kitchens include washer/dryers and many have dishwashers. A daily maid service is included at no additional charge. Full laundry/dry cleaning services are available. A dedicated Guests Services team provides 24 hours coverage and will be happy to organise tours, theatre tickets, restaurant bookings, taxis or chauffeur driven limousines and other services. Complimentary membership at Aquilla's Health Club is offered to all guests during their stay. Awarded 5 stars by the English Tourism Council.

Our inspector loved: *The stylish comfortable apartments which are perfect for the long stay guest in an ideal location.*

The Carlton Tower

ON CADOGAN PLACE, LONDON SW1X 9PY

In the heart of Knightsbridge, overlooking the private, leafy gardens of Cadogan Place, this 5-star luxury hotel successfully combines ultra modern convenience and facilities with traditional hospitality. The ideal city venue for the leisure and business visitor alike, Harrods and some of the capital's most fashionable shops are within walking distance and the bright lights of the West End and the financial areas of The City can be reached by a short taxi ride or tube journey. Beautifully furnished and decorated, an understated elegance pervades the hotel. The stylish and spacious bedrooms, including 59 suites and a Presidential Suite on the 18th floor, are equipped with every amenity and comfort expected from a leading hotel, such as air conditioning, modem access and fax machine. All rooms offer memorable London views. Arguably London's finest, the 184m² Presidential Suite offers unmatched accommodation and boasts a private sauna, enhanced security and the highest level of personalized service. The hotel is proud of its eclectic mix of restaurants and bars: the Rib Room & Oyster Bar is an acknowledged gourmet delight for those who enjoy the finest steaks. Extensive facilities at the rooftop health club include a tropical, glass-domed, 20m, stainless steel swimming pool.

Our inspector loved: *The health club & spa with some of the best views over London.*

Directions: A 3-minute walk from Knightsbridge tube station (Piccadilly Line). Take Sloane Street/Brompton Road station exit, turn right down Sloane Street then left into Cadogan Place.

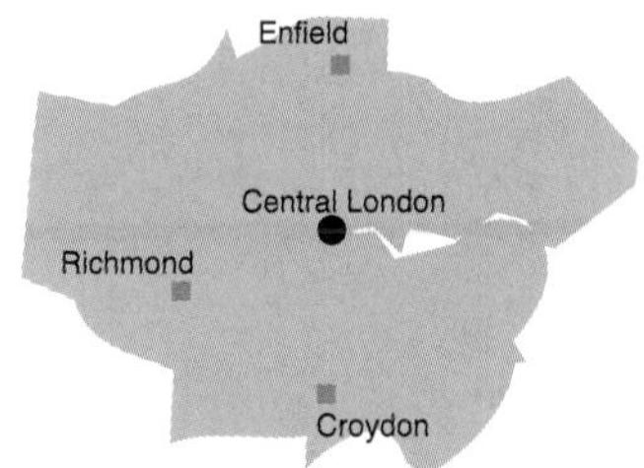

Web: www.johansens.com/carltontower
E-mail: JCTinfo@jumeirah.com
Tel: 0870 381 9326
International: +44 (0)20 7235 1234
Fax: +44 (0)20 7235 9129

Price Guide: (excluding VAT)
single £335
double/twin £335

SPA

The Lowndes Hotel

21 Lowndes Street, Knightsbridge, London SW1X 9ES

The Lowndes Hotel is a stylish boutique hotel which boasts 78 bedrooms and is ideally situated in London's residential Belgravia, just minutes from Hyde Park, fashionable Sloane Street and Duke of York Square. Classical contemporary décor combines effortlessly with modern comforts and rich fabrics to create a homely and inviting atmosphere. The hotel is ideal for business or pleasure alike and is renowned for its highly personalised service levels from the attentive team of staff. The Library, located on the ground floor, is perfect for small boardroom meetings, private dinners and cocktail receptions for up to 30 people. Many of the bedrooms have balconies overlooking fashionable Halkin Arcade and the choice of spacious suites will tempt the most discerning traveller. In the relaxed surrounds of Citronelle restaurant savour delicious Mediterranean cuisine and al-fresco dining on the outdoor terrace. Alternatively dine at The Lowndes Hotel's sister property, The Carlton Tower, and enjoy an eclectic mix of restaurants and bars, as well as a rooftop health club and spa. Highlights include a tropical water garden and 20m stainless steel swimming pool set in a beautiful glass atrium. The Lowndes' central location enables easy access by foot, public transport or taxi to London's major tourist attractions including the West End and the City.

Directions: The nearest underground tube stations are Knightsbridge, Hyde Park Corner and Sloane Square.

Web: www.johansens.com/lowndes
E-mail: contact@lowndeshotel.com
Tel: 0870 381 9285
International: +44 (0)20 7823 1234
Fax: 020 7235 1154

Price Guide: (room only, excluding VAT)
double £280-£315
suite £380-£530

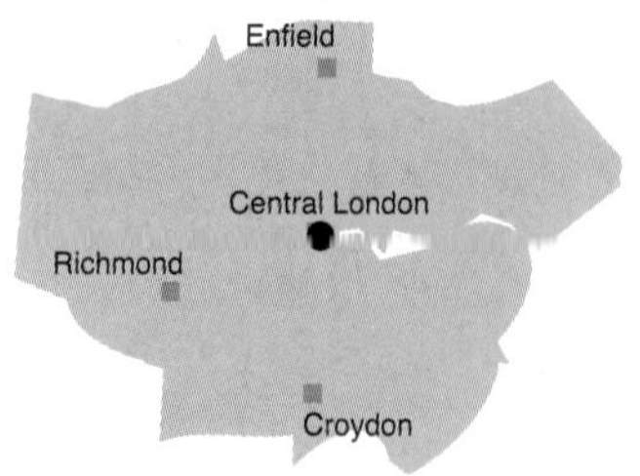

Our inspector loved: *The chef's homemade shortbread – delicious!*

 78   35     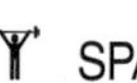 SPA 

The Royal Park

3 Westbourne Terrace, Lancaster Gate, Hyde Park, London W2 3UL

Situated on the doorstep of Hyde Park, this exquisite hotel comprises of 3 Grade II listed Georgian town houses, lovingly restored to their 1840's elegance. There are 48 charming bedrooms, decorated in stunning Regency colours that truly enhance the antique furniture, luxurious linens and handmade beds. Each room boasts a splendid antique writing desk, as well as the latest technology including flatscreen television and broadband Internet access. The hotel is adorned with delightful Georgian and Victorian antique pieces, carefully selected by Jonty Hearnden of "The Antiques Roadshow." Upon arrival, guests enter the glorious marble chequered reception with roaring log fire and receive a complimentary glass of sherry or whiskey. Although there is no restaurant, an excellent room service menu is available and breakfast can be served in guests' rooms or in the drawing room. Complimentary traditional English tea is served in the afternoon and a glass of champagne, with canapés, may be enjoyed in the evening. For small meetings the Green Room can accomodate 10 people. Oxford Street and Notting Hill are both within walking distance.

Our inspector loved: *The new patio garden and beautiful bedrooms.*

Directions: The nearest underground tube station is Lancaster Gate. The hotel is a 2-minute walk from the Heathrow Express at Paddington Station.

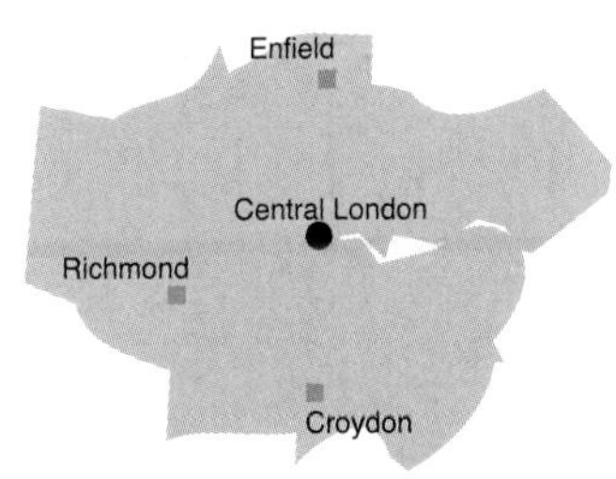

Web: www.johansens.com/royalpark
E-mail: info@theroyalpark.com
Tel: 0870 381 9289
International: +44 (0)20 7479 6600
Fax: 020 7479 6601

Price Guide: (weekend rates incl VAT)
single £120–£165
double £140–£190
suite £210–£295

Dorset Square Hotel

39 DORSET SQUARE, MARYLEBONE, LONDON NW1 6QN

Directions: Left from Marylebone tube or right from Baker street tube – the hotel is just minutes from each.

Web: www.johansens.com/dorsetsquare
E-mail: info@dorsetsquare.co.uk
Tel: 0870 381 8488
International: +44 (0)20 7723 7874
Fax: 020 7724 3328

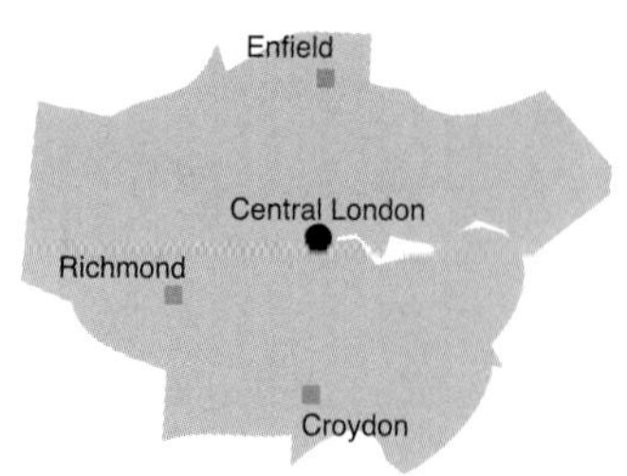

Price Guide: (excluding VAT)
single £150
dorset/superior £220
regency/de luxe £250
suite £350

One of the first boutique hotels in London, this little gem of a hotel is in a prime location for all that the west end has to offer. Set in a leafy square that was the original site for Thomas Lord's cricket ground, this Regency town house has been lovingly restored and designed to offer the ultimate in comfort and charm with a chic London edge. Each of the 37 bedrooms has been perfectly appointed to offer the latest amenities such as air conditioning, modem ports, and the marble bathrooms are equipped to an extremely high standard. The award winning Potting Shed and Bar is a delight – light and airy and exuding character with an array of terracotta pots along one wall. The cuisine is a selection of modern British. For those who prefer to remain in the luxury of their bedrooms there is also the wonderful "bedroom picnic" – a basket laden with cold meats, fresh fruits, cheeses and pastries and chilled champagne. Live Jazz nights are held every Friday The Thomas Lord meeting room with large plasma screen, natural daylight and air condition rooms is ideal for small meetings of up to 10 people. Madame Tussauds, the Planetarium and Regent's Park zoo are all within 2 minutes walk, and the shops of Oxford Street, Baker Street and even Bond Street are not far away. Theatreland is only a few minutes away, and the city is easily accessible by tube.

Our inspector loved: *The divine Potting Shed restaurant.*

 37  10     

47 Park Street

MAYFAIR, LONDON W1K 7EB

Passing through the grand, twin-pillared entranceway and tall, double-opening doors it is evident that this is a luxurious, discrete and intimate hotel, an exclusive residence for those wishing to avail themselves of the best that London can offer. In a superb location on the edge of Park Lane and Hyde Park, the hotel is surrounded by lovely Georgian terraces, leafy squares and the quiet back streets of Mayfair. The fashionable shopping areas of Bond Street, Knightsbridge and Oxford Street are a short walk away and the West End is easily accessible. Built in 1929 as a private home for the first Baron Milford, beautifully appointed accommodation has been combined with a sense of intimacy and belonging. Each of the one and two-bedroomed spacious and comfortably furnished guest suites feature restful décor, elegant drapes, antique furniture, fully-equipped kitchen, generous dining area and lounge, marble bathroom with power shower, satellite television, DVD and 3 telephone lines. Exceptional services on offer include: a discreet and uncompromising Concierge team, 24-hour reception, twice daily maid service, grocery pre-stocking, in-house florist, personal shopping service and limousine service. An abundance of prestigious restaurants are nearby, including the renowned Le Gavroche, whilst 24-hour room service enables friends or business associates to be entertained in style and privacy.

Our inspector loved: *This elegant hotel in a perfect location.*

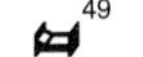

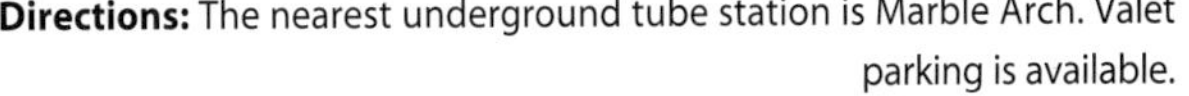

Directions: The nearest underground tube station is Marble Arch. Valet parking is available.

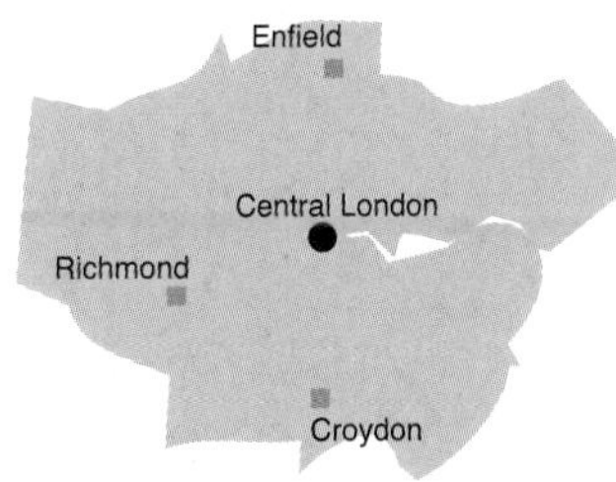

Web: www.johansens.com/parkstreet
E-mail: reservations@47parkstreet.com
Tel: 0870 381 9282
International: +44 (0)20 7491 7282
Fax: 020 7491 7281

Price Guide:
suite £330 – £600

Brown's Hotel

ALBEMARLE STREET, LONDON W1S 4BP

Directions: The nearest underground station is Green Park. Valet parking is available.

Web: www.johansens.com/brownsmayfair
E-mail: reservations.brownshotel@rfhotels.com
Tel: 0870 381 8403
International: +44 (0)20 7493 6020
Fax: 020 7493 9381

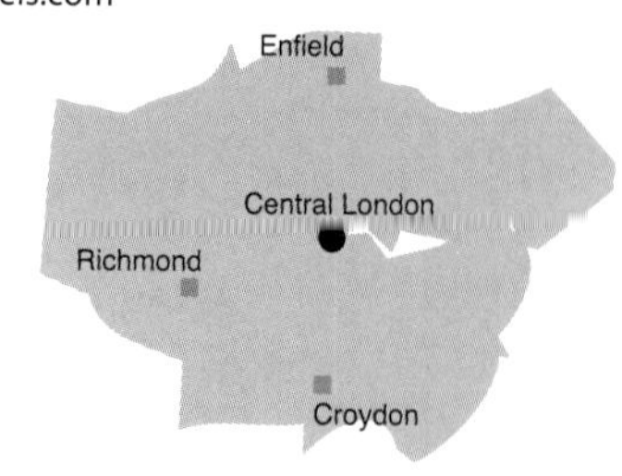

Price Guide:
(Excluding breakfast and VAT)
king/twin from £325
suite from £850

One of the most eagerly awaited hotel relaunches, the famous Brown's Hotel reopens in Autumn 2005 after a staggering £19 million refurbishment programme. Brown's has become legendary over the years as the first quintessential English luxury hotel, and great care has been taken to preserve its statesmanly heritage. Olga Polizzi has designed the interior with an objective to retain the hotel's inherent English charm by cleverly incorporating original wood panelling and gilt mirrors with modern, fresh colour schemes, mosaic tiles, delightful antique pieces and natural materials. With an unbeatable location, in the heart of Mayfair, the hotel is a stone's throw from the world famous shops of Bond Street, whilst London's theatreland and many restaurants and bars are a short walk away. New additions to the hotel include the Donovan Bar that will pay homage to British photographer Terence Donovan with a display of his famous black and white prints adorning the walls, and The Grill, formerly Restaurant 1837, which will serve a delicate balance of traditional English favourites with a contemporary, international twist. Brown's English Tea Room has served the most famous afternoon tea in London for many years, and with an improved menu, will ensure that guests on any myriad of diets will be able to savour afternoon tea in this beautiful and much-loved hotel.

 117  M 120      SPA 

Pembridge Court Hotel

34 Pembridge Gardens, London W2 4DX

This gracious Victorian town house has been lovingly restored to its former glory whilst providing all the modern facilities demanded by today's discerning traveller. The 20 rooms, all of which have air conditioning, are individually decorated with pretty fabrics and the walls adorned with an unusual collection of framed fans and Victoriana. The charming and tranquil sitting room is as ideal for a quiet drink and light snacks as it is for a small informal meeting. There is also a small boardroom and sitting room on the lower ground floor. The Pembridge Court is renowned for the devotion and humour with which it is run. Its long serving staff and its famous cat "Churchill" assure you of a warm welcome and the very best in friendly, personal service. Over the years the hotel has built up a loyal following amongst its guests, many of whom regard it as their genuine "home from home" in London. The Pembridge is situated in quiet tree-lined gardens in Londons' trendy Notting Hill Gate. The area is colourful and full of life with lots of great pubs and restaurants and the biggest antiques market in the world at nearby Portobello Road.

Our inspector loved: *The cosy "at home" feel of the sitting room and the collection of Victorian fans.*

Directions: Pembridge Gardens is a small turning off Notting Hill Gate/Bayswater Road, just 2 minutes from Portobello Road Antiques Market.

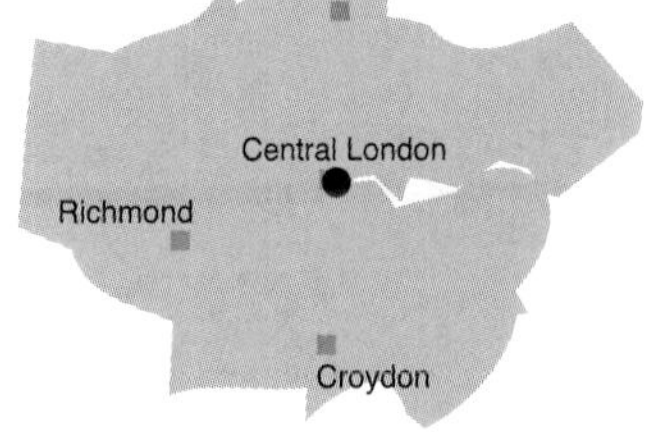

Web: www.johansens.com/pembridgecourt
E-mail: reservations@pemct.co.uk
Tel: 0870 381 8808
International: +44 (0)20 7229 9977
Fax: 020 7727 4982

Price Guide:
(inclusive of English breakfast & VAT)
single £130–£170
double/twin £190–£200

The Mandeville Hotel

MANDEVILLE PLACE, LONDON W1U 2BE

Situated in fashionable Marylebone Village, within a few minutes' walk from the shops and art galleries of Oxford Street, Bond Street and Mayfair, as well as the famous auction houses of Sothebys and Christies, this sophisticated hotel exudes style and modern opulence. Highly personalised service and attention to detail ensure that each guest feels at home. The elegant interior design places an emphasis on luxurious comfort and sense of space; magnificent original paintings adorn the walls alongside opulent fabrics and comfortable chairs. All the bedrooms are uniquely decorated with the most up-to-date conveniences and marble bathrooms are equipped with power showers. The penthouse attic suite has its own private terrace, attic bathroom and separate entrance. Red, yellow, green and silver tones enhance the cosy atmosphere of the hotel's stunning saloon, which features an eye-catching silver and glass bar and dark brown suede banquettes. Guests can savour the light bites and mouth-watering finger platters on offer. The superb restaurant has a theatrical theme and bold colour schemes designed by world famous Interior Designer, Stephen Ryan. Delicious modern British cuisine is on the menu accompanied by fine wines. Due to its central location, The Mandeville Hotel is ideal for exploring the many delights of London.

Our inspector loved: *The vibrant, silver and glass bar.*

Directions: The nearest underground station is Bond Street, which is a 5-minute walk away from the hotel.

Web: www.johansens.com/mandeville
E-mail: info@mandeville.co.uk
Tel: 0870 381 8344
International: +44 (0)20 7935 5599
Fax: 020 7935 9588

Price Guide:
single £275
double/twin £325
suite £500

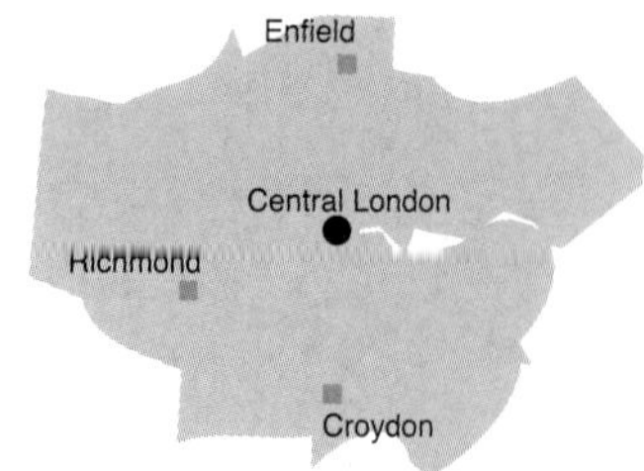

The Richmond Gate Hotel and Restaurant

RICHMOND HILL, RICHMOND-UPON-THAMES, SURREY TW10 6RP

This former Georgian country house stands on the crest of Richmond Hill close to the Royal Park and Richmond Terrace with its commanding views over the River Thames. The 68 stylishly furnished en-suite bedrooms, many with air-conditioning, combine every comfort of the present with the elegance of the past and include several luxury four-poster rooms and suites. Exceptional and imaginative cuisine, complemented by an extensive wine list offering over 100 wines from around the world is served in the sophisticated surroundings of the Gates On The Parks Restaurant. Weddings, business meetings and private dining events can be arranged in a variety of rooms. The beautiful Victorian walled garden provides for summer relaxation. Cedars Health and Leisure Club is accessed through the hotel and includes a 20-metre pool, 6-metre spa, sauna, steam room, aerobics studio, cardiovascular and resistance gymnasia and a health and beauty suite. Richmond is close to London and the West End yet in a country setting. The Borough offers a wealth of visitor attractions, including Hampton Court Palace, Wimbledon, Twickenham Rugby Stadium, Syon House and Park and the Royal Botanic Gardens at Kew.

***Our inspector loved:** The impressive refurbishment undertaken by the enthusiastic new owners.*

68 60 SPA

Directions: Opposite the Star & Garter Home at the top of Richmond Hill.

Web: www.johansens.com/richmondgate
E-mail: richmondgate@foliohotels.com
Tel: 0870 381 8855
International: +44 (0)20 8940 0061
Fax: 020 8332 0354

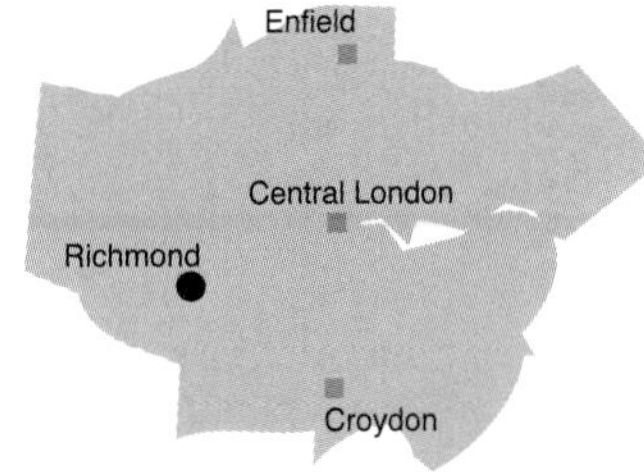

Price Guide:
single £140–£200
double/twin £150–£220
suite from £230

THE CRANLEY

10 BINA GARDENS, SOUTH KENSINGTON, LONDON SW5 0LA

Standing in a quiet, tree-lined street in the heart of Kensington, this charming and sophisticated Victorian town house is an ideal city venue for the leisure and business visitor alike, blending traditional style and service with 21st-century technology. Furnished with beautiful antiques and hand-embroidered linen fabrics, The Cranley has an understated elegance. Striking colour combinations and stone used throughout the bedrooms and reception areas are derived from the original floor in the entrance hall. Recently completely refurbished, The Cranley's bedrooms are now among some of the most comfortable in the Capital. All are delightfully decorated and have king-sized, four-poster or half-tester canopied beds. Each room is light, air-conditioned and has facilities ranging from antique desk, 2 direct dial telephone lines and voicemail to broadband connection. The luxury bathrooms have traditional Victorian-style fittings combined with a lavish use of warm limestone. Guests can enjoy copious continental breakfasts, complimentary English afternoon tea and an evening help-yourself apéritif with canapés. Many of London's attractions are within easy walking distance, including the shops and restaurants of Knightsbridge and the Kings Road.

Our inspector loved: *The four-poster beds and glorious fabrics.*

Directions: The nearest underground stations are Gloucester Road and South Kensington.

Web: www.johansens.com/cranley
E-mail: info@thecranley.com
Tel: 0870 381 8456
International: +44 (0)20 7373 0123
Fax: 020 7373 9497

Price Guide:
single £180
double/twin £220
suite £350

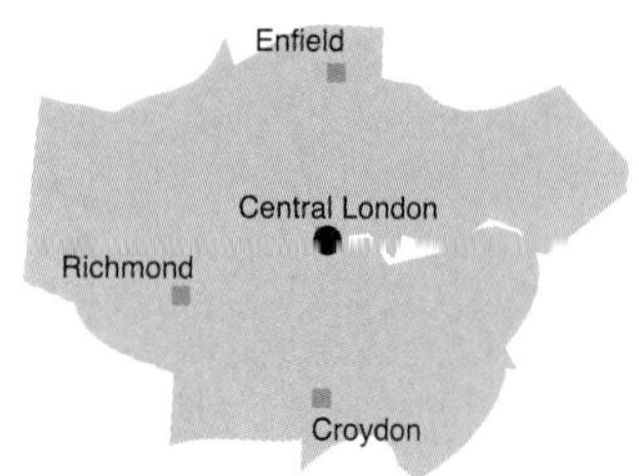

NUMBER SIXTEEN

16 SUMNER PLACE, LONDON SW7 3EG

Freshly refurbished behind an immaculate pillared façade, Number Sixteen, winner of Condé Nast Johansens Most Excellent London Hotel in 2004, and situated in the heart of South Kensington, is surrounded by some of London's best restaurants, bars, shops and museums. Harrods, Knightsbridge shopping, Hyde Park and the Victoria & Albert Museum are all just a short walk away. Although the area has a buzzy, cosmopolitan character, the hotel is a haven of calm and seclusion. In winter an open fire and honesty bar in the drawing room entices with its warmth, whilst in summer the conservatory, where breakfast is served, opens onto an award-winning private garden. The library is ideal for greeting friends or holding an informal business meeting. The 42 bedrooms are individually designed and decorated in a modern English style complete with crisp Frette bedlinen and white, hand-embroidered bedspreads. Each is appointed with facilities expected by the modern traveller, including mini-bar, personal safe and direct dial telephone with voice mail and modem point. Staff are friendly and attentive ensuring that guests are looked after almost as if they were staying in a private home. South Kensington underground station is just a 2-minute walk away, providing easy access to the West End and the City and a direct link to Heathrow Airport.

Our inspector loved: *The new conservatory and very pretty garden.*

Directions: Sumner Place is off the Old Brompton Road near Onslow Square.

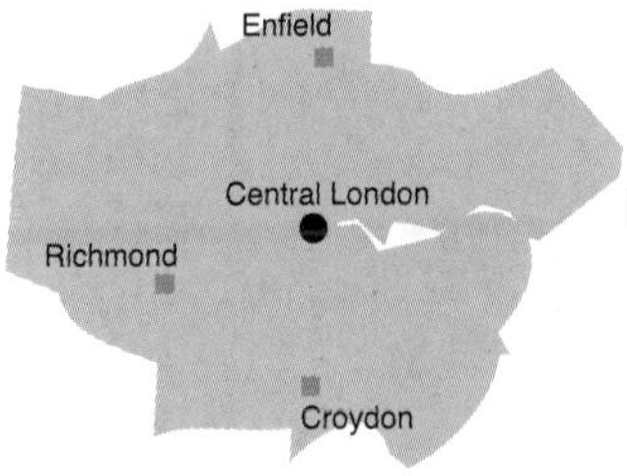

Web: www.johansens.com/numbersixteen
E-mail: sixteen@firmdale.com
Tel: 0870 381 8771
International: +44 (0)20 7589 5232
Fax: 020 7584 8615

Enfield
Central London
Richmond
Croydon

Price Guide: (room only excluding VAT)
single from £95
double/twin £170–£250

SOFITEL ST JAMES

6 WATERLOO PLACE, LONDON SW1Y 4AN

Located on the corner of Waterloo Place and Pall Mall, this imposing Grade II listed building is the former home of the Cox's and King's bank and has been carefully renovated to create an elegant 5-star hotel. Sofitel acquired the majority of the original artwork from the bank, which is now proudly displayed and balanced out by contemporary design. Bedrooms and suites are sophisticated and equipped with ultra-modern technology, and in the bathrooms black and white marble harmonises with granite tops and chrome fittings. The elegant Rose Lounge is the ideal place for a traditional afternoon tea amidst an eclectic mix of colours and styles, whilst the St James Bar offers the largest selection of Champagnes and cigars in London. French flair and refined cuisine are the hallmark of the buzzing Brasserie Roux. Guests can enjoy a pampering session in the hotel's fitness and massage centre complete with treatment rooms and steam room. The hotel's conference and banqueting facilities comprise of 8 rooms including a state-of-the-art boardroom with private dining room as well as a banqueting suite for up to 170 people. Numerous of London's major attractions, such as Trafalgar Square, Piccadilly Circus and the theatre district, are just around the corner.

Our inspector loved: *The majestic marbled reception lobby and the sophisticated St James bar.*

Directions: The nearest underground station is Piccadilly Circus.

Web: www.johansens.com/stjames
E-mail: H3144@accor.com
Tel: 0870 381 9185
International: +44 (0)20 7747 2200
Fax: +44 (0) 20 7747 2210

Price Guide:
single from £275
double from £320
suite £430-£1,200

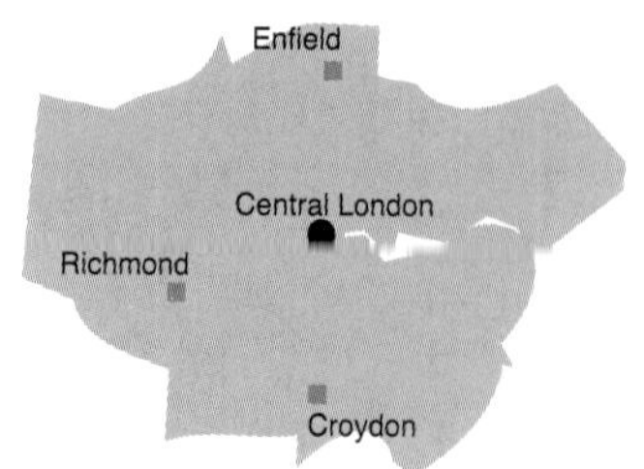

DOLPHIN SQUARE

DOLPHIN SQUARE, CHICHESTER STREET, LONDON SW1V 3LX

Centrally located in large, exquisite gardens bordered by the River Thames and Westminster, this quiet oasis is decorated with contemporary style and offers discreet service. The 148 suites offer a classical or modern décor with subtle colour co-ordinated design. The suites have a compact, well-equipped kitchen, yet 24-hour room service and a full range of facilities are available. Guests can enjoy delicious international cuisine in the informal Brasserie, and the Clipper Bar is a fun and stylish venue for a drink and chat. The restaurant, Allium, is an exciting venue under the direction of internationally renowned chef patron Anton Edelmann (formerly of The Savoy). The menu features contemporary European cuisine with an emphasis placed on flavours and simplicity in a relaxed but sophisticated atmosphere. A selection of Anton Edelmann's menus is also available for private dining. A variety of shops in Dolphin Square provide for guests' every need, including a newsagent, chemist, hair salon and travel agent. The extensive facilities at Zest! Health & Fitness Spa include an 18m indoor swimming pool, a fully-equipped gym, exercise studio, tennis court, squash courts, croquet lawn, sauna and steam rooms and numerous health and beauty treatments. There are superb facilities for celebrations of any size, and excellent business and corporate services.

Our inspector loved: *The extensive leisure facilities and great spa.*

Directions: The closest underground station is Pimlico.

Web: www.johansens.com/dolphinsquare
E-mail: reservations@dolphinsquare.org
Tel: 0870 381 8483
International: +44 (0)20 7834 3800
Fax: 020 7798 8735

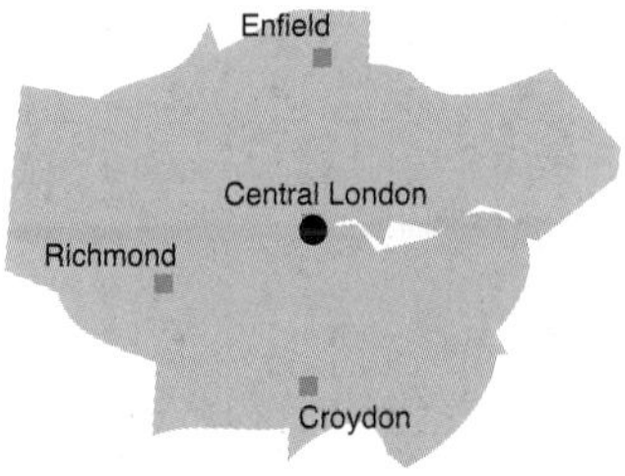

Enfield
Central London
Richmond
Croydon

Price Guide:
studio suite double/twin £195
1 bedroom suite £215–£450
2 bedroom suite £350
3 bedroom suite £450

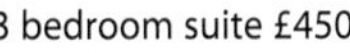

51 Buckingham Gate

51 BUCKINGHAM GATE, WESTMINSTER, LONDON SW1E 6AF

Close to Buckingham Palace, St James's Park and the Houses of Parliament, 51 Buckingham Gate is contemporary style and luxury on a grand scale. This attractive Victorian town house offers everything the discerning guest could wish for: privacy, relaxation and superb service delivered by multilingual staff which includes a team of Ivor Spencer trained butlers. Guests have a choice of dining options: Quilon, offering southern coastal Indian cuisine, Bank Westminster, Zander Bar and The Library. There are 82 suites and apartments, ranging from junior suites to the 5-bedroom Prime Minister's Suite, which combine contemporary interior design with luxury hotel facilities. De luxe suites offer award-winning bathrooms, whilst designated Ivor Spencer Suites have 16-hour personal butler service, limousine pick-up and an exclusive range of special amenities. Each suite provides sophisticated technology including 2-line speaker telephones, high-speed Internet access, fax/copier/printer, CD and DVD player. Fully-equipped kitchens as well as 24-hour room service are available. A team of talented chefs is also at hand to prepare private dinners. Guests can enjoy the exclusive spa, which offers Sodashi spa treatments, and a fully-equipped gymnasium at the Club at St James Court.

Our inspector loved: *The fabulous spa and luxurious suites at this award-winning hotel.*

Directions: The nearest underground stations are St James's Park and Victoria.

Web: www.johansens.com/buckinghamgate
E-mail: info@51-buckinghamgate.co.uk
Tel: 0870 381 8301
International: +44 (0)20 7769 7766
Fax: 020 7828 5909

Price Guide:
suites £405–£975

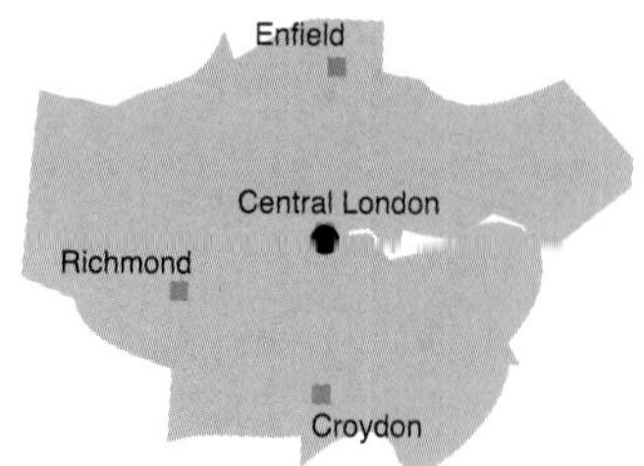

CANNIZARO HOUSE

WEST SIDE, WIMBLEDON COMMON, LONDON SW19 4UE

Cannizaro House is a captivating Georgian mansion set amidst green sweeping lawns, an ornamental lake and beautiful formal gardens on the edge of Wimbledon Common. Peaceful surroundings create an atmosphere of country living whilst the traditional hospitality of friendly staff make guests feel most welcome. With a long and distinguished history, this elegant hotel has been host to several famous people including King George III, Oscar Wilde, William Pitt and Henry James. Sumptuous interiors are appointed with fine antiques, guilded mirrors and ornate fireplaces, and individually decorated bedrooms are extremely luxurious; some have four-poster beds and views over the grounds and Cannizaro Park. Gentle colour schemes are complemented by opulent fabrics, crisp sheets and rich woodwork. Award-winning modern and classical cuisine is of the finest quality. Afternoon tea may be served on the sunny terrace, and the chic drawing room serves cocktails and apéritifs. Several intimate rooms are available for meetings and private dining, including the elegant Queen Elizabeth Room, a popular venue for wedding ceremonies. Ideally located for trips to London city centre and the West End with its many tourist attractions, museums, art galleries and theatres.

Our inspector loved: *The south-facing, lavender-filled terrace overlooking the extensive grounds.*

Directions: The nearest tube and British Rail station is Wimbledon.

Enfield
Central London
Richmond
Croydon

Web: www.johansens.com/cannizarohouse
E-mail: info@cannizarohouse.com
Tel: 0870 381 8402
International: +44 (0)208 879 1464
Fax: 020 8970 2753

Price Guide: (room only):
double/twin from £156
feature room from £184

Didsbury House

DIDSBURY PARK, DIDSBURY VILLAGE, MANCHESTER M20 5LJ

Directions: Exit the M56 at junction 1 and take the A34 towards Manchester. At the traffic lights turn left onto the A5145 towards Didsbury. At the 2nd set of traffic lights turn right into Didsbury Park. The hotel is on the left.

Web: www.johansens.com/didsburyhouse
E-mail: enquiries@didsburyhouse.co.uk
Tel: 0870 381 8481
International: +44 (0)161 448 2200
Fax: 0161 448 2525

Price Guide:
single £135–£300
double/twin £145–£300
suite £195–£300

This stylish and contemporary small boutique hotel, in a leafy south Manchester suburb, is a careful refurbishment and extension of a Grade II listed, mid-19th-century Victorian villa and coach house. It is the second town house hotel concept to be opened in the city by Eamonn and Sally O'Loughlin, the first being the acclaimed Eleven Didsbury Park. Their new hotel, just 100 yards away, is double the size and twice as stunning. It seduces guests immediately as they enter its beautiful hallway. The superb original carved wooden staircase carries the eye up to a magnificent stained-glass window. Ornate ceilings and architraves, polished wooden floors and warm décor dominate the luxurious public rooms. The exquisite and romantic attic suite has separate his and hers cast-iron roll-top baths and his and hers seats in a huge shower and steam cubicle, whilst in every gorgeous en-suite bedroom the bath fits 2. A top floor footbridge spans a central atrium and a charming lounge with ostrich-egg sized lights and pewter bar leads onto a secluded courtyard furnished with a restful and imaginative combination of steel, bamboo and water features. Gym, steam room and face, body and holistic treatments are available in the SO Spa. Breakfast and a room service menu are available in the evenings, but complimentary transport is provided for dining out.

Our inspector loved: *The original 18th-century staircase set in front of the stained-glass window.*

Etrop Grange

THORLEY LANE, MANCHESTER AIRPORT, GREATER MANCHESTER M90 4EG

Hidden away near Manchester Airport lies Etrop Grange, a beautiful country house hotel and restaurant. The original house was built in 1780 and more than 200 years on has been lovingly restored. Today, the hotel enjoys a fine reputation for its accommodation, where the luxury, character and sheer elegance of the Georgian era are evident in every feature. The magnificent award-winning restaurant offers a well balanced mix of traditional and modern English cuisine, complemented by an extensive selection of fine wines. Attention to detail ensures personal and individual service. In addition to the obvious advantage of having an airport within walking distance, the location of Etrop Grange is ideal in many other ways. With a comprehensive motorway network and InterCity stations minutes away, it is accessible from all parts of the UK. Entertainment for visitors ranges from the shopping, sport and excellent nightlife offered by the city of Manchester to golf, riding, clay pigeon shooting, water sports and outdoor pursuits in the immediate countryside. Cheshire also boasts an abundance of stately homes, museums and historical attractions.

Our inspector loved: *The complimentary chauffeur service to Manchester Airport.*

Directions: Leave M56 at junction 5 towards Manchester Airport. Follow signs for Terminal 2. Go up the slip road. At roundabout take first exit, take immediate left and hotel is 400yds on the right.

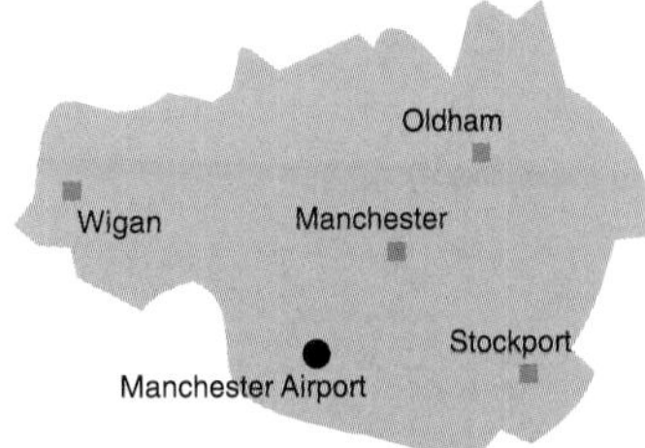

Web: www.johansens.com/etropgrange
E-mail: etropgrange@corushotels.com
Tel: 0870 381 8507
International: +44 (0)161 499 0500
Fax: 0161 499 0790

Price Guide:
single £89–£179
double/twin £99–£209
suites £136–£240

Hope Street Hotel

40 HOPE STREET, LIVERPOOL L1 9DA

Recently voted onto Condé Nast Traveller's list of the "World's 50 Coolest Hotels", this is Liverpool's first boutique-style hotel, and is a statement in stunning contemporary design. Ideally located in the cultural quarter, the hotel stands between the city's 2 cathedrals and a stone's throw from its theatres and concert halls. The bedrooms have been carefully designed with elegant, modern features and the latest technology. Beautiful wooden floors are warmed by underfloor heating, and vast king-size beds lie opposite wall-mounted plasma screens, accessorised with Egyptian cotton. The Residents' Lounge is a sophisticated nightspot with oak and slate floor and leather seating, and the restaurant, the award winning London Carriage Works has a reputation for Liverpool's most sought after tables. Fine dining and the more informal brasserie are separated by dramatic shards of glass; each serves a menu that uses the freshest local ingredients to create innovative cuisine. Guests wishing to enjoy the hotel's proximity to the theatres may benefit from the excellent pre and post-theatre dinner menu that is available each evening. There are boardroom and seminar rooms equipped with up-to-date, audio-visual equipment that can accommodate anything from fashion shows to film screenings.

Our inspector loved: *This new and stylish hotel nestled between both Cathedrals in the cultural centre of Liverpool.*

Directions: From the M62 follow the brown signs to Cathedrals. Hope Street runs between both Cathedrals. The hotel entrance is on Hope Place.

Web: www.johansens.com/hopestreethotel
E-mail: sleep@hopestreethotel.co.uk
Tel: 0870 381 8306
International: +44 (0)151 709 3000
Fax: 0151 709 2454

Price Guide:
King £125–£155
Studio £190
suite £225–£315

The Hoste Arms

THE GREEN, BURNHAM MARKET, KING'S LYNN, NORFOLK PE31 8HD

There are few places that feel so utterly comfortable in their surroundings. The Hoste Arms has been skilfully developed by Paul and Jeanne Whittome over several years but it's historic roots dating back to 1720 have never been compromised. Even the rather splendidly named 'Zulu Wing' echoes the comfort, style and attention to detail that its entrepreneurial owners manage so instinctively. A team of 12 bright young chefs create wonderful dishes and menus in a kitchen environment so impressive that it would be the envy of any restaurant in the country. A 300 bin wine list features some of the world's best wines at bargain prices and a new extensive cellar has recently been opened to offer yet another dimension to the experience of this wonderful place. The bedrooms and suites are well appointed and comfortable, featuring Egyptian cotton. Some have air conditioning. The Hoste Arms is well situated to cater for a variety of interests; located in Burnham Market (Chelsea-at-Sea), with its unique line of 40 privately owned shops, there are also several stately homes in the area such as Holkham Hall, Houghton Hall and Sandringham. For nature lovers there are bird sanctuaries, boat trips and miles of unspoilt sandy beaches. Golf enthusiasts have Hunstanton, Brancaster and Cromer.

Our inspector loved: *The Zulu Wing.*

Directions: Burnham Market is 2 miles from A149 on B1155.

Web: www.johansens.com/hostearms
E-mail: reception@hostearms.co.uk
Tel: 0870 381 8415
International: +44 (0)1328 738777
Fax: 01328 730103

Price Guide:
single £82–£145
doubles £102–£190
suites £142–£228

Congham Hall

GRIMSTON, KING'S LYNN, NORFOLK PE32 1AH

Dating from the mid-18th century, this stately manor house is set in acres of parkland, orchards and gardens. The conversion from country house to luxury hotel in 1982 was executed with care to enhance the elegance of the classic interiors. The hotel's renowned herb garden grows over 700 varieties of herb, many are used by the chef to create modern English dishes with the accent on fresh local produce and fish from the local Norfolk markets. The hotel's hives even produce the honey for your breakfast table. The beautiful flower displays, homemade pot pourri and roaring log fires blend together to create a welcoming and relaxing atmosphere A programme of events ranging from gardening, antiques and wine masterclasses are now available. Congham Hall is the ideal base from which to tour the spectacular beaches of the north Norfolk coastline, Sandringham, Burnham Market and Holkham Hall.

Our inspector loved: *The wonderful herb garden.*

Directions: Go to the A149/A148 interchange northeast of King's Lynn. Follow the A148 towards Sandringham/Fakenham/ Cromer for 100 yards. Turn right to Grimston. The hotel is then 2 miles on the left

Web: www.johansens.com/conghamhall
E-mail: info@conghamhallhotel.co.uk
Tel: 0870 381 8443
International: +44 (0)1485 600250
Fax: 01485 601191

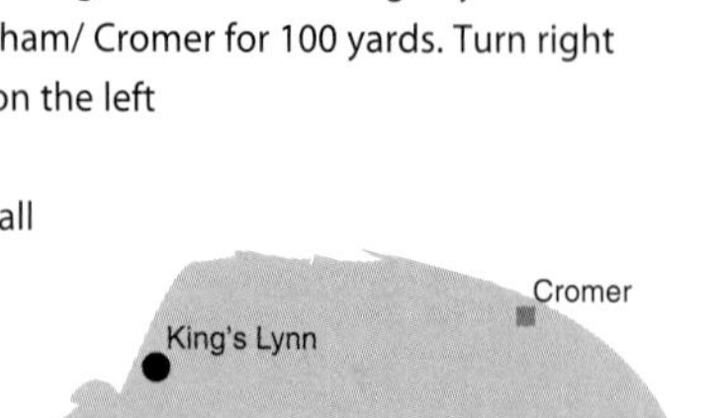

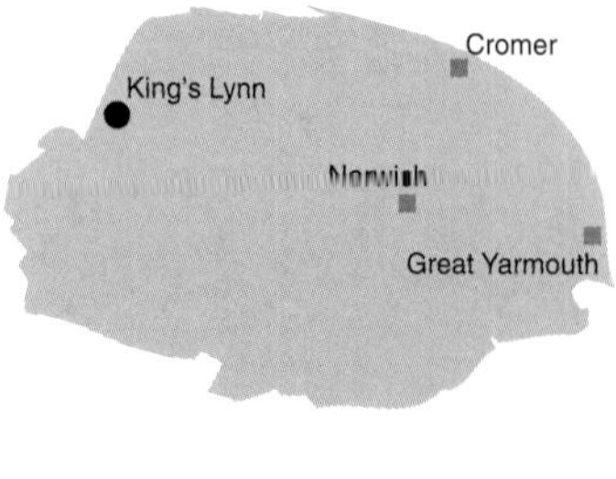

Price Guide:
single from £105
double/twin from £185
suites from £300

Park Farm Country Hotel & Leisure

HETHERSETT, NORWICH, NORFOLK NR9 3DL

Park Farm Country Hotel & Leisure occupies a secluded location in beautifully landscaped grounds south of Norwich, once the second greatest city in England. All the bedrooms have been sympathetically converted from traditional and new buildings. There are executive rooms for additional comfort, with four-poster beds and Jacuzzi baths. A superb leisure complex to suit all ages has been carefully incorporated alongside the original Georgian house to include heated swimming pool, sauna, steam room, solarium, spa bath, gymnasium, aerobics studio and a beauty therapy area. Due to the hotel's continuous upgrading policy, the highly regarded restaurant has been refurbished with elegant style and attractive colours and the bar has undergone a complete renovation to reflect a modern design, emphasising space and comfort. Conference facilities cater for up to 120 candidates (24-hour and daily delegate rates available). This is an ideal location for wedding receptions. The Norfolk broads, the coast, Norwich open market, castle museum and cathedral are nearby. A self-catering apartment, "Tumbrils," with private walled garden, is situated within the grounds.

Our inspector loved: *The friendly atmosphere and "buzz" in the conservatory and bar.*

Directions: By road, just off the A11 on the B1172. 8 miles from Norwich Airport, 6 miles from Norwich rail station and 5 miles from Norwich bus station.

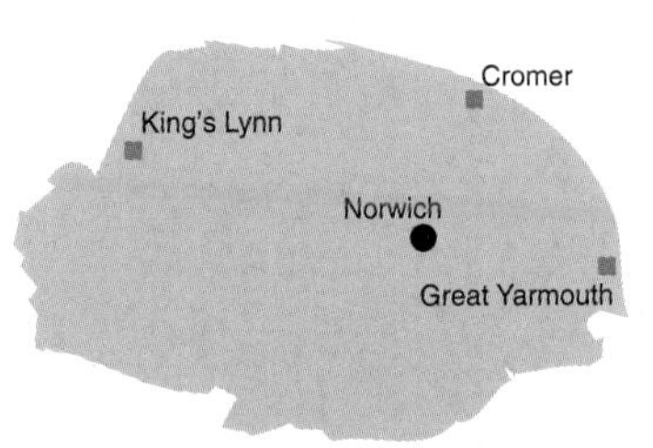

Web: www.johansens.com/parkfarm
E-mail: enq@parkfarm-hotel.co.uk
Tel: 0870 381 8800
International: +44 (0)1603 810264
Fax: 01603 812104

Price Guide:
single £95-£130
double/twin £122-£170
suites £175-£185

42 120 SPA

Fawsley Hall

FAWSLEY, NEAR DAVENTRY, NORTHAMPTONSHIRE NN11 3BA

Set in the beautiful Northamptonshire countryside and surrounded by acres of rolling parkland with lakes, landscaped by Capability Brown, Fawsley Hall combines the charm and character of a gracious manor with the facilities and comforts of a modern hotel. The original Tudor Manor House opened as a hotel in 1998 but many traces of its illustrious past have been retained, such as the vaulted hall and Queen Elizabeth I chamber. 43 wonderfully decorated rooms offer a range of Tudor, Georgian, Victorian and "classic modern"styles, many of which include four-poster beds. The Knightley Restaurant has established a reputation as being the finest in Northamptonshire and the Old Laundry Bar provides delicious light meals at lunchtime. The hotel's spa in the Georgian cellar includes a beauty salon, fitness studio, steam, sauna and spa bath. 5 conference and syndicate rooms can accommodate up to 80 delegates and the attractive Salvin Suite can seat up to 140 for a private banquet or wedding reception. Places of historic interest include: Sulgrave Manor, ancestral home of George Washington; Althorp; Canons Ashby, Blenheim Palace; Silverstone; Towcester Racecourse; an Elizabethan manor house and Warwick Castle. Oxford and Stratford-upon-Avon are nearby.

Our inspector loved: *The Great Hall with its paintings, fireplace and fine furnishings.*

Directions: Fawsley Hall can be reached by the M40, junction 11 or the M1, junction16. Both are 10 miles from the hotel.

Web: www.johansens.com/fawsleyhall
E-mail: reservations@fawsleyhall.com
Tel: 0870 381 8516
International: +44 (0)1327 892000
Fax: 01327 892001

Price Guide:
single from £145
double/twin from £185
suite from £350

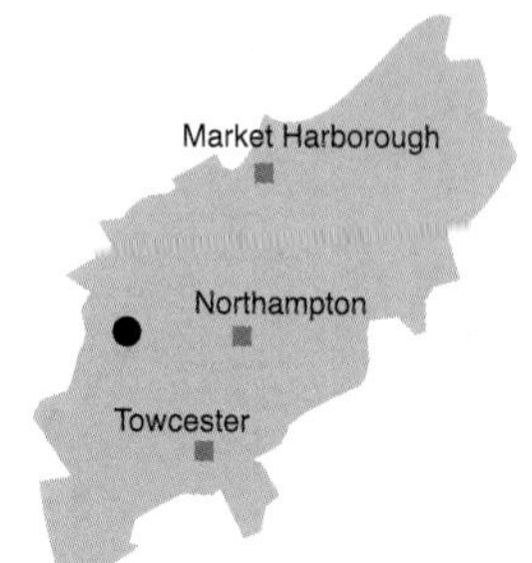

NEW

Rushton Hall

RUSHTON, NEAR KETTERING, NORTHAMPTONSHIRE NN14 1RR

This stunning Grade I listed building was built in the 16th century by Sir Thomas Tresham and a number of well-known aristocratic families have added to the structure over the years. Lying amidst beautifully manicured grounds, and approached by a long sweeping drive through imposing wrought-iron gates, the grand façade is guaranteed to impress arriving guests, and there can be few more spectacular destinations for an event, wedding or a simple weekend getaway. Great care has been taken with the design of the hotel, and the beautiful linen fold panelling and original flooring are complemented by comfortable, stylish furnishings and long, elegant drapes. Many of the bathrooms feature roll-top baths and luxurious fittings. The public rooms are stunning, ranging from the spectacular Great Hall, with vaulted ceiling and beautiful bay window overlooking the grounds, to the more intimate library and delightful drawing room. Outside, the grounds provide wonderful photographic opportunities; the balcony overlooks the 16th-century courtyard and the magnificent 400-year old stone seat boasts a magnificent view of the world famous triangular lodge. Within easy access of Market Harborough, Leicester and Northampton, the Hall is ideally located for motorway routes and trains into Kings Cross and St Pancras.

Directions: Take the A14 and exit at junction 7. Take the A43 then the A6003 towards Corby Until Rushton. Turn left just after the bridge.

Market Harborough
Northampton
Towcester

Web: www.johansens.com/rushtonhall
E-mail: enquiries@rushtonhall.com
Tel: 0870 381 8383
International: +44 (0)1536 713001
Fax: 01536 713010

Price Guide:
single/double from £100
suite £140–£300

Our inspector loved: *The fabulous Elizabethan Great Hall.*

 20     150     

WHITTLEBURY HALL

WHITTLEBURY, NEAR TOWCESTER, NORTHAMPTONSHIRE NN12 8QH

Whittlebury Hall is a modern building that successfully combines the elegance of classic Georgian architecture with contemporary furnishings and fabrics to create a truly fabulous hotel. The spacious bedrooms are tastefully decorated with modern touches and thoughtful extras; 3 superbly appointed, individually-styled suites have a whirlpool spa bath and shower. Guests may enjoy an apèritif in the aptly named Silverstone Bar where an array of motor racing memorabilia adorns the walls, before sampling the flavours of the informal Italian menu and wine list at Bentleys. Alternatively, the relaxed Astons Restaurant presents meals that blend classic and contemporary cuisine. The 2 AA Rosette-awarded Murrays Restaurant, offers the latest in food trends and fashion. The management training centre comprises 14 suites, 32 syndicate rooms, 6 meeting rooms and a lecture room for up to 450 delegates. Extensive facilities at The Spa and The Leisure Club include a range of heat and ice experiences, a gym, swimming pool and treatment suite where over 60 treatments are available for body, mind and soul. Adjacent to the Hall is the independently owned Whittlebury Park golf course, which offers preferred rates to guests. Motor racing enthusiasts can enjoy racing action at nearby Silverstone. Warwick Castle, Towcester racecourse and Oxford are all easily accessed by car.

Our inspector loved: *The spacious relaxing main lounge.*

Directions: 11 miles from the M1, junction 15A and 17 miles from the M40, junction 10.

Web: www.johansens.com/whittleburyhall
E-mail: sales@whittleburyhall.co.uk
Tel: 0870 381 8995
International: +44 (0)1327 857857
Fax: 01327 857867

Price Guide:
single £135
double/twin £170
suite £270

Marshall Meadows Country House Hotel

BERWICK-UPON-TWEED, NORTHUMBERLAND TD15 1UT

Marshall Meadows can truly boast that it is England's most northerly hotel, just a quarter of a mile from the Scottish border, an ideal base for those exploring the rugged beauty of Northumberland. A magnificent Georgian mansion standing in 15 acres of woodland and formal gardens, Marshall Meadows today is a luxurious retreat, with a country house ambience – welcoming and elegant. It has a burn and small waterfall with attractive woodland walks. This is not a large hotel; there are just 19 bedrooms, each individually designed. Restful harmonious colour schemes, comfortable beds and the tranquillity of its surroundings ensure a good night's sleep! The lounge is delightful, with traditional easy chairs and sofas, overlooking the patio. Ideal for summer afternoon tea. The congenial Duck & Grouse Bar stocks a range of whiskies, beers and fine wines. Marshall Meadows has a galleried restaurant where diners enjoy local game, fresh seafood and good wine. Private dining facilities are also available. Excellent golf, fishing and historic Berwick-on-Tweed are nearby. Short breaks are available throughout the year.

Our inspector loved: *The peaceful country setting in close proximity to the sea and its coastal walks.*

Directions: A1 heading North, take Berwick by-pass and at Meadow House roundabout, head towards Edinburgh. After 300 yards, turn right, indicated by white sign – the hotel is at the end of small side road.

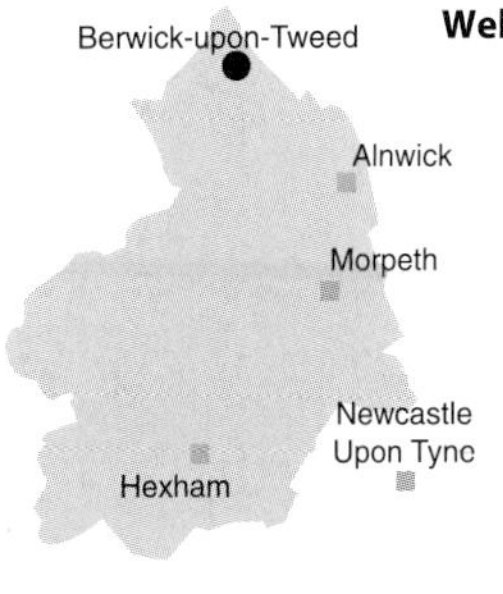

Berwick-upon-Tweed
Alnwick
Morpeth
Newcastle Upon Tyne
Hexham

Web: www.johansens.com/marshallmeadows
E-mail: stay@marshallmeadows.co.uk
Tel: 0870 381 8721
International: +44 (0)1289 331133
Fax: 01289 331438

Price Guide:
single £90–£105
double/twin £115–£150
suite £150–£175

19 M 180

Tillmouth Park

CORNHILL-ON-TWEED, NEAR BERWICK-UPON-TWEED, NORTHUMBERLAND TD12 4UU

This magnificent mansion house, built in 1882 using stones from nearby Twizel Castle, offers the same warm welcome to visitors today as when it was an exclusive private house. Tillmouth Park is situated in 15 acres of mature parkland gardens above the river Till. The generously sized bedrooms are individually designed with period and antique furniture, and are fully appointed with bathrobes, toiletries, hairdryer and trouser press. Most bedrooms offer spectacular views of the surrounding countryside. The wood-panelled, 2 AA Rosette, restaurant serves a fine table d'hôte menu offering contemporary British cuisine, whilst the Bistro is less formal. A well-chosen wine list and a vast selection of malt whiskies complement the cuisine. The elegant, galleried main hall offers country house comfort with open log fires. Tillmouth Park is ideally situated for country pursuits, with fishing on the Tweed and Till and clay shooting available on the grounds. The area also abounds in fine golf courses. Coldstream and Kelso are within easy reach; the Northumbrian coast and Berwick are 15 minutes away, and Flodden Field, Lindisfarne and Holy Island are nearby. There are many stately homes to visit in the area including Floors, Manderston, Paxton and the spectacular Alnwick Garden Project.

Our inspector loved: *The magnificent galleried main hall.*

Directions: Tillmouth Park is on the A698 Coldstream to Berwick-upon-Tweed road.

Web: www.johansens.com/tillmouthpark
E-mail: reception@tillmouthpark.f9.co.uk
Tel: 0870 381 8948
International: +44 (0)1890 882255
Fax: 01890 882540

Price Guide:
single £90–£145
twin/double £120–£190

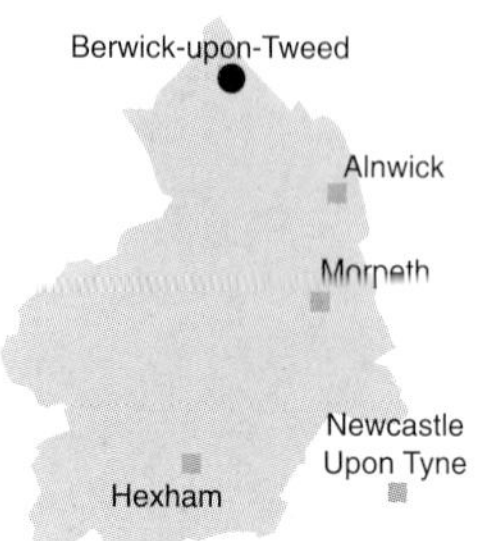

15 50

Matfen Hall

MATFEN, NEWCASTLE-UPON-TYNE, NORTHUMBERLAND NE20 0RH

Originally built in 1830 by Sir Edward Blackett, Matfen Hall has been carefully restored by Sir Hugh and Lady Blackett. This magnificent family seat lies in the heart of some of Northumberland's most beautiful countryside offering splendid facilities for conferences, weddings and leisure breaks. The Great Hall is awe-inspiring with its stained-glass windows, massive pillars and stone floors, whilst each of the bedrooms has its own individual character, combining modern features with traditional opulence. A huge open fireplace adds charm to the elegantly furnished Drawing Room and the unique Library and Print Room restaurant serves contemporary English cuisine which has been awarded 2 AA Rosettes. The Hall enjoys stunning views of the championship golf course, laid out on a classic parkland landscape with manicured greens and fairways flanked by majestic trees. Rated as one of the finest in the North East, it provides a pleasurable test for players of all abilities; there is also a 9-hole par 3 golf course. The spa is the only one in the world to offer Versace body treatments. Other amenities include a 16m swimming pool, 5 treatment suites featuring a VIP twin treatment room, crystal steam, salt grotto, herbal sauna, ice fountain and gym with latest Technogym equipment. Scenic coastal, rural and ancient sites are a drive away and Newcastle is a 20-minute journey. Special breaks are available.

Our inspector loved: *Having a relaxing pamper day in the leisure spa.*

Directions: From the A1 take the A69 towards Hexham. At Heddon-on-the-Wall take the B6318 towards Chollerford and travel 7 miles, then turn right to Matfen.

Web: www.johansens.com/matfenhall
E-mail: info@matfenhall.com
Tel: 0870 381 8724
International: +44 (0)1661 886500
Fax: 01661 886055

Price Guide:
single from £125–£170
double from £150–£260

53 120 SPA

Colwick Hall Hotel

COLWICK PARK, RACECOURSE ROAD, NOTTINGHAM, NOTTINGHAMSHIRE NG2 4BH

Directions: Colwick Hall Hotel is situated 2 miles from the city centre. Follow the brown signs for Nottingham Racecourse.

Web: www.johansens.com/colwickhall
E-mail: reservations@colwick-hall.co.uk
Tel: 0870 381 8594
International: +44 (0)115 950 0566
Fax: 0115 924 3797

Price Guide:
single £100–£160
double/twin £140–£180
suite £220–£280

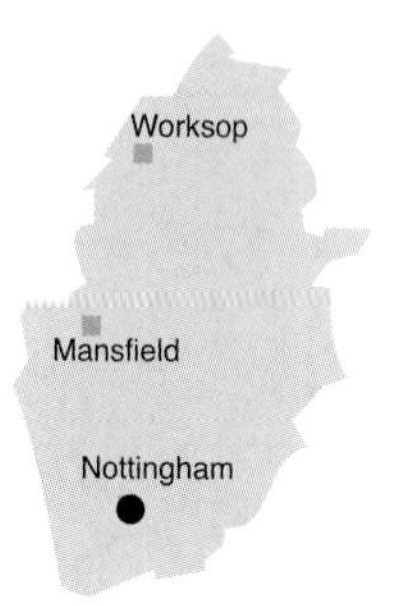

There can be few more spectacular settings than this magnificent Palladian-style Georgian country mansion set in acres of parkland overlooking Nottingham Racecourse. Approached via a long sweeping carriage drive, this Grade II listed building has a fascinating history, and it is only in recent years that it has been restored to such elegant splendour. The beautiful grounds have made the hall a prominent destination for functions and summer parties for a number of years; the landscaped lawns and ornamental fountains are unrivalled backdrops for photographs. New for September 2005 are 16 supremely luxurious bedrooms and suites. Each retains the proportions of the original 19th-century building and is consequently extremely spacious with equally generous bathrooms. The original plasterwork and coving has been fully restored and each room features an original cast-iron fireplace and grate, and is furnished with the ultimate elegance and style. The Georgetown Restaurant, with stunning cherub-painted ceiling, is situated in the exquisite front dining room and has a winning formula of delicious award-winning cuisine within an exotic Malaysian inspired setting. The flavours of the Malaysian Malays, Mandarin Chinese and Tamil Indians are all brought together under one roof, and the local house cocktail, the Singapore Sling, is rapidly gaining acclaim.

Our inspector loved: *The gorgeous Georgetown restaurant.*

Lace Market Hotel

29-31, HIGH PAVEMENT, THE LACE MARKET, NOTTINGHAM, NOTTINGHAMSHIRE NG1 1HE

Occupying a prime location in Nottingham's city centre, just yards from the most fashionable shopping area and the National Arena, this privately owned boutique hotel offers guests outstanding hospitality and service. The property has a large clientele from amongst the music industry and celebrity A-list, which is not surprising since the Lace Market boasts luxurious accommodation, stylish conference rooms, a gastro pub, an upmarket brasserie and chic cocktail bar all under one roof. The 42 bedrooms are individually designed and furnished with sumptuous bedding, unique artwork and indulgent en-suite facilities carefully selected to create a calming ambience in which to unwind. Serving classic French brasserie fayre, the sophisticated Merchants brasserie provides a delectable dining experience and guests may continue their evening with drinks in the trendy Saint Bar. Although this property is centrally based, arriving by car is not a problem with free, on-street overnight parking available and a convenient multi-storey car park located in the neighbouring road. Whilst visitors to Lace Market will find plenty to do in and around Nottingham they can also enjoy complimentary access to nearby Holmes Place Health Club with indoor pool, full gym facilities and fitness classes.

Our inspector loved: *The "in house" traditional Cock & Hoop pub complete with real ales. You can go "out" without leaving the hotel.*

 42   35    

Directions: Head for the city centre and use Stoney Street NCP car park.

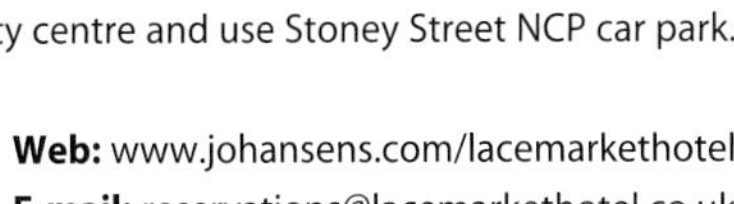

Web: www.johansens.com/lacemarkethotel
E-mail: reservations@lacemarkethotel.co.uk
Tel: 0870 381 9325
International: +44 (0)115 852 3232
Fax: 0115 852 3223

Price Guide: (room only)
small single £90
double/twin £112–£139
superior £179
studios £229

Restaurant Sat Bains with Rooms

TRENTSIDE, LENTON LANE, NOTTINGHAM, NG7 2SA

Directions: Take M1, jct 24, follow A453 for Nottingham. Stay in the middle lane when approaching the flyover, signposted Lenton Industrial Estate. Turn left at the roundabout then left again. The hotel is then signposted.

Web: www.johansens.com/satbains
E-mail: info@restaurantsatbains.net
Tel: 0870 381 8351
International: +44 (0)115 986 6566
Fax: 0115 986 0343

Price Guide:
single from £114
double from £129
suite from £265

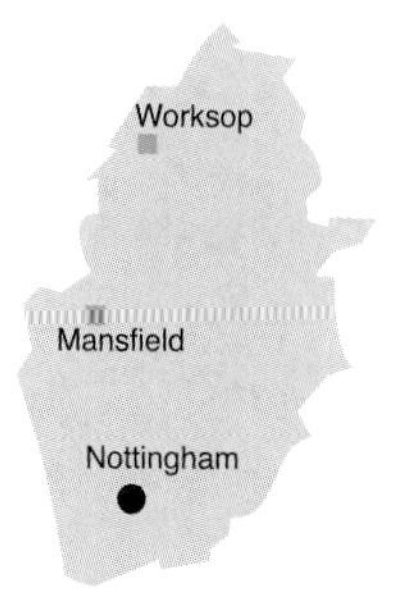

Michelin Star chef and Roux Scholar Sat Bains has introduced his unique characteristics and flavour to this newly acquired and completely refurbished country-style hotel, situated in a delightfully peaceful and secluded position on the banks of the River Trent, just 2 miles from Nottingham city centre. A former Victorian farmhouse, this attractive restaurant with rooms offers menus of gastronomic excellence and the highest quality rated hotel in the region. The food is superb: evening meals such as coquelet 'cooked in hay' accompanied by black pudding and pea purée, roast squab pigeon with candied carrots, potato terrine, celery purée, grapefruit, chocolate and roast Cornish turbot, coco beans, mussels, vanilla, lemon confit are more than enough to satisfy the most discerning diner. As an accompaniment, guests may choose from the extensive wine list of 150 bins, including many excellent New World vintages. The 8 luxurious bedrooms are individually designed and extremely comfortable. The Charles II room has a four-poster, open fireplace and private patio. The Renaissance room boasts a king-size bed and Jacuzzi whilst the Louis XV has walk-in wardrobes and separate lounge. Special accommodation and gastronomic packages are available, and a select cookery school that, over one day, explains and teaches the restaurant's cuisine techniques.

Our inspector loved: *The new bar area with its lovely leather chairs.*

The Bay Tree Hotel

SHEEP STREET, BURFORD, OXON OX18 4LW

The Bay Tree is a lovely old Tudor hotel which offers every modern facility. The oak-panelled rooms have huge stone fireplaces and a galleried staircase leads upstairs from the raftered hall. All the pretty bedrooms are en-suite, three of them furnished with four-poster beds and 2 of the 5 suites have half-tester beds. In the summer, guests can enjoy the delightful walled gardens, featuring landscaped terraces of lawn and flower beds. A relaxing atmosphere is enhanced by the staff's attentive service in the flagstoned dining room where the head chef's creative cuisine is complemented by a comprehensive selection of fine wines. Light meals are served in a country-style bar. Burford, often described as the gateway to the Cotswolds, is renowned for its assortment of antique shops and the Tolsey Museum of local history. The Bay Tree Hotel makes a convenient base for day trips to Stratford-upon-Avon, Stow-on-the-Wold and Blenheim Palace. Golf, clay pigeon shooting and riding can be arranged locally.

Our inspector loved: *The many charming nooks and crannies of this delightful hotel.*

Directions: Burford is on the A40 between Oxford and Cheltenham. Proceed halfway down the hill into Burford, turn left into Sheep Street and The Bay Tree Hotel is 30 yards on your right. Car parking is available.

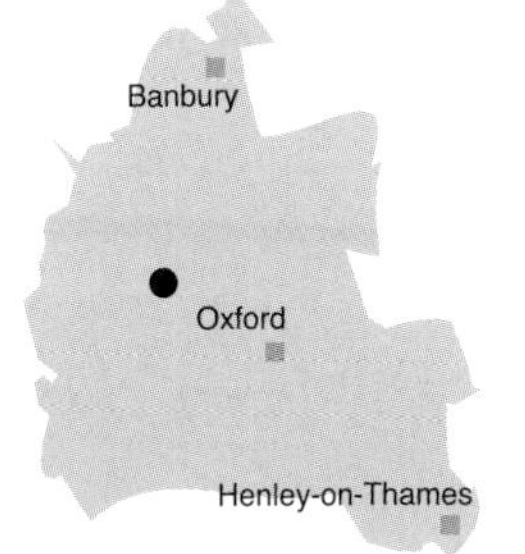

Web: www.johansens.com/baytree
E-mail: info@baytreehotel.info
Tel: 0870 381 8347
International: +44 (0)1993 822791
Fax: 01993 823008

Price Guide:
single £119
double/twin £165–£205
suite £195–£250

Phyllis Court Club

MARLOW ROAD, HENLEY-ON-THAMES, OXFORDSHIRE RG9 2HT

Founded in 1906 by the owner of the house and a group of friends and London businessmen, the Club has an intriguing history spanning 6 centuries and involving royal patronage. Phyllis Court occupies an unrivalled position on the banks of the Thames and overlooking the Henley Royal Regatta course. Phyllis Court prides itself on retaining the traditions of its illustrious past, whilst guests today who now stay in this fine historic residence can enjoy high standards of up-to-date hospitality. Oliver Cromwell slept here and he built the embankment wall; and it was here that William II held his first Royal Court. Years later, when the name Henley became synonymous with rowing, they came as patrons of the Royal Regatta: Prince Albert, King George V and Edward, Prince of Wales. The character of the place remains unaltered in its hallowed setting, but the comfortable bedrooms, the restaurant, the "cellar" and the entire complement of amenities are of the latest high quality. Residents become temporary members as the dining room and bar are open to members only. Ideal for meetings, functions,wedding parties and leisure breaks.

Our inspector loved: *Its splendid riverside location.*

Directions: M40, junction 4 to Marlow or M4, junction 8/9 then follow signposts to Henley-on-Thames. Phyllis Court is on the A4155 between Henley and Marlow.

Web: www.johansens.com/phylliscourt
E-mail: enquiries@phylliscourt.co.uk
Tel: 0870 381 8822
International: +44 (0)1491 570500
Fax: 01491 570528

Price Guide:
single £112
twin/double £131

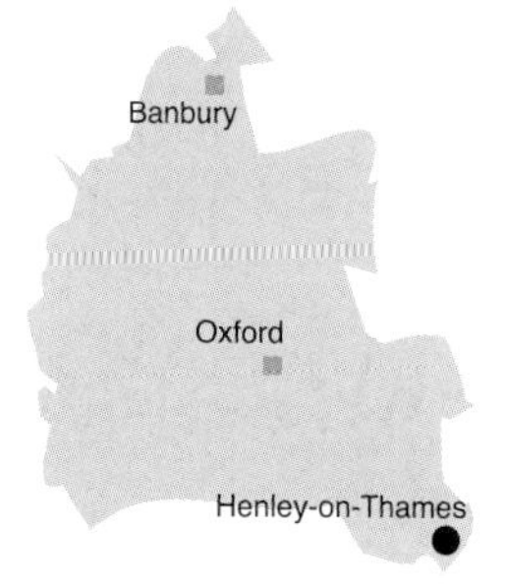

The Cotswold Lodge Hotel

66A BANBURY ROAD, OXFORD OX2 6JP

Situated in a tree-lined road, just 1 mile from Oxford, this attractive Victorian building, which has been restored in the style of a comfortable country house, is an ideal location for tourists and those on business looking for a welcoming and relaxed environment. The pleasantly decorated bedrooms range in style from traditional country house, courtyard and "cottagey" to the more conventional. There are also 10 special suites named after some of Oxford's famous colleges. The Scholars bar is ideal for a light lunch or pre-dinner drink and during winter, log fires enhance the cosy ambience. The more formal Sixty Six A restaurant serves seasonal menus using the freshest ingredients as well as a delicious selection of local produce alongside an extensive wine list to complement each dish. The Cotswold Lodge happily caters for many occasions including business meetings, conferences and weddings, and is a convenient base for visits to Oxford and beyond. Weekend breaks are available with much to do such as punting on the river, enjoying an "Inspector Morse" tour, going to the theatre, a game of golf and visiting nearby Woodstock and Blenheim. The hotel is glad to help with any arrangements.

Our inspector loved: *This country house hotel in the midst of Oxford.*

49 100

Directions: From M40 junction 8, take A40 or junction 9. Take A34 for Oxford. At Banbury Road roundabout take the direction of and continue through Summertown. The hotel is on the left at junction with Norham Road.

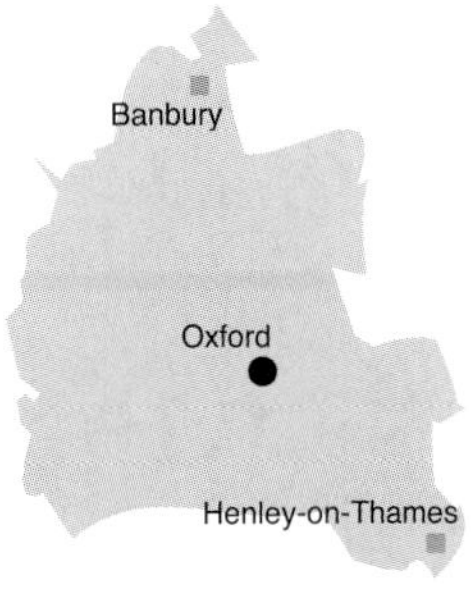

Web: www.johansens.com/cotswoldlodge
E-mail: info@cotswoldlodgehotel.co.uk
Tel: 0870 381 8450
International: +44 (0)1865 512121
Fax: 01865 512490

Price Guide:
single £125
double/twin £175
suite from £295

LE MANOIR AUX QUAT' SAISONS

GREAT MILTON, OXFORDSHIRE OX44 7PD

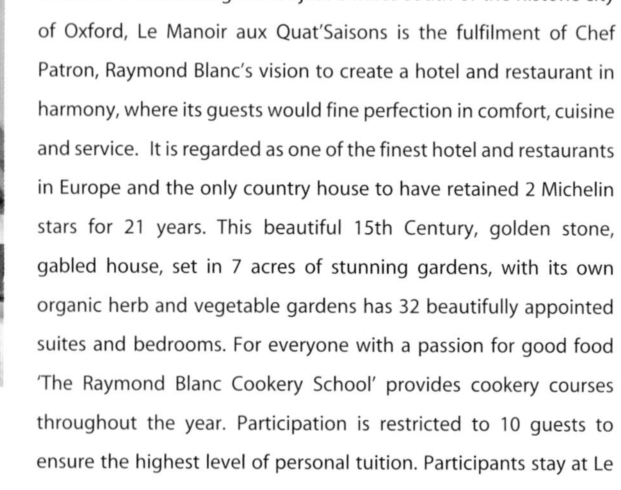

Situated in secluded grounds just 8 miles south of the historic city of Oxford, Le Manoir aux Quat'Saisons is the fulfilment of Chef Patron, Raymond Blanc's vision to create a hotel and restaurant in harmony, where its guests would fine perfection in comfort, cuisine and service. It is regarded as one of the finest hotel and restaurants in Europe and the only country house to have retained 2 Michelin stars for 21 years. This beautiful 15th Century, golden stone, gabled house, set in 7 acres of stunning gardens, with its own organic herb and vegetable gardens has 32 beautifully appointed suites and bedrooms. For everyone with a passion for good food 'The Raymond Blanc Cookery School' provides cookery courses throughout the year. Participation is restricted to 10 guests to ensure the highest level of personal tuition. Participants stay at Le Manoir and their partners are welcome to stay free of charge although their meals and drinks are charged for separately.

Our inspector loved: *The very special feeling of this extraordinary hotel and restaurant.*

Directions: From London, M40 and turn off at jct 7 (A329 to Wallingford). From the North, leave M40 at jct 8A and follow signs to Wallingford (A329). After 1½ miles, turn right, follow the brown signs for Le Manoir aux Quat' Saisons.

Web: www.johansens.com/lemanoirauxquatsaisons
E-mail: lemanoir@blanc.co.uk
Tel: 0870 381 8682
International: +44 (0)1844 278881
Fax: 01844 278847
USA/Canada Toll free: 1-800-393-5364

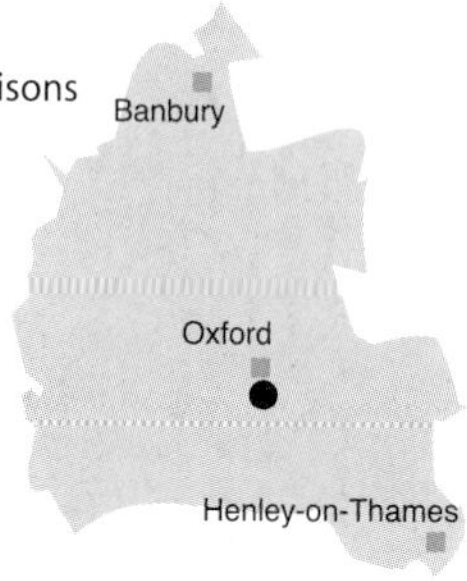

Banbury
Oxford
Henley-on-Thames

Price Guide:
double/twin £360–£595

FALLOWFIELDS

KINGSTON BAGPUIZE WITH SOUTHMOOR, OXON OX13 5BH

Fallowfields, home to Begum Aga Khan, dates back more than 300 years. Updated and extended throughout the decades, this is an extremely comfortable, welcoming and spacious country house hotel brimming with character. Set in 2 acres of tranquil, pretty gardens and surrounded by 10 acres of grassland, Oxford is easily accessible, 10 miles away. Each of the guest rooms is large and traditionally decorated, and some boast four-poster or coroneted beds. The drawing room and bar are elegant and relaxing, and even cosier in winter months with crackling log fires. The light and airy restaurant, recipient of 3 RAC dining awards, has a fresh and varied menu, and lends itself to many occasions such as a romantic evening, celebration, weekend treat or important business dinner. The library is also available for private dining. The peaceful ambience of the hotel also provides an ideal environment for high-level strategy and senior management retreats. With its convenient proximity to Oxford, the A34 and M40, Fallowfields is an excellent base for the corporate guest visiting the area or a perfect location for leisure guests wishing to explore the many cultural attractions and outdoor pursuits nearby such as theatres, stately homes and glorious walks along the Thames Path or Vale of the White Horse.

Our inspector loved: *The welcoming and comfortable feel of this lovely*

Directions: Take the Kingston Bagpuize exit on the A420 Oxford to Swindon. Fallowfields is at the west end of Southmoor, just after the Longworth sign.

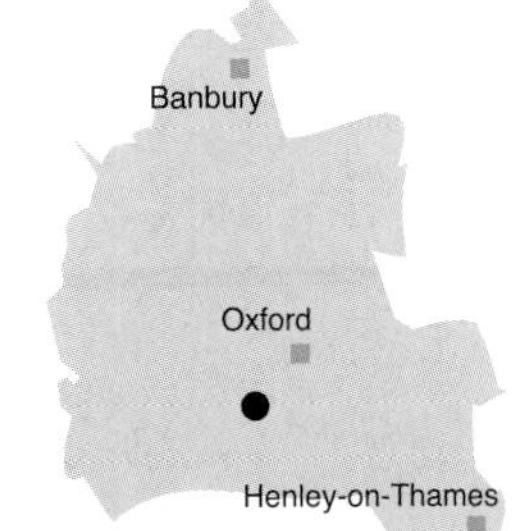

Web: www.johansens.com/fallowfields
E-mail: stay@fallowfields.com
Tel: 0870 381 8513
International: +44 (0)1865 820416
Fax: 01865 821275

Price Guide:
single £95–£145
double £120–£170

Weston Manor

WESTON-ON-THE-GREEN, OXFORDSHIRE OX25 3QL

Imposing wrought-iron gates flanked by sculptured busts surmounting tall grey stone pillars lead into the impressive entrance to this delightful manor house, the showpiece of the lovely village of Weston-on-the Green since the 11th century. The ancestral home of the Earls of Abingdon and Berkshire, and once the property of Henry VIII, today Weston Manor is a popular venue for weddings and corporate occasions. Standing regally in 12 acres of colourful gardens, the manor has been restored to an exceptional country house hotel with comfortable accommodation and attentive service from which leisure and business visitors can discover the delights of the nearby Cotswold countryside, Oxford, Woodstock, Blenheim Palace and Broughton Castle. Many of the individual bedrooms, including 4 in a cottage and 16 in the coach-house, feature antique furniture; all have garden views and private bathrooms. The restaurant, a magnificent vaulted and oak-panelled Baronial Hall, serves 2 AA Rosette-awarded cuisine; dining in such historic splendour is very much the focus of a memorable stay. The 7 versatile meeting rooms, including the Baronial Hall, have natural daylight and are ideal for exclusive use day and residential conferences and team-building events. There is a croquet lawn and secluded, heated outdoor swimming pool.

Our inspector loved: *The impressive approach and pretty surroundings.*

Directions: From the M40, exit at junction 9 onto the A34 towards Oxford. Leave the A34 at the first junction, towards Middleton Stoney. At the mini roundabout turn right onto the B430. The hotel is approx 500m on the left.

Web: www.johansens.com/westonmanor
E-mail: lesliewood@westonmanor.co.uk
Tel: 0870 381 8981
International: +44 (0)1869 350621
Fax: 01869 350901

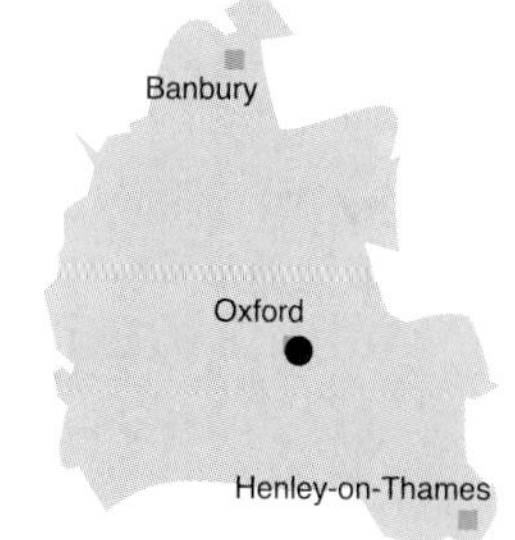

Price Guide:
single £99
double/twin £124
suite £195

The Springs Hotel & Golf Club

NORTH STOKE, WALLINGFORD, OXFORDSHIRE OX10 6BE

The Springs is a fine old country house which dates from 1874 and is set deep in the heart of the beautiful Thames Valley, yet within easy reach of the motorway networks. One of the first houses in England to be built in the Mock Tudor style, it stands in 6 acres of glorious grounds. The hotel's large south-facing windows overlook a spring-fed lake, from which it takes its name. Many of the comfortable bedrooms and suites offer beautiful views over the lake and lawns, whilst others overlook the quiet woodland that surrounds the hotel. Private balconies provide patios for summer relaxation. The Lakeside restaurant has an intimate atmosphere inspired by its gentle décor and the lovely view of the lake. The award-winning restaurant's menu takes advantage of fresh local produce and a well-stocked cellar of international wines provides the perfect accompaniment to a splendid meal. Leisure facilities include an 18-hole par 72 golf course, clubhouse and putting green, a swimming pool, sauna and touring bicycles. Facilities are as ideal for the corporate guest and teambuilding events as they are for a relaxing break. Oxford, Blenheim Palace and Windsor are nearby and the hotel is conveniently located for racing at Newbury and Ascot as well as the Royal Henley Regatta. Themed weekends are available.

Our inspector loved: *The charming, comfortable hotel with a wide range of attractions.*

Directions: From the M40 take exit 6 onto B4009, through Watlington to Benson; turn left onto A4074 towards Reading. After 2 miles go right onto B4009. The hotel is ½ mile further on the right.

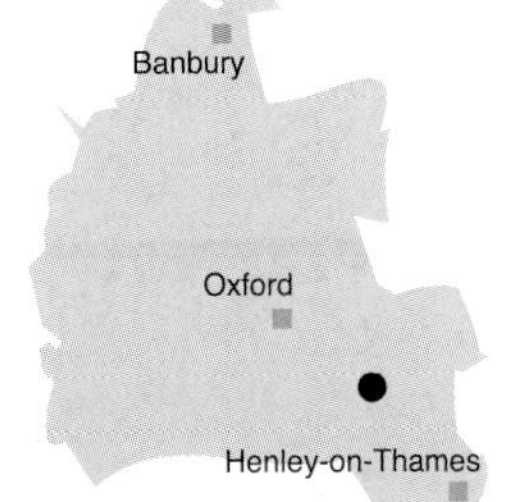

Web: www.johansens.com/springshotel
E-mail: info@thespringshotel.com
Tel: 0870 381 8904
International: +44 (0)1491 836687
Fax: 01491 836877

Price Guide:
single from £95
double/twin from £110
suite from £155

The Feathers

MARKET STREET, WOODSTOCK, OXFORDSHIRE OX20 1SX

Directions: From London leave the M40 at junction 8; from Birmingham leave at junction 9. Take A44 and follow the signs to Woodstock. The hotel is on the left.

Web: www.johansens.com/feathers
E-mail: enquiries@feathers.co.uk
Tel: 0870 381 8519
International: +44 (0)1993 812291
Fax: 01993 813158

Price Guide:
single £115
double/twin £135–£185
suite £200–£275

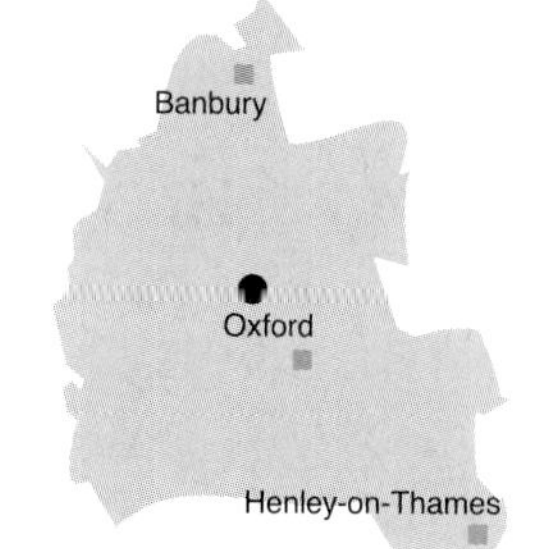

The 17th century Feathers is a privately owned and run town house hotel, situated in the centre of Woodstock, a few miles from Oxford. Woodstock is one of England's most attractive country towns, constructed mostly from Cotswold stone and with some buildings dating from the 12th century. In the hotel, antiques, log fires and traditional English furnishings lend character and charm. There are 20 bedrooms, all of which have private bathrooms and showers. If a beauty treat or massage appeals visit "Preen", the hotels relaxation room. There is also private dining and a boardroom. Public rooms, including the drawing room and study, are intimate and comfortable. The small garden is a delightful setting for a light lunch or afternoon tea and guests can enjoy a drink in the cosy courtyard bar, which has an open fire in winter. The antique-panelled restaurant is internationally renowned for its fine cuisine, complemented by a high standard of service and AA Rosette. The menu changes frequently and offers a wide variety of dishes, using the finest local ingredients. Blenheim Palace is just around the corner. The Cotswolds and the dreaming spires of Oxford are a short distance away. Special offers and weekend breaks are available

Our inspector loved: *The pretty bedrooms, welcoming bar and popular restaurant.*

HAMBLETON HALL

HAMBLETON, OAKHAM, RUTLAND LE15 8TH

Winner of Johansens Most Excellent Country Hotel Award 1996, Hambleton Hall, originally a Victorian mansion, celebrates its 25th Anniversary after opening as a hotel. Since then its renown has continually grown. It enjoys a spectacular lakeside setting in a charming and unspoilt area of Rutland. The hotel's tasteful interiors have been designed to create elegance and comfort, retaining individuality by avoiding a catalogue approach to furnishing. Delightful displays of flowers, an artful blend of ingredients from local hedgerows and the London flower markets colour the bedrooms. In the Michelin-Starred restaurant, chef Aaron Patterson and his enthusiastic team offer a menu which is strongly seasonal. Grouse, Scottish ceps and chanterelles, partridge and woodcock are all available at just the right time of year, accompanied by the best vegetables, herbs and salads from the Hall's garden. The Croquet Pavilion, a 2-bedroom suite with living room and breakfast room is a luxurious addition to the accommodation options. For the energetic there are lovely walks around the lake and opportunities for tennis and swimming, golf, riding, bicycling, trout fishing, and sailing. Burghley House and Belton are nearby, as are the antique shops of Oakham, Uppingham and Stamford.

Our inspector loved: *Overall the impeccable service; in particular the beautiful Fern bedroom.*

Directions: In the village of Hambleton, signposted from the A606, 1 mile east of Oakham.

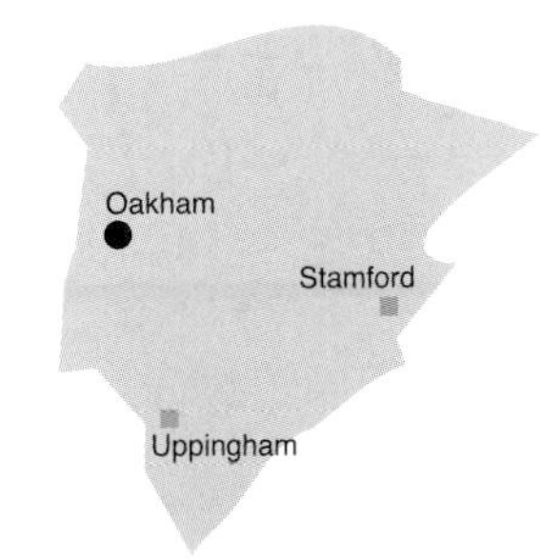

Web: www.johansens.com/hambletonhall
E-mail: hotel@hambletonhall.com
Tel: 0870 381 8582
International: +44 (0)1572 756991
Fax: 01572 724721

Price Guide:
single from £165
double/twin £195–£360
suite £500–£600

Dinham Hall

LUDLOW, SHROPSHIRE SY8 1EJ

Directions: Ludlow is approached via the A49. Dinham Hall is in the centre of town overlooking the castle.

Web: www.johansens.com/dinhamhall
E-mail: info@dinhamhall.co.uk
Tel: 0870 381 8482
International: +44 (0)1584 876464
Fax: 01584 876019

Price Guide:
single £95–£210
double/twin £140–£240

This 18th-century family home has been transformed into an elegant hotel effortlessly blending period décor with modern comforts. The 12 en-suite bedrooms, housed in either the main building or in the cottage within the grounds, feature ornate chandeliers and fine fabrics. Dinham Hall is a gastronome's delight, and the new lunchtime restaurant, with its varied menu, is a joy to sample. Aiming to bridge the gap between staple pub dishes and formal cuisine, the new menu has a strong Mediterranean influence and dishes include pappardelle with baby artichoke and parmesan and free range chicken with chorizo and a red pepper coulis. The established evening restaurant continues to serve seasonal dishes making good use of local produce in a smart, relaxed atmosphere. The fascinating town of Ludlow offers a wonderful mix of history, specialised antique dealers and is host to a burgeoning contemporary arts scene with talented furniture makers, crafts people and artists frequenting the area. Race enthusiasts should make time to visit the nearby course. Special mid-week rates for guests staying and dining at the hotel can be arranged upon request.

Our inspector loved: *The new lunchtime restaurant with its varied menu. Dining at Dinham Hall is always enjoyable.*

12 M 20

Albrighton Hall and Spa

Ellesmere Road, Shrewsbury, Shropshire SY4 3AG

This handsome and stately house stands in 15 acres of beautifully manicured grounds, just 5 minutes from the pretty town of Shrewsbury. Recently the subject of a staggering £5.5 million transformation, it is now fully restored to its original splendour and is fully equipped for the 21st-century guest. The entire hotel has been refurbished and updated to offer an additional 15 bedrooms and suites, carefully developed from a listed building in the grounds, as well as 6 conference and meeting rooms and 4 syndicate rooms. The M6 is only a 30-minute drive away and consequently Albrighton Hall and Spa is highly accessible from all areas of the UK, ideal for conferences, weddings and banquets. The glorious bar overlooks the gardens and lake, and the refreshing and modern approach to food is gaining the oak-panelled dining room a rapidly renowned reputation. The redesigned spa is quite spectacular and an absolute must for any guest visiting the Hall; the swimming pool has now been joined by the rock sauna, bio sauna, laconium, steam room and aroma grotto. First-class treatments are also available. Some of the country's top tourist attractions are nearby such as Shrewsbury Castle and Ironbridge Museum.

***Our inspector loved:** The sheer diversity offered in the newly refurbished Albrighton Hall, great variety whilst retaining an intimate ambience as well.*

Directions: Exit the M54 at Shrewsbury and take the A49 towards Whitchurch. At the second roundabout, take the A5124/A528 towards Ellesmere and follow the brown sign for Albrighton Hall.

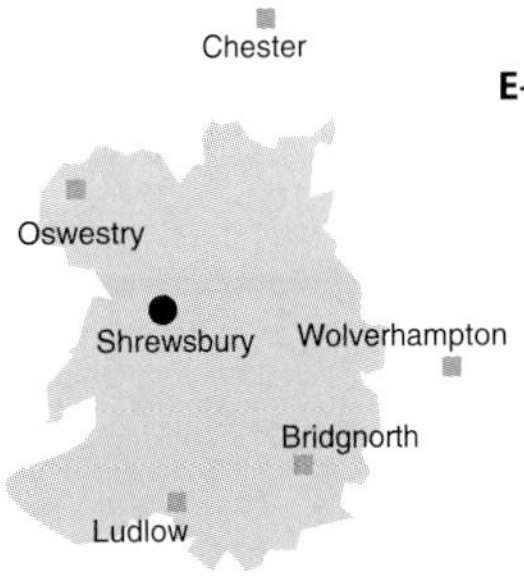

Chester
Oswestry
Shrewsbury
Wolverhampton
Bridgnorth
Ludlow

Web: www.johansens.com/albrighton
E-mail: albrighton@macdonald-hotels.co.uk
Tel: 0870 381 8602
International: +44 (0)1939 291000
Fax: 01939 291123

Price Guide:
room rates from £160

STON EASTON PARK

STON EASTON, BATH, SOMERSET BA3 4DF

The internationally renowned hotel, Ston Easton Park, is a Grade I Palladian mansion of notable distinction. A showpiece for some exceptional architectural and decorative features of its period, it dates from 1739 and has recently undergone extensive restoration, offering a unique opportunity to enjoy the opulent splendour of the 18th century. A high priority is given to the provision of friendly and unobtrusive service. The hotel has won innumerable awards for its décor, service and food. Jean Monro, an acknowledged expert on 18th-century decoration, supervised the design and furnishing of the interiors, complementing the original features with choice antiques, paintings and objets d'art. Fresh, quality produce, delivered from all parts of Britain, is combined with herbs and vegetables from the Victorian kitchen garden to create English and French dishes. To accompany your meal, a wide selection of rare wines and old vintages is stocked in the house cellars. The grounds, landscaped by Humphry Repton in 1793, consist of romantic gardens and parkland. The 17th-century Gardener's Cottage, close to the main house on the wooded banks of the River Norr, provides private suite accommodation.

Our inspector loved: *The feeling of a bygone era – the peace, seclusion and magnificent location.*

Directions: 11 miles south of Bath on the A37 between Bath and Wells.

Web: www.johansens.com/stoneastonpark
E-mail: info@stoneaston.co.uk
Tel: 0870 381 8916
International: +44 (0)1761 241631
Fax: 01761 241377

Price Guide:
single from £120
double/twin £150–£395
four-poster £210–£395

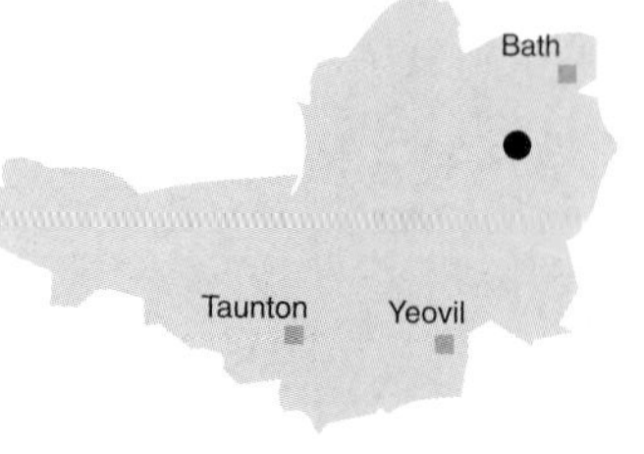

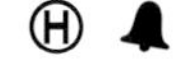

MOUNT SOMERSET COUNTRY HOUSE HOTEL

HENLADE, TAUNTON, SOMERSET TA3 5NB

This elegant Regency residence, awarded 2 Rosettes and 3 stars, stands high on the slopes of the Blackdown Hills, overlooking miles of lovely countryside. The Hotel is rich in intricate craftsmanship and displays fine original features. Its owners have committed themselves to creating an atmosphere in which guests can relax, confident that all needs will be catered for. The bedrooms are sumptuously furnished and many offer views over the Quantock Hills. All of the bedrooms have luxurious bathrooms and some have spa baths. Light lunches, teas, coffees and home-made cakes can be enjoyed in the beautifully furnished drawing room, whilst in the restaurant the finest food and wines are served. A team of chefs work together to create dishes which exceed the expectations of the most discerning gourmet. Places of interest nearby include Glastonbury Abbey, Wells Cathedral and Exmoor. Special breaks are available throughout the year.

Our inspector loved: *The superb upgraded en-suites complementing the beautiful bedrooms.*

Directions: At the M5 exit at junction 25, join the A358 towards Ilminster. Just past Henlade turn right at the sign for Stoke St. Mary. At the T-junction turn left, the Hotel drive is 150 yards on the right.

Web: www.johansens.com/mountsomerset
E-mail: info@mountsomersethotel.co.uk
Tel: 0870 381 8750
International: +44 (0)1823 442500
Fax: 01823 442900

Price Guide:
single from £105–£120
double/twin from £145–£175
suites £195–£220

11 60

Bindon Country House Hotel

LANGFORD BUDVILLE, WELLINGTON, SOMERSET TA21 0RU

Occupying a glorious location in 7 acres of tranquil gardens and woodland, this property offers guests a peaceful retreat from a hectic life. Bindon is the quintessential country house hotel with croquet on the lawn, a delightful rose garden and a rediscovered Victorian orangery. Some parts of the building date back to the 17th century, and when current owners Mark and Lynn Jaffa purchased the property in 1996 they undertook a painstaking restoration process to create the wonderful hotel that stands today. The 12 luxurious bedrooms are light, airy and spacious; each has its own character yet enjoys the same sumptuous fabrics, exquisite linens and pampering bathrooms. Acclaimed Head Chef Mike Davies, formerly head chef of a 2 AA Rosette-awarded restaurant and colleague of Head Chef of the Year, Phil Vickery, creates traditional, English dishes with a strong focus on seasonal produce that results in a daily changing table d'hôte menu and seasonally changing à la carte. After a satisfying meal guests may adjourn to the oak-panelled Wellington Bar to enjoy drinks in front of the cosy open fire. Local places of interest include Exmoor, Exeter, Wells, Dartmoor, Bath and Glastonbury with Langford Heath Nature Reserve just a 5-minute walk away. Short breaks from £150, including dinner are available. Exclusive use of the hotel can be arranged on a full, partial or self-catering basis.

Directions: 15 minutes from M5, jct 26 drive to Wellington and take B3187 to Langford Budville. Go through the village then right towards Wiveliscombe, right again at the junction and pass Bindon Farm. After 450 yards turn right.

Web: www.johansens.com/bindoncountryhouse
E-mail: stay@bindon.com
Tel: 0870 381 8364
International: +44 (0)1823 400070
Fax: 01823 400071

Price Guide:
single from £95
double/twin £115–£215
suite from £145

Our inspector loved: *This tucked away retreat offering all.*

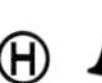

Hoar Cross Hall Spa Resort

HOAR CROSS, NR YOXALL, STAFFORDSHIRE DE13 8QS

The only spa resort in a stately home in England. Surrounded by 90 acres of beautiful countryside, lakes and exquisite formal and continental gardens with water features, exotic plants and beautiful flowers, Hoar Cross Hall is a secluded haven and the perfect venue for those who want a peaceful environment in which to be pampered. Oak panelling, tapestries, rich furnishings and paintings adorn the interior. A stunning Jacobean staircase leads to luxurious bedrooms, all with crown tester or four-poster beds and elegant design. Penthouses have private saunas and balconies overlooking the treetops. Breathtaking gilded ceilings and William Morris wallpaper in the original ballroom set the scene for the dining room, where a superb à la carte menu is offered. A tasty breakfast and buffet lunch is served in the Plantation Restaurants overlooking the pools. There are unlimited ways in which visitors can de-stress at Hoar Cross Hall; yoga, meditation, tai chi, pilates, dance classes and aqua-aerobics are all available and outdoor pursuits include tennis, croquet, archery and a golf academy with 9 hole par 3 golf course and driving range. Trained professionals are ready to assist and the spa consists of hydrotherapy baths, flotation therapy, saunas, an extensive gymnasium, steam rooms, water grottos, saunariums, aromatherapy room, aerobics and yoga suites .

Our inspector loved: *The balance of excellent meals and welcoming restaurant combined with serious facilities. Relaxed but so professional.*

Directions: From Lichfield turn off the A51 onto the A515 towards Ashbourne. Go through Yoxall and turn left to Hoar Cross.

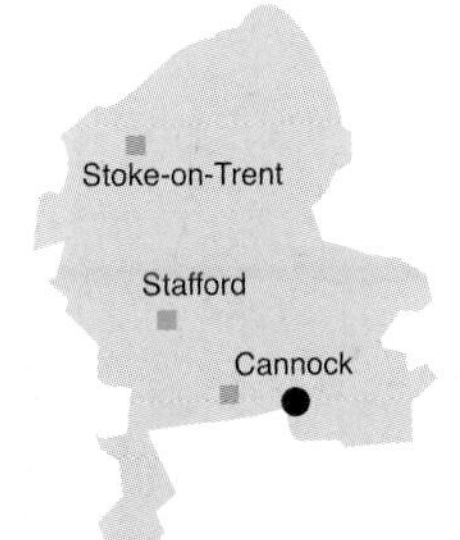

Web: www.johansens.com/hoarcrosshall
E-mail: info@hoarcross.co.uk
Tel: 0870 381 8598
International: +44 (0)1283 575671
Fax: 01283 575652

Price Guide: (fully inclusive of spa treatments, breakfast, lunch and dinner)
single £168-£218
double/twin £236-£356
suite £358–£418

99 160 16 SPA

Brudenell Hotel

THE PARADE, ALDEBURGH, SUFFOLK IP15 5BU

This delightful hotel is the epitome of a charming contemporary seaside hideaway with a light, airy and relaxed ambience. Informal décor and comfortable furnishings complement the occasional piece of driftwood, and welcoming staff attend to your every need. The AA Rosette awarded restaurant is situated immediately on the seafront and has the feel of an ocean liner. Fresh fish and grills is the speciality. The interior has been cleverly arranged so that the majority of guests can enjoy a stunning panoramic sea view. Decorated in a fresh modern style the spacious bedrooms are well-equipped and many offer either a sea, marsh or river view. Aldeburgh has something for everybody - scenic walks past pastel-coloured houses and fishermen's huts, superb boutique shopping, highly acclaimed restaurants and the annual Aldeburgh Festival. Thorpeness is an unusual and interesting village to explore and also has a splendid golf course. For those interested in history, there are many historic buildings, castles and an abbey in the area. The marshes are a haven for wading birds and birdwatchers or for the more adventurous there is horse riding, archery and rally karting. Access to the hotel is very easy for the less mobile and there is a lift.

Our inspector loved: *Watching the sun glistening on the waves from so many windows.*

Directions: Take the M25, junction 28 onto the A12, then take the A1094 to Aldeburgh. The hotel is on the seafront at the south end of town.

Web: www.johansens.com/brudenell
E-mail: info@brudenellhotel.co.uk
Tel: 0870 381 9182
International: +44 (0)1728 452071
Fax: 01728 454082

Price Guide:
single £65-£100
double £102-£208

Ravenwood Hall Country Hotel & Restaurant

ROUGHAM, BURY ST EDMUNDS, SUFFOLK IP30 9JA

Nestling within 7 acres of lovely lawns and woodlands deep in the heart of Suffolk lies Ravenwood Hall. Now an excellent country house hotel, this fine Tudor building dates back to 1530 and retains many of its original features. The restaurant, still boasting the carved timbers and huge inglenook from Tudor times, creates a delightfully intimate atmosphere in which to enjoy imaginative cuisine. The menu is a combination of adventurous and classical dishes, featuring some long forgotten English recipes. The Hall's extensive cellars are stocked with some of the finest vintages, along with a selection of rare ports and brandies. A cosy bar offers a less formal setting in which to enjoy some unusual meals. Comfortable bedrooms are furnished with antiques, reflecting the historic tradition of the Hall, although each is equipped with every modern facility. A wide range of leisure facilities is available for guests, including a croquet lawn and heated swimming pool. There are golf courses and woodland walks to enjoy locally; hunting and shooting can be arranged. Places of interest nearby include the famous medieval wool towns of Lavenham and Long Melford; the historic cities of Norwich and Cambridge are within easy reach, as is Newmarket, the home of horse racing.

Our inspector loved: *The huge inglenook fireplaces and the informal reminders of a private country estate.*

Directions: 2 miles east of Bury St Edmunds off the A14.

Web: www.johansens.com/ravenwoodhall
E-mail: enquiries@ravenwoodhall.co.uk
Tel: 0870 381 8849
International: +44 (0)1359 270345
Fax: 01359 270788

Price Guide:
single £87.50–£118.50
double/twin £113.50–£170

HINTLESHAM HALL

HINTLESHAM, IPSWICH, SUFFOLK IP8 3NS

The epitome of grandeur, Hintlesham Hall is a house of evolving styles: its splendid Georgian façade belies its 16th-century origins, to which the red-brick Tudor rear of the hall is a testament. The Stuart period also left its mark, in the form of a magnificent carved oak staircase leading to the north wing of the hall. The combination of styles works extremely well, with the lofty proportions of the Georgian reception rooms contrasting with the timbered Tudor rooms. The décor throughout is superb – all rooms are individually appointed in a discriminating fashion. Iced mineral water, toiletries and towelling robes are to be found in each of the comfortable bedrooms. The herb garden supplies many of the flavours for the well-balanced menu which will appeal to the gourmet and the health-conscious alike, complemented by a 300-bin wine list. Bounded by 175 acres of rolling countryside, leisure facilities include an associated 18-hole championship golf course. The Health Club offers a new state-of-the-art gymnasium, sauna, steam room, spa bath, tennis and croquet. A full range of E'spa products and services are available in the beauty suite by arrangement. Guests can also explore Suffolk's 16th-century wool merchants' villages, its pretty coast, Constable country and Newmarket

Our inspector loved: *The new refurbishment programme.*

Directions: Hintlesham Hall is 4 miles west of Ipswich on the A1071 Sudbury road.

Web: www.johansens.com/hintleshamhall
E-mail: reservations@hintleshamhall.com
Tel: 0870 381 8595
International: +44 (0)1473 652334
Fax: 01473 652463

Price Guide:
single £110–£195
double/twin £140–£280
suite £350–£495

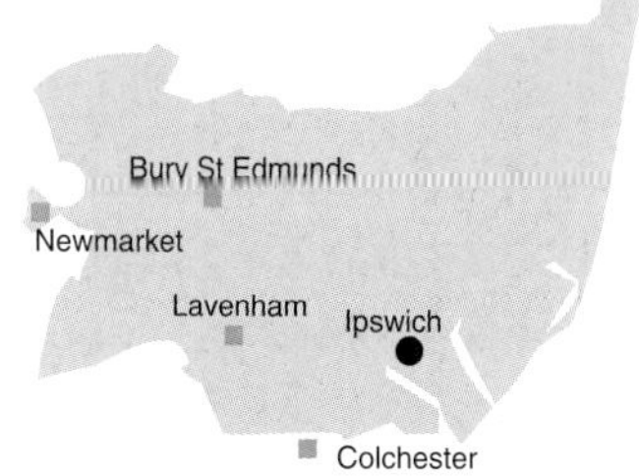

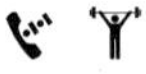
SPA

The Swan Hotel

HIGH STREET, LAVENHAM, SUDBURY, SUFFOLK CO10 9QA

Welcoming travellers since 1400 this medieval hotel stands within the heart of the Tudor village of Lavenham. Modern luxury sits comfortably alongside the 15th-century oak beams, panelled walls, flagged floors, log fires and inglenook fires, and the discovery of Medieval wall paintings have influenced the style of the interior, which features mementoes of England's early history hanging on the walls, such as the oldest surviving map of England, circa 1250. Each of the 51 en suite bedrooms has been decorated in calming colour schemes, with natural fabrics evoking the town's wool trade history. Lounge areas invite guests to relax in a soothing atmosphere surrounded by peace and traquillity and the Old Bar, with its brick floor, provides a welcoming retreat. The friendly and refined dining room prides itself on serving imaginative cuisine, created from fresh Suffolk and Norfolk produce accompanied by a comprehensive wine list. During the summer months guests may wish to dine al fresco in the courtyard. 3 large rooms can accommodate executive conferences and are equipped with state-of-the-art facilities and an experienced conference team are on-hand to help. Weddings can also be catered for. The Swan Hotel is a perfect base from which to enjoy an abundance of history, culture and unspoilt countryside.

Our inspector loved: *The Medieval wall paintings.*

Directions: From the A14 at Bury St Edmunds, take the A134 towards Sudbury. Turn onto the A1141 for Lavenham.

Web: www.johansens.com/theswanlavenham
E-mail: info@theswanatlavenham.co.uk
Tel: 0870 381 9280
International: +44 (0)1787 247477
Fax: 01787 248286

Bury St Edmunds
Newmarket
Lavenham
Ipswich
Colchester

Price Guide:
single £90–£100
double/twin £140–£195
suite £210

The Crown and Castle

ORFORD, WOODBRIDGE, SUFFOLK IP12 2LJ

Owned and run by food writer Ruth Watson and her husband, David, this charming red-brick hotel is idyllically located on the market square in Orford, a village overlooking the Alde estuary. Relaxed and informal surroundings ensure that guests feel at home, and friendly staff are always on hand to help. Stylish and well-equipped bedrooms are extremely comfortable. Garden rooms (in some of which dogs can stay) are spacious, and decorated in cool, neutral tones to create a serene ambience. The Trinity bistro is an award-winning restaurant with fantastic artworks, rich rust-coloured French velvet banquettes, and mellow wooden flooring. Good home-cooking embraces dishes ranging from Orford lobster and beef fillet carpaccio to Asian-style quail and Suffolk lamb. During the summer guests can sit and enjoy an aperitif, tapas or coffee on the flower-filled terrace, with a great view of the Norman keep just yards away. Snape Maltings, home to the Aldeburgh Festival, is just a few miles from Orford, as well as the nature reserves and unspoilt beaches of the Suffolk Heritage Coast. Short breaks and special packages are available.

Our inspector loved: *The nude painting in the restaurant!*

Directions: Signed from the A12, north of Woodbridge.

Web: www.johansens.com/crownandcastle
E-mail: info@crownandcastle.co.uk
Tel: 0870 381 8597
International: +44 (0)1394 450205

Price Guide:
single from £72
double £90–£145

The Swan Hotel

MARKET PLACE, SOUTHWOLD, SUFFOLK IP18 6EG

Rebuilt in 1659, following the disastrous fire that destroyed most of the town, The Swan Hotel was remodelled in the 1820s, with further additions made in 1938. The hotel provides every modern amenity and the current extensive refurbishment programme has ensured that a contemporary, stylish sophistication exudes throughout. The refined yet relaxed environment and friendly staff guarantees a most comfortable stay. Many of the bedrooms in the main hotel offer a glimpse of the sea, whilst the stylish garden rooms are clustered around the old bowling green. The elegant Drawing Room is perfect for quiet relaxation; the Reading Room and Southwold Room are also ideal for private functions. The daily menu, created from local produce and organic ingredients, offers dishes ranging from simple, delicious fare through the English classics to the chef's personal specialities as well as a full à la carte menu. An exciting selection of Adnams' wines from all over the world is offered. Southwold is bounded on 3 sides by creeks, marshes and the River Blyth; a paradise for birdwatchers and nature lovers. Little has changed in the town for a century, built around a series of greens there is a fine church, lighthouse and golf course close by. Music lovers flock to nearby Snape Maltings for the Aldeburgh Festival. Dr Hauschka beauty therapy treatments are now available at the hotel.

Directions: Southwold is off the A12 Ipswich–Lowestoft Road. The Swan Hotel is in the town centre.

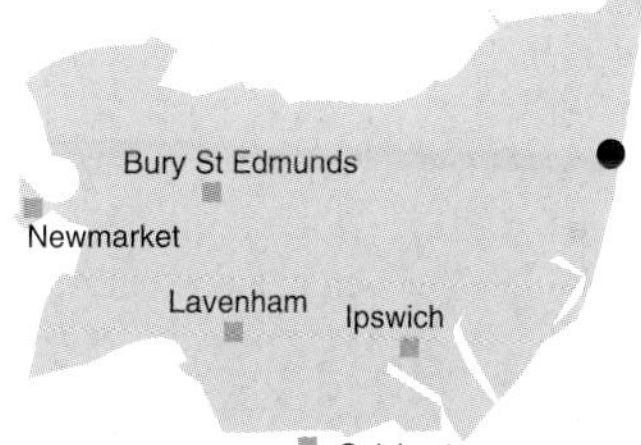

Web: www.johansens.com/swansouthwold
E-mail: swan.hotel@adnams.co.uk
Tel: 0870 381 8929
International: +44 (0)1502 722186
Fax: 01502 724800

Price Guide:
single from £78
double/twin from £134
suite from £196

Our inspector loved: *The refurbished bedrooms especially The Admirals.*

Seckford Hall

WOODBRIDGE, SUFFOLK IP13 6NU

Seckford Hall dates from 1530 and it is said that Elizabeth I once held court here. Furnished as a private house with many fine period pieces, the panelled rooms, beamed ceilings, carved doors and great stone fireplaces are set against the splendour of English oak. Local delicacies such as the house speciality, lobster, feature on the à la carte menu. The original minstrels gallery can be viewed in the banqueting hall, which is now a conference and function suite designed in-keeping with the general style. The Courtyard area was converted from a giant Tudor tithe barn, dairy and coach house; it now incorporates 10 charming cottage-style suites and a modern leisure complex, which includes a heated swimming pool, exercise machines, spa bath and beauty salon. Alternatively, guests may use the Internet Café where Internet access and office equipment is available. Set in 34 acres of tranquil parkland with sweeping lawns and a willow-fringed lake, guests may stroll about the grounds or simply relax in the attractive terrace garden. Equipment can be hired for the 18-hole golf course or a gentle walk along the riverside to picturesque Woodbridge, with its tide mill, antique shops and yacht harbours can be enjoyed. Visit the Sutton Hoo burial ship site and new museum and the Constable country and Suffolk coast nearby.

Our inspector loved: *Being inspired at the first sight of this beautiful Tudor building with its chimney's and flanking topiary.*

Directions: Remain on the A12 Woodbridge bypass until the blue and white hotel sign.

Web: www.johansens.com/seckfordhall
E-mail: reception@seckford.co.uk
Tel: 0870 381 8890
International: +44 (0)1394 385678
Fax: 01394 380610

Price Guide:
single £85–£130
double/twin £130–£200
suite £170–£200

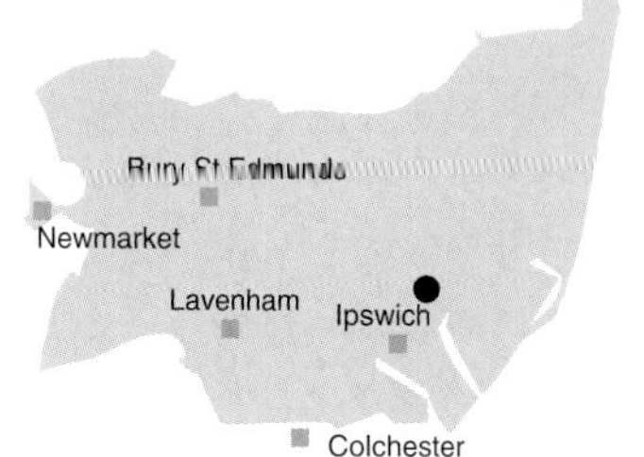

PENNYHILL PARK HOTEL & THE SPA

LONDON ROAD, BAGSHOT, SURREY GU19 5EU

Surrounded by 120 acres of peaceful parkland and a challenging 9-hole golf course, this carefully restored Victorian manor house offers a unique atmosphere and the intimacy of a private country estate with an extremely high level of luxury, service and facilities. Built in 1849, this 5-star hotel is an imposing and prestigious sight with the deep green and russet colours of summer and autumn, and ivy highlighting the majesty of its exterior walls and beautifully framing lead-paned, pillared windows. Exuding dignity and elegance, as befits its original intent of the 19th-century, there is a friendly and welcoming intimacy throughout. Guest rooms blend the refined character of the past with the comfort of the present and are individually designed with soft, warm-toned traditional décor enhanced by fine antiques and paintings. Tantalising cuisine is served in the cosy Latymer Restaurant, with its low beamed ceiling, and huge York stone fireplace. St James Restaurant features a marble floor, tall centrepiece statue and dual aspect views. The imaginative menus are essentially English with a French influence. Outdoor activities include clay pigeon shooting, fishing in the hotel lake, archery, tennis and croquet. The Spa offers an unrivalled experience in the UK and boasts 8 pools, 11 thermal cabins, experience showers, massage chairs, a fitness suite and 21 treatment rooms.

Directions: From the M3 take exit 3 then the A322 towards Bracknell. Turn left onto the A30 signposted to Camberley. ¾ mile after Bagshot turn right 50 yards past the Texaco garage.

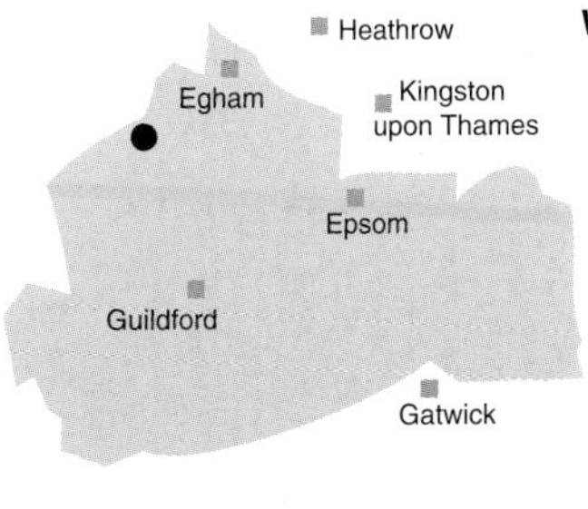

Heathrow
Egham
Kingston upon Thames
Epsom
Guildford
Gatwick

Web: www.johansens.com/pennyhillpark
E-mail: enquiries@pennyhillpark.co.uk
Tel: 0870 381 8815
International: +44 (0)1276 471774
Fax: 01276 473217

Price Guide:
single from £212
double/twin from £230
suite from £412

Our inspector loved: *The sheer magnificence of this hotel.*

Great Fosters

STROUDE ROAD, EGHAM, SURREY TW20 9UR

Directions: M25/J13, head for Egham and watch for brown Historic Buildings signs.

Web: www.johansens.com/greatfosters
E-mail: enquiries@greatfosters.co.uk
Tel: 0870 381 8569
International: +44 (0)1784 433822
Fax: 01784 472455

Price Guide:
single from £120
double/twin from £155
suite from £245

Probably built as a Royal hunting lodge in Windsor Forest, very much a stately home since the 16th century, today Great Fosters is a prestigious hotel within half an hour of both Heathrow Airport and central London. Its past is evident in the mullioned windows, tall chimneys and brick finials, whilst the Saxon moat – crossed by a Japanese bridge – surrounds 3 sides of the formal gardens, complete with topiary, statuary and a charming rose garden. Inside are fine oak beams and panelling, Jacobean chimney pieces, superb tapestries and a rare oakwell staircase leading to the Tower. Some of the guest rooms are particularly magnificent – one Italian styled with gilt furnishings and damask walls, others with moulded ceilings, beautiful antiques and Persian rugs. Guests relax in the bar before enjoying good English and French cooking and carefully selected wines in The Oak Room. Celebrations, meetings and weddings take place in the elegant Orangery and impressive Tithe Barn. Great Fosters is close to polo in Windsor Great Park, racing at Ascot, golf at Wentworth, boating in Henley and pageantry at Windsor Castle, Runnymede and Hampton Court.

Our inspector loved: *The magnificent modern tapestry in the dining room so perfectly complementing the outstanding architectural details of this ancient building.*

Lythe Hill Hotel & Spa

PETWORTH ROAD, HASLEMERE, SURREY GU27 3BQ

Cradled by the Surrey foothills in a tranquil setting is the enchanting Lythe Hill Hotel & Spa. It is an unusual cluster of ancient buildings – parts of which date from the 14th century. While most of the beautifully appointed accommodation is in the more recently converted part of the hotel, there are 5 charming bedrooms in the Tudor House, including the Henry VIII room with a four-poster bed dated 1614. There are 2 delightful restaurants: the Auberge de France offers classic French cuisine in the oak-panelled room which overlooks the lake and parklands, and the 'Dining Room' has the choice of imaginative English fare. An exceptional wine list offers over 200 wines from more than a dozen countries. The hotel boasts a splendid leisure facility called Amarna (which was voted hotel spa of the year) within the grounds of the hotel. It has a 16 x 8 metre swimming pool, steam room and sauna, gym, hairdressing, treatment rooms and a nail bar. National Trust hillside adjoining the hotel grounds provides interesting walks and views over the surrounding countryside. The area is steeped in history, with the country houses of Petworth, Clandon and Uppark to visit as well as racing at Goodwood and polo at Cowdray Park. Brighton and the south coast are only a short drive away.

Our inspector loved: *The clever use of real English oak in the new reception area.*

Directions: Lythe Hill lies about $1\frac{1}{2}$ miles from the centre of Haslemere, east on the B2131.

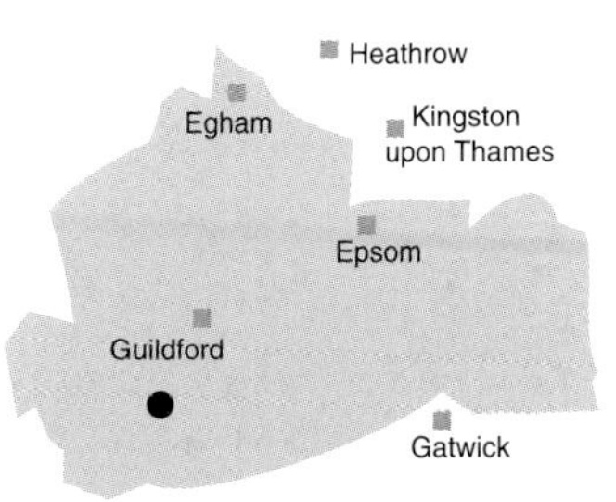

Web: www.johansens.com/lythehill
E-mail: lythe@lythehill.co.uk
Tel: 0870 381 8709
International: +44 (0)1428 651251
Fax: 01428 644131

Price Guide: (room only)
double £160–£295
suite £260–£350

FOXHILLS

STONEHILL ROAD, OTTERSHAW, SURREY KT16 0EL

This magnificent 400-acre estate is a delightful environment for any discerning traveller, whatever their interests may be. Named after the 18th-century foreign secretary, Charles James Fox, Foxhills comprises a large Manor House, elegant suites, 3 golf courses, numerous tennis courts, indoor and outdoor swimming pools, 2 restaurants and a host of health and fitness facilities including a gymnasium and beauty salon. The 42 bedrooms (soon to be 70), located in a superb courtyard setting, are the essence of comfort; elegantly furnished and offering all the latest amenities, they are designed in a number of styles; some have gardens whilst others are on 2 floors. The 2 restaurants pride themselves on their culinary excellence. Inside the Manor itself, the award-winning restaurant serves fine cuisine and is renowned for the Sunday buffet – a gourmet's delight! The sport and health facilities at Foxhills are particularly impressive and with 20 qualified instructors on hand, guests may wish to acquire a new skill such as racquetball or T'ai Chi. Those wishing to be pampered will enjoy the sauna, steam room and the fine beauty salon. Awarded 4-stars by the AA.

Our inspector loved: *The smiling helpful staff – the objective here is that everyone goes away happier than when they arrived.*

Directions: From M25 Jct 11, follow signs to Woking. After a dual carriageway, turn left into Guildford Road. 3rd exit at roundabout and immediately right into Foxhills Road. Turn left at the end of the road, Foxhills is on the right.

Web: www.johansens.com/foxhills
E-mail: reservations@foxhills.co.uk
Tel: 0870 381 8530
International: +44 (0)1932 704500
Fax: 01932 874762

Price Guide: (room only)
double/twin from £170
suite from £225

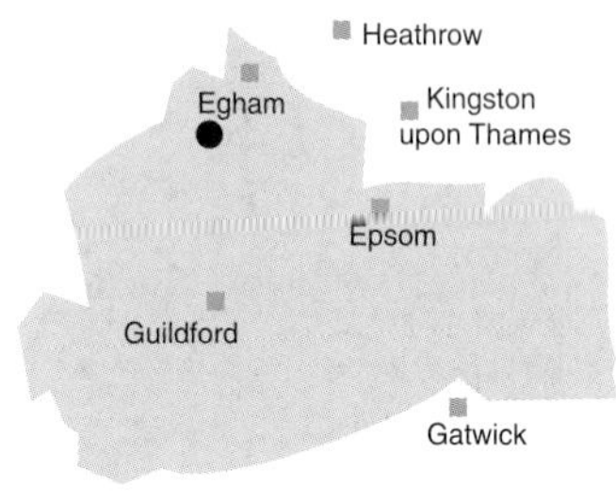

Nutfield Priory Hotel and Spa

NUTFIELD, NEAR REDHILL, SURREY RH1 4EL

Built in 1872 as a country retreat for Joshua Fielden MP, this striking Victorian gothic mansion is set high on Nutfield Ridge with panoramic views of the Surrey and Sussex countryside. Recent improvements have created wonderful treatment rooms, including a hyalite bath in the refurbished health spa and a completely redesigned contemporary café. The spacious bedrooms have been thoroughly modernized and luxuriously decorated with new furnishings and fabrics. The romantic Cloisters restaurant has also undergone a major redesign; leading interior designer John Minshaw has cleverly integrated deep chocolate and subtle beige hues with original natural stonework to create a simple yet cosmopolitan look. This sophisticated theme continues through the imaginative menu and fine English fare. For leisure pursuits, guests need not venture far. The Nutfield Priory Health Club and Spa houses 2 squash courts, a fully-equipped gym, an indoor pool and exercise studio. For those seeking complete relaxation, the spa offers a steam room, saunas, sunbeds and a wide range of pampering treatments. This delightful property is within easy reach of London and the home counties and is a perfect location for a memorable wedding or corporate function. The Gibson Room and Fielden Suite can be adapted to suit small or large gatherings and the grounds provide a glorious backdrop.

Our inspector loved: *The new bedrooms and renovated health club.*

Directions: Nutfield Priory is on the A25 between Redhill and Godstone and can be reached easily from junctions 6 and 8 of the M25. From Godstone, the Priory is on the left just after the village.

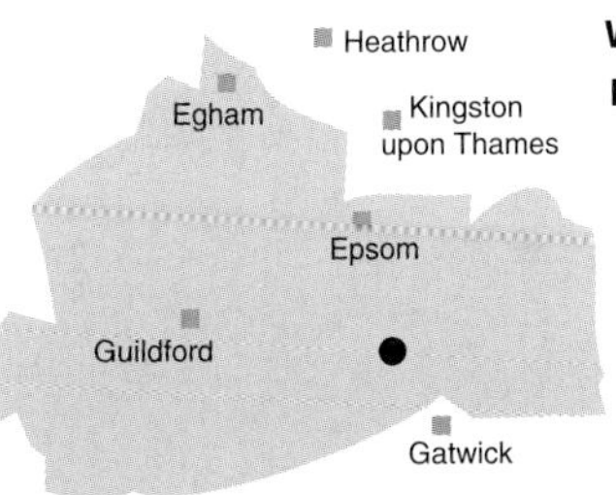

Web: www.johansens.com/nutfieldpriory
E-mail: nutfieldpriory@handpicked.co.uk
Tel: 0870 381 8775
International: +44 (0)1737 824400
Fax: 01737 823321

Price Guide:
single from £160
double/twin from £185
suite from £255

Oatlands Park Hotel

146 OATLANDS DRIVE, WEYBRIDGE, SURREY KT13 9HB

Directions: From the M25, junction 11 follow signs to Weybridge. Follow the A317 through the High Street into Monument Hill to the mini-roundabout. Turn left into Oatlands Drive and the hotel is 50 yards on left.

Web: www.johansens.com/oatlandspark
E-mail: info@oatlandsparkhotel.com
Tel: 0870 381 8779
International: +44 (0)1932 847242
Fax: 01932 84[illegible]

Price Guide: (room only)
single £80–£202
double/twin £113–£224
suite from £150–£230

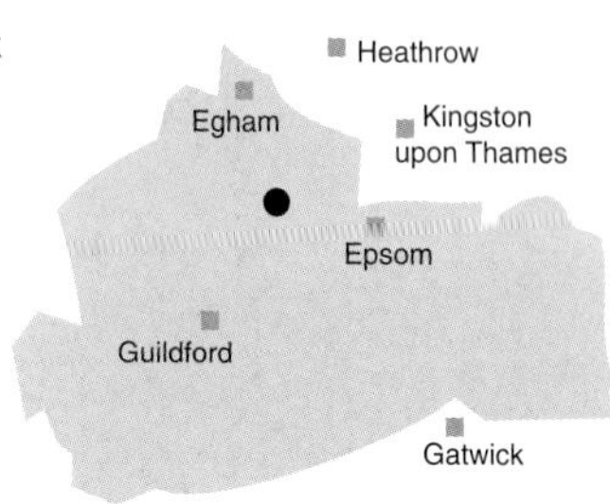

Set in acres of picturesque parkland, Oatlands Park Hotel stands in the heart of the Surrey countryside, overlooking the Broadwater Lake. 30 minutes from London, with easy access to Heathrow and Gatwick Airports, the hotel is a short distance from the M25 and 10 minutes from Webridge Railway Station. Records of the Oatlands estate show that the hotel has many royal connections; Elizabeth I and Stuart kings spent time in residence here, and Henry VIII's Hampton Court is only 5 miles away. The present mansion dates from the late 18th century and became a hotel in 1856. Although catering for the modern traveller, with experienced, approachable staff on-hand to aid conference planning, corporate hospitality or simply a restful stay, the hotel's historic character has been retained. Accommodation ranges from superior to large de luxe rooms and suites, and the recently refurbished Broadwater Restaurant has been beautifully decorated in a traditional style. A creative à la carte menu is offered and a traditional roast is served every Sunday lunchtime. The award-winning meeting rooms and smaller syndicate rooms are fitted with air conditioning and modern facilities including ADSL and WiFi connections. Leisure activities include tennis courts and a 9-hole, par 3 golf course.

Our inspector loved: *The grandeur and style in the dining room.*

 144   300       

The PowderMills

POWDERMILL LANE, BATTLE, EAST SUSSEX TN33 0SP

The PowderMills is an 18th-century listed country house skilfully converted into an elegant hotel. Originally the site of a famous gunpowder works, reputed to make the finest gunpowder in Europe during the Napoleonic wars, the beautiful and tranquil grounds are set amidst 150 acres of parks, lakes and woodlands, and feature a 7-acre specimen fishing lake. Wild geese, swans, ducks, kingfishers and herons abound. Situated close to the historic town of Battle, the hotel adjoins the famous battlefield of 1066, and guests can enjoy a leisurely walk through woodlands and fields to the Abbey. The hotel has been carefully furnished with locally acquired antiques and paintings, and on cooler days log fires burn in the entrance hall and drawing room. There is a range of 40 individually decorated en-suite bedrooms and junior suites in keeping with the style of the house, many with four-poster beds. Fine classical cooking by chef James Penn is served in the 2 AA Rosette-awarded Orangery Restaurant, whilst light meals and snacks are available in the library and conservatory. The location is an ideal base from which to explore the beautiful Sussex and Kent countryside.

Our inspector loved: *The wonderfully relaxed atmosphere and the stunning setting between the lakes.*

Directions: From centre of Battle take the Hastings road south. After ¼ mile turn right into Powdermill Lane. After a sharp bend, the entrance is on the right; cross over the bridge and lakes to reach the hotel.

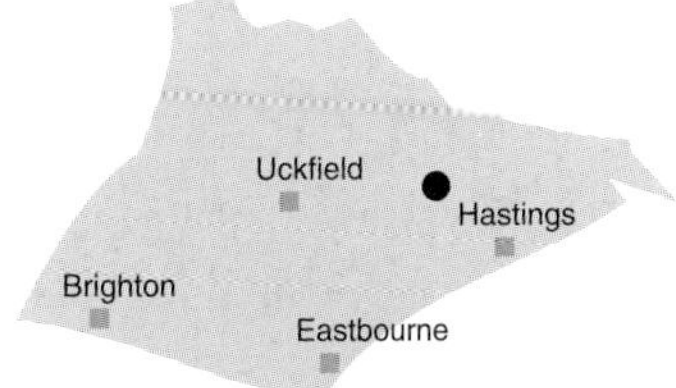

Web: www.johansens.com/powdermills
E-mail: powdc@aol.com
Tel: 0870 381 8835
International: +44 (0)1424 775511
Fax: 01424 774540

Price Guide:
single from £95
double/twin from £120

THE GRAND HOTEL

KING EDWARD'S PARADE, EASTBOURNE, EAST SUSSEX BN21 4EQ

The Grand Hotel is a fine property, steeped in history, which evokes the charm and splendour of the Victorian era. The majestic façade complements the elegant interior whilst the reception rooms are beautifully appointed with rich fabrics and ornaments. Many of the 152 bedrooms are of vast proportions: all being refurbished to include every comfort with attractive bathrooms. The hotel has numerous areas in which to relax and a good choice of restaurants and bars. The Mirabelle in particular achieves exceptional standards of fine dining. The array of new leisure facilities includes both indoor and outdoor pools, gymnasium, sauna, solarium, spa bath, steam room, snooker tables and a hair salon and 8 beauty rooms. Guests may choose to try the nearby racquet and golf clubs. For the meeting organiser, the hotel offers an impressive range of rooms which can cater for a number of business purposes from a board meeting for 12 to a larger conference for up to 300 delegates. Those seeking a peaceful retreat will be pleased with the tranquil atmosphere of Eastbourne. Pastimes include walks along the Downs, sea fishing and trips to the 2 nearby theatres.

Our inspector loved: *The outstanding levels of service at this rare truly grand coastal hotel.*

Directions: From London take A22 to the south coast and follow signs to Eastbourne, or take the M25 to join the M23 towards Brighton. Take A27 to Lewes then to Eastbourne. The Hotel is at the western end of the seafront.

Web: www.johansens.com/grandeastbourne
E-mail: reservations@grandeastbourne.com
Tel: 0870 381 8560
International: +44 (0)1323 412345
Fax: 01323 412233

Price Guide:
single £135–£420
double/twin £165–£290
suite £330–£450

152 300 SPA

Ashdown Park Hotel and Country Club

WYCH CROSS, FOREST ROW, EAST SUSSEX RH18 5JR

Ashdown Park is a grand, rambling 19th-century mansion overlooking almost 200 acres of landscaped gardens to the forest beyond. Built in 1867, the hotel is situated within easy reach of Gatwick Airport, London and the South Coast and provides the perfect backdrop for every occasion, from a weekend getaway to a honeymoon or business convention. The hotel is subtly furnished throughout to satisfy the needs of escapees from urban stress. The 106 en-suite bedrooms are beautifully decorated – several with elegant four-poster beds, all with up-to-date amenities. The Anderida restaurant offers a thoughtfully compiled menu and wine list, complemented by discreetly attentive service in soigné surroundings. Guests seeking relaxation can retire to the indoor pool, steam room and sauna, pamper themselves with a massage, before using the solarium, or visiting the beauty salon. Alternatively, guests may prefer to amble through the gardens and nearby woodland paths; the more energetic can indulge in tennis, croquet or use the Fitness Studio and Beauty Therapy. There is also an indoor driving range, a lounge/bar and an 18-hole par 3 golf course with an outdoor driving range.

Our inspector loved: *The exceptional level of customer service throughout the hotel.*

Directions: East of A22 at Wych Cross traffic lights on road signposted to Hartfield.

Web: www.johansens.com/ashdownpark
E-mail: reservations@ashdownpark.com
Tel: 0870 381 8325
International: +44 (0)1342 824988
Fax: 01342 826206

Price Guide:
single £135–£325
double/twin £165–£220
suite £285–£355

HORSTED PLACE COUNTRY HOUSE HOTEL

LITTLE HORSTED, EAST SUSSEX TN22 5TS

Directions: The hotel entrance is on the A26 just short of the junction with the A22, 2 miles south of Uckfield and signposted towards Lewes.

Web: www.johansens.com/horstedplace
E-mail: hotel@horstedplace.co.uk
Tel: 0870 381 8609
International: +44 (0)1825 750581
Fax: 01825 750459

Price Guide:
double/twin from £130
suite from £220

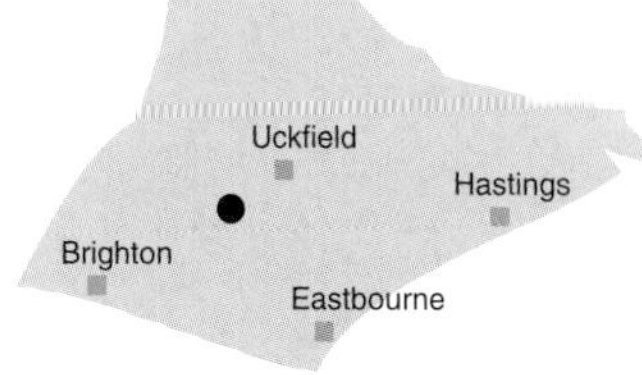

Horsted Place enjoys a splendid location amid the peace of the Sussex Downs. This magnificent Victorian Gothic Mansion, which was built in 1851, overlooks the East Sussex National golf course and boasts an interior predominantly styled by the celebrated Victorian architect, Augustus Pugin. In former years the Queen and Prince Philip were frequent visitors. Guests today are invited to enjoy the excellent service offered by a committed staff. Since the turn of 2001, and under new management, the bedrooms have been refurbished to provide luxurious décor and every modern comfort, whilst all public areas have been refurbished and upholstered. Dining at Horsted is guaranteed to be a memorable experience. Chef Allan Garth offers a daily fixed price menu as well as the seasonal à la carte menu. The Terrace Room is an elegant and airy private function room, licenced for weddings for up to 100 guests. The smaller Morning Room and Library are ideal for boardroom-style meetings and intimate dinner parties, and the self-contained management centre offers privacy and exclusivity for business meetings in a contemporary setting. Places of interest nearby include Royal Tunbridge Wells, Lewes and Glyndebourne. For golfing enthusiasts there is the East Sussex National Golf Club, one of the finest golf complexes in the world.

Our inspector loved: *The essential feel of a real country house.*

Newick Park

NEWICK, NEAR LEWES, EAST SUSSEX BN8 4SB

This magnificent Grade II listed Georgian country house, set in over 200 acres of breathtaking parkland and landscaped gardens, overlooks the Longford River and lake and the South Downs. Whilst situated in a convenient location near to the main road and rail routes and only 30 minutes away from Gatwick Airport, Newick Park maintains an atmosphere of complete tranquillity and privacy. The en-suite bedrooms are decorated in a classic style and contain elegant antique furnishings. The exquisite dining room offers a wide choice of culinary delights, carefully devised by the Head Chef, Chris Moore. The convivial bar complements the restaurant with its delicate style and understated elegance. The friendly staff ensure that guests receive a warm welcome and an outstanding level of comfort. The house and grounds are ideal for weddings or conferences and may be hired for exclusive use by larger groups. The Dell gardens, planted primarily in Victorian times, include a rare collection of Royal Ferns. Vibrant and diverse colours saturate the lawns during the changing seasons, courtesy of the various flowers and shrubs encompassing the gardens. The activities on the estate itself include fishing, shooting and tennis, whilst nearby distractions include the East Sussex Golf Club,racing at Goodwood and Glyndebourne Opera House.

Directions: The nearest motorway is the M23, jct 11.

Web: www.johansens.com/newickpark
E-mail: bookings@newickpark.co.uk
Tel: 0870 381 8762
International: +44 (0)1825 723633
Fax: 01825 723969

Price Guide:
single from £125
double/twin from £165

Our inspector loved: *The quite stunning setting of this country house.*

RYE LODGE

HILDER'S CLIFF, RYE, EAST SUSSEX TN31 7LD

Directions: Take A259 or A268 to Rye. Follow Town Centre signs - go through Landgate Arch (Historic stone archway built 1326) Hotel is 100 yards on right. (Nearest Motorway Junction 10 M20)

Web: www.johansens.com/ryelodge
E-mail: info@ryelodge.co.uk
Tel: 0870 381 8367
International: +44 (0)1797 223838
Fax: 01797 223585

Price Guide:
single from £85
double £140–£200

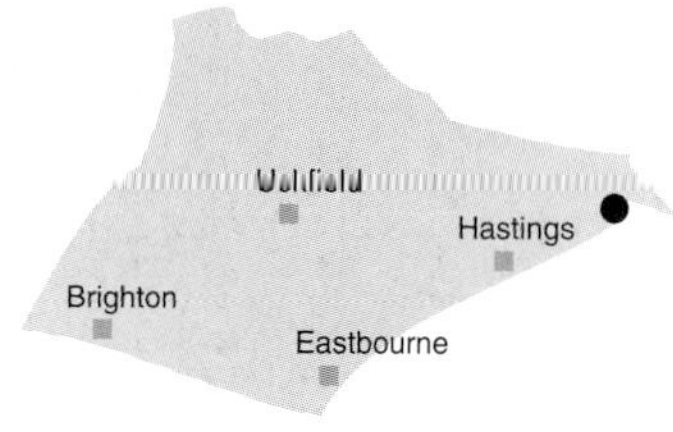

Rye Lodge is a traditional, historical hotel in the beautiful town of Rye with stunning views across the Estuary and Romney Marshes. Ideally located close to the High Street, it is surrounded by quaint shops, tea rooms, pubs and restaurants. Almost the entire town has been marked a conservation area of historical interest; its entrance gate was built in 1326. The interior of the hotel pays homage to its historical exterior with beautiful décor and relaxing colour schemes that complement its cosy atmosphere. Luxurious bedrooms are spacious with every modern convenience. Dining in the Terrace Restaurant is a delightful experience: its high ceiling, large windows and elegant Regency-style furniture creates a romantic ambience in which to savour delicious dinners by candlelight whilst enjoying the lovely views of the terrace gardens and Estuary. The hotel's Venetian Leisure Centre is a great place to unwind with its aromatherapy steam cabinet, sauna and heated indoor swimming pool. Rye is also well known for its hauntings: a ghostly monk is said to parade the hotel's car park and although the owners of 12 years have never seen this cowled spectre, the lands surrounding Rye Lodge were once chapel gardens and monastic cloisters. Bird lovers will relish the coast and marshes nearby.

Our inspector loved: *The immaculate presentation of this comfortable hotel; service is the keynote.*

Dale Hill

TICEHURST, NEAR TUNBRIDGE WELLS, EAST SUSSEX TN5 7DQ

Situated in over 350 acres of fine grounds, high on the Kentish Weald, the newly refurbished Dale Hill combines the best in golfing facilities with the style and refinement desired by discerning guests. The décor is enhanced by soft coloured fabrics and carpets, creating a summery impression throughout the year. Golfers have the choice of 2 18-hole courses, a gently undulating 6,093 yards par 70 and a new, challenging championship standard course designed by former US Masters champion Ian Woosnam. Just a 20-minute drive away, under the same ownership as the hotel, is the Nick Faldo designed Chart Hills course hailed as "the best new course in England". Packages allow guests to play both championship courses. Diners enjoy glorious views in a choice of restaurants where traditional award-winning cuisine is complemented by a fine wine list and service. The fully equipped health club features a heated swimming pool and a range of health and fitness facilities. Dale Hill is only a short drive from Tunbridge Wells and its renowned Pantiles shopping walk. Also nearby are medieval Scotney Castle, which dates back to 1380, Sissinghurst, a moated Tudor castle with gardens and Bewl Water, renowned for fly-fishing and water sports.

Our inspector loved: *The attention to every detail – the hotel positively sparkles.*

35 M 150

Directions: From the M25, junction 5, follow the A21 to Flimwell. Then turn right onto the B2087. Dale Hill is on the left.

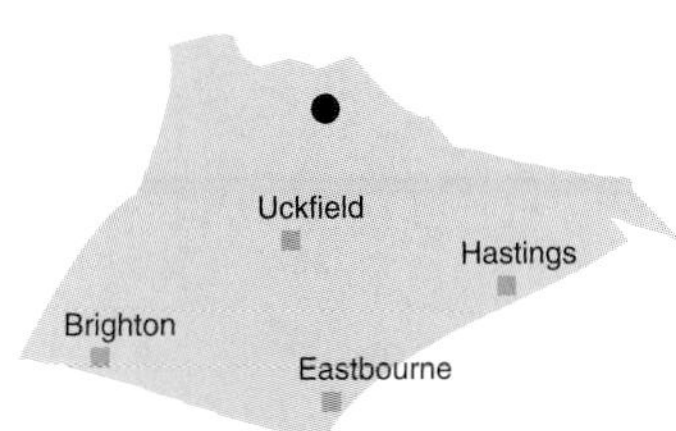

Web: www.johansens.com/dalehill
E-mail: info@dalehill.co.uk
Tel: 0870 381 8471
International: +44 (0)1580 200112
Fax: 01580 201249

Price Guide:
single £90–£110
double/twin £110–£180
suites £170-£210

AMBERLEY CASTLE

AMBERLEY, NEAR ARUNDEL, WEST SUSSEX BN18 9LT

Winner of the Johansens Award for Outstanding Excellence and Innovation, Amberley Castle boasts an amazing history spanning over 900 years. Set between the rolling South Downs and the peaceful expanses of the Amberley Wildbrooks, its towering battlements give breathtaking views and massive 14th-century curtain walls and the mighty portcullis bear silent testimony to a fascinating past. Proprietors, Joy and Martin Cummings, have transformed this medieval fortress into a unique country castle hotel. They offer a warm, personal welcome and their hotel provides the ultimate in contemporary luxury, whilst retaining an atmosphere of timelessness. 5 distinctive suites were added recently in the Bishopric by the main gateway. Each room is individually designed and has its own Jacuzzi bath. The exquisite 12th-century Queen's Room is the perfect setting for the creative cuisine of head chef James Peyton and his team. Amberley Castle is a natural first choice for romantic or cultural weekends, sporting breaks or confidential executive meetings. Roman ruins, antiques, stately homes, castle gardens, horse-racing and history "everywhere" you look, all within a short distance. It is easily accessible from London and the major air and channel ports.

Our inspector loved: *Everyone's dream of their castle in the country.*

Directions: Amberley Castle is on the B2139, off the A29 between Bury and Storrington. Look out for the Union flag, which clearly marks the driveway.

Web: www.johansens.com/amberleycastle
E-mail: info@amberleycastle.co.uk
Tel: 0870 381 8312
International: +44 (0)1798 831992
Fax: 01798 831998

Price Guide: (room only)
double/twin £155–£375
suite £285–£375

Bailiffscourt Hotel & Health Spa

CLIMPING, WEST SUSSEX BN17 5RW

Bailiffscourt is a perfectly preserved "medieval" house, built in the 1930s using authentic material salvaged from historic old buildings. Gnarled 15th-century beams and gothic mullioned windows combine to recreate a home from the Middle Ages. Set in 30 acres of beautiful pastures and walled gardens, this is a wonderful sanctuary in which to relax or work. Bedrooms are individually decorated and luxuriously furnished, many offer four-poster beds, open log fires and beautiful views over the surrounding countryside. The restaurant serves a varied menu and summer lunches can be taken al fresco in a rose-clad courtyard or in the walled garden; a list of well-priced wines accompanies meals. Private dining rooms are available for weddings, conferences and meetings, and companies can hire the hotel as their "country house" for 2 or 3 days. Bailiffscourt is surrounded by tranquil pastureland and an award-winning health spa featuring an outdoor Californian hot tub, indoor spa pool, sauna, steam room, gym, hammocks and 6 beauty therapy rooms offering 50 Mediterranean treatments. 2 tennis courts and a croquet lawn completes the on-site leisure facilities, whilst a private pathway leads 100yds down to Climping beach, ideal for windsurfing and morning walks. Arundel Castle and Chichester and Goodwood are nearby for classic car driving.

Directions: 3 miles south of Arundel, off the A259.

Gatwick
East Grinstead
Midhurst
Chichester
Brighton

Web: www.johansens.com/bailiffscourt
E-mail: bailiffscourt@hshotels.co.uk
Tel: 0870 381 8333
International: +44 (0)1903 723511
Fax: 01903 723107

Price Guide:
single from £175
double £195–£305
suite £345–£460

Our inspector loved: *The superb spa in its tranquil garden setting.*

THE MILLSTREAM HOTEL

BOSHAM, NR CHICHESTER, WEST SUSSEX PO18 8HL

A village rich in heritage, Bosham is depicted in the Bayeux Tapestry and King Harold is thought to be buried, alongside King Canute's, daughter in the local Saxon church. Moreover, sailors from the world over navigate their way to Bosham, which is a yachtsman's idyll on the banks of Chichester Harbour. The Millstream, just 300 yards from the harbour, consists of a restored 18th-century malthouse and adjoining cottages linked to The Grange, a small English manor house. Individually furnished bedrooms are complemented by chintz fabrics and pastel décor. The bar, drawing room and the restaurant are all most stylishly refurbished. A stream meanders past the front of the beautiful gardens. Cross the bridge to the 2 delightful new suites in "Waterside" the thatched cottage. Whatever the season, care is taken to ensure that the composition and presentation of the dishes reflect high standards. An appetising luncheon menu is offered and includes local seafood specialities such as: dressed Selsey crab, the Millstream's own home-smoked salmon and grilled fresh fillets of sea bass. During the winter, good-value "Hibernation Breaks" are available.

Our inspector loved: *The stylish new gazebo and its enchanting water feature beside the old mill stream.*

Directions: South of the A259 between Chichester and Havant.

Web: www.johansens.com/millstream
E-mail: info@millstream–hotel.co.uk
Tel: 0870 381 8739
International: +44 (0)1243 573234
Fax: 01243 573459

Price Guide:
single £89–£115
double/twin £135–£169
suite £185–£209

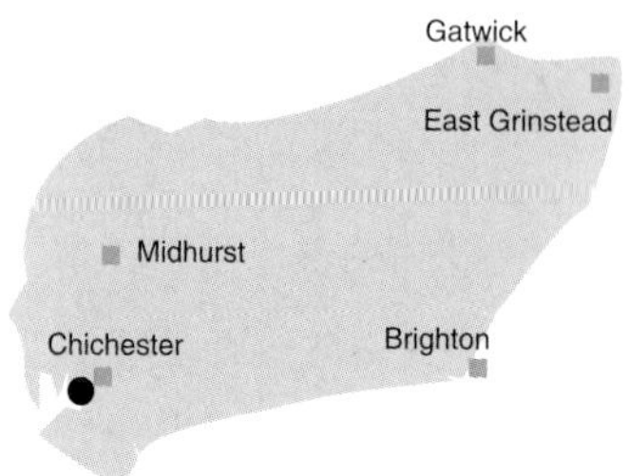

OCKENDEN MANOR

OCKENDEN LANE, CUCKFIELD, WEST SUSSEX RH17 5LD

Set in 9 acres of grounds in the centre of the Tudor village of Cuckfield on the Southern Forest Ridge, this hotel is an ideal base from which to discover Sussex and Kent, the Garden of England. First recorded in 1520, Ockenden Manor has become a hotel of great charm and character. The bedrooms all have their own individual identity: climb your private staircase to Thomas or Elizabeth, look out across the glorious Sussex countryside from Victoria's bay window or choose Charles, with its handsome four-poster bed. The elegant wood-panelled restaurant with its beautiful handpainted ceiling is the perfect setting in which to enjoy the chef's innovative cooking. An outstanding, extensive wine list offers, for example, a splendid choice of first-growth clarets. Spacious and elegantly furnished, the Ockenden Suite welcomes private lunch and dinner parties. A superb conservatory is part of the Ockenden Suite, this opens on to the lawns, where marquees can be set up for summer celebrations. The gardens of Nymans, Wakehurst Place and Leonardslee are nearby, as is the opera at Glyndebourne.

Our inspector loved: *The all-enveloping embrace of this supremely comfortable country house.*

Directions: In the centre of Cuckfield on the A272. Less than 3 miles east of the A23.

Web: www.johansens.com/ockendenmanor
E-mail: reservations@ockenden-manor.com
Tel: 0870 381 8780
International: +44 (0)1444 416111
Fax: 01444 415549

Price Guide:
single from £105
double/twin from £155
suite from £295

22 M 50

THE ANGEL HOTEL

NORTH STREET, MIDHURST, WEST SUSSEX GU29 9DN

The Angel Hotel is a stylishly restored 16th century coaching inn which has earned widespread praise from its guests, the national press and guidebooks. Sympathetically renovated to combine contemporary comfort with original character, The Angel bridges the gap between town house bustle and country house calm. To the front, a handsome Georgian façade overlooks the High Street, while at the rear, quiet rose gardens lead to the parkland and ruins of historic Cowdray Castle. There are 28 bedrooms, all offering private bathrooms and modern amenities. Individually furnished with antiques, many rooms feature original Tudor beams. The newly created Bistro style restaurant offers an excellent value contemporary menu. For corporate guests the hotel offers two attractive meeting rooms, a business suite, presentation aids and secretarial services. Racegoers will find it very convenient for Goodwood and theatregoers for the internationally acclaimed Chichester Festival Theatre. The historic market town of Midhurst is well placed for visits to Petworth House, Arundel Castle and the South Downs.

Our inspector loved: *This haven of town centre hospitality with its fine dining room and busy brasserie.*

Directions: From the A272, the hotel is on the left as the town centre is approached from the east.

Web: www.johansens.com/angelmidhurst
E-mail: info@theangelmidhurst.co.uk
Tel: 0870 381 8314
International: +44 (0)1730 812421
Fax: 01730 815928

Price Guide:
single £80–£115
double/twin £110–£150

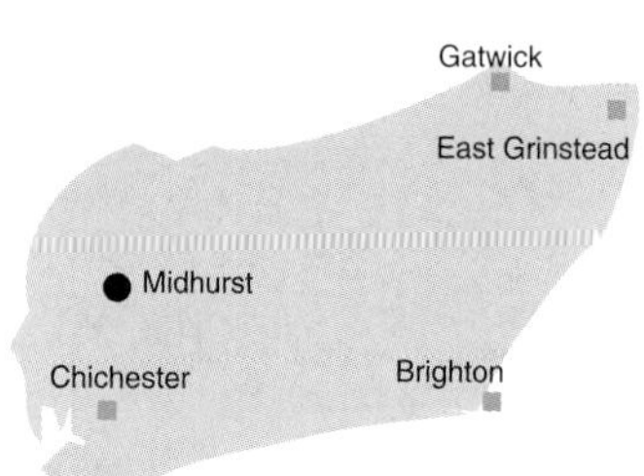

THE SPREAD EAGLE HOTEL & HEALTH SPA

SOUTH STREET, MIDHURST, WEST SUSSEX GU29 9NH

Dating from 1430, when guests were first welcomed here, The Spread Eagle Hotel is one of England's oldest hotels and is steeped in history; rich in charms, retaining many period features. Those wishing to be pampered will enjoy the superb fitness facilities and excellent standard of service. Located in either the main building or the market house, the 39 en-suite bedrooms, some with four-poster beds, are well-appointed with soft furnishings and fine ornaments. A roaring log fire attracts guests into the historic lounge bar, ideal for relaxing in the afternoons or enjoying an apéritif. Sumptuous modern British cuisine may be savoured in the candle-lit restaurant, complemented by an extensive wine list. Weddings, banquets and meetings are held in the Jacobean Hall and Polo Room. The Aquila Health Spa is an outstanding facility featuring a blue tiled swimming pool as its centrepiece. A Scandinavian sauna, Turkish steam room, hot tub, fitness centre and a range of beauty treatments, aromatherapy and massage are also offered. The stately homes at Petworth, Uppark and Goodwood are all within a short drive, with Chichester Cathedral, the Downland Museum and Fishbourne Roman Palace among the many local attractions. Cowdray Park Polo Club is only 1 mile away.

Our inspector loved: *The combination of ancient beams and panelling with the popular and friendly spa.*

Directions: Midhurst is on the A286 between Chichester and Milford.

Web: www.johansens.com/spreadeaglemidhurst
E-mail: reservations@spreadeagle-midhurst.com.
Tel: 0870 381 8903
International: +44 (0)1730 816911
Fax: 01730 815668

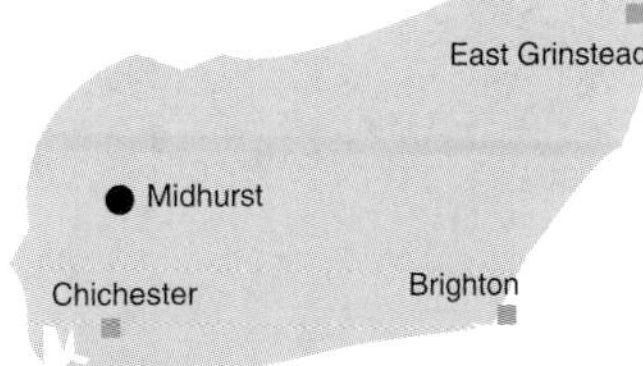

Price Guide:
single £89–£194
double/twin £99–£228

Ghyll Manor

HIGH STREET, RUSPER, NEAR HORSHAM, WEST SUSSEX RH12 4PX

Set in a pretty village in the heart of deepest Sussex countryside and surrounded by 50 acres of gardens and parkland, this elegant 17th-century manor is the ideal location for a relaxing break. The hotel consists of the original manor house, the more modern converted Stable Mews, 2 cottage suites and 8 beautifully furnished luxury bedrooms. All rooms are individually decorated; many boast traditional features including beamed ceilings and four-poster beds, and one room even has a tester bed with canopy. Superb food prepared, with only the freshest of local produce, is served in the Benedictine restaurant, winner of the Les Routiers Gold Key of Excellence for 4 consecutive years. Just 20 minutes from Gatwick Airport, Ghyll Manor, with its choice of 3 meeting rooms and first-class service, is the ideal location for conferences, whilst a dedicated team is on-hand to co-ordinate weddings. Guests can enjoy numerous walks such as the South Downs Way, and visit a number of fascinating National Trust properties and internationally renowned gardens such as Leonardslee and Wakehurst Place. London is only an hour's train journey away, as is the bustling city of Brighton with its mix of historical attractions, infamous piers and great shopping.

Our inspector loved: *the stylish new cocktail bar and the flowers everywhere – this hotel has its own resident florist.*

Directions: Leave the M23 at junction 11 and follow the A264 to Horsham. Turn off at the roundabout signed Faygate and Rusper.

Web: www.johansens.com/ghyllmanor
E-mail: ghyll.manor@csma.uk.com
Tel: 0870 381 9331
International: +44 (0)845 345 3426
Fax: 01293 871419

Price Guide:
single from £108
double/twin from £156

THE VERMONT HOTEL

CASTLE GARTH, NEWCASTLE-UPON-TYNE, TYNE & WEAR NE1 1RQ

The Vermont is Newcastle's only 4-star independent hotel, located next to the Castle, overlooking the Cathedral and the Tyne and Millennium Bridges. This impressive 12 storey, Manhattan-style tower boasts an unrivalled city centre position; a short walk to the main shopping centre, theatres, galleries, universities and main railway station. It has direct access to the Quayside and on site complimentary car parking. The 101 bedrooms and suites are a combination of classical and modern design with 24-hour service expected from a luxury hotel. 7 luxuriously appointed meeting rooms are available for special business occasions and private dining. The Bridge Restaurant is located at the Castle Garth level with spectacular views of the Tyne Bridge, alternatively there is the Redwood Bar, with its fireplace and sofas, open until very late. For those wishing to sample the atmosphere of the famous Quayside, Martha's Bar & Courtyard on the ground floor is the entrance to Newcastle's nightlife. The Vermont is the ideal base from which to explore Newcastle's excellent shops as well as the surrounding areas of Northumberland, Durham and The Borders

Our inspector loved: *Peaceful luxury next to the castle in the centre of Newcastle.*

Directions: Close to the A1(M), and 7 miles from Newcastle International Airport. Contact hotel for detailed directions.

Whitley Bay
Newcastle upon Tyne
Sunderland

Web: www.johansens.com/vermont
E-mail: info@vermont-hotel.co.uk
Tel: 0870 381 8962
International: +44 (0)191 233 1010
Fax: 0191 233 1234

Price Guide:
single/double from £110
suites from £240

101 M 200

NAILCOTE HALL

NAILCOTE LANE, BERKSWELL, NEAR SOLIHULL, WARWICKSHIRE CV7 7DE

Nailcote Hall is a charming Elizabethan country house hotel set in 15 acres of gardens and surrounded by Warwickshire countryside. Built in 1640, the house was used by Cromwell during the Civil War and was damaged by his troops prior to the assault on Kenilworth Castle. Ideally located in the heart of England, Nailcote Hall is within 15 minutes' drive of the castle towns of Kenilworth and Warwick, Coventry Cathedral, Birmingham International Airport/Station and the NEC. Situated at the centre of the Midlands motorway network, Birmingham city centre, the ICC and Stratford-upon-Avon are less than 30 minutes away. Leisure facilities include indoor swimming pool, gymnasium, solarium and sauna. Outside there are all-weather tennis courts, pétanque, croquet, a challenging 9-hole par-3 golf course and putting green (host to the British Championship Professional Short Course Championship). In the intimate Tudor surroundings of the Oak Room restaurant, chef will delight guests with superb cuisine, whilst the cellar boasts an extensive choice of international wines. En-suite bedrooms offer luxury accommodation and elegant facilities are available for conferences, private dining and corporate hospitality.

Our inspector loved: *The atmospheric Mulberry bedroom in the oldest part of the hotel and its view of the beautiful gardens.*

Directions: Situated 6 miles south of Birmingham International Airport/ NEC on the B4101 Balsall Common–Coventry road.

Web: www.johansens.com/nailcotehall
E-mail: info@nailcotehall.co.uk
Tel: 0870 381 8752
International: +44 (0)2476 466174
Fax: 02476 470720

Price Guide:
single £175
double/twin £190
suite £190–£295

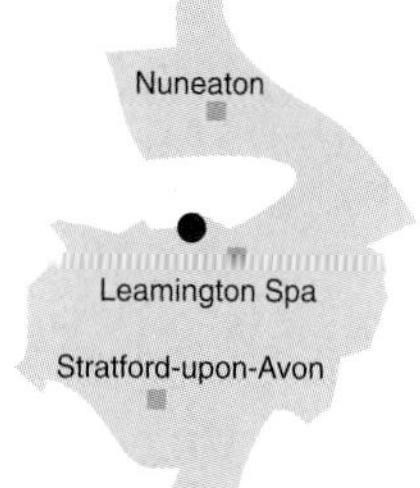

The Peacock Hotel

149 Warwick Road, Kenilworth, Warwickshire CV8 1HY

Set in the heart of the Warwickshire countryside this captivating hotel provides a peaceful retreat for guests whilst also enjoying a central location with easy access to many major attractions. The bold and vibrant décor throughout the property reflects the colours of a peacock, and an efficient, unobtrusive service is provided by the hotel staff. The en-suite accommodation is beautifully appointed and has been furnished to the highest standards for the ultimate comfort of guests. Club rooms are themed in Colonial 1920s style, embellished with sepia prints, Persian rugs, and chandeliers. The Peacock Hotel offers visitors a choice of 3 award-winning restaurants, all of which enjoy an excellent reputation locally and nationally and serve a wonderful variety of dishes. The menu at Coconut Lagoon is influenced by the cuisine of southern India, the Malabar Room is famed for its fine European dishes and extensive selection of cocktails, whilst the Colonial ballroom setting at Raffles is perfect for savouring the exquisite Malaysian cuisine. This property is ideally situated for visits to Stratford-upon-Avon, Warwick Castle, Cadbury World, the National Sea Life Centre and the lively city of Birmingham.

Our inspector loved: *The elegant décor and furnishings in the bedrooms.*

Directions: From Jct 15 M40 follow A46 north towards M69, exit from A46 at the A452 for Kenilworth town centre. Located on the right hand side after St Johns Church.

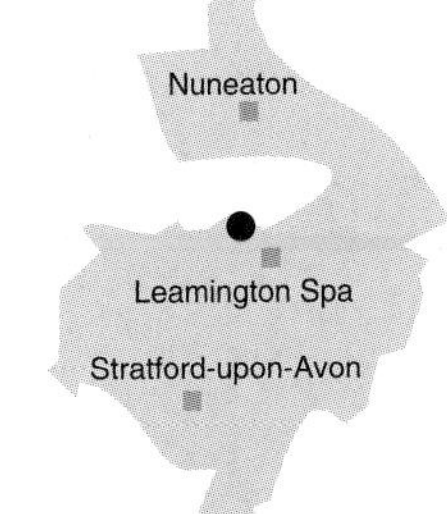

Web: www.johansens.com/peacockhotel
E-mail: reservations@peacockhotel.com
Tel: 0870 381 8397
International: +44 (0)1926 851156
Fax: 01926 864500

Price Guide:
single £52–£100
double/twin £59–£100
family £65–£110
feature club £72–£120

WARWICKSHIRE - LEAMINGTON SPA

Mallory Court

HARBURY LANE, BISHOPS TACHBROOK, LEAMINGTON SPA, WARWICKSHIRE CV33 9QB

Surrounded by 10 acres of attractive gardens, Mallory Court boasts a truly stunning backdrop across the beautiful Warwickshire countryside and is just a stone's throw away from Stratford-upon-Avon and Warwick Castle. Offering every home comfort, arriving guests are enveloped by the welcoming and tranquil ambience. Guests may begin their evening sipping champagne on the terrace before setting off to visit the Royal Shakespeare Theatre. During the winter season, afternoon tea may be enjoyed in the comfortable lounges beside the burning log fires. The 29 luxurious rooms are enhanced by thoughtful finishing touches and stunning views across the grounds. Modern, English-style dishes are served in the elegant restaurant where chef is happy to create tailor-made menus. Diners may begin with roasted Skye scallops, chicken with Avruga caviar served with marinated cucumber and oyster jus, followed by braised shoulder and roasted fillet of Lighthorne lamb with Provençal vegetables, ending with a hot passion fruit soufflé. In the summer of 2005 will be the opening of the new brasserie. This is an ideal venue for weddings and business meetings. Luxury leisure breaks and exclusive use of the hotel are available.

Our inspector loved: *The impeccable gardens and the sheer luxury and style of the interior furnishings and bedrooms.*

Directions: 2 miles south of Leamington Spa on Harbury Lane, just off the B4087 Bishops Tachbrook-Leamington Spa Road. Harbury Lane runs from the B4087 towards Fosse Way. M40, Jct13 from London/Jct14 from Birmingham.

Web: www.johansens.com/mallorycourt
E-mail: reception@mallory.co.uk
Tel: 0870 381 8713
International: +44 (0)1926 330214
Fax: 01926 451714

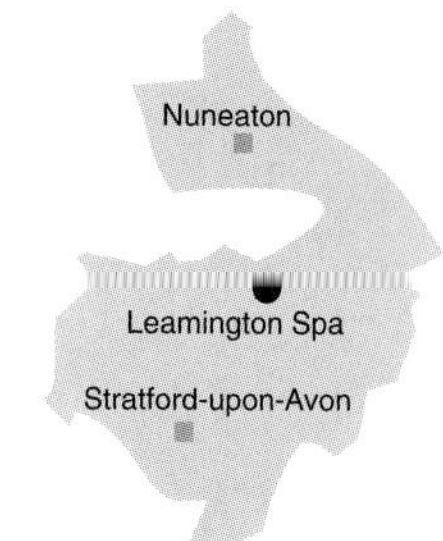

Price Guide:
double (single occupancy) from £125
double from £135
master rooms from £270

Alveston Manor

CLOPTON BRIDGE, STRATFORD-UPON-AVON, WARWICKSHIRE CV37 7HP

Legend has it that the first performance of Shakespeare's A Midsummer's Night Dream was given under the ancient cedar tree standing in the grounds of this historic and charming hotel. Alveston Manor is conveniently situated on the south side of the River Avon a short walk from the town centre. With its wood-framed façade, leaded windows, pointed roof peaks and tall, ornate chimneys it is an imposing sight to visitors and passing travellers. The interior is enhanced by tasteful décor, rich furnishings, antiques, fine pictures and striking floral displays. There is also a delightful, delicate aroma created by years of polish on original oak panelling and an Elizabethan staircase. The en-suite bedrooms are fitted to a high standard, with many of the bedrooms being situated in the adjoining modern Warwick and Charlecote Wings. A selection of suites and feature rooms are located in the original Manor House. Pre-dinner apéritifs can be sipped in an intimate cocktail bar before the enjoyment of a superbly prepared dinner. Guests can relax in total peace and enjoy an appealing period charm that sympathetically encompasses every modern day comfort or take advantage of the hotel's Vital Health, Fitness & Beauty Club which features an indoor pool, gymnasium, sauna, steam room and 6 beauty treatment rooms.

Our inspector loved: *The combination of Tudor panelling, Elizabethan staircase and the up-to-the-minute facilities.*

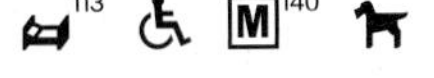

113 140 SPA

Directions: Exit the M40, junction 15 and take the A46 and A439 towards Stratford. Join the one-way system towards Banbury and Oxford. Alveston Manor is at the junction of A422/A3400

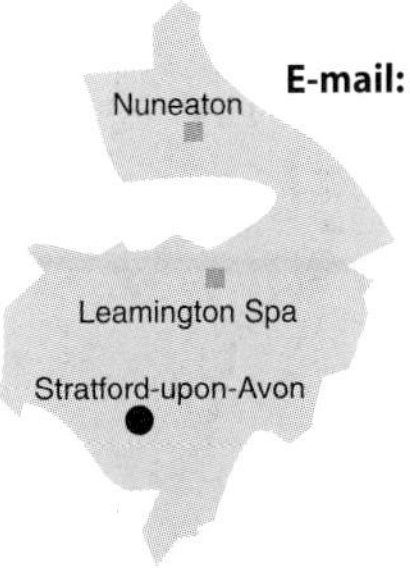

Nuneaton
Leamington Spa
Stratford-upon-Avon

Web: www.johansens.com/alvestonmanor
E-mail: sales.alvestonmanor@macdonald-hotels.co.uk
Tel: 0870 381 8310
International: +44 (0)1789 205478
Fax: 01789 414095

Price Guide:
single from £70
double/twin from £140
suite from £190

Ettington Park

ALDERMINSTER, STRATFORD-UPON-AVON, WARWICKSHIRE CV37 8BU

The foundations of Ettington Park date back at least 1000 years. Mentioned in the Domesday Book, Ettington Park rises majestically over 40 acres of Warwickshire parkland, surrounded by terraced gardens and carefully tended lawns, where guests can wander at their leisure to admire the pastoral views. The interiors are beautiful, their striking opulence enhanced by flowers, beautiful antiques and original paintings. Amid these elegant surroundings guests can relax totally, pampered with every luxury. On an appropriately grand scale, the 48 bedrooms and superb leisure complex, comprising an indoor heated swimming pool, spa bath, and sauna, make this a perfect choice for the sybarite. The menu reflects the best of English and French cuisine, served with panache in the dining room, with its elegant 18th-century rococo ceiling and 19th-century carved family crests. The bon viveur will relish the fine wine list. Splendid conference facilities are available: the panelled Long Gallery and 12th-century chapel are both unique venues. Clay pigeon shooting, archery and fishing can be arranged on the premises.

Our inspector loved: *The stunning neo-gothic building and its grounds.*

Directions: From M40 junction 15 (Warwick) take A46, A439 signposted Stratford, then left-hand turn onto A3400. Ettington Park is 5 miles south of Stratford-upon-Avon off the A3400.

Web: www.johansens.com/ettingtonpark
E-mail: ettingtonpark@handpicked.co.uk
Tel: 0870 381 8508
International: +44 (0)1789 450123
Fax: 01789 450472

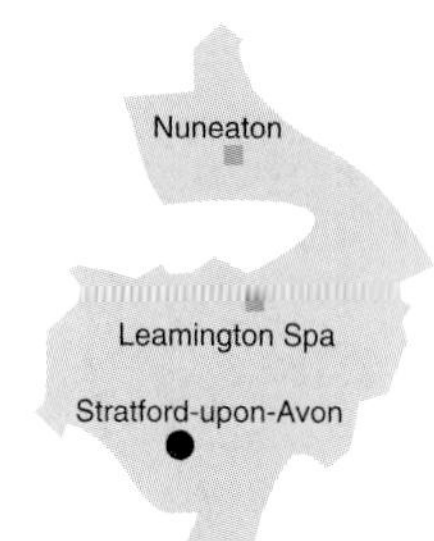

Price Guide:
single from £125
double/twin from £147
suite from £267

48 96

Billesley Manor

BILLESLEY, ALCESTER, NR STRATFORD-UPON-AVON, WARWICKSHIRE B49 6NF

This magnificent 4-star 16th-century Manor House is set in 11 acres of its own private parkland and has a unique topiary garden and sun terrace. Centuries of history and tradition with Shakespearian connection welcome guests to this beautiful hotel. Billesley Manor has 72 beautiful bedrooms, including four-poster rooms and suites, all of which are en-suite and many with stunning gardens views. Cuisine of the highest standard is served in the Stuart restaurant, awarded 2 AA Rosettes. A selection of rooms for private dining are available for family, friends or business guests. The Cedar Barns offer a new dimension in conference facilities incorporating state-of-the-art equipment in unique and impressive surroundings. A new spa incorporates an impressive indoor heated swimming pool, gym, beauty treatment rooms, sauna, steam room, solarium and healthy eating bistro. Tennis courts, croquet lawn and activity field are also available. The organisation of corporate events such as clay pigeon shooting, archery and quad biking are also on offer. Weekend breaks are available – ideal for visiting the Royal Shakespeare Theatre, Warwick Castle, Ragley Hall and the Cotswolds. Situated in the heart of England, minutes away from Shakespeare's Stratford-upon-Avon and only 23 miles from Birmingham International Airport, the hotel can be easily accessed by air, rail and road.

Directions: Leave M40 at exit 15, follow A46 towards Evesham and Alcester. 4 miles beyond Stratford-upon-Avon turn right to Billesley.

Web: www.johansens.com/billesley
E-mail: bookings@billesleymanor.co.uk
Tel: 0870 381 8363
International: +44 (0)1789 279955
Fax: 01789 764145

Price Guide:
single £125
double/twin £180
suite £250

Our inspector loved: *As ever the geometrically precise topiary garden.*

The Glebe at Barford

CHURCH STREET, BARFORD, WARWICKSHIRE CV35 8BS

Directions: M40 exit Junction 15 A429 signed Barford & Wellesbourne. Turning left at mini-roundabout, the hotel is on the right just past the church.

Web: www.johansens.com/glebeatbarford
E-mail: sales@glebehotel.co.uk
Tel: 0870 381 8548
International: +44 (0)1926 624218
Fax: 01926 624625

Price Guide:
single £105
double/twin £125
suite £160

Nuneaton
Leamington Spa
Stratford-upon-Avon

"Glebe" means belonging to the Church, which explains why this beautiful Georgian country house is in a unique and quiet position next to the church in Barford, an attractive village in Warwickshire. It is a Grade II listed building, dating back to 1820, with an unusual central atrium and surrounded by gardens. The bedrooms are spacious, comfortable and peaceful. They have all the accessories expected by today's travellers. The restaurant is in an elegant conservatory, green plants adding cool colour. There are excellent table d'hôte and à la carte menus and the wine list has been carefully selected to complement the dishes. The Glebe is an ideal venue for private celebrations and corporate events as it has several well-equipped conference rooms – the Bentley Suite seats 120 people for a banquet and the Directors Suite, with leather armchairs, is ideal for a discreet strategy meeting. Those wishing to be pampered will be pleased with the beauty and sunbed room. Guests appreciate the Glebe Leisure Club with a pool, gymnasium, sauna, steam room and spa facilities. They can play tennis and golf nearby. Ideally situated for Warwick and Stratford races.

Our inspector loved: *The splendid Cedar tree dominating the gravelled forecourt.*

ARDENCOTE MANOR HOTEL, COUNTRY CLUB & SPA

LYE GREEN ROAD, CLAVERDON, NR WARWICK, WARWICKSHIRE CV35 8LS

Under private ownership, this former Gentlemen's residence, which was built around 1860, has been sympathetically refurbished and substantially extended to provide a luxury hotel with all modern amenities and comforts, whilst retaining its traditional elegance and appealing intimacy. Set in 42 acres of landscaped grounds in the heart of Shakespeare country, it offers beautifully appointed en-suite accommodation – many rooms have glorious views of the lake and gardens – fine cuisine and extensive sports and leisure facilities, including indoor pool and spa bath, outdoor whirlpool, sauna and steamrooms, squash and tennis courts, fully equipped gymnasia and a 9-hole golf course. The Ardencote Spa is also at the disposal of guests, offering an extensive range of relaxing and holistic treatments. Ardencote Manor's award-winning restaurant, the lakeside Lodge, offers an exciting and innovative menu. Places of interest nearby include the NEC, Warwick Castle (discounted tickets available through hotel), Stratford-upon-Avon and the Cotswolds. Weekend breaks available.

Our inspector loved: *Enjoying the award-winning cuisine sitting in the Lodge restaurant looking at the lake.*

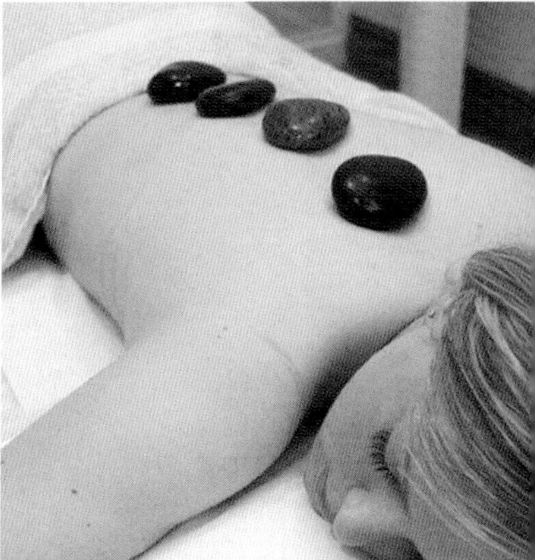

Directions: From M40 follow signs to Henley-in-Arden. Lye Green Road is off A4189 Henley-in-Arden/Warwick Road at Claverdon Village Green.

Web: www.johansens.com/ardencote
E-mail: hotel@ardencote.com
Tel: 0870 381 8320
International: +44 (0)1926 843111
Fax: 01926 842646

Price Guide:
single from £105
double from £120
suite £225

75 M 300 SPA

Wroxall Abbey Estate

BIRMINGHAM ROAD, WROXALL, NEAR WARWICK, WARWICKSHIRE CV35 7NB

Nestled in 27 acres of beautifully landscaped gardens within the glorious Warwickshire countryside, Wroxall Abbey Estate is something quite unique. Once the country seat of Sir Christopher Wren, this stunning collection of listed buildings now offers some of the finest hotel and conference facilities. In its entirety, the estate comprises 70 individually designed bedrooms, 15 meeting rooms, a collection of public rooms, a bistro, bar, restaurants and marquee. There is somewhere to suit every occasion, be it the elegant mansion, the courtyard building, with landmark clock tower, or the stunning 500m^2 marquee of flexible entertaining space. The country house-style bedrooms are carefully appointed; each has every modern comfort and amenity. Many have four-poster beds and original marble fireplaces, whilst the bathrooms boast separate walk-in showers and whirlpool baths. There is an extensive, first-class range of dining options: the elegant Sonnets restaurant, the informal Bistro, classic Broadwood Bar or the Garden Lounge. Furthermore, the panelled snooker room and bar, as well as the indoor pool complex, have been recently refurbished to exemplary standards. Sir Christopher Wren's chapel has some breathtaking displays of stained glass windows; there can be few more romantic places to exchange wedding vows.

Our inspector loved: *Sonnets restaurant: the wood panelling and the food.*

Directions: From the M42, exit at junction 5 onto the A4141 to Knowle. Continue towards Warwick for approximately 10 miles and drive through Chadwick End. The entrance to Wroxall Abbey Estate is on the right, 2 miles further on.

Web: www.johansens.com/wroxallcourt
E-mail: info@wroxallestate.com
Tel: 0870 381 9013
International: +44 (0)1926 484470
Fax: 01926 485206

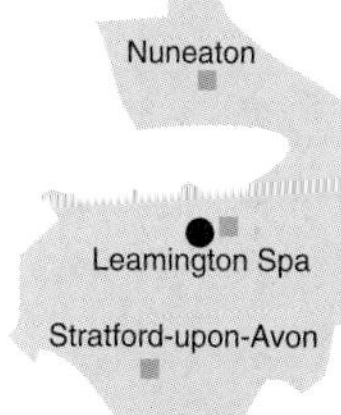

Price Guide:
single £79–£150
double/twin £99–£399

 70   300    SPA    

Lucknam Park, Bath

COLERNE, CHIPPENHAM, WILTSHIRE SN14 8AZ

For over 250 years Lucknam Park has been a focus of fine society and aristocratic living, something guests will sense immediately upon their approach along the mile-long avenue lined with beech trees. Built in 1720, this magnificent Palladian mansion is situated just 6 miles from Bath on the southern edge of the Cotswolds. The delicate aura of historical context is reflected in fine art and antiques dating from the late Georgian and early Victorian periods. Award winning food can be savoured in the elegant restaurant, at tables laid with exquisite porcelain, silver and glassware, accompanied with wines from an extensive cellar. Set within the walled gardens of the hotel is the spa, comprising an indoor pool, sauna, steam room, whirlpool spa, gymnasium, beauty salon and snooker room. Numerous activities can be arranged on request, including hot-air ballooning, golf and archery. The Lucknam Park Equestrian Centre, which is situated on the estate, welcomes complete beginners and experienced riders and takes liveries. Bowood House, Corsham Court and Castle Combe are all nearby. Lucknam Park is a member of Relais & Châteaux.

Our inspector loved: *The stunning refurbishment throughout. Beautiful fabrics and 18th century furniture.*

Directions: 15 minutes from M4, junctions 17 and 18, located between A420 and A4 near the village of Colerne.

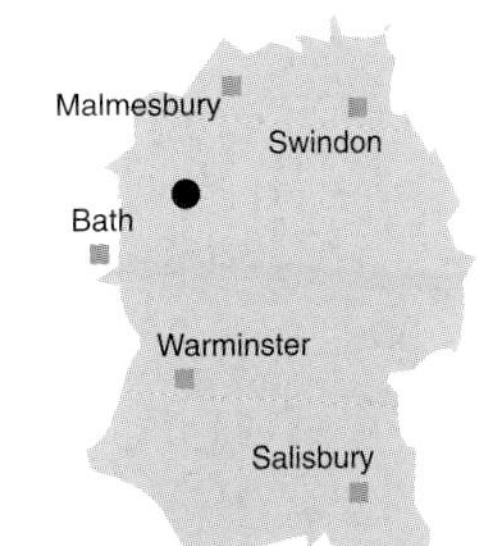

Web: www.johansens.com/lucknampark
E-mail: reservations@lucknampark.co.uk
Tel: 0870 381 8707
International: +44 (0)1225 742777
Fax: 01225 743536

Price Guide: (room only)
single/double/twin from £195
suite from £510

41 50 SPA

THE RECTORY HOTEL

CRUDWELL, NEAR MALMESBURY, WILTSHIRE SN16 9EP

Surrounded by a large garden, and with a grand entrance, Victorian pond and Cotswold stone walls, this picturesque hotel was originally a 14th-century home and has a welcoming atmosphere enhanced by friendly, professional staff. Following a recent refurbishment, the ground floor has been decorated in a contemporary style that cleverly complements the flagstone floors, open fireplaces and existing lush décor of the cosy rooms. The exceptional modern conveniences provide all the comforts of home whilst retaining a grandeur of a bygone era. All the en-suite bedrooms are individually and luxuriously furnished; some have window seats overlooking the landscaped gardens and larger bedrooms benefit from four-poster beds and spa baths. The award-winning 3 AA Rosette cuisine uses mostly organic ingredients and is lovingly created by the hotel's brigade of chefs headed by Peter Fairclough, who is a member of the prestigious Master Chefs of Great Britain. There are 2 dining locations: the formal, oak-panelled restaurant, with beams and period detail, and the airy, light Conservatory, which is perfect for private lunches and dinner parties. Apéritifs and coffee may be served by the pond, weather permitting, and during summer, lunch and dinner may be taken in the garden. Guests can explore Bath, the surrounding Cotswold towns and countryside.

Our inspector loved: *The pretty gardens and Victorian pool.*

Directions: From the M4, junction17 take the A429 to Cirencester. The hotel is opposite The Plough, next to the church.

Web: www.johansens.com/therectoryhotel
E-mail: info@therectoryhotel.co.uk
Tel: 0870 381 8786
International: +44 (0)1666 577194
Fax: 01666 577853

Price Guide.
single £85–£120
double/twin £95–£130
suite £145

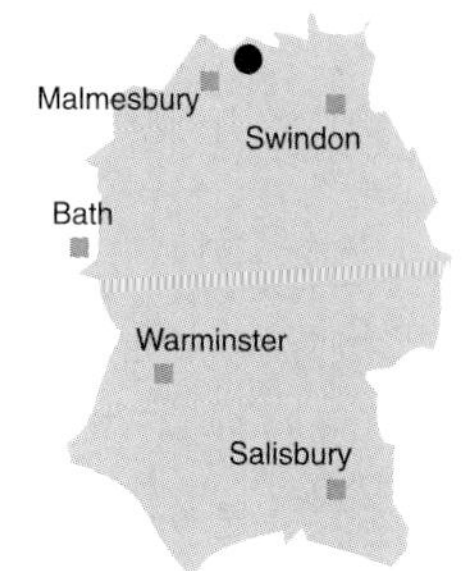

WHATLEY MANOR

EASTON GREY, MALMESBURY, WILTSHIRE SN16 0RB

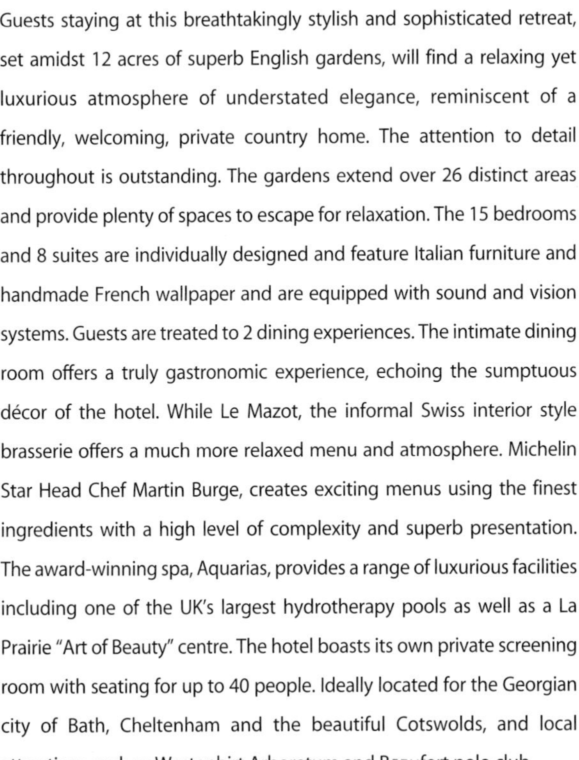

Guests staying at this breathtakingly stylish and sophisticated retreat, set amidst 12 acres of superb English gardens, will find a relaxing yet luxurious atmosphere of understated elegance, reminiscent of a friendly, welcoming, private country home. The attention to detail throughout is outstanding. The gardens extend over 26 distinct areas and provide plenty of spaces to escape for relaxation. The 15 bedrooms and 8 suites are individually designed and feature Italian furniture and handmade French wallpaper and are equipped with sound and vision systems. Guests are treated to 2 dining experiences. The intimate dining room offers a truly gastronomic experience, echoing the sumptuous décor of the hotel. While Le Mazot, the informal Swiss interior style brasserie offers a much more relaxed menu and atmosphere. Michelin Star Head Chef Martin Burge, creates exciting menus using the finest ingredients with a high level of complexity and superb presentation. The award-winning spa, Aquarias, provides a range of luxurious facilities including one of the UK's largest hydrotherapy pools as well as a La Prairie "Art of Beauty" centre. The hotel boasts its own private screening room with seating for up to 40 people. Ideally located for the Georgian city of Bath, Cheltenham and the beautiful Cotswolds, and local attractions such as Westonbirt Arboretum and Beaufort polo club.

Our inspector loved: *The beautiful bedrooms, space and magnificent spa.*

Directions: The hotel is situated off the B4040, 8 miles from junction 17 of the M4 motorway. 2 hours from London.

Web: www.johansens.com/whatley
E-mail: reservations@whatleymanor.com
Tel: 0870 381 9197
International: +44 (0)1666 822888
Fax: 01666 826120

Price Guide:
single/double/twin from £275
suite from £650

Howard's House

TEFFONT EVIAS, SALISBURY, WILTSHIRE SP3 5RJ

Directions: From London, turn left off A303. 2 miles after the Wylye intersection follow signs to Teffont and on entering the village join the B3089. Howard's House is signposted.

Web: www.johansens.com/howardshouse
E-mail: enq@howardshousehotel.com
Tel: 0870 381 8627
International: +44 (0)1722 716392
Fax: 01722 716820

Price Guide:
single £105
double/twin £165–£185

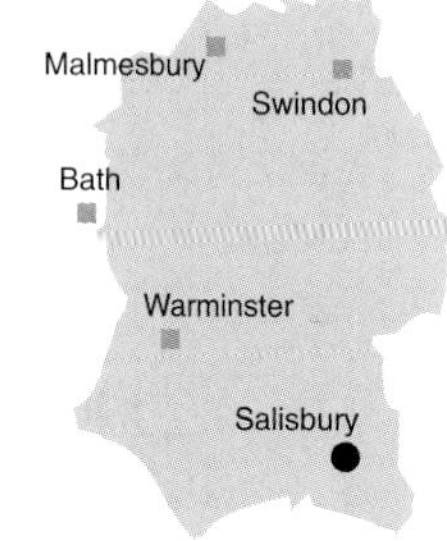

Tucked away in the depths of rural Wiltshire and surrounded by 2 acres of beautiful gardens the fragrance of jasmine exudes through the open windows of the House and the tinkling of the fountain in the lily pond can be gently heard. This charming small country house hotel, run by Noële Thompson, is located in the quintessential English hamlet of Teffon Evias, just 9 miles from Stonehenge. Howard's House is a haven of tranquillity for those seeking to escape the noise and stress of the modern world. The bedrooms are delightfully appointed, with additional touches of fresh fruit, homemade biscuits, plants and up-to-date magazines. The 3 AA Rosette-awarded restaurant is the height of elegance and serves modern British cuisine providing dishes of national acclaim. Cooked with flair and imagination and using home-grown and the best local produce, alfresco dining can be enjoyed during the summer. During winter guests may curl up by the genuine log fire with a good book and a glass of vintage port. Whatever the time of year you are guaranteed the ultimate in country house hospitality. Howard's House is ideally situated for visiting Stonehenge, Old Sarum, Salisbury Cathedral, Wilton House and Stourhead Gardens.

***Our inspector loved:** The friendly welcome and relaxed atmosphere.*

THE PEAR TREE AT PURTON

CHURCH END, PURTON, SWINDON, WILTSHIRE SN5 4ED

Dedication to service is the hallmark of this excellent honey-coloured stone hotel nestling in the Vale of the White Horse between the Cotswolds and Marlborough Downs. Owners Francis and Anne Young are justly proud of its recognition by the award of the RAC's Blue Ribbon for excellence. Surrounded by rolling Wiltshire farmland, The Pear Tree sits majestically in 7½ acres of tranquil grounds on the fringe of the Saxon village of Purton, famed for its unique twin towered Parish Church and the ancient hill fort of Ringsbury Camp. Each of the 17 individually and tastefully decorated bedrooms and suites is named after a character associated with the village, such as Anne Hyde, mother of Queen Mary II and Queen Anne. All are fitted to a high standard and have digital television, hairdryer, trouser press, a safe and a host of other luxuries. The award-winning conservatory restaurant overlooks colourful gardens and is the perfect setting in which to enjoy good English cuisine prepared with style and flair. Cirencester, Bath, Oxford, Avebury, Blenheim Palace, Sudeley Castle and the Cotswolds are all within easy reach.

Our inspector loved: *A friendly welcome with great food and lovely grounds.*

Directions: From M4 exit 16 follow signs to Purton and go through the village until reaching a triangle with Spar Grocers opposite. Turn right up the hill and the Pear Tree is on the second left after the Tithe Barn.

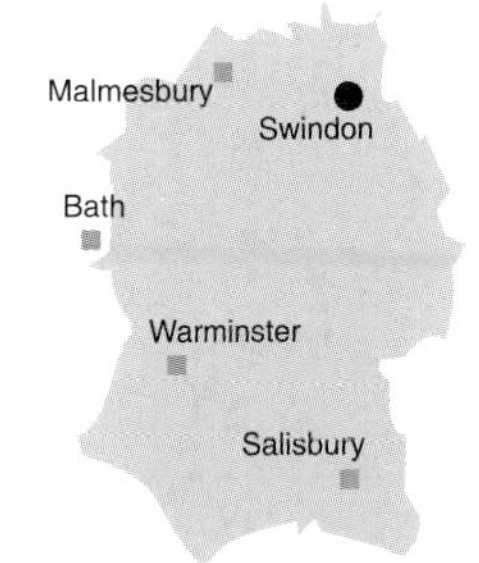

Web: www.johansens.com/peartree
E-mail: relax@peartreepurton.co.uk
Tel: 0870 381 8806
International: +44 (0)1793 772100
Fax: 01793 772369

Price Guide:
single £110
double/twin £110–£135
suites £135

17 M 50

Bishopstrow House

WARMINSTER, WILTSHIRE BA12 9HH

Bishopstrow House is the quintessential Georgian mansion. It combines the intimacy of a grand country hotel retreat with all the benefits of modern facilities and the luxury of the Bishopstrow Spa, which offers a superb range of beauty, fitness and relaxation therapies in addition to Perry Carson's hair styling. A Grade II listed building, Bishopstrow House was built in 1817 and has been sympathetically extended to include indoor and outdoor heated swimming pools, a gymnasium and a sauna. The attention to detail is uppermost in the library, drawing room and conservatory with their beautiful antiques and Victorian oil paintings. The bedrooms are grandly furnished; some have opulent marble bathrooms and whirlpool baths. Skilfully prepared modern British food is served in the Mulberry Restaurant, with lighter meals available in the Mulberry Bar and the conservatory which overlooks 27 acres of gardens. There is fly fishing on the hotel's private stretch of the River Wylye, golf at 5 nearby courses, riding, game and clay pigeon shooting. Longleat House, Wilton House, Stourhead, Stonehenge, Bath, Salisbury and Warminster are within easy reach.

Our inspector loved: *The Oval bedroom – spacious, luxurious and with a beautiful view.*

Directions: Bishopstrow House is south east of Warminster on the B3414 from London via the M3.

Web: www.johansens.com/bishopstrowhouse
E-mail: enquiries@bishopstrow.co.uk
Tel: 0870 381 8365
International: +44 (0)1985 212312
Fax: 01985 216769

Price Guide:
single £99
double/twin £160–£245
suite from £330

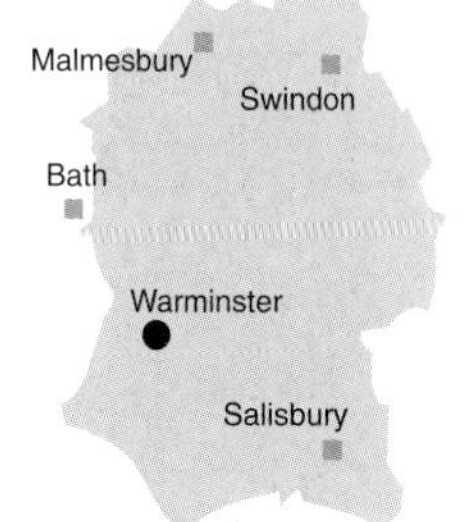

THE ELMS

ABBERLEY, WORCESTERSHIRE WR6 6AT

Built in 1710 by a pupil of Sir Christopher Wren, and converted into a country house hotel in 1946, The Elms has achieved an international reputation for excellence spanning the past half century. Standing impressively between Worcester and Tenbury Wells, this fine Queen Anne mansion is surrounded by beautiful meadows, woodland, hop fields and orchards of cider apples and cherries of the Teme Valley, whose river runs crimson when in flood from bank-side soil tinged with red sandstone. Further to a careful refurbishment in 2005, each of the 16 main house and 5 coach house bedrooms has its own character and provides magnificent views across the landscaped gardens. Guests can enjoy pre-dinner drinks in a comfortable, panelled bar before adjourning to the handsomely furnished restaurant, awarded 2 Rosettes, to be served with sophisticated and imaginative dishes prepeared by Head Chef Daren Bale, complemented by fine wines. The surrounding countryside is ideal for walking, fishing, shooting, golf and horse racing. Within easy reach are the attractions of the market town of Tenbury Wells, Hereford with mappa mundi (oldest map in the world), Witley Court, Bewdley and the ancient city of Worcester with its cathedral, county cricket ground and porcelain factory.

Our inspector loved: *The whole setting: the building, the grounds and the view.*

Directions: From the M5, exit at junction 5 (Droitwich) or junction 6 (Worcester) then take the A443 towards Tenbury Wells. The Elms is 2 miles after Great Witley. Do not take Abberley village turning.

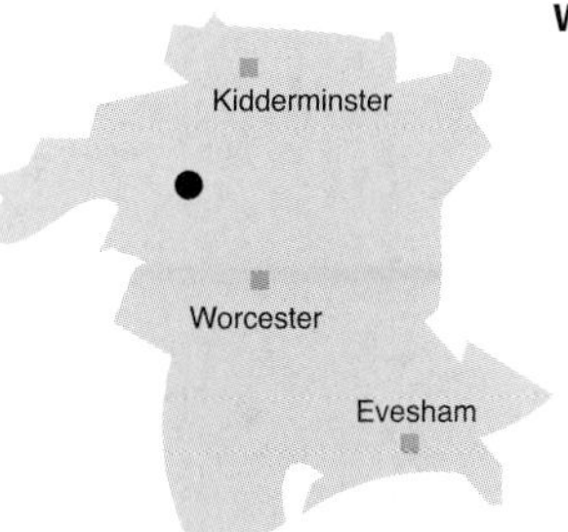

Web: www.johansens.com/elmsworcester
E-mail: info@theelmshotel.co.uk
Tel: 0870 381 8304
International: +44 (0)1299 896666
Fax: 01299 896804

Price Guide:
single £70–£145
double/twin £90–£180

The Broadway Hotel

THE GREEN, BROADWAY, WORCESTERSHIRE WR12 7AA

The Broadway Hotel stands proudly in the centre of the picturesque Cotswold village of Broadway where every stone evokes memories of Elizabethan England. Once used by the Abbots of Pershore, the hotel was formerly a 16th-century house, as can be seen by its architecture which combines the half timbers of the Vale of Evesham with the distinctive honey-coloured and grey stone of the Cotswolds. It epitomises a true combination of Olde Worlde charm and modern day amenities with friendly, efficient service. All bedrooms provide television, telephone and tea and coffee making facilities. Traditional English dishes and a peaceful ambience are offered in the beamed Courtyard Restaurant. There is an impressive variety of à la carte dishes complemented by good wines. The congenial Jockey Club bar is a pleasant place to enjoy a drink. The hotel overlooks the village green at the bottom of the main street where guests can browse through shops offering an array of fine antiques. On a clear day, 13 counties of England and Wales can be viewed from Broadway Tower. Snowhill, Burford, Chipping Campden, Bourton-on-the-Water, Stow-on-the-Wold and Winchcombe as well as larger Cheltenham, Worcester and Stratford are within easy reach.

Our inspector loved: *The glorious open wood burning stove in the galleried lounge.*

Directions: From London M40 to Oxford, A40 to Burford, A429 through Stow-on-the-Wold, then A44 to Broadway.

Web: www.johansens.com/broadwayworcestershire
E-mail: info@broadwayhotel.info
Tel: 0870 381 8381
International: +44 (0)1386 852401
Fax: 01386 853879

Price Guide:
single £80–£105
double £130–£165

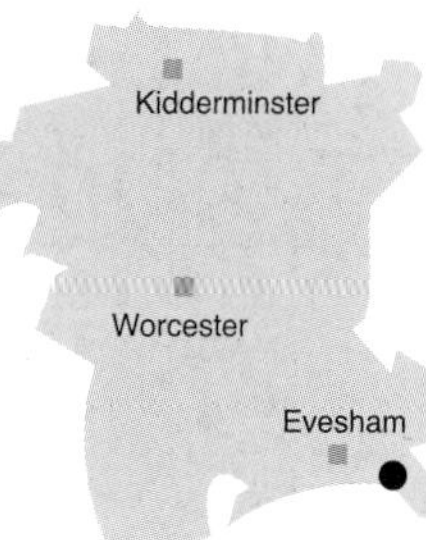

DORMY HOUSE

WILLERSEY HILL, BROADWAY, WORCESTERSHIRE WR12 7LF

Dormy House aims to be a home-away-from-home and with its cosy rooms, mouth-watering cuisine, postcard pretty landscape and above all, unstuffy service and ambience, guests will wish this was their own abode. This converted farmhouse dates back to the 17th century and the light stone walls, discreet alcoves and log fires create an inviting atmosphere, which is enhanced by the warm but unobtrusive welcome from the friendly staff. The 48 individually appointed bedrooms are decorated in a quintessential English style and feature rich fabrics, carved headboards and plump scatter cushions. Enjoy the locally-sourced produce served in The Dining Room or al fresco on the new terrace; the gastropub menu in the Barn Owl bar is popular. Activities abound and include relaxing in the sauna and steam room, a round of bar billiards in the games room, swinging a golf club or mallet on the 9-hole putting green or croquet lawn or walking in the circular routes. Cheltenham, Worcester and Stratford-Upon-Avon are nearby, alternatively there is the beautiful Cotswolds countryside on the doorstep. Broadway and Chipping Campden are popular daytrip options.

***Our inspector loved:** The cuisine, whether in the main dining room or al fresco on the new terrace.*

Directions: The hotel is ½ mile off the A44 between Moreton-in-Marsh and Broadway. Take the turning signposted Saintbury and the hotel is the first building on the left past the picnic area.

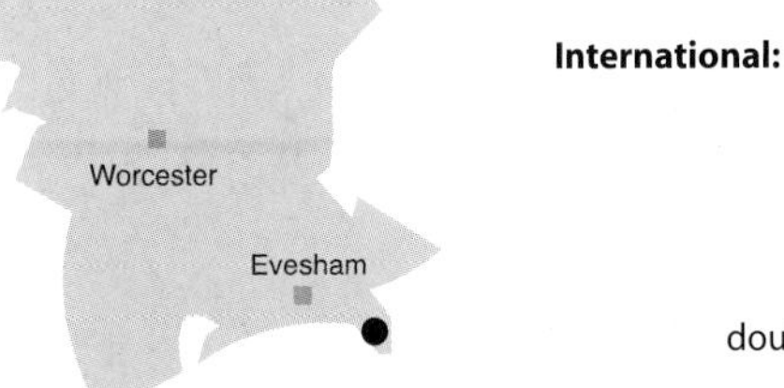

Web: www.johansens.com/dormyhouse
E-mail: reservations@dormyhouse.co.uk
Tel: 0870 381 8487
International: +44 (0)1386 852711
Fax: 01386 858636

Price Guide:
single £115
double/twin £155–£195
suite from £205

THE LYGON ARMS

BROADWAY, WORCESTERSHIRE WR12 7DU

Directions: Set in the heart of Broadway.

Web: www.johansens.com/lygonarms
E-mail: info@the-lygon-arms.co.uk
Tel: 0870 381 9190
International: +44 (0)1386 852255
Fax: 01386 858611

Price Guide:
single from £145
double/twin from £195
suite from £445

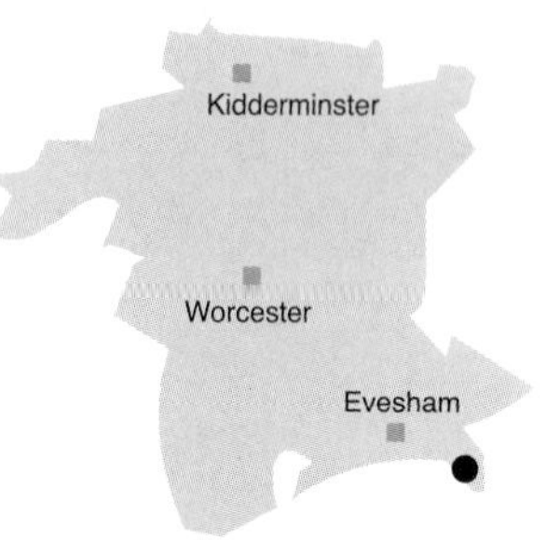

The Lygon Arms, a magnificent 16th-century building with numerous historical associations, stands in Broadway, acclaimed by many as the prettiest village in England, in the heart of the North Cotswolds. Over the years much restoration has been carried out, emphasising the outstanding period features, such as original 17th-century oak panelling and an ancient hidden stairway. All the bedrooms are individually and tastefully furnished and offer guests every modern luxury, combined with the elegance of an earlier age. The Great Hall, complete with a 17th-century minstrels' gallery and the smaller private dining rooms provide a fine setting for a well-chosen and imaginative menu. Conference facilities including the state-of-the-art Torrington Room are available for up to 80 participants. Guests can enjoy a superb range of leisure amenities in The Lygon Arms Spa, including all-weather tennis, indoor pool, spa bath, gymnasium, billiard room, beauty salons, steam room and saunas. Golf can be arranged locally. The many Cotswold villages, Stratford-upon-Avon, Oxford and Cheltenham are nearby, whilst Broadway itself is a paradise for the antique collector.

Our inspector loved: *The absolute wealth of literally hundreds of pieces of antique furniture in the hotel.*

Buckland Manor

BUCKLAND, NEAR BROADWAY, WORCESTERSHIRE WR12 7LY

The warm glow of Buckland Manor's golden Cotswold stone exterior blends beautifully with the colourful flowers and green shades of the glorious grounds, serving as an appetiser to visitors of the tranquil luxury and history inside those weather-beaten walls. A manor house on the site was first mentioned in the records of Gloucester Abbey in 600AD when the Abbot received it as a gift from Kynred, ruler of Mercia and chief king of the 7 kingdoms of England. Managed by Nigel Power, Buckland retains gracious living and tradition, with the addition of all modern comforts and best service. Guests can relax before log fires in 2 delightfully decorated lounges, one with lovely panelling and a beamed ceiling. The 13 excellently decorated en-suite bedrooms are furnished with luxury fittings and accessories. Some have four-poster beds and fireplaces and all bathrooms use water drawn from the Manor's own spring. Views over the grounds with their small waterfalls, outdoor pool, tennis courts, putting green and croquet lawns are spectacular. The dining room is an oasis of calm, and chef Adrian Jarrad prepares delicious, award-winning cuisine. Broadway Golf Club, Cheltenham race course, Stratford, Stow-on-the-Wold, Warwick and Blenheim are nearby. Buckland Manor is a member of Relais & Châteaux hotels.

Our inspector loved: *The glory of the gardens and the mellow yellow Cotswold stone.*

Directions: From the M40, exit at junction 8. Take the A40 to Burford, the A424 to Broadway and then the B4632 signposted Winchcombe to Buckland.

Web: www.johansens.com/bucklandmanor
E-mail: info@bucklandmanor.co.uk
Tel: 0870 381 9175
International: +44 (0)1386 852626
Fax: 01386 853557

Price Guide:
single £240-£430
double £250-£440

Brockencote Hall

CHADDESLEY CORBETT, NR KIDDERMINSTER, WORCESTERSHIRE DY10 4PY

The Brockencote estate consists of 70 acres of landscaped grounds surrounding a magnificent hall. There is a gatehouse, half-timbered dovecote, lake, some fine European and North American trees and an elegant conservatory. The estate dates back over three centuries and the style of the building reflects the changes which have taken place in fashion and taste. The hotel has been awarded 3 AA Red Stars, 4 RAC dining awards and is Heart of England Tourist Board Midlands Hotel of the Year silver award 2004. At present, the interior combines classical architectural features with contemporary creature comforts. As in most country houses, each of the bedrooms is different: all have their own character, complemented by tasteful furnishings and décor. The friendly staff provide a splendid service under the supervision of owners Alison and Joseph Petitjean. The Hall specialises in traditional French cuisine with occasional regional and seasonal specialities. Brockencote Hall is an ideal setting for those seeking peace and quiet in an unspoilt corner of the English countryside. Located a few miles south of Birmingham, it is convenient for business people and sightseers alike and makes a fine base for touring historic Worcestershire. Special rates available Sunday to Thursday.

Our inspector loved: *The beautifully panelled "library", dining and meeting room and its outlook over the grounds.*

Directions: Exit 4 from M5 or exit 1 from M42 (southbound). Brockencote Hall is set back from A448 at Chaddesley Corbett between Bromsgrove and Kidderminster.

Web: www.johansens.com/brockencotehall
E-mail: info@brockencotehall.com
Tel: 0870 381 8382
International: +44 (0)1562 777876
Fax: 01562 777872

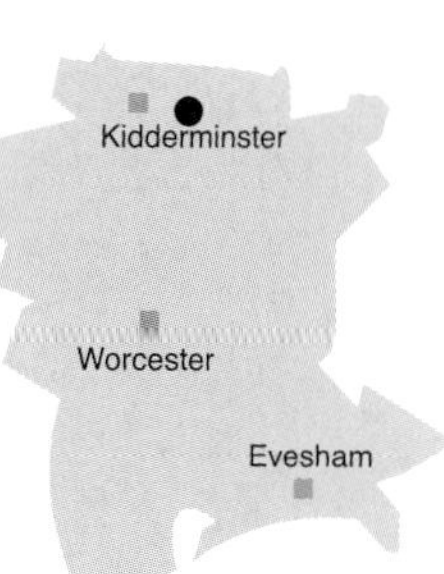

Price Guide:
single £89–£149.50
double/twin £116–£180

THE EVESHAM HOTEL

COOPER'S LANE, OFF WATERSIDE, EVESHAM, WORCESTERSHIRE WR11 1DA

It is the somewhat unconventional atmosphere at the Evesham Hotel that stays in the memory. Originally a Tudor farmhouse, the hotel was extended and converted into a Georgian mansion house in 1809. Unusually, it combines an award-winning welcome for families with the relaxed but efficient style required by business users. For the past 30 years it has been successfully run by the Jenkinson family. Each of the 40 en-suite bedrooms is furnished complete with a teddy bear and a toy duck for the bath. The restaurant offers delicious cuisine from a very imaginative and versatile menu, accompanied by a somewhat unique "Euro-sceptic" wine list (everything but French and German!) offering 100 different grape varieties. The drinks selection is an amazing myriad. The indoor swimming pool has a seaside theme. The peace of the 2½ acre garden belies the hotel's proximity to the town – a 5-minute walk away. In the gardens are 6 300-year-old mulberry trees and a magnificent cedar of Lebanon, planted in 1809. The hotel is a good base from which to explore the Cotswolds, Stratford-upon-Avon and the Severn Valley. Closed at Christmas.

Our inspector loved: *So much! The atmosphere, the themed bedrooms (safari, Egyptian, Chinese etc) the "saucy seaside" swimming pool, the food, the unique wine list and range of drinks...*

Directions: Cooper's Lane lies just off Waterside (the River Avon).

Kidderminster

Worcester

Evesham

Web: www.johansens.com/evesham
E-mail: reception@eveshamhotel.com
Tel: 0870 381 8510
International: +44 (0)1386 765566
Fax: 01386 765443

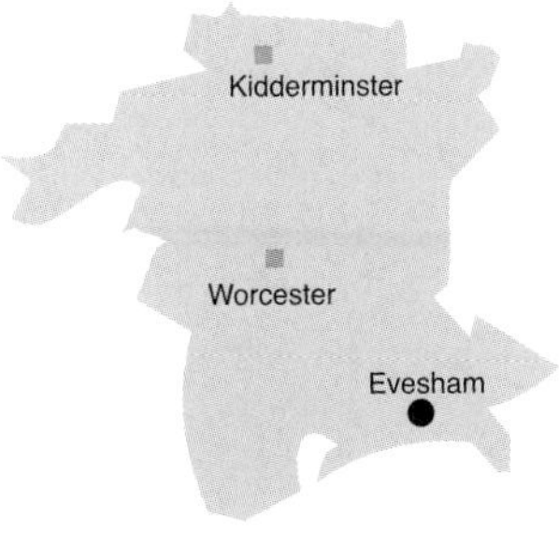

Price Guide:
single £78–£92

double/twin £124
family suite £168

Wood Norton Hall

WOOD NORTON, EVESHAM, WORCESTERSHIRE WR11 4WN

Directions: The hotel stands on the A44 Worcester Road, 3 miles north of the town centre.

Web: www.johansens.com/woodnortonhall
E-mail: info@wnhall.co.uk
Tel: 0870 381 9154
International: +44 (0)1386 425780
Fax: 01386 425781

Price Guide:
single £130-£230
double/twin £150-£200
suite £200-£230

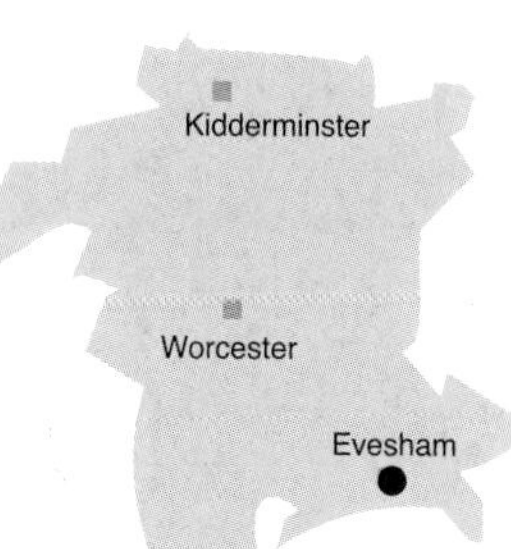

Wood Norton Hall is a glorious Grade II listed Victorian country house standing in 170 acres of beautiful Worcestershire countryside. A short drive from the historic market town of Evesham, 8 miles from Broadway and the Cotswolds with Stratford-upon-Avon only 15 miles away. French connections date back to 1872 and culminated in the wedding of Princess Louise of Orléans and Prince Charles of Bourbon in 1907. Original fleur-de-lys carved oak panelling lines the walls; grand fireplaces, elegant furniture and beautiful tapestries add comfort and colour. The en-suite rooms are furnished to the highest standards. The ground floor public rooms reflect the grandeur of the Victorian era with voluptuous window drapes framing views to the Vale of Evesham and the River Avon. The award-winning Le Duc's Restaurant provides the perfect ambience to savour a fine culinary tradition. The hall has 8 rooms suitable for conferences and private banquets and is an ideal venue for incentive programmes. Extensive leisure facilities include a billiard room, fitness suite and golf at a nearby international course.

Our inspector loved: *The magnificent oak panelling and banisters throughout the main building.*

The Cottage in the Wood

HOLYWELL ROAD, MALVERN WELLS, WORCESTERSHIRE WR14 4LG

The Malvern Hills, once the home and inspiration for England's great composer, Sir Edward Elgar, are the setting for The Cottage in the Wood. With its spectacular outlook across the Severn Valley, this unique hotel won acclaim from the Daily Mail for having the best view in England. The main house was originally the Dower House to the Blackmore Park estate and accommodation is offered here and in Beech Cottage, an old scrumpy house – and the magnificent new building, "The Pinnacles", named after the hill that rises above, which houses 19 of the traditional-styled bedrooms, many with patios or balconies and giving the best view of all. Owned and run by 2 generations of the Pattin family, the atmosphere is genuinely warm and relaxing. A regularly changing modern English menu is complemented by an almost obsessional wine list of 600 bins. If this causes any over-indulgence, guests can walk to the tops of the Malvern Hills direct from the hotel grounds. Good touring base for the Cotswolds, Forest of Dean, black and white villages and many historic houses and castles. Nearby are the Three Counties Showground and the Cathedral cities of Worcester, Gloucester and Hereford.

***Our inspector loved:** Enjoying the food and the relaxing décor in the dining room while taking in the panoramic view.*

Directions: 3 miles south of Great Malvern on A449, turn into Holywell Road by post box and hotel sign. Hotel is 250 yards on right.

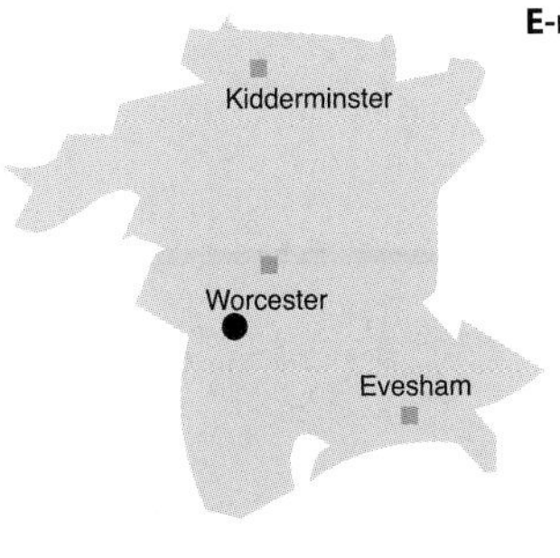

Web: www.johansens.com/cottageinthewood
E-mail: reception@cottageinthewood.co.uk
Tel: 0870 381 8452
International: +44 (0)1684 575859
Fax: 01684 560662

Kidderminster
Worcester
Evesham

Price Guide:
single £79–£105
double/twin £99–£175

WILLERBY MANOR HOTEL

WELL LANE, WILLERBY, HULL, EAST YORKSHIRE HU10 6ER

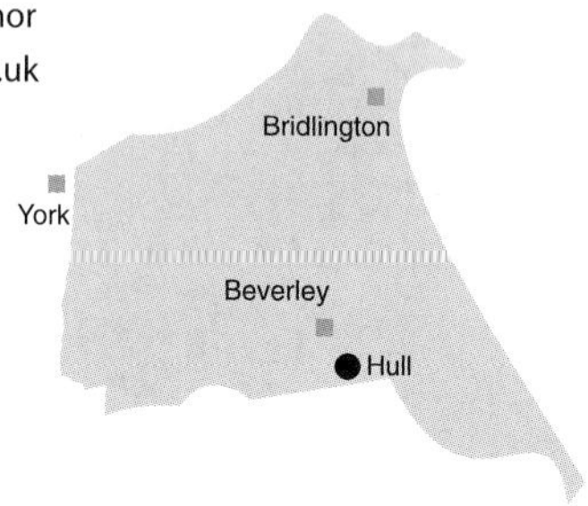

Originally the home of the Edwardian shipping merchant, Sir Henry Salmon, Willerby Manor was bought in the early 1970s by John Townend, a Wine Merchant from Hull. The elegance of the hotel, as it stands today, is testament to the careful work of the Townend family over the years. Furnished in a stylish manner, the public rooms are the essence of comfort. The 50 bedrooms are beautifully decorated with colour co-ordinated fabrics and soft furnishings. Every modern amenity is provided as well as an array of thoughtful extras such as fresh floral arrangements. Restaurant Icon serves modern English food, which is complemented by an extensive well-chosen wine list from the House of Townend. A more informal ambience pervades the Everglades Brasserie where guests may savour bistro-style meals and beverages. Fitness enthusiasts will be delighted with the well-equipped Health Club which includes a 19 metre swimming pool, spacious gymnasium, whirlpool spa bath, an exercise studio with daily classes and a beauty treatment room. The hotel is in a convenient location for those wishing to explore the cities of Hull and York.

Our inspector loved: *Having a relaxing swim in the large pool before dinner.*

Directions: Take the M62 towards Hull, which runs into the A63, turn off onto the A164 in the direction of Beverley. Follow the signs to Willerby and then Willerby Manor.

Web: www.johansens.com/willerbymanor
E-mail: willerbymanor@bestwestern.co.uk
Tel: 0870 381 8998
International: +44 (0)1482 652616
Fax: 01482 653901

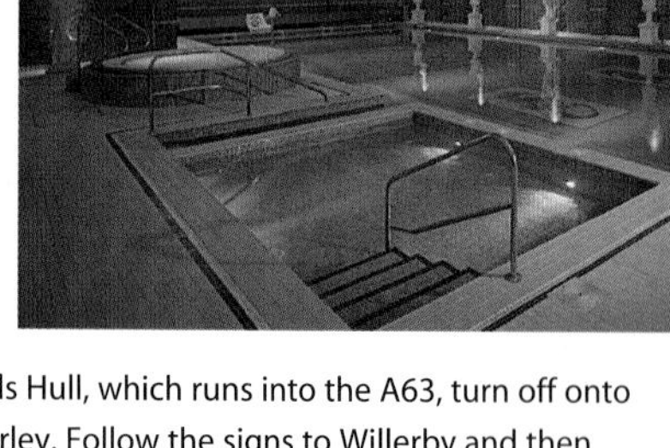

Price Guide:
single £52–£104
double/twin £82–£133

50 400 SPA

THE DEVONSHIRE ARMS COUNTRY HOUSE HOTEL

BOLTON ABBEY, SKIPTON, NORTH YORKSHIRE BD23 6AJ

The Devonshire reflects its charming setting in the Yorkshire Dales: a welcome escape from a busy and crowded world, peace and quiet, beautiful countryside – the perfect place in which to relax. The hotel is owned by the Duke and Duchess of Devonshire and is set in rolling parkland on their 30,000-acre Bolton Abbey Estate in the Yorkshire Dales National Park. The Dowager Duchess of Devonshire personally supervises the decoration of the interiors which include antiques and paintings from their family home at Chatsworth. Fine dining led by Michelin Star Executive Head Chef Michael Wignall in the elegant Burlington Restaurant is complemented by an outstanding award-winning wine list. Alternatively there is the less informal atmosphere of The Devonshire Brasserie and Bar with its lively décor and contemporary art. The Devonshire Club housed in a converted 17th-century barn offers a full range of leisure, health and beauty therapy facilities. There is plenty to do and see on the hotel's doorstep from exploring the ruins of the 12th-century Augustinian Bolton Priory to fly fishing on the river Wharfe. Managing Director, Jeremy Rata, together with General Manager, Eamonn Elliott, lead an enthusiastic team committed to providing a high standard of service and hospitality.

Our inspector loved: *The unique glass-fronted wine rooms offering a choice of over 2000 bins of fine and rare wines.*

Directions: Off the A59 Skipton–Harrogate road at junction with the B6160

Web: www.johansens.com/devonshirearms
E-mail: reservations@thedevonshirearms.co.uk
Tel: 0870 381 8480
International: +44 (0)1756 718111
Fax: 01756 710564

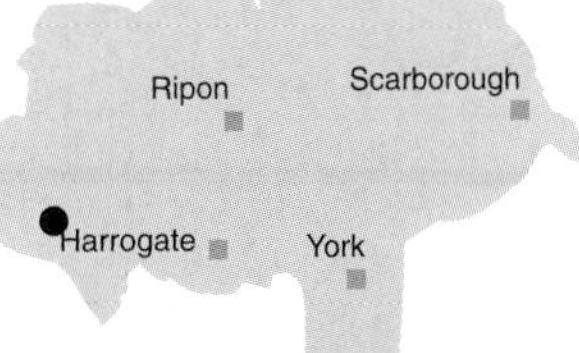

Price Guide:
single £165–£350
double/twin £195–£350
suite £380

40 90 SPA

Grants Hotel

SWAN ROAD, HARROGATE, NORTH YORKSHIRE HG1 2SS

Towards the end of the last century, Harrogate became fashionable among the gentry, who came to "take the waters" of the famous spa. Today's visitors have one advantage over their Victorian counterparts – they can enjoy the hospitality of Grants Hotel, the creation of Pam and Peter Grant. Their friendly welcome, coupled with high standards of service, ensures a pleasurable stay. All bedrooms are attractively decorated and have en-suite bathrooms. Downstairs, guests can relax in the comfortable lounge or take refreshments out to the terrace gardens. Drinks and light meals are available at all times from Harry Grant's Bar and dinner is served in the French café-style Chimney Pots Bistro, complete with brightly coloured check blinds and cloths and lots of humorous Beryl Cook pictures. Cuisine is basically traditional rustic with a smattering of Oriental influence complemented by the mouth-watering home-made puddings. Located less than 5 minutes' walk from Harrogate's Conference and Exhibition Centre, Grants offers its own luxury meeting and syndicate rooms, the Herriot Suite. The Royal Pump Room Museum and the Royal Baths Assembly Rooms are nearby. Guests have free use of The Academy Health and Leisure Club. Super value breaks available.

Our inspector loved: *The Beryl Cook pictures in the Bistro.*

Directions: Swan Road is in the centre of Harrogate, off the A61 to Ripon.

Web: www.johansens.com/grants
E-mail: enquiries@grantshotel-harrogate.com
Tel: 0870 381 8562
International: +44 (0)1423 560666
Fax: 01423 502550

Price Guide:
single £99–£115
double/twin £110–£160
suites £168

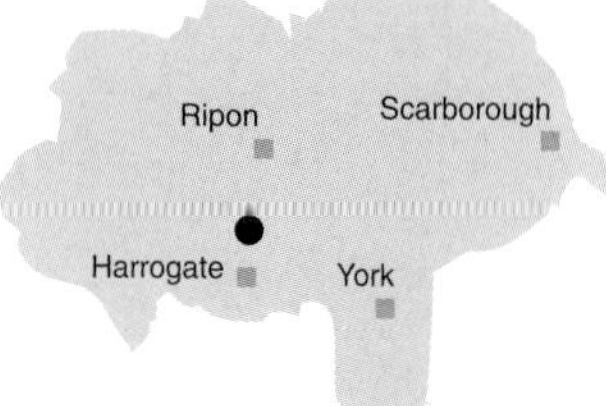

Rudding Park

FOLLIFOOT, HARROGATE, NORTH YORKSHIRE HG3 1JH

Rudding Park's award-winning hotel is just 2 miles from Harrogate town centre. Its setting is superb, surrounded by 230 acres of parkland. The hotel has an elegant façade and entrance, approached by a sweeping driveway. The Regency period house offers fine conference and banqueting rooms, whilst the adjoining hotel has been brilliantly designed and built to harmonise with the original mansion. A warm welcome awaits guests in the pleasant foyer, with its big fireplace and easy chairs. The bedrooms are spacious, with contemporary cherry wood furniture, relaxing colour schemes, many modern accessories and lovely views over the estate. Guests can relax in the Mackaness Drawing Room. The stylish 2 AA Rosette Clocktower Restaurant and Bar are inviting and on sunny days they extend onto the terrace. The food is delicious and the wine list extensive. Leisure facilities are excellent – there is an 18-hole par 72 parkland golf course which has played host to the PGA Mastercard tour series. The golf academy and driving range are ideal for lessons and practice. Hotel guests are welcome to use a local award-winning gym and health club.

Our inspector loved: *The enthusiastic and helpful staff with their attention to detail.*

Directions: Rudding Park is accessible from the A1 north or south, via the A661, just off the A658.

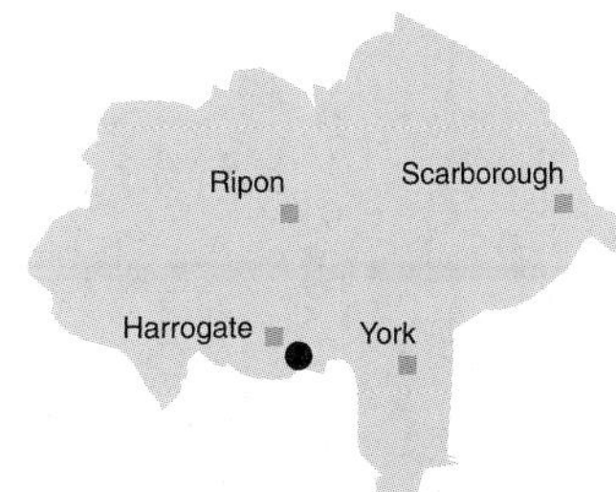

Web: www.johansens.com/ruddingpark
E-mail: sales@ruddingpark.com
Tel: 0870 381 8879
International: +44 (0)1423 871350
Fax: 01423 872286

Price Guide:
single £140–£170
double/twin £160–£190
suite £260–£320

Hob Green Hotel and Restaurant

MARKINGTON, HARROGATE, NORTH YORKSHIRE HG3 3PJ

Set in 870 acres of farm and woodland this charming "country house" hotel is only a short drive from the spa town of Harrogate and the ancient city of Ripon. The restaurant has an excellent reputation locally with only the finest fresh local produce being used, much of which is grown in the hotel's own garden. The interesting menus are complemented by an excellent choice of sensibly priced wines. All 12 bedrooms have been individually furnished and tastefully equipped to suit the most discerning guest. The drawing room and hall, warmed by log fires in cool weather, are comfortably furnished with the added attraction of fine antique furniture, porcelain and pictures. Situated in the heart of some of Yorkshire's most dramatic scenery, the hotel offers magnificent views of the valley beyond from all the main rooms. York is only 23 miles away. There is a wealth of cultural and historical interest nearby with Fountains Abbey and Studley Royal water garden and deer park a few minutes' drive. The Yorkshire Riding Centre is in Markington Village. Simply relax in this tranquil place where your every comfort is catered for. Special breaks available.

Our inspector loved: *Strolling around the large lovingly tended Victorian walled herb, vegetable and cutting flower garden.*

Directions: Turn left signposted Markington off the A61 Harrogate to Ripon road, the hotel is 1 mile after the village on the left.

Web: www.johansens.com/hobgreen
E-mail: info@hobgreen.com
Tel: 0870 381 8600
International: +44 (0)1423 770031
Fax: 01423 771589

Price Guide:
single £95–£115
double/twin £110–£145
suite £135–£165

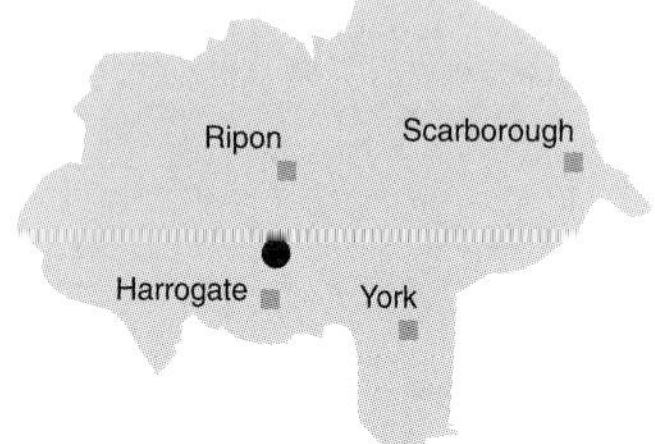

THE BOAR'S HEAD HOTEL

THE RIPLEY CASTLE ESTATE, HARROGATE, NORTH YORKSHIRE HG3 3AY

Imagine relaxing in a luxury hotel at the centre of a historic, private country estate in England's incredibly beautiful North Country. The Ingilby family who have lived in Ripley Castle for 28 generations invite you to enjoy their hospitality at The Boar's Head Hotel. There are 25 luxury bedrooms, individually decorated and furnished, most with king-sized beds. The restaurant's menu is outstanding, presented by a creative and imaginative kitchen brigade and complemented by a wide selection of reasonably priced, good quality wines. There is a welcoming bar serving traditional ales straight from the wood and popular bar meal selections. When staying at The Boar's Head, guests can enjoy complimentary access to the delightful walled gardens and grounds of Ripley Castle, which include the lakes and a deer park. A conference at Ripley is a different experience – using the idyllic meeting facilities available in the Castle, organisers and delegates alike will appreciate the peace and tranquillity of the location, which also offers opportunities for all types of leisure activity in the Deer Park.

Our inspector loved: *The historic Ripley Castle and the pretty village of Ripley.*

Directions: Ripley is very accessible, just 10 minutes from the conference town of Harrogate, 20 minutes from the motorway network and Leeds/Bradford Airport, and 40 minutes from the City of York.

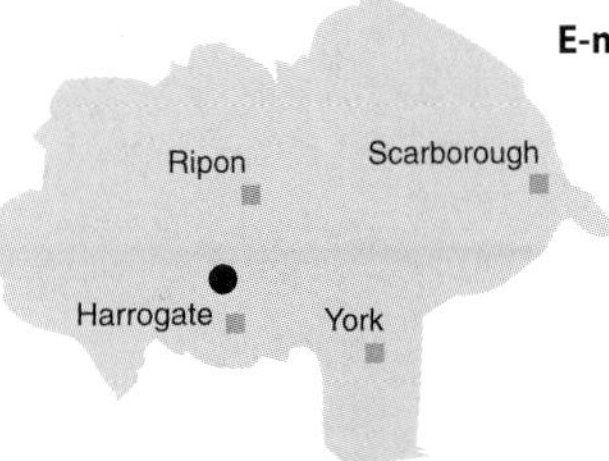

Web: www.johansens.com/boarsheadharrogate
E-mail: reservations@boarsheadripley.co.uk
Tel: 0870 381 8370
International: +44 (0)1423 771888
Fax: 01423 771509

Price Guide:
single £105–£130
double £125–£160

25 150

SIMONSTONE HALL

HAWES, NORTH YORKSHIRE DL8 3LY

Fine cuisine, comfort, peace and tranquillity combine with breathtaking scenery to make any stay at Simonstone Hall totally memorable. This former 18th-century hunting lodge has been lovingly restored and furnished with antiques to create an idyllic retreat for its guests.The hall stands in beautiful landscaped gardens with an adjacent 14,000 acres of grouse moors and upland grazing. Many period features have been retained such as the panelled dining room, mahogany staircase with ancestral stained glass windows and a lounge with ornamental fireplace and ceilings. The bedrooms are of the highest standards and offer every modern comfort including four-poster and sleigh beds. In the restaurant, guests savour the freshest local produce presented with flair and imagination, whilst enjoying stunning views across Upper Wensleydale. An excellent wine list is available to complement any dish. Traditional and Thai cuisine is served in the Game Tavern and The Orangery which provide a particularly warm and informal atmosphere. Simonstone Hall, with its fine views, is the perfect base for enjoying and exploring the hidden Yorkshire Dales. The area abounds with ancient castles, churches and museums. Hardraw Force, England's highest single drop waterfall, which can be heard from the gardens, is only a walk away.

Our inspector loved: *The wonderful setting with stunning views across Upper Wensleydale.*

Directions: Hawes is on A684. Turn north on Buttertubs Pass towards Muker. Simonstone Hall is ½ mile on the left.

Web: www.johansens.com/simonstonehall
E-mail: email@simonstonehall.demon.co.uk
Tel: 0870 381 8895
International: +44 (0)1969 667255
Fax: 01969 667741

Price Guide:
single £55–£100
double/twin £110–£180

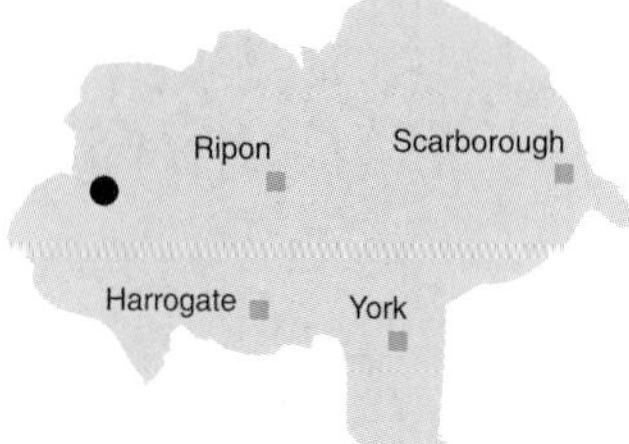

The Feversham Arms Hotel

HELMSLEY, NORTH YORKSHIRE YO62 5AG

This former mid-19th-century coaching inn, standing in the heart of an attractive market town nestling beneath the southern rim of the North Yorkshire moors, has been carefully redeveloped and furnished to create a relaxing retreat. The highest standards of hospitality and service are provided in a casual ambience where elements of the inn's past and present mingle in complete harmony. Mousey Thompson furniture and traditional soft leather sofas and armchairs feature comfortably next to Julia Burns' contemporary paintings. The 19 en-suite bedrooms, including 7 suites, are individually decorated and have every home-from-home facility. Dining is an experience: each dish is presented with flair and imagination, with the emphasis on game, lamb and the freshest of seafood from nearby Whitby. Guests can enjoy their meals in the lovely conservatory restaurant, in front of open fires in either of the delightfully decorated lounges or, on fine summer days, on the poolside terrace. As well as the outdoor pool the hotel has a tennis court. Places of interest nearby include Byland and Rievaulx Abbeys, Helmsley Castle, Castle Howard and Nunnington Hall.

Our inspector loved: *The unique dining experience in the conservatory restaurant, which overlooks the swimming pool and tennis court.*

Directions: From A1 take A64, then take the York north bypass (A1237) and then B1363. Alternatively, from A1 take A168 signposted Thirsk, then A170.

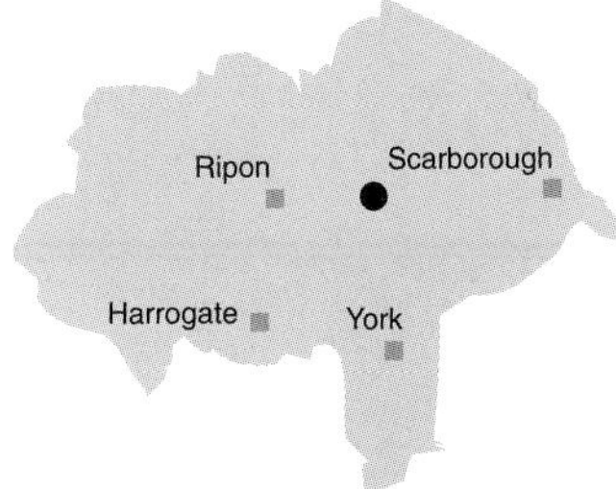

Web: www.johansens.com/fevershamarms
E-mail: info@fevershamarmshotel.com
Tel: 0870 381 9283
International: +44 (0)1439 770766
Fax: 01439 770346

Price Guide:
single £120–£190
double/twin £130–£160
suite £200

THE PHEASANT

HAROME, HELMSLEY, NORTH YORKSHIRE YO62 5JG

The Pheasant, rich in oak beams and open log fires, offers 2 types of accommodation, some in the hotel and some in a charming, 16th-century thatched cottage. The Binks family, who built the hotel and now own and manage it, have created a friendly atmosphere which is part of the warm Yorkshire welcome that awaits all guests. The bedrooms and suites are brightly decorated in an attractive cottage style, and are all complete with en-suite facilities. Traditional English cooking is the speciality of the restaurant; many of the dishes are prepared using local fresh fruit and vegetables. During summer, guests may relax on the terrace overlooking the pond. An indoor heated swimming pool is an added attraction. Other sporting activities available locally include swimming, riding, golf and fishing. York is a short drive away, as are a host of historic landmarks including Byland and Rievaulx Abbeys and Castle Howard of Brideshead Revisited fame. Also nearby is the magnificent North York Moors National Park. Dogs by arrangement. Closed Christmas, January and February.

***Our inspector loved:** The friendly and relaxed ambience in this family-run hotel.*

Directions: From Helmsley, take the A170 towards Scarborough; after ¼ mile turn right for Harome. The hotel is near the church in the village.

Web: www.johansens.com/pheasanthelmsley
Tel: 0870 381 8821
International: +44 (0)1439 771241
Fax: 01439 771744

Price Guide: (including 5-course dinner)
single £73–£80
double/twin £146–£160

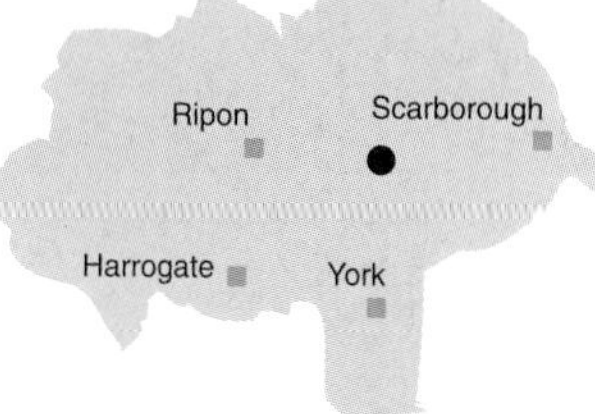

THE ROYAL HOTEL

ST NICHOLAS STREET, SCARBOROUGH, NORTH YORKSHIRE YO11 2HE

The AA and RAC 3 Star Royal Hotel has had a long and colourful history since its construction during the peak of Regency elegance in the 1830s, and remains a centrepiece overlooking the South Bay in England's oldest resort town. Many illustrious guests have passed through its doors including Winston Churchill, Charles Laughton and the playwright Alan Ayckbourn, all of whom have suites named after them. Offering a wide range of comfortable contemporary accommodation, en-suite rooms combine the modern and traditional and some have wonderful views over the harbour and the bay. A varied table d'hôte menu, with à la carte options, is served in the grand setting of the Dining Room, whilst traditional teas and light refreshments are on offer in the extensive lounges and Theatre Bar. A new continental-style café, Café Bliss, means visitors can enjoy a selection of delicacies indoors or al fresco. Once a spa town, Scarborough is close to the North Yorkshire Moors National Park and provides an excellent base for touring the local area, as well as enjoying its own features such as the Victorian Spa Complex.

Our inspector loved: *The original Regency Atrium with its elegant main staircase.*

Directions: From the A1/M1 take A64, continue to the town on Seamer Road. Turn onto Falsgrave towards the town centre. Turn right at the railway station then left at traffic lights and roundabout. The hotel is before the Town Hall.

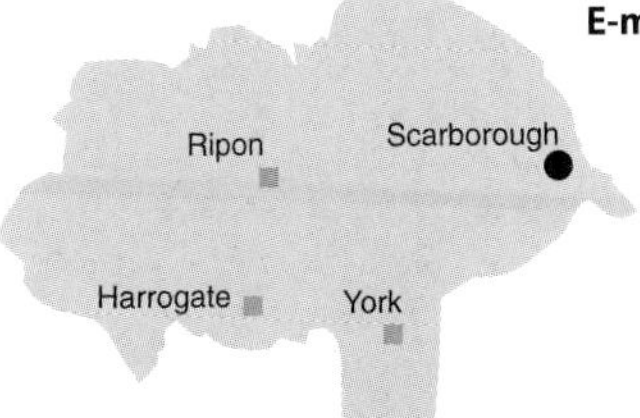

Web: www.johansens.com/royalscarborough
E-mail: royalhotel@englishrosehotels.co.uk
Tel: 0870 381 9277
International: +44 (0)1723 364333
Fax: 01723 371780

Price Guide:
single £65-£80
double £125-£185
suite £200-£350

HACKNESS GRANGE

NORTH YORK MOORS NATIONAL PARK, SCARBOROUGH, NORTH YORKSHIRE YO13 0JW

The attractive Georgian Hackness Grange country house lies at the heart of the dramatic North York Moors National Park – miles of glorious countryside with rolling moorland and forests. Set in acres of private grounds, overlooking a tranquil lake, home to many species of wildlife, Hackness Grange is a haven of peace and quiet for guests. There are charming bedrooms in the gardens, courtyard and the main house. For leisure activities, guests can enjoy 9-hole pitch 'n' putt golf, tennis and an indoor heated swimming pool. Hackness Grange is an ideal meeting location for companies wishing to have exclusive use of the hotel for VIP gatherings. The attractive Derwent Restaurant with its scenic views, is the setting for lunch and dinner. Here you will enjoy creatively prepared delicious cuisine, which is partnered by a wide choice of international wines. When you choose to stay at Hackness Grange you will find you have chosen well – a peaceful and relaxing location with so much to see and do: for example, visit Great Ayton, where Captain Cook first worked as a farm labourer.

Our inspector loved: *The ducks and wildlife around the lake.*

Directions: Take A64 York road until left turn to Seamer on to B1261, through to East Ayton and Hackness.

Web: www.johansens.com/hacknessgrange
E-mail: hacknessgrange@englishrosehotels.co.uk
Tel: 0870 381 8578
International: +44 (0)1723 882345
Fax: 01723 882391

Price Guide:
single from £65
double/twin £125–£180
suite from £190

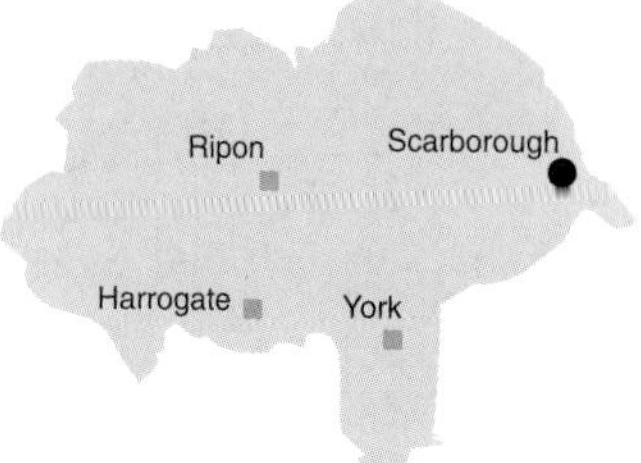

Wrea Head Country Hotel

SCALBY, NR SCARBOROUGH, NORTH YORKSHIRE YO13 0PB

Wrea Head Country Hotel is an elegant, beautifully refurbished Victorian country house built in 1881 and situated in 14 acres of wooded and landscaped grounds on the edge of the North York Moors National Park, just 3 miles from Scarborough. The house is furnished with antiques and paintings, and the oak-panelled front hall with its inglenook fireplace with blazing log fires in the winter, is very welcoming. All the bedrooms are individually decorated, with most having delightful views of the gardens. The elegant Four Seasons Restaurant is renowned for serving the best traditional English fare using fresh local produce and has a reputation for outstanding cuisine. There are attractive meeting rooms, each with natural daylight, ideal for private board meetings and training courses requiring privacy and seclusion. Scarborough is renowned for its cricket, music and theatre. Wrea Head is a perfect location from which to explore the glorious North Yorkshire coast and country, and special English Rose breaks are offered throughout the year.

Our inspector loved: *The large collection of Pietro Annigoni paintings in the main hall.*

Directions: Follow the A171 north from Scarborough, past the Scalby Village, until the hotel is signposted. Follow the road past the duck pond and then turn left up the drive.

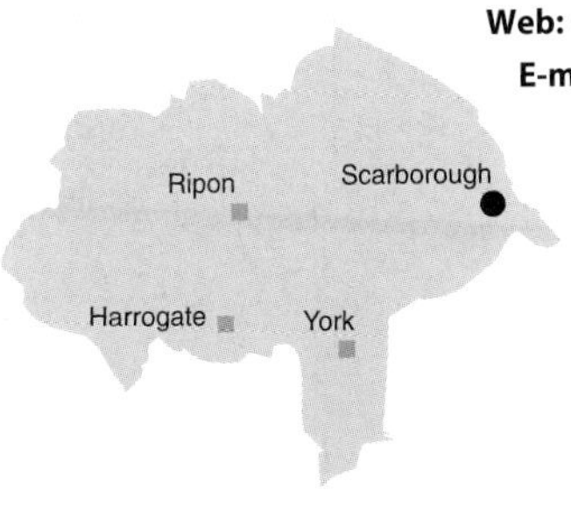

Ripon
Scarborough
Harrogate
York

Web: www.johansens.com/wreaheadcountry
E-mail: wreahead@englishrosehotels.co.uk
Tel: 0870 381 9012
International: +44 (0)1723 378211
Fax: 01723 355936

Price Guide:
single from £75
double/twin £130–£195
suite from £195

20 M 40

JUDGES COUNTRY HOUSE HOTEL

KIRKLEVINGTON HALL, KIRKLEVINGTON, YARM, NORTH YORKSHIRE TS15 9LW

Stunningly located within 31 acres of idyllic landscaped gardens and woodlands, this gracious country house hotel is a haven of peace. Its charm and welcoming atmosphere create a sense of intimacy, whilst the warmth of the hotel's luxurious interior design makes it perfect for relaxing and unwinding from the stresses of daily life. Beautiful public rooms are elegantly decorated with opulent fabrics, and guests are surrounded by books, stunning paintings and antiques. The sumptuous bedrooms are extremely comfortable; each includes a foot spa, and a pet goldfish on display. Some guest rooms have Jacuzzi baths and each evening there is a turndown service. Attention to detail and expertly chosen décor enhance the feeling of luxury. A mouth-watering 6-course meal is served in the Conservatory Restaurant, accompanied by the finest of wines. Private dining is available, perfect for parties or the family. The hotel's location makes it ideal for exploring the North East, whilst local attractions include the historic city of Durham, various castles and museums, the races at York and Sedgefield, Croft motor racing circuit and walking in the Cleveland Hills. Various adventure activities can also be organised including horse riding, canoeing, cycling, go karting, off roading and quad biking as well as many others.

Our inspector loved: *The friendly, attentive staff and pet goldfish in every bedroom.*

Directions: From the A19 take the A67 Yarm exit, Judges is 1½ miles along the A67 on the left after Kirklevington village.

Web: www.johansens.com/judges
E-mail: enquiries@judgeshotel.co.uk
Tel: 0870 381 9165
International: +44 (0)1642 789000
Fax: 01642 782878

Price Guide:
single £139–£153
double/twin £164–£179

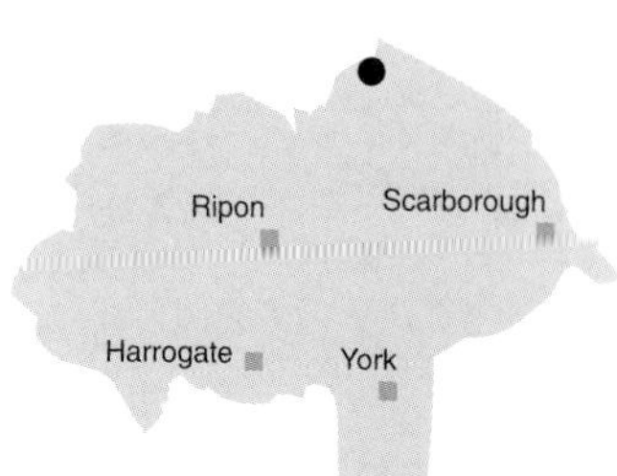

The Grange Hotel

1 CLIFTON, YORK, NORTH YORKSHIRE YO30 6AA

Set near the ancient city walls, just a short walk from the world-famous Minster, this sophisticated Regency town house has been carefully restored and its spacious rooms richly decorated. Beautiful stone-flagged floors lead to the classically styled reception rooms. The flower-filled Morning Room is welcoming, with its deep sofas and blazing fire in the winter months. Double doors between the panelled library and drawing room can be opened up to create a dignified venue for parties, wedding receptions, meetings or business entertaining. Prints, antiques and English chintz in the bedrooms reflect the proprietor's careful attention to detail. The Ivy Restaurant has an established reputation for first-class gastronomy, incorporating the best in modern British and European cuisine. The Seafood Bar has two murals depicting racing scenes. The Brasserie is open for lunch Monday to Saturday and dinner every night until after the theatre closes most evenings. For conferences, a computer and fax are available as well as secretarial services. Brimming with history, York's list of attractions includes the National Railway Museum, the Jorvik Viking Centre and the medieval Shambles.

Our inspector loved: *The stunning orchid arrangement in the York stone-paved front hall.*

Directions: The Grange Hotel is on the A19 York–Thirsk road, 400 yards from the city centre.

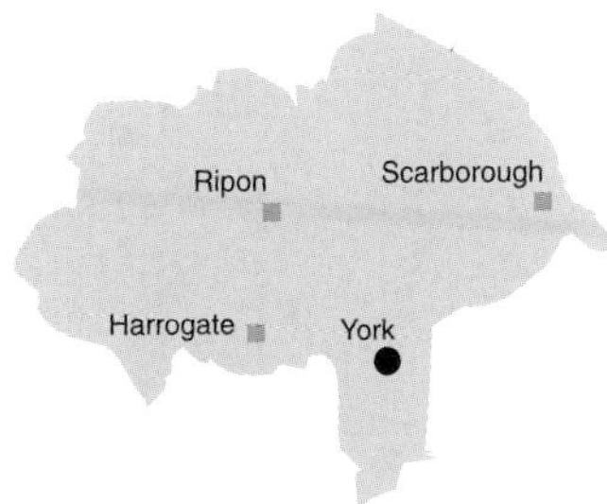

Web: www.johansens.com/grangeyork
E-mail: info@grangehotel.co.uk
Tel: 0870 381 8561
International: +44 (0)1904 644744
Fax: 01904 612453

Price Guide:
single £115–£170
double/twin £145–£210
suite £260

MIDDLETHORPE HALL HOTEL, RESTAURANT & SPA

BISHOPTHORPE ROAD, YORK, NORTH YORKSHIRE YO23 2GB

Middlethorpe Hall is a delightful William III house, built in 1699 for Thomas Barlow, a wealthy merchant and was for a time the home of Lady Mary Wortley Montagu, the 18th-century diarist. The house has been immaculately restored by Historic House Hotels, who have decorated and furnished it in its original style and elegance. There are beautifully designed bedrooms and suites in the main house and the adjacent 18th-century courtyard and a health and fitness spa with pool and treatment rooms. The restaurant, which has been awarded 3 Rosettes from the AA, offers the best in contemporary English cooking. Middlethorpe Hall, which was awarded by the York Tourism Bureau, Hotel of the Year 2005, stands in 26 acres of parkland and overlooks York Racecourse yet is only 1½ miles from the medieval city of York with its fascinating museums, restored streets and world-famous Minster. From Middlethorpe you can visit Yorkshire's famous country houses, like Castle Howard, Beningbrough and Harewood, the ruined Abbeys of Fountains and Rievaulx and explore the magnificent Yorkshire Moors. Helmsley, Whitby and Scarborough are nearby. Special breaks available.

Our inspector loved: *The Spa which is situated in the adjacent cottages and the organic walled garden.*

Directions: Take A64 (T) off A1 (T) near Tadcaster, follow signs to York West, then smaller signs to Bishopthorpe.

Web: www.johansens.com/middlethorpehall
E-mail: info@middlethorpe.com
Tel: 0870 381 8731
International: +44 (0)1904 641241
Fax: 01904 620176

Price Guide:
single £115–£160
double/twin £185–£310
suite from £260–£400

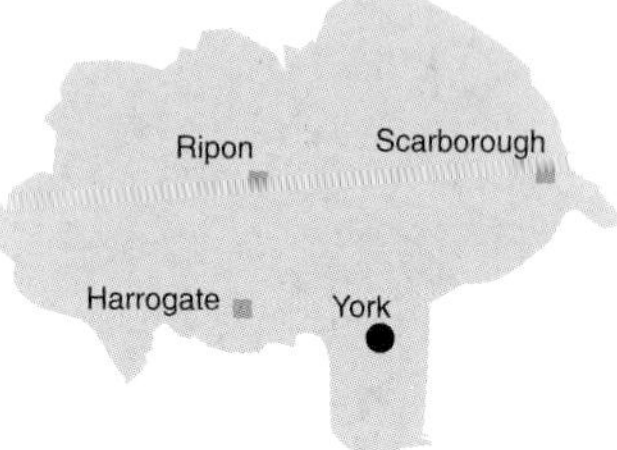

29 56 8 SPA

THE WORSLEY ARMS HOTEL

HOVINGHAM, NEAR YORK, NORTH YORKSHIRE YO62 4LA

The Worsley Arms is an attractive stone-built Georgian spa hotel in the heart of Hovingham, a pleasant and unspoilt Yorkshire village with a history stretching back to Roman times. The hotel, which overlooks the village green and is set amid delightful gardens, was built in 1841 by the baronet Sir William Worsley and is now owned and personally run by Anthony and Sally Finn. Hovingham Hall, home of the Worsley family and birthplace of the Duchess of Kent, is nearby. Elegant furnishings and open fires create a welcoming atmosphere. The spacious sitting rooms are an ideal place to relax over morning coffee or afternoon tea. The award-winning restaurant offers creatively prepared dishes, including game from the estate, cooked and presented with flair. Guests can visit the wine cellar to browse or choose their wine for dinner. The Cricketers bar provides a more informal setting to enjoy modern cooking at its best. The en-suite bedrooms range in size some with views over the pretty village green. There is plenty to do nearby, including tennis, squash, jogging, golf and scenic walks along nature trails. Guests can explore the beautiful Dales, the North Yorkshire Moors and the spectacular coastline or discover the abbeys, stately homes and castles nearby. Special breaks available.

Our inspector loved: *Walking around the wine cellar choosing the wine for dinner.*

Directions: Hovingham is on the B1257, 8 miles from Malton and Helmsley. 20 minutes north of York.

Web: www.johansens.com/worsleyarms
E-mail: worsleyarms@aol.com
Tel: 0870 381 9011
International: +44 (0)1653 628234
Fax: 01653 628130

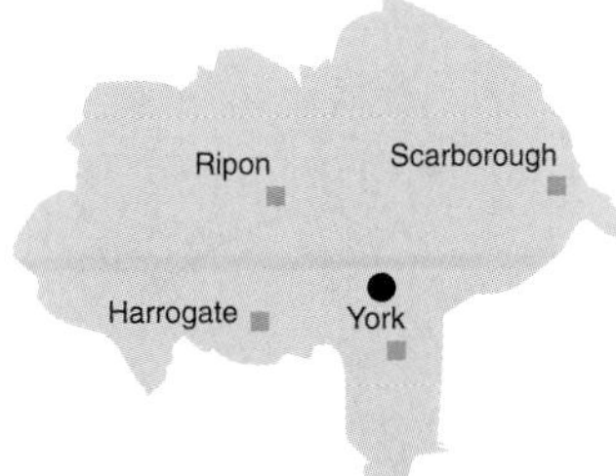

Price Guide:
single £80–£95
double/twin £110–£175

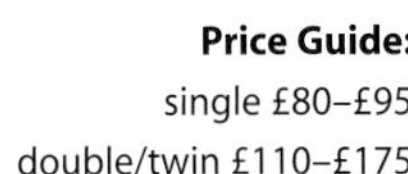

Monk Fryston Hall Hotel

MONK FRYSTON, NORTH YORKSHIRE LS25 5DU

A short distance from the A1 and almost equal distance from Leeds and York, this mellow old manor house hotel, built in 1740, is ideal for tourists, business people and those looking for an invitingly secluded spot for a weekend break. The mullioned and transom windows and the family coat of arms above the doorway are reminiscent of Monk Fryston's fascinating past. In 1954 the Hall was acquired by the late Duke of Rutland, who has created an elegant contemporary hotel, whilst successfully preserving the strong sense of heritage and tradition. The bedrooms, ranging from cosy to spacious, have private en-suite bathrooms and are appointed to a high standard. A generous menu offers a wide choice of traditional English dishes with something to suit all tastes. From the Hall, the terrace leads down to an ornamental Italian garden which overlooks a lake and is a delight to see at any time of year. Wedding receptions are held in the oak-panelled Haddon Room with its splendid Inglenook fireplace. The Rutland Room provides a convenient venue for meetings and private parties. York is 17 miles, Leeds 13 miles and Harrogate 18 miles away.

***Our inspector loved:** The oak-panelled front hall and bar with open fires in the winter.*

Directions: The Hall is 3 miles off the A1, on the A63 towards Selby in the centre of Monk Fryston.

Web: www.johansens.com/monkfrystonhall
E-mail: reception@monkfryston-hotel.co.uk
Tel: 0870 381 8741
International: +44 (0)1977 682369
Fax: 01977 683544

Price Guide:
single £95–£165
double/twin £120–£180

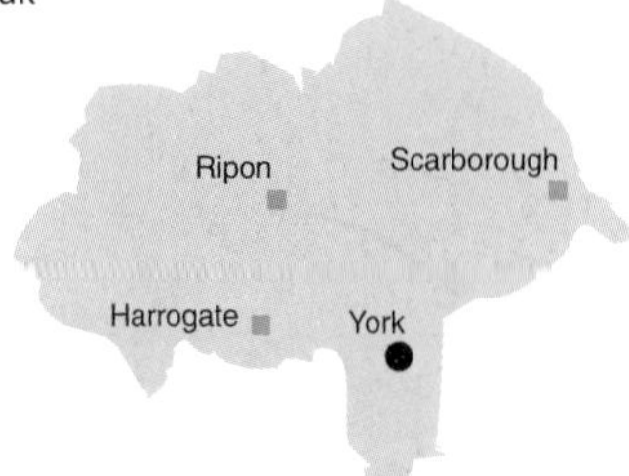

WHITLEY HALL HOTEL

ELLIOTT LANE, GRENOSIDE, SHEFFIELD, SOUTH YORKSHIRE S35 8NR

Carved into the keystone above one of the doors is the date 1584, denoting the start of Whitley Hall's lengthy country house tradition. In the bar is a priest hole, which may explain the local belief that a tunnel links the house with the nearby 11th-century church. In the 18th century, the house was a prestigious boarding school, with Gothic pointed arches and ornamentation added later by the Victorians. Attractively refurbished, Whitley Hall is now a fine hotel with all the amenities required by today's visitors. Stone walls and oak panelling combine with richly carpeted floors and handsome decoration. A sweeping split staircase leads to the bedrooms, all of which have en- suite bathrooms. Varied yet unpretentious cooking is served in generous portions and complemented by a wide choice from the wine cellar, including many clarets and ports. Peacocks strut around the 20 acre grounds, which encompass rolling lawns, mature woodland and 2 ornamental lakes. Banquets and private functions can be held in the conference suite.

Our inspector loved: *The peacocks fanning their tails in the garden.*

Directions: Leave M1 at junction 35, following signs for Chapeltown (A629), go down hill and turn left into Nether Lane. Go right at traffic lights, then left opposite Arundel pub, then immediately right into Whitley Lane. At fork turn right into Elliott Lane; hotel is on left.

Web: www.johansens.com/whitleyhall
E-mail: reservations@whitleyhall.com
Tel: 0870 381 8993
International: +44 (0)114 245 4444
Fax: 0114 245 5414

Price Guide:
single £70–£110
double/twin £92–£135

20 70

Holdsworth House Hotel & Restaurant

HOLDSWORTH, HALIFAX, WEST YORKSHIRE HX2 9TG

Holdsworth House is a beautiful grade II Jacobean manor house, 3 miles north of Halifax in the heart of Yorkshire's West Riding. Built in 1633, it was acquired by the Pearson family over 40 years ago. With care, skill and professionalism they have created a hotel and restaurant of considerable repute. The interior, with its polished oak panelling and open fireplaces, has been carefully preserved and embellished with fine antiques and paintings. The comfortable lounge opens onto a pretty courtyard and overlooks the parterre and gazebo. The restaurant, with its 2 AA Rosettes, comprises 3 beautifully furnished rooms, ideal for private dinner parties. Exciting modern English and continental cuisine is meticulously prepared and presented using local produce, complemented by a thoughtfully compiled wine list. Each cosy bedroom has its own style, from the split-level suites to the interconnecting rooms for families. This is the perfect base from which to explore the Pennines, the Yorkshire Dales and Haworth, home of the Brontë family. Weekend breaks available.

Our inspector loved: *The cosy, oak-panelled, award-winning restaurant.*

Directions: From M1 Jct42 take M62 west to Jct26. Follow A58 to Halifax (ignore signs to town centre). At Burdock Way roundabout take A629 to Keighley; after 1½ miles go right into Shay Lane; hotel is a mile on right.

Web: www.johansens.com/holdsworthhouse
E-mail: info@holdsworthhouse.co.uk
Tel: 0870 381 8603
International: +44 (0)1422 240024
Fax: 01422 245174

Price Guide:
single £97.50–£155
double/twin £140 –£190
suite £155–£190

42 The Calls

42 THE CALLS, LEEDS, WEST YORKSHIRE LS2 7EW

42 the Calls is a remarkable, award-winning hotel situated in the heart of Leeds, yet peacefully set in a quiet location alongside the river. Originally a corn mill, this unique hotel takes advantage of many of the original features of the mill, incorporating impressive beams, girders and old machinery into the décor. Each of the 41 bedrooms is imaginatively decorated in an individual style using beautiful fabrics and expert interior design to create a wonderful sense of harmony. Handmade beds and armchairs, a plethora of eastern rugs and extremely lavish bathrooms enhance the feeling of comfort and luxury including interactive plasma television screens. There is an excellent choice of restaurants in the vicinity, including the world renowned Michelin starred Pool Court at 42 next door and the stylish Brasserie 44. The hotel does offer round the clock room service or guests may dine in 2 of the city's restaurants and simply sign their lunch or dinner to their hotel bill. Shops, offices, galleries and theatres are all within a few minutes' walk from the hotel.

Our inspector loved: *The innovative design of the hotel and the privacy hatches for room service.*

Directions: M621, jct 3. Follow City Centre and West Yorkshire Playhouse signs then turn left after Tetley's Brewery then left again onto the City Centre Loop, following City signs. Take jct 15 and The Calls is immediately ahead.

Leeds
Bradford
Halifax
Huddersfield

Web: www.johansens.com/42thecalls
E-mail: hotel@42thecalls.co.uk
Tel: 0870 381 8737
International: +44 (0)113 244 0099
Fax: 0113 234 4100

Price Guide:
single £124–£194
double/twin £163–£249
suite from £238

41 75

CHEVIN COUNTRY PARK HOTEL

YORKGATE, OTLEY, WEST YORKSHIRE LS21 3NU

A quite unique hotel – you would probably need to travel to Scandinavia to discover a similar hotel to Chevin Park. Built entirely of Finnish logs and surrounded by birch trees, it is set in 50 acres of lake and woodland in the beauty spot of Chevin Forest Park. The spacious, carefully designed bedrooms are tastefully furnished with pine and some have patio doors leading to the lakeside gardens. In addition, there are several luxury lodges tucked away in the woods, providing alternative accommodation to the hotel bedrooms. Imaginative and appetising meals are served in the beautiful balconied restaurant, which overlooks the lake. Chevin Lodge offers conference facilities in the Woodlands Suite which is fully equipped for all business requirements. The Leisure Club has a 11 x 7 metres swimming pool, spa bath, sauna, solarium and gym. Also available are beauty treatments and holistic therapies. There is also a games room, all- weather tennis court and jogging trails that wind through the woods. Leeds, Bradford and Harrogate are within 20 minutes' drive. Special weekend breaks are available.

Our inspector loved: *This small piece of Finland set in Yorkshire.*

Directions: From A658 between Bradford and Harrogate, take the Chevin Forest Park road, then left into Yorkgate for Chevin Park.

Web: www.johansens.com/chevinlodge
E-mail: reception@chevinlodge.co.uk
Tel: 0870 381 8426
International: +44 (0)1943 467818
Fax: 01943 850335

Price Guide:
single £65–£150
double/twin £110–£180

49 120 SPA

Wood Hall

TRIP LANE, LINTON, NR WETHERBY, WEST YORKSHIRE LS22 4JA

Off the A1/M1 link about 15 miles due west of York, built of stone from the estate, Wood Hall, part of the Hand Picked Hotel Group, is an elegant Georgian country house overlooking the River Wharfe. Its grounds, over 100 acres in all, are approached along a private drive that winds through a sweep of parkland. Wood Hall has had a complete transformation after an extensive refurbishment, and now offers a modern, light and luxurious haven, which combines traditional hospitality. The sumptuously furnished drawing room and the oak-panelled bar, with its gentlemen's club atmosphere, lead off the grand entrance hall. Gastronomes will relish the excellent menu, which combines contemporary Anglo-French style with attractive presentation. The mile-long private stretch of the Wharfe offers up trout and barbel to the keen angler, while miles of walks and jogging paths encompass the estate. There is a spa including a swimming pool, spa bath, steam room, gymnasium and treatment salon. Near to the National Hunt racecourse at Wetherby, York, Harrogate, Leeds, the Dales and Harewood House are only a short distance away. Special breaks available.

Our inspector loved: *The stunning view of the hotel as you drive up the long driveway.*

Directions: From Wetherby, take the A661 towards Harrogate. Take turning for Sicklinghall and Linton, then left for Linton and Wood Hall. Turn right opposite the Windmill public house; hotel is $1\frac{1}{2}$ miles further on.

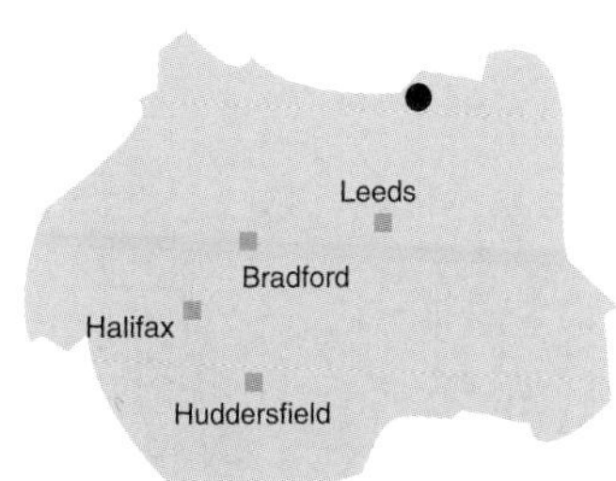

Web: www.johansens.com/woodhall
E-mail: woodhall@handpicked.co.uk
Tel: 0870 381 9004
International: +44 (0)1937 587271
or 0800 9 177 877
Fax: 01937 584353

Price Guide:
single from £120
double/twin from £210

44 140 SPA

Channel Islands

Recommendations in the Channel Islands appear on pages 292-293

For further information on the Channel Islands, please contact:

Visit Guernsey
PO Box 23, St Peter Port, Guernsey GY1 3AN
Tel: +44 (0)1481 723552
Internet: www.visitguernsey.com

Jersey Tourism
Liberation Square, St Helier, Jersey JE1 1BB
Tel: +44 (0)1534 500777
Internet: www.jersey.com

Sark Tourism
The Visitors Centre, The Avenue, Sark, GY9 0SA
Tel: +44 (0)1481 832345
Internet: www.sark.info

Herm Tourist Office
The White House Hotel, Herm Island via Guernsey GY1 3HR
Tel: +44 (0)1481 722377
Internet: www.herm-island.com

or see pages 376-378 for details of
local attractions to visit during your stay.

Images from www.britainonview.com

THE ATLANTIC HOTEL AND OCEAN RESTAURANT

LE MONT DE LA PULENTE, ST BRELADE, JERSEY JE3 8HE

Directions: From the airport turn right at the roundabout towards St Brelade (B36). At the traffic lights turn right towards St Ouen's Bay (A13) then right into La Rue de la Sergente (B35). Look out for the hotel sign on your right.

Web: www.johansens.com/atlantic
E-mail: info@theatlantichotel.com
Tel: 0870 381 8330
International: +44 (0)1534 744101
Fax: 01534 744102

Price Guide:
single £145–£190
double/twin £190–£295
suite £295–£490

This is a stunning luxury hotel that offers elegance, grace, comfort, exquisite cuisine and impeccable service. It is excellent in every way, from majestic interior pillars and magnificent wood panelling to sumptuous furnishings, warm décor and perfect location. The Atlantic stands regally in 3 acres of private grounds alongside La Moye Golf Course overlooking the 5-mile sweep of St Ouen's Bay. A multi-million pound refurbishment of the hotel including the enlargement of bedrooms and remodelling of the building's exterior to give a marine flavour, has resulted in even more venue quality and the hotel's elevation to 5-Sun status by Jersey Tourism. No expense has been spared in refurbishing the bedrooms, suites and garden studios. Tastefully decorated, they offer occupants the highest standard of facilities and comfort together with splendid views of the sea or the golf course. Most prestigious and stylish is the spacious Atlantic Suite with its own entrance hall, living room, guest cloakroom and service pantry in addition to the en suite master bedroom. The delightful, award-winning restaurant overlooks the open-air swimming pool and sun terrace. Excellent and imaginative menus showcase the Modern British cuisine with the emphasis on seafood and fresh local produce.

***Our inspector loved:** The exquisite new Ocean Restaurant – setting exciting new trends in style.*

The Club Hotel and Spa

GREEN STREET, ST HELIER, JERSEY JE2 4UH

The island of St Helier is a breathtaking retreat, dominated by long sandy beaches and intimate bays, and the young Club Hotel and Spa embraces its relationship with these beautiful surroundings. Designed with a contemporary elegance and sense of understated luxury, the serene and tranquil ambience is reflected by the gentle tidal coastline. There are 38 guest rooms and 8 suites; each is furnished to an exceptionally high standard and equipped with the very latest LCD TVs and CD players, whilst the bathrooms have granite surfaces with power showers and sumptuous bathrobes. The Bohemia Restaurant is rapidly gaining an excellent reputation, and has recently been awarded a Michelin Star and 3 AA Rosettes. Fronted by a chic and popular bar, there is a sophisticated atmosphere that complements the fine dining and impeccable, unobtrusive service. The exclusive Club Spa offers an exceptional variety of treatments that are marine-based and harvested in the local gulf of St Malo. Guests are encouraged to savour a slower pace and maximise the benefits of the treatments on offer, as well as enjoying the salt water pool, Rasul Room, salt cabin and herbal steam room. Invigorated and refreshed, guests may wish to explore the island, and abundance of activities such as diving, surfing and sailing. Alternatively, there are numerous beautiful countryside walks.

Directions: On leaving the airport join the B36 heading for St Helier. At roundabout join the A12 to St Helier then onto A1 for approximately 3½ miles. Continue through the traffic lights towards and into the tunnel. On exiting the tunnel take the second left into Green Street. The hotels is 100 yards on the left.

Airport
St Saviour
St Brelade
St Helier

Web: www.johansens.com/theclubjersey
E-mail: reservations@theclubjersey.com
Tel: 0870 381 8313
International: +44 (0)1534 876500
Fax: 01534 720371

Price Guide:
double/twin from £195
suite from £325

Our inspector loved: *Its town centre location, and magnificent spa.*

 46   30        SPA 

IRELAND

Recommendations in Ireland appear on pages 296-315

For further information on Ireland, please contact:

The Irish Tourist Board
(Bord Fáilte Eíreann)
Baggot Street Bridge
Dublin 2
Tel: +353 (0)1 602 4000
Internet: www.ireland.ie

Northern Ireland Tourist Information
Belfast Welcome Centre
47 Donegall Place
Belfast, BT1 5AD
Tel: +44 (0)28 9024 6609
Internet: www.gotobelfast.com

or see pages 376-378 for details of local attractions to visit during your stay.

Images from Fáilte Ireland

Bushmills Inn Hotel

9 DUNLUCE ROAD, BUSHMILLS, CO ANTRIM, BT57 8QG, NORTHERN IRELAND

Originally built as a Coaching Inn, with the oldest part dating back to the 1600s, the Bushmills Inn was the last stop for weary travelers on their way to the Giant's Causeway, now a world heritage site. It was here they would stop to sample the whiskey that made the village internationally famous - dating back to 1608, Bushmills is the world's oldest distillery. This faithfully restored hotel, rescued from near dereliction in 1987 and now incorporating the adjoining Mill House has received numerous awards and epitomises the true spirit of Ulster hospitality. Public rooms are varied and cosy with stripped pine and peat fires. A magnificent wooden staircase leads to a gallery displaying stunning paintings of the Causeway Coast. In the old hay loft, with its original oak beams there's a snug, complete with stove fire and comfortable chairs, where books are tucked into the nooks and crannies. The Mill House accommodates most of the bedrooms, all imaginatively designed in traditional style with discretely hidden modern conveniences. Explore the rugged staggered coastline with its wide sandy beaches, picturesque harbours, craggy cliffs and ruined castles. The area boasts seven quality golf courses including the classic dunes setting at Royal Portrush, consistently ranked amongst the world's top 10 courses. The hotel, in the midst of these famous links courses, was voted Irelands Golf Hotel of the Year in 2003.

Our inspector loved: *The authenticity and uniqueness of this lovely inn.*

Directions: Situated 2 miles from Giant's Causeway on the A2 in the village of Bushmills as you cross the river.

Web: www.johansens.com/bushmills
E-mail: mail@bushmillsinn.com
Tel: 0870 381 9315
International: +44 (0)28 2073 3000
Fax:+44 (0)28 2073 2048

Price Guide:
Mill House double/twin £138–£248
Coaching Inn
small single £68
double/twin £88–£98

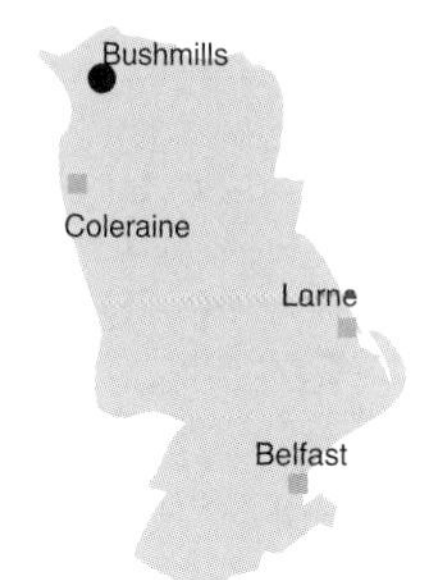

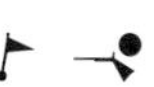

Gregans Castle

BALLYVAUGHAN, CO CLARE, IRELAND

This wonderful, family-run hotel dates back to the 1600s, and today owners Simon and Frederieke Haden welcome guests into its warm, comfortable atmosphere. Careful attention to detail is very much in evidence, from the blazing turf fires to the antique furniture, and the collection of Raymond Piper paintings of local flora. Each of the bedrooms and suites is individually decorated in a relaxing country house style, and public rooms such as the Corkscrew Room and Drawing Room offer conducive areas for enjoying a book, board game or apéritif before dinner. The bay views from the dining room are stunning, and in summer a beautiful light is created by the rays of the setting sun travelling across Galway Bay and striking the limestone mountains. Burren lamb and beef and fresh Atlantic fish appear on the menu daily. Local organic produce is used when available. The Burren is a unique terrain, and provides a home to many rare and rich Alpine and Arctic flowers. Nearby country roads are ideal for cycling and horse riding, whilst beaches and hills are simply waiting to be walked upon. Many golf courses including Lahinch and Doonbeg GC are within easy reach. Only 1 hour from Shannon Airport.

Our inspector loved: *The view over to Ballyvaughan Bay.*

Directions: From Shannon airport take the N18 to Ennis, then N85 to "Fountain Cross" then R476 and R480 to Gregans. From Galway take N18, then N67 to Ballyvaughan. Follow the N67 out of the village and Gregans Castle can be found on the left approx 3 miles away.

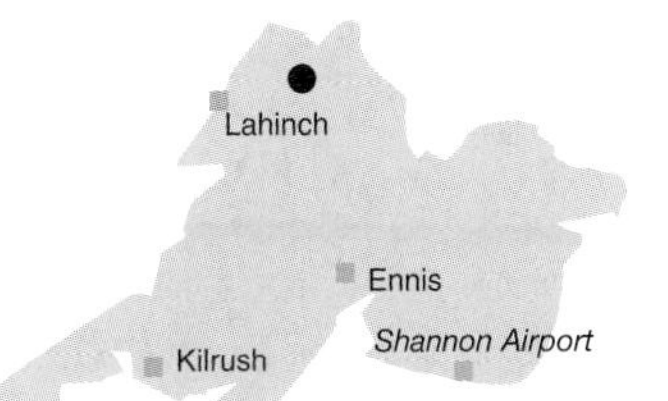

Web: www.johansens.com/gregans
E-mail: stay@gregans.ie
Tel: 00 353 65 7077005
Fax: 00 353 65 7077111

Price Guide: (Euro)
single from €120
double/twin from €170
suite from €250

Dromoland Castle

NEWMARKET-ON-FERGUS, SHANNON AREA, CO CLARE

Dating from the 16th century, Dromoland Castle is one of the most famous baronial castles in Ireland. Dromoland was the ancestral seat of the O'Briens, direct descendants of Irish King Brian Boru. Reminders of its past are everywhere: in the splendid wood and stone carvings, magnificent panelling, oil paintings and romantic gardens. The 100 en-suite guest rooms and suites are all beautifully furnished. Stately halls and an elegant dining room are all part of the Dromoland experience. The Dromoland International Centre is one of Europe's most comprehensive conference venues, hosting groups of up to 450. Classical cuisine is prepared by award-winning chef David McCann. Dromoland's 18-hole golf course, designed by Ron Kirby & JB Carr, this over 6850-yard championship course roams through woodland and around lakes with subtlety and sensitivity. Fishing, clay pigeon shooting and full Health and Beauty Centre are all available on the estate, whilst activities nearby include horse riding and golf on some of Ireland's other foremost courses. The castle is an ideal base from which to explore this breathtakingly beautiful area. Member of Preferred Hotels & Resorts World Wide.

Our inspector loved: *The unique Dromoland experience in a stunning setting.*

Directions: Take the N18 to Newmarket-on-Fergus, go 2 miles beyond the village and the hotel entrance is on the right-hand side. 8 miles from Shannon Airport

Web: www.johansens.com/dromolandcastle
E-mail: sales@dromoland.ie
Tel: 00 353 61 368144
Fax: 00 353 61 363355

Price Guide: (Euro) (room only)
single/double €225–€573
suite €471–€955

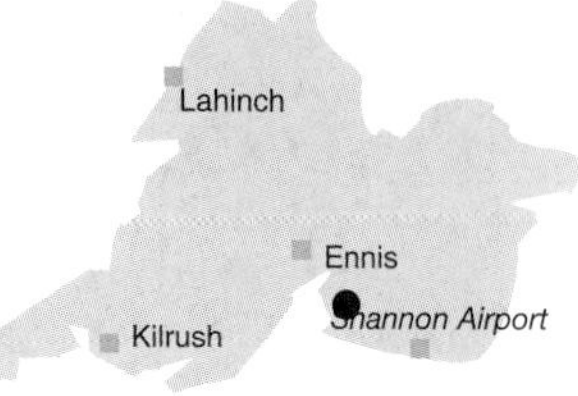

Longueville House & Presidents' Restaurant

MALLOW, CO CORK, IRELAND

Longueville House is a listed Heritage Georgian manor, built circa1720 and set amidst 500 acres of wooded estate in the heart of Blackwater Valley. Its authentic architectural features and superbly appointed suites and guest rooms offer peaceful sanctuary and a taste of Ireland from the early part of the 18th century. Within the timeless elegance of the Presidents' Restaurant, the finest contemporary French and Irish cuisine is served. The hotel is virtually self-sufficient - a tradition that has remained largely unaltered for almost 300 years - by using fresh produce from the estate's farm, gardens and river, which are expertly prepared and presented under the expert eye of chef and host William O'Callaghan. There is an extensive wine list, with choices from the Old and New Worlds. A "residential" wedding service, in the style of a private house party, can be arranged, including accommodation for guests, a full Irish breakfast and dinner served in the recently restored Victorian conservatory. Consultations and details can be organised by appointment. Personalised corporate events can also be catered for. Amenities on the estate include fly-fishing, winter game and clay pigeon shooting, and Cork Racecourse is just over a kilometre away.

Our inspector loved: *The tranquil atmosphere created by the O'Callaghan family.*

Directions: Longueville House is 3 miles west of Mallow on the N72 to Killarney. Take the Ballclough junction on the right-hand side and the hotel entrance is 100 yards on the left.

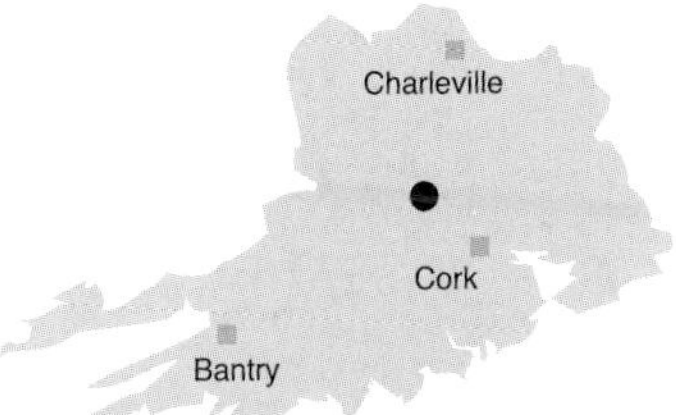

Web: www.johansens.com/longuevillehouse
E-mail: info@longuevillehouse.ie
Tel: 00 353 22 47156
Fax: 00 353 22 47459

Charleville
Cork
Bantry

Price Guide: (Euro)
single from €90
double/twin from €148

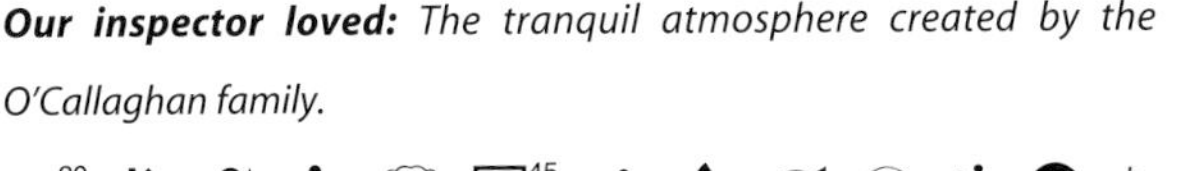

Rathmullan House

RATHMULLAN, LETTERKENNY, CO DONEGAL, IRELAND

Delightfully situated above the shores of peaceful Lough Swilly this attractive former manor is a sanctuary of comfort and relaxation, and an ideal base for exploring the wild and beautiful county of Donegal. Built as a summer house for a Belfast banking family in the 1800s and excellently run as a country hotel by the Wheeler family since 1963, Rathmullan House has all the charm, graciousness and good taste of the 19th-century era. Prize-winning, tree-shaded gardens, leading to a clean sandy beach, provide total serenity and the opportunity to breath fresh Irish air whilst absorbing the dramatic surrounding scenery making this an ideal venue for weddings and small conferences. Inside are 3 elegant sitting-rooms with tall ceilings, marble fireplaces, deep and soft sofas and chairs, fine antiques, oil paintings and overflowing bookcases. The bedrooms vary in décor and facilities, ranging from simple garret rooms for families to luxurious superior rooms with balconies overlooking the garden and Lough Swilly. The dining room, with unusual tented ceiling, is renowned for good food and generous, award-winning breakfasts. Leisure facilities include an indoor heated swimming pool and steam rooms, 2 all-weather tennis courts and a croquet lawn. Nearby are 4 challenging golf courses, deep sea and wreck fishing, boat trips, sailing, horse riding, mountain climbing and miles of beaches to stroll along.

Our inspector loved: *The warmth of welcome to children.*

Directions: From Dublin take the N2 and A5. From Belfast take the A6. Drive to Letterkenny and take the road to Ramelton. At the bridge in Ramelton turn right towards Rathmullan. Go through the village and head north. The entrance to the hotel is just beyond the chapel .

Web: www.johansens.com/rathmullanhouse
E-mail: info@rathmullanhouse.com
Tel: 00 353 74 915 8188
Fax: 00 353 74 915 8200

Price Guide: (Euro)
single from €80
double/twin from €160
superior from €200

Merrion Hall Hotel

54-56 Merrion Road, Ballsbridge, Dublin 4

This exclusive Edwardian property is located close to the RDS Convention centre just minutes from downtown Dublin. Merrion Hall shares its neighbourhood with the world's embassies in the fashionable Ballsbridge area of Dublin City. Executive bedrooms, some with four-poster suites, offer air conditioning, whirlpool spas and all the modern comforts expected by the discerning traveller. The hotel's library stocks a fine selection of Irish and international literature, whilst afternoon teas and fine wines are served in the main drawing room. A feature of this Edwardian town house is a very special breakfast, which can be enjoyed in the conservatory, overlooking the terraced garden. There are also numerous restaurants within a short stroll of the hotel, leaving guests utterly spoilt for choice. Near to Lansdowne Road, it is linked to major tourist sites and the business district by the DART electric train. There is a direct luxury coach link to and from Dublin airport. For the corporate guests there is a boardroom, meeting rooms, business facilities and wireless internet access. Residents have complimentary parking on the grounds. The hotel can arrange golfing packages and scenic tours. A member of Ireland's Manor House Hotels

Our inspector loved: *The convenient location of this Edwardian house.*

Directions: From the city centre take Merrion Road; the hotel is on the left- hand side overlooking the RDS Convention Centre.

Web: www.johansens.com/merrionhall
E-mail: merrionhall@iol.ie
Tel: 00 353 1 668 1426
Fax: 00 353 1 668 4280

Price Guide: (Euro)
single €106–€139
double/twin €139–€189
de luxe €169–€249
garden suites €239–€349

24 60

Cashel House

CASHEL, CONNEMARA, CO GALWAY, IRELAND

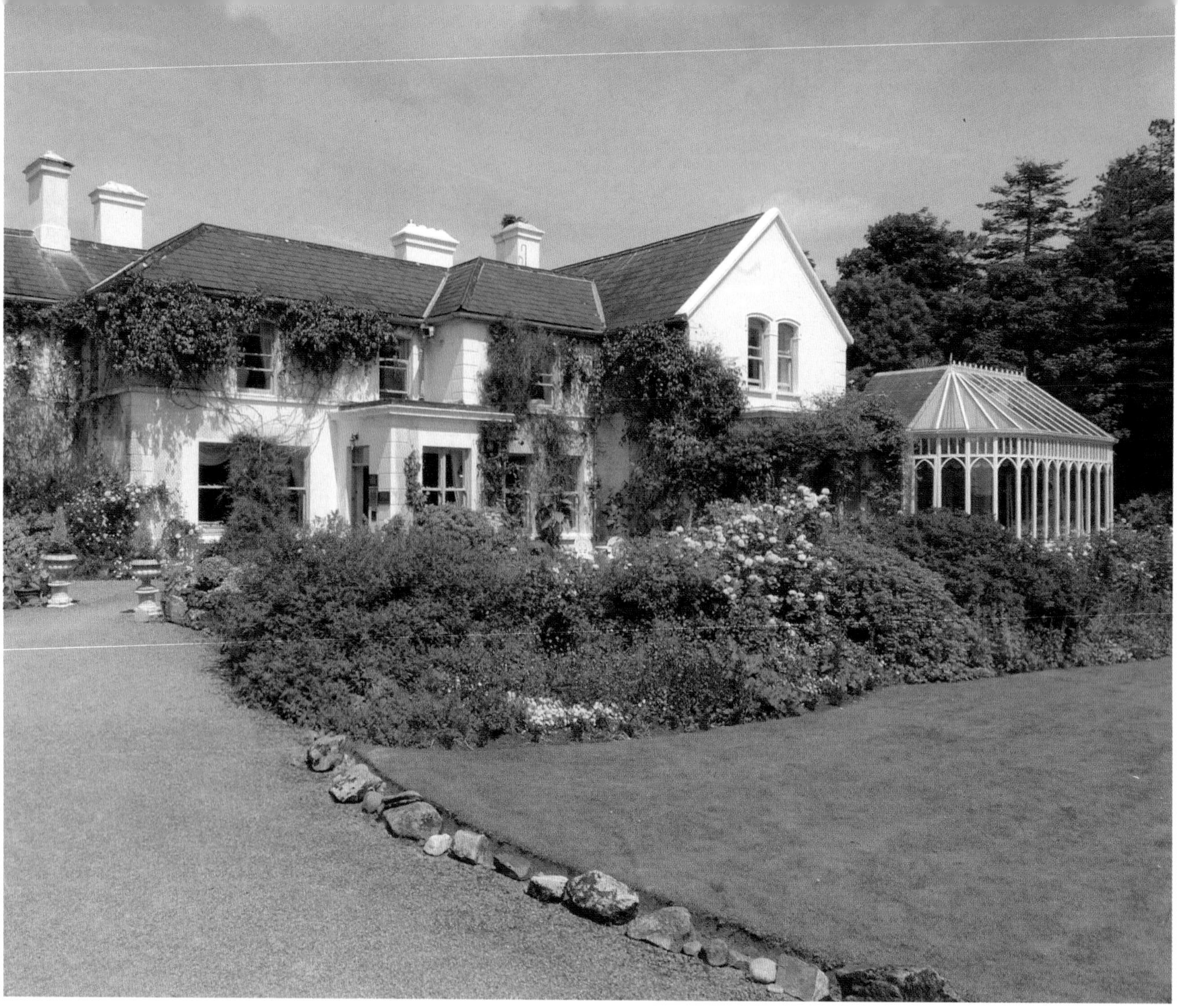

Directions: Travel south off the N59 - Galway Clifden Road. Continue for 1 mile east of Recess then turn left.

Web: www.johansens.com/cashelhouse
E-mail: info@cashel-house-hotel.com
Tel: 00 353 95 31001
Fax: 00 353 95 31077

Price Guide: (Euro)
single €85–€125
double/twin €170–€250
suite €230–€310

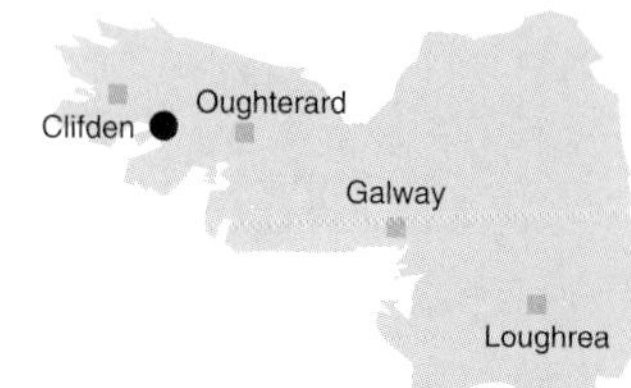

Delightfully situated at the head of Cashel Bay on Ireland's unspoilt west coast, this gleaming white hotel, with the beautiful contrasting backdrop of green-coated Cashel Hill, is a sheltered sanctuary of peace and comfort where guests can relax, unwind and rejuvenate. Built by the owners' great, great grandfather as a family home for Captain Thomas Hazel, an English landowner, it is surrounded by 50 acres of award-winning gardens featuring exotic and exquisite flowering shrubs, secluded woodland walks and clear, tinkling streams. The very welcoming proprietors Dermot and Kay McEvilly, offer luxury, tranquillity and privacy, and nothing is too much trouble. Turf and log fires glow in public areas where the furnishings and décor are the epitome of good taste and comfort. Bedrooms and suites have everything the discerning visitor requires and overlook the hill or garden. In the dining room, Dermot and Kay oversee the preparation and serving of the appetising and imaginative dishes from the constantly changing menu. The emphasis is on local seafood, lamb, beef, game and home-grown vegetables, complemented by a carefully chosen wine list. Visitors may enjoy the hard tennis court, visit the Stud Farm in the grounds or take a swim in the private beach. Golf, climbing, sea, river and lake fishing can be arranged.

Our inspector loved: *The beautiful 50-acre garden.*

Renvyle House Hotel

CONNEMARA, CO GALWAY, IRELAND

Renvyle House Hotel has occupied its rugged, romantic position on Ireland's west coast for over 4 centuries. Set between mountains and sea on the unspoilt coast of Connemara, this hardy, beautiful building with its superlative views over the surrounding countryside is just an hour's drive from Galway or Sligo. Originally constructed in 1541, Renvyle has been an established hotel for over 100 years, witnessing in that time a procession of luminaries through its doors – Augustus John, Lady Gregory, Yeats and Churchill, drawn no doubt by an atmosphere as warm and convivial then as it is today. Renvyle now welcomes visitors with turf fires glowing in public areas, wood-beamed interiors and comfortable, relaxed furnishings in the easy rooms. The bedrooms are comfortably appointed and all have been refurbished in the past 3 years. In the dining room, meals from a constantly-changing menu are served with emphasis on local fish and Renvyle lamb. In the grounds activities include tennis, croquet, riding, bowls and golf. Beyond the hotel, there are walks in the heather-clad hills, or swimming and sunbathing on empty beaches.

Our inspector loved: *The new rooms and additions to this Connemara hotel.*

Directions: On the N59 from Galway turn right at Recess, take the Letterfrack turning to Tully Cross and Renvyle is signposted.

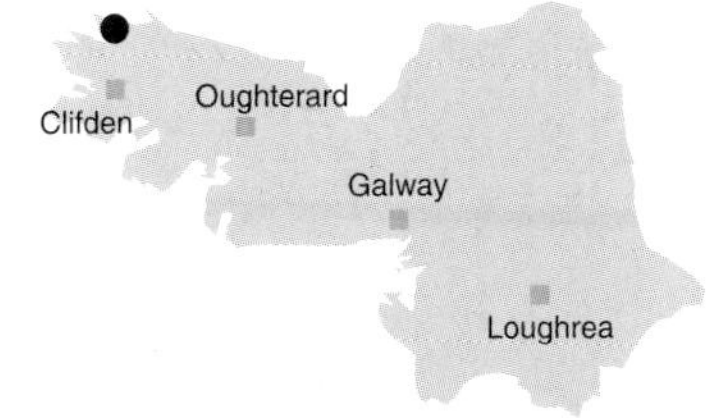

Web: www.johansens.com/renvylehouse
E-mail: info@renvyle.com
Tel: 00 353 95 43511
Fax: 00 353 95 43515

Price Guide: (Euro)
single €40
double/twin €80

PARK HOTEL KENMARE & SÁMAS

KENMARE, CO. KERRY, IRELAND

Directions: The hotel is in the centre of Kenmare on the N70 or the N71, just 27 miles away from Kerry International Airport.

Web: www.johansens.com/parkkenmare
E-mail: info@parkkenmare.com
Tel: 00 353 64 41200
Fax: 00 353 64 41402

Price Guide: (Euro)
double €206–€770

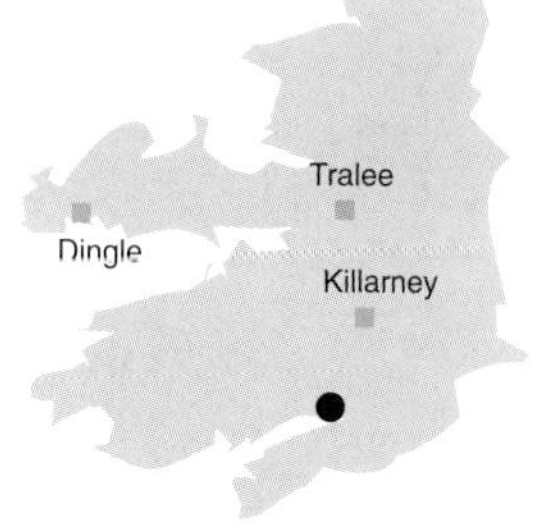

"Mystical," "magical," "wonderful" and "green" are some of the words one would use in relation to describing Ireland. Due to SÁMAS, a Deluxe Destination Spa at the applauded Park Hotel Kenmare, the word "holistic" can be added. Adjoining the hotel and staffed by a professional team, the Spa offers over 60 Holistic treatments combined with heat experiences and relaxation to rejuvenate body, mind and spirit. There are both male and female spas to meet individual, distinctive requirements. Retaining the character and ambience of a past era, the Park Hotel Kenmare combines elegant accommodation and superb amenities with glorious countryside views and is holder of numerous awards, including Egon Ronay and AA 'Hotel of the Year', AA Three Rosettes, RAC Gold Ribbon and Condé Nast Gold List. Bedrooms and suites are furnished in traditional style with fine antiques and objects d'art and have every modern amenity. The elegant dining room, with silver-laden sideboards and views over the terraced gardens, offers acclaimed seasonal à la carte and set dinner menus with a leaning towards local seafood. The hotel has its own 12-seat cinema, tennis and croquet. Adjacent is Kenmare Golf Club's 18-hole parkland course and within easy reach are numerous championship links courses.

***Our inspector loved:** Feeling totally relaxed after a SÀMAS experience.*

   SPA      

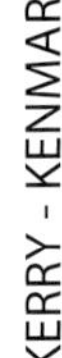

Sheen Falls Lodge

KENMARE, CO. KERRY, IRELAND

Voted AA Hotel of the Year and one of Ireland's most romantic, opulent hotels, Sheen Falls Lodge is a haven set within 300 acres of woodlands and crystal, cascading waterfalls. This gracious mansion evokes the atmosphere of a country house, and boasts spacious, luxurious bedrooms with fine linens, restful décor and magnificent views. The differing panoramas of Kenmare Bay and the Sheen waterfalls can be enjoyed from the Sun Lounge, Billiard Room and Library, which holds over 1,200 books. Log fires, sumptuous seating and attentive service complete the essence of utter relaxation. A 5-minute walk along a private avenue, winding down to the water's edge, leads to the Little Hay and Garden thatched cottages. These secluded hideaways are extremely comfortable and offer ultimate privacy. The Green cottage is ideal for families, golfing and corporate visitors; cottage guests may use the hotel's facilities. Enjoy Oscar's bistro, with its Mediterranean influenced menu or the elegant La Cascade, the hotel's signature restaurant, followed by an evening tour of the wine cellar and sample a fine port or whiskey with the sommelier. Activities on the estate include salmon and trout fishing, walking, cycling and hiking. The spa, with Jacuzzi and pool, provides a variety of treatments, and there are several excellent golf courses, the Beara Peninsula and the Ring of Kerry nearby.

Directions: From Kenmare follow N71 in the direction of Glengarrif and turn left after the Suspension Bridge. Dublin airport is about 5 hours drive away, Shannon airport is 2½ hours travelling time, Cork airport is approx 1¼ hours and Kerry airport is 50 minutes away.

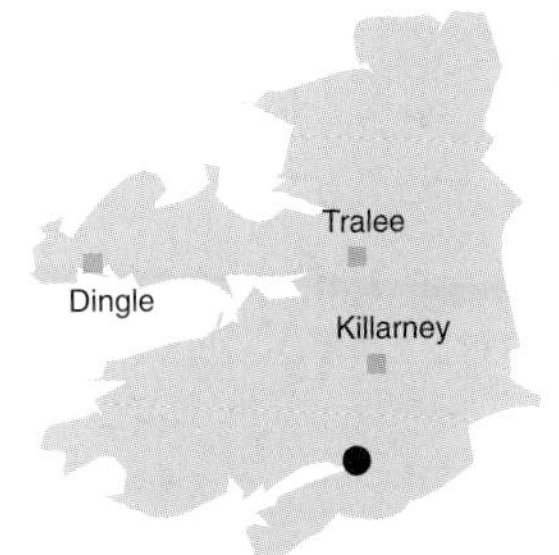

Web: www.johansens.com/sheenfallslodge
E-mail: info@sheenfallslodge.ie
Tel: 00 353 64 41600
Fax: 00 353 64 41386

Price Guide: (Euro)
Deluxe Room €275–€425

Our inspector loved: *Sitting on the terrace watching the waterfalls.*

66 120 SPA

CAHERNANE HOUSE HOTEL

MUCKROSS ROAD, KILLARNEY, CO KERRY, IRELAND

Directions: 1 mile from the town centre on the Muckross Road.

Web: www.johansens.com/cahernane
E-mail: info@cahernane.com
Tel: 00 353 64 31895
Fax: 00 353 64 34340

Price Guide: (Euro)
single €130
double €210
suite €340

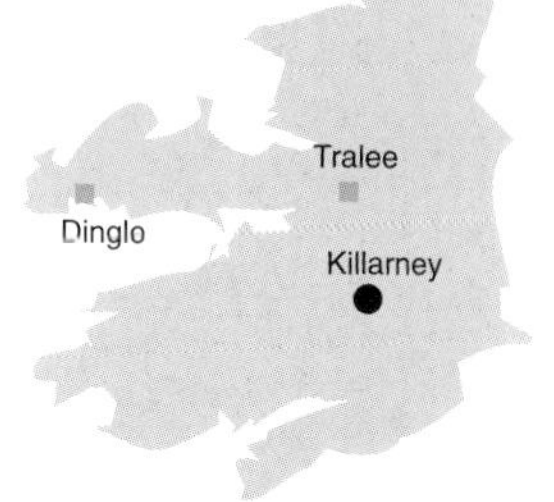

A shady tunnel of greenery frames the ¼-mile long drive leading to the welcoming entrance doors at this historic house, a place of peace and tranquillity where time moves at a calming, slow pace. A delightful, family-run hotel, Cahernane is the former home of the Earls of Pembroke and dates back to the 17th century. Standing in gorgeous parklands on the edge of Killarney's National Park, this is a designated area of outstanding beauty with an untamed landscape of lakes, mountains, woodland walks and gardens where giant rhododendrons and tropical plants grow in abundance. The Browne family pride themselves on their hospitality and attentive service that ensures guests enjoy the hotel's charm and grace. Each of the individually designed bedrooms and suites is elegantly furnished, tastefully decorated and has a lovely bathroom; some boast a Jacuzzi. Recipient of 2 AA Rosettes, 3 RAC Ribbons and the RAC White Ribbon, Herbert Room restaurant offers à la carte and table d'hôte menus prepared by chef Pat Karney, whilst less formal dining is enjoyed in the Cellar Bar. The Wine Cellar forms the backdrop to the Cellar Bar and stocks a comprehensive selection. A new spa and conference facility, as well as additional luxury suites, are due to open in 2006. Challenging golf courses, a variety of outdoor pursuits and national treasures such as Muckross House and Ross Castle are within easy reach.

Our inspector loved: *The homely feel and attention to residents' comfort.*

 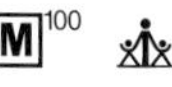        

Parknasilla Hotel

GREAT SOUTHERN HOTEL, PARKNASILLA, CO. KERRY, IRELAND

County Kerry has an equitable climate from the warm Gulf Stream. Parknasilla is a splendid Victorian mansion surrounded by extensive parkland and subtropical gardens leading down to the seashore. New arrivals appreciate the graceful reception rooms which, like the luxurious bedrooms, look out on the mountains, across the verdant countryside or down to Kenmare Bay. Wonderful damask and chintz harmonize with the period furniture and thoughtful 'extras' have been provided. The bathrooms are lavishly appointed. George Bernard Shaw's many visits are reflected in the names of the inviting Doolittle Bar and the elegant Pygmalion Restaurant. The sophisticated menus always include fish fresh from the sea and the international wine list will please the most discerning guests. Corporate activities and private celebrations are hosted in the traditional Shaw Library or handsome Derryquin Suite. Leisure facilities abound: a private 12-hole golf course with challenging championship courses close by, horse riding, water sports, sailing, clay pigeon shooting and archery. Parknasilla has 7 recommended walks through the estate and its own boat for cruises round the coast. Indoors there is a superb pool, sauna, steam room, Jacuzzi, hot tub, hydrotherapy seaweed baths, aromatherapy and massage

Our inspector loved: *The sensitive modernisation of this Victorian favourite.*

84 80 SPA

Directions: The hotel is south west of Killarney off N70.

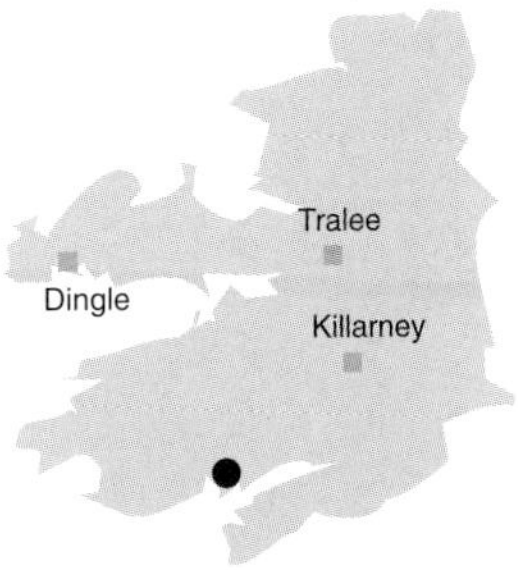

Tralee
Dingle
Killarney

Web: www.johansens.com/parknasilla
E-mail: res@parknasilla-gsh.com
Tel: 00 353 1 2144800
Fax: 00 353 64 45323
UK Freephone: 0800 7316107

Price Guide: (Euro) (room only)
single/double/twin €150–€250
suite €500

Ballygarry House

KILLARNEY ROAD, TRALEE, CO KERRY, IRELAND

Elegantly and stylishly decorated with rich warm colours, fine antiques and fresh flowers, this charming hotel with its peaceful ambience immediately makes guests feel at ease. The floral displays extend outside to the entrance and amidst the six acres of lawned gardens. Situated at the foot of the Kerry Mountains, Ballygarry House has been a family-run hotel for the past 50 years, and owner Padraig McGillicuddy does everything to help make guests feel at home. The en-suite guest rooms are individually designed and beautifully appointed to ensure a feeling of generous space, whilst fluffy white bathrobes, luxury toiletries and antique furnishings create an atmosphere of tranquillity. Dining is a delight in the elegant restaurant where soft tones, crisp white linen and garden views enhance the gastronomic experience. A chat with locals may be enjoyed in the cosy bar or relax in the soft, easy chairs in the fire-warmed drawing room. Activities include walking, angling and shooting. Due to open in February 2006, Spa "Nádúr" will be a super new addition. True to its name this "natural" spa speaks of unspoilt landscapes, the pure organic ingredients of the spa products and the genuine nature of the spa therapists. In addition to the vast selection of treatments available, a visit to the relaxation room, crystal steam rooms and outdoor hot tub will be a must.

Directions: 2 miles from the Tralee town centre on the Killarney Road.

Web: www.johansens.com/ballygarryhouse
E-mail: info@ballygarryhouse.com
Tel: 00 353 66 7123322
Fax: 00 353 66 7127630

Price Guide: (Euro)
single €115–€130
double/twin €160–€190
suite €190–€250

Our inspector loved: *The individually designed spacious bedrooms.*

Killashee House Hotel & Villa Spa

KILLASHEE, NAAS, CO KILDARE, IRELAND

A tall, slim bell tower with steeple peak and an elaborate grey stone Jacobean-style façade, are eye-catching impressions as this prestigious hotel is approached along an elegant curved driveway. Once through the imposing arched entrance door a world of opulence, comfort and tranquillity awaits. Killashee House Hotel & Villa Spa was originally a hunting lodge built in the 1860s for an influential family named Moore, whose coat of arms is visible on the walls. It is a glorious, gracious retreat surrounded by 80 acres of gardens and woodland located 30 minutes from Dublin. Many of the individually designed bedrooms and suites have four-poster beds and stunning views over the gardens and, weather permitting, the Wicklow Mountains. Bedrooms are full of character that reflects the elegance and refinement of the Victorian period, combined with modern amenities and high-tech services expected by today's guest. Traditional Irish and Mediterranean cuisine can be enjoyed in the award-winning Turner's restaurant. For those wishing to work up an appetite or to relax prior to dining, the Country Club and Villa Spa with 25m pool and 18 luxurious treatment rooms offer the ultimate in fitness and pampering, including Elemis, Thalgo & Cellcosmet treatments. Curragh, Punchestown and Naas racecourses, and several championship golf courses are within easy reach.

Our inspector loved: *The large and luxurious new rooms.*

Directions: 30 minutes from Dublin on the N7/M7 to Naas, then 1 mile along R448 Kilcullen Road.

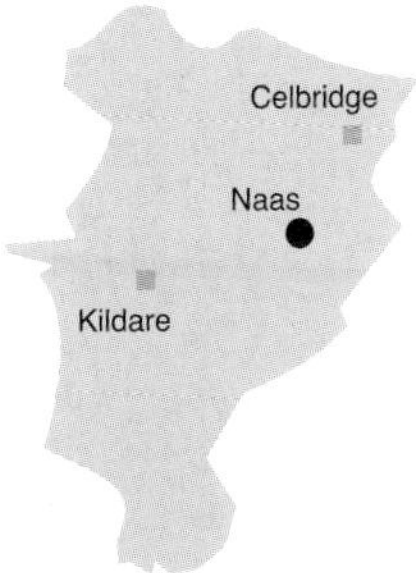

Web: www.johansens.com/killashee
E-mail: reservations@killasheehouse.com
Tel: 00 353 45 879277
Fax: 00 353 45 879266

Price Guide: (Euro) (per person sharing)
single from €144
double/twin from €99
classic from €125
suites €107.50–€247.50

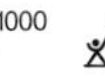

Mount Juliet Conrad

THOMASTOWN, CO KILKENNY, IRELAND

Directions: 16 miles from Kilkenny on the N9 via N10.

Web: www.johansens.com/mountjuliet
E-mail: info@mountjuliet.ie
Tel: 00 353 56 777 3000
Fax: 00 353 56 777 3019

Price Guide: (Euro)
single from €150
double/twin from €230
suite €450

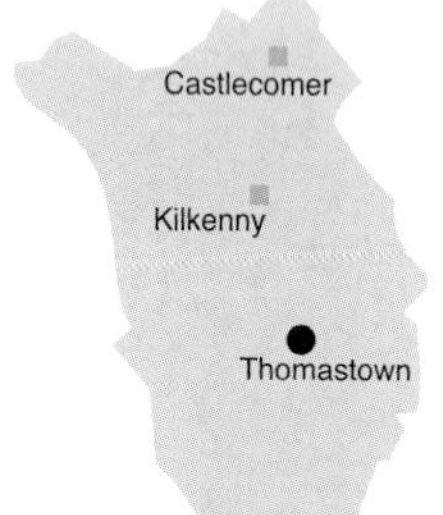

Mount Juliet Conrad is an architectural gem, a magnificent 18th-century Georgian mansion standing proudly on the banks of the River Nore in the heart of a lush 1,500-acre estate. The entrance doorway leads into an impressive hall featuring elaborate stucco work with bas-reliefs on walls and ceilings. A feeling of opulence pervades all reception rooms, the bars recall a glorious equestrian past whilst the homeliness of the library and drawing rooms provide comfortable venues for relaxation. Afternoon tea or a pre-dinner glass of champagne can be enjoyed in the elegant Majors Room. Jewel in the crown, however, is the exquisite Lady Helen Dining Room, famed for its original stucco plasterwork, pastoral views and superb cuisine. The 32 en-suite guest rooms are individually designed and are full of the character and charm that reflects the quiet good taste and refinement of the Georgian period. Centre of activity for guests is Hunters Yard, which is situated on the edge of a championship golf course, host to the American Express World Golf Championships in 2002 and 2004. The Hunters Yard is the epicentre of the estate's sporting and leisure life and offers stylish dining in Kendals Restaurant and 16 "Club" style rooms which offer direct access to the hotels sybaritic spa. For guests who require a greater degree of space and privacy, there are 10 lodges located beside the magnificent Rose Gardens.

***Our inspector loved:** The outstanding golf corse and sporting facilities.*

Glin Castle

GLIN, CO LIMERICK, IRELAND

Home to the 29th Knight of Glin and Madam FitzGerald, Glin Castle has received accolades from all over the world, and maintains a reputation as one of the most unique places to stay in Ireland. The present castle was built with entertaining in mind in the late 18th century and has been sympathetically restored for modern day guests. Its famous collections of Irish furniture and paintings, built up over the centuries, fill reception rooms, whilst family portraits and photographs adorn the walls and mahogany side tables. Beautiful features are endless; the Corinthian pillars and rare flying staircase of the entrance hall, the Sitting Room's crackling fire, the Drawing Room with its 6 long windows overlooking the croquet lawn, the library with its secret bookcase doorway. Each of the sumptuous bedrooms is furnished with period pieces including rugs, chaise longues, and chintz covered beds. Those at the back look across the garden and those at the front have views of the River Shannon. The castle stands within 500 acres of grounds which comprise formal gardens, a series of follies, a parade of yew trees and a walled garden that supplies the hotel kitchen with fresh fruit and vegetables for its good Irish country house cooking, as well as fresh flowers for the rooms.

Our inspector loved: *The aristocratic opulence of this wonderful castle home.*

Directions: From Ennis and Shannon airport via N68 take the ferry from Kilimer. Alternatively take the N69 from Limerick.

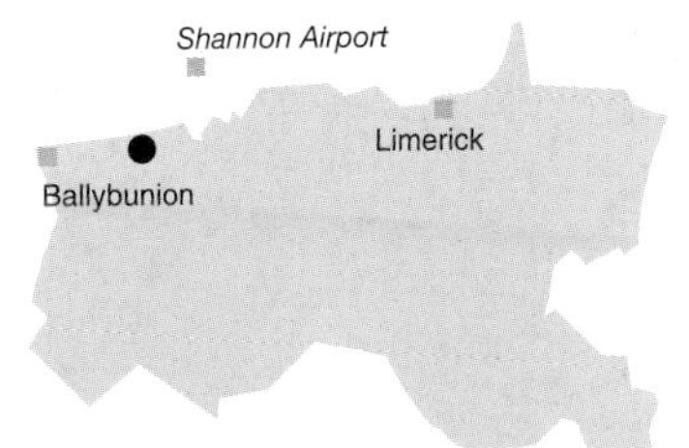

Web: www.johansens.com/glincastle
E-mail: knight@iol.ie
Tel: 00 353 68 34173
Fax: 00 353 68 34364

Price Guide: (Euro)
standard €280
superior €360
de luxe €440

Ashford Castle

CONG, CO MAYO

Ashford Castle is set on the northern shores of Lough Corrib amidst acres of beautiful gardens and forests. Once the country estate of Lord Ardilaun and the Guinness family, it was transformed into a luxury hotel in 1939. The castle's Great Hall is lavishly decorated with rich panelling, fine period pieces, objets d'art and masterpiece paintings. Guest rooms are of the highest standards and many feature high ceilings, enormous bathrooms and delightful lake views. The main dining room offers superb continental and traditional menus, while the gourmet restaurant, The Connaught Room, specialises in excellent French cuisine. Before and after dinner in the Dungeon Bar guests are entertained by a harpist or pianist. Ashford Castle offers a full range of country sports, including fishing on Lough Corrib, clay pigeon shooting, riding, an exclusive 9-hole golf course and Ireland's only school of falconry. The hotel has a modern health centre comprising a whirlpool, sauna, steam room, fully equipped gymnasium and conservatory. Ashford is an ideal base for touring the historic West of Ireland, places like Kylemore Abbey, Westport House and the mediaeval town of Galway. A member of Leading Hotels of the World.

Our inspector loved: *The stunning views across Lough Corrib.*

Directions: 30 minutes from Galway on the shore of Lough Corrib, on the left when entering the village of Cong.

Web: www.johansens.com/ashfordcastle
E-mail: ashford@ashford.ie
Tel: 00 353 94 95 46003
Fax: 00 353 94 95 46260

Price Guide: (Euro)
single/twin/double €215–€515
stateroom/suite €570–€995

KNOCKRANNY HOUSE HOTEL & SPA

KNOCKRANNY, WESTPORT, CO MAYO, IRELAND

It would be difficult to better the views from Knockranny House Hotel & Spa: overlooking the majestic Croagh Patrick Mountain towering over the little heritage town of Westport and the calm waters of Clew Bay. Standing in secluded landscaped gardens, this privately owned, Victorian-style hotel has all the opulent charm of a bygone era coupled with facilities expected by today's discerning visitor. Each of the sumptuous, spacious bedrooms is tastefully furnished, warmly decorated and has every home comfort. Deluxe rooms offer king-size beds, spa baths, robes, slippers, DVD and CD players. Executive Suites are equally luxurious with four-poster beds and lounge areas. La Fougère Restaurant serves eclectic menus featuring superb modern Irish cuisine, and the Drawing Room and Foyer, each furnished with antiques and plush seats, are ideal for those seeking peace and serenity. The Conservatory and Library boast panoramic views, and are popular with guests favouring afternoon tea or a social chat over a drink. The new, state-of-the-art Spa Salveo, is centred around a beautifully designed vitality pool with spectacular, Roman-style marble columns. A serail mud chamber, hammam massage and dry floatation are just 3 of the exotic and pampering experiences on offer in 12 treatment rooms.

Our inspector loved: *Feeling totally relaxed after a hammam massage in Spa Salveo.*

Directions: Turn left off the N60 before entering Westport town. A complimentary bottle of house wine and chocolates is available for guests staying 2 nights or more.

Web: www.johansens.com/knockranny
E-mail: info@khh.ie
Tel: 00 353 98 28600
Fax: 00 353 98 28611

Price Guide: (Euro)
single from €125
double/twin from €190
suite from €250

54 500 SPA

Nuremore Hotel and Country Club

CARRICKMACROSS, CO MONAGHAN, IRELAND

Directions: The hotel is ideally located on the main N2 Road, between Dublin and Monaghan. Just 45 minutes drive from Dublin Airport and 75 minutes drive from Belfast.

Web: www.johansens.com/nuremore
E-mail: nuremore@eircom.net
Tel: 00 353 42 9661438
Fax: 00 353 42 9661853

Price Guide: (Euro)
single €150–€200
double/twin €220–€280
suite from €250–€300

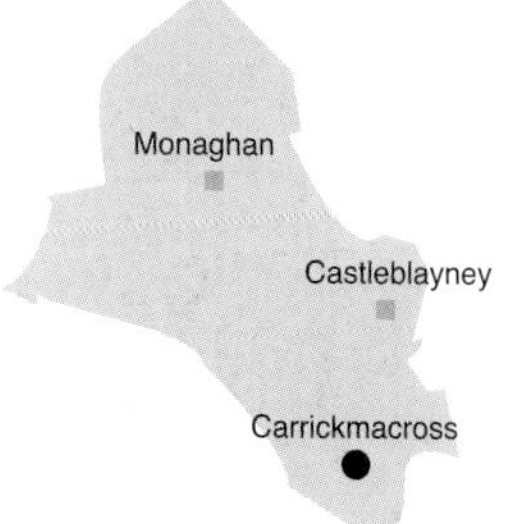

Nestling on the outskirts of Carrickmacross, Nuremore Hotel and Country Club is set in 200 acres of rolling countryside with beautifully landscaped gardens. Its wide range of facilities include a swimming pool, tennis courts, treatment rooms and a health club featuring a gymnasium, spa bath, sauna and steam room. The hotel's renowned 18-hole championship golf course makes superb use of the surrounding lakes and landscape and has been described as one of the most picturesque parkland courses in the country. Resident professional, Maurice Cassidy, is on hand to offer advice and tuition. All 72 bedrooms and suites are beautifully appointed to ensure a generous feeling of personal space and guests can sample the classic European cuisine with Irish and French influences, prepared by award-winning chef Raymond McArdle, "Georgina Campbell's Ireland" Chef of the Year 2005. The restaurant has won Bushmill Guide's Best Ulster Restaurant 2005/06, been listed in Food & Wine magazine and it also features in the Bridgestone Guide to Ireland's best 100 restaurants. The impressive conference centre constantly evolves to ensure it remains at the cutting edge for business events. Conference and syndicate rooms boast natural lighting, AV equipment, air conditioning, fax and ISDN lines. A dedicated conference team ensures that all functions run smoothly.

Our inspector loved: *The extensive sporting and health facilities.*

72 500 SPA

 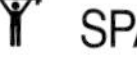      

MARLFIELD HOUSE

GOREY, CO WEXFORD, IRELAND

Staying at Johansens award-winning Marlfield House is a memorable experience. Set in 34 acres of woodland and gardens, this former residence of the Earl of Courtown preserves the Regency lifestyle in all its graciousness. Built in 1820 and situated just 55 miles south of Dublin, it is recognised as one of the finest country houses in Ireland and is supervised by its welcoming hosts and proprietors, Raymond and Mary Bowe and their daughters Margaret and Laura. The State Rooms have been built in a very grand style and have period fireplaces where open fires burn even in cooler weather. All of the furniture is antique and the roomy beds are draped with sumptuous fabrics. The bathrooms are made of highly polished marble and some have large freestanding bathtubs. There is an imposing entrance hall, luxurious drawing room and an impressive curved Richard Turner conservatory. The kitchen's gastronomic delights have earned it numerous awards. Located 2 miles from fine beaches and within easy reach of many golf courses, including Courtown, Seafield, Woodenbridge, Druids Glen, The European Club and Coolattin, the house is central to many touring high points: Glendalough, Waterford Crystal and Powerscourt Gardens and the medieval city of Kilkenny. Closed mid-December to the end of January.

Our inspector loved: *The instant calming influence caused by the Bowe family's devotion to quality.*

Directions: On the Gorey–Courtown road, just over a mile east of Gorey.

Web: www.johansens.com/marlfieldhouse
E-mail: info@marlfieldhouse.ie
Tel: 00 353 55 21124
Fax: 00 353 55 21572

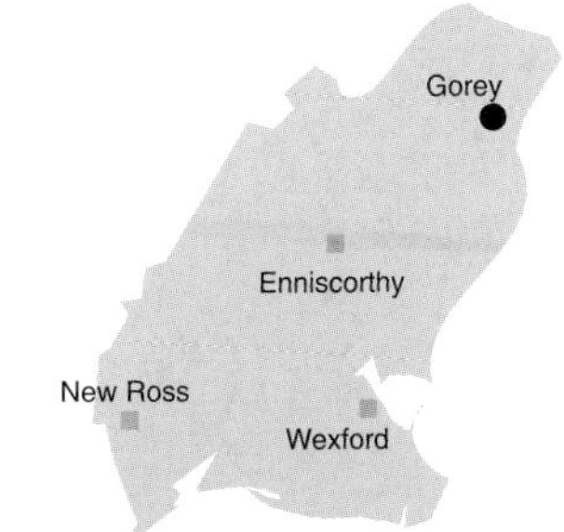

Price Guide: (Euro)
single from €130
double/twin from €235
state rooms from €425

SCOTLAND

Recommendations in Scotland appear on pages 318-351

For further information on Scotland, please contact:

Visit Scotland
Ocean Point 1, 94 Ocean Drive, Edinburgh, EH6 6JH
Tel: +44 (0)131 332 2433
Internet: www.visitscotland.com

or see pages 376-378 for details of local attractions to visit during your stay.

Images from www.britainonview.com

DARROCH LEARG

BRAEMAR ROAD, BALLATER, ABERDEENSHIRE AB35 5UX

4 acres of leafy grounds surround Darroch Learg, situated on the side of the rocky hill which dominates Ballater. The hotel, which was built in 1888 as a fashionable country residence, offers panoramic views over the golf course, River Dee and Balmoral Estate to the fine peaks of the Grampian Mountains. All bedrooms are individually furnished and decorated, providing modern amenities. The reception rooms in Darroch Learg are similarly elegant and welcoming, a comfortable venue in which to enjoy a relaxing drink. Log fires create a particularly cosy atmosphere on chilly nights. The beautifully presented food has been awarded 3 AA Rosettes. A wide choice of wines, a former winner of the AA "Wine List of the Year for Scotland" and finalist in the Condé Nast Johansens Taittinger Wine List Award 2005, complements the cuisine, which is best described as modern and Scottish in style. To perfect the setting, there is a wonderful outlook south towards the hills of Glen Muick. The wealth of outdoor activities on offer include walking, riding, mountain-biking, loch and river fishing, gliding and skiing. The surrounding areas are interesting with an old ruined Kirk and ancient Celtic stones. A few miles away stands Balmoral Castle, the Highland residence of the British sovereign.

Our inspector loved: *The personal attention of the charming owners and staff, wonderful understated food, wine and décor.*

Directions: At the western edge of Ballater on the A93.

Web: www.johansens.com/darrochlearg
E-mail: info@darrochlearg.co.uk
Tel: 0870 381 8477
International: +44 (0)13397 55443
Fax: 013397 55252

Price Guide:
single £65–£80
double/twin £130–£160

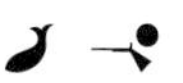

Pittodrie House Hotel

CHAPEL OF GARIOCH, BY INVERURIE, ABERDEENSHIRE AB51 5HS

Situated in 2,400 acres of private estate with Bennachie as its backdrop, this Baronial-style mansion has foundations that date back to the 15th century. Half of the hotel is still owned by its ancestral family, and the public rooms with cosy log fires have undergone an impressive refurbishment. Enchanting old oil paintings adorn the walls, and the immaculate restaurant features crisp white linen and fresh flowers. Interesting daily changing menus are based on finest locally sourced produce and ingredients grown in the hotel's walled garden, and include delights such as marinated venison, braised shank of Highland lamb and roasted fillet of prime Scottish beef with Stornoway black pudding. 16 of the bedrooms are a recent addition to the hotel, whilst the 11 original rooms are currently being redecorated. The hotel's outstanding facilities make this an ideal location for corporate entertainment and events; packages can be individually arranged upon request. As well as the function rooms and audio-visual equipment available, there is a multitude of on-site activities to choose from, including off-road driving, paint-balling, whisky tastings – there are 180 malts to choose from – falconry displays, murder mystery parties and helicopter flights. Numerous places of historic interest such as standing stones, Fyvie Castle and Haddo House & Gardens can be found nearby.

Directions: Take the A96 for 6 miles north west. The hotel is signposted on the road to Chapel of Garioch, a further 11/2 miles left off the main road.

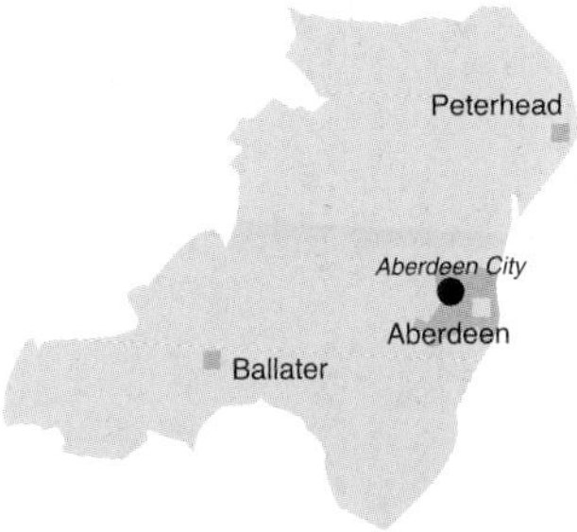

Peterhead
Aberdeen City
Aberdeen
Ballater

Web: www.johansens.com/pittodriehouse
E-mail: pittodrie@macdonald.hotels.co.uk
Tel: 0870 381 8377
International: +44 (0)1467 681744
Fax: 01467 681648

Price Guide:
single £85–£149
double/twin £130–£159

Our inspector loved: *The grand public rooms in this historic house.*

 27   130       

Loch Melfort Hotel & Restaurant

ARDUAINE, BY OBAN, ARGYLL PA34 4XG

Directions: From Oban take the A816 south for 19 miles. From Loch Lomond area follow A82 then A83, finally A816 north to Arduaine.

Web: www.johansens.com/lochmelfort
E-mail: reception@lochmelfort.co.uk
Tel: 0870 381 8699
International: +44 (0)1852 200233
Fax: 01852 200214

Price Guide: (including dinner)
double/twin £118-£178
superior £138–£218

Spectacularly located on the west coast of Scotland, the Loch Melfort Hotel is a quiet hideaway on Asknish Bay, with the awe-inspiring backdrop of woodlands and the magnificent mountains of Argyll. Friendly staff attend to every need and there is a warm, welcoming atmosphere. Spacious bedrooms are lavishly appointed with bold bright fabrics, comfortable furnishings and have large patio windows overlooking the islands of Jura, Shuna and Scarba. The award-winning restaurant, which has breathtaking views stretching as far as the eye can see, is perfect for a romantic meal. Guests may feast on the sumptuous fresh local fish, shellfish and meat complemented by an extensive selection of fine wines. There is also a mouth-watering array of home-made desserts, delicious ice creams and Scottish cheeses. Skerry Bistro serves informal meals, lunches, suppers and afternoon teas. Outdoor activities include fishing, sailing, riding, windsurfing, walking and mountain biking. Visitors can explore the nearby islands and local places of interest include Mull, Kilchoan Castle, Castle Stalker and the stunning Dunstaffnage Castle (home of Clan Campbell). The Arduaine Gardens, situated adjacent to the hotel, are extremely beautiful and home to a diversity of plants and trees from all over the world. The Marine Sanctuary and Kilmartin Glen are well worth a visit.

Our inspector loved: *The super views and great food.*

ARDANAISEIG

KILCHRENAN BY TAYNUILT, ARGYLL PA35 1HE

This romantic small luxury hotel, built in 1834, stands alone in a setting of almost surreal natural beauty at the foot of Ben Cruachan. Directly overlooking Loch Awe and surrounded by wild wooded gardens, Ardanaiseig is evocative of the romance and history of the Highlands. Skilful restoration has ensured that this lovely old mansion has changed little since it was built. The elegant drawing room has log fires, bowls of fresh flowers, superb antiques, handsome paintings and marvellous views of the islands in the Loch and of faraway mountains. The traditional library, sharing this outlook, is ideal for postprandial digestifs. The charming bedrooms are peaceful, appropriate to the era of the house, yet equipped thoughtfully with all comforts. True Scottish hospitality is the philosophy of the Ardanaiseig Restaurant, renowned for its inspired use of fresh produce from the Western Highlands. Chef, Gary Goldie won a gold award in the "hotelreviewscotland" 2005 awards. The wine list is magnificent. Artistic guests enjoy the famous 100-acre Ardanaiseig gardens and nature reserve, filled with exotic shrubs and trees brought back from the Himalayas over the years. Brilliant rhododendrons and azaleas add a riot of colour. The estate also offers fishing, boating, tennis and croquet (snooker in the evenings) and exhilarating hill or lochside walks.

Directions: Reaching Taynuilt on the A85, take the B845 to Kilchrenan. Turn left at Kilchronan Inn and continue to the end of the road

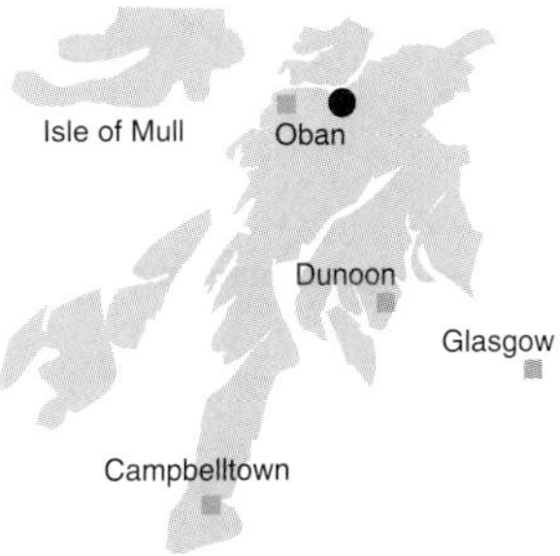

Isle of Mull, Oban, Dunoon, Glasgow, Campbelltown

Web: www.johansens.com/ardanaiseig
E-mail: ardanaiseig@clara.net
Tel: 0870 381 8319
International: +44 (0)1866 833333
Fax: 01866 833222

Price Guide:
single £80–£125
double/twin £108–£276

Our inspector loved: *The feeling of complete escape and excellent food.*

 16   28         

CAMERON HOUSE

LOCH LOMOND G83 8QZ

Directions: From Glasgow Airport, follow M8 towards Greenock, leave at jct 30, go over Erskine Toll Bridge. Join A82 towards Loch Lomond and Crianlarich. Approx 14 miles on, at Balloch roundabout, carry straight on. Hotel is 1 mile on the right.

Web: www.johansens.com/cameronhouse
E-mail: reservations@cameronhouse.co.uk
Tel: 0870 381 8588
International: +44 (0)1389 755565
Fax: 01389 759522

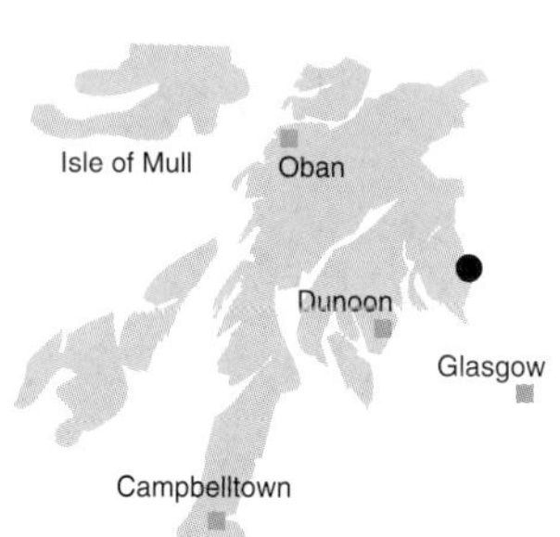

Price Guide:
single £178–£208
double/twin £245–£275
suite £395–£495

Set amidst 108 acres of countryside on the southern shores of Loch Lomond, in the Trossachs, with views of Ben Lomond and beyond, this 5-star resort is the perfect destination for business and leisure travellers. Once the home of the illustrious Smollett family, the house has been sympathetically restored to provide an elegant, timeless ambience. Bedrooms are luxuriously appointed and suites have four-poster beds with panoramic views over the loch. There are various dining options including the elegant 3 AA Rosette Georgian Room Restaurant and the more informal Smolletts Restaurant, whilst traditional afternoon tea is served in the Drawing Room. Casual dining can be enjoyed in the stylish Marina Restaurant and Bar, a contemporary restaurant centred around an open kitchen. Leisure facilities include a large lagoon-style swimming pool, sauna, steam room, Turkish bath and spa bath as well as gym, tennis, children's club, and a range of treatments at the Éspa health and beauty salon. There is golf on the "Wee Demon" 9-hole golf course, quad biking, clay pigeon shooting and numerous water sports on the loch. A golf course and spa, located close to the hotel, are due to open soon; guests will take a water taxi from the front of the hotel to reach it. The hotel's 46ft motor cruiser, the Celtic Warrior, can be hired for private cruises, weddings, various celebrations and small business meetings.

***Our inspector loved:** The location and food, which is just the best around.*

         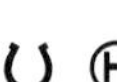 

STONEFIELD CASTLE

TARBERT, LOCH FYNE, ARGYLL PA29 6YJ

Nestled within 60 acres of its own woodland garden, Stonefield Castle stands high on the Kintyre peninsula overlooking the craggy Argyll coastline and Loch Fyne. Famed for their fisheries and smoke-houses this area has much to be proud of and guests sitting in the restaurant will have a heady combination of exemplary Scottish cuisine and the most spectacular scenery on the West Coast. The Castle was built in 1837 and stands today as a fine example of Scottish Baronial architecture, with long elegant windows, gothic turrets and imposing castellations. Each of its 33 bedrooms has been carefully designed to ensure that this period elegance is retained and indeed some of the original pieces of furniture remain in the hotel. The woodland gardens at Stonefield lure horticulturalists from far and wide to see its rare examples of exotic rhododendrons and shrubs. In fact Stonefield has the United Kingdom's second largest collection of Himalayan rhododendrons. The spectacular scenery of the local countryside makes this a stunning backdrop for summer walks or cosy autumn retreats.

Our inspector loved: *Some of the finest views and gardens in Scotland.*

Directions: Take the A82 from Glasgow along Loch Lomond side, then the A83 at Tarbert towards Campbelltown. The hotel is 10 miles past Lochgilphead on left hand side

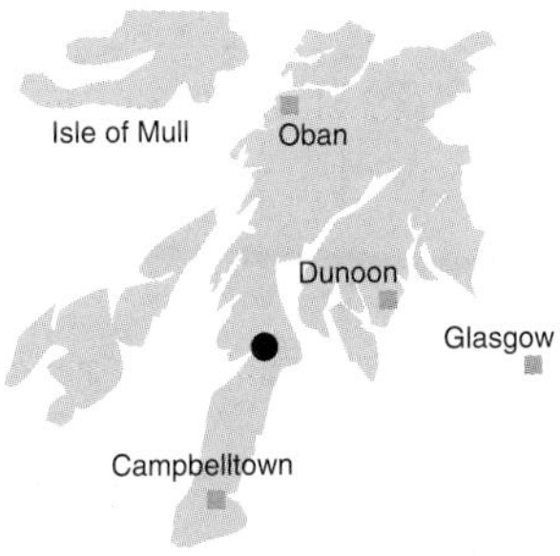

Isle of Mull
Oban
Dunoon
Glasgow
Campbelltown

Web: www.johansens.com/stonefield
E-mail: enquiries@stonefieldcastle.co.uk
Tel: 0870 381 8918
International: +44 (0)1880 820836
Fax: 01880 820929

Price Guide:
single £90–£125
double/twin £180–£200
suite £250

 33   120     

Balcary Bay Hotel

AUCHENCAIRN, NR CASTLE DOUGLAS, DUMFRIES & GALLOWAY DG7 1QZ

Enjoying a very warm climate due to its proximity to the Gulf Stream, Balcary Bay is one of Scotland's more romantic and secluded hideaways, yet only ½ hour from the bustling market town of Dumfries. As you sit in the lounge overlooking Balcary Bay, the calling of birds and the gently lapping waves compete for your attention. Guests will be greeted by genuine Scottish hospitality, which includes the provision of modern facilities with a traditional atmosphere, imaginatively prepared local delicacies such as lobsters, prawns and salmon, plus the reassuring intimacy of a family-run hotel. This hotel is a true haven for those wishing to get away from their hectic lives and an ideal break for a romantic weekend. This exciting corner of Scotland offers numerous great coastal and woodland walks, whilst nearby are several 9 and 18-hole golf courses at Colvend, Kirkcudbright, Castle Douglas, Southerness and Dumfries. There are also salmon rivers and trout lochs, sailing, shooting, riding and bird-watching facilities. The area abounds with National Trust historic properties and gardens. Seasonal short breaks and reduced inclusive rates are available for 3 and 7 night stays.

Our inspector loved: *The views from this hotel, which complete the feeling of total escape.*

Directions: Located off the A711 Dumfries–Kirkcudbright road, 2 miles out of Auchencairn on the Shore Road.

Web: www.johansens.com/balcarybay
E-mail: reservations@balcary-bay-hotel.co.uk
Tel: 0870 381 8334
International: +44 (0)1556 640217/640311
Fax: 01556 640272

Price Guide:
single £65
double/twin £115–£135

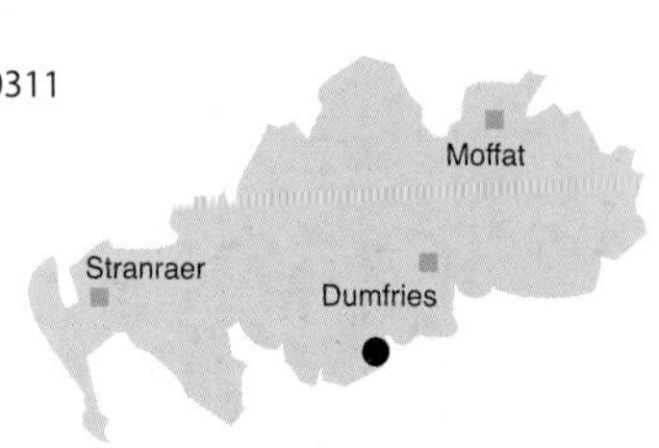

Cally Palace Hotel

GATEHOUSE OF FLEET, DUMFRIES & GALLOWAY DG7 2DL

Set in over 150 acres of forest and parkland, on the edge of Robert Burns country, this 18th-century country house has been restored to its former glory by the McMillan family, the proprietors since 1981. On entering the hotel, guests will initially be impressed by the grand scale of the interior. 2 huge marble pillars support the original moulded ceiling of the entrance hall. All the public rooms have ornate ceilings, original marble fireplaces and fine reproduction furniture. Combine these with grand, traditional Scottish cooking and you have a hotel par excellence. Awarded 1 Rosette for cuisine, Cally Palace offers a delightful dining experience enhanced by the atmospheric piano playing every evening. The 55 en-suite bedrooms have been individually decorated. Some are suites with a separate sitting room; others are large enough to accommodate a sitting area. An indoor leisure complex, completed in the style of the marble entrance hall, includes heated swimming pool, Jacuzzi and saunas. The hotel has an all-weather tennis court, a putting green, croquet and a lake. Also, for hotel guests' use only, is an 18-hole golf course, par 71, length 6,062 yards set around the lake in the grounds. Special weekend breaks are available out of season. Closed January and mid week in February.

***Our inspector loved:** The grandeur and comfort of the building combined with the friendly staff make this a real gem.*

Directions: 60 miles west of Carlisle, turn right off the A75 to Gatehouse of Fleet. The hotel entrance is on the left after approximately 1 mile just before the village.

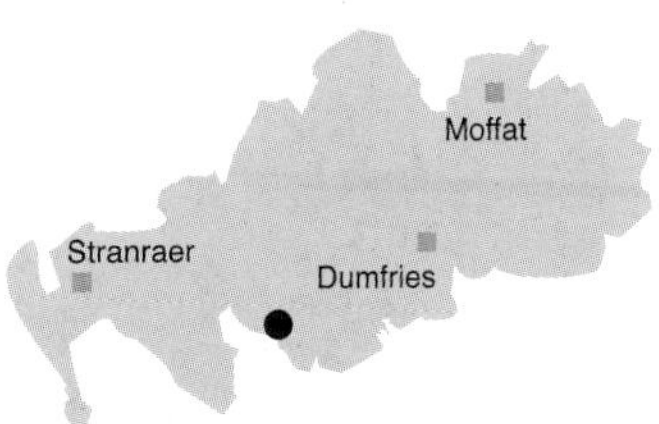

Moffat
Stranraer
Dumfries

Web: www.johansens.com/callypalace
E-mail: info@callypalace.co.uk
Tel: 0870 381 8401
International: +44 (0)1557 814341
Fax: 01557 814522

Price Guide: (including dinner, minimum 2-night stay)
single £94–£138
double/twin £178–£202

Kirroughtree House

NEWTON STEWART, WIGTOWNSHIRE DG8 6AN

Directions: From the A75 Dumfries to Stranraer road. 1 mile east of Newton Stewart turn on to the A712 towards New Galloway. The hotel entrance is 250 metres on the left.

Web: www.johansens.com/kirroughtreehouse
E-mail: info@kirroughtreehouse.co.uk
Tel: 0870 381 8659
International: +44 (0)1671 402141
Fax: 01671 402425

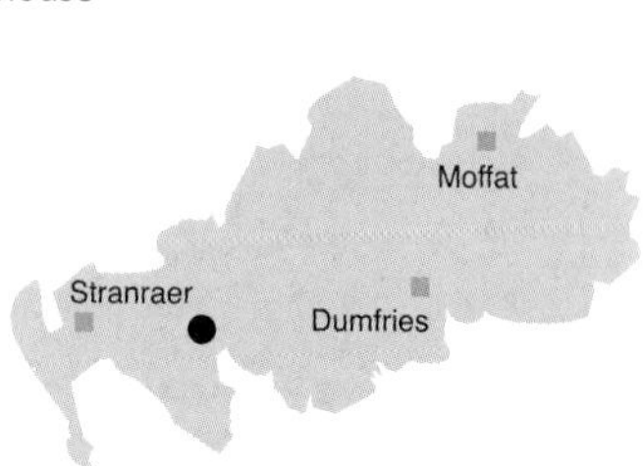

Price Guide:
single £90–£115
double/twin £160–£200
suite £210

A previous winner of the Johansens Most Excellent Service Award and the Good Hotel Guide's Scottish Hotel of the Year, Kirroughtree House is situated in the foothills of the Cairnsmore of Fleet, on the edge of Galloway Forest Park. Standing in 8 acres of landscaped gardens, guests can relax and linger over the spectacular views. Built by the Heron family in 1719, the oak-panelled lounge, with open fireplace, reflects the style of that period. From the lounge rises the original staircase, where Robert Burns often recited his poems. Each bedroom is well furnished; guests may choose to spend the night in one of the hotel's spacious de luxe bedrooms with spectacular views over the surrounding countryside. Many guests are attracted by Kirroughtree's culinary reputation, awarded 2 AA rosettes – only the finest produce is used to create meals of originality and finesse. An ideal venue for small meetings, family parties and weddings; exclusive use of the hotel can be arranged. Pitch and putt and croquet can be enjoyed in the grounds and the hotel's position makes it an ideal base for great walking expeditions. Residents can play golf on the many local courses and also have use of the exclusive 18-hole course at Cally Palace. Trout and salmon fishing, shooting and deer stalking during the season can all be organised. Short breaks available.

Our inspector loved: *The classic elegance and exceptional service.*

The Bonham

35 DRUMSHEUGH GARDENS, EDINBURGH EH3 7RN

This award-winning, boutique-style hotel is situated just a few minutes walk from the West End of Edinburgh and is equally suitable for a restful weekend or a high-intensity business trip. Many of the original Victorian features of the 3 converted town houses have been maintained. The interior has been designed to create a contemporary ambience within the classic timelessness of a Victorian town house. Each room has been elegantly and dramatically created with modern furniture and art, using rich, bold colours to produce tasteful oversized abundance throughout. The Bonham offers a traditional feel with a modern twist, coupled with impeccable standards and individuality. Purely for pleasure, each of the 48 bedrooms offers 55 channel cable TV, a mini-bar and e-TV, which provides a complete PC capability, Internet and E-mail access as well as DVD video and CD player. The Events Room is a perfect setting for a range of select meetings and private dining. Restaurant at The Bonham, the most timeless contemporary restaurant in Edinburgh, serves distinct European inspired cuisine which is complemented by provocative wines. Along with its famous castle and numerous shops, Edinburgh houses Scotland's national galleries and some splendid museums.

Our inspector loved: *The design and décor of the hotel make it surely one of the coolest in Edinburgh.*

Directions: The Hotel is situated in the city centre's West End.

Web: www.johansens.com/bonham
E-mail: reserve@thebonham.com
Tel: 0870 381 8373
International: +44 (0)131 274 7400
Fax: 0131 274 7405

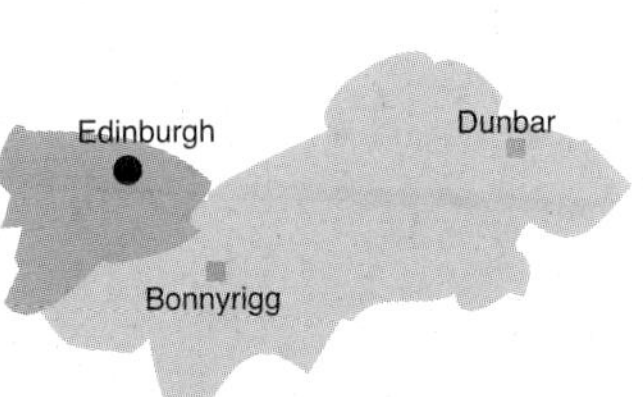
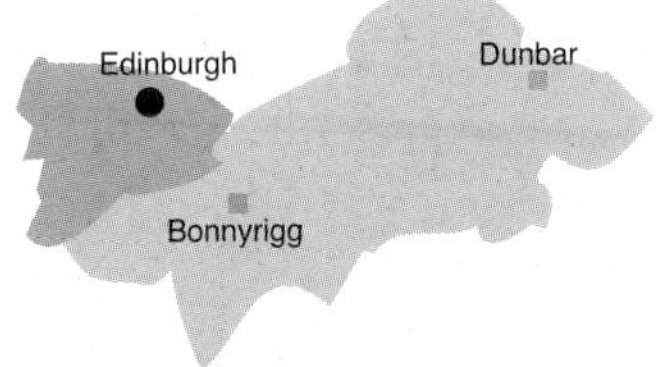

Price Guide:
single: £108–£165
double/twin £127–£195
suprior double/twin £168–£245
suites £221–£350

BRUNTSFIELD HOTEL

69 BRUNTSFIELD PLACE, EDINBURGH EH10 4HH

This elegant Victorian town house first became a hotel in the 1920s and has maintained a reputation for its special charm and character ever since. Located just a few minutes from the hustle and bustle of the city centre, guests arriving here will relish the peace and tranquillity of its setting overlooking the leafy Bruntsfield Links, one of Edinburgh's oldest golfing areas and now an elegant park. The traditional Victorian architecture is mirrored inside the building with carefully decorated bedrooms and lounges to ensure that a welcoming ambience of warmth and comfort is maintained throughout the hotel. Many of the 71 carefully appointed bedrooms have delightful views, either of the Links or Edinburgh Castle and beyond towards the Old Town; there are also a number of larger rooms with 4-poster beds. The hotel offers 2 dining settings: the Cardoon restaurant with its relaxed-style and atmosphere, which serves an award-winning selection of freshly prepared dishes using local produce, and the less formal Kings Bar, a popular meeting place which is open all day for drinks, light meals, snacks and coffees. Bruntsfield Hotel is the ideal base from which to explore the vibrant and cosmopolitan Scottish capital with its excellent shopping, wonderful historic sites and many festivals.

Our inspector loved: *The different dining options and the great outlook over a grass meadow despite being in the city centre.*

Directions: Join the A702 city bypass, exit at Lothianburn to Bruntsfield Place. The hotel overlooks Bruntsfield Links Park.

Web: www.johansens.com/bruntsfield
E-mail: reservations@thebruntsfield.co.uk
Tel: 0870 381 8388
International: +44 (0)131 229 1393
Fax: 0131 229 5634

Price Guide:
single £79-£120
double/twin £120-£250

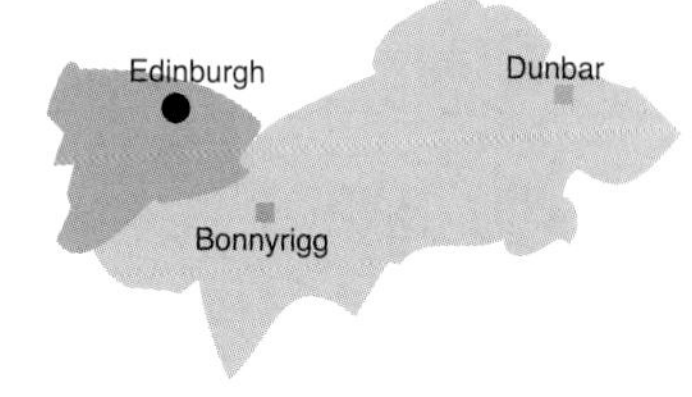

CHANNINGS

15 SOUTH LEARMONTH GARDENS, EDINBURGH EH4 1EZ

Channings is located on a quiet cobbled street only 10 minutes' walk from the centre of Edinburgh, with easy access to the shops on Princes Street and the timeless grandeur of Edinburgh Castle. The hotel, formerly 5 Edwardian town houses, retains its original features, which have been restored with flair and consideration, and the atmosphere is like that of an exclusive country club. With an ambience of country-style tranquillity, guests can relax in one of the fully refurbished lounges with coffee or afternoon tea served by the friendliest of staff. For those who like to browse, the hotel has an interesting collection of antique prints, furniture, objets d'art, periodicals and books. The atmosphere is perfect for discreet company meetings, small conferences and private or corporate events, which may be held. These may take place in the oak-panelled Library or Kingsleigh. The restaurant offers a varied eating experience. Hubert Lamort Head Chef, has developed an impressive repertoire of Mediterranean inspired dishes. His sound product knowledge results in a colourful menu combining traditional ingredients with simplistic, modern twists.

Our inspector loved: *The location; in the heart of Edinburgh yet overlooking green grass and with the friendliest of staff.*

Directions: Go north-west from Queensferry Street, over Dean Bridge on to Queensferry Road. Take the 3rd turning on the right down South Learmonth Avenue, then turn right at the end into South Learmonth Gardens.

Edinburgh
Dunbar
Bonnyrigg

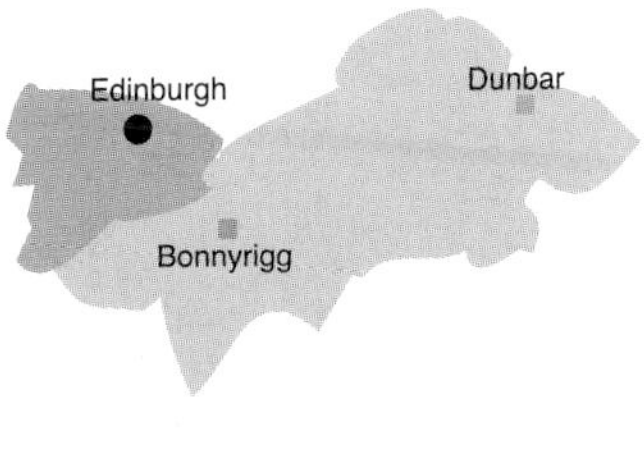

Web: www.johansens.com/channings
E-mail: reserve@channings.co.uk
Tel: 0870 381 8413
International: +44 (0)131 274 7401
Fax: 0131 274 7405

Price Guide:
single £101–£160
double/twin £131–£230
four poster/suite £187–£275

THE EDINBURGH RESIDENCE

7 ROTHESAY TERRACE, EDINBURGH EH3 7RY,

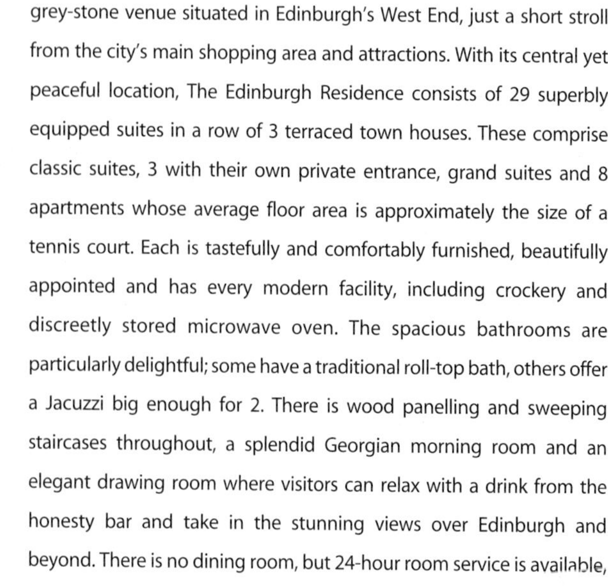

Space, luxury, privacy and convenience can be enjoyed at this stylish, grey-stone venue situated in Edinburgh's West End, just a short stroll from the city's main shopping area and attractions. With its central yet peaceful location, The Edinburgh Residence consists of 29 superbly equipped suites in a row of 3 terraced town houses. These comprise classic suites, 3 with their own private entrance, grand suites and 8 apartments whose average floor area is approximately the size of a tennis court. Each is tastefully and comfortably furnished, beautifully appointed and has every modern facility, including crockery and discreetly stored microwave oven. The spacious bathrooms are particularly delightful; some have a traditional roll-top bath, others offer a Jacuzzi big enough for 2. There is wood panelling and sweeping staircases throughout, a splendid Georgian morning room and an elegant drawing room where visitors can relax with a drink from the honesty bar and take in the stunning views over Edinburgh and beyond. There is no dining room, but 24-hour room service is available, and just a short walk away is the Residence's sister restaurant, The Bonham, whose European-inspired cuisine has earned it a high reputation. Small private or corporate events can be accommodated.

Our inspector loved: *This stylish and relaxed alternative to a traditional hotel; great service with great style.*

Directions: From the West End of Princes Street head towards West Register Street. Princes Street becomes Rutland Place then Shandwich Place. Turn right into Coates Crescent then right again into Walker Street. Walker Street turns into Drumsheugh Gardens. Turn left at Rothesay Terrace.

Web: www.johansens.com/edinburghres
E-mail: reserve@theedinburghresidence.com
Tel: 0870 381 8913
International: +44 (0)131 274 7403
Fax: 0131 274 7405

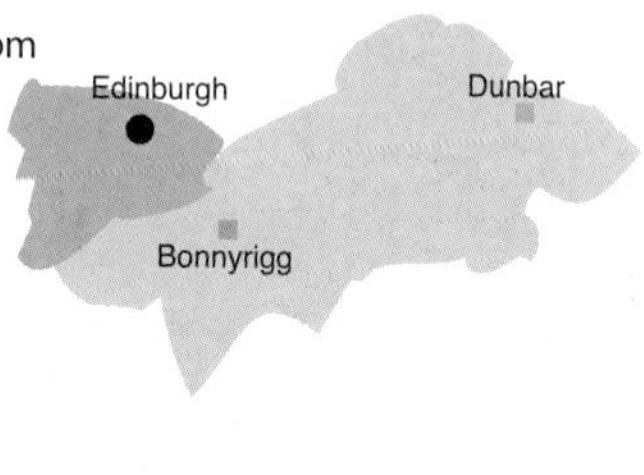

Edinburgh · Dunbar · Bonnyrigg

Price Guide:
suite £135–£280
town house apartment £260–£395

29

15

NUMBER TEN WITH CHRISTOPHER NORTH HOUSE

6 & 10 GLOUCESTER PLACE, EDINBURGH EH3 6EF

Behind its graceful grey-stone façade highlighted by tall, colourfully draped windows and slender, decorative wrought-iron pavement railings this lovely old house is the epitome of elegance and style. Surrounded by similarly attractive architecture it stands serenely in the splendid residential area of Edinburgh's New Town, a short walk from Princes Street and the business district of Charlotte Square. Originally the home of poet, writer and moral philosopher Christopher North, who lived here from 1823 to 1854, the house has been tastefully refurbished and extended over the years, and today it is an attractive boutique-style residence with a contemporary ambience that blends superbly into the classic timelessness of a Georgian town house. Many original features have been retained in lounges and bedrooms, which have been delightfully decorated and furnished to ensure a welcoming atmosphere of warmth and comfort. Each en-suite guest room is individually designed to appeal to the most discerning leisure or business traveller. Home-from-home comforts include television, direct dial telephone, tea and coffee making tray and baby listening service. Guests can enjoy pre-dinner drinks in the friendly Mozart Kaffee Haus before sampling the Bacchus restaurant's delicious and varied menu.

***Our inspector loved:** The warm and personal welcome and the lovely new suites in Number Ten.*

 29     

Directions: In the heart of Georgian Edinburgh, only 5 minutes walk from Princes Street, down Charlotte Square to Moray Place and the hotel.

Web: www.johansens.com/christophernorth
E-mail: reservations@christophernorth.co.uk
Tel: 0870 381 9310
International: +44 (0)131 225 2720
Fax: 0131 220 4706

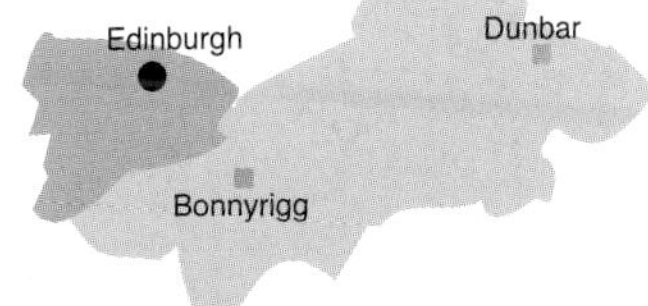

Price Guide:
single £88–£110
double/twin £120–£160
Executive double £120–£180
Executive suite £160–£240

EDINBURGH

THE HOWARD

34 GREAT KING STREET, EDINBURGH EH3 6QH

Directions: From Queen Street turn north into Dundas Street, then take the third right into Great King Street. The hotel is on the left.

Web: www.johansens.com/howardedinburgh
E-mail: reserve@thehoward.com
Tel: 0870 381 8626
International: +44 (0)131 274 7402
Fax: 0131 274 7405

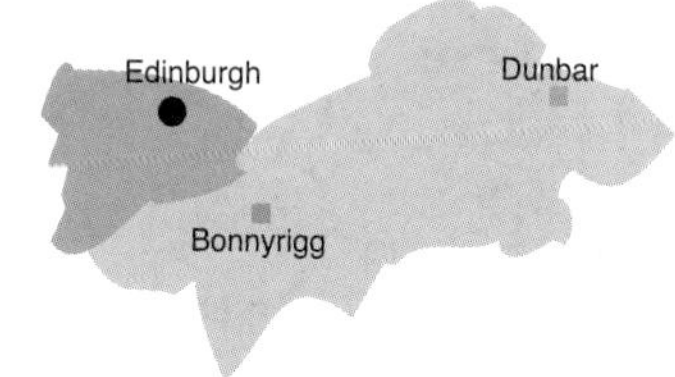

Price Guide:
single £108–£210
double/twin £180–£275
suite £243–£395
grand suite £273–£395

Situated in the heart of Edinburgh, with good connections by train and easily accessible from Edinburgh Airport, this 5-star hotel, originally built as a private house, ensures that each guest is made to feel special and experiences traditional Georgian pampering as if a guest in a private home. Visitors take a step back in time at The Howard where attention to detail and attentive service is paramount. A team of butlers will take care of guests' unpacking, serve afternoon tea and will even arrange a social itinerary for exploring nearby Edinburgh, with its chic designer boutiques just a 10-minute walk away in George Street. Some of the 17 individually decorated bedrooms boast free-standing roll-top baths, Jacuzzi and a power or double shower; 3 suites feature exclusive terraced gardens and private entrances. 24-hour room service is available and dinner, selected from the à la carte menu, may be served in the comfort of guests' bedrooms by their personal butler. Alternatively, dining at The Atholl is an unforgettable experience where the talented team of chefs create meticulously prepared cuisine. This is an elegant Georgian setting ideal for personal entertaining , private corporate gatherings and civil wedding ceremonies.

Our inspector loved: *The most discreet personal service and the incredible consideration to detail.*

GLASSOW

One Devonshire Gardens

1 DEVONSHIRE GARDENS, GLASGOW, G12 0UX

Only 10 minutes from the city centre, One Devonshire Gardens is set in the heart of Glasgow's fashionable West End with its tree-lined terraces and Victorian mansions. Quite simply for those who expect and appreciate the finest of standards, this multi-award-winning hotel is situated in a series of converted period townhouses offering luxurious accommodation and exquisite cuisine. It's all about individuality, and all 35 bedrooms have their own distinctive identity, imaginative and unusual use of classic and contemporary furnishings. Public areas reflect the grandeur of a bygone era with antiques and original Scottish artwork throughout, and guests are entrusted to old-fashioned values of genuine personal service in relaxing comfort and style. The terraced garden is perfect for afternoon teas on a sunny day or pre-dinner drinks on a balmy evening. The hotel has an air-conditioned residents-only gym, equipped with a range of cardio and resistance equipment, together with cardio-theatre; a personal trainer can be organised. Guests can enjoy a range of in-room spa treatments and can request a personalized yoga instructor in the comfort of their own room, both by prior arrangement. 2 dining options are offered including the hotel's award-winning fine dining 2 AA Rosette No 5 Restaurant, and Room Glasgow offering classic cuisine with a contemporary twist.

Our inspector loved: *The incredible effort made to add those little touches that make this hotel the very best there is.*

Directions: From the M8 take junction 17 and follow signs for the A82 Dumbarton/Kelvinside (Great Western Road).

Web: www.johansens.com/onedevonshire
E-mail: reservations@onedevonshiregardens.com
Tel: 0870 381 9146
International: +44 (0)141 3392001
Fax: 0141 3371663

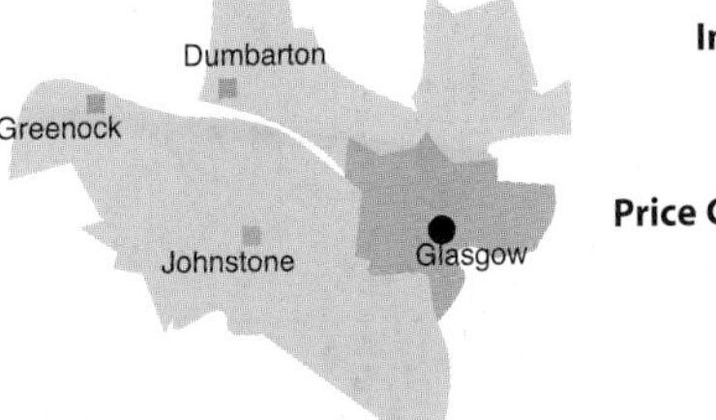

Price Guide: (Continental breakfast £12, full Scottish breakfast £17)
double £135-£295
town house suite from £365

ROYAL MARINE HOTEL

GOLF ROAD, BRORA, SUTHERLAND KW9 6QS

Directions: A 1-hour drive from Inverness. Travel north on the A9, signposted Wick. In Brora cross the bridge and turn right. The hotel is 100 yards on the left.

Web: www.johansens.com/royalmarine
E-mail: info@highlandescape.com
Tel: 0870 381 9133
International: +44 (0)1408 621252
Fax: 01408 621181

Price Guide:
single £79
double £120-£160

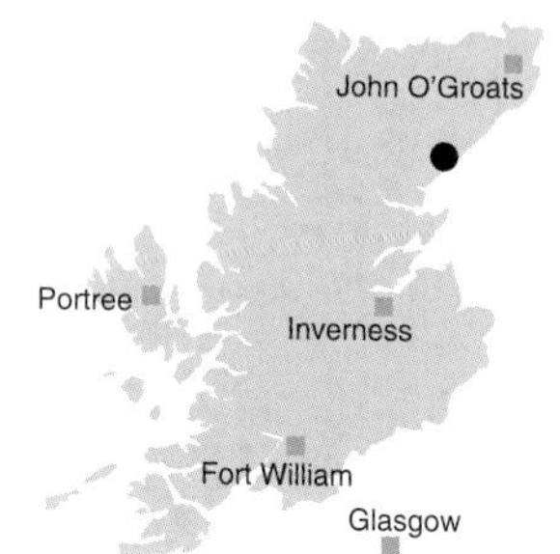

Overlooking the mouth of River Brora, Royal Marine Hotel, designed by Sir Robert Lorimer in 1913, has undergone great restoration to its original antique furniture, woodwork and panelling. Passing under the wooden arches of the entrance hall and ascending the grand staircase, guests step back in time to refined living of a bygone era. All 22 en-suite bedrooms offer modern comfort whilst retaining the ambience of early 20th-century elegance, and the new luxury additions of 24, two bedroomed apartments with magnificent views over Brora Golf Course and the Dornoch Firth. Scottish cuisine is served in the Sir Robert Lorimer Dining Room where fresh seafood, local salmon, meat and game, are all on the menu, complemented by a varied wine list. Less formal meals are taken in Hunter's Bistro where a fine selection of malt whiskies can be sampled and the Garden Room Café Bar in the Leisure Club also serves lighter snacks all day. The Leisure Club features an indoor swimming pool, gymnasium, sauna, steam room and Jacuzzi. There are several golf courses nearby, including Royal Dornoch and the Brora Championship course is just a 1-minute walk from the hotel. Sea angling, walking and hawking expeditions can all be arranged. The hotel maintains 2 fishing boats on Loch Brora, which are available for hire.

Our inspector loved: *This very traditional hotel with excellent facilities and great golf on the doorstep.*

Inverlochy Castle

TORLUNDY, FORT WILLIAM PH33 6SN

Set amidst gorgeous scenery in the foothills of Ben Nevis, Inverlochy was built in 1863 by the first Lord Abinger, and as a visitor in 1873 Queen Victoria wrote of it, "I never saw a lovelier or more romantic spot." Today, with new manager, Norbert Lieder, the castle is a splendid hotel. A massive reception room has Venetian crystal chandeliers, a Michaelangelo-style ceiling and a handsome staircase leading through to 3 elaborately decorated dining rooms and the Drawing Room, which has views over the castle's private loch and recently underwent a designer makeover. Spacious bedrooms, all with individual furnishings, offer every comfort. Michelin-starred chef Matt Gray, continues to create menus featuring modern British cuisine using the finest local ingredients including local game, hand picked wild mushrooms and scallops from the Isle of Skye. Various outdoor activities are available to guests, such as golf, clay pigeon shooting, guided walking, fly fishing for brown trout, pony trekking and tennis. Stunning places of landscape and history await exploration nearby: the mountains of Glencoe, the falls at Glen Nevis, the monument at Glenfinnan and many more.

Our inspector loved: *The Victorian splendour combining tasteful, contemporary grandeur, great wines and wonderful food.*

Directions: 3m north-east of Fort William on the A82.

Web: www.johansens.com/inverlochy
E-mail: info@inverlochy.co.uk
Tel: 0870 381 9278
International: +44 (0)1397 702177
Fax: 01397 702953

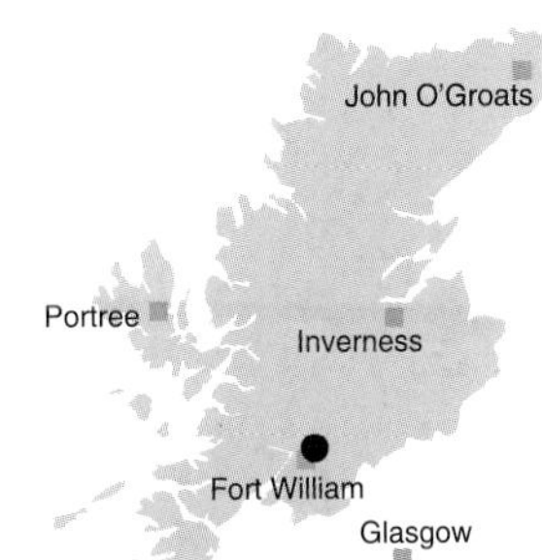

Price Guide:
single £220-£580
double £300-£495
suite £470-£580

Muckrach Lodge Hotel & Restaurant

DULNAIN BRIDGE, BY GRANTOWN-ON-SPEY, INVERNESS-SHIRE PH26 3LY

Set in 10 acres of landscaped grounds and surrounded by the woods and farms of Muckrach estate, this former sporting lodge has a relaxed ambience with an awe-inspiring backdrop of Cairngorms National Park. Quality of service is paramount in this welcoming hotel, where a comfortable atmosphere has been lovingly created with plump sofas, log fires and vases of fresh flowers, and the new self-catering unit, formerly the annex rooms, provides total privacy. The finest quality beef, lamb, game, fish and shellfish are locally sourced and served in the hotel's excellent 2 AA Rosette restaurant, with its distinguished cellar of fine wines and rare malts. There is a large selection of books, magazines and games to enjoy by the fireside or, for the more energetic, the beautiful National Park offers stunning mountains, heather moors, ancient forests and sparkling lochs in the valley of the River Spey. Muckrach Lodge is the ideal base for touring the Highlands, Loch Ness, Royal Deeside and the picturesque Moray coastal villages. The Malt Whisky and Castle Trails are extremely interesting and Strathspey's turbulent history can be discovered by visiting the area's cathedrals, forts and museums. The area is renowned for its rare natural history and offers superb golf with Royal Dornoch, Nairn, Boat of Garten and many others. Alternatively, fishing, riding and watersports are available.

Our inspector loved: *The relaxed style and the absence of pretentiousness.*

Directions: Muckrach Lodge is 3 miles South West of Grantown-on-Spey on the B9102 and A95, through Dulnain Bridge Village on the A938.

Web: www.johansens.com/muckrachlodge
E-mail: stay@muckrach.co.uk
Tel: 0870 381 8751
International: +44 (0)1479 851257
Fax: 01479 851325

Price Guide:
single £65–£85
double/twin £130–£170
good value short breaks available

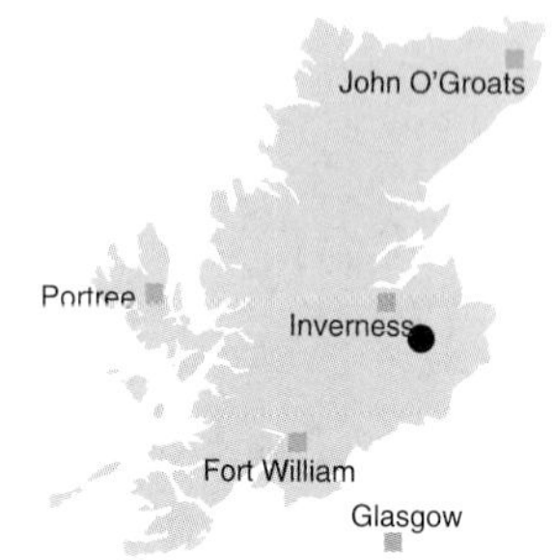

Kincraig House Hotel

INVERGORDON, ROSS-SHIRE, SCOTLAND IV18 0LF

Built in 1820, this historic country house is full of character and is set within 5 acres of its own elevated gardens with picturesque views over the Cromarty Firth. Inverness Airport is only 35 minutes away, and some of Scotland's finest golf courses, beaches and scenery are situated on the doorstep. The hotel has 15 bedrooms, all with en-suite facilities, each with its own distinct charm. Four-poster beds, moulded ceilings and elegant fireplaces retain a period feel, whilst the lounge has oak panelled walls that add warmth and atmosphere to this fine buiding. The restaurant overlooking the gardens has a relaxed atmosphere and offers guests the chance to enjoy some excellent cuisine. Service is friendly and unobtrusive, with the lounge an exceptional and popular spot amongst regular guests wishing to enjoy a Dalmore malt whisky after dinner from the local distillery. The beautiful Loch Ness, Isle of Skye and Inverness the Highland capital are all within easy access of the hotel.

Our inspector loved: *The beautiful period features.*

Directions: Located on the A9, on the left-hand side 2 miles north of the turn off signposted Alness and Invergordon.

Web: www.johansens.com/kincraighouse
E-mail: info@kincraig-house-hotel.co.uk
Tel: 0870 381 9323
International: +44 (0)1349 852587
Fax: 01349 852193

Price Guide:
single £55–£65
double £90–£170

BUNCHREW HOUSE HOTEL

INVERNESS IV3 8TA

This splendid 17th-century Scottish mansion, "Hotel on the Shore", is set amidst 20 acres of landscaped gardens and woodlands on the shores of the Beauly Firth. Guests can enjoy breathtaking views of Ben Wyvis and the Black Isle, while just yards from the house the sea laps at the garden walls. Bunchrew has been carefully restored to preserve its heritage, whilst still giving its guests the highest standards of comfort and convenience. A continual schedule of refurbishment is on-going. The bedrooms are beautifully furnished and decorated to enhance their natural features. The elegant panelled drawing room is the ideal place to relax at any time, and during winter log fires lend it an added appeal which has given the hotel 4-star status. In the candle-lit restaurant the traditional cuisine includes prime Scottish beef, fresh lobster and langoustines, locally caught game and venison and freshly grown vegetables which has been rewarded with 2 AA Rosettes. A carefully chosen wine list complements the menu. Local places of interest include Cawdor Castle, Loch Ness, Castle Urquhart and a number of beautiful glens. For those who enjoy sport there is skiing at nearby Aviemore, sailing, cruising, golf, shooting and fishing.

Our inspector loved: *The cosy charm and splendid shore location.*

Directions: From Inverness follow signs to Beauly, Dingwall on the A862. 1 mile from the outskirts of Inverness the entrance to the hotel is on the right.

Web: www.johansens.com/bunchrewhouse
E-mail: welcome@bunchrew-inverness.co.uk
Tel: 0870 381 8393
International: +44 (0)1463 234917
Fax: 01463 710620

Price Guide:
single £95–£160
double/twin £140–£220

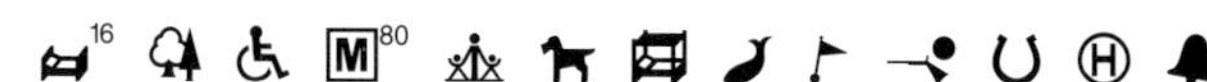

Culloden House

CULLODEN, INVERNESS, INVERNESS-SHIRE IV2 7BZ

A majestic circular drive leads to the splendour of this handsome Georgian mansion, battle headquarters of Bonnie Prince Charlie 253 years ago. 3 miles from Inverness, this handsome Palladian country house stands in 40 acres of beautiful gardens and peaceful parkland roamed by roe deer. Princes past and present and guests from throughout the world have enjoyed the hotel's ambience and hospitality. Rich furnishings, sparkling chandeliers, impressive Adam fireplaces and ornate plaster reliefs add to the grandness of the hotel's luxurious, high-ceilinged rooms. The bedrooms are appointed to the highest standard, many having four-poster beds and Jacuzzis. 4 non-smoking suites are in the Pavilion Annex, which overlooks a 3-acre walled garden and 2 in the West Pavilion. In the Dining Room guests can savour superb cuisine prepared by chef Michael Simpson, who trained at Gleneagles Hotel and the Hamburg Conference Centre. There is an outdoor tennis court and indoor sauna. Shooting, fishing and pony-trekking can be arranged, while nearby are Cawdor Castle, the Clava Cairns Bronze Age burial ground and Culloden battlefield. AA 4 stars and 2 Rosettes, Scottish Tourist Board 4 stars.

Our inspector loved: *The elegant exterior and great comfort and service once inside.*

Directions: Leave Inverness on the A96 towards Aberdeen and take the right turn off to Culloden. The hotel is signposted on the left ¾ mile after turning.

Web: www.johansens.com/cullodenhouseinverness
E-mail: info@cullodenhouse.co.uk
Tel: 0870 381 9137
International: +44 (0)1463 790461
Fax: 01463 792181

Price Guide:
single £155–£189
double £210–£260
suite £260–£290

Cuillin Hills Hotel

PORTREE, ISLE OF SKYE IV51 9QU

Directions: Skye can be reached by bridge from Kyle of Localsh or by ferry from Mallaig or Glenelg. From Portree take the A855 to Staffin. After ½ mile take the road to Budhmor.

Web: www.johansens.com/cuillinhills
E-mail: info@cuillinhills-hotel-skye.co.uk
Tel: 0870 381 8467
International: +44 (0)1478 612003
Fax: 01478 613092

Price Guide:
single £55–£75
double/twin £110–£230

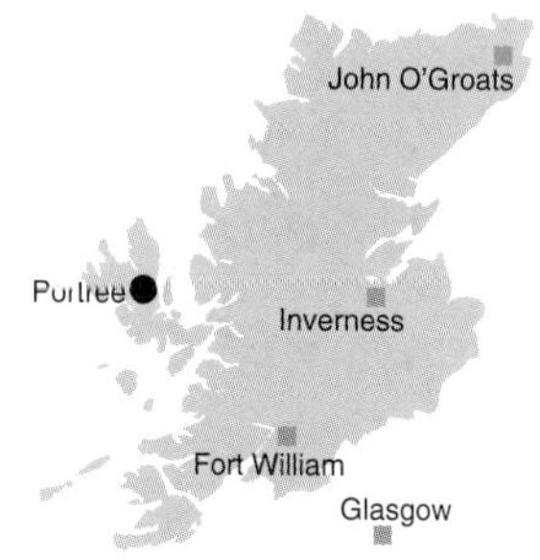

Spectacular views of the majestic Cuillin Mountains and Portree Bay on the beautiful Isle of Skye make this hotel the perfect choice for any discerning visitor. Originally built in the 1870s as a hunting lodge, Cuillin Hills Hotel benefits from 15 acres of private mature grounds, which create a secluded setting and tranquil atmosphere. Quality and comfort is a priority, reflected in the beautiful furniture and décor of the lounge, where guests can relax in front of the log fire and sample the extensive choice of malt whiskys. Spacious bedrooms are elegantly furnished and decorated to the highest standard with all modern conveniences. Imaginative and traditional cuisine combine to create award-winning delights, which are served in the stylish restaurant overlooking the bay. Guests may feast on highland game, lobster, scallops and other deliciously fresh local produce as well as tasty homemade desserts. An interesting selection of informal meals is served in the bar. The island's rich history can be discovered through its castles, museums and visitor centres. There is an abundance of beautiful unspoilt coastal paths and woodland walks nearby. The town of Portree is a mere 10 minutes' walk away.

Our inspector loved: *The panoramic position of this well-kept, friendly hotel.*

Loch Torridon Country House Hotel

Torridon, by Achnasheen, Wester-Ross IV22 2EY

Loch Torridon is gloriously situated at the foot of wooded mountains on the shores of the loch from which it derives its name. Built as a shooting lodge for the first Earl of Lovelace in 1887, in a 58-acre estate containing formal gardens, mature trees and resident Highland cattle. Today, Daniel and Rohaise Rose-Bristow welcome guests into their home offering the best in Highland hospitality. Awarded Top 200 status in the AA and 3 Red Stars, the hotel has 18 bedrooms which are luxuriously decorated. The Victorian kitchen garden provides chef, Kevin Broome, with fresh herbs, salad and a variety of fruits and vegetables. Dinner is served from 7pm - 8.45pm where an extensive fine dining table d'hôte menu is offered. Guests may begin with white bean and barley slice, wrapped in home cured wild sea salmon with garden beetroot and Marjoram fondue followed by roast fillet and braised aromatic belly free-range Highland pork, chickpea and olive casserole, shallot mash, jus of pork. Providing a seasonal alternative, dinner is also served in the more informal Ben Damph Bar and Restaurant with rooms where alternative accommodation is available. Outdoor pursuits: archery; mountain biking; clay pigeon shooting; a huge choice of low and high level walks; boating; fishing; and the opportunity to watch otters, seals and whales.

Our inspector loved: *The highly appropriate hotel legend, "where spirits soar and eagles fly."*

Directions: The hotel is 10 miles from Kinlochewe on the A896. Do not turn off to Torridon village.

Web: www.johansens.com/lochtorridon
E-mail: enquiries@lochtorridonhotel.com
Tel: 0870 381 9136
International: +44 (0)1445 791242
Fax: 01445 712253

Price Guide:
single £67–£116
double/twin £116–£348
master suite £212–£348

DALHOUSIE CASTLE AND SPA

NR EDINBURGH, BONNYRIGG EH19 3JB

For over 700 years Dalhousie Castle has nestled in beautiful parkland, providing warm Scottish hospitality. There are fascinating reminders of a rich and turbulent history, such as the 2 AA Rosette Vaulted Dungeon Restaurant; a delightful setting in which to enjoy classical French and traditional Scottish "Castle Cuisine". 15 of the 29 Castle bedrooms are historically themed and include the James VI, Mary Queen of Scots, Robert the Bruce and William Wallace. The "de Ramseia" suite houses the 500-year-old "Well". There are also 7 en-suite bedrooms in the 100-year-old Lodge. Five carefully renovated function rooms provide a unique setting for conferences for up to 120 delegates, banquets and weddings for up to 100 guests. Extensive parking and a helipad are on site. Dalhousie Castle is only 7 miles from Edinburgh city centre and just 14 miles from the International Airport. The Castle has a Scottish Tourist Board 4 Star classification. The Aqueous Spa includes a hydro pool, Laconium, Ottoman and treatment rooms. The Orangery Restaurant, overlooking the South Esk River, offers contemporary Scottish/European dining. Activities including Dalhousie Castle Falconry with its own mews where guests can enjoy a private display and learn to fly Eagles, Owls, Hawks and Falcons. Clay pigeon shooting can be arranged given prior notice as well as golf at nearby courses.

Our inspector loved: *If you shun modern, soulless accommodation in favour of a bit of up-market sophistication this is the place for you.*

Directions: From Edinburgh on city by pass take the city by pass south to the A7, through Newtongrange. Turn right at the junction onto B704, hotel is ³/₄ mile and well signposted.

Web: www.johansens.com/dalhousiecastle
E-mail: info@dalhousiecastle.co.uk
Tel: 0870 381 8472
International: +44 (0)1875 820153
Fax: 01875 821936

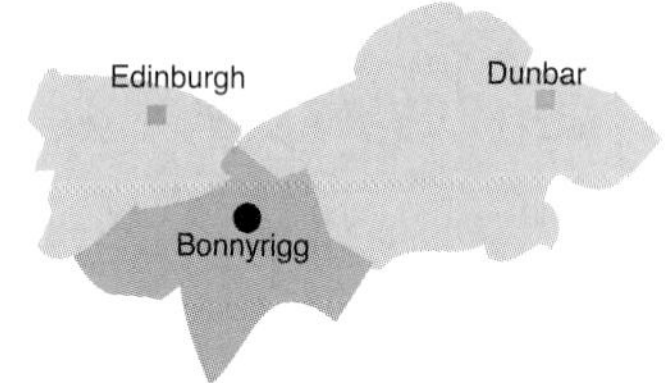

Price Guide:
single from £130
double from £175

GLENEAGLES

AUCHTERARDER, PERTHSHIRE PH3 1NF

Known as the "great palace in the glen" this luxurious hotel nestles in the heart of the Ochil Hills on the edge of the Highlands in the White Muir of Auchterarder. From its Georgian-style windows and lush green grounds guests can marvel at views of Ben Lomond and the Grampians. The Gleneagles Hotel is enveloped by clean, crisp air and an artistic landscape capped by an ever-changing sky of blue, violet and autumnal gold. It is a haven of comfort and impeccable service. The interior has been redesigned and refurbished with 21st-century amenities, whilst offering the charm and atmosphere of a Scottish country house. The elegant public rooms are enhanced by superb antique furniture. The 256 bedrooms and 13 suites have every home-from-home comfort, in subtle, yet dramatic colours with sensual fabrics and spacious bathrooms. Many have stunning views across Gleneagles' lawns, estate and golf courses. Guests may dine in the sophisticated Strathearn and Michelin-starred Andrew Fairlie restaurants, whilst a cosy bar serves light lunches and afternoon teas. Championship golf facilities and a variety of country sports and pursuits can be enjoyed. Superb leisure facilities. Less than 50 miles from Edinburgh and Glasgow Airports.

Our inspector loved: *This ever-improving star of Scottish hotels, great food options, polished service and everything to do, golf especially.*

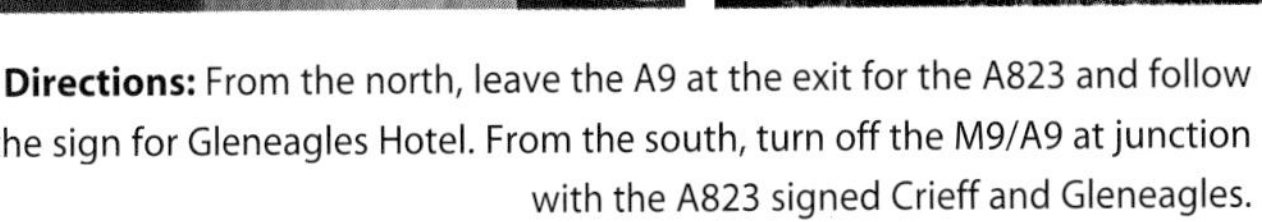

Directions: From the north, leave the A9 at the exit for the A823 and follow the sign for Gleneagles Hotel. From the south, turn off the M9/A9 at junction with the A823 signed Crieff and Gleneagles.

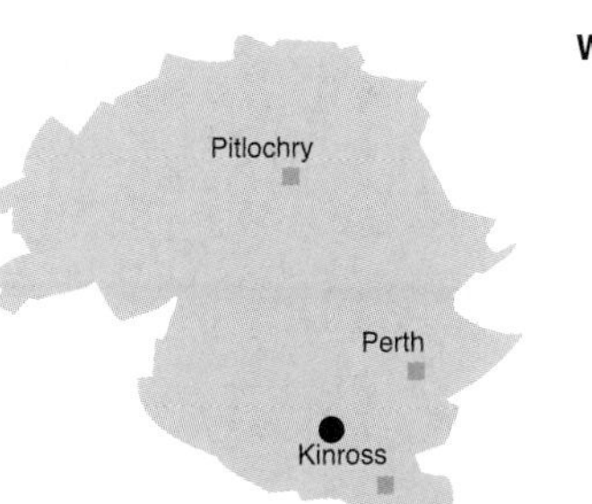

Web: www.johansens.com/gleneagles
E-mail: resort.sales@gleneagles.com
Tel: 0870 381 8553
International: +44 (0)1764 662231
Fax: 01764 662134

Price Guide:
double/twin £355–£500
suite £830–£1,800

The Royal Hotel

MELVILLE SQUARE, COMRIE, PERTHSHIRE PH6 2DN

Set in an area of outstanding natural beauty, this former inn was once frequented by personalities such as Rob Roy McGregor and Queen Victoria, whose stay bestowed the name of The Royal Hotel on Comrie's major inn. Its homely yet luxurious and elegant atmosphere is enhanced by open log fires, period furnishings and genuine Highland hospitality provided by the cheerful staff and the Milsom family, who also own the Tufton Arms Hotel, Appleby. The 11 bedrooms have been individually designed and show exceptional attention to detail. Alternatively, guests may rent the apartment within the grounds, which accommodates up to 6 people. An ideal place to unwind, the comfortable Lounge Bar is popular for pre-dinner drinks, which include a choice of over 130 whiskies. Scottish cuisine and fine wines are enjoyed in the conservatory-style Brasserie or the more intimate Royal Restaurant, where chef David Milsom and his team, awarded an AA Rosette, create delicious dishes based on fresh local produce. Located amidst superb walking country, guests may take gentle walks in the nearby Glens and across the hills and moorlands. The hotel has its own stretch of the river Earn for fishing, and fowl or clay pigeon shooting can be arranged. Comrie is surrounded by excellent golf courses from scenic Highland layouts to idyllic parkland settings, such as the famous Gleneagles.

Our inspector loved: *This modern inn "par excellence".*

Directions: Located in the centre of the village, on the A85.

Web: www.johansens.com/royalcomrie
E-mail: reception@royalhotel.co.uk
Tel: 0870 381 8875
International: +44 (0)1764 679200
Fax: 01764 679219

Price Guide:
single £75
double £120
suite £160

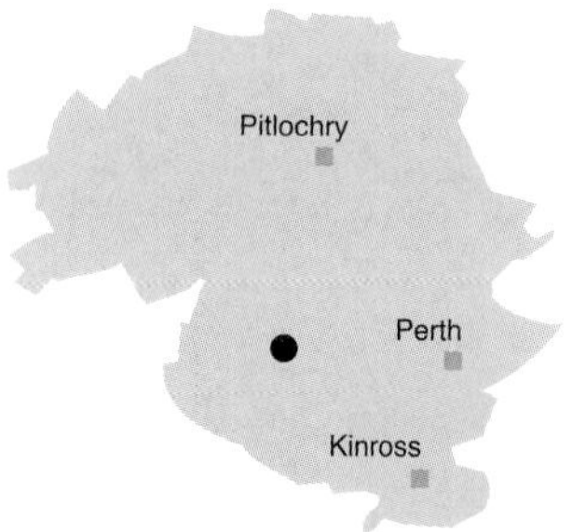

KINNAIRD

KINNAIRD ESTATE, BY DUNKELD, PERTHSHIRE PH8 0LB

With a panoramic vista across the Tay Valley, Kinnaird is surrounded by a beautiful 9,000-acre estate, ideally situated for those seeking a relaxing break or enthusiasts of outdoor pursuits. Built in 1770 this Edwardian mansion boasts 8 individually decorated bedrooms with exquisite fabrics, deep cushioned sofas, gas log fires and opulent bathrooms. In the courtyard are 2 cottages furbished to the same high standard and 4 more cottages located in secluded spots boasting panoramic views. Throughout the house, rare pieces of antique furniture, china and fine paintings abound. The panelled Cedar room is the essence of comfort and enjoys a large open fire where guests enjoy pre-dinner drinks or unwind next door at the full-size billiard table. The newly refurbished restaurant, The Ashtree, with its hand-painted Italian frescoes and ornate fireplace, serves modern classical cuisine created by award-winning chef Trevor Brooks. The well stocked wine cellar maintains an extensive range of wine, liqueurs and malt whiskies. The tranquil beauty room, the Retreat, offers many beauty and holistic treatments including reflexology, aromatherapy and manicures. Other activities include walking, salmon and brown trout fishing, bird-watching, pheasant and partridge shooting, deer stalking and croquet. This historic house holds a civil licence; the gardens are perfect for picturesque photographs.

Our inspector loved: *The spacious rooms, elegance, and amazing food.*

Directions: 2 miles north of Dunkeld on the A9 then take the B898 for 4½ miles.

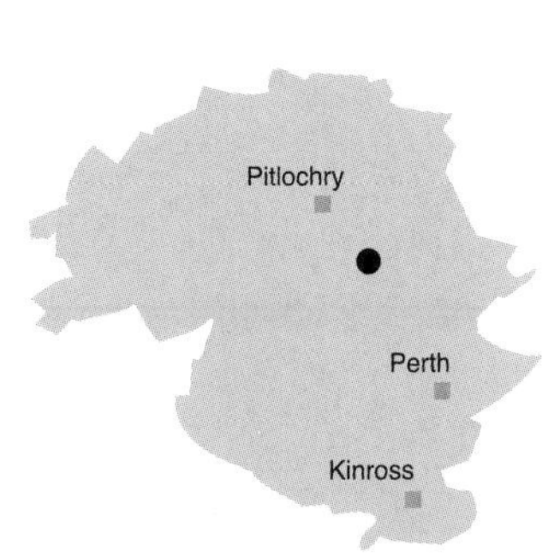
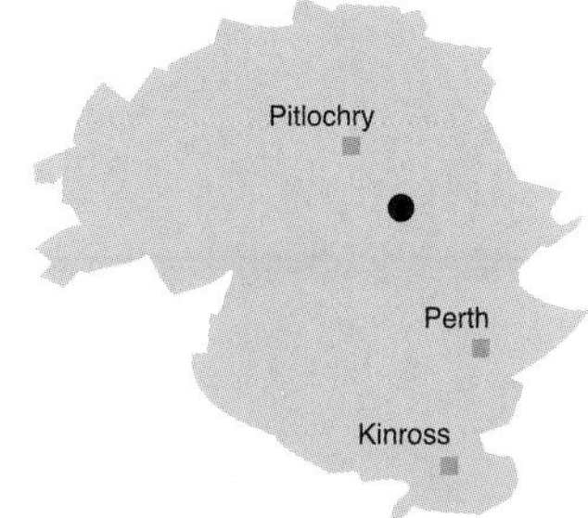

Web: www.johansens.com/kinnaird
E-mail: enquiry@kinnairdestate.com
Tel: 0870 381 9124
International: +44 (0)1796 482440
Fax: 01796 482289

Price Guide: (including dinner)
double/twin £350–£525
winter rates £325 or £275 for 2 or more nights

Ballathie House Hotel

KINCLAVEN, STANLEY, PERTHSHIRE PH1 4QN

Set in an estate overlooking the River Tay near Perth, Ballathie House Hotel offers Scottish hospitality in a house of character and distinction. Dating from 1850, this mansion has a French baronial façade and handsome interiors. Overlooking lawns which slope down to the riverside, the drawing room is an ideal place to relax with coffee and the papers or to enjoy a malt whisky after dinner. The premier bedrooms are large and elegant, whilst the standard rooms are designed in a cosy, cottage style. On the ground floor there are several bedrooms suitable for guests with disabilities. Local ingredients such as Tay salmon, Scottish beef, seafood and piquant soft fruits are used by chef, Kevin MacGillivray, winner of the title Scottish Chef of the Year 1999–2000, to create menus catering for all tastes. The hotel has 2 Rosettes for fine Scottish cuisine. Activities available on the estate include salmon fishing, river walks, croquet and putting. The new Riverside Rooms are ideal for both house guests or sportsmen. The area has many good golf courses. Perth, Blairgowrie and Edinburgh are within an hour's drive. STB 4 star and AA 3 Red Stars (Top 200). Dogs are permitted in certain rooms only. 2 day breaks from £95, including dinner.

Our inspector loved: *Something of the grand hotel in rural Perthshire, with polished service and classic comforts.*

Directions: From the A93 at Beech Hedges, follow the signs for Kinclaven and Ballathie or take the A9 and turn right 2 miles north of Perth,at the sign for Stanley. The hotel is well signposted from this point and lies 10 miles north of Perth.

Web: www.johansens.com/ballathiehouse
E-mail: email@ballathiehousehotel.com
Tel: 0870 381 8337
International: +44 (0)1250 883268
Fax: 01250 883396

Price Guide:
single £79–£89
double/twin £158–£220
suite £228–£250

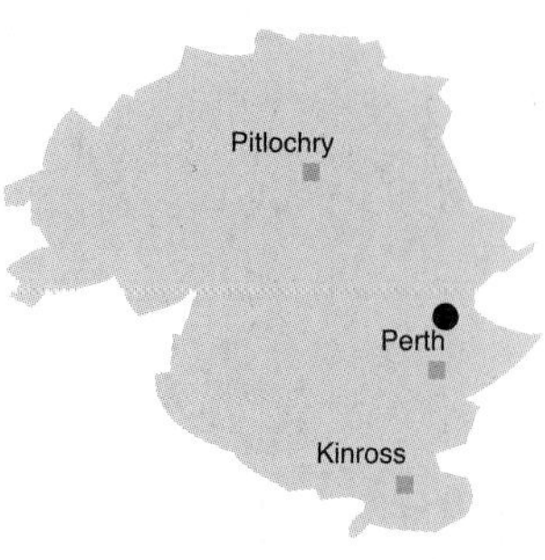

The Roxburghe Hotel & Golf Course

KELSO, BY KELSO, ROXBURGHSHIRE TD5 8JZ

The Roxburghe Hotel & Golf Course reflects the warm, friendly atmosphere one would expect when staying with friends in a beautiful home rather than merely checking into a hotel. Owned by the Duke of Roxburghe, the hotel nestles privately amidst woodlands on the banks of the River Teviot, and as a working country estate it offers some of the best salmon fishing found on the River Tweed. This is also reflected in the dining: renowned for the quality of its fish, meat and game, local produce is used to superb effect by highly-acclaimed chef, Keith Short, and is complemented by fine wines from the Duke's own cellar. Many of the 22 bedrooms have been personally and individually designed by the Duchess herself, some of which have four-poster beds and log fires. Surrounding the hotel is the magnificent golf course, the fifth top inland course in Scotland, home to the Charles Church Scottish Seniors Open and designed by Dave Thomas. However, The Roxburghe is not just about golf, other leisure activities include shooting for pheasant, partridge and grouse, clay-pigeon shooting, mountain biking,croquet and woodland walks; there is also a health and beauty suite. Organised visits to the Duke's home, Floors Castle, can be arranged in the summer months.

Directions: The hotel is at Heiton, just off the A698 Kelso–Jedburgh road.

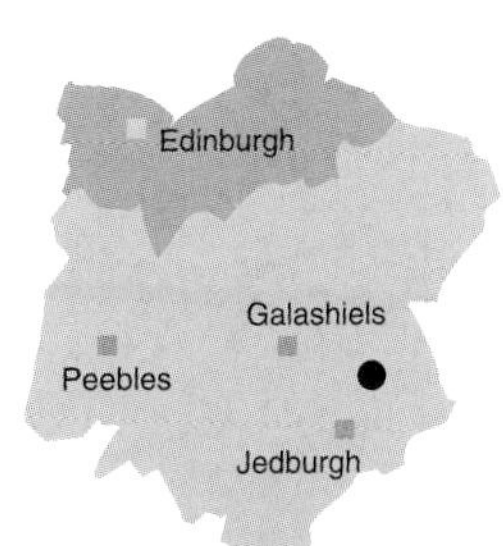

Web: www.johansens.com/roxburghekelso
E-mail: hotel@roxburghe.net
Tel: 0870 381 8873
International: +44 (0)1573 450331
Fax: 01573 450611

Price Guide:
single £120-£145
double/twin £145-£185
four-poster £205-£230
suite £235-£280

Our inspector loved: *A championship golf course on the doorstep.*

Cringletie House

EDINBURGH ROAD, PEEBLES EH45 8PL

A distinguished baronial mansion set within 28 acres, Cringletie House is the epitome of style and fine country living. Elegant turrets combine with the traditional red Borders' sandstone to capture the quiet dignity of a bygone era. All of the beautifully appointed bedrooms have been individually decorated and boast breathtaking views over the surrounding Peebleshire countryside. The splendid panelled dining room has an impressive carved oak and marble fireplace, many original artworks and an eye catching hand painted ceiling depicting a heavenly classical scene. Highly acclaimed cuisine is created with flair and imagination with menus designed around the fruits and vegetables available in Scotland's only 17th-century walled kitchen garden. Specialities include deliciously prepared fresh game and fish. Guests can play outdoor chess or boule in the woodland garden, attempt the 9-hole putting green, play lawn croquet or simply stroll around the manicured lawns and lush woodlands surrounding the hotel. Fishing is available on the River Tweed and for golf lovers there is an excellent golf course in Peebles. Other activities such as archery, shooting, quad biking and hot air ballooning can be arranged. Cringletie is a good base from which to explore the rich historical and cultural heritage of the Borders and is only 30 minutes from Edinburgh.

Directions: Take the A703 from Edinburgh towards Peebles. The hotel is on the right approximately 2 miles south of Eddleston village

Web: www.johansens.com/cringletiehouse
E-mail: enquiries@cringletie.com
Tel: 0870 381 9279
International: +44 (0)1721 725750
Fax: 01721 725751

Price Guide:
single £100-£120
double/twin £140–£280

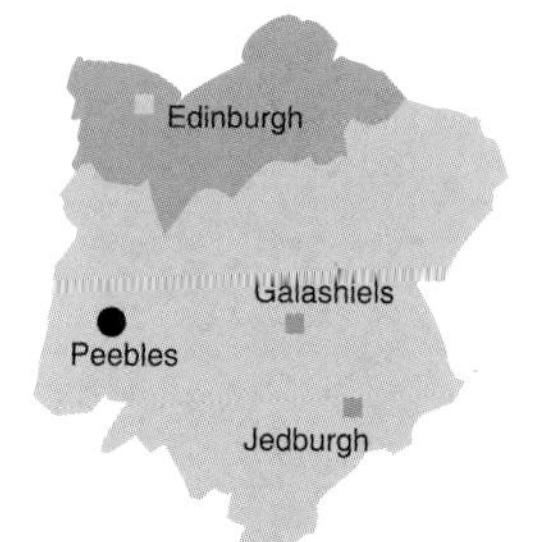

Our inspector loved: *The attention to detail shown by the new owners.*

Dryburgh Abbey Hotel

ST BOSWELLS, MELROSE, SCOTTISH BORDERS TD6 0RQ

This is quintessential Scotland with its russet and yellow moorlands, cool green pastures, rivers running with princely salmon, darting trout and hillsides speckled with sheep whose wool is used to produce the world famous Borderlands tweed. Dryburgh Abbey Hotel stands in the heart of this glorious, Sir Walter Scott countryside just 5 miles south east of the small historic town of Melrose, which nestles in the shelter of the 3 peaks of lovely Eildon Hills. Beautifully restored, this delightful old country house is superbly located on the banks of the River Tweed next to the ruins of the 12th-century abbey from which it takes its name, home to the tombs of the novelist Sir Walter Scott and Field Marshal Earl Haig, the British Army's Commander-in-Chief during World War I. Solid and traditional on the outside, the interior of the hotel is grand and opulent with all the luxuries and modern comforts expected from a leading leisure and business residence. Bedrooms are elegantly furnished and decorated, well equipped and proffer superb views. 2 lounges offer peaceful relaxation and guests can choose to dine in style in the tranquil setting of the Tweed Restaurant overlooking the river, alternatively there is the bistro-style ambience of the Courtyard Bar. Indoor swimming pool, shooting and fishing by arrangement.

Our inspector loved: *The great backdrop of the abbey ruins and River Tweed.*

Directions: Take the A68 from Edinburgh to St Boswells then turn onto the B6404. Continue on this road for 2 miles then turn left onto the B6356 signposted Scott's view and Earlston. The hotel entrance is approximately 2 miles further on this road.

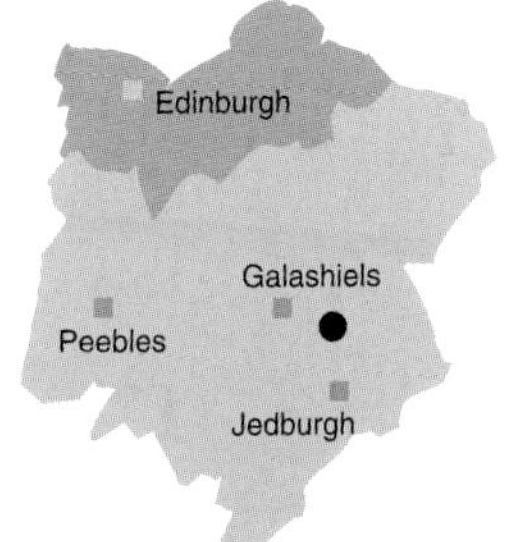

Web: www.johansens.com/dryburghabbey
E-mail: enquiries@dryburgh.co.uk
Tel: 0870 381 9311
International: +44 (0)1835 822261
Fax: 01835 823945

Price Guide:
single £63.50–£103.50
double/twin £60–£80

Glenapp Castle

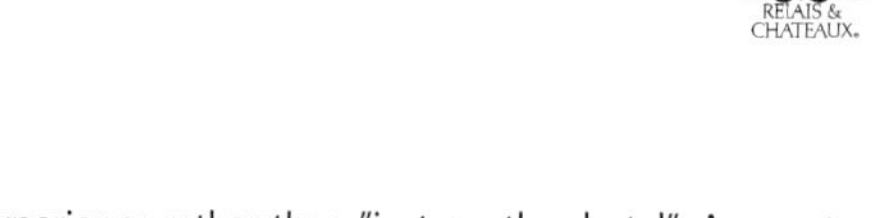

BALLANTRAE, SCOTLAND KA26 0NZ

Glenapp is an experience rather than "just another hotel". As you turn through the castle gates, Glenapp stands proudly in front of you; imposing, exciting and inviting. The owners, Fay and Graham Cowan, offer a truly Scottish welcome to their glorious Ayrshire home. They bought Glenapp in a state of neglect and spent six years refurbishing it to combine the requirements of the discerning guest with the classic style of the house. No expense has been spared, from the stone fireplaces carved with the family crest to the Castle's own monogrammed china. Head Chef Matt Weedon will prepare exciting, innovative 6-course gourmet dinners using local produce, and fruit, vegetables and herbs straight from the garden. The castle retains many original features as well as personally selected oil paintings and antique furnishings throughout bedrooms, lounges and oak panelled hallways. The 17 en-suite bedrooms are spacious, individually decorated, and furnished to the highest standards, all offering either views of the garden or coastline. The 30-acre gardens contain many rare trees and shrubs and an impressive Victorian glasshouse and walled garden. Tennis and croquet are available in the grounds. Guests may play golf on the local courses including championship courses, and shoot or fish on local estates.

Our inspector loved: *Everything about it - now in its 7th year yet it gets better and better.*

Directions: Glenapp Castle is approximately 15 miles north of Stranraer or 35 miles south of Ayr on A77.

Web: www.johansens.com/glenappcastle
E-mail: enquiries@glenappcastle.com
Tel: 0870 381 8551
International: +44 (0)1465 831212
Fax: 01465 831000

Price Guide: (including dinner)
luxury double/twin from £365
suite from £425
master room from £495

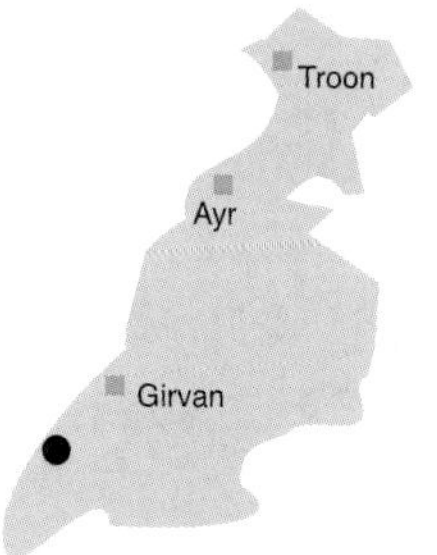

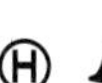

Buchanan Arms Hotel & Leisure Club

DRYMEN, STIRLINGSHIRE G63 0BQ

With its warm welcome, attractive décor, comfortable furnishings and superb setting this is a haven of relaxation that attracts guests time and time again. Built and opened in 1752 as a droving inn this sparkling white-fronted hotel, highlighted by attractive roof peaks and a large half-moon shaped roadside window, stands in the heart of a picturesque conservation village between the vibrant city of Glasgow and historic town of Stirling, just about 3 miles from the scenic beauty of the eastern edge of Loch Lomond. It is the perfect location for touring city, town and countryside and within easy reach are Balloch Castle, Glengoyne Distillery and the magnificent Trossachs. The Buchanan Arms Hotel has been sympathetically and skillfully restored to provide a comfortable, timeless grace that exudes a blend of character and charm combined with 21st-century facilities. Each of the 52 guest rooms are individually designed, delightfully decorated and offer the highest standard of amenities and thoughtful little comforts. True Scottish hospitality is the philosophy of the hotel's attentive staff, particularly in the Tapestries Restaurant where courteous service presents creatively prepared dishes featuring the freshest of local produce. Leisure facilities include a swimming pool, sauna, spa, gymnasium, squash courts and health and beauty suite.

Directions: From Glasgow (17 miles) follow signs to Aberfoyle on the A81. At Bearsden Cross roundabout take the A809 to Drymen.

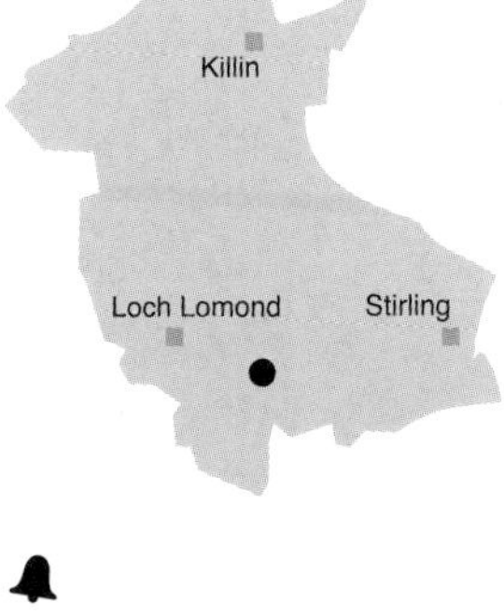

Web: www.johansens.com/buchananarms
E-mail: enquiries@buchananarms.co.uk
Tel: 0870 381 9301
International: +44 (0)1360 660588
Fax: 01360 660943

Price Guide:
single £85–£115
double £130–£190

Our inspector loved: *The great location for Loch Lomond and Trossachs.*

  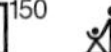      

CONDÉ NAST JOHANSENS
J
RECOMMENDED

Wales

Recommendations in Wales appear on pages 354-370

For further information on Wales, please contact:

Wales Tourist Board
Brunel House, 2 Fitzalan Road, Cardiff CF24 0UY
Tel: +44 (0)29 2049 9909
Web: www.visitwales.com

North Wales Tourism
77 Conway Road, Colwyn Bay, Conway LL29 7LN
Tel: +44 (0)1492 531731
Web: www.nwt.co.uk

Mid Wales Tourism
The Station, Machynlleth, Powys SY20 8TG
Tel: (Freephone) 0800 273747
Web: www.visitmidwales.co.uk

South West Wales Tourism Partnership
The Coach House, Aberglasney, Carmarthenshire SA32 8QH
Tel: +44 (0)1558 669091
Web: www.swwtp.co.uk

or see pages 376-378 for details of local attractions to visit during your stay.

Images from www.britainonview.com

Llechwen Hall

LLANFABON, NR ABERCYNON, CARDIFF, MID GLAMORGAN CF37 4HP

Directions: Exit the M4 at junction 32 and follow the A470 towards Merthyr Tydfil for approximately 11 miles. Join the A472 towards Nelson and then the A4054 towards Cilfynydd. The hotel is on the left after ½ mile.

Web: www.johansens.com/Llechwenhall
E-mail: llechwen@aol.com
Tel: 0870 381 8698
International: +44 (0)1443 742050
Fax: 01443 742189

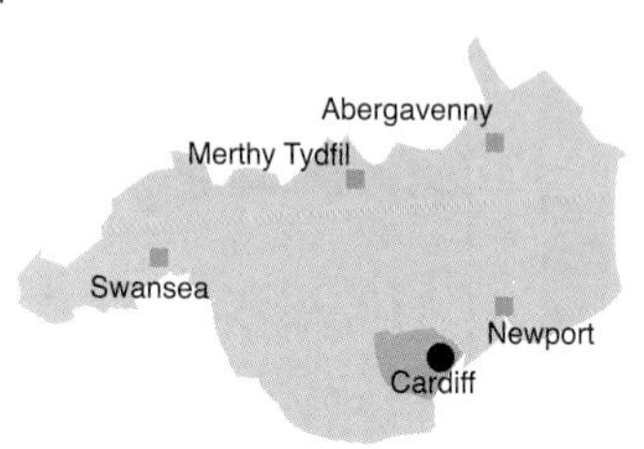

Price Guide:
single £54.50–£65.50
double/twin £75–£106

Visitors step back in time when they enter this lovely 17th-century Welsh Long-House with its Victorian frontage standing in 6 acres of mature gardens on the hillside overlooking the Aberdare and Merthyr valleys. There are 4-foot thick walls with narrow embrasures, low ceilings, stout-blackened oak beams, huge fireplaces and stone-roofed outbuildings. Careful restoration and sympathetic refurbishment over the years has created a 3-star country house hotel with an award-winning restaurant. The 20 superbly appointed bedrooms are individually decorated and furnished to provide a truly comfortable environment. Guests have a choice of restaurants for memorable dining. Outstanding, freshly prepared cusine, with seasonal changes to the menu, is served either in the intimate atmosphere of the oak-beamed restaurant in part of the original Welsh Long-House or in the light and airy Victorian dining room with its stunning views across the valleys. Pre and after-dinner drinks can be enjoyed in an elegant cocktail lounge. The hotel is just a 20 minute drive from Cardiff and 15 minutes from the foothills of the Brecon Beacons.

Our inspector loved: *The spacious and well appointed bedrooms and spectacular setting in 6 acres of wooded gardens.*

Falcondale Mansion Hotel

LAMPETER, DYFED SA48 7RX

The recent winner of a number of accolades in the hotel trade, Falcondale Mansion Hotel is rapidly gaining an excellent reputation and putting this charming area of Wales firmly on the map. Lying on the outskirts of Lampeter, it is ideally located to enjoy the many coastal walks and unspoilt beaches that lie in the region as well as a number of National Trust properties and the fishing port of Aberaeron with its delightfully painted houses. Lampeter is a charming university town: St David's College is the third oldest university after Oxford and Cambridge and has many interesting small shops. There is a reliable bus service to and from Lampeter, and good road links to Cardiff Airport. The hotel is an elegant Italianate mansion set in14 acres of secluded countryside with a wonderful mix of ornamental woods and sweeping elegant lawns. An idyllic setting for weddings and parties or for a tranquil and romantic getaway, there are 20 guest rooms, and recent refurbishment has ensured that they are stylishly decorated with accompanying luxurious bathrooms. With a Welsh head chef supported by an English, French and South African team, the cuisine creates imaginative arrangements of traditional Welsh favourites with an international flavour, and is deserving of its recent recognition.

Our inspector loved: *Now in its fourth year of Hutton ownership, Falcondale Mansion Hotel is blossoming*

Directions: Exit the M4 and take the A485 towards Carmarthen. Turn left at the T-junction to Lampeter and drive through the town towards Cardigan. Turn right just before the Murco petrol garage into the South Drive.

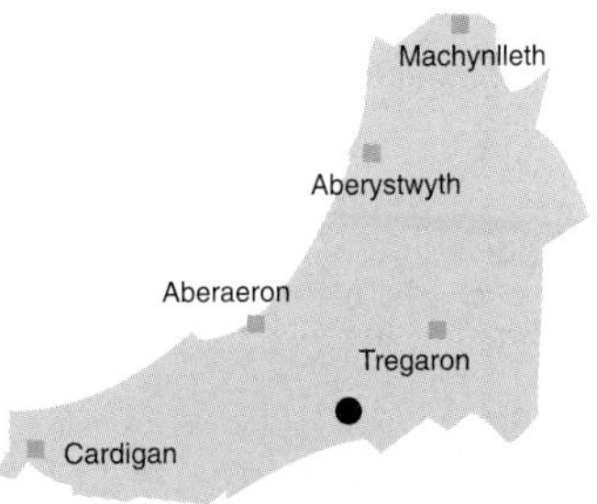

Web: www.johansens.com/falcondale
E-mail: info@falcondalehotel.com
Tel: 0870 381 9235
International: +44 (0)1570 422910
Fax: 01570 423559

Price Guide:
single from £95
double/twin from £130

 20     70    

Ynyshir Hall

EGLWYSFACH, MACHYNLLETH, CEREDIGION SY20 8TA

Once owned by Queen Victoria, Ynyshir Hall is a captivating Georgian manor house that perfectly blends modern comfort and old-world elegance. Its 12 acres of landscaped gardens are set alongside the Dovey Estuary, one of Wales's most outstanding areas of natural beauty. The hotel is surrounded by the Ynyshir Bird Reserve. Hosts Rob and Joan Reen offer guests a warm welcome and ensure a personal service, the hallmark of a good family-run hotel. Period furniture and opulent fabrics enhance the 9 charming bedrooms. The suites, including a four-poster room and ground floor room, are particularly luxurious. The interior features antiques, contemporary colour schemes, oriental rugs and original paintings, created by Rob, an acclaimed artist. With its calm, elegant atmosphere, the candle-lit restaurant provides the perfect backdrop for a sublime culinary experience. Chef Adam Simmonds, formerly of Le Manoir Aux Quat' Saisons, creates dishes prepared with superb local ingredients such as wild sea bass, Cardigan Bay lobster and tender Welsh mountain lamb, complemented by a fine wine list of over 300 bins from all over the world. Awarded The Catey's Independent Hotel of the Year 2002, Welsh Hotel of the Year 2001 and 4 Rosettes by the AA. Condé Nast Johansens award nomination 2005. Landmarks include Cader Idris, Wales's 2nd highest mountain. Closed in January.

Directions: Off main road between Aberystwyth and Machynlleth.

Web: www.johansens.com/ynyshirhall
E-mail: info@ynyshir–hall.co.uk
Tel: 0870 381 9020
International: +44 (0)1654 781209
Fax: 01654 781366

Price Guide:
single £110–£180
double/twin £125–£180
suite £210–£275

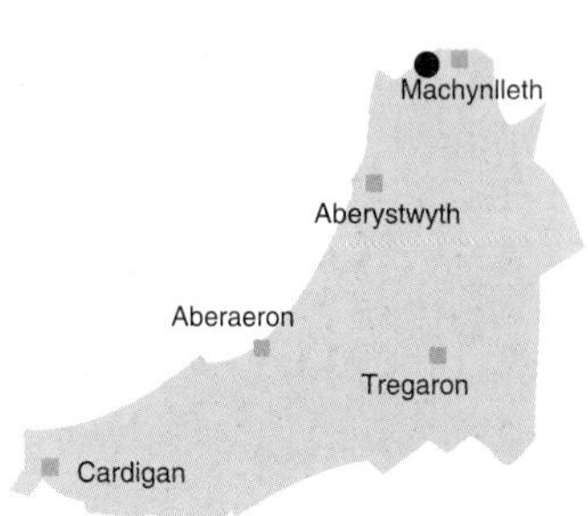

Our inspector loved: *The superb dining in the restaurant – totally delicious.*

       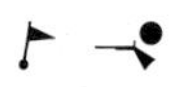  

Bodysgallen Hall & Spa

LLANDUDNO, NORTH WALES LL30 1RS

Nestling in 200 acres of magnificent parkland to the south of Llandudno and west of Pydew Mountain, Grade I listed Bodysgallen Hall & Spa exudes a mixture of history, great comfort and sophistication. With spectacular views of Snowdonia and Conwy Castle it provides all that is best in country house hospitality and expectations. Bodysgallen has grown and developed from a 13th-century fortified tower into one of the grandest family houses in Wales and is now a superb, charismatic hotel. Large, beautiful gardens include a 17th-century parterre of box hedges filled with scented herbs, a rockery with cascade, a superbly restored formal walled rose garden and several follies. Within these beautiful grounds is a cluster of 16 self-contained cottages, for guests requiring total privacy. The 19 comfortable bedrooms inside the house, are individually and stylishly furnished and are non-smoking. All guest accommodation has the latest facilities, with selected Sky TV channels in most of the rooms and some have air conditioning. The antique furnished entrance hall and first-floor drawing rooms, with large fireplaces and splendid oak panelling, are particularly appealing, as are the 2 dining rooms where 3 AA Rosette award-winning head chef John Williams serves imaginative cuisine. A short walk through the garden takes guests to the health and fitness spa with indoor swimming pool.

Directions: On the A470, 1 mile from the intersection with the A55. Llandudno is a mile further on the A470.

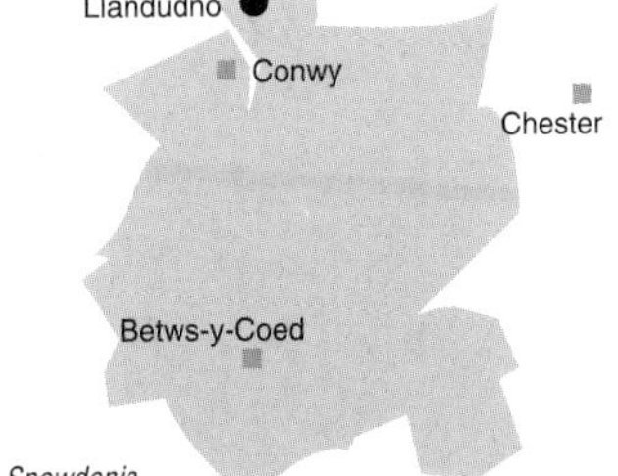

Web: www.johansens.com/bodysgallenhall
E-mail: info@bodysgallen.com
Tel: 0870 381 8372
International: +44 (0)1492 584466
Fax: 01492 582519

Price Guide:
single from £125
double/twin from £175
suite from £195

Our inspector loved: *This enchanting, historic hall, so calm, wonderful.*

35 50 8 SPA

St Tudno Hotel & Restaurant

NORTH PROMENADE, LLANDUDNO, NORTH WALES LL30 2LP

Directions: The hotel is located on the promenade opposite the pier entrance and gardens. Car parking and garages are available for up to 12 cars.

Web: www.johansens.com/sttudno
E-mail: sttudnohotel@btinternet.com
Tel: 0870 381 8907
International: +44 (0)1492 874411
Fax: 01492 860407

Price Guide:
single from £75
double/twin £94–£220
suite from £260

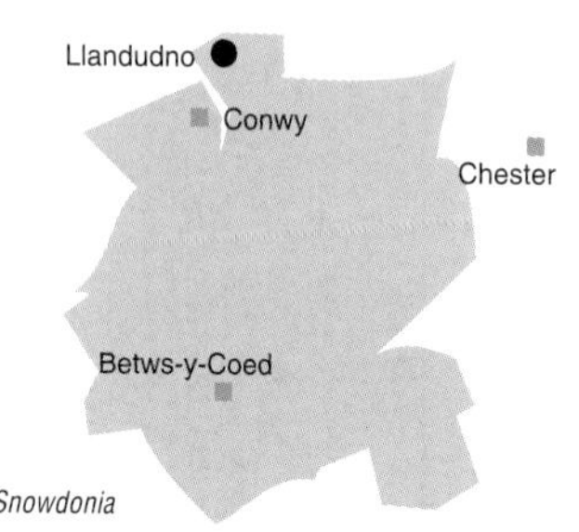

Without doubt one of the most delightful small hotels to be found on the coast of Britain, St Tudno Hotel & Restaurant, a former winner of the Johansens Hotel of the Year Award for Excellence, offers a very special experience. The hotel has been elegantly and lovingly furnished with meticulous attention to detail, and provides a particularly warm welcome generated by the Bland family over the past 34 years. Each beautifully co-ordinated bedroom has been individually designed with many thoughtful extras; half are equipped with spa baths. The bar lounge and sitting room, which overlook the sea, have an air of Victorian charm, and the Rosette award-winning, air-conditioned Terrace Restaurant is regarded as one of Wales' leading restaurants. This AA Red Star Hotel has won a host of other prestigious awards: Best Seaside Resort Hotel in Great Britain (Good Hotel guide); Welsh Hotel of the Year; Runner up for Johansens Tattinger Wine List Award 2004; the AA's Wine Award for Wales 2004 and even an accolade for having the Best Hotel Loos in Britain! St Tudno is ideally situated for visits to Snowdonia, Conwy and Caernarfon Castles, and glorious winter walks on the Great Orme, Bodnant Gardens and Anglesey. Llandudno's excellent theatre is only a short walk away. Golf, riding, dry-slope skiing and tobogganing can all be enjoyed locally, and the hotel has a heated indoor pool.

***Our inspector loved:** This intimate seafront hotel, a pleasure for all seasons.*

WILD PHEASANT HOTEL

BERWYN ROAD, LLANGOLLEN, DENBIGHSHIRE LL20 8AD

Some of the most spectacular scenery in Wales lies along the tranquil Vale of Llangollen, threaded by the River Dee. The stunning Horseshoe Pass meaders between the mountains of Llantysilio and Eglwyseg, and these, with the heights of Berwyn and Castell Dinas Branis, provide an impressive backdrop to the town. Wild Pheasant Hotel is a short walk from the centre of this town, famous for the scene of the International Musical Eisteddfod, which is held every July and attracts 120,000 visitors. Dating back to the 19th century, this highly acclaimed hotel has been sympathetically updated, renovated and extended to provide a luxury retreat with all modern amenities and an eclectic blend of contemporary and traditional design. Guest rooms retain country house charm and the atmosphere of a bygone era whilst offering every home comfort; most have spectacular views. En-suite bedrooms, in the original part of the hotel, combine tradition, style and comfort; 2 have four-poster beds. Space and good taste are the hallmarks of the 15 luxury rooms in the new wing extension; 1 of the 3 penthouse suites has a hot tub on its balcony. Excellent dining options include a Rosette-awarded restaurant and the more informal Bistro Bar. Fully-equipped spa and comprehensive conference facilities are available.

Our inspector loved: *The excellent range of bedrooms from traditional simplicity to opulent modernity. True value for money.*

46 M 200 SPA

Directions: From the north take the M6 then the M56 to Chester. Follow the A483 past Wrexham and take the A5 to Langollen. From the south take the M6 then the M54 past Shrewsbury onto the A5 to Langollen.

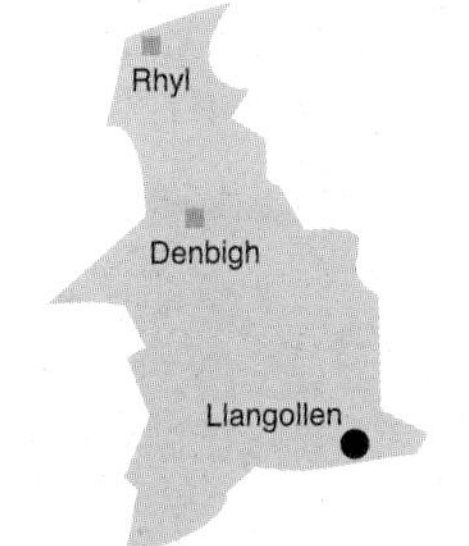

Web: www.johansens.com/wildpheasant
E-mail: wild.pheasant@talk21.com
Tel: 0870 381 8633
International: +44 (0)1978 860629
Fax: 01978 861837

Price Guide:
single £42–£84
double/twin £84–£168
suite £208–£248

Palé Hall

PALÉ ESTATE, LLANDDERFEL, BALA, GWYNEDD LL23 7PS

Directions: Situated off the B4401 Corwen to Bala Road, Palé Hall is 4 miles from Llandrillo.

Web: www.johansens.com/palehall
E-mail: enquiries@palehall.co.uk
Tel: 0870 381 8799
International: +44 (0)1678 530285
Fax: 01678 530220

Price Guide:
single £80–£140
double/twin £115–£200

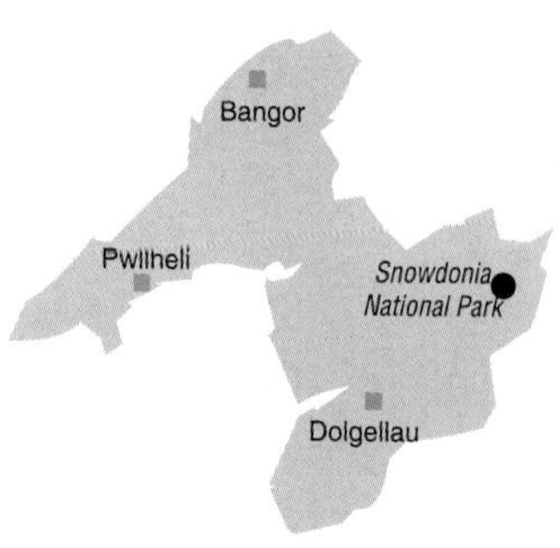

Set in acres of peaceful, tranquil woodland on the edge of Snowdonia National Park, Palé Hall is a magnificent building, beautifully preserved, and provides the opportunity to sample a true country house lifestyle. Shooting parties are a regular occurrence on the surrounding estates, whilst fishing on the Dee is available on site. A venture with Land Rover Experience also enables guests to experience off-road driving in their preferred choice of 4-wheel drive, whilst the less adventurous can walk for miles on the beautiful Palé estate. The staff at Palé Hall carefully maintain the beautiful period interior of the building including the gallieried staircase and painted ceilings, which have survived largely due to the house's unusual electricity system. Supplied by a turbine powered by water, Palé's 18 electric fires were left burning during 22 years of unoccupancy! Queen Victoria and Winston Churchill have stayed at the Hall. The 17 individually designed suites with luxurious bathrooms, one of which features a steam shower, have breathtaking views of the surrounding scenery. The 2 AA Rosette-awarded restaurant serves seasonal table d'hôte menus complemented by a fine wine selection. Exclusive use is available for conferences, product launches and weddings. Smoking is not permitted in the hotel.

Our inspector loved: *The entire Palé Hall experience - so relaxing.*

PENMAENUCHAF HALL

PENMAENPOOL, DOLGELLAU, GWYNEDD LL40 1YB

Climbing the long tree lined driveway you arrive at Penmaenuchaf Hall to behold its idyllic setting. With stunning panoramic views across the spectacular Mawddach Estuary and wooded mountain slopes in the distance, this handsome Victorian mansion is truly an exceptional retreat. Set within the Snowdonia National Park, the 21-acre grounds encompass lawns, a formal sunken rose garden, a water garden and woodland. The beautiful interiors feature oak and mahogany panelling, stained-glass windows, log fires in winter, polished Welsh slate floors and freshly cut flowers. There are 12 non-smoking luxurious bedrooms, some with four-poster and half-tester beds and all with interesting views. In the restaurant guests can choose from an imaginative menu prepared with the best seasonal produce and complemented by an extensive list of wines. An elegant panelled dining room can be used for private dinners or meetings. Penmaenuchaf Hall is perfect for a totally relaxed holiday. For recreation, guests can fish for trout and salmon along 10miles of the Mawddach River, try mountain biking or take part in a range of water sports. They can also enjoy scenic walks, visit sandy beaches and historic castles and take trips on narrow-gauge railways. Special offers for early booking are available.

Our inspector loved: *The continued evolution of this tranquil hotel, which is always a great pleasure for a light lunch or overnight stay.*

Directions: The hotel is off the A493 Dolgellau–Tywyn road, about 2 miles from Dolgellau.

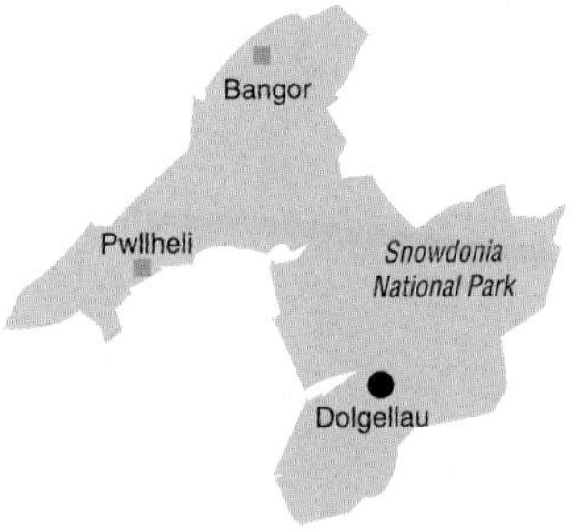

Bangor
Pwllheli
Snowdonia National Park
Dolgellau

Web: www.johansens.com/penmaenuchafhall
E-mail: relax@penhall.co.uk
Tel: 0870 381 8813
International: +44 (0)1341 422129
Fax: 01341 422787

Price Guide:
single £75–£135
double/twin £130–£200

Llansantffraed Court Hotel

LLANVIHANGEL GOBION, ABERGAVENNY, MONMOUTHSHIRE NP7 9BA

Llansantffraed Court is a perfect retreat from the fast pace of modern life. This elegant Georgian-style country house hotel, part of which dates back to the 14th century, is set in spacious grounds on the edge of the Brecon Beacons and the Wye Valley. Guests are provided with the highest level of personal, yet unobtrusive service. Most of the tastefully decorated and luxuriously furnished bedrooms offer views over the hotel's gardens and ornamental trout lake. While one has a four-poster bed, others feature oak beams and dormer windows. An excellent reputation is enjoyed by the 2 AA Rosette restaurant; the menus reflect the changing seasons and the availability of fresh local produce. Exquisite cuisine is complemented by fine wines. Afternoon tea can be taken in the lounge, where guests enjoy a blazing log fire during the cooler months and savour the views of the South Wales countryside. A range of excellent facilities is available for functions, celebrations and meetings. Llansantffraed Court is an ideal base for exploring the diverse history and beauty of this area and there are plenty of opportunities to take advantage of energetic or relaxing pursuits, including golf, trekking, walking, and salmon and trout fishing.

Our inspector loved: *This elegant Georgian hotel surrounded by rolling parkland as far as the eye can see.*

Directions: From M4 J24 (Via A449) off B4598 (formerly A40 old road) Leave A40 D/C at Abergavenny or Raglan. Follow signs to Clytha and the hotel is approx 4½ miles away.

Web: www.johansens.com/llansantffraedcourt
E-mail: reception@llch.co.uk
Tel: 0870 381 8697
International: +44 (0)1873 840678
Fax: 01873 840674

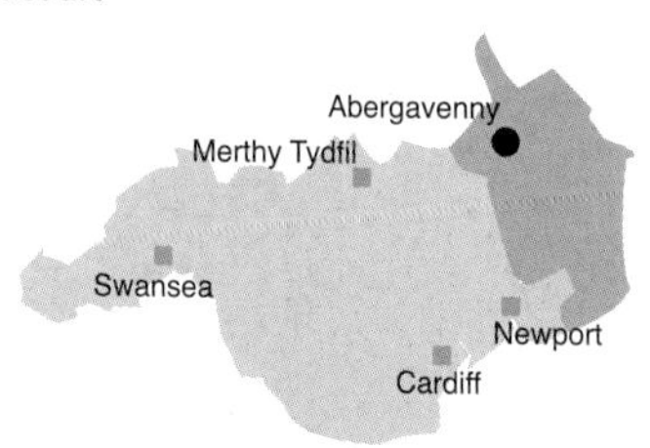

Price Guide:
single from £95
double/twin from £115
suites £160

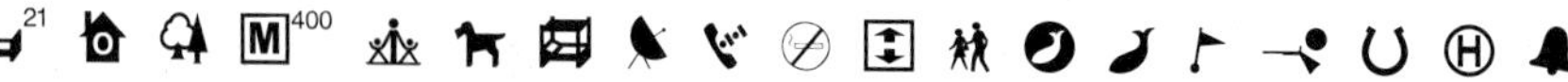

ALLT-YR-YNYS HOTEL

WALTERSTONE, NEAR ABERGAVENNY, HR2 0DU

Nestling in the foothills of the Black Mountains, on the fringes of the Brecon Beacons National park, Allt-yr-Ynys is an impressive Grade II 16th-century manor house hotel. The Manor was the home of the Cecil family whose ancestry dates back to Rhodri Mawr, King of Wales in the 8th century. A more recent Cecil was Lord Burleigh, Chief Minister to Queen Elizabeth I, portrayed by Sir Richard Attenborough in the recent film, "Elizabeth". Features of this interesting past still remain and include moulded ceilings, oak panelling and beams and a 16th-century four-poster bed in the Jacobean suite. However, whilst the charm and the character of the period remains, the house has been sympathetically adapted to provide all the comforts expected of a modern hotel. The former outbuildings have been transformed into spacious and well-appointed guest bedrooms. Fine dining is offered in the award-winning restaurant and the conference/function suite accommodates up to 200 guests. Facilities include a heated pool, Jacuzzi, clay pigeon shooting range and private river fishing. Pastimes include exploring the scenery, historic properties and plethora of tourist attractions.

Our inspector loved: *The spacious individually decorated bedrooms, all with glorious secluded views of the countryside.*

Directions: 5 miles north of Abergavenny on A465 Abergavenny/ Hereford trunk road, turn west at Old Pandy Inn in Pandy. After 400 metres turn right down lane at grey/green barn. The hotel is on the right after 400 metres.

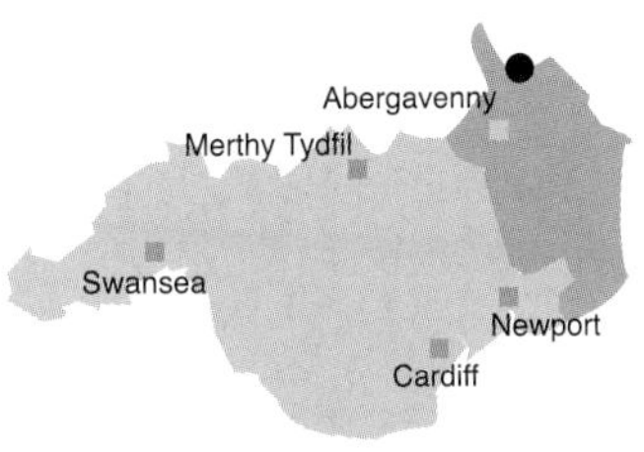

Web: www.johansens.com/alltyrynys
E-mail: reception@allthotel.co.uk
Tel: 0870 381 8309
International: +44 (0)1873 890307
Fax: 01873 890539

Price Guide: (per room)
single £110
double/twin £120–£160
suite from £150

Warpool Court Hotel

ST DAVID'S, PEMBROKESHIRE SA62 6BN

Originally built as St David's Cathedral Choir School in the 1860s, Warpool Court enjoys spectacular scenery at the heart of the Pembrokeshire National Park, with views over the coast and St Bride's Bay to the islands beyond. First converted to a hotel over 40 years ago, continuous refurbishment has ensured all its up-to-date comforts are fit for the new century. All 25 bedrooms have immaculate en-suite facilities of which 14 enjoy sea views. The 2 AA Rosette restaurant enjoys a splendid reputation. Imaginative menus, including vegetarian, offer a wide selection of modern and traditional dishes. Local produce, including Welsh lamb and beef, is used whenever possible, with crab, lobster, sewin and sea bass caught just off the coast. Salmon and mackerel are smoked on the premises. The hotel gardens are ideal for a peaceful stroll or an after-dinner drink in the summer. There is a covered heated swimming pool (open April to the end of October) and an all-weather tennis court in the grounds. A path from the hotel leads straight on to the Pembrokeshire Coastal Path, with its rich variety of wildlife and spectacular scenery. Boating and water sports are available locally. St David's Peninsula offers a wealth of history and natural beauty and has inspired many famous artists. Closed in January.

Our inspector loved: *The spectacular views of the coast from the dining room complementing the superb 2 Rosette cuisine.*

Directions: The hotel is signposted from St David's town centre.

Web: www.johansens.com/warpoolcourt
E-mail: info@warpoolcourthotel.com
Tel: 0870 381 8968
International: +44 (0)1437 720300
Fax: 01437 720676

Price Guide:
single £95–£115
double/twin £160–£230

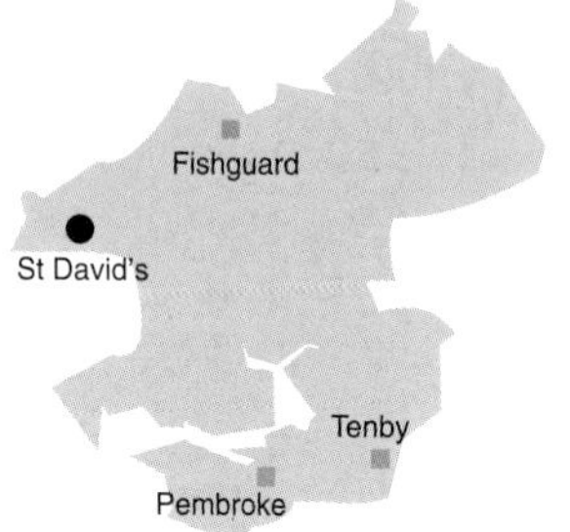

Penally Abbey

PENALLY, TENBY, PEMBROKESHIRE SA70 7PY

Built on the site of an ancient abbey, this listed country house stands in 5 acres of garden and woodland on the edge of Pembrokeshire National Park. It is an impressive hotel with wisteria-clad stone walls enhanced by decorative windows through which guests enjoy panoramic views over the gardens to Carmathen Bay and Caldey Island. Penally Abbey comprises 3 limestone buildings, all delightfully furnished to combine the best of the old with the modern. Abbey House, the original house, is reminiscent of a country seat: a superbly proportioned lounge features an Adams fireplace, comfortable leather Chesterfields and family photographs. Enchanting bedrooms are adorned with period pieces, and a sun-catching conservatory leads to the garden terrace. Adjoining is the intimate and quaint Coach House, a converted stable block, with 4 bedrooms decorated in a cottage style; each room has it own entrance. Next door is the newly renovated and uncluttered St Deiniol's Lodge; bedrooms feature urban chic, rich wooden furniture, leather sofas and marble bathrooms. High coved ceilings, large ogee head windows, hand-carved fireplaces and crystal chandeliers heighten the relaxing ambience of the restaurant where fresh seasonal delicacies are enjoyed. Water skiing, surfing and sailing can be arranged nearby.

Our inspector loved: *The romantic location, and outstanding accommodation ranging from classic contemporary to period four posters.*

Directions: Penally Abbey is situated adjacent to the church on Penally village green.

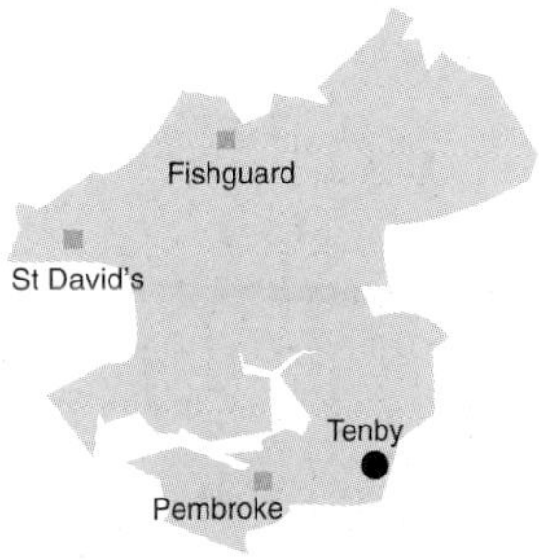

Web: www.johansens.com/penallyabbey
E-mail: penally.abbey@btinternet.com
Tel: 0870 381 8810
International: +44 (0)1834 843033
Fax: 01834 844714

Price Guide:
single £120
double/twin £130–£160
suite £185

LAMPHEY COURT HOTEL

LAMPHEY, NR TENBY, PEMBROKESHIRE SA71 5NT

Idyllically located for enjoying spectacular coastal walks and the pretty resorts of Tenby and Saundersfoot, Lamphey Court Hotel is a welcoming country house with excellent facilities. The well-proportioned, richly decorated public rooms are in-keeping with the era when the house was built. The attractive bedrooms offer an extremely high standard of comfort; family suites are located in a former coach house with generously sized rooms and extra space for families. The formal, candlelit Georgian restaurant offers a dinner menu featuring locally caught fish such as Teifi salmon and freshwater Bay lobster. The light and airy Conservatory Restaurant provides a more informal alternative for lunch and lighter meals. Guests may take advantage of the hotel's modern leisure spa, with its large indoor swimming pool overlooking the gardens and floodlit tennis courts, spa pool, saunas and a gymnasium. Skilled therapists provide a range of treatments. The Pembrokeshire National Park offers an unprecedented choice of activities close by including golf, sailing, fishing and cycling. Alternatively, visit the medieval Bishop's Palace located within the hotel grounds.

Our inspector loved: *The extensive leisure centre offering an indoor swimming pool, well equipped gymnasium, hairdresser, sauna and solarium.*

Directions: From M4 to Carmarthen links with M5, M50 and major trunk roads. From Carmarthen follow A40 to St Clears, then follow the A477 towards Pembroke. Turn left at Milton Village for Lamphey and watch for sign at the crossroads

Web: www.johansens.com/courtpembroke
E-mail: info@lampheycourt.co.uk
Tel: 0870 381 8675
International: +44 (0)1646 672273
Fax: 01646 672480

Price Guide:
single £80–£100
double/twin £115–£160

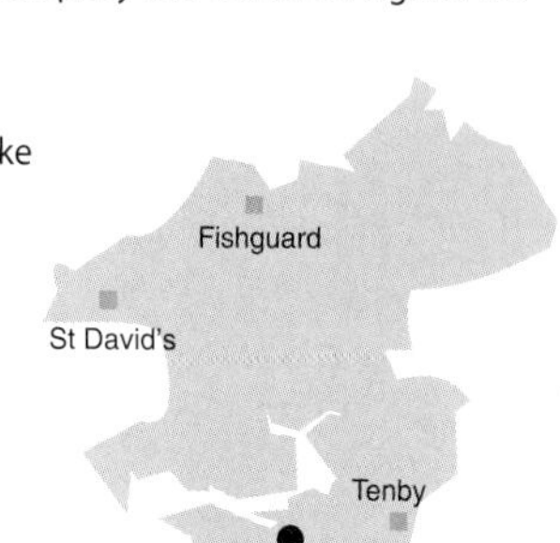

LLANGOED HALL

LLYSWEN, BRECON, POWYS LD3 0YP

With a spectacular location by the Brecon Beacons and the Black Mountains and close to the world book centre of Hay-on-Wye, Llangoed Hall has been transformed into a luxurious but welcoming hideaway. Guests in search of a home-away-from-home will be impressed with General Manager Calum Milne's attention to detail and the discreet and professional service from his attentive staff. A timeless and understated elegance pervades the property, which is enhanced by Sir Bernard Ashley's exclusive Elanbach fabrics and the 23 exquisitely refurbished bedrooms that feature cast iron baths, Roberts radios and 17th-century antique mirrors. An eclectic collection of art adorns the interior and is sure to delight true enthusiasts. In the recently redecorated restaurant, head chef Sean Ballington serves local produce including Welsh lamb and salmon whilst the resident wine expert, Regine Ashley, selects accompanying vintages from a distinguished list. Corporate groups in search of a private location can hire Llangoed Hall on an exclusive basis. Outside, the maze has been restored to its former glory and the beautiful gardens complement the breathtaking surrounds. Fishing, rock-climbing and 4x4 driving are some of the many activities that can be enjoyed nearby.

Our inspector loved: *The newly refurbished rooms, which enhance this splendid property - the maze is fun too!*

Directions: 9 miles west of Hay and 11 miles north of Brecon on the A470. Bristol and Cardiff Airports just under an hour away.

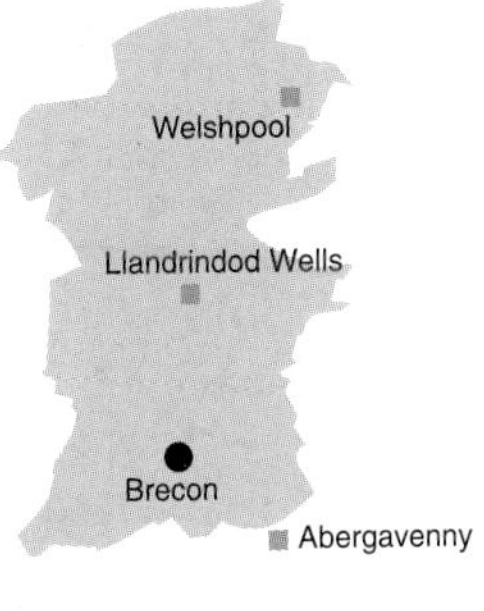

Welshpool
Llandrindod Wells
Brecon
Abergavenny

Web: www.johansens.com/llangoedhall
E-mail: enquiries@llangoedhall.com
Tel: 0870 381 8696
International: +44 (0)1874 754525
Fax: 01874 754545

Price Guide:
single from £140
double/twin from £180
suite from £340

Gliffaes Country House Hotel

CRICKHOWELL, POWYS NP8 1RH

Standing 150 feet above River Usk this delightful and elegant hotel is a rare haven of peace and tranquillity. Gliffaes is a large Italianate house, which has been run as a hotel by the same family since 1948. The hotel has moved with the times and all the 22 bedrooms have been much improved lately, but it has lost nothing of its Country House charm and character. The hotel has 33 acres of mature woodlands and beautiful gardens with many fine specimen trees, in addition there are 2½ miles of wild brown trout and salmon fishing at your disposal. Tuition and guides can be arranged. An afternoon of tennis or croquet provides the ideal excuse for a lazy afternoon tea on the terrace, whilst you gaze at the river and the hills beyond. Located in the Brecon Beacons National Park means that there is almost limitless opportunities for year round walking, riding and cycling in the unspoilt countryside with the added attraction of a log fire and a good dinner after a day in the outdoors. Those less active may fancy a trip to nearby Hay-on-Wye, with its many second hand book and print shops or a visit to some of the nearby Castles or perhaps to the Elan Valley to watch the Red Kites feeding. There can be few prettier venues for a few days away in this most tranquil of spots.

Our inspector loved: *Enjoying a relaxing drink on the terrace overlooking River Usk - blissful.*

Directions: Gliffaes is signposted from the A40, 2½ miles west of Crickhowell.

Web: www.johansens.com/gliffaescountryhouse
E-mail: calls@gliffaeshotel.com
Tel: 0870 381 8557
International: +44 (0)1874 730371
Fax: 01874 730463

Price Guide:
single from £57–£77.50
double/twin £119–£170

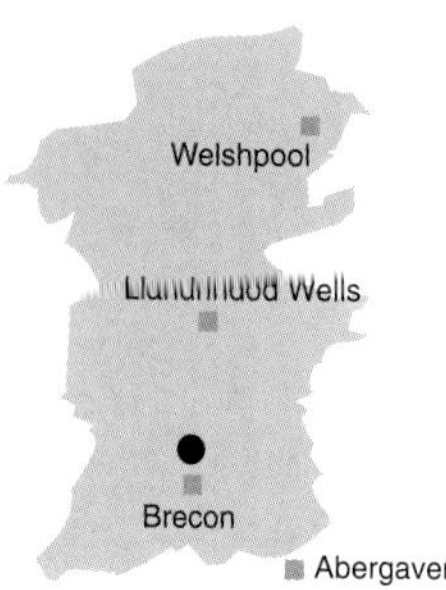

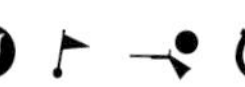

Lake Vyrnwy Hotel

LAKE VYRNWY, MONTGOMERYSHIRE SY10 0LY

Lush forest, wild moorland, rugged mountains and shimmering lake; this stunning country house hotel boasts breathtaking views in all directions. An idyllic haven for country-lovers, Lake Vyrnwy Hotel is set within 24,000 acres of the Vyrnwy Estate, on the hillsides of the Berwyn Mountain Range, easily accessible from the Northwest, Midlands and London. Each of the comfortable guest rooms is individually decorated and some have Jacuzzis, balconies and luxury four-poster beds fitted with sumptuous linen. Guests may dine in the unpretentious atmosphere of the AA Rosette awarded Tower Restaurant whilst enjoying fine contemporary cuisine. The emphasis is placed on fresh local produce, in fact, the hotel houses a small farm for the production of lamb. With its superb location the hotel offers 9 interesting and diverse leisure activities, making it an ideal location for conferences or corporate team-building exercises. Exhilarating white water rafting, rock climbing, 4-wheel driving, clay shooting, archery and fishing can all be arranged. There is something for everybody and tailor-made packages for any occasion can be organised.

Our inspector loved: *The spectacular views from the dining room, a truly relaxing experience.*

Directions: From Shrewsbury take the A458 to Welshpool, then turn right onto the B4393 just after Ford (signposted to Lake Vyrnwy 28 miles).

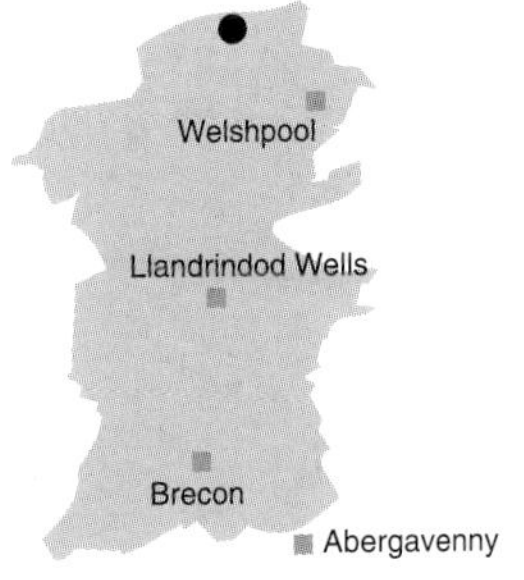

Web: www.johansens.com/lakevyrnwy
E-mail: res@lakevyrnwy.com
Tel: 0870 381 8671
International: +44 (0)1691 870 692
Fax: 01691 870 259

Price Guide:
single £90–£155
double/twin £120–£190
suite £190–£220

35 120

THE LAKE COUNTRY HOUSE AND SPA

LLANGAMMARCH WELLS, POWYS LD4 4BS

A trout leaping up from a serene lake, carpets of wild flowers bobbing in the breeze and badgers ambling by the woods nearby are all sights to be savoured at this glorious country house, surrounded by 50 acres of unspoilt grounds. This hidden gem in Powys, Mid Wales, is a haven for wildlife enthusiasts with over 100 bird-nesting boxes within the grounds and ample opportunities for salmon and trout fishing and horse-riding. Decadent lounges with fine antiques, sumptuous sofas and rich paintings invite guests to discover this charming property, and the bedrooms are individually appointed with period furnishings, scatter cushions and ornate mirrors. In 2006, the accommodation will be further enhanced with the launch of 12 new suites. Traditional Welsh teas are served in the drawing room by roaring log fires in the winter or beneath the chestnut tree in the summer and Welsh cakes, light chocolate sponges and melting scones with homemade jams and cream are some of the many treats to savour. Fresh produce and herbs from the garden are used in the Condé Nast Johansens award-winning restaurant whilst the superb wine list boasts over 300 choices. In addition to the outdoor pursuits and the historic sights nearby, the new spa, gym and swimming pool complex, is situated by the lake providing an inspired setting for those wishing to unwind.

***Our inspector loved:** This unspoilt, special place - idyllic in every season.*

Directions: From the A483 follow signs to Llangammarch Wells and then to the hotel.

Web: www.johansens.com/lakecountryhouse
E-mail: info@lakecountryhouse.co.uk
Tel: 0870 381 8668
International: +44 (0)1591 620202
Fax: 01591 620457

Price Guide:
single £120
double/twin £160–£200
suite £200–£250

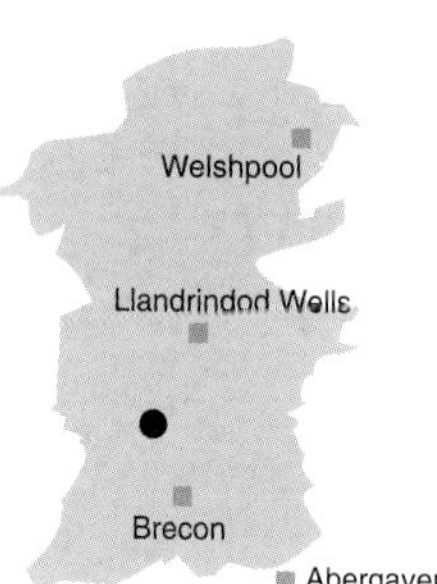

MINI LISTINGS COUNTRY HOUSES

Condé Nast Johansens are delighted to recommend over 230 country houses, small hotels and inns across Great Britain & Ireland. Call 0800 269 397 or see the order forms on page 425 to order Guides.

England

Bath & North East Somerset

Bellplot House Hotel & Thomas's Restaurant - High Street, Chard, Somerset TA20 1QB. Tel: 0870 381 8339

The County Hotel - 18/19 Pulteney Road, Bath, Somerset BA2 4EZ. Tel: 0870 381 8455

Dorian House - One Upper Oldfield Park, Bath BA2 3JX. Tel: 0870 381 8650

The Ring O' Roses - Stratton Road, Holcombe, Near Bath BA3 5EB. Tel: 0870 381 9181

Bedfordshire

Cornfields Restaurant & Hotel - Wilden Road, Colmworth, Bedfordshire MK44 2NJ. Tel: 0870 381 8340

Mill House Restaurant With Rooms - Mill House, Mill Road, Sharnbrook, Bedfordshire MK44 1NP. Tel: 0870 381 9189

Berkshire

▼

Cantley House - Milton Road, Wokingham, Berkshire RG40 5QG. Tel: 0870 381 9233

The Christopher Hotel - High Street, Eton, Windsor, Berkshire SL4 6AN. Tel: 0870 381 8526

The Cottage Inn - Maidens Green, Winkfield, Berkshire SL4 4SW. Tel: 0870 381 9234

The Crab at Chieveley - Wantage Road, Newbury, Berkshire RG20 8UE. Tel: 0870 381 8318

The Inn on the Green - The Old Cricket Common, Cookham Dean, Berkshire SL6 9NZ. Tel: 0870 381 8639

The Leatherne Bottel Riverside Restaurant - The Bridleway, Goring-on-Thames, Berkshire RG8 0HS. Tel: 0870 381 8685

Stirrups Country House Hotel - Maidens Green, Bracknell, Berkshire RG42 6LD. Tel: 0870 381 9238

Buckinghamshire

Bull & Butcher - Turnville, Oxon RG9 6QU. Tel: 0870 381 8451

The Dinton Hermit - Water Lane, Ford, Aylesbury, Buckinghamshire HP17 8XH. Tel: 0870 381 9295

The Ivy House - London Road, Chalfont-St-Giles, Buckinghamshire HP8 4RS. Tel: 0870 381 9236

Cheshire

Broxton Hall - Whitchurch Road, Broxton, Chester, Cheshire CH3 9JS. Tel: 0870 381 8387

Willington Hall Hotel - Willington, Near Tarporley, Cheshire CW6 0NB. Tel: 0870 381 8999

Cornwall

Chandlers Waterside Apartment - 30A Passage Street, Fowey, Cornwall PL23 1DE. Tel: 0870 381 9204

Cormorant on the River, Hotel & Riverside Restaurant - Golant By Fowey, Cornwall PL23 1LL. Tel: 0870 381 8446

Eden-Gate Apartments - The Old Town Hall, St Blazey, Cornwall PL24 2NH. Tel: 0870 381 9191

Highland Court Lodge - Biscovey Road, Biscovey, Near St Austell, Cornwall PL24 2HW. Tel: 0870 381 9290

The Hundred House Hotel & Fish in the Fountain Restaurant - Ruan Highlanes, Near Truro, Cornwall TR2 5JR. Tel: 0870 381 9205

Porth Avallen Hotel - Sea Road, Carlyon Bay, St Austell, Cornwall PL25 3SG. Tel: 0870 381 9366

Primrose Valley Hotel - Primrose Valley, Porthminster Beach, St Ives, Cornwall TR26 2ED. Tel: 0870 381 9377

Tredethy House - Helland Bridge, Wadebridge, Cornwall PL30 4QS. Tel: 0870 381 9142

Tregea Hotel & Estuary Restaurant - 16-18 High Street, Padstow, Cornwall PL28 8BB. Tel: 0870 381 8541

Trehellas House Hotel & Restaurant - Washaway, Bodmin, Cornwall PL30 3AD. Tel: 0870 381 8953

Trelawne Hotel - The Hutches Restaurant - Mawnan Smith, Nr Falmouth, Cornwall TR11 5HT. Tel: 0870 381 8954

Trevalsa Court Country House Hotel & Restaurant - School Hill, Mevagissey, St Austell, Cornwall PL26 6TH. Tel: 0870 381 8955

Wisteria Lodge & Country Spa - Boscundle, Tregrehan, St Austell, Cornwall PL25 3RJ. Tel: 0870 381 9183

Cumbria

Broadoaks Country House - Bridge Lane, Troutbeck, Windermere, Cumbria LA23 1LA. Tel: 0870 381 8380

Crosby Lodge Country House Hotel - High Crosby, Crosby-on-Eden, Carlisle, Cumbria CA6 4QZ. Tel: 0870 381 8461

Dale Head Hall Lakeside Hotel - Thirlmere, Keswick, Cumbria CA12 4TN. Tel: 0870 381 8470

Fayrer Garden House Hotel - Lyth Valley Road, Bowness-on-Windermere, Cumbria LA23 3JP. Tel: 0870 381 8517

Gilpin Lodge - Crook Road, Windermere, Cumbria LA23 3NE. Tel: 0870 381 8546

Grizedale Lodge - Grizedale Forest, Hawkshead, Ambleside, Cumbria LA22 0QL. Tel: 0870 381 9342

Lake House Hotel - Lake Road, Waterhead Bay, Ambleside, Cimbria LA22 0HD. Tel: 0870 381 8492

The Leathes Head - Borrowdale, Keswick, Cumbria CA12 5UY. Tel: 0870 381 8686

Linthwaite House Hotel - Crook Road, Bowness-on-Windermere, Cumbria LA23 3JA. Tel: 0870 381 8694

Nent Hall Country House Hotel - Alston, Cumbria CA9 3LQ. Tel: 0870 381 9210

The Queen's Head Hotel - Main Street, Hawkshead, Cumbria LA22 0NS. Tel: 0870 381 8844

Sawrey House Country Hotel & Restaurant - Near Sawrey, Hawkshead, Ambleside, Cumbria LA22 0LF. Tel: 0870 381 8886

Swinside Lodge Hotel - Grange Road, Newlands, Keswick, Cumbria CA12 5UE. Tel: 0870 381 8933

Temple Sowerby House Hotel and Restaurant - Temple Sowerby, Penrith, Cumbria CA10 1RZ. Tel: 0870 381 8942

Underwood - The Hill, Millom, Cumbria LA18 5EZ. Tel: 0870 381 8959

West Vale Country House & Restaurant - Far Sawrey, hawkshead, Ambleside, Cumbria LA22 0LQ. Tel: 0870 381 9378

The Wheatsheaf at Brigsteer - Brigsteer, Kendal, Cumbria LA8 8AN. Tel: 0870 381 8495

Derbyshire

The Chequers Inn - Froggatt Edge, Hope Valley, Derbyshire S32 3ZJ. Tel: 0870 381 8422

Dannah Farm Country House - Bowman's Lane, Shottle, Nr Belper, Derbyshire DE56 2DR. Tel: 0870 381 8476

The Plough Inn - Leadmill Bridge, Hathersage, Derbyshire S30 1BA. Tel: 0870 381 8827

The Wind in the Willows - Derbyshire Level, Glossop, Derbyshire SK13 7PT. Tel: 0870 381 9001

Devon

Browns Hotel, Wine Bar & Brasserie - 80 West Street, Tavistock, Plymouth, Devon PL19 8AQ. Tel: 0870 381 8386

Combe House Hotel & Restaurant - Gittisham, Honiton, Nr Exeter, Devon EX14 3AD. Tel: 0870 381 8440

▼

The Edgemoor - Haytor Road, Bovey Tracey, South Devon TQ13 9LE. Tel: 0870 381 8499

The Galley Restaurant with Rooms & Spa - 41 Fore Street, Topsham, Exeter EX3 0HU. Tel: 0870 381 9307

Heddon's Gate Hotel - Martinhoe, Parracombe, Barnstaple, Devon EX31 4PZ. Tel: 0870 381 8549

Hewitt's - Villa Spaldi - North Walk, Lynton, Devon EX35 6HJ. Tel: 0870 381 8593

Mini Listings Country Houses

Condé Nast Johansens are delighted to recommend over 230 country houses, small hotels and inns across Great Britain & Ireland.
Call 0800 269 397 or see the order forms on page 425 to order Guides.

▼

Home Farm Hotel - Wilmington, Nr Honiton, Devon EX14 9JR. Tel: 0870 381 8604

Ilsington Country House Hotel - Ilsington Village, Near Newton Abbot, Devon TQ13 9RR. Tel: 0870 381 8635

Kingston House - Staverton, Totnes, Devon TQ9 6AR. Tel: 0870 381 8655

The New Inn - Coleford, Crediton, Devon EX17 5BZ. Tel: 0870 381 8757

Percy's Country Hotel & Restaurant - Coombeshead Estate, Virginstow, Devon EX21 5EA. Tel: 0870 381 8817

Dorset

The Bridge House Hotel - Prout Bridge, Beaminster, Dorset DT8 3AY. Tel: 0870 381 8379

Chandlers Hotel - 4 Westerhall Road, Weymouth, Dorset DT4 7SZ. Tel: 0870 381 8453

The Grange At Oborne - Oborne, Nr Sherborne, Dorset DT9 4LA. Tel: 0870 381 9240

Kemps Country Hotel & Restaurant - East Stoke, Wareham, Dorset BH20 6AL. Tel: 0870 381 8647

La Fleur de Lys - Bleke Street, Shaftesbury, Dorset SP7 8AW. Tel: 0870 381 8454

Langtry Manor - Derby Road, East Cliff, Bournemouth, Dorset BH1 3QB. Tel: 0870 381 8681

The Lord Bute - 181/185 Lymington Road, Highcliffe On Sea, Christchurch, Dorset BH23 4JS. Tel: 0870 381 9341

The Poachers Inn - Piddletrenthide, Dorchester, Dorset DT2 7QX. Tel: 0870 381 8580

Yalbury Cottage Hotel - Lower Bockhampton, Dorchester, Dorset DT2 8PZ. Tel: 0870 381 9015

Essex

The Crown House - Great Chesterford, Saffron Walden, Essex CB10 1NY. Tel: 0870 381 8465

The Pump House Apartment - 132 Church Street, Great Burstead, Essex CM11 2TR. Tel: 0870 381 8842

Gloucestershire

Bibury Court - Bibury Court, Bibury, Gloucestershire GL7 5NT. Tel: 0870 381 8360

Charlton Kings Hotel - Charlton Kings, Cheltenham, Gloucestershire GL52 6UU. Tel: 0870 381 8416

Lower Brook House - Blockley, Nr Moreton-in-marsh, Gloucestershire GL56 9DS. Tel: 0870 381 9297

The Malt House - Broad Campden, Gloucestershire GL55 6UU. Tel: 0870 381 8714

Theroyalisthotel - Digbeth Street, Stow-on-the-Wold, Gloucestershire GL54 1BN. Tel: 0870 381 8566

Three Choirs Vineyards Estate - Newent, Gloucestershire GL18 1LS. Tel: 0870 381 8946

The Wild Duck Inn - Drakes Island, Ewen, Cirencester, Gloucestershire GL7 6BY. Tel: 0870 381 8997

Hampshire

Langrish House - Langrish, Nr Petersfield, Hampshire GU32 1RN. Tel: 0870 381 8679

The Mill At Gordleton - Silver Street, Hordle, Nr Lymington, New Forest, Hampshire SO41 6DJ. Tel: 0870 381 8558

The Nurse's Cottage - Station Road, Sway, Lymington, New Forest, Hampshire SO41 6BA. Tel: 0870 381 8774

Thatched Cottage Hotel & Restaurant - 16 Brookley Road, Brockenhurst, New Forest, Hampshire SO42 7RR. Tel: 0870 381 8943

Herefordshire

Ford Abbey - Pudleston, Nr Leominster, Herefordshire HR6 0RZ. Tel: 0870 381 9144

Glewstone Court - Near Ross-on-Wye, Herefordshire HR9 6AW. Tel: 0870 381 8556

Moccas Court - Moccas, Herefordshire HR2 9LH. Tel: 0870 381 8406

The Pilgrim Hotel - Much Birch, Hereford HR2 8HJ. Tel: 0870 381 9335

Rhydspence Inn - Whitney-on-Wye, Near Hay-on-Wye, Herefordshire HR3 6EU. Tel: 0870 381 9156

The Verzon - Hereford Road, Trumpet, Nr Ledbury, Herefordshire HR8 2PZ. Tel: 0870 381 9348

Wilton Court Hotel - Wilton, Ross-on-Wye, Herefordshire HR9 6AQ. Tel: 0870 381 9000

Hertfordshire

Redcoats Farmhouse Hotel and Restaurant - Redcoats Green, Near Hitchin, Hertfordshire SG4 7JR. Tel: 0870 381 8851

The White House and Lion & Lamb Bar & Restaurant - Smiths Green, Dunmow Road, Takeley, Bishop's Stortford, Hertfordshire CM22 6NR. Tel: 0870 381 9334

Isle of Wight

Rylstone Manor - Rylstone Gardens, Shanklin, Isle of Wight PO37 6RE. Tel: 0870 381 8882

The Wellington Hotel - Belgrave Road, Ventnor, Isle of Wight PO38 1JH. Tel: 0870 381 9320

Kent

Little Silver Country Hotel - Ashford Road, St Michaels, Tenterden, Kent TN30 6SP. Tel: 0870 381 8424

Romney Bay House Hotel - Coast Road, Littlestone, New Romney, Kent TN28 8QY. Tel: 0870 381 8863

Wallett's Court Hotel & Spa - West Cliffe, St Margaret's-at-Cliffe, Dover, Kent CT15 6EW. Tel: 0870 381 8966

Lancashire

Ferrari's Restaurant & Hotel - Thornley, Longridge, Preston, Lancashire PR3 2TB. Tel: 0870 381 8459

The Inn at Whitewell - Forest Of Bowland, Clitheroe, Lancashire BB7 3AT. Tel: 0870 381 8638

Springfield House Hotel - Wheel lane, Pilling, Near Preston PR3 6HL. Tel: 0870 381 9213

Tree Tops Country House Restaurant & Hotel - Southport Old Road, Formby, Nr Southport, Lancashire L37 0AB. Tel: 0870 381 8950

Leicestershire

▼

Abbots Oak Country House - Abbots Oak, Warren Hills Road, Near Coalville, Leicestershire LE67 4UY. Tel: 0870 381 8303

Horse & Trumpet - Old Green, Medbourne, Near Market Harborough, Leicestershire LE16 8DX. Tel: 0870 381 9340

Manners Arms - Croxton Road, Knipton, Grantham, Lincolnshire NG32 1RH. Tel: 0870 381 8429

Rothley Court Hotel - Westfield lane, Rothley, Leicestershire LE7 7LG. Tel: 0870 381 9339

Sysonby Knoll Hotel - Asfordby Road, Melton Mowbray, Leicestershire LE13 0HP. Tel: 0870 381 9352

Lincolnshire

Bailhouse Hotel - 34 Bailgate, Lincoln, Lincolnshire LN1 3AP. Tel: 0870 381 9212

The Crown Hotel - All Saints Place, Stamford, Lincolnshire PE9 2AG. Tel: 0870 381 8464

The Dower House Hotel - Manor Estate, Woodhall Spa, Lincolnshire LN10 6PY. Tel: 0870 381 9214

The Lea Gate Inn - Leagate Road, Coningsby, Lincolnshire LN4 4RS. Tel: 0870 381 8684

Mini Listings Country Houses

Condé Nast Johansens are delighted to recommend over 230 country houses, small hotels and inns across Great Britain & Ireland. Call 0800 269 397 or see the order forms on page 425 to order Guides.

Washingborough Hall - Church Hill, Washingborough, Lincoln LN4 1BE. Tel: 0870 381 8971

Merseyside

Racquet Club - Hargreaves Building, 5 Chapel Street, Liverpool L3 9AA. Tel: 0870 381 9287

Norfolk

Beechwood Hotel - Cromer Road, North Walsham, Norfolk NR28 0HD. Tel: 0870 381 8353

Broom Hall Country Hotel - Richmond Road, Saham Toney, Thetford, Norfolk IP25 7EX. Tel: 0870 381 8384

Brovey Lair - Carbrooke Road, Ovington, Thetford, Norfolk IP25 6SD. Tel: 0870 381 8385

Elderton Lodge Hotel & Langtry Restaurant - Gunton Park, Thorpe Market, Nr North Walsham, Norfolk NR11 8TZ. Tel: 0870 381 8502

The Gin Trap Inn - 6 High Street, Ringstead, Hunstanton, Norfolk PE36 5JU. Tel: 0870 381 9376

The Great Escape Holiday Company - Docking, Kings Lynn, Norfolk PE31 8LY. Tel: 0870 381 8568

▼

Idyllic Cottages At Vere Lodge - South Raynham, Fakenham, Norfolk NR21 7HE. Tel: 0870 381 8961

The Kings Head Hotel - Great Bircham, King's Lynn, Norfolk PE31 6RJ. Tel: 0870 381 9203

The Moat House - Rectory Lane, Hethel, Norwich NR14 8HD. Tel: 0870 381 9317

The Neptune Inn & Restaurant - 85 Old Hunstanton Road, Old Hunstanton, Norfolk PE36 6HZ. Tel: 0870 381 9374

The Norfolk Mead Hotel - Coltishall, Norwich, Norfolk NR12 7DN. Tel: 0870 381 8764

The Old Rectory - 103 Yarmouth Road, Norwich, Norfolk NR7 0HF. Tel: 0870 381 8784

The Stower Grange - School Road, Drayton, Norwich, Norfolk NR8 6EF. Tel: 0870 381 8921

Northamptonshire

The Falcon Hotel - Castle Ashby, Northamptonshire NN7 1LF. Tel: 0870 381 8512

The New French Partridge - Horton, Near Northampton, Northamptonshire NN7 2AP. Tel: 0870 381 9201

The Windmill at Badby - Main Street, Badby, Daventry, Northamptonshire NN11 3AN. Tel: 0870 381 9002

Northumberland

The Otterburn Tower - Otterburn, Northumberland NE19 1NS. Tel: 0870 381 8796

Waren House Hotel - Waren Mill, Bamburgh, Northumberland NE70 7EE. Tel: 0870 381 8967

Nottinghamshire

Cockliffe Country House Hotel - Burnt Stump Country Park, Burnt Stump Hill, Nottinghamshire NG5 8PQ. Tel: 0870 381 8435

Langar Hall - Langar, Nottinghamshire NG13 9HG. Tel: 0870 381 8676

The Saracens Head Hotel - Market Place, Southwell, Nottinghamshire NG25 0HE. Tel: 0870 381 9337

Oxfordshire

Burford House - 99 High Street, Burford, Oxfordshire OX18 4QA. Tel: 0870 381 9211

Duke Of Marlborough Country Inn - Woodleys, Woodstock, Oxford OX20 1HT. Tel: 0870 381 9219

The Jersey Arms - Middleton Stoney, Oxfordshire OX25 4AD. Tel: 0870 381 8644

The Kings Head Inn & Restaurant - The Green, Bledington, Nr Kingham, Oxfordshire OX7 6XQ. Tel: 0870 381 8654

The Spread Eagle Hotel - Cornmarket, Thame, Oxfordshire OX9 2BW. Tel: 0870 381 8902

Rutland

Barnsdale Lodge - The Avenue, Rutland Water, Near Oakham, Rutland LE15 8AH. Tel: 0870 381 8342

Shropshire

The Hundred House Hotel, Norton - Bridgnorth Road, Norton, Nr Shifnal, Telford, Shropshire TF11 9EE. Tel: 0870 381 8629

Pen-Y-Dyffryn Country Hotel - Rhydycroesau, Near Oswestry, Shropshire SY10 7JD. Tel: 0870 381 8809

Soulton Hall - Nr Wem, Shropshire SY4 5RS. Tel: 0870 381 8899

Somerset

Ashwick Country House Hotel - Dulverton, Somerset TA22 9QD. Tel: 0870 381 8327

Beryl - Wells, Somerset BA5 3JP. Tel: 0870 381 8358

Compton House - Townsend, Axbridge, Somerset BS26 2AJ. Tel: 0870 381 8441

Farthings Hotel & Restaurant - Hatch Beauchamp, Somerset TA3 6SG. Tel: 0870 381 8515

Glencot House - Glencot Lane, Wookey Hole, Nr Wells, Somerset BA5 1BH. Tel: 0870 381 8552

Karslake County House & Restaurant - Halse Lane, Winsford, Exmoor National Park, Somerset TA24 7JE. Tel: 0870 381 9134

Porlock Vale House - Porlock Weir, Somerset TA24 8NY. Tel: 0870 381 8830

Tarr Farm Inn - Tarr Steps, Dulverton, Exmoor National Park TA22 9PY. Tel: 0870 381 8463

Three Acres Country House - Three Acres, Brushford, Dulverton, Somerset TA22 9AR. Tel: 0870 381 9229

Staffordshire

Somerford Hall - Brewood, Staffordshire ST19 9DQ. Tel: 0870 381 9120

Suffolk

The Brome Grange Hotel - Brome, Eye, Suffolk IP23 8AP. Tel: 0870 381 9299

▼

Clarice House - Horringer Court, Horringer Road, Bury St Edmunds Suffolk IP29 5PH. Tel: 0870 381 8431

Surrey

Chase Lodge - 10 Park Road, Hampton Wick, Kingston-upon-Thames, Surrey KT1 4AS. Tel: 0870 381 8419

Stanhill Court Hotel - Stan Hill Road, Charlwood, Nr Horley, Surrey RH6 0EP. Tel: 0870 381 8908

East Sussex

The Hope Anchor Hotel - Watchbell Street, Rye, East Sussex TN31 7HA. Tel: 0870 381 8607

West Sussex

The Chequers at Slaugham - Slaugham, Nr Handcross, West Sussex RH17 6AQ. Tel: 0870 381 8421

Mini Listings Country Houses

Condé Nast Johansens are delighted to recommend over 230 country houses, small hotels and inns across Great Britain & Ireland.
Call 0800 269 397 or see the order forms on page 425 to order Guides.

Crouchers Country Hotel & Restaurant - Birdham Road, Apuldram, Near Chichester, West Sussex PO20 7EH. Tel: 0870 381 8462

The Mill House Hotel - Mill Lane, Ashington, West Sussex RH20 3BX. Tel: 0870 381 8735

The Old Tollgate Restaurant and Hotel - The Street, Bramber, Steyning, West Sussex BN44 3WE. Tel: 0870 381 8789

Warwickshire

Nuthurst Grange - Hockley Heath, Warwickshire B94 5NL. Tel: 0870 381 8776

Wiltshire

The Castle Inn - Castle Combe, Wiltshire SN14 7HN. Tel: 0870 381 8361

▼

The George Inn - Longbridge Deverill, Warminster, Wiltshire BA12 7DG. Tel: 0870 381 8542

The Lamb at Hindon - High Street, Hindon, Wiltshire SP3 6DP. Tel: 0870 381 9208

The Old Manor Hotel - Trowle, Near Bradford on Avon, Wiltshire BA14 9BL. Tel: 0870 381 8782

Stanton Manor Hotel & Gallery Restaurant - Stanton Saint Quintin, Near Chippenham, Wiltshire SN14 6DQ. Tel: 0870 381 8910

Widbrook Grange - Widbrook, Bradford-on-Avon, Nr Bath, Wiltshire BA15 1UH. Tel: 0870 381 8996

Worcestershire

The Boot Inn - Radford Road, Flyford Flavell, Worcestershire WR7 4BS. Tel: 0870 381 9319

Colwall Park - Colwall, Near Malvern, Worcestershire WR13 6QG. Tel: 0870 381 8437

The Old Rectory - Ipsley Lane, Ipsley, Near Redditch, Worcestershire B98 0AP. Tel: 0870 381 9169

The Old Windmill - Withybed Lane, Inkberrow, Worcestershire WR7 4JL. Tel: 0870 381 9167

▼

Riverside Restaurant and Hotel - The Parks, Offenham Road, Near Evesham, Worcestershire WR11 8JP. Tel: 0870 381 9298

The White Lion Hotel - High Street, Upton-upon-Severn, Nr Malvern, Worcestershire WR8 0HJ. Tel: 0870 381 8989

North Yorkshire

The Austwick Traddock - Austwick, Via Lancaster, North Yorkshire LA2 8BY. Tel: 0870 381 8331

The Boar's Head Hotel - The Ripley Castle Estate, Harrogate, North Yorkshire HG3 3AY. Tel: 0870 381 8370

The Devonshire Fell - Burnsall, Skipton, North Yorkshire BD23 6BT. Tel: 0870 381 8554

Dunsley Hall - Dunsley, Whitby, North Yorkshire YO21 3TL. Tel: 0870 381 8494

Hob Green Hotel and Restaurant - Markington, Harrogate, North Yorkshire HG3 3PJ. Tel: 0870 381 8600

The Red Lion - By The Bridge At Burnsall, Near Skipton, North Yorkshire BD23 6BU. Tel: 0870 381 8850

Stow House Hotel - Aysgarth, Leyburn, North Yorkshire DL8 3SR. Tel: 0870 381 8920

West Yorkshire

Hey Green Country House Hotel - Waters Road, Marsden, West Yorkshire HD7 6NG. Tel: 0870 381 8652

Channel Islands

Herm Island

The White House - Herm Island, Guernsey, Channel Islands GY1 3HR. Tel: 0870 381 8988

Sark

Aval du Creux Hotel - Harbour Hill, Sark, Guernsey, Channel Islands GY9 0SB. Tel: 0870 381 9173

La Sablonnerie - Little Sark, Sark, Channel Islands GY9 0SD. Tel: 0870 381 8666

Jersey

Eulah Country House - Mont Cochon, St Helier, Jersey, Channel Islands JE2 3JA. Tel: 0870 381 8509

Ireland

Galway

Ross Lake House Hotel - Rosscahill, Oughterard, Co Galway, Ireland. Tel: 00 353 91 550109

Zetland Country House Hotel - Cashel Bay, Connemara, Co Galway, Ireland. Tel: 00 353 95 31111

Kerry

Emlagh House - Dingle, Co Kerry, Ireland. Tel: 00 353 66 915 2345

Sligo

Coopershill House - Riverstown, Co Sligo, Ireland. Tel: 00 353 71 9165108

Scotland

Angus

Castleton House Hotel - Glamis, By Forfar, Angus DD8 1SJ. Tel: 0870 381 8411

Argyll & Bute

Ballachulish House - Ballachulish, Argyll PH49 4JX. Tel: 0870 381 8336

The Frog At Dunstaffnage Bay - Dunstaffnage Marina, Connel, By Oban, Argyll PA37 1PX. Tel: 0870 381 8533

Highland Cottage - Breadalbane Street, Tobermory, Isle of Mull PA75 6PD. Tel: 0870 381 9184

Ptarmigan House - The Fairways, Tobermory PA75 6PS. Tel: 0870 381 9343

Mini Listings Country Houses

Condé Nast Johansens are delighted to recommend over 230 country houses, small hotels and inns across Great Britain & Ireland.
Call 0800 269 397 or see the order forms on page 425 to order Guides.

Clackmannanshire

Castle Campbell Hotel - 11 Bridge Street, Dollar, Clackmannanshire FK14 7DE. Tel: 0870 381 9232

Dumfries & Galloway

Fernhill Hotel - Heugh Road, Portpatrick DG9 8TD. Tel: 0870 381 8521

Fife

▼

The Barns at Kingsbarns - 5 Main Street, Kingsbarns, Fife KY16 8TA. Tel: 0870 381 9370

Highland

Corriegour Lodge Hotel - Loch Lochy, By Spean Bridge, Inverness-shire PH34 4EB. Tel: 0870 381 8447

The Cross at Kingussie - Tweed Mill Brae, Ardbroilach Road, Kingussie, Inverness-shire PH21 1LB. Tel: 0870 381 9349

Forss House Hotel - Forss, Near Thurso, Caithness KW14 7XY. Tel: 0870 381 8321

Hotel Eilean Iarmain - Sleat, Isle of Skye IV43 8QR. Tel: 0870 381 8619

Ruddyglow Park - Loch Assynt, By Lairg, Sutherland IV27 4HB. Tel: 0870 381 8457

The Steadings at The Grouse & Trout - Flichity, Farr, South Loch Ness, Inverness IV2 6XD. Tel: 0870 381 9138

Toravaig House Hotel - Knock Bay, Sleat, Isle of Skye IV44 8RE. Tel: 0870 381 9344

Moray

Knockomie Hotel - Grantown Road, Forres, Morayshire IV36 2SG. Tel: 0870 381 8663

Perth & Kinross

Cairn Lodge Hotel - Orchil Road, Auchterarder, Perthshire PH3 1LX. Tel: 0870 381 9284

The Four Seasons Hotel - St Fillans, Perthshire PH6 2NF. Tel: 0870 381 8528

Monachyle Mhor - Balquhidder, By Lochearnhead, Perthshire FK19 8PQ. Tel: 0870 381 9231

Scottish Borders

Castle Venlaw - Edinburgh Road, Peebles EH45 8QG. Tel: 0870 381 8410

South Ayrshire

Culzean Castle - The Eisenhower Apartment - Maybole, Ayrshire KA19 8LE. Tel: 0870 381 8469

Wales

Anglesey

Ye Olde Bulls Head Inn - Castle Street, Beaumaris, Anglesey LL58 8AP. Tel: 0870 381 9017

Cardiff

The Inn at the Elm Tree - St Brides, Wentlooge, Nr Newport NP10 8SQ. Tel: 0870 381 8637

Carmarthenshire

Ty Mawr Country Hotel - Brechfa, Carmarthenshire SA32 7RA. Tel: 0870 381 9318

Ceredigion

Conrah Country House Hotel - Rhydgaled, Chancery, Aberystwyth, Ceredigion SY23 4DF. Tel: 0870 381 8444

Ty Mawr Mansion Country House - Cilcennin, Lampeter SA48 8DB. Tel: 0870 381 8572

Conwy

Sychnant Pass House - Sychnant Pass Road, Conwy LL32 8BJ. Tel: 0870 381 8936

Tan-Y-Foel Country House - Capel Garmon, Nr Betws-y-Coed, Conwy LL26 0RE. Tel: 0870 381 8938

Glamorgan

Egerton Grey - Porthkerry, Nr Cardiff, Vale Of Glamorgan CF62 3BZ. Tel: 0870 381 8501

Gwynedd

Bae Abermaw - Panorama Hill, Barmouth, Gwynedd LL42 1DQ. Tel: 0870 381 8332

Hotel Maes-Y-Neuadd - Talsarnau, Near Harlech, Gwynedd LL47 6YA. Tel: 0870 381 9332

Llwyndu Farmhouse - Llanaber, Nr Barmouth, Gwynedd LL42 1RR. Tel: 0870 381 9143

Plas Dolmelynllyn - Ganllwyd, Dolgellau, Gwynedd LL40 2HP. Tel: 0870 381 8825

Porth Tocyn Country House Hotel - Abersoch, Pwllheli, Gwynedd LL53 7BU. Tel: 0870 381 8832

Monmouthshire

▼

The Bell At Skenfrith - Skenfrith, Monmouthshire NP7 8UH. Tel: 0870 381 8354

The Crown At Whitebrook - Whitebrook, Monmouthshire NP25 4TX. Tel: 0870 381 8563

Parva Farmhouse and Restaurant - Tintern, Chepstow, Monmouthshire NP16 6SQ. Tel: 0870 381 8803

Pembrokeshire

The Gower Hotel & Orangery Restaurant - Milford Terrace, Saundersfoot, Pembrokeshire SA69 9EL. Tel: 0870 381 9149

Wolfscastle Country Hotel & Restaurant - Wolf's Castle, Haverfordwest, Pembrokeshire SA62 5LZ. Tel: 0870 381 9162

Powys

Glangrwyney Court - Glangrwyney, Nr Crickhowell, Powys NP8 1ES. Tel: 0870 381 8547

Swansea

Fairyhill - Reynoldston, Gower, Near Swansea SA3 1BS. Tel: 0870 381 9321

HISTORIC HOUSES, CASTLES & GARDENS

Incorporating Museums & Galleries

We are pleased to feature over 150 places to visit during your stay at a Condé Nast Johansens recommended hotel.

England

Bedfordshire

Cecil Higgins Art Gallery - Castle Lane, Bedford, Bedfordshire MK40 4AF. Tel: 01234 211222

Woburn Abbey - Woburn, Bedfordshire MK17 9WA. Tel: 01525 290666

Berkshire

Anderton house - The Landmark Trust, Shottesbrooke, Maidenhead, Berkshire SL6 3SW. Tel: 01628 825920

Dolbelydr - The Landmark Trust, Shottesbrooke, Maidenhead, Berkshire SL6 3SW. Tel: 01628 825920

Old Campden House - The Landmark Trust, Shottesbrooke, Maidenhead, Berkshire SL6 3SW. Tel: 01628 825920

▼

Taplow Court - Berry Hill, Taplow, Nr Maidenhead, Berkshire SL6 0ER. Tel: 01628 591209

Buckinghamshire

Doddershall Park - Quainton, Aylesbury, Buckinghamshire HP22 4DF. Tel: 01296 655238

Hughenden Manor - High Wycombe, Buckinghamshire HP14 4LA. Tel: 01494 755573

Nether Winchendon House - Nr Aylesbury, Buckinghamshire HP18 0DY. Tel: 01844 290199

Waddesdon Manor - Waddesdon, Nr Aylesbury, Buckinghamshire HP18 0JH. Tel: 01296 653211

Cambridgeshire

Ely Cathedral - The Chapter House, The College, Ely, Cambrideshire CB7 4DL. Tel: 01353 667735

Octavia Hill's Birthplace House - 1 South Brink Place, Wisbech, Cambridgeshire PE13 1JE. Tel: 01945 476358

Oliver Cromwell's House - 29 St Mary's Street, Ely, Cambridgeshire CB7 4HF. Tel: 01353 662062

Peterborough Cathedral - The Chapter Office, Minster Precincts, Peterborough, Cambridgeshire PE1 1XS. Tel: 01733 343342

The Manor - Hemingford Grey, Cambridgeshire PE28 9BN. Tel: 01480 463134

Cheshire

Arley Hall & Gardens - Arley, Northwich, Cheshire CW9 6NA. Tel: 01565 777353

Dorfold Hall - Nantwich, Cheshire CW5 8LD. Tel: 01270 625245

Gawsworth Hall - Gasworth, Macclesfield, Cheshire SK11 9RN. Tel: 01260 223456

Norton Priory Museum & Gardens - Tudor Road, Manor Park, Cheshire WA7 1SX. Tel: 01928 569895

Rode Hall - Church Lane, Scholar Green, Cheshire ST7 3QP. Tel: 01270 873237

Tabley House Stately Home - Tabley House, Knutsford, Cheshire WA16 0HB. Tel: 01565 750151

Co Durham

Auckland Castle - Bishop Auckland, Co Durham DL14 7NR. Tel: 01388 601627

Raby Castle - Staindrop, Darlington, Co Durham DL2 3AH. Tel: 01833 660207 / 660202

Cumbria

Isel Hall - Cockermouth, Cumbria CA13 0QG. Tel: x Directory

Mirehouse & Keswick - Mirehouse, Keswick, Cumbria CA12 4QE. Tel: 01768 772287

Muncaster Castle - Ravenglass, Cumbria CA18 1RQ. Tel: 01229 717614

Windermere Steamboat Centre - Rayrigg Road, Windermere, Cumbria LA23 1BN. Tel: 01539 445565

Derbyshire

Haddon Hall - Bakewell, Derbyshire DE45 1LA. Tel: 01629 812855

Hardwick Hall - Doe Lea, Chesterfield, Derbyshire S44 5QJ. Tel: 01246 850430

Melbourne Hall & Gardens - Melbourne, Derbyshire DE73 1EN. Tel: 01332 862502

Renishaw Hall Gardens - Renshaw Park, Renshaw, Sheffield, Derbyshire S21 3WB. Tel: 01246 432310

Devon

Bowringsleigh - Kingbridge, Devon. Tel: 01548 852014

Downes Estate at Crediton - Crediton, Devon. Tel: 01392 439046

Haldon Belvedere/ Lawrence Castle - Higher Ashton, Nr Dunchideock, Exeter, Devon. Tel: 01392 833668

Dorset

Cranborne Manor Garden - Cranborne, Wimborne, Dorset BH21 5PP. Tel: 01725 517248

Lulworth Castle - The Lulworth Estate, East Lulworth, Wareham, Dorset BH20 5QS. Tel: 01929 400352

Mapperton - Mapperton, Beaminster, Dorset DT8 3NR. Tel: 01308 862645

Moignes Court - Owermoigne, Dorset. Tel: 01305 853 479

Essex

Ingatestone Hall - Hall Lane, Ingatestone, Essex CM4 9NR. Tel: 01277 353010

The Gardens of Easton Lodge - Warwick House, Easton Lodge, Essex CM6 2BB. Tel: 01371 876979

Gloucestershire

Cheltenham Art Gallery & Museum - Clarence Street, Cheltenham, Gloucestershire GL50 3JT. Tel: 01242 237431

Hardwicke Court - Gloucester, Gloucestershire GL2 4RS. Tel: 01452 720212

Nature In Art - Wallsworth Hall, Main A38, Twigworth, Gloucestershire GL2 9PA. Tel: 01452 731422

Sezincote - Moreton-in-Marsh, Gloucestershire GL56 9AW. Tel: 01386 700444

Hampshire

Avington Park - Winchester, Hampshire SO21 1DB. Tel: 01962 779260

Beaulieu - John Montagu Building, Beaulieu, Hampshire SO42 7ZN. Tel: 01590 612345

Beaulieu Vineyard and Gardens - Beaulieu Estate, John Montagu Building, Beaulieu, Hampshire SO42 7ZN. Tel: 01590 612345

Breamore House & Museum - Breamore, nr Fordingbridge, Hampshire SP6 2DF. Tel: 01725 512468

Broadlands - Romsey, Hampshire SO51 9ZD. Tel: 01794 505010

Gilbert White's House and The Oates Museum - Selborne, Hampshire GU34 3JH. Tel: 01420 511275

Greywell Hill House - Greywell, Hook, Hampshire RG29 1DG. Tel: 01256 7035 65

Herefordshire

Eastnor Castle - Eastnor, Ledbury, Herefordshire HR8 1RL. Tel: 01531 633160

Kentchurch Court - Kentchurch, Nr Pontrilas, Hereford, Herefordshire HR2 0DB. Tel: 01981 240228

Kinnersley Castle - Kinnersley, Herefordshire HR3 6QF. Tel: 01544 327407

Hertfordshire

Ashridge - Ringshall, Berkhamsted, Hertfordshire HP4 1NS. Tel: 01442 843491

Mill Green Museum and Mill - Mill Green Museum and Mill, Mill Green, Hatfield, Hertfordshire AL9 5PD. Tel: 01707 271362

St. Pauls Walden Bury - Hitchin, Hertfordshire SG4 8BP. Tel: 01438 871218/871229

Welwyn Roman Baths - Welwyn Bypass, Welwyn, Hertfordshire AL6 9HT. Tel: 01707 271362

Isle of Wight

Deacons Nursery - Moor View, Godshill, Isle of Wight PO38 3HW. Tel: 01983 840750

Newport Roman Villa - Cypress Road, Newport, Isle of Wight PO30 1HE. Tel: 01983 529720

Kent

Cobham Hall - Cobham, Kent DA12 3BL. Tel: 01474 823371

Finchcocks, Living Museum of Music - Goudhurst, Kent TN17 1HH. Tel: 01580 211702

Graham Clarke Up the Garden Studio - Green Lane, Boughton Monchelsea, Maidstone, Kent ME17 4LF. Tel: 01622 743938

Groombridge Place Gardens & Enchanted Forest - Groombridge, Tunbridge Wells, Kent TN3 9QG. Tel: 01892 861444

Hever Castle & Gardens - Edenbridge, Kent TN8 7NG. Tel: 01732 865224

Knole - Sevenoaks, Kent TN15 0RP. Tel: 01732 450608

Leeds Castle - Maidstone, Kent ME17 1PL. Tel: 01622 765400

Mount Ephraim Gardens - Hernhill, Nr Faversham, Kent ME13 9TX. Tel: 01227 751496

Penshurst Place & Gardens - Penshurst, Nr Tonbridge, Kent TN11 8DG. Tel: 01892 870307

The Grange - Ramsgate, Kent. Tel: 01628 825920

The New College of Cobham - Cobhambury Road, Graves End, Kent DA12 3BG. Tel: 01474 814280

Lancashire

Stonyhurst College - Stonyhurst, Clitheroe, Lancashire BB7 9PZ. Tel: 01254 826345

Townhead House - Slaidburn, Via CLitheroe, Lancashire BBY 3AG. Tel: 01772 421566

Liverpool

Knowsley Hall - Prescot, Liverpool L32 4AF. Tel: 0151 489 4437 / 0468 698640

London

Handel House Museum - 25 Brook Street, London W1K 4HB. Tel: 020 7495 1685

Pitzhanger Manor House - Walpole Park, Mattock Lane, Ealing, London W5 5EQ. Tel: 020 8567 1227

Sir John Soane's Museum - 13 Lincoln's Inn Fields, London WC2A 3BP. Tel: 020 7405 2107

Westminster Abbey - Broad Sanctuary, London SW1P 3PA. Tel: 020 7222 5152

Middlesex

Syon Park - London Road, Brentford, Middlesex TW8 8JF. Tel: 020 8560 0882

Norfolk

Fairhaven Woodland and Water Garden - School Road, South Walsham, Norwich, Norfolk NR13 6EA. Tel: 01603 270449

Hoveton Hall Gardens - Hoveton, Wroxham, Norfolk NR12 8RJ. Tel: 01603 782798

Mannington Hall - Saxthorpe, Norwich, Norfolk NR11 7BB. Tel: 01263 584175

Walsingham Abbey Grounds - c/o The Estate Office, Little Walsingham, Norfolk NR22 6BP. Tel: 01328 820259 / 820510

Wolterton and Mannington Estate - Mannington Hall, Norwich, Norfolk NR11 7BB. Tel: 01263 584175

Northamptonshire

Cottesbrooke Hall and Gardens - Cottesbrooke, Northampton, Northamptonshire NN6 8PF. Tel: 01604 505808

Haddonstone Show Garden - The Forge House, Church Lane, East Haddon, Northamptonshire NN6 8DB. Tel: 01604 770711

▼

Alnwick Castle - Alnwick, Northumberland NE66 1NQ. Tel: 01665 510777 / 511100

Chipchase Castle - Chipchase, Wark on Tyne, Hexham, Northumberland NE48 3NT. Tel: 01434 230203

Paxton House & Country Park - Berwick-upon-Tweed, Northumberland TD15 1SZ. Tel: 01289 386291

Seaton Delaval Hall - Seaton Sluice, Whitley Bay, Northumberland NE26 4QR. Tel: 0191 237 1493 / 0786

Nottinghamshire

Newstead Abbey House and Grounds - Linby, Nottinghamshire NG15 8GE. Tel: (0623) 793557

Papplewick Hall - Papplewick, Nottingham, Nottinghamshire NG15 8FE. Tel: 0115 963 3491

Oxfordshire

Fawley Court - Marian Fathers Historic House & Museum - Marlow Road, Henley-On-Thames, Oxfordshire RG9 3AE. Tel: 01491 574917

Kingston Bagpuize House - Kingston Bagpuize, Abingdon, Oxfordshire OX13 5AX. Tel: 01865 820259

Mapledurham House - Mapledurham, Nr Reading, Oxfordshire RG4 7TR. Tel: 01189 723350

Wallingford Castle Gardens - Castle Street, Wallingford, Oxfordshire. Tel: 01491 835373

Shropshire

Coleham Pumping Station - Longden Coleham, Shrewsbury, Shropshire SY3 7DN. Tel: 01743 362947

Hawkstone Park & Follies - Weston-under-Redcastle, Shrewsbury, Shropshire SY4 5UY. Tel: 01939 200 611

Hodnet Hall Gardens - Hodnet, Market Drayton, Shropshire TF9 3NN. Tel: 01630 685786

Shrewsbury Castle & Shropshire Regimental Museum - Castle Street, Shrewsbury, Shropshire SY1 2AT. Tel: 01743 358516

Shrewsbury Museum & Art Gallery - Barker Street, Shrewsbury, Shropshire SY1 1QH. Tel: 01743 361196

Weston Park - Weston-under-Lizard, Nr Shifnal, Shropshire TF11 8LE. Tel: 01952 852100

Somerset

Cothay Manor & Gardens - Cothay Manor, Greenham, Nr Wellington, Somerset TA21 OJR. Tel: 01823 672283

East Lambrook Manor Garden - South Petherton, Somerset TA13 5HL. Tel: 01460 240328

Great House Farm - Wells Road, Theale, Wedmore, Somerset BS28 4SJ. Tel: 01934 713133

Hestercombe House Gardens - Cheddon Fitzpaine, Taunton, Somerset TA2 8LG. Tel: 01823 413923

Number One Royal Crescent - Bath Preservation Trust, Bath, Somerset BA1 2LR. Tel: 01225 428126

Orchard Wyndham - Williton, Taunton, Somerset TA4 4HH. Tel: 01984 632309

Robin Hood's Hut - Halswell, Somerset. Tel: 01628 825920

Staffordshire

Izaak Walton's Cottage - Shallowford, nr. Stafford, Staffordshire ST15 OPA. Tel: 01785 760 278

Stafford Castle - Newport Road, Stafford, Staffordshire ST16 1DJ. Tel: 01785 257 698

The Ancient High House - Greengate Street, Stafford, Staffordshire ST16 2JA. Tel: 01785 223181

Whitmore Hall - Whitmore, Newcastle-under-Lyme, Staffordshire ST5 5HW. Tel: 01782 680478

Suffolk

Ancient House - Clare, Suffolk CO10 8NY. Tel: 01628 825920

Freston Tower - Suffolk. Tel: 01628 825920

Kentwell Hall - Long Melford, Suffolk CO10 7JS. Tel: 01787 310207

Mechanical Music Museum & Bygones - Blacksmith Road, Cotton, Nr Stowmarket, Suffolk IP14 4QN. Tel: 01449 613876

Newbourne Hall - Newbourne, Nr. Woodbridge, Suffolk IP12 4NP. Tel: 01473 736764

Otley Hall - Hall Lane, Otley, Ipswich, Suffolk IP6 9PA. Tel: 01473 890264

Shrubland Park Gardens - Shrubland Estate, Coddenham, Ipswich, Suffolk IP6 9QQ. Tel: 01473 830221

Surrey

Albury Park - Albury, Guildford, Surrey GU5 9BB. Tel: (01483) 202964

Claremont House - Claremont Drive, Esher, Surrey KT10 9LY. Tel: 01372 467841

Goddards - Abinger Common, Dorking, Surrey RH5 6TH. Tel: 01628 825920

Guildford House Gallery - 155, High Street, Guildford, Surrey GU1 3AJ. Tel: 01483 444740

Loseley Park - Estate Office, Guildford, Surrey GU3 1HS. Tel: 01483 304440

▼

Painshill Landscape Garden - Portsmouth Road, Cobham, Surrey KT11 1JE. Tel: 01932 868113

Sussex

Royal Pavilion - Brighton, Sussex BN1 1EE. Tel: 01273 290900

East Sussex

Charleston - Firle, East Sussex BN8 6LL. Tel: 01323 811626

Firle Place - The Estate Office, Lewes, East Sussex BN8 6NS. Tel: 01273 858043

Garden and Grounds of Herstmonceux Castle - Herstmonceux Castle, Hailsham, East Sussex BN27 1RN. Tel: 01323 833816

Merriments Gardens - Hurst Green, EastSussex TN19 7RA. Tel: 01580 860666

Wilmington Priory - Wilmington, Nr Eastbourne, East Sussex BN26 5SW. Tel: 01628 825920

West Sussex

Borde Hill Garden - Balcombe Road, West Sussex RH16 1XP. Tel: 01444 450326

Denmans Garden - Clock House, Denmans, Fontwell, West Sussex BN18 0SU. Tel: 01243 542808

Goodwood House - Goodwood, Chichester, West Sussex PO18 0PX. Tel: 01243 755000

High Beeches Gardens - High Beeches, Handcross, West Sussex RH17 6HQ. Tel: 01444 400589

Leonardslee - Lakes & Gardens - Lower Beeding, Horsham, West Sussex RH13 6PP. Tel: 01403 891212

Parham House and Gardens - Parham Park , Nr Pulborough, West Sussex RH20 4HS. Tel: 01903 742021

Weald and Downland Open Air Museum - Singleton, Chichester, West Sussex PO21 4JU. Tel: 01243 811363

West Dean Gardens - West Dean, Chichester, West Sussex PO18 0QZ. Tel: 01243 818210

Worthing Museum & Art Gallery - Chapel Road, Worthing, West Sussex BN11 1HP. Tel: 01903 239999

Warwickshire

Arbury Hall - Nuneaton, Warwickshire CV10 7PT. Tel: 024 7638 2804

Ragley Hall - Alcester, Warwickshire B49 5NJ. Tel: 01789 762090

Shakespeare Houses - The Shakespeare Centre, Henley Street, Stratford-upon-Avon, Warwickshire CV37 6QW. Tel: 01789 204016

West Midlands

Barber Institute of Fine Arts - The University of Birmingham, Edgbaston, Birmingham, West Midlands B15 2TS. Tel: 0121 414 7333

The Birmingham Botanical Gardens and Glasshouses - Westbourne Road, Edgbaston, Birmingham, West Midlands B15 3TR. Tel: 0121 454 1860

Wiltshire

Hamptworth Lodge - Landford, Salisbury, Wiltshire SP5 2EA. Tel: 01794 390215

Longleat - Warminster, Wiltshire BA12 7NW. Tel: 01985 844400

Salisbury Cathedral - Visitor Services, 33 The Close, Salisbury, Wiltshire SP1 2EJ. Tel: 01722 555120

Worcestershire

Harvington Hall - Harvington, Kidderminister, Worcester DY10 4LR. Tel: 01562 777846

Little Malvern Court - Nr Malvern, Worcestershire WR14 4JN. Tel: 01684 892988

Spetchley Park Gardens - Spetchley Park, Worcester, Worcester WR5 1RS. Tel: 01453 810303

North Yorkshire

Duncombe Park - Helmsley, York, North Yorkshire YO62 5EB. Tel: 01439 770213

Fountains Abbey & Studley Royal - Ripon, North Yorkshire HG4 3DY. Tel: 01765 608888

Kiplin Hall - Nr Scorton, Richmond, North Yorkshire. Tel: 01748 818178

Newburgh Priory - Coxwold, North Yorkshire YO61 4AS. Tel: 01347 868435

Newby Hall & Gardens - Ripon, North Yorkshire HG4 5AE. Tel: 01423 322583

Ripley Castle - Ripley Castle Estate, Harrogate, North Yorkshire HG3 3AY. Tel: 01423 770152

Skipton Castle - Skipton, North Yorkshire BD23 1AQ. Tel: 01756 792442

The Forbidden Corner - The Tupgill Park Estate, Coverham, Middleham, North Yorkshire DL8 4TJ. Tel: 01969 640638

West Yorkshire

Bramham Park - Estate Office, Bramham Park, Wetherby, West Yorkshire LS23 6ND. Tel: 01937 846000

Bronte Parsonage Museum - Church Street, Haworth, Keighley, West Yorkshire BD22 8DR. Tel: 01535 642323

Ledston Hall - Hall Lane, Ledstone, West Yorkshire WF10 3BB. Tel: 01423 523 423

Northern Ireland

Co Antrim

Ballance House - 118a Lisburn Road, Glenavy, Co Antrim BT28 4NY. Tel: 02892 648492

Co Down

Mount Stewart House, Garden and Temple - Newtownards, Co Down BT22 2AD. Tel: 028 427 88387/028 427 88487

Seaforde Gardens - Seaforde, Downpatrick, Co Down BT30 8PG. Tel: 028 4481 1225

Ireland

Co Cork

Bantry House & Gardens - Bantry, Co. Cork. Tel: + 353 2 750 047

Co Offaly

Birr Castle Demesne - Birr, Co. Ofaly. Tel: + +353 509 20336

Co Kildare

The Irish National Stud, Japanese Gardens & St Fiachra's Garden - Tully, Kildare Town, Co Kildare. Tel: +353 45 521617

Co Waterford

Lismore Castle - Lismore, Co Waterford. Tel: +353 58 54424

Co Wexford

Kilmokea Country Manor & Gardens - Great Island, Campile, Co Wexford. Tel: +353 51 388109

Co Wicklow

Humewood Castle - Kiltegan, Co. Wicklow. Tel: +353 508 73215

Mount Usher Gardens - Ashford, Co Wicklow. Tel: +353 404 40205

Scotland

Aberdeenshire

Craigston Castle - Turriff, Aberdeenshire AB53 5PX. Tel: 01888 551228

Argyll & Bute

Ardkinglas Estate - Argyll & Bute. Tel: 01499 600261

Ayrshire

Auchinleck - Ochiltree, Ayrshire. Tel: 01628 825920

Kelburn Castle and Country Centre - Kelburn, Fairlie (Nr Largs), Ayrshire KA29 0BE. Tel: 01475 568685

Sorn Castle - Sorn, Mauchline, Ayrshire KA5 6HR. Tel: 0141 942 6460

Borders

▼

Abbotsford - Melrose, Borders TD6 9BQ. Tel: 01896 752043

Dumfries

Drumlanrig Castle, Gardens and Country Park - Nr Thornhill, Dumfries DG3 4AQ. Tel: 01848 330248

Fife

Cambo Gardens - Cambo Estate, Kingbarns, St. Andrews, Fife KY16 8QD. Tel: 01333 450054

Isle of Skye

Armadale Castle, Gardens & Museum of the Isles 01401 - Armadale, Sleat, Isle of Skye IV45 8RS. Tel: 01471 844305

Kincardineshire

Arbuthnott House and Garden - Arbuthnott, Laurencekirk, Kincardineshire AB30 1PA. Tel: 01561 361226

Orkney Islands

Balfour Castle - Shapinsay, Orkney Islands KW17 2DL. Tel: 01856 711282

Peebles

Traquair House - Innerleithen, Peebles EH44 6PW. Tel: 01896 830323

Scottish Borders

Bowhill House & Country Park - Bowhill, Selkirk, Scottish Borders TD7 5ET. Tel: 01750 22204

Manderston - Duns, Berwickshire, Scottish Borders TD11 3PP. Tel: 01361 882636

Strathclyde

Mount Stuart House and Gardens - Mount Stuart, Isle of Bute, Strathclyde PA20 9LR. Tel: 01700 503877

West Lothian

Hopetoun House - South Queensferry, West Lothian EH30 9SL. Tel: 0131 331 2451

Newliston - Kirkliston, West Lothian EH29 9EB. Tel: 0131 333 3231

Wigtownshire

Ardwell Estate Gardens - Ardwell House, Stranraer, Wigtownshire DG9 9LY. Tel: 01776 860227

Wales

Ceridigion

Pembroke Castle - Pembroke, Dyfed, Ceridigion SA71 4LA. Tel: 01646 681510

Flintshire

Golden Grove - Llanasa, Nr. Holywell, Flintshire CH8 9NA. Tel: 01745 854452

Pembrokeshire

St Davids Cathedral - The Deanery, The Close, St. David's, Pembrokeshire SA62 6RH. Tel: 01437 720199

Powys

The Judge's Lodging - Broad Street, Presteigne, Powys LD8 2AD. Tel: 01544 260650

South Glamorgan

CADW - Plas Carew, Unit 5/7 Cefn Coed, Parc Nantgarw, Cardiff, South Glamorgan CF15 3QQ . Tel: 029 2050 0200

France

Chateau Royal D'Amboise - Chateau Royal, B.P. 271, 37403 Amboise, 37403. Tel: 00 33 2 47 57 00 98

Mini Listings Europe

Condé Nast Johansens are delighted to recommend over 380 properties across Europe and The Mediterranean.
Call 0800 269 397 or see the order forms on page 425 to order guides.

Austria

KÄRNTEN (VELDEN)
Seeschlössl Velden, Klagenfurter Strasse 34, 9220 Velden, Austria. Tel: +43 4274 2824

VORARLBERG (LECH AM ARLBERG)
Sporthotel Kristiania, Omesberg 331, 6764 Lech am Arlberg, Austria. Tel: +43 5583 25 610

Belgium

ANTWERP
Firean Hotel, Karel Oomsstraat 6, 2018 Antwerp, Belgium. Tel: +32 3 237 02 60

BRUGES
Hotel Die Swaene, 1 Steenhouwersdijk (Groene Rei), 8000 Bruges, Belgium. Tel: +32 50 34 27 98

KNOKKE~HEIST
Romantik Hotel du Dragon, Albertlaan 73, 8300 Knokke~Heist, Belgium. Tel: +32 50 63 05 80

KORTRIJK
Grand Hotel Damier, Grote Markt 41, 8500 Kortrijk, Belgium. Tel: +32 56 22 15 47

MALMÉDY
Hostellerie Trôs Marets, Route des Trôs Marets 2, 4960 Malmédy, Belgium. Tel: +32 80 33 79 17

POPERINGE
Hotel Recour, Guido Gezellestraat 7, 8970 Poperinge, Belgium . Tel: +32 57 33 57 25

TURNHOUT
Ter Driezen, 18 Herentalsstraat, 2300 Turnhout, Belgium. Tel: +32 14 41 87 57

Croatia

DUBROVNIK
Grand Villa Argentina, Frana Supila 14, 20000 Dubrovnik, Croatia. Tel: +385 20 44 0555

TROGIR
Villa Lavandula, Put Salduna 3, 21220 Trogir, Croatia. Tel: +385 21 798 330

Cyprus

▼
PAPHOS
Elysium, Queen Verenikis Street, PO Box 60701, 8107 Paphos, Cyprus. Tel: +357 26 844 444

Czech Republic

(PRAGUE)
Art Hotel Prague, Nad Královskou Oborou 53, 170 00 Prague 7, Czech Republic. Tel: +420 233 101 331

(PRAGUE)
Bellagio Hotel Prague, U Milosrdnych 2, 110 00 Prague 1, Czech Republic. Tel: +420 221 778 999

(PRAGUE)
Hotel Alchymist Residence, Trziste 19, Malá Strana, 11800 Prague, Czech Republic. Tel: +420 257 286 011 016

(PRAGUE)
Hotel Hoffmeister & Lily Wellness and Spa, Pod Bruskou 7, Malá Strana, 11800 Prague 1, Czech Republic. Tel: +420 251 017 111

(PRAGUE)
Nosticova Residence, Nosticova 1, Malá Strana, 11800 Prague, Czech Republic. Tel: +420 257 312 513 16

(PRAGUE)
Romantik Hotel U Raka, Cerninská 10/93, 11800 Prague 1, Czech Republic. Tel: +420 2205 111 00

Estonia

PÄRNU
Ammende Villa , Mere Pst 7, 80010 Pärnu, Estonia. Tel: +372 44 73 888

TALLINN
Domina City Hotel, Vana Posti 11/13, 10146 Tallinn, Estonia. Tel: +372 681 3900

France

ALSACE~LORRAINE (COLMAR)
Hostellerie Le Maréchal, 4 Place Six Montagnes Noires, Petite Venise, 68000 Colmar, France. Tel: +33 3 89 41 60 32

ALSACE~LORRAINE (COLMAR)
Hôtel Les Têtes, 19 Rue des Têtes, 68000 Colmar, France. Tel: +33 3 89 24 43 43

ALSACE~LORRAINE (CONDÉ NORTHEN)
Domaine de la Grange de Condé, 41 rue des Deux Nied, 57220 Condé Northen, France. Tel: +33 3 87 79 30 50

ALSACE~LORRAINE (GÉRARDMER - VOSGES)
Hostellerie Les Bas Rupts Le Chalet Fleuri, 181 Route de la Bresse, 88400 Gérardmer, Vosges, France. Tel: +33 3 29 63 09 25

ALSACE~LORRAINE (GUEBWILLER)
Hostellerie St Barnabé, 68530 Murbach - Buhl, Guebwiller, France. Tel: +33 3 89 62 14 14

ALSACE~LORRAINE (JUNGHOLTZ)
Les Violettes, Thierenbach, 68500 Jungholtz, France. Tel: +33 3 89 76 91 19

ALSACE~LORRAINE (OBERNAI)
Hotel à la Cour d'Alsace, 3 Rue de Gail, 67210 Obernai, France. Tel: +33 3 88 95 07 00

ALSACE~LORRAINE (ROUFFACH)
Château d'Isenbourg, 68250 Rouffach, France. Tel: +33 3 89 78 58 50

ALSACE~LORRAINE (STRASBOURG - OSTWALD)
Château de L'Ile, 4 Quai Heydt, 67540 Ostwald, France. Tel: +33 3 88 66 85 00

ALSACE~LORRAINE (STRASBOURG)
Romantik Hotel Beaucour-Baumann, 5 Rue des Bouchers, 67000 Strasbourg, France. Tel: +33 3 88 76 72 00

ALSACE~LORRAINE (THIONVILLE)
Romantik Hotel L'Horizon, 50 Route du Crève~Cœur, 57100 Thionville, France. Tel: +33 3 82 88 53 65

BRITTANY (BILLIERS)
Domaine de Rochevilaine, Pointe de Pen Lan, 56190 Billiers, France. Tel: +33 2 97 41 61 61

BRITTANY (LA GOUESNIÈRE - SAINT~MALO)
Château de Bonaban, 35350 La Gouesnière, France. Tel: +33 2 99 58 24 50

BRITTANY (LA ROCHE~BERNARD)
Domaine de Bodeuc, Route Saint Dolay, La Roche~Bernard, 56130 Nivillac, France. Tel: +33 2 99 90 89 63

BRITTANY (MOËLAN~SUR~MER)
Manoir de Kertalg, Route de Riec~Sur~Belon, 29350 Moëlan~sur~Mer, France. Tel: +33 2 98 39 77 77

BRITTANY (SAINT MALO - PLEVEN)
Manoir du Vaumadeuc, 22130 Pleven, France. Tel: +33 2 96 84 46 17

BRITTANY (TREBEURDEN)
Ti Al Lannec, 14 Allée de Mézo~Guen, BP 3, 22560 Trebeurden, France. Tel: +33 2 96 15 01 01

BURGUNDY - FRANCHE~COMTÉ (AVALLON)
Château de Vault de Lugny, 11 Rue du Château, 89200 Avallon, France. Tel: +33 3 86 34 07 86

BURGUNDY - FRANCHE~COMTÉ (CHOREY~LES~BEAUNE)
Ermitage de Corton, R.N. 74, 21200 Chorey~les~Beaune, France. Tel: +33 3 80 22 05 28

BURGUNDY - FRANCHE~COMTÉ (POLIGNY)
Hostellerie des Monts de Vaux, Les Monts de Vaux, 39800 Poligny, France. Tel: +33 3 84 37 12 50

BURGUNDY - FRANCHE~COMTÉ (VOUGEOT)
Château de Gilly, Gilly~les~Cîteaux, 21640 Vougeot, France. Tel: +33 3 80 62 89 98

CHAMPAGNE ~ ARDENNES (TINQUEUX - REIMS)
L'Assiette Champenoise, 40 Avenue Paul Vaillant Couturier, 51430 Tinqueux - Reims, France. Tel: +33 3 26 84 64 64

CHAMPAGNE~ARDENNES (ETOGES)
Château d'Etoges, 51270 Etoges~en~Champagne, France. Tel: +33 3 26 59 30 08

CHAMPAGNE~ARDENNES (FÈRE~EN~TARDENOIS)
Château de Fère, 02130 Fère~en~Tardenois, France. Tel: +33 3 23 82 21 13

CHAMPAGNE~ARDENNES (SAINTE PREUVE)
Domaine du Château de Barive, 02350 Sainte-Preuve, France. Tel: +33 3 23 22 15 15

CÔTE D'AZUR (AUPS)
Bastide du Calalou, Village de Moissac-Bellevue, 83630 Aups, France. Tel: +33 4 94 70 17 91

CÔTE D'AZUR (ÈZE VILLAGE)
Château Eza, Rue de la Pise, 06360 Èze Village, France. Tel: +33 4 93 41 12 24

CÔTE D'AZUR (GRASSE)
Bastide Saint Mathieu, 35 Chemin de Blumenthal, 06130 Saint Mathieu, Grasse, France. Tel: +33 4 97 01 10 00

CÔTE D'AZUR (LE RAYOL - CANADEL~SUR~MER)
Le Bailli de Suffren, Avenue des Américains, Golfe de Saint~Tropez, 83820 Le Rayol - Canadel~Sur~Mer, France. Tel: +33 4 98 04 47 00

CÔTE D'AZUR (MENTON)
Grand Hotel des Ambassadeurs, 3 rue Partouneaux, 06500 Menton, France. Tel: +33 93 28 75 75

Mini Listings Europe

Condé Nast Johansens are delighted to recommend over 380 properties across Europe and The Mediterranean.
Call 0800 269 397 or see the order forms on page 425 to order guides.

CÔTE D'AZUR (RAMATUELLE)
La Ferme d'Augustin, Plage de Tahiti, 83350 Ramatuelle, Near Saint~Tropez, France. Tel: +33 4 94 55 97 00

CÔTE D'AZUR (SAINT~PAUL~DE~VENCE)
Le Mas d'Artigny, Route de la Colle, 06570 Saint~Paul~de~Vence, France. Tel: +33 4 93 32 84 54

CÔTE D'AZUR (SAINT~PAUL~DE~VENCE)
Le Mas de Pierre, Route des Serres, 06570 Saint~Paul~de~Vence. Tel: +33 4 93 59 00 10

CÔTE D'AZUR (SAINT~RAPHAËL)
La Villa Mauresque, 1792 route de la Corniche, 83700 Saint~Raphaël, France. Tel: +33 494 83 02 42

CÔTE D'AZUR (VENCE)
Hôtel Cantemerle, 258 Chemin Cantemerle, 06140 Vence, France. Tel: +33 4 93 58 08 18

LOIRE VALLEY (AMBOISE)
Château de Pray, Route de Chargé, 37400 Amboise, France. Tel: +33 2 47 57 23 67

LOIRE VALLEY (AMBOISE)
Le Choiseul, 36 Quai Charles Guinot, 37400 Amboise, France. Tel: +33 2 47 30 45 45

▼

LOIRE VALLEY (AMBOISE)
Le Manoir Les Minimes, 34 Quai Charles Guinot, 37400 Amboise, France. Tel: +33 2 47 30 40 40

LOIRE VALLEY (LANGEAIS)
Château de Rochecotte, 37130 Saint~Patrice, (Near Langeais) France. Tel: +33 2 47 96 16 16

LOIRE VALLEY (LES BEZARDS)
Auberge des Templiers, Les Bezards, 45290 Boismorand, France. Tel: +33 2 38 31 80 01

LOIRE VALLEY (REIGNAC~SUR~INDRE)
Le Château de Reignac, 19 Rue Louis de Barberin, 37310 Reignac~sur~Indre, France. Tel: +33 2 47 94 14 10

LOIRE VALLEY (SAINT~AMOND MONTROND)
Château de la Commanderie, Farges Allichamps, 18200 Saint~Amand de Montrond, France. Tel: +33 2 48 61 04 19

LOIRE VALLEY (SAINTE~MAURE~DE~TOURAINE)
Hostellerie des Hauts de Sainte Maure, 2-4 avenue du Général-de-Gaulle, 37800 Sainte~Maure~de~Touraine, France. Tel: +33 2 47 65 50 65

LOIRE VALLEY (SAUMUR - CHÊNEHUTTE~LES~TUFFEAUX)
Le Prieuré, 49350 Chênehutte~Les~Tuffeaux, France. Tel: +33 2 47 30 45 45

LOIRE VALLEY (TOURS - LUYNES)
Domaine de Beauvois, Le Pont Clouet, Route de Cléré~les~Pins, 37230 Luynes, France. Tel: +33 2 47 55 50 11

LOIRE VALLEY (TOURS - MONTBAZON)
Château d'Artigny, 37250 Montbazon, France. Tel: +33 2 47 34 30 30

LOIRE VALLEY (TOURS - MONTBAZON)
Domaine de La Tortinière, Route de Ballan~Miré, 37250 Montbazon, France. Tel: +33 2 43 79 32 20

MIDI~PYRÉNÉES (CARCASSONNE~FLOURE)
Château de Floure, 1, Allée Gaston Bonheur, 11800 Floure, France. Tel: +33 4 68 79 11 29

MIDI~PYRÉNÉES (MIREPOIX)
Relais Royal, 8 Rue Maréchal Clauzel, 09500 Mirepoix, France. Tel: +33 5 61 60 19 19

NORMANDY (CAMBREMER)
Château les Bruyeres, Route du Cadran, 14340 Cambremer, France. Tel: +33 2 31 32 22 45

NORMANDY (ETRETAT)
Domaine Saint Clair, Le Donjon, Chemin de Saint Clair, 76790 Etretat, France. Tel: +33 2 35 27 08 23

NORMANDY (FECAMP - SASSETOT)
Château de Sassetot, 76540 Sassetot~Le~Mauconduit, France. Tel: +33 2 35 28 00 11

NORMANDY (HONFLEUR - CRICQUEBOEUF)
Manoir de la Poterie, Chemin Paul Ruel, 14113 Cricqueboeuf, France. Tel: +33 2 31 88 10 40

NORTH - PICARDY (ALBERT)
Hôtel Royal Picardie, Avenue du Général Leclerc, 80300 Albert, France. Tel: +33 3 22 75 37 00

NORTH - PICARDY (BETHUNE - GOSNAY)
La Chartreuse du Val Saint Esprit, 62199 Gosnay, France. Tel: +33 3 21 62 80 00

NORTH - PICARDY (CALAIS - RECQUES~SUR~HEM)
Château de Cocove, 62890 Recques~sur~Hem, France. Tel: +33 3 21 82 68 29

NORTH - PICARDY (DOULLENS - REMAISNIL)
Château de Remaisnil, 80600 Remaisnil, France. Tel: +33 3 22 77 07 47

NORTH - PICARDY (LILLE)
Carlton Hotel, Rue de Paris, 59000 Lille, France. Tel: +33 3 20 13 33 13

NORTH PICARDY (LIGNY~EN~CAMBRÉSIS)
Château de Ligny, 2 rue Pierre Curie, 59191 Ligny~en~Cambrésis, France. Tel: +33 3 27 85 25 84

PARIS (CHAMPS~ELYSÉES)
Hôtel de Sers, 41 Avenue Pierre 1er de Serbie, 75008 Paris, France. Tel: +33 1 53 23 75 75

PARIS (CHAMPS~ELYSÉES)
Hôtel San Régis, 12 Rue Jean Goujon, 75008 Paris, France. Tel: +33 1 44 95 16 16

PARIS (CHAMPS~ELYSÉES)
La Trémoille, 14 Rue de la Trémoille, 75008 Paris, France. Tel: +33 1 56 52 14 00

PARIS (CONCORDE)
Hôtel de Crillon, 10, Place de La Concorde, 75008 Paris, France. Tel: +33 1 44 71 15 00

PARIS (ETOILE - PORTE MAILLOT)
Hotel Duret, 30 rue Duret, 75116 Paris, France. Tel: +33 1 45 00 42 60

PARIS (ÉTOILE - PORTE MAILLOT)
La Villa Maillot, 143 Avenue de Malakoff, 75116 Paris, France. Tel: +33 1 53 64 52 52

PARIS (INVALIDES)
Hôtel Le Tourville, 16 Avenue de Tourville, 75007 Paris, France. Tel: +33 1 47 05 62 62

PARIS (JARDIN DU LUXEMBOURG)
Le Relais Médicis, 23 Rue Racine, 75006 Paris, France. Tel: +33 1 43 26 00 60

PARIS (JARDIN DU LUXEMBOURG)
Le Sainte~Beuve, 9 Rue Sainte~Beuve, 75006 Paris, France. Tel: +33 1 45 48 20 07

PARIS (MADELEINE)
Hôtel Le Lavoisier, 21 rue Lavoisier, 75008 Paris, France. Tel: +33 1 53 30 06 06

PARIS (MADELEINE)
Hôtel Opéra Richepanse, 14 Rue du Chevalier de Saint-George, 75001 Paris, France. Tel: +33 1 42 60 36 00

PARIS (SAINT~GERMAIN)
Hotel Duc de Saint~Simon, 14 rue de Saint-Simon, 75007 Paris, France. Tel: +33 1 44 39 20 20

PARIS (SAINT~GERMAIN)
Hôtel Le Saint~Grégoire, 43 Rue de L'Abbé Grégoire, 75006 Paris, France. Tel: +33 1 45 48 23 23

PARIS REGION (BARBIZON)
Hostellerie du Bas-Breau, 22 Rue Grande, 77630 Barbizon, France. Tel: +33 1 60 66 40 05

PARIS REGION (GRESSY~EN~FRANCE - CHANTILLY)
Le Manoir de Gressy, 77410 Gressy~en~France, Chantilly, Near Roissy, Charles de Gaulles Airport, Paris, France. Tel: +33 1 60 26 68 00

PARIS REGION (SAINT GERMAIN EN LAYE)
Cazaudehore la Forestière, 1 Avenue du Président Kennedy, 78100 Saint Germain en Laye, France. Tel: +33 1 30 61 64 64

PARIS REGION (SAINT SYMPHORIEN~LE~CHÂTEAU)
Château d'Esclimont, 28700 Saint Symphorien~Le~Château, France. Tel: +33 2 37 31 15 15

PARIS REGION (VERSAILLES - HOUDAN)
Château de Berchères, 18 rue de Château, 28260 Berchères~sur~Vesgre, France. Tel: +33 2 37 82 28 22

POITOU~CHARENTE (LA ROCHELLE)
Hotel "Residence de France", 43 Rue Minage, 17000 La Rochelle, France. Tel: +33 5 46 28 06 00

POITOU~CHARENTES (COGNAC - CHÂTEAUBERNARD)
Château de L'Yeuse, 65 Rue de Bellevue, Quartier de L'Echassier, 16100 Châteaubernard, France. Tel: +33 5 45 36 82 60

POITOU~CHARENTES (MASSIGNAC)
Domaine des Etangs, 16310 Massignac, France. Tel: +33 5 45 61 85 00

POITOU~CHARENTES (MOSNAC NEAR JONZAC)
Moulin du Val de Seugne, Marcouze, 17240 Mosnac, France. Tel: +33 5 46 70 46 16

PROVENCE (AIX~EN~PROVENCE)
Le Pigonnet, 5 Avenue du Pigonnet, 13090 Aix~en~Provence, France. Tel: +33 4 42 59 02 90

PROVENCE (ARLES)
L'Hôtel Particulier, 4 rue de la Monnaie, 13200 Arles, France. Tel: +33 4 90 52 51 40

PROVENCE (BAGNOLS-SUR-CÈZE)
Château de Montcaud, Combe, 30200 Sabran, France. Tel: +33 4 66 89 60 60

PROVENCE (GORDES)
Les Mas des Herbes Blanches, Joucas, 84220 Gordes, France. Tel: +33 4 90 05 79 79

PROVENCE (LES~BAUX~DE~PROVENCE)
Mas de l'Oulivié, Les Arcoules, 13520 Les~Baux~de~Provence, France. Tel: +33 4 90 54 35 78

PROVENCE (PORT CAMARGUE)
Le Spinaker, Pointe de la Presqu'île, Port Camargue, 30240 Le Grau~du~Roi, France. Tel: +33 4 66 53 36 37

PROVENCE (SAINTES~MARIES~DE~LA~MER)
Mas de La Fouque, Route du Petit Rhône, 13460 Saintes~Maries~de~La~Mer, France. Tel: +33 4 90 97 81 02

PROVENCE (SAINT~RÉMY~DE~PROVENCE)
Château des Alpilles, Route Départementale 31, Ancienne Route du Grès, 13210 Saint~Rémy~de~Provence, France. Tel: +33 4 90 92 03 33

Mini Listings Europe

Condé Nast Johansens are delighted to recommend over 380 properties across Europe and The Mediterranean.
Call 0800 269 397 or see the order forms on page 425 to order guides.

RHÔNE~ALPES (CONDRIEU)
Le Beau Rivage, 2 rue du Beau-Rivage, 69420 Condrieu, France. Tel: +33 4 74 56 82 82

RHÔNE~ALPES (DIVONNE~LES~BAINS)
Château de Divonne, 01220 Divonne~les~Bains, France. Tel: +33 4 50 20 00 32

RHÔNE~ALPES (DIVONNE~LES~BAINS)
Le Domaine de Divonne Casino, Golf & Spa Resort, Avenue des Thermes, 01220 Divonne~les~Bains, France. Tel: +33 4 50 40 34 34

RHÔNE~ALPES (LES GÊTS)
Chalet Hôtel La Marmotte, 61 Rue du Chêne, 74260 Les Gêts, France. Tel: + 33 4 50 75 80 33

RHÔNE~ALPES (LYON)
La Tour Rose, 22 Rue du Boeuf, 69005 Lyon, France. Tel: +33 4 78 92 69 10

RHÔNE~ALPES (MEGÈVE)
Le Fer à Cheval, 36 route du Crêt d'Arbois, 74120 Megève, France. Tel: +33 4 50 21 30 39

RHÔNE~ALPES (SCIEZ~SUR~LÉMAN)
Château de Coudrée, Domaine de Coudrée, Bonnatrait, 74140 Sciez~sur~Léman, France. Tel: +33 4 50 72 62 33

SOUTH WEST (BIARRITZ)
Hôtel du Palais, 1 Avenue de L'Impératrice, 64200 Biarritz, France. Tel: +33 5 59 41 64 00

SOUTH-WEST (SAINT~JEAN~DE~LUZ)
Grand Hôtel, 43 Boulevard Thiers, 64500 Saint~Jean~de~Luz, France. Tel: +33 5 59 26 35 36

WESTERN LOIRE (CHALLAIN~LA~POTERIE)
Château de Challain, 49440 Challain~la~Potherie, France. Tel: +33 2 41 92 74 26

WESTERN LOIRE (CHAMPIGNÉ - ANGERS)
Château des Briottières, 49330 Champigné, France. Tel: +33 2 41 42 00 02

Great Britain

ENGLAND (BERKSHIRE)
The French Horn, Sonning on Thames, Berkshire RG4 6TN, England. Tel: +44 (0)1189 692 204

ENGLAND (CHESHIRE)
Hillbark Hotel, Royden Park, Frankby, Wirral CH48 1NP, England. Tel: +44 (0)151 625 2400

ENGLAND (DERBYSHIRE)
The Peacock at Rowsley, Rowsley, Near Matlock, Derbyshire DE4 2EB, England. Tel: +44 (0)1629 733518

ENGLAND (DEVON)
Bovey Castle, North Bovey, Dartmoor National Park, Devon TQ13 8RE, England. Tel: +44 (0)1647 445 016

ENGLAND (DORSET)
The Priory Hotel, Church Green, Wareham, Dorset BH20 4ND, England. Tel: +44 (0)1929 551 666

ENGLAND (EAST SUSSEX)
Ashdown Park Hotel and Country Club, Wych Cross, Forest Row, East Sussex, RH18 5JR, England. Tel: +44 (0)1342 824988

ENGLAND (EAST SUSSEX)
The Grand Hotel, King Edward's Parade, Eastbourne, East Sussex, BN21 4EQ, England. Tel: +44 (0)1323 412345

ENGLAND (EAST SUSSEX)
Rye Lodge, Hilder's Cliff Rye, East Sussex, TN31 7LD, England. Tel: +44 (0)1797 223838

ENGLAND (HAMPSHIRE)
Tylney Hall, Rotherwick, Hook, Hampshire, RG27 9AZ, England. Tel: +44 (0)1256 764881

ENGLAND (HEREFORDSHIRE)
Castle House, Castle Street, Hereford, Herefordshire, HR1 2NW, England. Tel: +44 (0)1432 356321

ENGLAND (HEREFORDSHIRE)
Ford Abbey, Pudleston, Near Leominster, Herefordshire HR6 0RZ, England. Tel: +44 (0)1568 760700

ENGLAND (KENT)
Eastwell Manor, Boughton Lees, Near Ashford, Kent, TN25 4HR, England. Tel: +44 (0)1233 213000

ENGLAND (LONDON)
The Carlton Tower, On Cadogan Place, London SW1X 9PY, England. Tel: +44 (0)20 7235 1234

ENGLAND (LONDON)
The Cranley, 10 Bina Gardens, South Kensington, London SW5 0LA, England. Tel: +44 (0)20 7373 0123

ENGLAND (LONDON)
The Lowndes Hotel, 21 Lowndes Street, Knightsbridge, London SW1X 9ES, England. Tel: +44 (0)20 7823 1234

ENGLAND (LONDON)
The Mayflower Hotel, 26-28 Trebovir Road, London SW5 9NJ, England. Tel: +44 (0)20 7370 0991

ENGLAND (LONDON)
Pembridge Court Hotel, 34 Pembridge Gardens, London W2 4DX, England. Tel: +44 (0)20 7229 9977

ENGLAND (LONDON)
The Royal Park, 3 Westbourne Terrace, Lancaster Gate, Hyde Park, London W2 3UL, England. Tel: +44 (0)20 7479 6600

ENGLAND (LONDON)
Twenty Nevern Square, 20 Nevern Square, London SW5 9PD, England. Tel: +44 (0)20 7565 9555

ENGLAND (NORTHAMPTONSHIRE)
Fawsley Hall, Fawsley, Near Daventry, Northamptonshire NN11 3BA, England. Tel: +44 (0)1327 892000

ENGLAND (OXFORDSHIRE)
Phyllis Court Club, Marlow Road, Henley-on-Thames, Oxfordshire, RG9 2HT, England. Tel: +44 (0)1491 570500

ENGLAND (STAFFORDSHIRE)
Hoar Cross Hall Health Spa Resort, Hoar Cross, Near Yoxall, Staffordshire DE13 8QS, England. Tel: +44 (0)1283 575671

ENGLAND (WEST SUSSEX)
Amberley Castle, Amberley, Near Arundel, West Sussex BN18 9LT, England. Tel: +44 (0)1798 831 992

ENGLAND (WORCESTERSHIRE)
Buckland Manor, Buckland, Near Broadway, Worcestershire WR12 7LY, England. Tel: +44 (0)1386 852626

SCOTLAND (HIGHLAND)
Knockomie Hotel, Grantown Road, Forres, Morayshire, IV36 2SG, Scotland. Tel: +44 (0)1309 673146

SCOTLAND (HIGHLAND)
Royal Marine Hotel, Golf Road, Brora, Sutherland, KW9 6QS, Scotland. Tel: +44 (0)1408 621252

SCOTLAND (INVERNESS-SHIRE)
Muckrach Lodge Hotel & Restaurant, Dulnain Bridge, By Grantown~on~Spey, Inverness-shire, PH26 3LY, Scotland. Tel: +44 (0)1479 851257

WALES (GWYNEDD)
Hotel Maes-Y-Neuadd, Talsarnau, Near Harlech, Gwynedd, LL47 6YA, Wales. Tel: +44 (0)1766 780200

Greece

ATHENS
Astir Palace Vouliagmeni, 40 Apollonos Street, 166 71 Vouliagmeni, Athens, Greece. Tel: +30 210 890 2000

ATHENS
Hotel Pentelikon, 66 Diligianni Street, 14562 Athens, Greece. Tel: +30 2 10 62 30 650

CHIOS
Argentikon, Kambos, 82100 Chio, Greece. Tel: +30 227 10 33 111

CORFU
Villa de Loulia, Peroulades, Corfu, Greece. Tel: +30 266 30 95 394

CRETE
Athina Luxury Villas, Ksamoudochori, Platanias, 73014 Chania, Crete, Greece. Tel: +30 28210 20960

▼

CRETE
Elounda Gulf Villas & Suites, Elounda, 72053 Crete, Greece. Tel: +30 28410 90300

CRETE
Elounda Peninsula All Suite Hotel, 72053 Elounda, Crete, Greece. Tel: +30 28410 68012

CRETE
Pleiades Luxurious Villas, Plakes, 72100 Aghios Nikolaos, Crete, Greece. Tel: +30 28410 90450

CRETE
St Nicolas Bay Hotel, PO Box 47, 72100 Aghios Nikolaos, Crete, Greece. Tel: +30 2841 025041

KAVALA
Imaret, 30-32 Poulidou Street, 65110 Kavala, Greece. Tel: +30 2510 620 151-55

LEFKADA
Pavezzo Country Retreat, Katouna, Lefkada, Greece. Tel: +30 264 50 717 82

MYKONOS
Apanema, Tagoo, Mykonos, Greece. Tel: +30 22890 28590

MYKONOS
Tharroe of Mykonos, Mykonos Town, Angelica, 84600 Mykonos, Greece. Tel: +30 22890 27370

RHODES
Melenos Lindos, Lindos, Rhodes, Greece. Tel: +30 224 40 32 222

SANTORINI
Alexander's Boutique Hotel of Oia, 84702 Oia, Santorini, Greece. Tel: +30 22860 71818

SANTORINI
Fanari Villas, Oia, 84702 Santorini, Greece. Tel: +30 22860 71007

SPETSES, NEAR ATHENS
Orloff Resort, Spetses Island, Old Harbour, 18050 Spetses, Greece. Tel: +30 229 807 5444

Ireland

DUBLIN
Aberdeen Lodge, 53-55 Park Avenue, Ballsbridge, Dublin 4, Ireland. Tel: +353 1 283 8155

Mini Listings Europe

Condé Nast Johansens are delighted to recommend over 380 properties across Europe and The Mediterranean.
Call 0800 269 397 or see the order forms on page 425 to order guides.

Italy

CAMPANIA (NAPLES)
Grand Hotel Parker's, Corso Vittorio Emanuele 135, 80121 Naples, Italy. Tel: +39 081 761 2474

CAMPANIA (RAVELLO)
Hotel Villa Maria, Via S. Chiara 2, 84010 Ravello (SA), Italy. Tel: +39 089 857255

CAMPANIA (SORRENTO)
Grand Hotel Cocumella, Via Cocumella 7, 80065 Sant'Agnello, Sorrento, Italy. Tel: +39 081 878 2933

EMILIA ROMAGNA (REGGIO EMILIA)
Hotel Posta (Historical Residence), Piazza del Monte, 2, 42100 Reggio Emilia, Italy. Tel: +39 05 22 43 29 44

EMILIA ROMAGNA (RICCIONE - RIVIERA ADRIATICA)
Hotel des Nations, Lungomare Costituzione 2, 47838 Riccione (RN), Italy. Tel: +39 0541 647878

LAZIO (CIVITA CASTELLANA)
Relais Falisco, Via Don Minzoni 19, 01033 Civita Castellana (VT), Italy. Tel: +39 0761 54 98

LAZIO (ORTE)
La Locanda della Chiocciola, Loc Seripola SNC, 01028 Orte, Italy. Tel: +39 0761 402 734

LAZIO (PALO LAZIALE - ROME)
La Posta Vecchia Hotel Spa, Palo Laziale, 00055 Ladispoli, Rome, Italy. Tel: +39 0699 49501

LAZIO (ROME)
FortySeven Hotel, Via L Petroselli 47, 00186 Rome, Italy. Tel: +39 066 787 816

LAZIO (ROME)
Hotel Aventino, Via San Domenico 10, 00153 Rome, Italy. Tel: +39 06 5745 231

LAZIO (ROME)
Hotel dei Borgognoni, Via del Bufalo 126 (Piazza di Spagna), 00187 Rome, Italy. Tel: +39 06 6994 1505

LAZIO (ROME)
Hotel dei Consoli, Via Varrone 2/d, 00193 Roma, Italy. Tel: +39 0668 892 972

LAZIO (ROME)
Hotel Fenix, Viale Gorizia 5/7, 00198 Rome, Italy. Tel: +39 06 8540 741

LIGURIA (FINALE LIGURE)
Hotel Punta Est, Via Aurelia 1, 17024 Finale Ligure (SV) Italy. Tel: +39 019 600611

LIGURIA (SANREMO COAST - DIANO MARINA)
Grand Hotel Diana Majestic, Via Oleandri 15, 18013 Diano Marina (IM), Italy. Tel: +39 0183 402 727

LIGURIA (SANTA MARGHERITA LIGURE)
Grand Hotel Miramare, Via Milite Ignoto, 30, 16038 Santa Margherita Ligure - Genova, Liguria, Italy. Tel: +39 0185 287013

LIGURIA (SESTRI LEVANTE)
Hotel Vis à Vis, Via della Chiusa 28, 16039 Sestri Levante (GE), Italy. Tel: +39 0185 42661

LOMBARDY (BELLAGIO - LAKE COMO)
Grand Hotel Villa Serbelloni, Via Roma 1, 22021 Bellagio, Lake Como, Italy. Tel: +39 031 950 216

LOMBARDY (CANTELLO - VARESE)
Albergo Madonnina, Largo Lanfranco da Ligurno 1, 21050 Cantello - Varese, Italy. Tel: +39 0332 417 731

LOMBARDY (LAKE GARDA - DESENZANO)
Park Hotel, Via Lungolago Cesare Battisti 19, 25015 Desenzano del Garda, Lake Garda, (BS) Italy. Tel: +39 030 914 3494

▼

LOMBARDY (LAKE GARDA - GARDONE RIVIERA)
Grand Hotel Gardone Riviera, Via Zanardelli 84, 25083 Gardone Riviera (BS), Lago di Garda, Italy. Tel: +39 0365 20261

LOMBARDY (LAKE GARDA - SALÒ)
Hotel Bellerive, Via Pietro da Salò 11, 25087 Salò (BS), Italy. Tel: +39 0365 520 410

LOMBARDY (MILAN - FRANCIACORTA)
L'Albereta Relais & Châteaux, Via Vittorio Emanuele 23, 25030 Erbusco (Bs), Italy. Tel: +39 030 7760 550

LOMBARDY (MILAN - MONZA)
Hotel de la Ville, Viale Regina Margherita 15, 20052 Monza (MI), Italy. Tel: +39 039 3942

LOMBARDY (MILAN)
Petit Palais maison de charme, Via Molino delle Armi 1, 20123 Milan, Italy. Tel: +39 02 584 891

PIEMONTE (ALAGNA - MONTE ROSA)
Hotel Cristallo, Piazza degli Alberghi, 13021 Alagna (VC), Italy. Tel: +39 0163 922 822/23

PIEMONTE (BELGIRATE - LAKE MAGGIORE)
Villa Dal Pozzo d'Annone, Strada Statale del Sempione 5, 28832 Belgirate (VB), Lake Maggiore, Italy. Tel: +39 0322 7255

PIEMONTE (CANNOBIO - LAKE MAGGIORE)
Hotel Pironi, Via Marconi 35, 28822 Cannobio, Lago Maggiore (VB), Italy. Tel: +39 0323 70624

PIEMONTE (STRESA - LAKE MAGGIORE)
Hotel Villa Aminta, Via Sempione Nord 123, 28838 Stresa (VB), Italy. Tel: +39 0323 933 818

PUGLIA (MARTINA FRANCA)
Relais Villa San Martino, Via Taranto, Zona G - 59, 74015 Martina Franca (TA), Italy. Tel: +39 080 480 5152

SARDINIA (ALGHERO)
Villa Las Tronas, Lungomare Valencia 1, 07041 Alghero (SS), Italy. Tel: +39 079 981 818

SARDINIA (GOLFO DI MARINELLA - PORTO ROTONDO)
Domina Palumbalza Sporting, Golfo di Marinella, 52 Porto Rotondo, 07026 Olbia (Sassari), Italy. Tel: +39 0789 32005

SARDINIA (PORTO CERVO - COSTA SHERALDA)
Grand Hotel Porto Cervo, Località Cala Grann, 07020 Porto Cervo (SS), Italy. Tel: +39 0789 91533

SARDINIA (S. MARGHERITA DI PULA - CAGLIARI)
Villa del Parco & Spa by Forte Village, SS 195, Km 39600, S. Margherita di Pula, 0910 Cagliari, Italy. Tel: +39 070 92171

SICILY (SALINA - AEOLIAN ISLANDS)
Hotel Signum, Via Scalo 15, Malfa, 98050 Salina (ME), Italy. Tel: +39 090 9844 222

SICILY (TAORMINA MARE)
Grand Hotel Atlantis Bay, Via Nazionale 161, Taormina Mare (ME), Italy. Tel: +39 0942 618 011

SICILY (TAORMINA MARE)
Grand Hotel Mazzarò Sea Palace, Via Nazionale 147, 98030 Taormina (ME), Italy. Tel: +39 0942 626 237

SICILY (TAORMINA RIVIERA - MARINA D'AGRO)
Baia Taormina Hotel & Spa, Statale dello Ionio, Km 39, 98030 Marina d'Agro, Taormina Riviera (ME), Italy. Tel: +39 0942 756 292

TRENTINO - ALTO ADIGE / DOLOMITES (COLFOSCO - CORVARA)
Art Hotel Cappella, Str. Pecei 17, Alta Badia - Dolomites, 39030 Colfosco - Corvara (BZ), Italy. Tel: +39 0471 836183

TRENTINO - ALTO ADIGE / DOLOMITES (FIÈ ALLO SCILIAR - BOLZANO)
Romantik Hotel Turm, Piazza della Chiesa 9, 39050 Fie' Allo Sciliar (Bz), Italy. Tel: +39 0471 725014

TRENTINO - ALTO ADIGE / DOLOMITES (NOVA LEVANTE - BOLZANO)
Posthotel Cavallino Bianco, Via Carezza 30, 39056 Nova Levante (Bz), Dolomites, Italy. Tel: +39 0471 613113

TUSCANY (AMBRA - CHIANTI ARETINO)
Le Case Del Borgo - Tuscan Luxury Living, Loc. Duddova, 52020 Ambra (Arezzo) Italy. Tel: +39 055 996 3340

TUSCANY (CASTAGNETO CARDUCCI)
Tombolo Talasso Resort, Via del Corallo 3, 57024 Marina di Castagneto Carducci (LI), Italy. Tel: +39 0565 74530

TUSCANY (FLORENCE - BORGO SAN LORENZO)
Monsignor Della Casa Country Resort, Via di Mucciano 16, 50032 Borgo San Lorenzo, Florence, Italy. Tel: +39 055 840 821

TUSCANY (FLORENCE)
Hotel Lorenzo Il Magnifico, Via Lorenzo Il Magnifico 25, 50129 Florence, Italy. Tel: +39 055 463 0878

TUSCANY (FLORENCE)
Marignolle Relais & Charme, Via di S Quirichino a Marignolle 16, 50124 Florence, Italy. Tel: +39 055 228 6910

TUSCANY (FLORENCE)
Villa Montartino, Via Gherardo Silvani 151, 50125 Florence, Italy. Tel: +39 055 223520

TUSCANY (LUCCA)
Albergo Villa Marta, Via del ponte Guasperini 873, San Lorenzo a Vaccoli, 55100 Lucca, Italy. Tel: +39 0583 37 01 01

TUSCANY (MONTEBENICHI - CHIANTI AREA)
Country House Casa Cornacchi, Loc. Montebenichi, 52021 Arezzo, Tuscany, Italy. Tel: +39 055 998229

TUSCANY (MONTEPULCIANO - SIENA)
Dionora, Via Vicinale di Poggiano, 53040 Montepulciano (Siena), Italy. Tel: +39 0578 717 496

TUSCANY (PIETRASANTA)
Albergo Pietrasanta - Palazzo Barsanti Bonetti, Via Garibaldi 35, 55045 Pietrasanta (Lucca), Italy. Tel: +39 0584 793 727

TUSCANY (PIEVESCOLA - SIENA)
Relais La Suvera (Dimora Storica), 53030 Pievescola - Siena, Italy. Tel: +39 0577 960 300

TUSCANY (PISA)
Hotel Relais Dell'Orologio, Via della Faggiola 12/14, 56126 Pisa, Italy. Tel: +39 050 830 361

TUSCANY (POGGI DEL SASSO - MAREMMA)
Castello di Vicarello, Loc. Vicarello, 58044 Poggi del Sasso (GR), italy. Tel: +39 0564 990 718

TUSCANY (PORTO ERCOLE - ARGENTARIO)
Il Pellicano Hotel & Spa, Loc. Sbarcatello, 58018 Porto Ercole (Gr), Tuscany, Italy. Tel: +39 0564 858111

TUSCANY (PORTOFERRAIO - ISOLA D'ELBA)
Hotel Villa Ottone, Loc. Ottone, 57037 Portoferraio (LI), Isola d'Elba, Italy. Tel: +39 0565 933 042

Mini Listings Europe

Condé Nast Johansens are delighted to recommend over 380 properties across Europe and The Mediterranean.
Call 0800 269 397 or see the order forms on page 425 to order guides.

TUSCANY (ROCCATEDERIGHI - GROSSETO)
Pieve di Caminino (Historical Residence), Via Prov. di Peruzzo, 58028 Roccatederighi - Grosseto, Italy. Tel: +39 0564 569 737

TUSCANY (SIENA - ASCIANO)
Hotel Borgo CasaBianca, Località Casabianca, 53041 Asciano (SI), Italy. Tel: +39 0577 704 362

TUSCANY (SIENA - MONTERIGGIONI - STROVE)
Castel Pietraio, Strada di Strove 33, 53035 Monteriggioni, Italy. Tel: +39 0577 300020

TUSCANY (SIENA - MONTERIGGIONI)
Hotel Monteriggioni, Via 1 Maggio 4, 53035 Monteriggioni (SI), Italy. Tel: +39 0577 305 009

TUSCANY (VERSILIA - FORTE DEI MARMI)
Hotel Byron, Viale A Morin 46, 55042 Forte dei Marmi (LU), Italy. Tel: +39 0584 787 052

TUSCANY (VERSILIA - VIAREGGIO)
Hotel Plaza e de Russie, Piazza d'Azeglio 1, 55049 Viareggio (LU), Italy. Tel: +39 0584 44449

UMBRIA (ASSISI)
Romantik Hotel Le Silve di Armenzano, 06081 Loc. Armenzano, Assisi (PG), Italy. Tel: +39 075 801 9000

UMBRIA (ASSISI)
San Crispino Historical Residence, Via Sant' Agnese 11, 06081 Assisi (PG), Italy.
Tel: Reservations Office +44 (0)1732 810 800

UMBRIA (CORTONA - PETRIGNANO)
Relais Alla Corte del Sole, Loc. I Giorgi, 06061 Petrignano del Lago (PG), Italy. Tel: +39 075 9689008

UMBRIA (DERUTA - PERUGIA)
L'Antico Forziere , Via della Rocca 2, 06051 Casalina Deruta (PG), Italy. Tel: +39 075 972 4314

UMBRIA (GUBBIO)
Castello di Petroia, Località Scritto di Gubbio, Petroia, 06020 Gubbio (Pg), Italy. Tel: +39 075 92 02 87

UMBRIA (ORVIETO - ALLERONA)
I Casali di Monticchio, Vocabolo Monticchio 34, 05011 Allerona, Orvieto (TR), Italy. Tel: +39 0763 62 83 65

UMBRIA (PERUGIA - PIEVE SAN QUIRICO)
Le Torri di Bagnara (Historical Residences), Strada della Bruna 8, 06080 Pieve San Quirico, Perugia, Italy. Tel: +39 075 579 2001 and +39 335 6408 549

UMBRIA (PERUGIA - PIEVE SAN QUIRICO)
Le Torri di Bagnara (Historical Residences), Strada della Bruna 8, 06080 Pieve San Quirico, Perugia, Italy. Tel: +39 075 579 2001 and +39 335 6408 549

UMBRIA (PERUGIA - SAN MARTINO)
Alla Posta dei Donini, Via Deruta 43, 06079 San Martino in Campo (PG), Italy. Tel: +39 075 609 132

UMBRIA (PERUGIA - UMBERTIDE)
Borgo Bastia Creti, Fa Spedalicchio, 06019 Umbertide (PG), Italy. Tel: Reservations Office +44 (0)1732 810 800

VALLE D'AOSTA (COURMAYEUR - MONT BLANC)
Mont Blanc Hotel Village, Localita La Croisette 36, 11015 La Salle (AO), Valle d'Aosta, Italy. Tel: +39 0165 864 111

VENETIA (BASSANO DEL GRAPPA)
Villa Ca' Sette, Via Cunizza da Romano 4, 36061 Bassano del Grappa, Italy. Tel: +39 0424 383350

VENETIA (GARDA - LAKE GARDA)
Villa Madrina, Via Paolo Veronese 1, 37016 Garda (VR), Italy. Tel: +39 045 6270 144

VENETIA (LAKE GARDA - BARDOLINO - VERONA)
Color Hotel, Via Santa Cristina 5, 37011 Bardolino (VR), Italy. Tel: +39 045 621 0857

VENETIA (LIDO DI JESOLO)
Park Hotel Brasilia, Via Levantina, 30017 Lido di Jesolo, Italy. Tel: +39 0421 380851

VENETIA (TREVISO - ASOLO)
Albergo Al Sole, Via Collegio 33, 31011 Asolo, Treviso, Italy. Tel: +39 0423 951 332

VENETIA (VALPOLICELLA - VERONA)
Relais La Magioca, Via Moron 3, 37024 Negrar - Valpolicella (VR), Italy. Tel: +39 045 600 0167

VENETIA (VENICE - LIDO)
Albergo Quattro Fontane - Residenza d'Epoca, Via Quattro Fontane 16, 30126 Lido di Venezia, Venice, Italy. Tel: +39 041 526 0227

VENETIA (VENICE)
Ca Maria Adele, Dorsoduro 111, 30123 Venezia, Italy. Tel: +39 041 52 03 078

VENETIA (VENICE)
Domina Prestige Giudecca, Corte Ferrando 409/C, Giudecca, 30133 Venice (Ve), Italy. Tel: +39 041 2960 168

VENETIA (VENICE)
Hotel Flora, San Marco 2283/A, 30124 Venetia, Italy. Tel: +39 041 52 05 844

VENETIA (VENICE)
Hotel Giorgione, SS Apostoli 4587, 30131 Venice, Italy. Tel: +39 041 522 5810

VENETIA (VENICE)
Hotel Sant' Elena Venezia, Calle Buccari 10, Sant' Elena, 30132 Veezia, Italy. Tel: +39 041 27 17 811

VENETIA (VENICE)
Londra Palace, Riva degli Schiavoni, 4171, 30122 Venice, Italy. Tel: +39 041 5200533

VENETIA (VENICE)
Novecento, San Marco 2683/84, 30124 Venezia, Italy. Tel: +39 041 24 13 765

VENETIA (VERONA)
Hotel Gabbia d'Oro (Historical Residence), Corso Porta Borsari 4A, 37121 Verona, Italy. Tel: +39 045 8003060

Latvia

JURMALA
TB Palace, Pilsonu Street 8, L2015, Latvia. Tel: +371 714 7094

RIGA
Hotel Bergs, Bergs Bazaar, Elizabetes Street 83/85, Riga, L1050, Latvia. Tel: +371 777 09 00

Lithuania

VILNIUS
Grotthuss Hotel, Ligoninės 7, 01134 Vilnius, Lithuania. Tel: +370 5 266 0322

VILNIUS
The Narutis Hotel, 24 Pilies Street, 01123 Vilnius, Lithuania. Tel: +370 5 2122 894

Luxembourg

REMICH
Hotel Saint~Nicolas, 31 Esplanade, 5533 Remich, Luxembourg. Tel: +352 2666 3

The Netherlands

AMSTERDAM
Ambassade Hotel, Herengracht 341, 1016 Amsterdam, The Netherlands. Tel: +31 20 5550222

SANTPOORT - AMSTERDAM
Duin & Kruidberg Country Estate, Duin en Kruidbergerweg 60, 2071 Santpoort, Haarlem, Amsterdam, The Netherlands. Tel: +31 23 512 1800

THE HAGUE
Le Méridien Hotel des Indes, Lange Voorhout 54-56, 2514 EG The Hague, The Netherlands. Tel: +31 70 36 12 345

Portugal

ALENTEJO (ÉVORA)
Convento do Espinheiro Heritage Hotel & Spa, Apartado 594, 7002-502 Évora, Portugal. Tel: +351 266 742 437

ALENTEJO (MÉRTOLA)
Estalagem São Domingos, Rua Dr Vargas, Mina de São Domingos, 7750-171 Mértola, Portugal. Tel: +351 286 640 000

ALENTEJO (REDONDO)
Convento de São Paulo, Aldeia da Serra, 7170 -120 Redondo, Portugal. Tel: +351 266 989 160

ALGARVE (LAGOS)
Villa Esmeralda, Porto de Mós, 8600 Lagos, Portugal. Tel: +351 282 760 430

ALGARVE (MONCARAPACHO)
Vila Monte, Sítio dos Caliços, Olhão, 8700-069 Moncarapacho, Portugal. Tel: +351 289 790 790

LISBON & TAGUS VALLEY (CASCAIS)
Albatroz Palace, Luxury Suites, Rua Frederico Arouca 100, 2750-353 Cascais, Lisbon, Portugal. Tel: +351 21 484 73 80

LISBON & TAGUS VALLEY (CASCAIS)
Hotel Cascais Mirage, Av Margina, No 8554, 2754-536 Cascais, Portugal. Tel: +351 210 060 600

LISBON & TAGUS VALLEY (LISBON)
As Janelas Verdes, Rua das Janelas Verdes 47, 1200-690 Lisbon, Portugal. Tel: +351 21 39 68 143

LISBON & TAGUS VALLEY (LISBON)
Hotel Britania, Rua Rodrigues Sampaio 17, 1150-278 Lisbon, Portugal. Tel: +351 21 31 55 016

MADEIRA (FUNCHAL)
Quinta da Bela Vista, Caminho do Avista Navios 4, 9000 Funchal, Madeira, Portugal. Tel: +351 291 706 400

MADEIRA (PONTA DO SOL)
Estalagem da Ponta do Sol, Quinta da Rochinha, 9360 Ponta do Sol, Madeira, Portugal. Tel: +351 291 970 200

OPORTO & NORTHERN PORTUGAL (PINHÃO)
Vintage House, Lugar da Ponte, 5085-034 Pinhão, Portugal. Tel: +351 254 730 230

▼

OPORTO & NORTHERN PORTUGAL (VIDAGO)
Vidago Palace Hotel & Golf, Parque de Vidago, 5425-307 Vidago, Portugal. Tel: +351 276 990 900

MINI LISTINGS EUROPE

Condé Nast Johansens are delighted to recommend over 380 properties across Europe and The Mediterranean.
Call 0800 269 397 or see the order forms on page 425 to order guides.

OPORTO & NORTHERN PORTUGAL (MARIALVA)
Casas do Côro, Marialvamed Turismo Histórico e Lazer Lda, Apartado 1, Marialva, 6430-081 Mêda, Portugal. Tel: +351 91 755 2020

Serbia & Montenegro

ST STEFAN
Villa Montenegro, 2 Vukice Mitrovic Str, 86312 St Stefan, Montenegro. Tel: +381 86 468 802

Spain

ANDALUCÍA (ARCOS DE LA FRONTERA)
Hacienda El Santiscal, Avda. El Santiscal 129 (Lago de Arcos), 11630 Arcos de La Frontera, Spain. Tel: +34 956 70 83 13

ANDALUCÍA (BENAHAVÍS-MARBELLA)
Gran Hotel Benahavis, Huerta de Rufino s/n, 29679 Benahavís, Málaga, Spain. Tel: +34 902 504 862

ANDALUCÍA (ESTEPONA)
Gran Hotel Elba Estepona & Thalasso Spa, Urb. Arena Beach, Ctra. Estepona-Cádiz 151, 29680 Estepona, Spain. Tel: +34 952 809 200

ANDALUCÍA (GAUCIN)
Hotel Casablanca, Celle Teodoro de Molina, No 12, 29480 Gaucin, Málaga, Spain. Tel: +34 952 151 019

ANDALUCÍA (GRANADA)
Barceló La Bobadilla *** GL,** Finca La Bobadilla, Apto. 144, 18300 Loja, Granada, Spain. Tel: +34 958 32 18 61

ANDALUCÍA (GRANADA)
El Ladrón de Agua, Carrera del Darro 13, 18010 Granada, Spain. Tel: +34 958 21 50 40

ANDALUCÍA (GRANADA)
Hospes Palacio de Los Patos, C/ Solarillo de Gracia 1, 18002 Granada, Andalucía, Spain. Tel: +34 958 53 57 90

ANDALUCÍA (GRANADA)
Hotel Casa Morisca, Cuesta de la Victoria 9, 18010 Granada, Spain. Tel: +34 958 221 100

ANDALUCÍA (GRANADA)
Hotel Palacio de Santa Inés, Cuesta de Santa Inés 9, 18010 Granada, Spain. Tel: +34 958 22 23 62

ANDALUCÍA (GRANADA)
Palacio de los Navas, Calle Navas 1, 18009 Granada, Spain. Tel: +34 958 21 57 60

ANDALUCÍA (MÁLAGA)
El Molino de Santillán, Ctra. de Macharaviaya, Km 3, 29730 Rincón de la Victoria, Málaga, Spain. Tel: +34 952 40 09 49

ANDALUCÍA (MARBELLA)
Gran Hotel Guadalpin Banús, c/Edgar Neville, s/n Nueva Andalucía, 29660 Marbella, Spain. Tel: +34 952 899 700

ANDALUCÍA (MARBELLA)
Gran Hotel Guadalpin Marbella, Blvd. Príncipe Alfonso de Hohenloe, S/N 29600 Marbella, Málaga, Spain. Tel: +34 952 899 400

ANDALUCÍA (MARBELLA)
Vasari Vacation Resort & Spa, Urb. La Alzambra, Edif. Vasari Center, 29660 Marbella, Málaga, Spain. Tel: +34 952 907 806

ANDALUCÍA (MIJAS)
Hacienda San Jose, Entrerios (Buzón 59), Mijas, Málaga, Spain. Tel: +34 952 119 494

ANDALUCÍA (MIJAS~COSTA)
Hotel Byblos Andaluz, Mijas Golf, 29650 Mijas~Costa, Málaga, Spain. Tel: +34 952 47 30 50

ANDALUCÍA (RONDA)
Hotel Molino del Arco, Partido de los Frontones s/n, 29400 Ronda, Málaga, Spain. Tel: +34 952 114 017

ANDALUCÍA (SEVILLA - ÉCIJA)
Hotel Palacio de Los Granados, Emilio Castelar 42, 41400 Écija, Sevilla, Spain. Tel: +34 955 905 344

ANDALUCÍA (SEVILLA - GUILLENA)
Hotel Cortijo Águila Real, Ctra. Guillena-Burguillos Km 4, 41210 Guillena, Sevilla, Spain. Tel: +34 955 78 50 06

ANDALUCÍA (SEVILLA - LAS CABEZAS)
Cortijo Soto Real, Ctra Las Cabezas - Villamartin Km 13, 41710 Utrera, Sevilla, Spain. Tel: +34 955 869 200

ANDALUCÍA (SEVILLA - OSUNA)
Palacio Marqués de la Gomera, C/ San Pedro 20, 41640 Osuna, Sevilla, Spain. Tel: +34 95 4 81 22 23

ANDALUCÍA (SEVILLA)
Hospes Hotel Las Casas Del Rey de Baeza, C/Santiago, Plaza Jesús de la Redención 2, 41003 Sevilla, Spain. Tel: +34 954 561 496

ANDALUCÍA (SOTOGRANDE)
Almenara Golf Hotel & Spa, A-7 (National Road), 11310 Sotogrande, Spain. Tel: + 34 902 18 18 36

ANDALUCÍA (TARIFA)
Cortijo el Aguilon, CN 340, km 68.3, Facinas, 11391 Tarifa (Cádiz), Spain. Tel: +34 637 424 251

ANDALUCÍA (ÚBEDA)
Palacio de la Rambla, Plaza del Marqués 1, 23400 Úbeda, Jaén, Spain. Tel: +34 953 75 01 96

ARAGÓN (TRAMACASTILLA)
Hotel El Privilegio de Tena, Calle Zacalera 1, Plaza Mayer, 22663 Tramacastilla de Tena, Huesca, Aragón, Spain. Tel: +34 974 487 206

ARAGÓN (VALDERROBRES)
La Torre del Visco, 44587 Fuentespalda, Teruel, Spain. Tel: +34 978 76 90 15

ASTURIAS (CANGAS DE ONÍS)
Hotel la Cepada, Avenida Contranquil s/n, 33550 Cangas de Onís, Spain. Tel: +34 985 84 94 45

▼

ASTURIAS (VILLAMAYOR)
Palacio de Cutre, La Goleta S/N, Villamayor, 33583 Infiesto, Asturias, Spain. Tel: +34 985 70 80 72

BALEARIC ISLANDS (IBIZA)
Atzaró Agroturismo, Ctra San Juan, Km 15, 07840 Santa Eulalia, Ibiza, Balearic Islands . Tel: +34 971 33 88 38

BALEARIC ISLANDS (IBIZA)
Can Lluc, Crta Santa Inés, km 2, 07816 San Rafael, Ibiza, Balearic Islands. Tel: +34 971 198 673

BALEARIC ISLANDS (IBIZA)
Cas Gasi, Apdo. Correos 117, 07814 Santa Gertrudis, Ibiza, Balearic Islands. Tel: +34 971 197 700

BALEARIC ISLANDS (MALLORCA)
Agroturismo Es Puig Moltó, Ctra. Pina-Montuiri, 07230 Montuiri, Mallorca, Balearic Islands. Tel: +34 971 18 17 58

BALEARIC ISLANDS (MALLORCA)
Ca's Xorc, Carretera de Deià, Km 56.1, 07100 Sóller, Mallorca, Balearic Islands. Tel: +34 971 63 82 80

BALEARIC ISLANDS (MALLORCA)
Gran Hotel Son Net, 07194 Puigpunyent, Mallorca, Balearic Islands. Tel: +34 971 14 70 00

BALEARIC ISLANDS (MALLORCA)
Hospes Hotel Maricel, Carretera d'Andratx 11, 07181 Cas Català, (Calvià) Mallorca, Balearic Islands. Tel: +34 971 707 744

BALEARIC ISLANDS (MALLORCA)
Hotel Can Simoneta, Ctra. de Artá a Canyamel km 8, Finca Torre de Canyamel, 07580 Capdepera, Mallorca, Balearic Islands. Tel: +34 971 816 110

BALEARIC ISLANDS (MALLORCA)
Hotel Dalt Murada, C/ Almudaina 6-A, 07001 Palma de Mallorca, Mallorca, Balearic Islands. Tel: +34 971 425 300

BALEARIC ISLANDS (MALLORCA)
Hotel Tres, C/ Apuntadores 3, 07012 Palma de Mallorca, Balearic Islands, Spain. Tel: +34 971 717 333

BALEARIC ISLANDS (MALLORCA)
La Moraleja Hotel, Urbanización Los Encinares s/n, 07469 Cala San Vicente, Mallorca, Balearic Islands. Tel: +34 971 534 010

BALEARIC ISLANDS (MALLORCA)
Palacio Ca Sa Galesa, Carrer de Miramar 8, 07001 Palma de Mallorca, Balearic Islands. Tel: +34 971 715 400

BALEARIC ISLANDS (MALLORCA)
Read's Hotel & Spa, Ca'n Moragues, 07320 Santa María, Mallorca, Balearic Islands. Tel: +34 971 14 02 62

BALEARIC ISLANDS (MALLORCA)
Valldemossa Hotel & Restaurant, Ctra. Vieja de Valldemossa s/n, 07170 Valldemossa, Mallorca, Balearic Islands. Tel: +34 971 61 26 26

CANARY ISLANDS (FUERTEVENTURA)
Hotel Elba Palace Golf, Urb. Fuerteventura Golf Club, Ctra. de Jandia, km11, 35610 Antigua, Fuerteventura, Canary Islands. Tel: +34 928 16 39 22

CANARY ISLANDS (FUERTEVENTURA)
Kempinski Hotel Atlantis Bahia Real, Avenida Grandes Playas s/n, 35660 Corralejo, Fuerteventura, Canary Islands. Tel: +34 928 53 64 44

CANARY ISLANDS (GRAN CANARIA)
Gran Hotel Lopesan Costa Meloneras, C/Mar Mediterráneo 1, 35100 Maspalomas, Gran Canaria, Canary Islands. Tel: +34 928 12 81 00

CANARY ISLANDS (GRAN CANARIA)
Gran Hotel Lopesan Villa Del Conde, C/Mar Mediterráneo 7, Urbanización Costa Meloneras, 35100 Maspalomas, Gran Canaria, Canary Islands. Tel: +34 928 141 717

CANARY ISLANDS (LANZAROTE)
Princesa Yaiza Suite Hotel Resort, Avenida Papagayo s/n, 35570 Playa Blanca, Yaiza, Lanzarote, Canary Islands. Tel: +34 928 519 222

CANARY ISLANDS (TENERIFE)
Abama, Carretera General TF-47, Km 9, 38687 Guía de Isora, Tenerife, Canary Islands. Tel: +34 922 865 444

CANARY ISLANDS (TENERIFE)
Gran Hotel Bahía del Duque Resort, C/ Alcalde Walter Paetzmann, s/n, 38660 Costa Adeje, Tenerife, Canary Islands. Tel: +34 922 74 69 00

CANARY ISLANDS (TENERIFE)
Gran Tacande Hotel & Spa, C/ Alcalde Walter Paetzmann s/n, Costa Adeje, 386170 Tenerife, Canary Islands. Tel: +34 922 746 400

CANARY ISLANDS (TENERIFE)
Hotel Jardín Tropical, Calle Gran Bretaña, 38670 Costa Adeje, Tenerife, Canary Islands. Tel: +34 922 74 60 00

Mini Listings Europe

Condé Nast Johansens are delighted to recommend over 380 properties across Europe and The Mediterranean.
Call 0800 269 397 or see the order forms on page 425 to order guides.

CANARY ISLANDS (TENERIFE)
Hotel Las Madrigueras, Golf Las Américas, 38660 Playa de Las Américas, Tenerife, Canary Islands. Tel: +34 922 77 78 18

CASTILLA LA MANCHA (TALAVERA DE LA REINA)
Finca Canturias, Alcaudete de la Jara, Ctra. Calera y Chozas, Km 12, 45662 Talavera de la Reina, Spain. Tel: +34 925 59 41 08

CASTILLA Y LEÓN (PALENCIA)
Posada de la Casa del Abad de Ampudia, Plaza Francisco Martín Gromaz 12, 34160 Ampudia (Palencia), Spain. Tel: +34 979 768 008

CASTILLA Y LEÓN (SALAMANCA)
Castillo de Buen Amor, Carretera National 630 Km 317, 6 Topas 37799, Salamanca, Spain. Tel: +34 923 355 002

CASTILLA Y LEÓN (SALAMANCA)
Hotel Rector, c/Rector Esperabé 10-Apartado 399, 37008 Salamanca, Spain. Tel: +34 923 21 84 82

CASTILLO Y LEÓN (SALAMANCA)
Hacienda Zorita, Carretera Salamanca-Ledesma, Km 8.7, 37115 Valderón, Spain. Tel: +34 923 129 400

CATALUÑA (ALCANAR)
Tancat de Codorniu, Ctra. N340, Km 1059, 43530 Alcanar, Spain. Tel: +34 977 737 194

CATALUÑA (BARCELONA)
Gallery Hotel, C/ Rosselló 249, 08008 Barcelona, Spain. Tel: +34 934 15 99 11

CATALUÑA (BARCELONA)
Gran Hotel La Florida, Carretera Vallvidrera al Tibidabo 83-93, 08035 Barcelona, Spain. Tel: +34 93 259 30 00

CATALUÑA (BARCELONA)
Hotel Casa Fuster, Passeig de Gràcia 132, 08008 Barcelona, Spain. Tel: +34 93 255 30 00

CATALUÑA (BARCELONA)
Hotel Claris, Pau Claris 150, 08009 Barcelona, Spain. Tel: +34 934 87 62 62

CATALUÑA (BARCELONA)
Hotel Duquesa de Cardona, Passeig Colon 12, 08002 Barcelona, Spain. Tel: +34 93 268 90 90

CATALUÑA (BARCELONA)
Hotel Omm, Rosselló 265, 08008 Barcelona, Spain. Tel: +34 93 445 40 00

CATALUÑA (BARCELONA)
Hotel Pulitzer, C/Bergara 8, 08002 Barcelona, Spain. Tel: +34 93 481 67 67

CATALUÑA (BOLVIR DE CERDANYA)
Torre del Remei, Camí Reial s/n, 17539 Bolvir de Cerdanya, Girona, Spain. Tel: +34 972 140 182

CATALUÑA (CALDERS)
Hotel Urbisol, Ctra. Manresa to Moià (N-141c), Km 20, 08279 Calders, Barcelona, Spain. Tel: +34 93 830 91 53

CATALUÑA (COSTA BRAVA)
Hotel Santa Marta, Playa de Santa Cristina, 17310 Lloret de Mar, Spain. Tel: +34 972 364 904

CATALUÑA (COSTA BRAVA)
Rigat Park & Spa Hotel, Av. America 1, Playa de Fenals, 17310 Lloret de Mar, Costa Brava, Gerona, Spain. Tel: +34 972 36 52 00

CATALUÑA (LA SELVA DEL CAMP)
Mas Passamaner, Camí de la Serra 52, 43470 La Selva del Camp (Tarragona), Spain. Tel: +34 977 766 333

CATALUÑA (ROSES)
Romantic Villa - Hotel Vistabella , Cala Canyelles Petites, PO Box 3, 17480 Roses (Gerona), Spain. Tel: +34 972 25 62 00

CATALUÑA (SITGES)
San Sebastian Playa Hotel, Calle Port Alegre 53, 08870 Sitges (Barcelona), Spain. Tel: +34 93 894 86 76

EXTREMADURA (ZAFRA)
Casa Palacio Conde de la Corte, Plaza Pilar Redondo 2, 06300 Zafra, Spain. Tel: +34 924 563 311

MADRID (MADRID)
Antiguo Convento, C/ de Las Monjas, s/n Boadilla del Monte, 28660 Madrid, Spain. Tel: + 34 91 632 22 20

MADRID (MADRID)
Gran Hotel Canarias, Plaza Cánovas del Castillo 4, 28014 Madrid, Spain. Tel: +34 91 420 2092

MADRID (MADRID)
Gran Meliá Fénix, Hermosilla 2, 28001 Madrid, Spain. Tel: +34 91 431 67 00

MADRID (MADRID)
Hotel Orfila, C/Orfila, No 6, 28010 Madrid, Spain. Tel: +34 91 702 77 70

MADRID (MADRID)
Hotel Quinta de los Cedros, C/Allendesalazar 4, 28043 Madrid, Spain. Tel: +34 91 515 2200

MADRID (MADRID)
Hotel Urban, Carrera de San Jerónimo 34, 28014 Madrid, Spain. Tel: +34 91 787 77 70

MADRID (MADRID)
Hotel Villa Real, Plaza de las Cortes 10, 28014 Madrid, Spain. Tel: +34 914 20 37 67

MADRID (MADRID)
Mirasierra Suites Hotel, C/ Alfredo Marquerie 43, 28034 Madrid, Spain. Tel: +34 91 727 79 00

PAIS VASCO (ARMINTZA)
Hotel Arresi, Portugane 7, 48620 Armintza, Spain. Tel: +34 94 68 79 208

VALENCIA (ALICANTE)
Hospes Amérigo, C/ Rafael Altamira 7, 03002 Alicante, Spain. Tel: +34 965 14 65 70

VALENCIA (ALICANTE)
Hotel Sidi San Juan & Spa, Playa de San Juan, 03540 Alicante, Spain. Tel: +34 96 516 13 00

VALENCIA (ALQUERIAS - CASTELLÓN)
Torre La Mina, C/ La Regenta 1, 12539 Alquerias-Castellón, Spain. Tel: +34 964 57 0180

VALENCIA (DÉNIA)
La Posada del Mar, Plaça de les Drassanes, s/n 03700 Dénia, Spain. Tel: +34 96 643 29 66

VALENCIA (VALENCIA)
Hospes Palau de la Mar, Navarro Reverter 14, 46004 Valencia, Spain. Tel: +34 96 316 2884

VALENCIA (VALENCIA)
Hotel Sidi Saler & Spa, Playa el Saler, 46012 Valencia, Spain. Tel: +34 961 61 04 11

VALENCIA (XÀTIVA)
Hotel Mont Sant, Subida Al Castillo, s/n Xàtiva, 46800 Valencia, Spain. Tel: +34 962 27 50 81

Switzerland

LUGANO
Villa Sassa, Via Tesserete 10, 6900 Lugano, Switzerland. Tel: +41 91 911 41 11

WEGGIS - LAKE LUCERNE
Park Hotel Weggis, Hertensteinstrasse 34, CH - 6353 Weggis, Switzerland. Tel: +41 41 392 05 05

Turkey

ANTALYA
Aspen Hotel, Mermerli Sokak No 25, Kaleiçi 07100 Antalya, Turkey. Tel: +90 242 247 0590

ANTALYA
The Marmara Antalya, Eski Lara Yolu No 136, Sirinyali, Antalya, Turkey. Tel: +90 242 249 3600

ANTALYA
Olympos Lodge, PO Box 38, Çirali, Kemer, Antalya, Turkey. Tel: +90 242 825 7171

ANTALYA
Renaissance Antalya Beach Resort & Spa, PO Box 654, 07004 Beldibi - Kemer, Antalya, Turkey. Tel: +90 242 824 84 31

ANTALYA
Tuvana Residence, Tuzcular Mahallesi, Karanlik Sokak 7, 07100 Kaleiçi - Antalya, Turkey. Tel: +90 242 247 60 15

▼

ANTALYA
Villa Mahal, PO Box 4 Kalkan, 07960 Antalya, Turkey. Tel: +90 242 844 32 68

BODRUM
Divan Bodrum Palmira, Kelesharim Caddesi 6, 48483 Bodrum, Turkey. Tel: +90 252 377 5601

BODRUM
The Marmara Bodrum, Suluhasan Caddesi, Yokusbasi, Mevkii No 18, PK 199, 48400 Bodrum, Turkey. Tel: +90 252 313 8130

BODRUM
The Queen Ada Hotel, Hasgoru Sokak, No 7, Torba, 48400 Bodrum, Turkey. Tel: +90 252 367 1598

ISTANBUL
Ansen 130 Suites & Restaurant, Mesrutiyet Caddesi Ansen 130, 34430 Tepebasi, Tünel, Istanbul, Turkey. Tel: +90 212 245 88 08

ISTANBUL
The Marmara Istanbul, Taksim Meydani, Taksim, 34437 Istanbul, Turkey. Tel: +90 212 251 4696

ISTANBUL
The Marmara Pera, Mesrutiyet Cad, Tepebasi, 34430 Istanbul, Turkey. Tel: +90 212 251 4646

ISTANBUL
Sumahan On The Water, Kuleli Caddesi No 51, Çengelköy, 34684 Istanbul, Turkey. Tel: +90 216 422 8000

İZMÍR
Sisus Hotel, Dalyanköy Yat Limani Mevkii, Çesme - İzmír, Turkey. Tel: +90 232 724 0330

MARMARIS
Golden Key Bördübet, Bördübet Mevkii, Marmaris, Turkey. Tel: +90 252 436 9230

MUSTAFAPASA
"Rose Mansions" - Sinasos Gül Konaklari, Sümer Sokak, Mustafapasa, Ürgüp, Turkey. Tel: +90 384 353 5486

ÜRGÜP
Sacred House, Karahandere Mahallesi, Barbaros Hayrettin, Sokak, No 25, 50400 Ürgüp, Turkey. Tel: +90 384 341 7102

Mini Listings The Americas

Condé Nast Johansens are delighted to recommend 285 properties across The Americas, Atlantic, Caribbean and Pacific.
Call 0800 269 397 or see the order forms on page 425 to order guides.

Recommendations in the U.S.A.

U.S.A. - ARIZONA (GREER)

Hidden Meadow Ranch
620 Country Road 1325, Greer, Arizona 85927
Tel: +1 928 333 1000
Fax: +1 928 333 1010
Web: www.johansens.com/hiddenmeadow

U.S.A. - ARIZONA (SCOTTSDALE)

The Hermosa Inn
5532 North Palo Cristi Road, Scottsdale, Arizona 85253
Tel: +1 602 955 8614
Fax: +1 602 955 8299
Web: www.johansens.com/hermosa

U.S.A. - ARIZONA (SEDONA)

Sedona Rouge Hotel & Spa
2250 West Highway 89A, Sedona, Arizona 86336
Tel: +1 928 203 4111
Fax: +1 928 203 9094
Web: www.johansens.com/sedonarouge

U.S.A. - ARIZONA (TUCSON)

Arizona Inn
2200 East Elm Street, Tucson, Arizona 85719
Tel: +1 520 325 1541
Fax: +1 520 881 5830
Web: www.johansens.com/arizonainn

U.S.A. - ARIZONA (TUCSON)

Tanque Verde Ranch
14301 East Speedway, Tucson, Arizona 85748
Tel: +1 520 296 6275
Fax: +1 520 721 9427
Web: www.johansens.com/tanqueverde

U.S.A. - ARIZONA (WICKENBURG)

Rancho de los Caballeros
1551 South Vulture Mine Road, Wickenburg, Arizona 85390
Tel: +1 928 684 5484
Fax: +1 928 684 9565
Web: www.johansens.com/caballeros

U.S.A. - CALIFORNIA (ATASCADERO)

The Carlton Hotel
6005 El Camino Real, Atascadero, California 93422
Tel: +1 805 461 5100
Fax: +1 805 461 5116
Web: www.johansens.com/carltoncalifornia

U.S.A. - CALIFORNIA (BEL AIR)

Hotel Bel-Air
701 Stone Canyon Road, Los Angeles, California 90077
Tel: +1 310 472 1211
Fax: +1 310 909 1611
Web: www.johansens.com/belair

U.S.A. - CALIFORNIA (BIG SUR)

Post Ranch Inn
Highway 1, P.O. Box 219, Big Sur, California 93920
Tel: +1 831 667 2200
Fax: +1 831 667 2512
Web: www.johansens.com/postranchinn

U.S.A. - CALIFORNIA (BIG SUR)

Ventana Inn and Spa
Highway 1, Big Sur, California 93920
Tel: +1 831 667 2331
Fax: +1 831 667 2419
Web: www.johansens.com/ventana

U.S.A. - CALIFORNIA (BORREGO SPRINGS)

La Casa del Zorro Desert Resort
3845 Yaqui Pass Road, Borrego Springs, California 92004
Tel: +1 760 767 5323
Fax: +1 760 767 5963
Web: www.johansens.com/zorrodesert

U.S.A. - CALIFORNIA (CARMEL VALLEY)

Stonepine Estate
150 East Carmel Valley Road, Carmel Valley, California 93924
Tel: +1 831 659 2245
Fax: +1 831 659 5160
Web: www.johansens.com/stonepine

U.S.A. - CALIFORNIA (CARMEL-BY-THE-SEA)

L'Auberge Carmel
Monte Verde at Seventh, Carmel-by-the-Sea, California 93921
Tel: +1 831 624 8578
Fax: +1 831 626 1018
Web: www.johansens.com/laubergecarmel

U.S.A. - CALIFORNIA (CARMEL-BY-THE-SEA)

The Tradewinds at Carmel
Mission Street at Third Avenue, Carmel-by-the-Sea, California 93921
Tel: +1 831 624 2776
Fax: +1 831 624 0634
Web: www.johansens.com/tradewinds

U.S.A. - CALIFORNIA (EUREKA)

The Carter House Inns
301 L Street, Eureka, California 95501
Tel: +1 707 444 8062
Fax: +1 707 444 8067
Web: www.johansens.com/carterhouse

U.S.A. - CALIFORNIA (GLEN ELLEN)

The Gaige House
13540 Arnold Drive, Glen Ellen, California 95442
Tel: +1 707 935 0237
Fax: +1 707 935 6411
Web: www.johansens.com/gaige

U.S.A. - CALIFORNIA (HEALDSBURG)

The Grape Leaf Inn
539 Johnson Street, Healdsburg, California 95448
Tel: +1 707 433 8140
Fax: +1 707 433 3140
Web: www.johansens.com/grapeleaf

U.S.A. - CALIFORNIA (KENWOOD)

The Kenwood Inn and Spa
10400 Sonoma Highway, Kenwood, California 95452
Tel: +1 707 833 1293
Fax: +1 707 833 1247
Web: www.johansens.com/kenwoodinn

U.S.A. - CALIFORNIA (LOS OLIVOS)

The Fess Parker Wine Country Inn
2860 Grand Avenue, Los Olivos, California 93441
Tel: +1 805 688 7788
Fax: +1 805 688 1942
Web: www.johansens.com/fessparker

Mini Listings The Americas

Condé Nast Johansens are delighted to recommend 285 properties across The Americas, Atlantic, Caribbean and Pacific.
Call 0800 269 397 or see the order forms on page 425 to order guides.

U.S.A. - CALIFORNIA (MENDOCINO)

The Joshua Grindle Inn

44800 Little Lake Road, Mendocino, California 95460
Tel: +1 707 937 4143
Fax: +1 801 751 4998
Web: www.johansens.com/joshuagrindle

U.S.A. - CALIFORNIA (MENDOCINO)

The Stanford Inn By The Sea

Coast Highway One & Comptche-Ukiah Road, Mendocino, California 95460
Tel: +1 707 937 5615
Fax: +1 707 937 0305
Web: www.johansens.com/stanford

U.S.A. - CALIFORNIA (MILL VALLEY)

Mill Valley Inn

165 Throckmorton Avenue, Mill Valley, California 94941
Tel: +1 415 389 6608
Fax: +1 415 389 5051
Web: www.johansens.com/millvalleyinn

U.S.A. - CALIFORNIA (MONTEREY)

Old Monterey Inn

500 Martin Street, Monterey, California 93940
Tel: +1 831 375 8284
Fax: +1 831 375 6730
Web: www.johansens.com/oldmontereyinn

U.S.A. - CALIFORNIA (NAPA VALLEY)

1801 First Inn

1801 First Street, Napa, California 94559
Tel: +1 707 224 3739
Fax: +1 707 224 3932
Web: www.johansens.com/1801inn

U.S.A. - CALIFORNIA (NAPA)

Milliken Creek

1815 Silverado Trail, Napa, California 94558
Tel: +1 707 255 1197
Fax: +1 707 255 3112
Web: www.johansens.com/milliken

U.S.A. - CALIFORNIA (OAKHURST)

Chateau du Sureau

48688 Victoria Lane, Oakhurst, California 93644
Tel: +1 559 683 6860
Fax: +1 559 683 0800
Web: www.johansens.com/chateausureau

U.S.A. - CALIFORNIA (OLEMA)

Olema Druids Hall

9870 Shoreline Highway One, Olema, California 94950
Tel: +1 415 663 8727
Fax: +1 415 663 1830
Web: www.johansens.com/olema

U.S.A. - CALIFORNIA (PASO ROBLES)

The Villa Toscana

4230 Buena Vista, Paso Robles, California 93446
Tel: +1 805 238 5600
Fax: +1 805 238 5605
Web: www.johansens.com/villatoscana

U.S.A. - CALIFORNIA (RANCHO SANTA FE)

The Inn at Rancho Santa Fe

5951 Linea del Cielo, Rancho Santa Fe, California 92067
Tel: +1 858 756 1131
Fax: +1 858 759 1604
Web: www.johansens.com/ranchosantafe

U.S.A. - CALIFORNIA (SAN DIEGO)

Tower 23 Hotel

4551 Ocean Boulevard, San Diego, California 92129
Tel: +1 858 270 2323
Fax: +1 858 274 2333
Web: www.johansens.com/tower23

U.S.A. - CALIFORNIA (SAN FRANCISCO BAY AREA)

Inn Above Tide

30 El Portal, Sausalito, California 94965
Tel: +1 415 332 9535
Fax: +1 415 332 6714
Web: www.johansens.com/innabovetide

U.S.A. - CALIFORNIA (SAN FRANCISCO)

Mandarin Oriental San Francisco

222 Sansome Street, San Francisco, California 94104-2792
Tel: +1 415 276 9888
Fax: +1 415 433 0289
Web: www.johansens.com/mandarinorientalsf

U.S.A. - CALIFORNIA (SAN FRANCISCO)

Union Street Inn

2229 Union Street, San Francisco, California 94123
Tel: +1 415 346 0424
Fax: +1 415 922 8046
Web: www.johansens.com/unionstreetsf

U.S.A. - CALIFORNIA (SANTA BARBARA)

Harbor View Inn

28 West Cabrillo Boulevard, Santa Barbara, California 93101
Tel: +1 805 963 0780
Fax: +1 805 963 7967
Web: www.johansens.com/harborview

U.S.A. - CALIFORNIA (SANTA YNEZ)

The Santa Ynez Inn

3627 Sagunto Street, Santa Ynez, California 93460-0628
Tel: +1 805 688 5588
Fax: +1 805 686 4294
Web: www.johansens.com/santaynez

U.S.A. - CALIFORNIA (SOLVANG)

Alisal Guest Ranch

1054 Alisal Road, Solvang, California 93463
Tel: +1 805 688 6411
Fax: +1 805 688 2510
Web: www.johansens.com/alisalguestranch

U.S.A. - CALIFORNIA (SONOMA)

Ledson Hotel & Harmony Club

480 First Street East, Sonoma, California 95476
Tel: +1 707 996 9779
Fax: +1 707 996 9776
Web: www.johansens.com/ledsonhotel

U.S.A. - CALIFORNIA (ST. HELENA)

Meadowood

900 Meadowood Lane, St. Helena, California 94574
Tel: +1 707 963 3646
Fax: +1 707 963 3532
Web: www.johansens.com/meadowood

U.S.A. - COLORADO (ASPEN)

The St. Regis Residences Aspen

315 East Dean Street, Aspen, Colorado 81611
Tel: +1 970 920 3300
Fax: +1 970 920 9555
Web: www.johansens.com/stregis

Mini Listings The Americas

Condé Nast Johansens are delighted to recommend 285 properties across The Americas, Atlantic, Caribbean and Pacific.
Call 0800 269 397 or see the order forms on page 425 to order guides.

U.S.A. - COLORADO (BOULDER)

The St. Julien Hotel & Spa

9th and Canyon (900 Walnut Street), Boulder, Colorado 80302
Tel: +1 720 406 9696
Fax: +1 720 406 9668
Web: www.johansens.com/stjulien

U.S.A. - COLORADO (CLARK)

The Home Ranch

P.O. Box 822, 54880 Routt Country Road 129, Clark, Colorado 80428
Tel: + 1 970 879 1780
Fax: +1 970 879 1795
Web: www.johansens.com/homeranch

U.S.A. - COLORADO (COLORADO SPRINGS)

The Broadmoor

P.O. Box 1439, 1 Lake Avenue, Colorado Springs, Colorado 80901-1439
Tel: +1 719 634 7711
Fax: +1 719 577 5700
Web: www.johansens.com/broadmoor

U.S.A. - COLORADO (DENVER)

Castle Marne

1572 Race Street, Denver, Colorado 80206
Tel: +1 303 331 0621
Fax: +1 303 331 0623
Web: www.johansens.com/castlemarne

U.S.A. - COLORADO (DUNTON)

Dunton Hot Springs

52068 West fork Road, Dunton, 81323 Colorado
Tel: +1 970 882 4800
Fax: +1 970 882 7475
Web: www.johansens.com/duntonhotsprings

U.S.A. - COLORADO (ESTES PARK)

Taharaa Mountain Lodge

3110 So. St. Vrain, Estes Park, Colorado 80517
Tel: +1 970 577 0098
Fax: +1 970 577 0819
Web: www.johansens.com/taharaa

U.S.A. - COLORADO (MANITOU SPRINGS)

Cliff House at Pikes Peak

306 Cañon Avenue, Manitou Springs, Colorado 80829
Tel: +1 719 685 3000
Fax: +1 719 685 3913
Web: www.johansens.com/thecliffhouse

U.S.A. - COLORADO (MONTROSE)

Elk Mountain Resort

97 Elk Walk, Montrose, Colorado 81401
Tel: +1 970 252 4900
Fax: +1 970 252 4913
Web: www.johansens.com/elkmountain

U.S.A. - COLORADO (STEAMBOAT SPRINGS)

Vista Verde Guest Ranch

P.O. Box 770465, Steamboat Springs, Colorado 80477
Tel: +1 970 879 3858
Fax: +1 970 879 1413
Web: www.johansens.com/vistaverderanch

U.S.A. - CONNECTICUT (GREENWICH)

Delamar Greenwlch Harbor

500 Steamboat Road, Greenwich, Connecticut 06830
Tel: +1 203 661 9800
Fax: +1 203 661 2513
Web: www.johansens.com/delamar

U.S.A. - CONNECTICUT (STONINGTON)

The Inn at Stonington

60 Water Street, Stonington, Connecticut 06378
Tel: 1 860 535 2000
Fax: 1 860 535 8193
Web: www.johansens.com/stonington

U.S.A. - DELAWARE (REHOBOTH BEACH)

Boardwalk Plaza Hotel

Olive Avenue & The Boardwalk, Rehoboth Beach, Delaware 19971
Tel: +1 302 227 7169
Fax: +1 302 227 0561
Web: www.johansens.com/boardwalkplaza

U.S.A. - DELAWARE (WILMINGTON)

The Inn at Montchanin

Route 100 & Kirk Road, Montchanin, Delaware 19710
Tel: +1 302 888 2133
Fax: +1 302 888 0389
Web: www.johansens.com/montchanin

U.S.A. - DISTRICT OF COLUMBIA (WASHINGTON)

The Hay Adams

Sixteenth & H Streets N.W., Washington D.C. 20006
Tel: +1 202 638 6600
Fax: +1 202 638 2716
Web: www.johansens.com/hayadams

U.S.A. - DISTRICT OF COLUMBIA (WASHINGTON)

The Madison

15th and M Streets, N.W., Washington D.C. 20005
Tel: +1 202 862 1600
Fax: +1 202 587 2696
Web: www.johansens.com/madison

U.S.A. - FLORIDA (DAYTONA BEACH SHORES)

The Shores Resort & Spa

2637 South Atlantic Avenue, Daytona Beach Shores, Florida 32118
Tel: +1 386 767 7350
Fax: +1 386 760 3651
Web: www.johansens.com/shoresresort

U.S.A. - FLORIDA (KEY WEST)

Simonton Court Historic Inn & Cottages

320 Simonton Street, Key West, Florida 33040
Tel: +1 305 294 6386
Fax: +1 305 293 8446
Web: www.johansens.com/simontoncourt

U.S.A. - FLORIDA (MARCO ISLAND/NAPLES)

Marco Beach Ocean Resort

480 South Collier Boulevard, Marco Island, Florida 34145
Tel: +1 239 393 1400
Fax: +1 239 393 1401
Web: www.johansens.com/marcobeach

U.S.A. - FLORIDA (MIAMI BEACH)

Bentley Beach Resort & Spa

101 Ocean Drive, Miami Beach, Florida 33139
Tel: +1 305 938 4600
Fax: +1 305 938 4601
Web: www.johansens.com/bentleybeach

U.S.A. - FLORIDA (NAPLES)

LaPlaya Beach & Golf Resort

9891 Gulf Shore Drive, Naples, Florida 34108
Tel: +1 239 597 3123
Fax: +1 239 597 8283
Web: www.johansens.com/laplaya

Mini Listings The Americas

Condé Nast Johansens are delighted to recommend 285 properties across The Americas, Atlantic, Caribbean and Pacific.
Call 0800 269 397 or see the order forms on page 425 to order guides.

U.S.A. - FLORIDA (ORLANDO)

Celebration Hotel

700 Bloom Street, Celebration, Florida 34747
Tel: +1 407 566 6000
Fax: +1 407 566 6001
Web: www.johansens.com/celebration

U.S.A. - FLORIDA (ORLANDO)

Portofino Bay Hotel

5601 Universal Boulevard, Orlando, Florida 32819
Tel: +1 407 503 1000
Fax: +1 407 503 1010
Web: www.johansens.com/portofinobay

U.S.A. - FLORIDA (ORLANDO)

The Villas of Grand Cypress

One North Jacaranda, Orlando, Florida 32836
Tel: +1 407 239 4700
Fax: +1 407 239 7219
Web: www.johansens.com/grandcypress

U.S.A. - FLORIDA (PALM COAST)

The Lodge at Ocean Hammock Resort

105 16th Road, Palm Coast, Florida 32137
Tel: +1 386 447 4600
Fax: +1 386 447 4601
Web: www.johansens.com/oceanhammock

U.S.A. - FLORIDA (PONTE VEDRA BEACH)

The Lodge & Club at Ponte Vedra Beach

607 Ponte Vedra Boulevard, Ponte Vedra Beach, Florida 32082
Tel: +1 904 273 9500
Fax: +1 904 273 0210
Web: www.johansens.com/ponteverdrabeach

U.S.A. - FLORIDA (SEAGROVE BEACH)

WaterColor Inn & Resort

34 Goldenrod Circle, Seagrove Beach, Florida 32459
Tel: +1 850 534 5000
Fax: +1 850 534 5001
Web: www.johansens.com/watercolor

U.S.A. - FLORIDA (ST. AUGUSTINE)

Casablanca Inn

24 Avenida Menendez, St. Augustine, Florida 32084
Tel: +1 904 829 0928
Fax: +1 904 826 1892
Web: www.johansens.com/casablanca

U.S.A. - FLORIDA (ST. PETE BEACH)

Don CeSar Beach Resort

3400 Gulf Boulevard, St. Pete Beach, Florida 33706
Tel: +1 727 360 1881
Fax: +1 727 367 3609
Web: www.johansens.com/doncesar

U.S.A. - GEORGIA (ADAIRSVILLE)

Barnsley Gardens Resort

597 Barnsley Gardens Road, Adairsville, Georgia 30103
Tel: +1 770 773 7480
Fax: +1 770 877 9155
Web: www.johansens.com/barnsleygardens

U.S.A. - GEORGIA (CUMBERLAND ISLAND)

Greyfield Inn

Cumberland Island, Georgia
Tel: +1 904 261 6408
Fax: +1 904 321 0666
Web: www.johansens.com/greyfieldinn

U.S.A. - GEORGIA (SAVANNAH)

The Ballastone

14 East Oglethorpe Avenue, Savannah, Georgia 31401-3707
Tel: +1 912 236 1484
Fax: +1 912 236 4626
Web: www.johansens.com/ballastone

U.S.A. - GEORGIA (SAVANNAH)

The Eliza Thompson House

5 West Jones Street, Savannah, Georgia 31401
Tel: +1 912 236 3620
Fax: +1 912 238 1920
Web: www.johansens.com/elizathompsonhouse

U.S.A. - GEORGIA (SAVANNAH)

The Gastonian

220 East Gaston Street, Savannah, Georgia 31401
Tel: +1 912 232 2869
Fax: +1 912 232 0710
Web: www.johansens.com/gastonian

U.S.A. - GEORGIA (SAVANNAH)

Kehoe House

123 Habersham Street, Savannah, Georgia 3140
Tel: +1 912 232 1020
Fax: +1 912 231 0208
Web: www.johansens.com/kehoehouse

U.S.A. - GEORGIA (SAVANNAH)

Mansion on Forsyth Park

700 Drayton Street, Savannah, Georgia 3140
Tel: +1 912 238 5158
Fax: +1 912 238 5146
Web: www.johansens.com/forsythpark

U.S.A. - HAWAII (BIG ISLAND)

The Palms Cliff House

28-3514 Mamalahoa Highway 19, P.O. Box 189, Honomu, Hawaii 96728-0189
Tel: +1 808 963 6076
Fax: +1 808 963 6316
Web: www.johansens.com/palmscliff

U.S.A. - HAWAII (BIG ISLAND)

Shipman House

131 Ka'iulani Street, Hilo, Hawaii 96720
Tel: +1 808 934 8002
Fax: +1 808 934 8002
Web: www.johansens.com/shipman

U.S.A. - HAWAII (MAUI)

Hotel Hana-Maui

5031 Hana Highway, Hana, Maui, Hawaii 96713
Tel: +1 808 248 8211
Fax: +1 808 248 7202
Web: www.johansens.com/hanamaui

U.S.A. - HAWAII (MAUI)

The Plantation Inn

174 Lahainaluna Road, Lahaina, Maui, Hawaii 96761
Tel: +1 808 667 9225
Fax: +1 808 667 9293
Web: www.johansens.com/plantationinn

U.S.A. - HAWAII (MOLOKAI)

The Lodge at Molokai Ranch

100 Maunaloa Highway, P.O. Box 259, Hawaii 96770
Tel: +1 808 660 2824
Fax: +1 808 552 2773
Web: www.johansens.com/molokailodge

Mini Listings The Americas

Condé Nast Johansens are delighted to recommend 285 properties across The Americas, Atlantic, Caribbean and Pacific.
Call 0800 269 397 or see the order forms on page 425 to order guides.

U.S.A. - IDAHO (MCCALL)

The Whitetail Club
501 West Lake Street, McCall, Idaho 83638
Tel: +1 208 634 2244
Fax: +1 208 634 7504
Web: www.johansens.com/whitetail

U.S.A. - LOUISIANA (NEW ORLEANS)

Hotel Maison De Ville
727 Rue Toulouse, New Orleans, Louisiana 70130
Tel: +1 504 561 5858
Fax: +1 504 528 9939
Web: www.johansens.com/maisondeville

U.S.A. - LOUISIANA (NEW ORLEANS)

The LaFayette Hotel
600 St. Charles Avenue, New Orleans, Louisiana 70130
Tel: +1 504 524 4441
Fax: +1 504 962 5537
Web: www.johansens.com/lafayette

U.S.A. - LOUISIANA (NEW ORLEANS)

Maison Perrier
4117 Perrier Street, New Orleans, Louisiana 70115
Tel: +1 504 897 1807
Fax: +1 504 897 1399
Web: www.johansens.com/perrier

U.S.A. - LOUISIANA (NEW ORLEANS)

The St. James Hotel
330 Magazine Street, New Orleans, Louisiana 70130
Tel: +1 504 304 4000
Fax: +1 504 569 0640
Web: www.johansens.com/stjames

U.S.A. - MAINE (BAR HARBOR)

Balance Rock Inn
21 Albert Meadow, Bar Harbor, Maine 04609-1701
Tel: +1 207 288 2610
Fax: +1 207 288 5534
Web: www.johansens.com/balancerock

U.S.A. - MAINE (GREENVILLE)

The Lodge At Moosehead Lake
Lily Bay Road, P.O. Box 1167, Greenville, Maine 04441
Tel: +1 207 695 4400
Fax: +1 207 695 2281
Web: www.johansens.com/lodgeatmooseheadlake

U.S.A. - MAINE (KENNEBUNKPORT)

The White Barn Inn
37 Beach Avenue, Kennebunkport, Maine 04043
Tel: +1 207 967 2321
Fax: +1 207 967 1100
Web: www.johansens.com/whitebarninn

U.S.A. - MAINE (PORTLAND)

Portland Harbor Hotel
468 Fore Street, Portland, Maine 04101
Tel: +1 207 775 9090
Fax: +1 207 775 9990
Web: www.johansens.com/portlandharbor

U.S.A. - MARYLAND (FROSTBURG)

Savage River Lodge
1600 Mt. Aetna Road, Frostburg, Maryland 21532
Tel: +1 301 689 3200
Fax: +1 301 689 2746
Web: www.johansens.com/savageriver

U.S.A. - MASSACHUSETTS (BOSTON)

The Charles Street Inn
94 Charles Street, Boston, Massachusetts 02114-4643
Tel: +1 617 314 8900
Fax: +1 617 371 0009
Web: www.johansens.com/charlesstreetinn

U.S.A. - MASSACHUSETTS (BOSTON)

Hotel Commonwealth
500 Commonwealth Avenue, Boston, Massachusetts 02215
Tel: +1 617 933 5000
Fax: +1 617 266 6888
Web: www.johansens.com/commonwealth

U.S.A. - MASSACHUSETTS (BOSTON)

The Lenox
61 Exeter Street at Boylston, Boston, Massachusetts 02116
Tel: +1 617 536 5300
Fax: +1 617 267 1237
Web: www.johansens.com/lenox

U.S.A. - MASSACHUSETTS (BOSTON)

Nine Zero hotel
90 Tremont Street, Boston, Massachusetts 02108
Tel: +1 617 772 5800
Fax: +1 617 772 5810
Web: www.johansens.com/ninezero

U.S.A. - MASSACHUSETTS (CAPE COD)

Chatham Bars Inn
Shore Road, Chatham, Cape Cod, Massachusetts 02633
Tel: +1 508 945 0096
Fax: +1 508 945 6785
Web: www.johansens.com/chathambarsinn

U.S.A. - MASSACHUSETTS (CAPE COD)

The Crowne Pointe Historic Inn & Spa
82 Bradford Street, Provincetown, Massachusetts 02657
Tel: +1 508 487 6767
Fax: +1 508 487 5554
Web: www.johansens.com/crownepointe

U.S.A. - MASSACHUSETTS (CAPE COD)

Wequassett Inn Resort and Golf Club
On Pleasant Bay, Chatham, Cape Cod, Massachusetts 02633
Tel: +1 508 432 5400
Fax: +1 508 430 3131
Web: www.johansens.com/wequassett

U.S.A. - MASSACHUSETTS (IPSWICH)

The Inn at Castle Hill
280 Argilla Road, Ipswich, Massachusetts 01938
Tel: +1 978 412 2555
Fax: +1 978 412 2556
Web: www.johansens.com/castlehill

U.S.A. - MASSACHUSETTS (LENOX)

Cranwell Resort, Spa & Golf Club
55 Lee Road, Route 20, Lenox, Massachusetts 01240
Tel: +1 413 637 1364
Fax: +1 413 637 4364
Web: www.johansens.com/cranwell

U.S.A. - MASSACHUSETTS (MARTHA'S VINEYARD)

Hob Knob Inn
128 Main Street, Edgartown, Massachusetts 02539
Tel: +1 508 627 9510
Fax: +1 508 627 4560
Web: www.johansens.com/hobknobinn

Mini Listings The Americas

Condé Nast Johansens are delighted to recommend 285 properties across The Americas, Atlantic, Caribbean and Pacific.
Call 0800 269 397 or see the order forms on page 425 to order guides.

U.S.A. - MASSACHUSETTS (MARTHA'S VINEYARD)

The Charlotte Inn
27 South Summer Street, Edgartown, Massachusetts 02539
Tel: +1 508 627 4151
Fax: +1 508 627 4652
Web: www.johansens.com/charlotte

U.S.A. - MASSACHUSETTS (MARTHA'S VINEYARD)

The Winnetu Inn & Resort at South Beach
31 Dunes Road, R.F.D. 270B, Edgartown, Massachusetts 02539
Tel: +1 978 443 1733
Fax: +1 978 443 0479
Web: www.johansens.com/winnetu

U.S.A. - MICHIGAN (MACKINAC ISLAND)

Hotel Iroquois on the Beach
298 Main Street, Mackinac Island, Michigan 49757
Tel: April - October +1 906 847 3321
Fax: +1 906 847 6274
Web: www.johansens.com/iroquoishotel

U.S.A. - MISSISSIPPI (JACKSON)

Fairview Inn
734 Fairview Street, Jackson, Mississippi 39202
Tel: +1 601 948 3429
Fax: +1 601 948 1203
Web: www.johansens.com/fairviewinn

U.S.A. - MISSISSIPPI (NATCHEZ)

Monmouth Plantation
36 Melrose Avenue, Natchez, Mississippi 39120
Tel: +1 601 442 5852
Fax: +1 601 446 7762
Web: www.johansens.com/monmouthplantation

U.S.A. - MISSISSIPPI (NESBIT)

Bonne Terre Country Inn
4715 Church Road West, Nesbit, Mississippi 38651
Tel: +1 662 781 5100
Fax: +1 662 781 5466
Web: www.johansens.com/bonneterre

U.S.A. - MISSISSIPPI (VICKSBURG)

Anchuca Historic Mansion & Inn
1010 First East Street, Vicksburg, Mississippi 39183
Tel: +1 601 661 0111
Fax: +1 601 661 0111
Web: www.johansens.com/anchuca

U.S.A. - MISSOURI (BRANSON)

Chateau on the Lake
415 North State Highway 265, Branson, Missouri 65616
Tel: +1 417 334 1161
Fax: +1 417 339 5566
Web: www.johansens.com/chateaulake

U.S.A. - MISSOURI (CLAYTON/ST.LOUIS)

Clayton on the Park
3025 Bonhomme Avenue, Clayton/St. Louis, Missouri 63105
Tel: +1 314 290 1500
Fax: +1 314 721 8588
Web: www.johansens.com/claytononthepark

U.S.A. - MISSOURI (KANSAS CITY)

Hotel Phillips
106 West 12th Street, Kansas City, Missouri 64105
Tel: +1 816 221 7000
Fax: +1 816 221 3477
Web: www.johansens.com/phillips

U.S.A. - MISSOURI (KANSAS CITY)

The Raphael Hotel
325 Ward Parkway, Kansas City, Missouri 64112
Tel: +1 816 756 3800
Fax: +1 816 802 2131
Web: www.johansens.com/raphael

U.S.A. - MISSOURI (RIDGEDALE)

Big Cedar Lodge
612 Devil's Pool Road, Ridgedale, Missouri 65739
Tel: +1 417 335 2777
Fax: +1 417 335 2340
Web: www.johansens.com/bigcedar

U.S.A. - MISSOURI (ST. LOUIS)

The Chase Park Plaza
212-232 North Kingshighway Boulevard, St. Louis, Missouri 63108
Tel: +1 314 633 3000
Fax: +1 314 633 1144
Web: www.johansens.com/chaseparkplaza

U.S.A. - MONTANA (BIG SKY)

The Big EZ Lodge
7000 Beaver Creek Road, Big Sky, Montana 59716
Tel: +1 406 995 7000
Fax: +1 406 995 7007
Web: www.johansens.com/bigez

U.S.A. - MONTANA (DARBY)

Triple Creek Ranch
5551 West Fork Road, Darby, Montana 59829
Tel: +1 406 821 4600
Fax: +1 406 821 4666
Web: www.johansens.com/triplecreek

U.S.A. - NEW HAMPSHIRE (JACKSON)

The Wentworth
Jackson Village, New Hampshire 03846
Tel: +1 603 383 9700
Fax: +1 603 383 4265
Web: www.johansens.com/wentworth

U.S.A. - NEW HAMPSHIRE (PLAINFIELD)

Home Hill
703 River Road, Plainfield, New Hampshire 03781
Tel: +1 603 675 6165
Fax: +1 603 675 5220
Web: www.johansens.com/homehill

U.S.A. - NEW HAMPSHIRE (WHITEFIELD)

Mountain View Grand Resort & Spa
Mountain View Road, Whitefield, New Hampshire 03598
Tel: +1 603 837 2100
Fax: +1 603 837 8884
Web: www.johansens.com/mountainview

U.S.A. - NEW MEXICO (ESPAÑOLA)

Rancho de San Juan
P.O. Box 4140, Highway 285, Española, New Mexico 87533
Tel: +1 505 753 6818
Fax: +1 505 753 6818
Web: www.johansens.com/ranchosanjuan

U.S.A. - NEW MEXICO (SANTA FE)

The Inn of The Five Graces
150 E Devargas Street, Santa Fe, New Mexico 87501
Tel: +1 505 992 0957
Fax: +1 505 955 0549
Web: www.johansens.com/fivegraces

Mini Listings The Americas

Condé Nast Johansens are delighted to recommend 285 properties across The Americas, Atlantic, Caribbean and Pacific.
Call 0800 269 397 or see the order forms on page 425 to order guides.

U.S.A. - NEW YORK (AURORA)

The Aurora Inn
391 Main Street, Aurora, New York 13026
Tel: +1 315 364 8888
Fax: +1 315 364 8887
Web: www.johansens.com/aurora

U.S.A. - NEW YORK (BANGALL)

The Inn at Bullis Hall
P.O. Box 630, Bangall (Stanfordville), New York 12506
Tel: +1 845 868 1665
Fax: +1 845 868 1441
Web: www.johansens.com/bullishall

U.S.A. - NEW YORK (BOLTON LANDING)

The Sagamore
110 Sagamore Road, Bolton Landing, New York 12814
Tel: +1 518 644 9400
Fax: +1 518 644 2851
Web: www.johansens.com/sagamore

U.S.A. - NEW YORK (BUFFALO)

The Mansion on Delaware Avenue
414 Delaware Avenue, Buffalo, New York 14202
Tel: +1 716 886 3300
Fax: +1 716 883 3923
Web: www.johansens.com/mansionondelaware

U.S.A. - NEW YORK (EAST AURORA)

Roycroft Inn
40 South Grove Street, East Aurora, New York 14052
Tel: +1 716 652 5552
Fax: +1 716 655 5345
Web: www.johansens.com/roycroftinn

U.S.A. - NEW YORK (GENEVA)

Belhurst
4069 Route 14 South, P.O. Box 609, Geneva,
New York 14456
Tel: +1 315 781 0201
Fax: +1 315 781 0201
Web: www.johansens.com/belhurst

U.S.A. - NEW YORK (LAKE PLACID)

Lake Placid Lodge
Whiteface Inn Road, New York 12946
Tel: +1 518 523 2700
Fax: +1 518 523 1124
Web: www.johansens.com/placid

U.S.A. - NEW YORK (NEW YORK CITY)

Hotel Plaza Athenee
37 East 64th Street, New York 10021
Tel: +1 212 734 9100
Fax: +1 212 772 0958
Web: www.johansens.com/athenee

U.S.A. - NEW YORK (NEW YORK CITY)

The Inn at Irving Place
56 Irving Place, New York, New York 10003
Tel: +1 212 533 4600
Fax: +1 212 533 4611
Web: www.johansens.com/irvingplace

U.S.A. - NEW YORK (NEW YORK CITY)

The Mark
Madison Avenue at East 77th Street, New York,
New York 10021
Tel: +1 212 744 4300
Fax: +1 212 744 2749
Web: www.johansens.com/themark

U.S.A. - NEW YORK (NEW YORK CITY)

Trump International Hotel
One Central Park West, New York 10023
Tel: +1 212 299 1000
Fax: +1 212 299 1150
Web: www.johansens.com/trumpintl

U.S.A. - NEW YORK (SARANAC LAKE)

The Point
Saranac Lake, New York 12983
Tel: +1 518 891 5674
Fax: +1 518 891 1152
Web: www.johansens.com/thepoint

U.S.A. - NEW YORK (TARRYTOWN)

The Castle On The Hudson
400 Benedict Avenue, Tarrytown, New York 10591
Tel: +1 914 631 1980
Fax: +1 914 631 4612
Web: www.johansens.com/hudson

U.S.A. - NEW YORK/LONG ISLAND (EAST HAMPTON)

The Baker House 1650
181 Main Street, East Hampton, New York 11937
Tel: +1 631 324 4081
Fax: +1 631 329 5931
Web: www.johansens.com/bakerhouse

U.S.A. - NEW YORK/LONG ISLAND (EAST HAMPTON)

The Mill House Inn
31 North Main Street, East Hampton, New York 11937
Tel: +1 631 324 9766
Fax: +1 631 324 9793
Web: www.johansens.com/millhouse

U.S.A. - NEW YORK/LONG ISLAND (SOUTHAMPTON)

1708 House
126 Main Street, Southampton, New York 11968
Tel: +1 631 287 1708
Fax: +1 631 287 3593
Web: www.johansens.com/1708house

U.S.A. - NORTH CAROLINA (ASHEVILLE)

Inn on Biltmore Estate
One Antler Hill Road, Asheville, North Carolina 28803
Tel: +1 828 225 1600
Fax: PLEASE SUPPLY
Web: www.johansens.com/biltimore

U.S.A. - NORTH CAROLINA (BEAUFORT)

The Cedars Inn
305 Front Street, Beaufort, North Carolina 28516
Tel: +1 252 728 7036
Fax: +1 252 728 1685
Web: www.johansens.com/cedarsinn

U.S.A. - NORTH CAROLINA (BLOWING ROCK)

Gideon Ridge Inn
202 Gideon Ridge Road, Blowing Rock,
North Carolina 28605
Tel: +1 828 295 3644
Fax: +1 828 295 4586
Web: www.johansens.com/gideonridge

U.S.A. - NORTH CAROLINA (CASHIERS)

Millstone Inn
119 Lodge Lane, Highway 64 West, Cashiers,
North Carolina 28717
Tel: +1 828 743 2737
Fax: +1 828 743 0208
Web: www.johansens.com/millstoneinn

MINI LISTINGS THE AMERICAS

Condé Nast Johansens are delighted to recommend 285 properties across The Americas, Atlantic, Caribbean and Pacific.
Call 0800 269 397 or see the order forms on page 425 to order guides.

U.S.A. - NORTH CAROLINA (DUCK)

The Sanderling
1461 Duck Road, Duck, North Carolina 27949
Tel: +1 252 261 4111
Fax: +1 252 261 1638
Web: www.johansens.com/sanderling

U.S.A. - NORTH CAROLINA (HIGHLANDS)

Old Edwards Inn and Spa
445 Main Street, Highlands, North Carolina 28741
Tel: +1 828 526 8008
Fax: +1 828 526 8301
Web: www.johansens.com/oldedwards

U.S.A. - NORTH CAROLINA (LAKE TOXAWAY)

The Greystone Inn
Greystone Lane, Lake Toxaway, North Carolina 28747
Tel: +1 828 966 4700
Fax: +1 828 862 5689
Web: www.johansens.com/greystoneinn

U.S.A. - NORTH CAROLINA (NEW BERN)

The Aerie Inn
509 Pollock Street, New Bern, North Carolina 28562
Tel: +1 252 636 5553
Fax: +1 252 514 2157
Web: www.johansens.com/aerieinn

U.S.A. - NORTH CAROLINA (PITTSBORO)

The Fearrington House
2000 Fearrington Village Center, Pittsboro, North Carolina 27312
Tel: +1 919 542 2121
Fax: +1 919 542 4202
Web: www.johansens.com/fearrington

U.S.A. - NORTH CAROLINA (RALEIGH - DURHAM)

The Siena Hotel
1505 E Franklin Street, Chapel Hill, North Carolina 27514
Tel: +1 919 929 4000
Fax: +1 919 968 8527
Web: www.johansens.com/siena

U.S.A. - NORTH CAROLINA (TRYON)

Pine Crest Inn
85 Pine Crest Lane, Tryon, North Carolina 28782
Tel: +1 828 859 9135
Fax: +1 828 859 9136
Web: www.johansens.com/pinecrestinn

U.S.A. - OHIO (CINCINNATI)

The Cincinnatian Hotel
601 Vine Street, Cincinnati, Ohio 45202-2433
Tel: +1 513 381 3000
Fax: +1 513 651 0256
Web: www.johansens.com/cincinnatian

U.S.A. - OKLAHOMA (BARTLESVILLE)

Inn at Price Tower
510 Dewey Avenue, Bartlesville, Oklahoma 74003
Tel: +1 918 336 1000
Fax: +1 918 336 7117
Web: www.johansens.com/pricetower

U.S.A. - OKLAHOMA (TULSA)

Hotel Ambassador
1345 South Main Street, Tulsa, Oklahoma 74119
Tel: +1 918 587 8200
Fax: +1 918 587 8208
Web: www.johansens.com/ambassador

U.S.A. - OREGON (ASHLAND)

The Winchester Inn & Restaurant
35 South Second Street, Ashland, Oregon 97520
Tel: +1 541 488 1113
Fax: +1 541 488 4604
Web: www.johansens.com/winchester

U.S.A. - OREGON (CANNON BEACH)

The Stephanie Inn
2740 South Pacific, P.O. Box 219, Cannon Beach, Oregon 97110
Tel: +1 503 436 2221
Fax: +1 503 436 9711
Web: www.johansens.com/stephanieinn

U.S.A. - OREGON (GOLD BEACH)

Tu Tu' Tun Lodge
96550 North Bank Rogue, Gold Beach, Oregon 97444
Tel: +1 541 247 6664
Fax: +1 541 247 0672
Web: www.johansens.com/tututun

U.S.A. - OREGON (PORTLAND)

The Benson Hotel
309 Southwest Broadway, Portland, Oregon 97205
Tel: +1 503 228 2000
Fax: +1 503 471 3920
Web: www.johansens.com/benson

U.S.A. - OREGON (PORTLAND)

The Heathman Hotel
1001 S.W. Broadway, Portland, Oregon 97205
Tel: +1 503 241 4100
Fax: +1 503 790 4100
Web: www.johansens.com/heatherman

U.S.A. - PENNSYLVANIA (BRADFORD)

Glendorn
1000 Glendorn Drive, Bradford, Pennsylvania 16701
Tel: +1 814 362 6511
Fax: +1 814 368 9923
Web: www.johansens.com/glendorn

U.S.A. - PENNSYLVANIA (FARMINGTON)

Nemacolin Woodlands
1001 LaFayette Drive, Farmington, Pennsylvania 15437
Tel: +1 724 329 8555
Fax: +1 724 329 6947
Web: www.johansens.com/nemacolin

U.S.A. - PENNSYLVANIA (HERSHEY)

Hershey Resort Hotel & Spa
100 West Hershey park Drive, Hershey, Pennsylvania 17033
Tel: +1 717 533 2171
Fax: +1 717 534 3165
Web: www.johansens.com/hersheyresort

U.S.A. - PENNSYLVANIA (LEOLA)

Leola Village Inn & Suites
38 Deborah Drive, Route 23, Leola, Pennsylvania 17540
Tel: +1 717 656 7002
Fax: +1 717 656 7648
Web: www.johansens.com/leolavillage

U.S.A. - PENNSYLVANIA (PHILADELPHIA)

Rittenhouse Square European Boutique
1715 Rittenhouse Square, Philadelphia, Pennsylvania 19103
Tel: +1 215 546 6500
Fax: +1 215 546 8787
Web: www.johansens.com/rittenhouse

MINI LISTINGS THE AMERICAS

Condé Nast Johansens are delighted to recommend 285 properties across The Americas, Atlantic, Caribbean and Pacific.
Call 0800 269 397 or see the order forms on page 425 to order guides.

U.S.A. - PENNSYLVANIA (SKYTOP)

Skytop Lodge
One Skytop, Skytop, Pennsylvania 18357
Tel: +1 800 345 7759
Fax: +1 570 595 8917
Web: www.johansens.com/skytop

U.S.A. - RHODE ISLAND (BLOCK ISLAND)

The Atlantic Inn
P.o. Box 1788, Block Island, Rhode Island 02807
Tel: +1 401 466 5883
Fax: +1 401 466 5678
Web: www.johansens.com/atlanticinn

U.S.A. - RHODE ISLAND (NEWPORT)

Chanler at Cliff Walk
117 Memorial Boulevard, Newport, Rhode Island 02840
Tel: +1 401 847 1300
Fax: +1 401 847 3620
Web: www.johansens.com/chanler

U.S.A. - RHODE ISLAND (NEWPORT)

La Farge Perry House
24 Kay Street, Newport, Rhode Island 02840
Tel: +1 877 736 1100
Web: www.johansens.com/lafargeperry

U.S.A. - RHODE ISLAND (PROVIDENCE)

Hotel Providence
311 Westminster Street, Providence, Rhode Island 02903
Tel: +1 401 861 8000
Fax: +1 401 861 8002
Web: www.johansens.com/providence

U.S.A. - SOUTH CAROLINA (CHARLESTON)

The Boardwalk Inn at Wild Dunes Resort
5757 Palm Boulevard, Isle of Palms, South Carolina 29451
Tel: +1 843 886 6000
Fax: +1 843 886 2916
Web: www.johansens.com/boardwalk

U.S.A. - SOUTH CAROLINA (CHARLESTON)

Charleston Harbor Resort & Marina
20 Patriots Point Road, Charleston, South Carolina 29464
Tel: +1 843 856 0028
Fax: +1 843 856 8333
Web: www.johansens.com/charlestonharbor

U.S.A. - SOUTH CAROLINA (CHARLESTON)

Woodlands Resort & Inn
125 Parsons Road, Summerville, South Carolina 29483
Tel: +1 843 875 2600
Fax: +1 843 875 2603
Web: www.johansens.com/woodlandssc

U.S.A. - SOUTH CAROLINA (KIAWAH ISLAND)

The Sanctuary at Kiawah Island
1 Sanctuary Beach Drive, Kiawah Island,
South Carolina 29455
Tel: +1 843 768 6000
Fax: +1 843 768 5150
Web: www.johansens.com/sanctuary

U.S.A. - SOUTH CAROLINA (PAWLEYS ISLAND)

Litchfield Plantation
Kings River Road, Box 290, Pawleys Island,
South Carolina 29585
Tel: +1 843 237 9121
Fax: +1 843 237 1041
Web: www.johansens.com/litchfieldplantation

U.S.A. - SOUTH CAROLINA (TRAVELERS REST)

La Bastide
10 Road Of Vines, Travelers Rest, South Carolina 29690
Tel: +1 864 836 8463
Fax: +1 864 836 4820
Web: www.johansens.com/labastide

U.S.A. - TENNESSEE (WALLAND)

Blackberry Farm
1471 West Millers Cove Road, Walland, Great Smoky Mountains, Tennessee 37886
Tel: +1 865 380 2260
Fax: +1 865 681 7753
Web: www.johansens.com/blackberryfarm

U.S.A. - TEXAS (AUSTIN)

The Mansion at Judges' Hill
1900 Rio Grande, Austin, Texas 78705
Tel: +1 512 495 1800
Fax: +1 512 691 4461
Web: www.johansens.com/judgeshill

U.S.A. - TEXAS (GLEN ROSE)

Rough Creek Lodge
P.O. Box 2400, Glen Rose, Texas 76043
Tel: +1 254 965 3700
Fax: +1 254 918 2570
Web: www.johansens.com/roughcreek

U.S.A. - TEXAS (GRANBURY)

The Inn on Lake Granbury
205 West Doyle Street, Granbury, Texas 76048
Tel: +1 817 573 0046
Fax: +1 817 573 0047
Web: www.johansens.com/lakegranbury

U.S.A. - TEXAS (HOUSTON)

The Lancaster Hotel
701 Texas Avenue, Houston, Texas 77002
Tel: +1 713 228 9500
Fax: +1 713 223 4528
Web: www.johansens.com/lancaster

U.S.A. - TEXAS (SAN ANTONIO)

The Beauregard House
215 Beauregard Street, San Antonio, Texas 78204
Tel: +1 210 222 1198
Fax: +1 210 222 9338
Web: www.johansens.com/beauregard

U.S.A. - UTAH (MOAB)

Sorrel River Ranch Resort & Spa
Highway 128, Mile 17, P.O. Box K, Moab, Utah 84532
Tel: +1 435 259 4642
Fax: +1 435 259 3016
Web: www.johansens.com/sorrelriver

U.S.A. - VERMONT (KILLINGTON)

Mountain Top Inn & Resort
195 Mountain Top Road, Chittenden, Vermont 05737
Tel: +1 802 483 2311
Fax: +1 802 483 6373
Web: www.johansens.com/mountaintopinn

U.S.A. - VERMONT (KILLINGTON)

Red Clover Inn
Woodward Road, Mendon, Vermont 05701
Tel: +1 802 775 2290
Fax: +1 802 773 0594
Web: www.johansens.com/redclover

Mini Listings The Americas

Condé Nast Johansens are delighted to recommend 285 properties across The Americas, Atlantic, Caribbean and Pacific.
Call 0800 269 397 or see the order forms on page 425 to order guides.

U.S.A. - VERMONT (WOODSTOCK)

Woodstock Inn & Resort

Fourteen The Green, Woodstock, Vermont 05091-1298
Tel: +1 802 457 1100
Fax: +1 802 457 6699
Web: www.johansens.com/woodstockinn

U.S.A. - VIRGINIA (CHARLOTTESVILLE)

200 South Street Inn

200 South Street, Charlottesville, Virginia 22902
Tel: +1 434 979 0200
Fax: +1 434 979 4403
Web: www.johansens.com/200southstreetinn

U.S.A. - VIRGINIA (STAUNTON)

Frederick House

28 North New Street, Staunton, Virginia 24401
Tel: + 1 540 885 4220
Fax: +1 540 885 5180
Web: www.johansens.com/frederickhouse

U.S.A. - VIRGINIA (WASHINGTON METROPOLITAN AREA)

Morrison House Hotel

116 South Alfred Street, Alexandria, Virginia 22314
Tel: +1 703 838 8000
Fax: +1 703 684 6283
Web: www.johansens.com/morrisonhouse

U.S.A. - WASHINGTON (BELLINGHAM)

The Chrysalis Inn & Spa

804 10th Street, Bellingham, Washington 98225
Tel: +1 360 756 1005
Fax: +1 360 647 0342
Web: www.johansens.com/chrysalis

U.S.A. - WASHINGTON (FRIDAY HARBOR)

Friday Harbor House

130 West Street, Friday Harbor, Washington 98250
Tel: +1 360 378 8455
Fax: +1 360 378 8453
Web: www.johansens.com/fridayharbor

U.S.A. - WASHINGTON (KIRKLAND)

Woodmark Hotel on Lake Washington

1200 Carillon Point, Kirkland, Washington 98033
Tel: +1 425 822 3700
Fax: +1 425 822 3699
Web: www.johansens.com/woodmark

U.S.A. - WASHINGTON (LEAVENWORTH)

Run of the River

9308 E. Leavenworth Road, Leavenworth,
Washington 98826
Tel: +1 509 548 7171
Fax: 1 509 548 7547
Web: www.johansens.com/runoftheriver

U.S.A. - WASHINGTON (QUINCY)

Cave B Inn at Sagecliffe

344 Silica Road N.W., Quincy, Washington 98848
Tel: +1 509 785 2283
Fax: +1 509 785 3670
Web: www.johansens.com/cavebinn

U.S.A. - WASHINGTON (SEATTLE)

Sorrento Hotel

900 Madison Street, Seattle, Washington 98104-1297
Tel: +1 206 622 6400
Fax: +1 206 343 6155
Web: www.johansens.com/sorrento

U.S.A. - WASHINGTON (SPOKANE)

The Davenport Hotel and Tower

10 South Post Street, Spokane, Washington 99201
Tel: +1 509 455 8888
Fax: +1 509 624 4455
Web: www.johansens.com/davenport

U.S.A. - WASHINGTON (UNION)

Alderbrook Resort & Spa

10 East Alderbrook Drive, Union, Washington 98592
Tel: +1 360 898 2200
Fax: +1 360 898 4610
Web: www.johansens.com/alderbrook

U.S.A. - WASHINGTON (WOODINVILLE)

The Herbfarm

14590 North East 145th Street, Woodinville,
Washington 98072
Tel: +1 425 485 5300
Fax: +1 425 424 2925
Web: www.johansens.com/herbfarm

U.S.A. - WASHINGTON (WOODINVILLE)

Willows Lodge

14580 N.E. 145th Street, Woodinville, Washington 98072
Tel: +1 425 424 3900
Fax: +1 425 424 2585
Web: www.johansens.com/willowslodge

U.S.A. - WISCONSIN (CHETEK)

Canoe Bay

P.O. Box 28, Chetek, Wisconsin 54728
Tel: +1 715 924 4594
Fax: +1 715 924 2078
Web: www.johansens.com/canoebay

U.S.A. - WYOMING (CHEYENNE)

Nagle Warren Mansion

222 East 17Th Street, Cheyenne, Wyoming 82001
Tel: +1 307 637 3333
Fax: +1 307 638 6879
Web: www.johansens.com/naglewarrenmansion

U.S.A. - WYOMING (DUBOIS)

Brooks Lake Lodge

458 Brooks Lake Road, Dubois, Wyoming 82513
Tel: +1 307 455 2121
Fax: +1 307 455 2221
Web: www.johansens.com/brookslake

U.S.A. - WYOMING (GRAND TETON NATIONAL PARK)

Jenny Lake Lodge

Inner Park Loop Road, Grand Teton National Park,
Wyoming 83013
Tel: +1 307 543 3300
Fax: +1 307 543 3358
Web: www.johansens.com/jennylake

U.S.A. - WYOMING (JACKSON HOLE)

Spring Creek Ranch

1800 Spirit Dance Road, Jackson Hole, Wyoming 83001
Tel: +1 307 733 8833
Fax: +1 307 733 1524
Web: www.johansens.com/springcreek

Mini Listings The Americas

Condé Nast Johansens are delighted to recommend 285 properties across The Americas, Atlantic, Caribbean and Pacific.
Call 0800 269 397 or see the order forms on page 425 to order guides.

Recommendations in Mexico

MEXICO - BAJA CALIFORNIA SUR (SAN JOSE DEL CABO)

Casa Natalia

Blvd. Mijares 4, San Jose Del Cabo, Baja California Sur 23400
Tel: +52 624 14 251 00
Fax: +52 624 14251 10
Web: www.johansens.com/casanatalia

MEXICO - BAJA CALIFORNIA SUR (SAN JOSE DEL CABO)

One & Only Palmilla

Km 7.5 Carretera Transpeninsular, San Jose Del Cabo, Baja California Sur 23400
Tel: +52 624 146 7000
Fax: +52 624 146 7001
Web: www.johansens.com/oneandonlypalmilla

MEXICO - COLIMA (COLIMA)

Hacienda de San Antonio

Municipio de Comala S/n, Colima 28450
Tel: +52 312 314 9554
Fax: +52 312 313 4254
Web: www.johansens.com/sanantonio

MEXICO - DISTRITO FEDERAL (MEXICO CITY)

Casa Vieja

Eugenio Sue 45, Polanco 11560, Distrito Federal
Tel: +52 55 82 82 0067
Fax: +52 55 52 81 3780
Web: www.johansens.com/casavieja

MEXICO - ESTADO DE MEXICO (MALINALCO)

Casa Limon

Rio Lerma 103, Barrio de Santa María, Malinalco, Estado de Mexico 524040
Tel: +52 714 702 56
Fax: +52 714 147 0619
Web: www.johansens.com/casalimon

MEXICO - GUANAJUATO (GUANAJUATO)

Quinta Las Acacias

Paseo de la Presa 168, Guanajuato, Guanajuato 36000
Tel: +52 473 731 1517
Fax: +52 473 731 1862
Web: www.johansens.com/acacias

MEXICO - GUANAJUATO (SAN MIGUEL DE ALLENDE)

La Puertecita Boutique Hotel

Santo Domingo 75 Col. Los Arcos, San Miguel de Allende, Guanajuato 37740
Tel: +52 415 152 5011
Fax: +52 415 152 5505
Web: www.johansens.com/lapuertacita

MEXICO - GUERRERO (ZIHUATANEJO)

Hotel Villa Del Sol

Playa La Ropa S/N, Zihuatanejo, Guerrero 40880
Tel: +52 755 555 5500
Fax: +52 755 554 2758
Web: www.johansens.com/villadelsol

MEXICO - JALISCO (PUERTA VALLARTA / COSTA ALEGRE)

Las Alamandas Resort

Carretera Barra de Navidad - Puerto Vallarta km 83.5, Col. Quemaro, Jalisco 48980
Tel: +52 322 285 5500
Fax: +52 322 285 5027
Web: www.johansens.com/lasalamandas

MEXICO - JALISCO (PUERTO VALLARTA)

Hacienda San Angel

Miramar 336, Col. Centro Puerto Vallarta, Jalisco 48300
Tel: +52 322 222 2692
Fax: +52 322 223 194
Web: www.johansens.com/sanangel

MEXICO - MICHOACÁN (MORELIA)

Hotel Los Juaninos

Morelos Sur 39, Centro, Morelia, Michoacán 58000
Tel: +52 443 312 00 36
Fax: +52 443 312 00 36
Web: www.johansens.com/juaninos

MEXICO - MICHOACÁN (MORELIA)

Hotel Virrey de Mendoza

Av. Madero Pte. 310, Centro Histórico, Morelia, Michoacán 58000
Tel: +52 44 33 12 08 59
Fax: +52 44 33 12 67 19
Web: www.johansens.com/hotelvirrey

MEXICO - MICHOACÁN (MORELIA)

Villa Montaña Hotel & Spa

Patzimba 201, Vista Bella, Morelia, Michoacán 58090
Tel: +52 443 314 02 31
Fax: +52 443 315 14 23
Web: www.johansens.com/montana

MEXICO - NAYARIT (NUEVO VALLARTA)

Grand Velas All Suites & Spa Resort

Av. Cocoteros 98 Sur, Nuevo Vallarta, Nayarit 63735
Tel: +52 322 226 8000
Fax: +52 322 297 2005
Web: www.johansens.com/grandvelas

MEXICO - OAXACA (OAXACA)

Casa Oaxaca

Calle García Vigil 407, Centro, Oaxaca, Oaxaca 68000
Tel: +52 951 514 4173
Fax: +52 951516 4412
Web: www.johansens.com/oaxaca

MEXICO - OAXACA (OAXACA)

Hacienda Los Laureles - Spa

Hidalgo 21, Oaxaca, Oaxaca 68020
Tel: +52 951 501 5300
Fax: +52 951 501 5301
Web: www.johansens.com/laureles

MEXICO - PUEBLA (CHOLULA)

La Quinta Luna

3 sur 702, San Pedro Cholula, Puebla 72760
Tel: +52 222 247 8915
Fax: +52 222 247 8916
Web: www.johansens.com/quintaluna

MEXICO - QUERÉTARO (QUERÉTARO)

La Casa de la Marquesa

Madero 41, Querétaro, Centro Histórico 7600
Tel: +52 442 212 0092
Fax: +52 442 212 0098
Web: www.johansens.com/marquesa

MEXICO - QUINTANA ROO (ISLA MUJERES)

Casa De Los Sueños

Lote 9A y 9B, A 200 MTS de Garrafon, Fracc Turquesa, Isla Mujeres, Quintana Roo 77400
Tel: +52 998 877 0651
Fax: +52 998 877 0708
Web: www.johansens.com/lossuenos

Mini Listings The Americas

Condé Nast Johansens are delighted to recommend 285 properties across The Americas, Atlantic, Caribbean and Pacific.
Call 0800 269 397 or see the order forms on page 425 to order guides.

MEXICO - SONORA (ALAMOS)

Hacienda de los Santos Resort and Spa
Calle Molina 8, Centro, Alamos, Sonora 85760
Tel: +52 647 428 0222
Fax: +52 647 428 0367
Web: www.johansens.com/lossantos

MEXICO - YUCATÁN (MÉRIDA)

Hacienda Xcanatun - Casa de Piedra
Carretera Mérida-Progreso, Km 12, Mérida, Yucatán 97300
Tel: +52 999 941 0273
Fax: +52 999 941 0319
Web: www.johansens.com/xcanatun

Recommendations in Central America

BELIZE - (SOUTH STANN CREEK)

Kanantik Reef & Jungle Resort
South Stann Creek, Belize
Tel: +501 520 8048
Fax: +501 520 8089
Web: www.johansens.com/kanantik

COSTA RICA - GUANACASTE (PLAYA CONCHAL)

Paradisus Playa Conchal
P.O. Box 232-5150, Guanacaste, Playa Conchal, Costa Rica
Tel: +506 654 4123
Fax: +506 654 4181
Web: www.johansens.com/paradisusplayaconchal

HONDURAS - ATLÁNTIDA (LA CEIBA)

The Lodge at Pico Bonito
A. P. 710, La Ceiba, Atlántida, C. P. 31101
Tel: +504 440 0388
Fax: +504 440 0468
Web: www.johansens.com/picobonito

Recommendations in South America

ARGENTINA - BUENOS AIRES (CAPITAL FEDERAL)

1555 Malabia House
Malabia 1555, Buenos Aires, C1414 DME
Tel: +54 11 4832 3345
Fax: +54 11 4832 3345
Web: www.johansens.com/malabiahouse

ARGENTINA - RIO NEGRO (BARILOCHE)

Hotel Pire-Hue ski in & ski out
Hotel Base Cerro Catedral, Bariloche R8400
Tel: +54 11 4807 8200
Fax: +54 29 4446 0039
Web: www.johansens.com/hotelpirehue

BRAZIL - BAHIA (PRAIA DO FORTE)

Praia do Forte Eco Resort & Thalasso Spa
Avenida do Farol, S/N Praia do Forte -
Mata de São João, Bahia
Tel: +55 71 36 76 40 00
Fax: +55 71 36 76 11 12
Web: www.johansens.com/praiadoforte

BRAZIL - BAHIA (SANTA CRUZ CABRÁLIA)

Toca do Marlin
Estrada BA-001 km 40.5, Santa Cruz Cabralia,
Bahia 45807-000
Tel: +55 73 36 71 5009
Fax: +55 73 36 71 5009
Web: www.johansens.com/tocadomarlin

BRAZIL - MINAS GERIAS (TIRADENTES)

Solar da Ponte
Praça das Mercês S/N, Tiradentes, Minas Gerais 36325-000
Tel: +55 32 33 55 12 55
Fax: +55 32 33 55 12 01
Web: www.johansens.com/solardaponte

BRAZIL - RIO DE JANEIRO (ANGRA DOS REIS)

Sítio do Lobo
Ponta do Lobo, Ilha Grande, Angra dos Reis, Rio de Janeiro
Tel: +55 21 2227 4138
Fax: +55 21 2267 7841
Web: www.johansens.com/sitiodolobo

BRAZIL - RIO DE JANEIRO (BÚZIOS)

Casas Brancas Boutique-Hotel & Spa
Alto do Humaitá 10, Armação dos Búzios, Rio de Janeiro
Tel: +55 22 2623 1458
Fax: +55 22 2623 2147
Web: www.johansens.com/casasbracas

BRAZIL - RIO DE JANEIRO (BÚZIOS)

Glenzhaus Lodge
Rua 1 - Quadra F - Lote 27/28, Armação dos Búzios,
Rio de Janeiro 28950-000
Tel: +55 21 2239 9933
Fax: +55 21 2274 1948
Web: www.johansens.com/glenzhaus

BRAZIL - RIO DE JANEIRO (MANGARATIBA)

Hotel Portobello Resort & Safari
Rodovia Rio-Santos, Km 438, Mangaratiba, Rio de Janeiro
23860-000
Tel: +55 21 27 89 80 00
Fax: +55 21 26 89 31 00
Web: www.johansens.com/portobelloresort

BRAZIL - RIO DE JANEIRO (PARATY)

Pousada Porto Imperial
Rua Tenente Francisco Antônio, S/N Paraty,
Rio de Janeiro 23970-000
Tel: +55 24 33 71 23 23
Fax: +55 24 33 71 21 11
Web: www.johansens.com/pousadaportoimperial

BRAZIL - RIO DE JANEIRO (PETRÓPOLIS)

Tankamana EcoResort
Estrada Julio Capua, S/N Vale do Cuiaba,
Itaipava - Petrópolis, Rio de Janeiro 25745-050
Tel: +55 24 2222 9181
Fax: +55 24 2222 9181
Web: www.johansens.com/tankamana

BRAZIL - RIO DE JANEIRO (RIO DE JANEIRO)

Hotel Marina All Suites
Av. Delfim Moreira, 696, Praia do Leblon,
Rio de Janeiro 22441-000
Tel: +55 21 2172 1001
Fax: +55 21 2172 1110
Web: www.johansens.com/marinaallsuites

BRAZIL - SÃO PAULO (CAMPOS DO JORDÃO)

Hotel Frontenac
Av. Dr. Paulo Ribas, 295 Capivari,
Campos do Jordão 12460-000
Tel: +55 12 3669 1000
Fax: +55 12 3669 1009
Web: www.johansens.com/frontenac

Mini Listings Atlantic / Caribbean

Condé Nast Johansens are delighted to recommend 285 properties across The Americas, Atlantic, Caribbean and Pacific.
Call 0800 269 397 or see the order forms on page 425 to order guides.

PERU - LIMA PROVINCIAS (YAUYOS)

Refugios Del Peru - Viñak Reichraming
Santiago de Viñak, Yauyos, Lima
Tel: +51 1 421 6952
Fax: +51 1 421 8476
Web: www.johansens.com/refugiosdelperu

ATLANTIC - BERMUDA (WARWICK)

Surf Side Beach Club
90 South Shore Road, Warwick
Tel: +1 441 236 7100
Fax: +1 441 236 9765
Web: www.johansens.com/surfside

Recommendations in the Atlantic

ATLANTIC - BAHAMAS (GRAND BAHAMA ISLAND)

Old Bahama Bay Resort
West End, Grand Bahama Island, Bahamas
Tel: +1 242 350 6500
Fax: +1 242 346 6546
Web: www.johansens.com/oldbahamabay

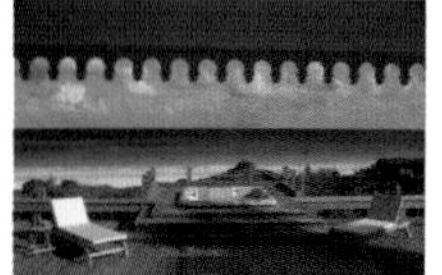

ATLANTIC - BAHAMAS (HARBOUR ISLAND)

Pink Sands
Chapel Street, Harbour Island
Tel: +1 242 333 2030
Fax: +1 242 333 2060
Web: www.johansens.com/pinksands

ATLANTIC - BERMUDA (DEVONSHIRE)

Ariel Sands
34 South Shore Road, Devonshire
Tel: +1 441 236 1010
Fax: +1 441 236 0087
Web: www.johansens.com/arielsands

ATLANTIC - BERMUDA (HAMILTON)

Rosedon Hotel
P.O. Box Hm 290, Hamilton Hmax
Tel: +1 441 295 1640
Fax: +1 441 295 5904
Web: www.johansens.com/rosedonhotel

ATLANTIC - BERMUDA (HAMILTON)

Waterloo House
P.O. Box H.M. 333, Hamilton H.M. B.X., Bermuda
Tel: +1 441 295 4480
Fax: +1 441 295 2585
Web: www.johansens.com/waterloohouse

ATLANTIC - BERMUDA (PAGET)

Horizons & Cottages
33 South Shore Road, Paget, P.G.04, Bermuda
Tel: +1 441 236 0048
Fax: +1 441 236 1981
Web: www.johansens.com/horizonscottages

ATLANTIC - BERMUDA (SOMERSET)

Cambridge Beaches
Kings Point, Somerset
Tel: +1 441 234 0331
Fax: +1 441 234 3352
Web: www.johansens.com/cambridgebeaches

ATLANTIC - BERMUDA (SOUTHAMPTON)

The Reefs
56 South Shore Road, Southampton
Tel: +1 441 238 0222
Fax: +1 441 238 8372
Web: www.johansens.com/thereefs

Recommendations in the Caribbean

CARIBBEAN - ANGUILLA (MAUNDAYS BAY)

Cap Juluca
Maundays Bay, Anguilla
Tel: +1 264 497 6666
Fax: +1 264 497 6617
Web: www.johansens.com/capjuluca

CARIBBEAN - ANTIGUA (ST. JOHN'S)

Blue Waters
P.O. Box 256, St. John's, Antigua
Tel: +44 870 360 12455
Fax: +44 870 360 1246
Web: www.johansens.com/bluewaters

CARIBBEAN - ANTIGUA (ST. JOHN'S)

Curtain Bluff
P.O. Box 288, Antigua
Tel: +1 268 462 8400
Fax: +1 268 462 8409
Web: www.johansens.com/curtainbluff

CARIBBEAN - ANTIGUA (ST. JOHN'S)

Galley Bay
Five Islands, P.O. Box 305, St. John's, Antigua
Tel: +1 954 481 8787
Fax: +1 954 481 1661
Web: www.johansens.com/galleybay

CARIBBEAN - ANTIGUA (ST. JOHN'S)

The Inn at English Harbour
P.o. Box 187, St. John's, Antigua
Tel: +1 268 460 1014
Fax: +1 268 460 1603
Web: www.johansens.com/innatenglishharbour

CARIBBEAN - BARBADOS (CHRIST CHURCH)

Little Arches
Enterprise Beach Road, Christ Church, Barbados
Tel: +1 246 420 4689
Fax: +1 246 418 0207
Web: www.johansens.com/littlearches

CARIBBEAN - BARBADOS (ST. JAMES)

Coral Reef Club
St. James, Barbados
Tel: +1 246 422 2372
Fax: +1 246 422 1776
Web: www.johansens.com/coralreefclub

CARIBBEAN - BARBADOS (ST. JAMES)

Lone Star
Mount Standfast, St. James, Barbados
Tel: +1 246 419 0599
Fax: +1 246 419 0597
Web: www.johansens.com/lonestar

Mini Listings Caribbean

Condé Nast Johansens are delighted to recommend 285 properties across The Americas, Atlantic, Caribbean and Pacific.
Call 0800 269 397 or see the order forms on page 425 to order guides.

CARIBBEAN - BARBADOS (ST. JAMES)

The Sandpiper
Holetown, St. James, Barbados
Tel: +1 246 422 2251
Fax: +1 246 422 0900
Web: www.johansens.com/sandpiper

CARIBBEAN - BARBADOS (ST. PETER)

Little Good Harbour
Shermans, St. Peter, Barbados
Tel: +1 246 439 3000
Fax: +1 246 439 2020
Web: www.johansens.com/goodharbour

CARIBBEAN - BONAIRE

Harbour Village Beach Club
Kaya Gobernador N. Debrot No. 71, Bonaire, Netherland Antilles
Tel: +1 305 567 9509
Fax: +1 305 648 0699
Web: www.johansens.com/harbourvillage

CARIBBEAN - BRITISH VIRGIN ISLANDS (TORTOLA)

Long Bay Beach Resort & Villas
Long Bay, Tortola, British Virgin Islands
Tel: +1 954 481 8787
Fax: +1 954 481 1661
Web: www.johansens.com/longbay

CARIBBEAN - CURAÇAO (WILLEMSTAD)

Avila Beach Hotel
Penstraat 130, Willemstad, Curaçao, Netherlands Antilles
Tel: +599 9 461 4377
Fax: +599 9 461 1493
Web: www.johansens.com/avilabeach

CARIBBEAN - GRENADA (ST. GEORGE'S)

Spice Island Beach Resort
Grand Anse Beach, P.O. Box 6, St. George's, Grenada
Tel: +1 473 444 4423/4258
Fax: +1 473 444 4807
Web: www.johansens.com/spiceisland

CARIBBEAN - JAMAICA (MONTEGO BAY)

Half Moon
Montego Bay, Jamaica
Tel: +1 876 953 2211
Fax: +1 876 953 2731
Web: www.johansens.com/halfmoongolf

CARIBBEAN - JAMAICA (MONTEGO BAY)

Round Hill Hotel and Villas
P.O. Box 64, Montego Bay, Jamaica
Tel: +1 876 956 7050
Fax: +1 876 956 7505
Web: www.johansens.com/roundhill

CARIBBEAN - JAMAICA (MONTEGO BAY)

Tryall Club
P.O. Box 1206, Montego Bay, Jamaica
Tel: +1 800 238 5290
Fax: +1 876 956 5673
Web: www.johansens.com/tryallclub

CARIBBEAN - JAMAICA (OCHO RIOS)

Sans Souci Resort & Spa
P.O. Box 103, Ocho Rios, St. Ann, Jamaica
Tel: +1 876 994 1206
Fax: +1 876 994 1544
Web: www.johansens.com/sanssouci

CARIBBEAN - MARTINIQUE (LE FRANCOIS)

Cap Est Lagoon Resort & Spa
97240 Le François, Martinique
Tel: +596 596 54 80 80
Fax: +596 596 54 96 00
Web: www.johansens.com/capest

CARIBBEAN - NEVIS (CHARLESTOWN)

The Hermitage
Figtree Parish, P.O. Box 497, Charlestown, Nevis
Tel: +1 869 469 3477
Fax: +1 869 469 2481
Web: www.johansens.com/hermitagenevis

CARIBBEAN - SAINT-BARTHÉLEMY (GUSTAVIA)

Carl Gustaf Hotel
BP 700, Rue des Normands, Gustavia, 97099 Saint-Barthélemy
Tel: +590 590 297 900
Fax: +590 590 278 237
Web: www.johansens.com/carlgustaf

CARIBBEAN - ST. LUCIA (CASTRIES)

The Body Holiday at LeSport
Cariblue Beach, Castries, St. Lucia
Tel: +1 758 457 7800
Fax: +1 758 450 0368
Web: www.johansens.com/lesport

CARIBBEAN - ST. LUCIA (CASTRIES)

Windjammer Landing Villa Beach Resort & Spa
Labrelotte Bay, Gros Islet, St. Lucia
Tel: +1 954 481 8787
Fax: +1 954 481 1661
Web: www.johansens.com/windjammerlanding

CARIBBEAN - ST. LUCIA (SOUFRIÈRE)

Anse Chastanet
Soufrière, St. Lucia
Tel: +1 758 459 7000
Fax: +1 758 459 7700
Web: www.johansens.com/ansechastanet

CARIBBEAN - ST. LUCIA (SOUFRIÈRE)

Ladera Resort
P.O. Box 225, Soufrière, St. Lucia
Tel: +1 758 459 7323
Fax: +1 758 459 5156
Web: www.johansens.com/ladera

CARIBBEAN - THE GRENADINES (MUSTIQUE)

Firefly
Mustique Island, St. Vincent & The Grenadines
Tel: +1 784 488 8414
Fax: +1 784 488 8514
Web: www.johansens.com/firefly

CARIBBEAN - THE GRENADINES (PALM ISLAND)

Palm Island
St. Vincent & The Grenadines
Tel: +1 954 481 8787
Fax: +1 954 481 1661
Web: www.johansens.com/palmisland

CARIBBEAN - TURKS & CAICOS (PROVIDENCIALES)

Grace Bay Club
P.O. Box 128, Providenciales, Turks & Caicos
Tel: +1 649 946 5050
Fax: +1 649 946 5758
Web: www.johansens.com/gracebayclub

Mini Listings Caribbean / Pacific

Condé Nast Johansens are delighted to recommend 285 properties across The Americas, Atlantic, Caribbean and Pacific.
Call 0800 269 397 or see the order forms on page 425 to order guides.

CARIBBEAN - TURKS & CAICOS (PROVIDENCIALES)

Parrot Cay

P.O. Box 164, Providenciales, Turks & Caicos
Tel: +1 649 946 7788
Fax: +1 649 946 7789
Web: www.johansens.com/parrotcay

CARIBBEAN - TURKS & CAICOS (PROVIDENCIALES)

Point Grace

P.O. Box 700, Providenciales, Turks & Caicos Islands
Tel: +1 649 946 5096
Fax: +1 649 946 5097
Web: www.johansens.com/pointgrace

CARIBBEAN - TURKS & CAICOS (PROVIDENCIALES)

Turks & Caicos Club

P.O. Box 687, Providenciales, Turks & Caicos
Tel: +1 649 946 5800
Fax: +1 649 946 5858
Web: www.johansens.com/turksandcaicos

Recommendations in the Pacific

PACIFIC - FIJI ISLANDS (DAVUI ISLAND)

Royal Davui

P.O. Box 3171, Lami, Fiji Islands
Tel: +679 330 7090
Fax: +679 331 1500
Web: www.johansens.com/royaldavui

PACIFIC - FIJI ISLANDS (LABASA)

Nukubati Island

P.O. Box 1928, Labasa, Fiji Islands
Tel: +61 2 93888 196
Fax: +61 2 93888 204
Web: www.johansens.com/nukubati

PACIFIC - FIJI ISLANDS (LAUTOKA)

Blue Lagoon Cruises

183 Vitogo Parade, Lautoka, Fiji Islands
Tel: +679 6661 622
Fax: +679 6664 098
UK Phone: 020 8544 1602
Web: www.johansens.com/bluelagooncruises

PACIFIC - FIJI ISLANDS (QAMEA ISLAND)

Qamea Resort & Spa

P.A. Matei, Tajeuni, Fiji Islands
Tel: +679 888 0220
Fax: +679 888 0092
Web: www.johansens.com/qamea

PACIFIC - FIJI ISLANDS (TOBERUA ISLAND)

Toberua Island Resort

P.O. Box 3332, Nausori, Fiji Islands
Tel: +679 347 2777
Fax: +679 347 2888
Web: www.johansens.com/toberuaisland

PACIFIC - FIJI ISLANDS (YASAWA ISLAND)

Yasawa Island Resort

P.O. Box 10128, Nadi Airport, Nadi, Fiji Islands
Tel: +679 672 2266
Fax: +679 672 4456
Web: www.johansens.com/yasawaisland

PACIFIC - FIJI ISLANDS (SAVU SAVU)

Jean-Michel Cousteau Fiji Islands Resort

Lesiaceva Point, Savu Savu, Fiji Islands
Tel: +415 788 5794
Fax: +415 788 0150
Web: www.johansens.com/jean-michelcousteau

PACIFIC - SAMOA (APIA)

Aggie Grey's Hotel

P.O. Box 67, Apia, Samoa
Tel: +685 228 80
Fax: +685 236 26 or 685 23203
Web: www.johansens.com/aggiegreys

PACIFIC - SAMOA (APIA)

Aggie Grey's Lagoon Beach Resort & Spa

P.O. Box 3267, Apia, Samoa
Tel: +685 45611
Fax: +685 45626
Web: www.johansens.com/aggiegreyslagoon

Index by Property

Index by Property

▼

Holbeck Ghyll Country House Hotel ..... Ambleside 62

▼

Inverlochy Castle ..... Fort William 335

▼

Mill End ..... Chagford 86

Index by Location

London

England

A

B

C

D

INDEX BY LOCATION

INDEX BY LOCATION

N

O

▼
Otley ....Chevin Country Park Hotel 288

P

R

S

▼
Stratford-Upon-Avon ....Billesley Manor..................................249

T

U

V

W

Y

Channel Islands

Northern Ireland

Ireland

Scotland

▼

Wales

▼

INDEX BY ACTIVITY

SPA Dedicated Spa facilities

England

Channel Islands

Ireland

▼

Scotland

Hotels with heated indoor swimming pool

England

▼

Index by Activity

Channel Islands

Ireland

Scotland

Wales

Outdoor pool

England

Channel Islands

Ireland

Golf course on-site

England

▼ **Ardencote Manor Hotel ...... Warwickshire 251**

Index by Activity

Ireland

Scotland

Wales

Fishing on-site

England

Ireland

Scotland

Wales

▼

Shooting on-site

England

Ireland

Scotland

Wales

M200 Conference facilities for 200 delegates or more

England

Ireland

Scotland

Wales

INDEX BY CONSORTIUM

Distinguished Hotels International

England

Ireland

Scotland

Pride Of Britain members

England

Channel Islands

Scotland

Wales

▼

Leading Hotels of the World

England

Ireland

Scotland

Small Luxury Hotels Of The World members

England

Channel Islands

Ireland

Scotland

Relais & Châteaux members

England

Ireland

Scotland

Wales

Ireland's Blue Book

N Ireland

Ireland

LONDON

Hotel location shown in red (hotel) or purple (spa hotel) with page number

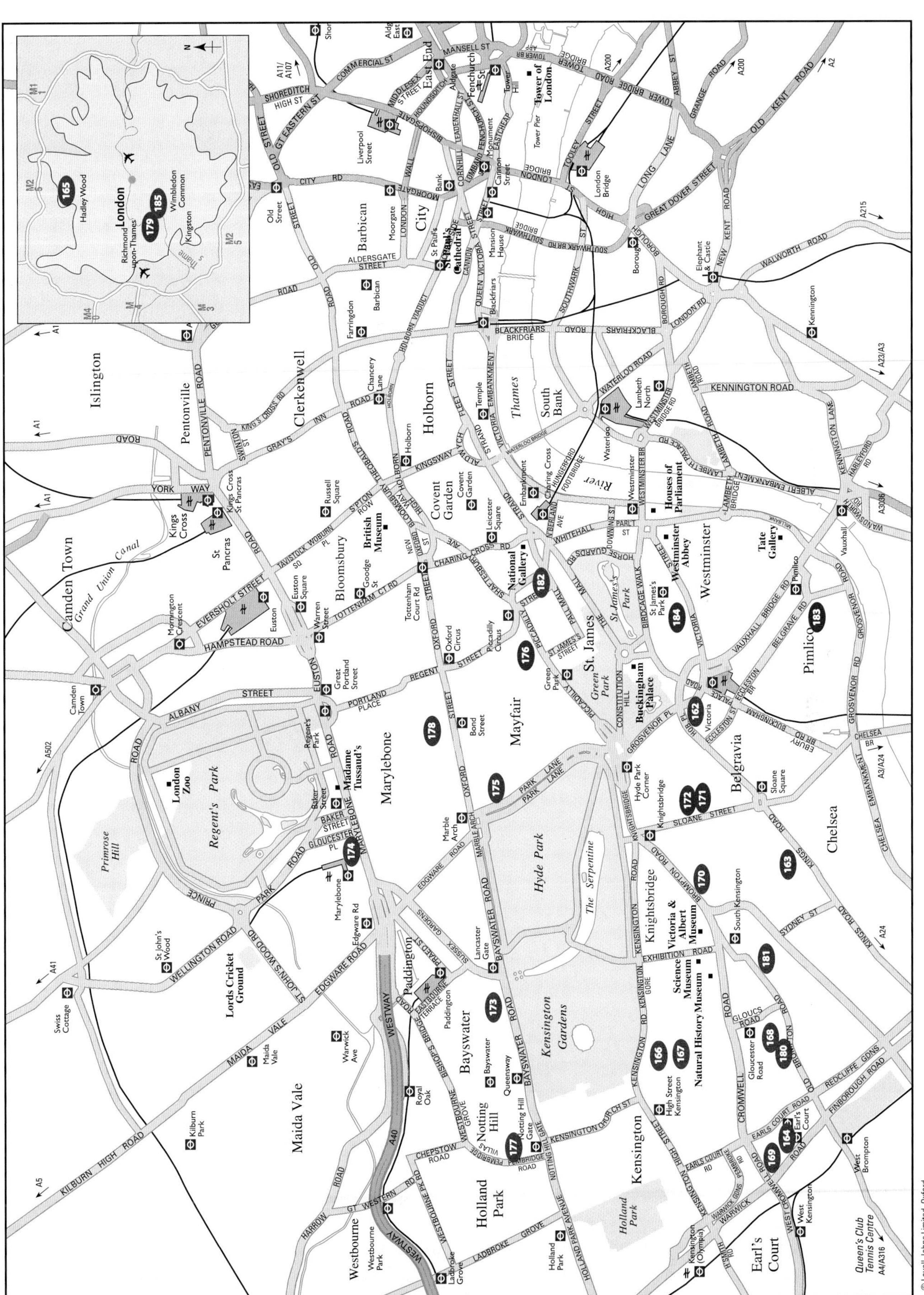

North West England

Hotel location shown in red (hotel) or purple (spa hotel) with page number

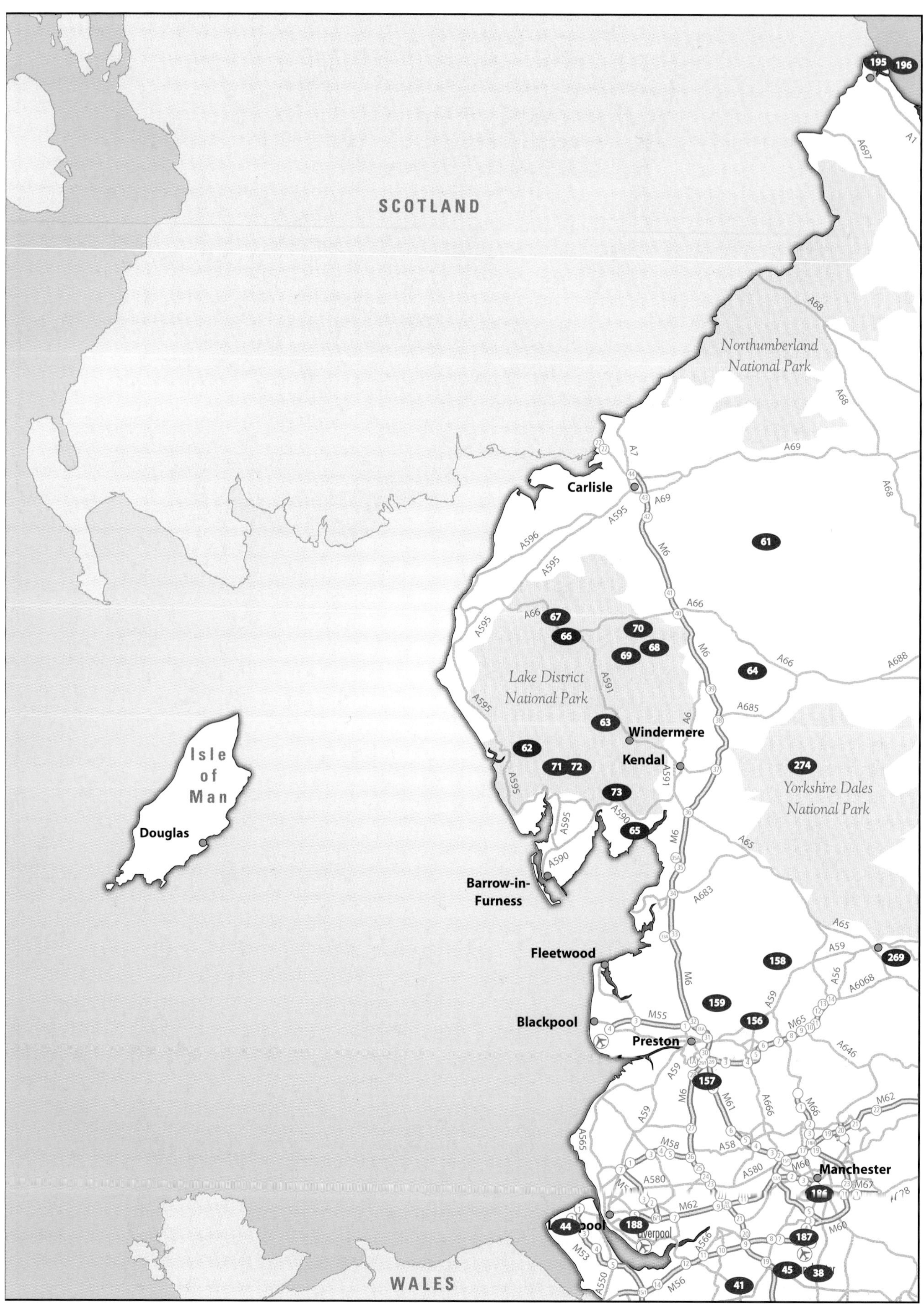

Hotel location shown in red (hotel) or purple (spa hotel) with page number

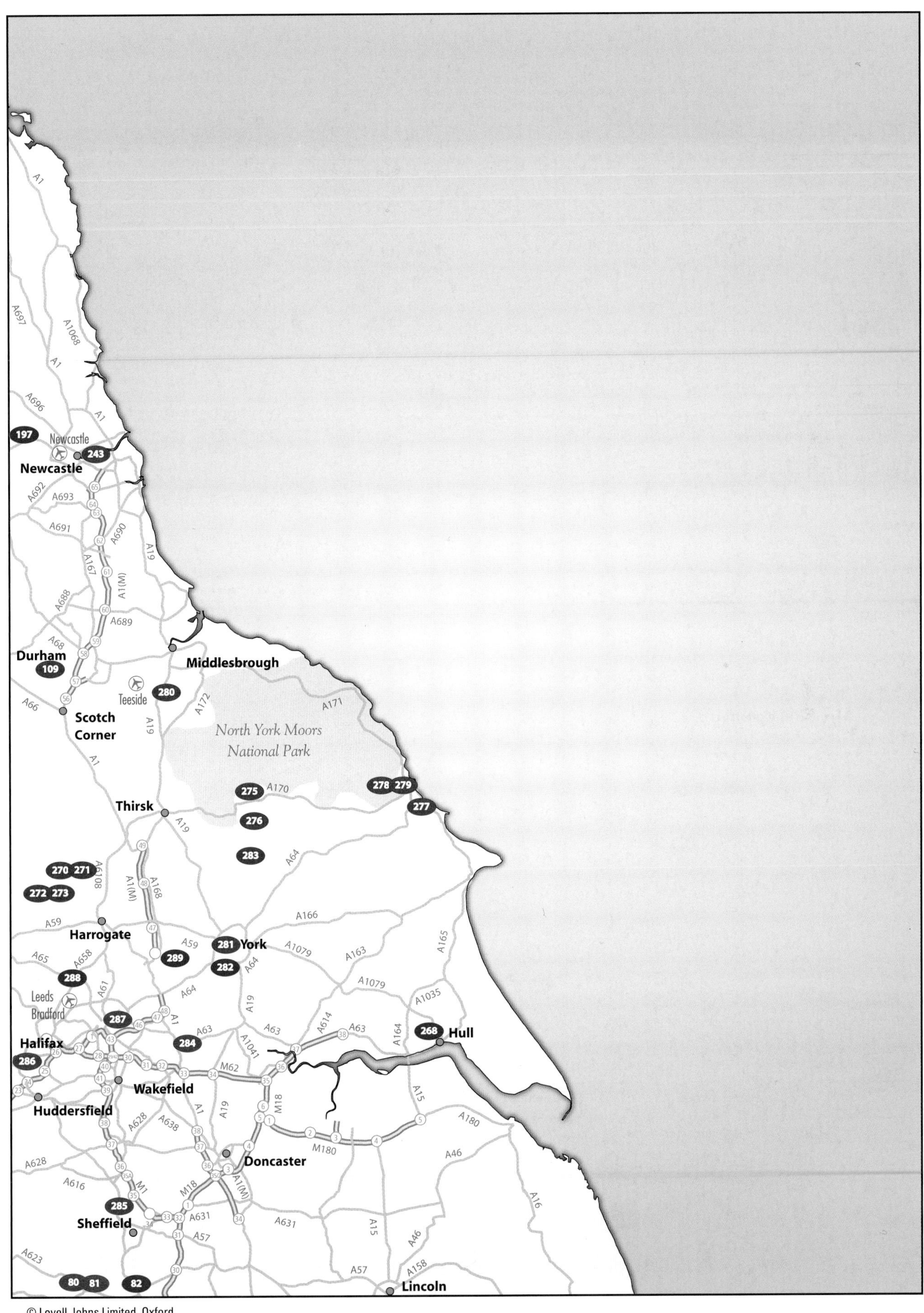

Central England

Hotel location shown in red (hotel) or purple (spa hotel) with page number

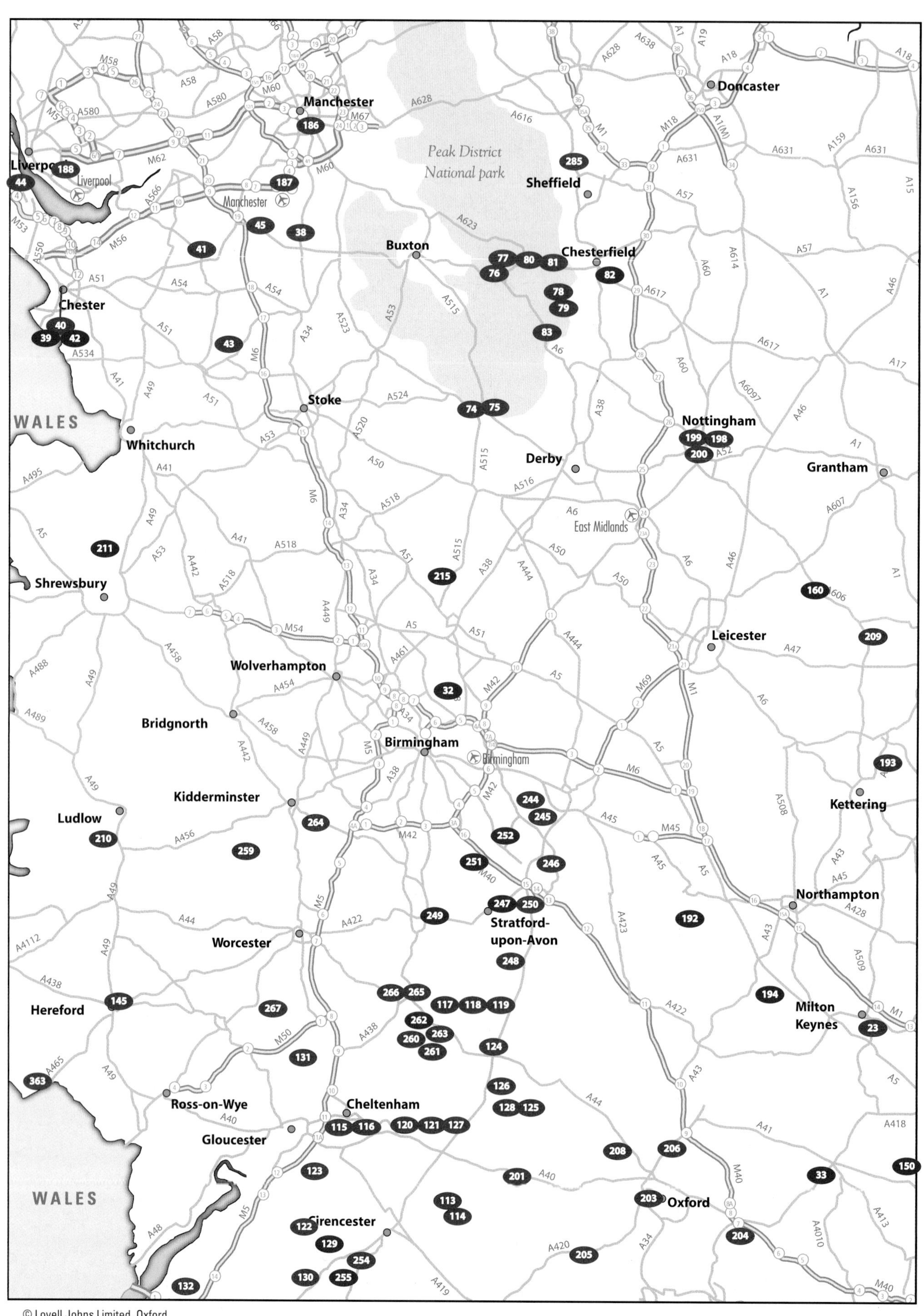

Eastern England

Hotel location shown in red (hotel) or purple (spa hotel) with page number

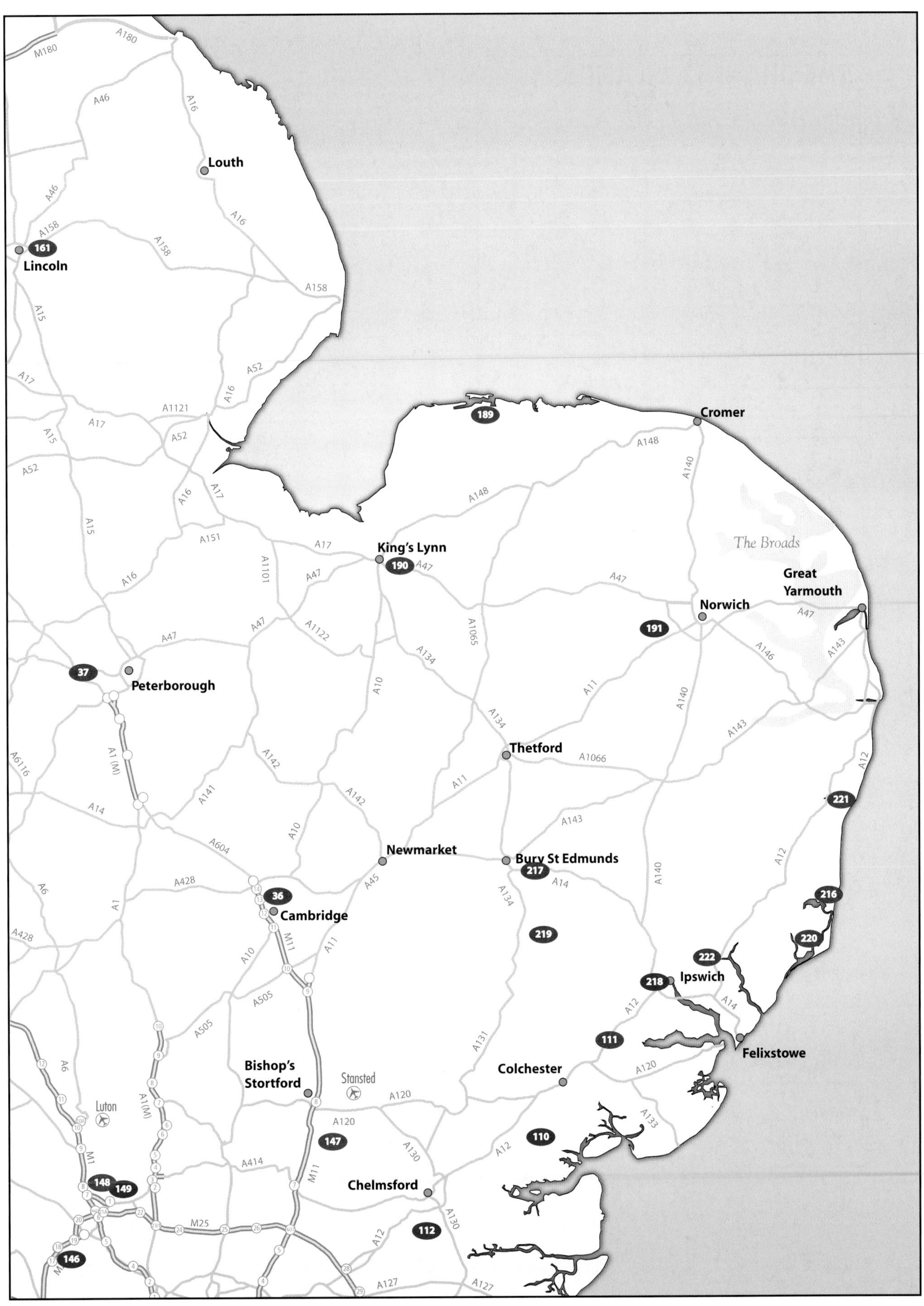

© Lovell Johns Limited, Oxford

Channel Islands & South West England

Hotel location shown in red (hotel) or purple (spa hotel) with page number

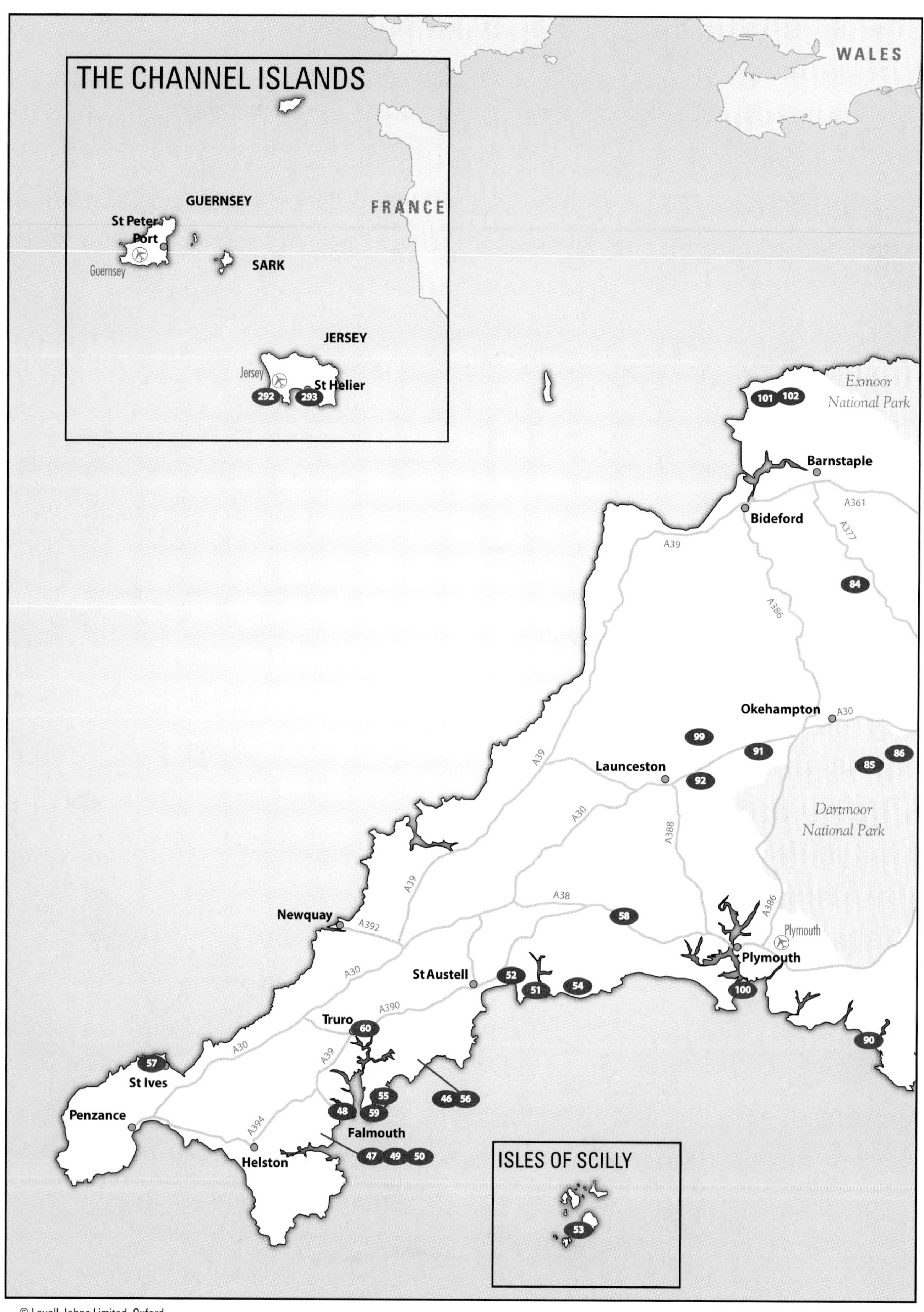

South West England

Hotel location shown in red (hotel) or purple (spa hotel) with page number

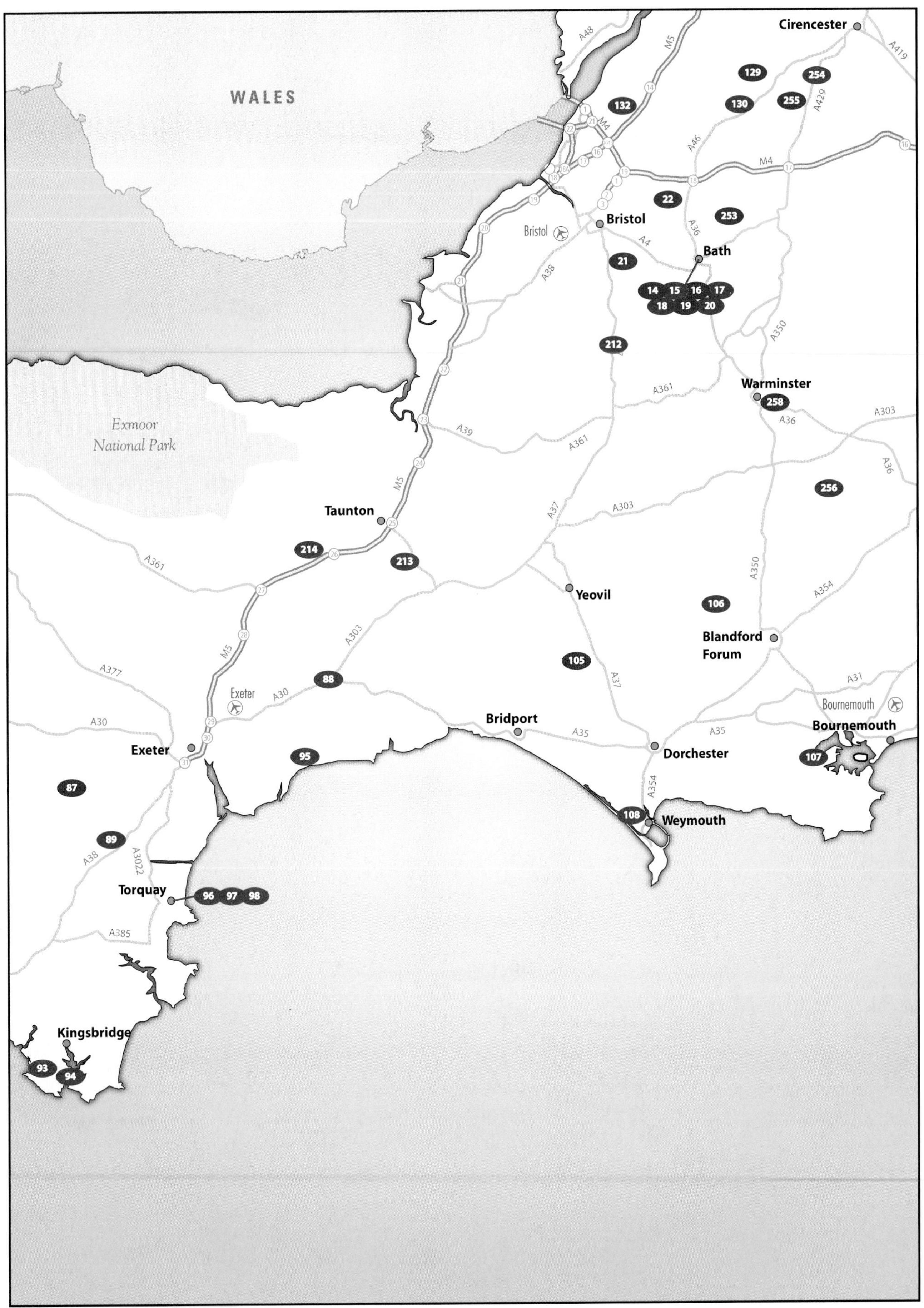

Southern England

Hotel location shown in red (hotel) or purple (spa hotel) with page number

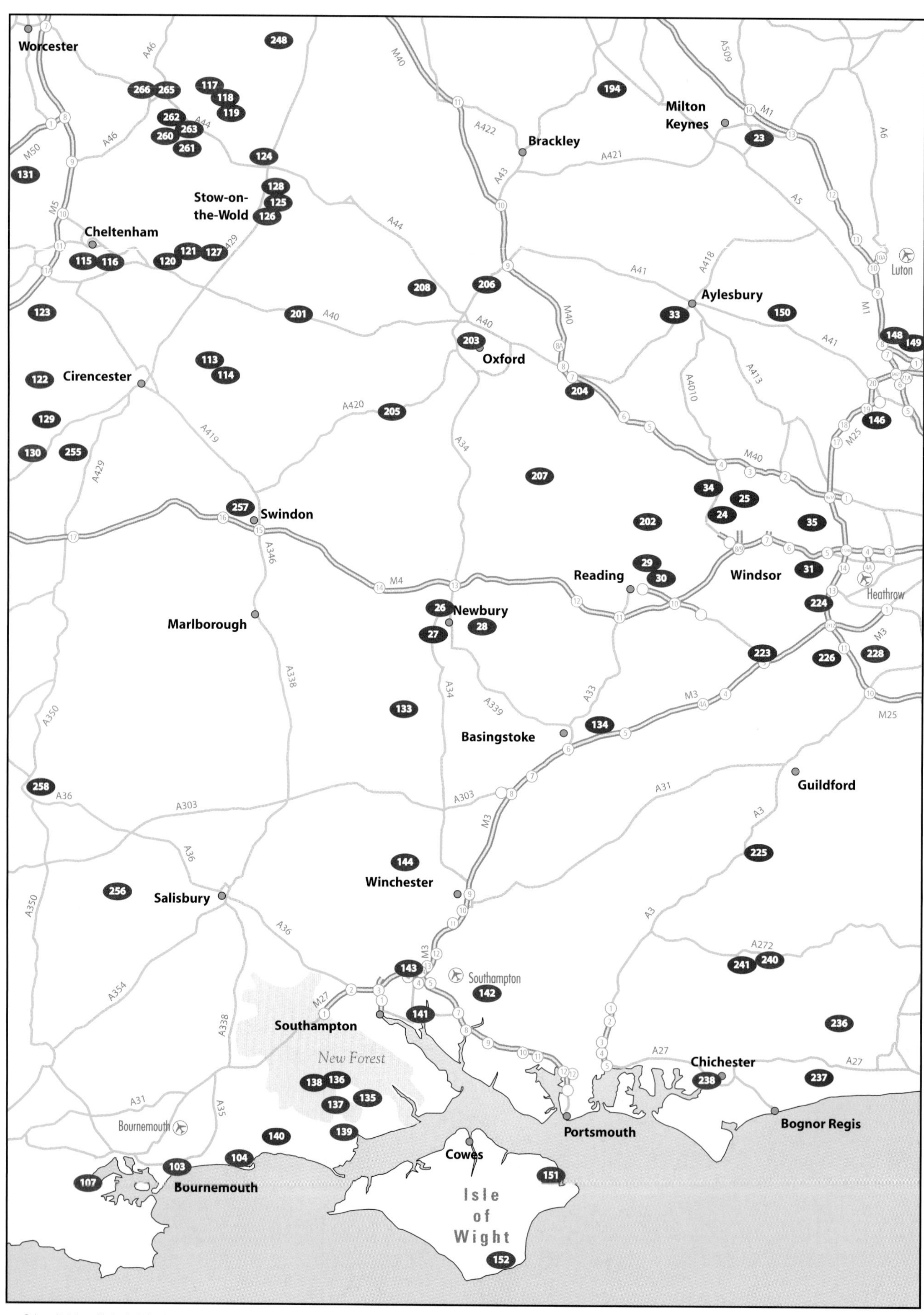

South East England

Hotel location shown in red (hotel) or purple (spa hotel) with page number

IRELAND

Hotel location shown in red (hotel) or purple (spa hotel) with page number

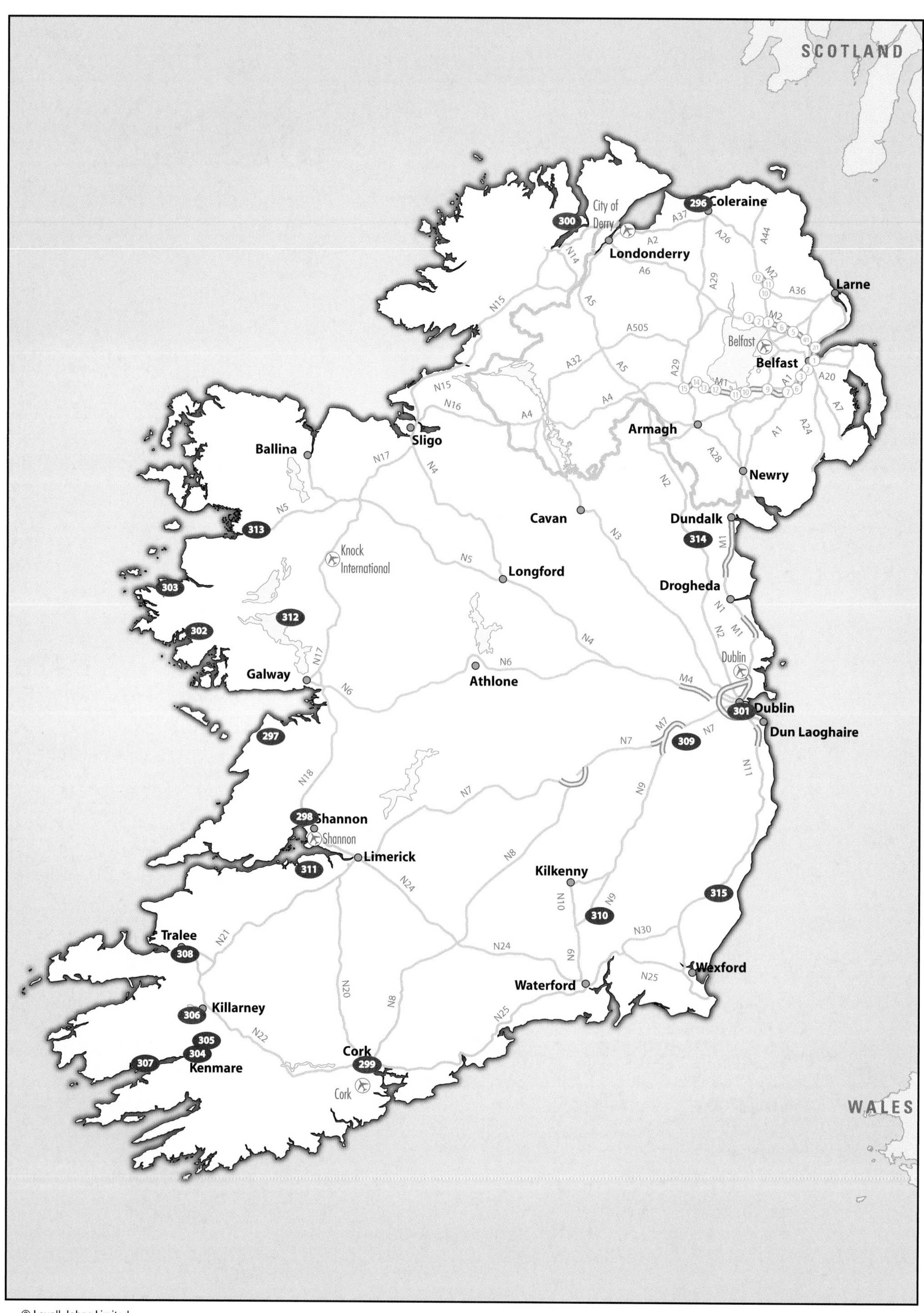

© Lovell Johns Limited,

SCOTLAND

Hotel location shown in red (hotel) or purple (spa hotel) with page number

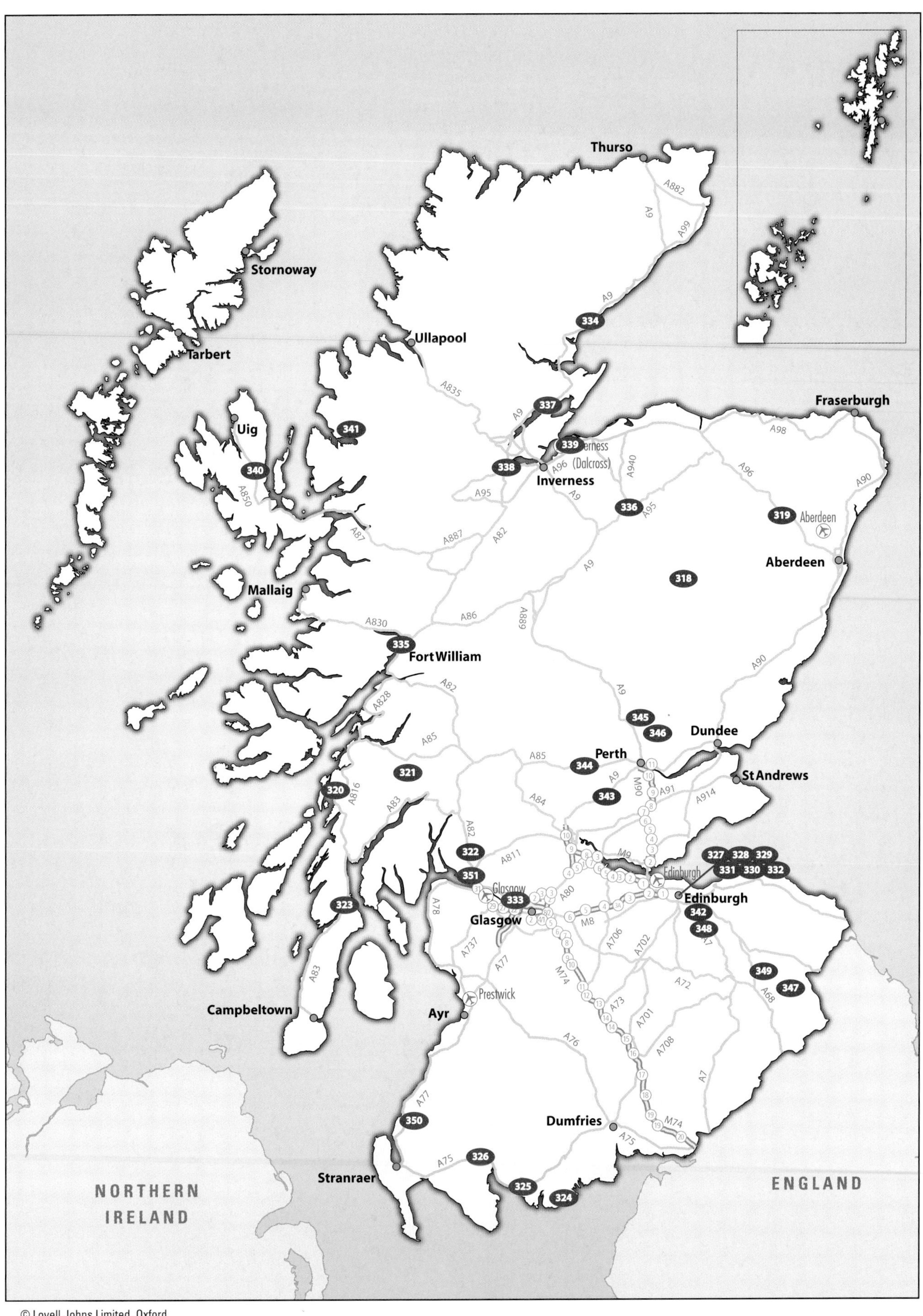

WALES

Hotel location shown in red (hotel) or purple (spa hotel) with page number

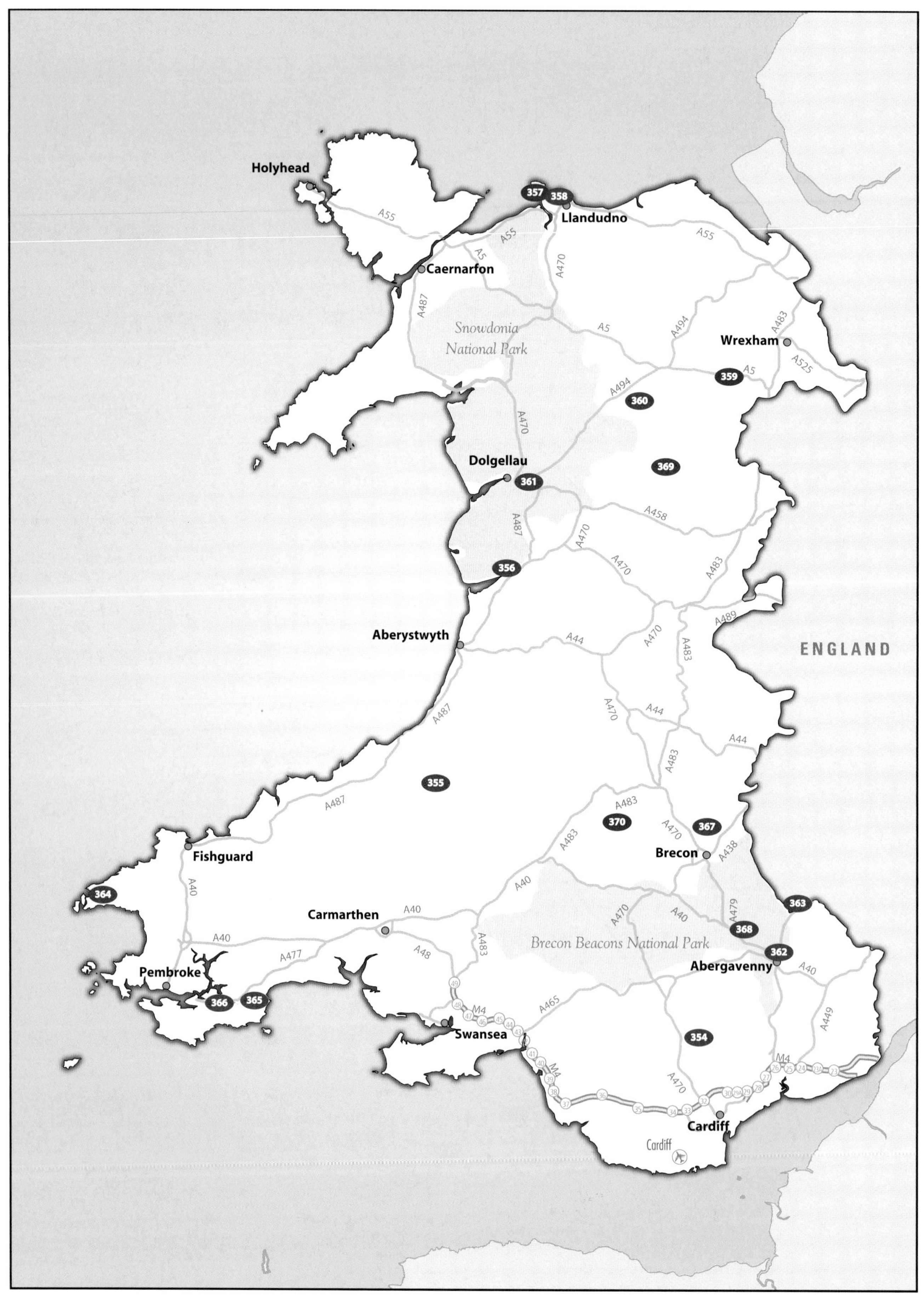

ORDER FORM

Up to £20 off when you order more than one Guide...

Order 4 Guides get £20 off, 3 Guides get £10 off, 2 Guides £5 off

Hotels & Spas
Great Britain & Ireland
£19.95

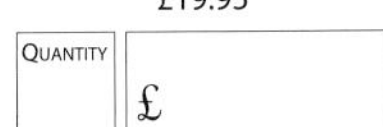

QUANTITY | £

Country Houses
Great Britain & Ireland
£16.95

QUANTITY | £

Hotels & Spas
Europe & Mediterranean
£16.95

QUANTITY | £

Hotels, Inns & Resorts
Americas, Caribbean,
Pacific, Atlantic - £14.95

QUANTITY | £

Business Venues
(published Feb 2006)
£25.00

QUANTITY | £

Save over £38 when you order the **The International Collection...**

The International Collection
£75.00

QUANTITY | £

a boxed presentation set of the four leisure Guides,

PLUS the Business Venues Guide,

PLUS our exclusive silver plated luggage tag.

A great offer for only £75 *(RRP £113.80)*

(Silver plated luggage tag RRP £15, presentation box RRP£5)

DISCOUNT - Discount does not apply to the International Collection 2 Guides = £5 off ☐ 3 Guides = £10 off ☐ 4 Guides = £20 off ☐

PACKING & DELIVERY - All UK Orders add £4.99 (Outside UK add £6 (per Guide) or £25 for The International Collection) £

GRAND TOTAL - Don't forget to deduct your discount £

☐ Please charge my Visa/Mastercard/Amex/Switch ☐ I enclose a cheque payable to Condé Nast Johansens

Card No.: Exp. Date: Issue No. (Switch only): Start Date:

Name: Signature:

Address:

Postcode: Tel: E-mail:

Please tick if you would like to receive information or offers from The Condé Nast Publications Ltd by telephone ☐ or SMS ☐ or E-mail ☐
Please tick if you would like to receive information or offers from other selected companies by telephone ☐ or SMS ☐ or E-mail ☐
Please tick this box if you prefer not to receive direct mail from The Condé Nast Publications Ltd ☐ and other reputable companies ☐

Mail to Condé Nast Johansens, FREEPOST (CB264), Eastbourne, BN23 6ZW (no stamp required)
or fax your order on 01323 649 350 or register online at www.cnjguides.co.uk quoting reference below

CALL OUR HOTLINE NOW ON FREEPHONE 0800 269 397
OR ORDER ONLINE AT www.cnjguides.co.uk ref: J006

GUEST SURVEY REPORT

Evaluate your stay in a Condé Nast Johansens Recommendation

Following your stay in a Condé Nast Johansens recommendation, please spare a moment to complete this Guest Survey Report. This is an important source of information for Johansens, to maintain the highest standards for our recommendations and to support our team of inspectors.

It is also the prime source of nominations for Condé Nast Johansens Awards for Excellence, which are made annually to those properties worldwide that represent the finest standards and best value for money in luxury, independent travel.

Your details

Name: __________

Address: __________

Postcode: __________

Telephone: __________

E-mail: __________

Your rating of the hotel

	Excellent	Good	Disappointing	Poor
Bedrooms	○	○	○	○
Public Rooms	○	○	○	○
Food/Restaurant	○	○	○	○
Service	○	○	○	○
Welcome/Friendliness	○	○	○	○
Value For Money	○	○	○	○

Hotel details

Name of hotel: __________

Location: __________

Date of visit: __________

Any other comments

If you wish to make additional comments, please write separately to the Publisher, Condé Nast Johansens Ltd, 6-8 Old Bond Street, London W1S 4PH

Please tick if you would like to receive information or offers from The Condé Nast Publications Ltd by telephone ☐ or SMS ☐ or E-mail ☐
Please tick if you would like to receive information or offers from other selected companies by telephone ☐ or SMS ☐ or E-mail ☐

Please return to **Condé Nast Johansens, FREEPOST (CB264), EASTBOURNE BN23 6ZW** (no stamp required) or alternatively send by fax on 01323 649350

GUEST SURVEY REPORT

Evaluate your stay in a Condé Nast Johansens Recommendation

Following your stay in a Condé Nast Johansens recommendation, please spare a moment to complete this Guest Survey Report. This is an important source of information for Johansens, to maintain the highest standards for our recommendations and to support our team of inspectors.

It is also the prime source of nominations for Condé Nast Johansens Awards for Excellence, which are made annually to those properties worldwide that represent the finest standards and best value for money in luxury, independent travel.

Your details

Name: __________

Address: __________

Postcode: __________

Telephone: __________

E-mail: __________

Your rating of the hotel

	Excellent	Good	Disappointing	Poor
Bedrooms	○	○	○	○
Public Rooms	○	○	○	○
Food/Restaurant	○	○	○	○
Service	○	○	○	○
Welcome/Friendliness	○	○	○	○
Value For Money	○	○	○	○

Hotel details

Name of hotel: __________

Location: __________

Date of visit: __________

Any other comments

If you wish to make additional comments, please write separately to the Publisher, Condé Nast Johansens Ltd, 6-8 Old Bond Street, London W1S 4PH

Please tick if you would like to receive information or offers from The Condé Nast Publications Ltd by telephone ☐ or SMS ☐ or E-mail ☐
Please tick if you would like to receive information or offers from other selected companies by telephone ☐ or SMS ☐ or E-mail ☐

Please return to **Condé Nast Johansens, FREEPOST (CB264), EASTBOURNE BN23 6ZW** (no stamp required) or alternatively send by fax on 01323 649350

ORDER FORM

Up to £20 off when you order more than one Guide...

Order 4 Guides get £20 off, 3 Guides get £10 off, 2 Guides £5 off

Hotels & Spas
Great Britain & Ireland
£19.95

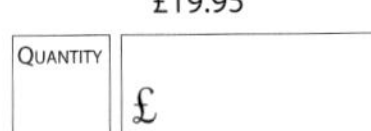

QUANTITY | £

Country Houses
Great Britain & Ireland
£16.95

QUANTITY | £

Hotels & Spas
Europe & Mediterranean
£16.95

QUANTITY | £

Hotels, Inns & Resorts
Americas, Caribbean,
Pacific, Atlantic - £14.95

QUANTITY | £

Business Venues
(published Feb 2006)
£25.00

QUANTITY | £

Save over £38 when you order the **The International Collection...**

The International Collection
£75.00

QUANTITY | £

a boxed presentation set of the four leisure Guides,

PLUS the Business Venues Guide,

PLUS our exclusive silver plated luggage tag.

A great offer for only £75 *(RRP £113.80)*

(Silver plated luggage tag RRP £15, presentation box RRP£5)

DISCOUNT - Discount does not apply to the International Collection 2 Guides = £5 off ☐ 3 Guides = £10 off ☐ 4 Guides = £20 off ☐

PACKING & DELIVERY - All UK Orders add £4.99 (Outside UK add £6 (per Guide) or £25 for The International Collection) £

GRAND TOTAL - Don't forget to deduct your discount £

☐ Please charge my Visa/Mastercard/Amex/Switch ☐ I enclose a cheque payable to Condé Nast Johansens

Card No.: Exp. Date: Issue No. (Switch only): Start Date:

Name: Signature:

Address:

Postcode: Tel: E-mail:

Please tick if you would like to receive information or offers from The Condé Nast Publications Ltd by telephone ☐ or SMS ☐ or E-mail ☐
Please tick if you would like to receive information or offers from other selected companies by telephone ☐ or SMS ☐ or E-mail ☐
Please tick this box if you prefer not to receive direct mail from The Condé Nast Publications Ltd ☐ and other reputable companies ☐

Mail to Condé Nast Johansens, FREEPOST (CB264), Eastbourne, BN23 6ZW (no stamp required)
or fax your order on 01323 649 350 or register online at www.cnjguides.co.uk quoting reference below

CALL OUR HOTLINE NOW ON FREEPHONE 0800 269 397
OR ORDER ONLINE AT www.cnjguides.co.uk ref: J006

GUEST SURVEY REPORT

Evaluate your stay in a Condé Nast Johansens Recommendation

Following your stay in a Condé Nast Johansens recommendation, please spare a moment to complete this Guest Survey Report. This is an important source of information for Johansens, to maintain the highest standards for our recommendations and to support our team of inspectors.

It is also the prime source of nominations for Condé Nast Johansens Awards for Excellence, which are made annually to those properties worldwide that represent the finest standards and best value for money in luxury, independent travel.

Your details

Name: __________

Address: __________

Postcode: __________

Telephone: __________

E-mail: __________

Hotel details

Name of hotel: __________

Location: __________

Date of visit: __________

Your rating of the hotel

	Excellent	Good	Disappointing	Poor
Bedrooms	❍	❍	❍	❍
Public Rooms	❍	❍	❍	❍
Food/Restaurant	❍	❍	❍	❍
Service	❍	❍	❍	❍
Welcome/Friendliness	❍	❍	❍	❍
Value For Money	❍	❍	❍	❍

Any other comments

If you wish to make additional comments, please write separately to the Publisher, Condé Nast Johansens Ltd, 6-8 Old Bond Street, London W1S 4PH

Please tick if you would like to receive information or offers from The Condé Nast Publications Ltd by telephone ☐ or SMS ☐ or E-mail ☐
Please tick if you would like to receive information or offers from other selected companies by telephone ☐ or SMS ☐ or E-mail ☐

Please return to **Condé Nast Johansens, FREEPOST (CB264), EASTBOURNE BN23 6ZW** (no stamp required) or alternatively send by fax on 01323 649350

GUEST SURVEY REPORT

Evaluate your stay in a Condé Nast Johansens Recommendation

Following your stay in a Condé Nast Johansens recommendation, please spare a moment to complete this Guest Survey Report. This is an important source of information for Johansens, to maintain the highest standards for our recommendations and to support our team of inspectors.

It is also the prime source of nominations for Condé Nast Johansens Awards for Excellence, which are made annually to those properties worldwide that represent the finest standards and best value for money in luxury, independent travel.

Your details

Name: __________

Address: __________

Postcode: __________

Telephone: __________

E-mail: __________

Hotel details

Name of hotel: __________

Location: __________

Date of visit: __________

Your rating of the hotel

	Excellent	Good	Disappointing	Poor
Bedrooms	❍	❍	❍	❍
Public Rooms	❍	❍	❍	❍
Food/Restaurant	❍	❍	❍	❍
Service	❍	❍	❍	❍
Welcome/Friendliness	❍	❍	❍	❍
Value For Money	❍	❍	❍	❍

Any other comments

If you wish to make additional comments, please write separately to the Publisher, Condé Nast Johansens Ltd, 6-8 Old Bond Street, London W1S 4PH

Please tick if you would like to receive information or offers from The Condé Nast Publications Ltd by telephone ☐ or SMS ☐ or E-mail ☐
Please tick if you would like to receive information or offers from other selected companies by telephone ☐ or SMS ☐ or E-mail ☐

Please return to **Condé Nast Johansens, FREEPOST (CB264), EASTBOURNE BN23 6ZW** (no stamp required) or alternatively send by fax on 01323 649350

ORDER FORM

Up to £20 off when you order more than one Guide...

Order 4 Guides get £20 off, 3 Guides get £10 off, 2 Guides £5 off

Hotels & Spas
Great Britain & Ireland
£19.95

QUANTITY | £

Country Houses
Great Britain & Ireland
£16.95

QUANTITY | £

Hotels & Spas
Europe & Mediterranean
£16.95

QUANTITY | £

Hotels, Inns & Resorts
Americas, Caribbean,
Pacific, Atlantic - £14.95

QUANTITY | £

Business Venues
(published Feb 2006)
£25.00

QUANTITY | £

Save over £38 when you order the **The International Collection...**

The International Collection
£75.00

QUANTITY | £

a boxed presentation set of the four leisure Guides,

PLUS the Business Venues Guide,

PLUS our exclusive silver plated luggage tag.

A great offer for only £75 *(RRP £113.80)*

(Silver plated luggage tag RRP £15, presentation box RRP£5)

DISCOUNT - Discount does not apply to the International Collection 2 Guides = £5 off ☐ 3 Guides = £10 off ☐ 4 Guides = £20 off ☐

PACKING & DELIVERY - All UK Orders add £4.99 (Outside UK add £6 (per Guide) or £25 for The International Collection) £

GRAND TOTAL - Don't forget to deduct your discount £

☐ Please charge my Visa/Mastercard/Amex/Switch ☐ I enclose a cheque payable to Condé Nast Johansens

Card No.: Exp. Date: Issue No. (Switch only): Start Date:

Name: Signature:

Address:

Postcode: Tel: E-mail:

Please tick if you would like to receive information or offers from The Condé Nast Publications Ltd by telephone ☐ or SMS ☐ or E-mail ☐
Please tick if you would like to receive information or offers from other selected companies by telephone ☐ or SMS ☐ or E-mail ☐
Please tick this box if you prefer not to receive direct mail from The Condé Nast Publications Ltd ☐ and other reputable companies ☐

Mail to Condé Nast Johansens, FREEPOST (CB264), Eastbourne, BN23 6ZW (no stamp required)
or fax your order on 01323 649 350 or register online at www.cnjguides.co.uk quoting reference below

CALL OUR HOTLINE NOW ON FREEPHONE 0800 269 397
OR ORDER ONLINE AT www.cnjguides.co.uk ref: J006

GUEST SURVEY REPORT

Evaluate your stay in a Condé Nast Johansens Recommendation

Following your stay in a Condé Nast Johansens recommendation, please spare a moment to complete this Guest Survey Report. This is an important source of information for Johansens, to maintain the highest standards for our recommendations and to support our team of inspectors.

It is also the prime source of nominations for Condé Nast Johansens Awards for Excellence, which are made annually to those properties worldwide that represent the finest standards and best value for money in luxury, independent travel.

Your details

Name:

Address:

Postcode:

Telephone:

E-mail:

Hotel details

Name of hotel:

Location:

Date of visit:

Your rating of the hotel

	Excellent	Good	Disappointing	Poor
Bedrooms				
Public Rooms				
Food/Restaurant				
Service				
Welcome/Friendliness				
Value For Money				

Any other comments

If you wish to make additional comments, please write separately to the Publisher, Condé Nast Johansens Ltd, 6-8 Old Bond Street, London W1S 4PH

Please tick if you would like to receive information or offers from The Condé Nast Publications Ltd by telephone ☐ or SMS ☐ or E-mail ☐
Please tick if you would like to receive information or offers from other selected companies by telephone ☐ or SMS ☐ or E-mail ☐

Please return to **Condé Nast Johansens, FREEPOST (CB264), EASTBOURNE BN23 6ZW** (no stamp required) or alternatively send by fax on 01323 649350

GUEST SURVEY REPORT

Evaluate your stay in a Condé Nast Johansens Recommendation

Following your stay in a Condé Nast Johansens recommendation, please spare a moment to complete this Guest Survey Report. This is an important source of information for Johansens, to maintain the highest standards for our recommendations and to support our team of inspectors.

It is also the prime source of nominations for Condé Nast Johansens Awards for Excellence, which are made annually to those properties worldwide that represent the finest standards and best value for money in luxury, independent travel.

Your details

Name:

Address:

Postcode:

Telephone:

E-mail:

Hotel details

Name of hotel:

Location:

Date of visit:

Your rating of the hotel

	Excellent	Good	Disappointing	Poor
Bedrooms				
Public Rooms				
Food/Restaurant				
Service				
Welcome/Friendliness				
Value For Money				

Any other comments

If you wish to make additional comments, please write separately to the Publisher, Condé Nast Johansens Ltd, 6-8 Old Bond Street, London W1S 4PH

Please tick if you would like to receive information or offers from The Condé Nast Publications Ltd by telephone ☐ or SMS ☐ or E-mail ☐
Please tick if you would like to receive information or offers from other selected companies by telephone ☐ or SMS ☐ or E-mail ☐

Please return to **Condé Nast Johansens, FREEPOST (CB264), EASTBOURNE BN23 6ZW** (no stamp required) or alternatively send by fax on 01323 649350

GUEST SURVEY REPORT

Evaluate your stay in a Condé Nast Johansens Recommendation

Following your stay in a Condé Nast Johansens recommendation, please spare a moment to complete this Guest Survey Report. This is an important source of information for Johansens, to maintain the highest standards for our recommendations and to support our team of inspectors.

It is also the prime source of nominations for Condé Nast Johansens Awards for Excellence, which are made annually to those properties worldwide that represent the finest standards and best value for money in luxury, independent travel.

Your details

Name: __________

Address: __________

__________ Postcode: __________

Telephone: __________

E-mail: __________

Hotel details

Name of hotel: __________

Location: __________

Date of visit: __________

Your rating of the hotel

	Excellent	Good	Disappointing	Poor
Bedrooms	❍	❍	❍	❍
Public Rooms	❍	❍	❍	❍
Food/Restaurant	❍	❍	❍	❍
Service	❍	❍	❍	❍
Welcome/Friendliness	❍	❍	❍	❍
Value For Money	❍	❍	❍	❍

Any other comments

If you wish to make additional comments, please write separately to the Publisher, Condé Nast Johansens Ltd, 6-8 Old Bond Street, London W1S 4PH

Please tick if you would like to receive information or offers from The Condé Nast Publications Ltd by telephone ☐ or SMS ☐ or E-mail ☐
Please tick if you would like to receive information or offers from other selected companies by telephone ☐ or SMS ☐ or E-mail ☐

Please return to **Condé Nast Johansens, FREEPOST (CB264), EASTBOURNE BN23 6ZW** (no stamp required)
or alternatively send by fax on 01323 649350

GUEST SURVEY REPORT

Evaluate your stay in a Condé Nast Johansens Recommendation

Following your stay in a Condé Nast Johansens recommendation, please spare a moment to complete this Guest Survey Report. This is an important source of information for Johansens, to maintain the highest standards for our recommendations and to support our team of inspectors.

It is also the prime source of nominations for Condé Nast Johansens Awards for Excellence, which are made annually to those properties worldwide that represent the finest standards and best value for money in luxury, independent travel.

Your details

Name: __________

Address: __________

__________ Postcode: __________

Telephone: __________

E-mail: __________

Hotel details

Name of hotel: __________

Location: __________

Date of visit: __________

Your rating of the hotel

	Excellent	Good	Disappointing	Poor
Bedrooms	❍	❍	❍	❍
Public Rooms	❍	❍	❍	❍
Food/Restaurant	❍	❍	❍	❍
Service	❍	❍	❍	❍
Welcome/Friendliness	❍	❍	❍	❍
Value For Money	❍	❍	❍	❍

Any other comments

If you wish to make additional comments, please write separately to the Publisher, Condé Nast Johansens Ltd, 6-8 Old Bond Street, London W1S 4PH

Please tick if you would like to receive information or offers from The Condé Nast Publications Ltd by telephone ☐ or SMS ☐ or E-mail ☐
Please tick if you would like to receive information or offers from other selected companies by telephone ☐ or SMS ☐ or E-mail ☐

Please return to **Condé Nast Johansens, FREEPOST (CB264), EASTBOURNE BN23 6ZW** (no stamp required)
or alternatively send by fax on 01323 649350